New Perspectives on

Microsoft® Office FrontPage® 2003

Comprehensive

Jessica Evans

THOMSON

COURSE TECHNOLOGY™

Australia • Canada • Mexico • Singapore • Spain • United Kingdom • United States

THOMSON

COURSE TECHNOLOGY

New Perspectives on Microsoft® Office FrontPage® 2003—Comprehensive

is published by Course Technology.

Managing Editor:
Rachel Goldberg

Senior Product Manager:
Kathy Finnegan

Senior Technology Product Manager:
Amanda Young Shelton

Product Managers:
Karen Stevens, Brianna Germain

Associate Product Manager:
Emilie Perreault

Editorial Assistant:
Shana Rosenthal

Marketing Manager:
Joy Stark

Developmental Editor:
Judy Adamski

QA Manuscript Reviewers:
John Freitas, Marc Spoto, Alex White, Christian Kunciw, Susan Whalen

Production Editor:
Summer Hughes

Composition:
GEX Publishing Services

Text Designer:
Steve Deschene

Cover Designer:
Nancy Goulet

Cover Artist:
Ed Carpenter
www.edcarpenter.net

Preface

Real, Thought-Provoking, Engaging, Dynamic, Interactive—these are just a few of the words that are used to describe the New Perspectives Series' approach to learning and building computer skills.

Without our critical-thinking and problem-solving methodology, computer skills could be learned but not retained. By teaching with a case-based approach, the New Perspectives Series challenges students to apply what they've learned to real-life situations.

Our ever-growing community of users understands why they're learning what they're learning. Now you can too!

See what instructors and students are saying about the best-selling New Perspectives Series:

"I have used books from the New Perspectives series for about ten years now. I haven't been able to find anything else that approaches their quality when it comes to covering intermediate and advanced software application topics."
— Karleen Nordquist, College of St. Benedict & St. John's University

"We have been using the New Perspectives Series for several years and are pleased with it. Step-by-step instructions, end-of-chaper projects, and color screenshots are positives."
— Michael J. Losacco, College of DuPage

...and about New Perspectives on Microsoft Office FrontPage 2003:

"I appreciate that the 'design' aspect is included in Tutorial 1. Often books either do not cover design principles at all or add them as an afterthought. I think that from the very beginning these issues need to be addressed."
— Kim Blosser, Blue Ridge Community College

"Overall, the text is excellent! Tutorial 4 is one of my favorite tutorials as this is where you can use shared borders, themes, photo galleries, and word art to make a project much easier to do and change it from an ordinary Web site to an extra-ordinary one."
— Fred Parce, Texas State Technical College Harlingen

www.course.com/NewPerspectives

Why *New Perspectives* will work for you

Context

Each tutorial begins with a problem presented in a "real-world" case that is meaningful to students. The case sets the scene to help students understand what they will do in the tutorial.

Hands-on Approach

Each tutorial is divided into manageable sessions that combine reading and hands-on, step-by-step work. Screenshots—now 20% larger for enhanced readability—help guide students through the steps. **Trouble?** tips anticipate common mistakes or problems to help students stay on track and continue with the tutorial.

Review

In New Perspectives, retention is a key component to learning. At the end of each session, a series of Quick Check questions helps students test their understanding of the concepts before moving on. And now each tutorial contains an end-of-tutorial summary and a list of key terms for further reinforcement.

Assessment

Engaging and challenging Review Assignments and Case Problems have always been a hallmark feature of the New Perspectives Series. Now we've added new features to make them more accessible! Colorful icons and brief descriptions accompany the exercises, making it easy to understand, at a glance, both the goal and level of challenge a particular assignment holds.

Reference

While contextual learning is excellent for retention, there are times when students will want a high-level understanding of how to accomplish a task. Within each tutorial, Reference Windows appear before a set of steps to provide a succinct summary and preview of how to perform a task. In addition, a complete Task Reference at the back of the book provides quick access to information on how to carry out common tasks. Finally, each book includes a combination Glossary/Index to promote easy reference of material.

Lab Assignments

Certain tutorials in this book contain Lab Assignments, which provide additional reinforcement of important skills in a simulated environment. These labs have been hailed by students and teachers alike for years as the most comprehensive and accurate on the market. Great for pre-work or remediation, the labs help students learn concepts and skills in a structured environment.

Student Online Companion

This book has an accompanying online companion Web site designed to enhance learning. This Web site includes:

- Lab Assignments for selected tutorials
- Student Data Files and PowerPoint presentations
- Links to Web sites for additional information

Certification

If you've used the New Perspectives FrontPage book in the past, you may have noticed the Microsoft Office Specialist logo on the cover. With this release, Microsoft has decided not to offer a certification exam for FrontPage 2003. Rest assured that this title contains the same comprehensive level of instruction you expect from New Perspectives.

www.course.com/NewPerspectives

Review

Apply

Reference Window

Task Reference

Reinforce

New Perspectives offers an entire system of instruction

The New Perspectives Series is more than just a handful of books. It's a complete system of offerings:

New Perspectives catalog

Our online catalog is never out of date! Go to the catalog link on our Web site to check out our available titles, request a desk copy, download a book preview, or locate online files.

Coverage to meet your needs!

Whether you're looking for just a small amount of coverage or enough to fill a semester-long class, we can provide you with a textbook that meets your needs.

- Brief books typically cover the essential skills in just 2 to 4 tutorials.
- Introductory books build and expand on those skills and contain an average of 5 to 8 tutorials.
- Comprehensive books are great for a full-semester class, and contain 9 to 12+ tutorials.
- Power Users or Advanced books are perfect for a highly accelerated introductory class or a second course in a given topic.

So if the book you're holding does not provide the right amount of coverage for you, there's probably another offering available. Go to our Web site or contact your Course Technology sales representative to find out what else we offer.

Instructor Resources

We offer more than just a book. We have all the tools you need to enhance your lectures, check students' work, and generate exams in a new, easier-to-use and completely revised package. This book's Instructor's Manual, ExamView testbank, PowerPoint presentations, data files, solution files, figure files, and a sample syllabus are all available on a single CD-ROM or for downloading at www.course.com.

How will your students master Microsoft Office?

SAM (Skills Assessment Manager) 2003 helps you energize your class exams and training assignments by allowing students to learn and test important computer skills in an active, hands-on environment. With SAM 2003, you create powerful interactive exams on critical Microsoft Office 2003 applications, including Word, Excel, Access, and PowerPoint. The exams simulate the application environment, allowing your students to demonstrate their knowledge and to think through the skills by performing real-world tasks. Designed to be used with the New Perspectives Series, SAM 2003 includes built-in page references so students can create study guides that match the New Perspectives textbooks you use in class. Powerful administrative options allow you to schedule exams and assignments, secure your tests, and run reports with almost limitless flexibility. Find out more about SAM 2003 by going to www.course.com or speaking with your Course Technology sales representative.

Distance Learning

Enhance your course with any of our online learning platforms. Go to www.course.com or speak with your Course Technology sales representative to find the platform or the content that's right for you.

www.course.com/NewPerspectives

About This Book

This book offers a case-based, problem-solving approach to learning Microsoft FrontPage 2003. Students will learn how to create and publish Web pages with links, graphics, tables, and frames.

- Updated for the new software! Includes features new to FrontPage 2003 such as custom link bars, custom themes, multiple browser preview, and Split view, which displays both the design and code views simultaneously.
- This edition features a new running tutorial case and two new case problems.
- Increased emphasis on design issues, including Web-safe colors, expanded coverage of fonts, and how to use various picture file formats.
- Includes a 120-day trial of the full version FrontPage 2003 software!

New to this edition!

- Larger screenshots!
- Sequential page numbering!
- New end-of-tutorial material provides additional conceptual review in the form of key terms and a tutorial summary.
- New labels and descriptions for the end-of-tutorial exercises make it easy for you to select the right exercises for your students.

Acknowledgments

I would like to thank several people who very carefully reviewed the published previous edition of this book and the manuscript as I developed it for this book for their excellent comments and suggestions: Joanne Walters, J Sargeant Reynolds Community College; Jay Human, Lexington CC; Fred Parce, Texas State Technical College Harlingen; and Kim Blosser, Blue Ridge Community College. Your many comments and suggestions were a great resource for me as I worked to improve this book's content and cases.

I have always been blessed to be a part of the best publishing team in the business. I would like to thank Rachel Goldberg, Managing Editor, who has been a terrific resource and a good friend over the years in addition to being a great leader of the New Perspectives Team; and Karen Stevens, Product Manager, who has provided support and much-needed encouragement during this book's development. I would also like to thank my Developmental Editor, Judy Adamski, for her constant support and wisdom and her willingness to go the extra mile to help me meet this book's fast-paced schedule. I have also been fortunate to have a great set of quality assurance testers on all of my projects, and this one is no different. Thank you to John Freitas, Marc Spoto, and Alex White for helping to improve this book and for carefully checking all of my solution files. Finally, I am grateful to Summer Hughes, Production Editor, for all of her efforts to ensure that this book was published quickly and accurately.

I would also like to acknowledge the contributions of my friends and neighbors, Brett and Shelly Greer and Scott and Carla Swenson, for allowing me to adapt and expand their successful Web sites and use them as new case problems in this book. The new cases in this edition are fun, interesting, and a true reflection of how real businesses use Web sites in today's economy.

And last but not least…I am fortunate to be surrounded by many people who support me in my personal and professional endeavors. To my husband, Richard and our daughter, Hannah, thank you for support, encouragement, love, and confidence and pride in what I do.

— Jessica Evans

www.course.com/NewPerspectives

Brief Contents

FrontPage

Table of Contents

New Perspectives on
Microsoft® Office FrontPage® 2003

Read This Before You Begin: Tutorials 1 & 2

To the Student

Data Disks

To complete the Tutorials, Review Assignments, and Case Problems in this book, you will need the starting student Data Files. Your instructor will either provide you with these Data Files or ask you to obtain them yourself.

The FrontPage Tutorials 1 and 2 require the folders shown in the next column to complete the Tutorials, Review Assignments, and Case Problems. You will need to copy these folders from a file server, a standalone computer, or the Web to the drive and folder where you will be storing your Data Files. Your instructor will tell you which computer, drive letter, and folders contain the files you need. You can also download the files by going to www.course.com; see the inside front cover for more information on downloading the files to your working folder, or ask your instructor or technical support person for assistance.

You will need to store your Data Files on a Zip disk, hard drive, or network drive that you can access. You will also need a location in which to create and save Web sites; the default location used in this book is C:\My Webs\[YourName], where "[YourName]" is your first and last names. You cannot complete this book using floppy disks.

▼ FrontPage
Tutorial.01
Tutorial.02

Course Labs

Tutorial 1 features two interactive Course Labs to help you understand Internet and hypermedia concepts. There are Lab Assignments at the end of Tutorial 1 that relate to these labs. Contact your instructor or technical support person for assistance in accessing these labs.

To the Instructor

The Data Files and Course Labs are available on the Instructor Resources CD for this title. Follow the instructions in the Help file on the CD-ROM to install the programs to your network or standalone computer. See the "To the Student" section above for information on how to set up the Data Files that accompany this text. To complete the tutorials in this book, students must have a Web browser, access to a Web server with the FrontPage 2002 Server Extensions or Windows SharePoint Services installed on it, and an Internet connection. You are granted a license to copy the Data Files and Course Labs to any computer or computer network used by students who have purchased this book.

System Requirements

If you are going to work through this book using your own computer, you need:

• **Computer System** Microsoft Windows 2000 Professional or higher, Microsoft FrontPage 2003, and Microsoft Office 2003 must be installed on your computer. (The screens shown in this book use Microsoft Windows XP Professional. If your computer has Microsoft Windows 2000 Professional, your screens will look slightly different.) This book assumes a typical installation of FrontPage 2003 and Office 2003.

The recommended browser for viewing Web pages is Internet Explorer 6.0 or higher.

• **Data Files** You will not be able to complete the tutorials or exercises in this book using your own computer until you have a set of Data Files.

• **Course Labs** See your instructor or technical support person to obtain the Course Lab software for use on your own computer.

www.course.com/NewPerspectives

Lab

Computer History Hypermedia

The Internet: World Wide Web

Student Data Files

To complete this tutorial, you will need the following Data Files. Additional Data Files needed to complete the end-of-tutorial exercises are listed with the Review Assignments and Case Problems.

Creating a Web Site

Creating the Web Site for the Sunshine Landscape & Garden Center

Case

Sunshine Landscape & Garden Center

Brett Kizer graduated from college with a master's degree in business administration. At first, he tried the traditional MBA career path and worked for a financial institution. He soon determined, however, that he was not going to be happy working in an office. When an opportunity arose for him to purchase an established garden center in the Texas Hill Country, he quickly came up with the resources to do so, and he and his wife, Shelly, became the owners of the Sunshine Landscape & Garden Center. Because Brett and Shelly knew very little about plants and landscaping when they bought the business, Brett took several courses at a local college to become more knowledgeable about his new role. In addition, he took the required course of study to become a licensed irrigator and acquired an existing business that installed commercial and residential irrigation systems. With the addition of irrigation to the nursery's existing services, Sunshine soon had several new commercial and residential clients and hired several employees to support the nursery's increase in services and sales.

A short time later, Brett purchased several computers with Microsoft Windows XP and Microsoft Office 2003 installed on them. He then computerized the nursery's accounting, inventory, and ordering systems. The transition from the previous owner's paper-based system to a computerized system helped Brett and Shelly better manage the nursery by eliminating inventory that did not sell well and increasing orders in those areas of the business that generated the most profits.

As part of his business plan, Brett wants to create a Web site for the center so he can provide information to the community about the services offered by the business. Because Sunshine's employees spend a good deal of time troubleshooting common gardening problems and counseling local residents about appropriate plants for the area, Brett also wants to make the Web site a resource for information about what

▼ **Tutorial.01**

▽ Tutorial folder

    link.doc

    list.doc

types of plants to install, when to plant them, how to maintain them, and other information that local residents frequently request from the nursery's expert employees. Brett hopes that the Web site will make it easy for Sunshine's customers to rely on the nursery for information and all their gardening needs.

In the several months since Brett hired you, you have been working in various positions at the nursery and have acquired a good sense of the overall operation of the business. In your capacity as a landscape designer, you have counseled residential and commercial customers about their landscaping needs, recommended plants to install, and helped customers troubleshoot various problems with new and existing landscaping. Brett thinks that you are an ideal candidate to manage the development of the new Web site because, in addition to your experience at the nursery, you have taken several college-level courses on Web site design and development. After considering several alternatives, you and Brett decide to use FrontPage to create, manage, and maintain the site. You will create the Web site and, at the same time, teach Brett how to use FrontPage so he will be able to utilize it in the future to contribute to and help maintain the site.

Session 1.1

The Internet: World Wide Web

Web Servers

The **Internet** is a large, worldwide collection of computer networks that are connected to one another. In a **network**, two or more computers are connected together for the purposes of sharing resources and communicating. Within a network, one computer is designated as the server, which functions as the network's central computer. The **network server**, or **host**, is a powerful computer that stores and distributes information and resources across the network to individual computers. The Internet is not a single, massive computer, but rather a collection of connected networks through which users exchange information. The Internet allows you to communicate and share data with people in the next office, across the street, or around the world.

The Internet's resources are organized in a **client/server architecture**. The server runs software that coordinates and communicates with the other computers connected to it. These other computers are called **clients**; a personal computer that is connected to the Internet is one example of a client. The server to which the client is connected stores information and processes the client's requests for that information. When a client requests information from a server, that request is transferred in the form of a file. The server then finds the information and returns it to the client, also in the form of a file. This file travels over the Internet from one server to another until it eventually reaches the client that requested it. Sometimes the file travels through many different servers before finally reaching this client.

To access the Internet, you need an account with an Internet service provider. An **Internet service provider (ISP)** is a business that provides a connection to the Internet for individuals, businesses, and organizations for a fee. An ISP might be a small, local business or a large, national provider such as EarthLink or America Online. Many colleges, universities, and large businesses have their own direct connections to the Internet and, in effect, act as their own ISP.

To function as a Web server, a server connected to the Internet must run special software that enables it to receive and execute clients' requests for Web pages. When you install Windows 2000 Professional or higher, you can also install Microsoft Internet Information Services, or IIS, which lets your computer function as a Web server. In this book, you will use IIS or a compatible server to process Web pages.

What Is FrontPage?

Microsoft FrontPage is a program that simplifies the development, maintenance, and publication of a Web site. A **Web site** consists of the Web pages, files, and folders that a business or organization presents via the Internet. You can use FrontPage to create, view, edit, and publish your Web site; insert and edit text, pictures, and photo galleries in your Web pages; import and export files; add, test, and repair hyperlinks to and within your pages; and generate a variety of reports about your Web site's function and usage. FrontPage also includes features that simplify Web site creation, such as templates for creating Web pages and built-in functions for processing Web pages on a server.

To create professional-looking Web pages, you don't need to be an experienced HTML programmer. **Hypertext Markup Language (HTML)** is the language that creates the **HTML documents** that a Web browser, such as Microsoft Internet Explorer or Netscape Navigator, interprets to display Web pages. You can create Web pages by learning HTML and using it to produce the necessary tags to create the content of a Web page and define its format. You can create an HTML document using an HTML authoring program or a text editor such as Notepad. Notepad does not insert any HTML tags into its document file. Instead, you must write and edit the tags yourself, and, therefore, you need to know each tag's name and its attributes. Writing HTML documents can prove tedious when you are creating a complex Web page. By contrast, FrontPage creates HTML tags automatically so you can create an HTML document without learning HTML. Regardless of the method you use to create a Web page, you can work with FrontPage to open and revise the Web page. The Student Online Companion page for Tutorial 1 has links to other programs that you can use to develop a Web site and resources for learning and understanding HTML.

In addition to creating the HTML document for you, FrontPage includes many features that make it easy to create Web pages and publish Web sites. When you publish a Web site, you transfer copies of the Web site's files and folders to a Web server or other location. If the location to which you have published your Web site is connected to the Internet, publishing the Web site makes it available to people using the Internet.

Web pages are usually classified into two categories: dynamic and static. A **static Web page** is one that displays information that does not change, such as text that describes a business, its address, and a map of the route to that business. A **dynamic Web page** is one that contains data that changes on a schedule, such as stock market and weather data, pricing changes made to a database, and forms that let you search a Web site for a specific keyword. When a Web page contains dynamic content, it must contain instructions to tell the Web server how to process it. A programmer can write small programs, called scripts, to provide these processing instructions. Instead of requiring its users to develop scripts to process dynamic content, you can publish a Web site to a Web server that uses a set of programs and script files called the **FrontPage Server Extensions** or **SharePoint Services**. The FrontPage Server Extensions and SharePoint Services are programs that run on a Web server and provide the processing instructions for dynamic Web pages. You will learn more about the FrontPage Server Extensions and SharePoint Services in Tutorial 6.

You can create and publish a FrontPage Web site on your computer, on a local area network, or on a Web server connected to the Internet. A **local area network (LAN)** is a group of computers that are located near one another and connected so as to share data, files, software, and hardware. By starting with a **disk-based Web site**, which lets you store and retrieve Web pages on a computer's disk drive, you will be able to test the Web site before making it accessible to Internet visitors. To access a disk-based Web site, you use a drive letter and the page's pathname with backslashes—for example, C:\My Webs\garden\index.htm. Some Web sites are created as disk-based Web sites on the developer's computer or on a LAN to control access to the site and to test its functionality. Because you must publish a Web site to a Web server running the FrontPage Server Extensions or SharePoint Services, the testing of more advanced features of a Web site, such as the ability to process forms or conduct searches, requires a server. A **server-based Web site** uses Web server software that is installed on either a client or a server. You open a server-based Web site by typing the prefix "http:"

and the file's pathname with forward slashes—for example, http://localhost/garden/index.htm. The computers in the offices of the Sunshine Landscape & Garden Center are configured in a LAN. You tell Brett that he can create a disk-based Web site and then publish it to his computer's server to test its functionality, appearance, and content. When he is satisfied that the Web site is complete and functioning correctly, he can publish it to the Web server at the ISP he has chosen to host it, making it accessible to Internet visitors. At that point, Brett would need to continue testing the site on the ISP's server to make sure that everything works as expected.

Before getting started on creating the actual Web site, you tell Brett that the most important first step is to plan the Web site's development. Using the five-part process that you'll teach Brett will ensure a successful site.

Developing a Web Site

The task of developing a Web site might be undertaken by an individual or by a team of people working together to meet certain established goals. A Web site often results from the efforts of a development team consisting of a copywriter, an editor, a graphic designer, a programmer, a systems administrator, and a marketing representative, with a Web design director, sometimes called a **webmaster**, as the team's coordinator. Figure 1-1 shows some of the general responsibilities of each team member. Individuals who own a small business or who have information to put on the Internet sometimes create and develop their own Web sites without the input from a team.

| Figure 1-1 | Web development team |

Graphic designer
develops the Web site's visual appearance and creates graphic images.

Marketing representative
establishes the Web site's goals and controls the organizational presence.

Copywriter and editor
prepares and evaluates content.

Web design director (webmaster)
manages Web development and coordinates team activities.

Systems administrator
knows Web server limitations, maintains system hardware, and manages security and access.

Programmer
creates HTML documents and develops server processing.

Regardless of who is responsible for developing a Web site, FrontPage makes it easy to perform the various activities required to create and maintain it because FrontPage generates the HTML documents as well as the scripts and other programs required to create your Web site. In addition, FrontPage includes a collection of clip-art images and other graphics that you can use to enhance your site's appearance. The Internet itself is also a great resource for beginning Web site developers, as many sites provide free graphics and scripts that you can use to enhance your own site. The Student Online Companion page for Tutorial 1 includes links to resources that provide graphics and other design information that you might find helpful when developing your own Web site.

Developing a Web site is a multitask process that includes the following activities:

- Defining the goal and purpose of the Web site
- Determining and preparing the Web site's contents
- Designing the Web site
- Building the Web site
- Testing the Web site

Your first objective is to meet with Brett to define the site's overall goal and purpose to ensure that the Web site you develop will meet the needs of its visitors.

Defining the Goal and Purpose of the Web Site

As the first step in creating a Web site, you must clearly define the site's goal and purpose. What do you want to achieve with your site? What will a Web site help you accomplish that other marketing media cannot? Who is your target audience? After meeting with Brett and several other key employees at the nursery, you determine that the Sunshine Landscape & Garden Center wants to develop a Web site that promotes the services provided by the nursery and offers information about products and plants sold at the nursery.

After agreeing on the Web site's goal and purpose, you meet with the people responsible for different services offered by the nursery, such as irrigation, landscape design, and rock work, to obtain the preliminary information necessary to begin developing the site. Specific factors to consider when planning a Web site include the following:

- **Primary intent:** What is the purpose of the Web site? Will you use the Web site to promote the business, accept online orders, or provide information?
- **Short- and long-term goals:** What specific goals should the Web site meet? For example, do you want to market your company's products to boost sales or to increase the company's visibility?
- **Intended audience:** Who do you want or expect to visit your Web site? What research have you completed to describe your site's target audience? What information does your audience need? Have you completed any research about the browsers your audience will use to access the Web site?

Most Web sites include multiple Web pages that are linked together in a hierarchy. The site's top-level page, called the **home page**, includes hyperlinks to the pages that appear at the next level. **Hyperlinks**, or **links**, are keywords, phrases, or pictures in a Web page that, when clicked using a mouse, connect to related information located in the same Web page, in the same Web site, or in another Web site. A hyperlink might open another Web page or play a video clip or a sound file. The process of using a hyperlink to connect to another location on the Internet is called linking. When you click a hyperlink with your mouse, you retrieve the hyperlink's file from the Web server on which it resides. Your Web browser then opens or plays this file on your computer.

**Computer
History
Hypermedia**

Figure 1-2 shows your notes after talking with several key employees at the nursery. Your Web site plan contains all the information you need to begin working on the Web site for the Sunshine Landscape & Garden Center.

Figure 1-2 ► Web site plan for Sunshine Landscape & Garden Center

Web Site Plan

Objectives

Develop a Web site that provides the following information:

- Descriptions of services available at the Sunshine Landscape & Garden Center, including landscape design, rock work, and irrigation, and photographs of completed projects

- Photographs and information about plants and other gardening supplies available for purchase at the nursery

- Seasonal suggestions about plants to install in the area and how to maintain them

- Answers to common gardening questions

- Seasonal suggestions about common gardening tasks to perform during the current month

Requirements

The following information is required to complete the Web site:

- Descriptions of landscape design, rock work, and irrigation services

- Information about plants, their care, and how to install them

- Monthly gardening feature

- Photographs of completed landscaping projects, plants and gardening supplies available for purchase, and different rocks and landscaping materials available

- Information about irrigation services

- The company's logo

Results

The Web site will contain the following main pages:

- Home page

- Garden Center page

- Landscape & Rock Work page

- Bulk Goods page

- Irrigation page

Determining and Preparing the Web Site's Contents

After completing your Web site plan, you are ready to begin developing the Web site's contents. You should gather relevant documents, workbooks, presentations, and other data that you might use or adapt for use in the Web site. As part of this step, you might need to revisit people who were involved in planning the Web site to see if they have material that you can use in your Web pages.

Content is the most fundamental aspect of Web design because the success of any Web site ultimately depends on the quality of its information.

Designing the Web Site

Your next step in developing a Web site is to design the site. In the commercial and competitive realm of the Web, good design is crucial. The overall layout and quality of the pictures and graphics in a Web page should enhance the page's contents and make it interesting for its users to view. Web site design is very different from the page designs you find in newspapers, magazines, and other print media. For example, it's fine in a print publication to include long blocks of text with few pictures or graphics. In a Web page, however, you need to use headings and graphics to make your content easy to view and read on a computer screen. In addition, you have to develop your site for users who view it with different Web browsers, operating systems, monitors, and screen resolutions. You also need to develop your site with individual users in mind. A site geared toward college-aged visitors should look very different than a site developed for seniors. Your selection of graphics, fonts, and other design elements can make the site look very appealing to your target audience or it can turn them away.

During the design stage, you should ask and answer questions related to your company's organizational image. What message is your company trying to convey? What distinguishes your organization from its competitors? Should the Web site be classic, stylish, or contemporary? You should also determine other factors that can influence the site's appearance. Depending on your target audience and Web site goals, these factors might include selecting a specific type style to use in your pages or developing custom graphics.

Armed with the answers to these questions, you can sketch a design of the site, including its individual pages. In this way, you can plan the relationships among Web pages before creating them and connecting them using hyperlinks. Figure 1-3 shows your plan for linking the pages in the Web site for the Sunshine Landscape & Garden Center. The plan specifies which Web pages you must create and the likely hyperlinks that will connect the Web pages.

Preliminary sketch of the Web site | **Figure 1-3**

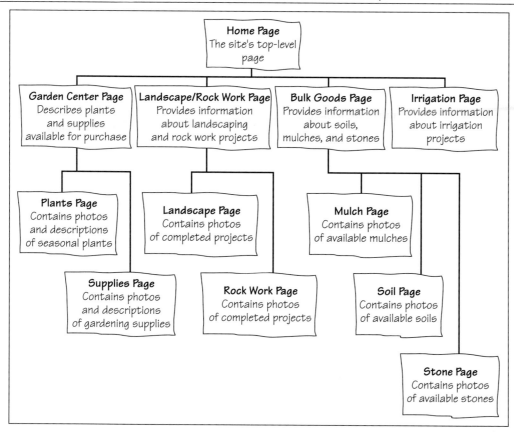

With your Web design plan in place, you can begin developing the Web pages. You will create all of the pages for the Web site as you work through the tutorials in this book.

Building the Web Site

As you transform your Web site's plan into a Web site, it is important to recognize that Internet Explorer and other popular Web browsers, such as Netscape Navigator, might display your pages in slightly different ways. When creating a Web site, you should always test your pages in different browsers to ensure that your pages will be displayed correctly. Fortunately, FrontPage includes an option that you can set before developing any Web pages to ensure compatibility with certain browsers and Internet technologies. For example, if your research indicates that your Web site will be viewed using both Internet Explorer and Netscape Navigator, you might choose to develop it with the settings enabled for creating pages that are supported by both browsers. When you set this option, FrontPage dims commands that are not supported by both browsers. If you do not have information about which browsers will access your site, you can ask your ISP or visit Internet Web sites that conduct browser research to learn more about popular Web browsers used by Internet visitors. The Student Online Companion page for Tutorial 1 includes links to companies that conduct research about the popularity of different Web browsers.

Another important consideration during this phase is that the best Web sites are visually appealing, convey information correctly and succinctly, and download quickly. Keep the following guidelines in mind while you are building a Web site:

- Know and adhere to the stated goals for the site as you decide how to present its information.
- Consider your audience's reaction to every piece of information and every picture to be included.
- Include components that download quickly. People often leave a site if downloading its pages takes too long. Large pictures can download slowly; if you must include them, provide an option to download them as separate Web pages.
- Make the site visually appealing. Strike a balance between a site design that is too simple and one that is chaotic. Make the text large enough for easy viewing, and use color and font variations to draw attention to items. However, don't use so many different fonts, colors, or features on a page that the excessive formatting becomes distracting.
- Organize your content into groups of related information. For example, if you are designing a Web site for a bookstore, arrange the material according to subject areas.
- Include appropriate navigation options, including hyperlinks that make it easy to return to the home page. Users should be able to move around easily within your site.
- Contact your ISP to inquire about any special naming conventions for your Web site and its pages. For example, some Web servers will only process pages with filenames that use all lowercase letters. Some ISPs also place restrictions on the use of spaces and special characters (such as $ and #) in filenames because some Web servers do not support files containing spaces and special characters in their filenames. Another common restriction is limiting filenames to eight characters. There might be other restrictions on the name of the home page, how to name the Web site's folder, and the features you can include in your Web site. The best way to plan for these types of conventions and restrictions is to know in advance about the filename conventions and restrictions that the ISP you choose to host your site will enforce. You tell Brett that a good rule of thumb is to use only lowercase letters in filenames and no spaces or special characters, and to limit the size of your filenames to eight characters. You will use these conventions when developing the Sunshine Landscape & Garden Center Web site.

Testing the Web Site

The final step in developing a Web site is to test it. This step includes verifying that all hyperlinks work correctly and that all multimedia files are available. You should thoroughly test a Web site before and after publishing it to a Web server. In these tutorials, you will test Web pages using FrontPage and a browser. It is also important to test your Web site using different browsers, and different versions of those browsers, to ensure that all pages function and appear correctly.

Starting FrontPage

Through the five-part Web development process, you and Brett identified a clear vision of the Web site to be developed for the Sunshine Landscape & Garden Center, and you are ready to begin creating the Web site. First, however, you need to start FrontPage and explore some important features of the FrontPage program window.

To start FrontPage:

1. Make sure that you know the location of the Data Files that you will use as you complete the tutorials in this book, and the location where you will create your Web sites.

   Trouble? You must have the FrontPage Data Files to complete the tutorials in this book. The "Read This Before You Begin" section of this book includes information about where to get the Data Files and how to use them.

   Trouble? The steps in this book are written for students who will create their Web sites in the following folder on their computer's hard drive: C:\My Webs\[StudentName], where "[StudentName]" is your first and last name. However, you can create your Web sites in any folder or on any network or server that supports FrontPage Web sites. If you are unsure of the location where you will create your Web sites for this book, ask your instructor or technical support person for assistance.

2. Click the **Start** button on the taskbar, point to **All Programs**, point to **Microsoft Office**, and then click **Microsoft Office FrontPage 2003** to start FrontPage. A blank Web page opens in the FrontPage program window. See Figure 1-4.

| Figure 1-4 | Microsoft FrontPage program window |

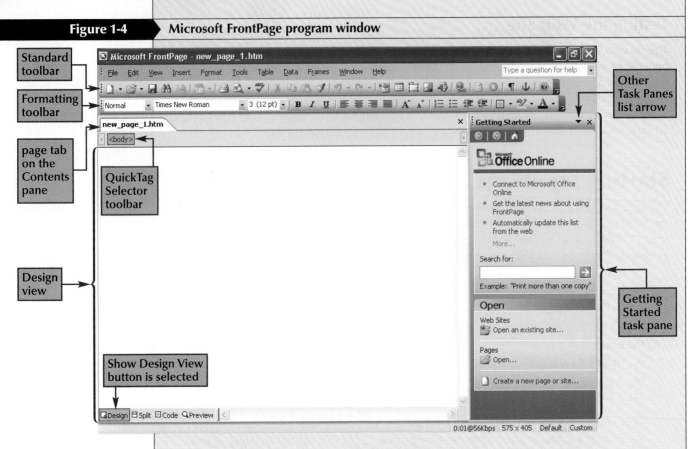

Trouble? If a User Name dialog box opens and asks you to enter your full name and initials, provide this information in the appropriate text boxes, and then click the OK button.

Trouble? If a dialog box opens and asks whether you would like to make FrontPage your default Web page editor, click the No button.

Trouble? If your Microsoft FrontPage 2003 title bar contains a path to a Web site (such as C:\My Webs\site), click File on the menu bar, and then click Close Site to close it. If you want to set FrontPage so that it doesn't automatically open the Web site that was open the last time FrontPage was used, click Tools on the menu bar, click Options, click the General tab, and then click the Open last Web automatically when FrontPage starts check box to clear it. Click the OK button to close the Options dialog box.

Trouble? If the Show Design View button shown in Figure 1-4 is not selected, you are in a different Page view. Click the Show Design View button to change to Design view.

Figure 1-4 shows the default FrontPage program window. Before creating the garden Web site, you want to tell Brett about some important FrontPage features.

When you first start FrontPage, a new Web page opens in the Design view window within the Contents pane. By default, this page is named new_page_1.htm. This filename appears as a tab at the top of the Contents pane. As you open and create other Web pages, their filenames will appear on new tabs. You can switch between Web pages by clicking these tabs.

The area below the tabs, called the **QuickTag Selector toolbar**, shows the HTML for the content in the Web page that contains the insertion point. Because you are viewing a Web page with no content, only the <body> tag appears on the QuickTag Selector toolbar. If you click an HTML tag on the QuickTag Selector toolbar, the text affected by that tag is selected in the Web page and you can use the QuickTag Selector toolbar to make changes to the selected text. This feature makes it easy for you to examine the HTML tags that format the selected text and to make changes to text affected by the tags.

When you first start FrontPage, the Getting Started task pane opens on the right side of your screen. You can use the options in the Getting Started task pane to search for Help on a specific topic, or to create or open a Web site or create or open a Web page. Clicking the Other Task Panes list arrow displays a list of other task panes, as shown in Figure 1-5. Notice that there are task panes for a variety of common tasks you might perform when working in a Web site, such as creating tables or inserting clip-art images. As you work in FrontPage, the task pane sometimes might close automatically so you can see more of the Web page on which you are working; you can close the task pane yourself by clicking the Close button on its title bar. In addition, as you work in FrontPage, different task panes might open automatically to provide shortcuts for working on the current task. The shortcuts available in the different task panes are also available through the menu commands and toolbar buttons.

Task pane options  Figure 1-5

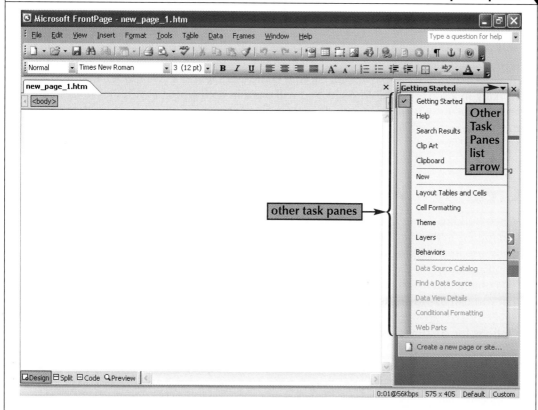

Finally, just as in other Office programs, you can customize the toolbars and menu bars in FrontPage so that the Standard and Formatting toolbars appear on one or two rows, and so that menus show your frequently used commands first. To change these settings, click Tools on the menu bar, click Customize, and then click the Options tab. If you want your screens to match the ones shown in this book, change your settings to match those shown in Figure 1-6.

Figure 1-6 ▶ **Customize dialog box**

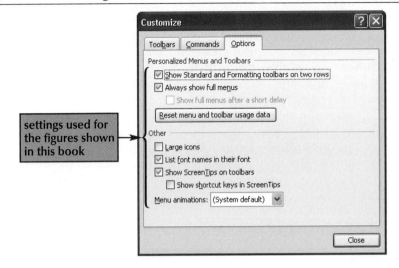

settings used for the figures shown in this book →

If you are storing the Web sites that you create in this book on your computer's hard drive, on a removable drive (such as a Zip drive), or on a network drive, you are working in a disk-based Web site. If you are storing your Web sites on a Web server, then you are working in a server-based Web site. You will work in both types of Web sites in this book. Your instructor or technical support person will advise you of any differences that you might encounter while working through the tutorials in this book and where to create your Web sites.

Creating a Web Site

When building a new Web site, you must first create a folder in which to store the files and folders in the site. A **Web folder** is a Windows folder, similar to a folder that you might use in other programs, but it is configured to store a Web site. You always use FrontPage to create the folder for your Web site. The Web site that you create depends on the content that it will contain. Figure 1-7 describes the various templates and wizards that you can use to create a new Web site.

Figure 1-7 ▶ **Options for creating a new FrontPage Web site**

Template or Wizard	Description
One Page Web Site	Creates a Web site that contains one blank page named index.htm or Default.htm, which becomes the site's home page
Corporate Presence Wizard	Creates a Web site with pages that a corporation might use
Customer Support Web Site	Creates a Web site that contains pages useful for companies providing customer support, particularly software companies
Database Interface Wizard	Creates a Web site that you can connect to a database in which you can add, view, update, and delete records
Discussion Web Site Wizard	Creates a Web site that contains a table of contents, full-text searching capability, and threads organized around a specific discussion topic
Empty Web Site	Creates a Web site that contains no pages
Import Web Site Wizard	Creates a Web site that contains pages imported from another location, such as another Web site or a hard drive

		Figure 1-7
Options for creating a new FrontPage Web site (continued)		

Template or Wizard	Description
Personal Web Site	Creates a Web site that an individual might use to publish pages about his or her interests and favorite Web sites
Project Web Site	Creates a Web site that contains a list of members, a schedule, status information, and a discussion archive related to a specific project
SharePoint Team Site	Creates a Web site with tools that group members can use to collaborate on a project, including a calendar, a library for storing shared documents, a tasks list, and a contacts list

Because you need to create a Web site that includes a home page for the Sunshine Landscape & Garden Center, you will use the One Page Web Site template. After creating the Web site, you will add pages and other content to it.

To create the garden Web site:

1. Click the **Other Task Panes** list arrow, and then click **New** to display the New task pane. This task pane contains options for creating new Web pages and Web sites. See Figure 1-8.

New task pane | Figure 1-8

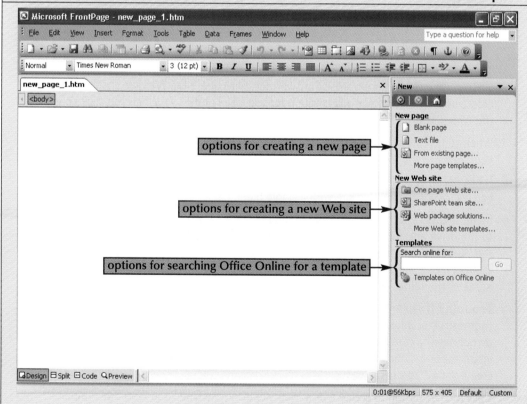

2. In the New Web site section of the New task pane, click **More Web site templates**. The Web Site Templates dialog box opens. See Figure 1-9.

Figure 1-9 **Web Site Templates dialog box**

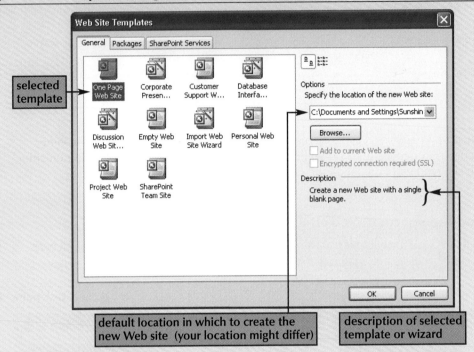

selected template

default location in which to create the new Web site (your location might differ)

description of selected template or wizard

The options in this dialog box let you create a new Web site using one of six templates, or you can use one of four wizards to answer questions about the Web site that you want to create and then FrontPage will create it for you (see Figure 1-7). When you click an icon in the Web Site Templates dialog box, its description appears in the Description section.

When you create a new Web site, you must select a template or wizard on which to base your new site and the location in which to store the Web site's files and folders.

3. If necessary, click the **One Page Web Site** icon. Notice that the Description box shows that you will create a new Web site with a single blank page.

4. Select the text in the Specify the location of the new Web site text box, type the path to the drive and folder where you will create your Web site, and then type the name of the Web site that you will create, **garden**. The path used in the figures in this book is C:\My Webs\[Student Name]\garden; "garden" is the name of the Web site and the name of the folder that will store the Web site's files.

Trouble? If you are storing your Web sites on a different drive or in a different folder, your instructor might provide you with a location different from that given in Step 4. You do not need to store your Data Files and your Web sites in the same location. Ask your instructor or technical support person for help if you are unsure of the location in which to create your Web sites.

5. Click the **OK** button to create a new Web site using the One Page Web Site template. FrontPage creates the garden Web site in the location you specified and closes the New task pane. When you create a new Web site, FrontPage creates some folders and hidden files that it uses to run the Web site. Because you used the One Page Web Site template to create the garden Web site, FrontPage also created a home page named index.htm. (If you created your Web site on a server, FrontPage names the home page Default.htm.) The garden Web site appears in Figure 1-10.

Web site in Folders view | **Figure 1-10**

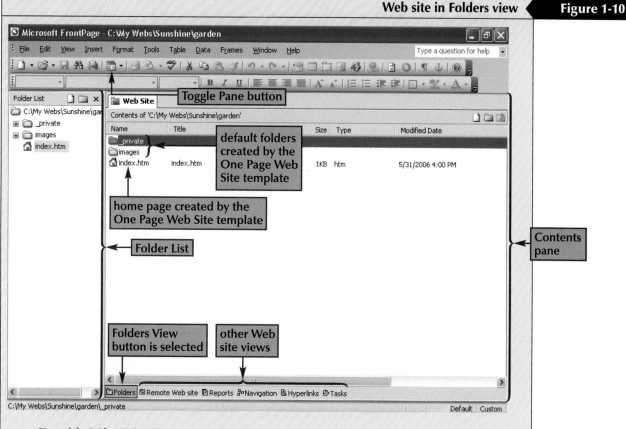

Trouble? If a dialog box opens and indicates that FrontPage must convert this folder to a FrontPage Web site, click the Yes button to continue.

Trouble? If your Folder List is hidden, click the Toggle Pane button 🗐 on the Standard toolbar to display it.

Notice that the FrontPage program window has a different appearance when it displays a Web site instead of just the Web page shown in Figure 1-4. A Web site is a collection of folders and files for an entire site, and not just a single Web page. Because a Web site is more complicated than a single Web page, FrontPage displays additional features to make it easy for you to view the entire contents of a Web site. Notice the Folder List that opens on the left side of your screen. The Folder List shows the root folder (also called the root Web) for the current Web site, which in this case is the garden folder. The garden folder includes two subfolders, _private and images, and the home page file, index.htm, that FrontPage created. The three buttons on the Folder List let you create a new Web page 🗋, create a new folder 📁, and close the Folder List ✕ . You can click the Toggle Pane button 🗐 on the Standard toolbar to open and close the Folder List. Displaying the Folder List is a matter of personal preference; you might want to keep it visible as you work in FrontPage so you can see all of the files and folders in your Web site. For this book, however, you will close the Folder List when you don't need it so you can see more of the Web page as you do your work.

The Contents pane shows the same information as the Folder List but provides details about the title, size, file type, last modification date, the name of the author who last modified the file, and optional comments about each file in the Web site (you might need to scroll the Contents pane to see all of these columns). Notice that the path to the current Web site appears on the Microsoft FrontPage 2003 title bar; your path might differ. Finally, the buttons at the bottom of the Contents pane let you change the Web site view and examine other details about the site's files, hyperlinks, and features. You will learn more about Web site views after you have added additional content and hyperlinks to the Web site.

When you used the One Page Web Site template to create the garden Web site, FrontPage created and saved the garden Web site's home page as **index.htm**. It's a good idea to check with the ISP you selected to host your Web site to find out if it has any file-name requirements for a site's home page. Other acceptable names are default.htm and home.htm, and some servers require different filename extensions, such as .html or .php, for a site's home page. A Web browser will recognize any of these files as a Web site's home page.

You tell Brett that when you first create a Web site, you should check the Web site's settings to verify that you are creating pages with features that are supported by the browsers that you expect to access the site. Because FrontPage lets you create features that are not supported by all Web browsers, it also includes options that let you disable certain features so you can easily refrain from using them in your Web site.

Specifying a Browser Version

You checked an Internet Web site that publishes Web browser studies and learned that Internet Explorer is the most popular Web browser used on the Internet. Netscape Navigator is also a popular browser, as are browsers used by different ISPs, such as America Online. FrontPage lets you specify one or more browsers and versions to target when creating your Web pages, so you can be sure that these target browsers can display the pages you will create. When you change the default authoring settings for a Web site, FrontPage will use those settings for all future Web sites that you create, unless you change them. Therefore, it is a good idea to check these settings for all new Web sites that you create to ensure their accuracy.

To change the authoring settings of the garden Web site:

1. Point to the **Authoring Settings** pane on the status bar. Figure 1-11 shows the word "Default" on this panel; your current setting might differ. When you point to the pane, a ScreenTip appears and displays information about the current authoring settings.

Using the Authoring Settings feature | **Figure 1-11**

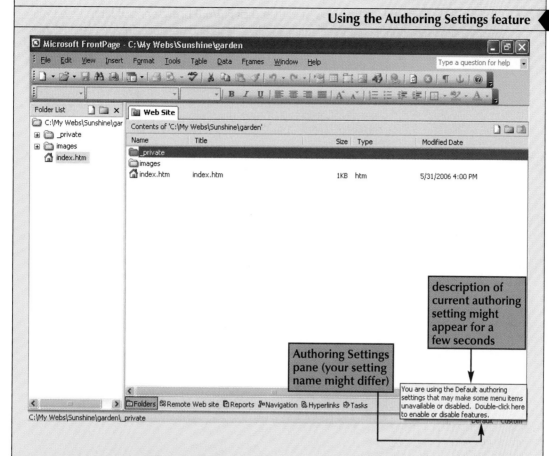

2. Double-click the **Authoring Settings** pane on the status bar. The Page Options dialog box opens with the Authoring tab selected. Read the message at the top of the Authoring tab, which indicates that changing these settings might disable some menu and dialog box options so as to ensure that Web sites you create will contain only those features supported by the browsers and options that you select. In the future, if you attempt to create a feature in a Web site and that feature's menu command is disabled, you can check the Web site's settings to see whether that feature has been disabled.

3. Click the **FrontPage and SharePoint technologies** list arrow, and then click **Custom**. You tell Brett that you will not use Generator and ProgID tags or downlevel image files in the garden Web site, so he can disable these features. You will use Author-time Web Components to create navigation bars and shared borders, so you will enable these options.

4. If necessary, click the **Generator and ProgID tags** check box and the **Downlevel image file** check box to deselect them; then make sure that every other check box in the FrontPage and SharePoint technologies section contains a check mark.

5. Click the **Browsers** list arrow, and then click **Microsoft Internet Explorer only**. FrontPage will allow you to use only those features supported by Internet Explorer. People who access the Web site using another Web browser will still be able to view its content, but the browser might not be able to display some features you have created. You'll identify these features for Brett as he creates the Web site.

6. Click the **Browser versions** list arrow, and then click **5.0/6.0 browsers and later**. When you specify a browser setting, FrontPage automatically selects and deselects Internet technologies that the selected browser(s) and version(s) support. As shown in Figure 1-12, FrontPage changes the settings in the dialog box to enable features supported by versions 5.0, 6.0, and later of the specified browser, Internet Explorer. If you need to change the default settings, you can click the check box for the technology that you want to enable or disable, at which time one or all of the settings for the browser and browser version would change to "Custom," indicating that you have customized the default authoring settings.

| Figure 1-12 | Authoring tab of the Page Options dialog box |

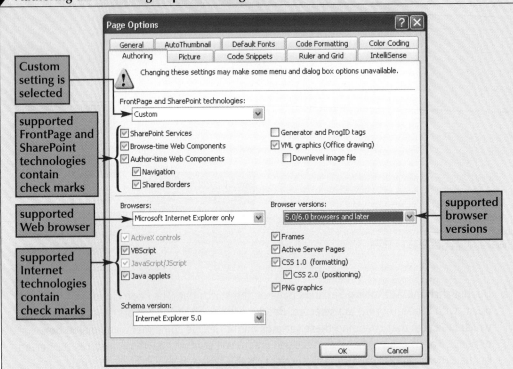

7. Click the **OK** button to close the dialog box. Notice that the Authoring Settings pane shows the "Custom" authoring setting and that the Browser Settings pane next to the Authoring Settings pane shows "IE 5.0/6.0+," which indicates custom authoring settings and support for Internet Explorer versions 5.0, 6.0, and higher.

Specifying a Page Size

If you have experience using the Internet on different computers with different monitors, you might already have discovered that Web pages don't have the same standard dimensions as sheets of paper. When you view a Web page on a computer, you might see the full page or need to use a scroll bar to view all of its contents. Figure 1-13 shows how a Web page might look to users with monitors set to different resolutions. The Web page on the left is being viewed in a browser that displays 640 × 480 pixels. The same Web page on the right is being viewed in a browser that displays 1024 × 768 pixels. A **pixel** is a single point of an image. For most monitors, you can use Windows to control the number of pixels that appear on the screen at the same time. For a monitor set to 640 × 480 resolution, you will see approximately 307,000 pixels on the screen at the same time—640 pixels on each of 480 lines. As you increase the resolution, you will see more pixels and more lines of the Web page. For this reason, monitors with high resolutions display more content.

Comparing the same Web page displayed at different resolutions ◀ **Figure 1-13**

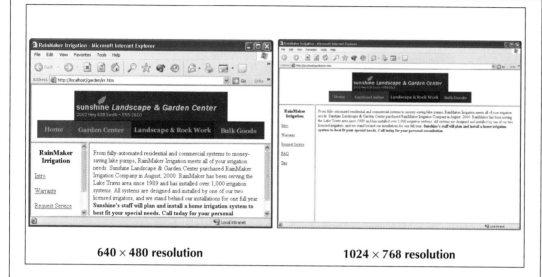

640 × 480 resolution   1024 × 768 resolution

Because people who view your Web pages will use different monitors with different resolutions, part of your testing process should include viewing your Web site using different computers and monitors. In addition, you can use FrontPage to set your default page size. For most Web sites, this page size (or resolution) is 800 × 600. FrontPage includes a feature that lets you set your default page size and change it to see how your site looks when viewed at different resolutions. Brett wants to set the page resolution now so the pages will already be optimized for people viewing the pages at 800 × 600 resolution. You will set the page size by opening the home page, but all other pages that you create in the Web site will use the same page size.

To open the home page and set the default page size:

1. Double-click **index.htm** in the Folder List. The home page, which contains no content yet, opens in Design view. Notice the Page Size pane on the status bar.

2. Click the **Page Size** pane to open a menu of preset sizes. The current page size appears at the top; your value might differ from what appears in Figure 1-14. This menu includes settings for the most commonly used browser settings. You can click a new setting or click Modify Page Sizes to open the Modify Page Sizes dialog box, where you can add, modify, and reset the commonly used settings.

Figure 1-14 | **Home page in Design view**

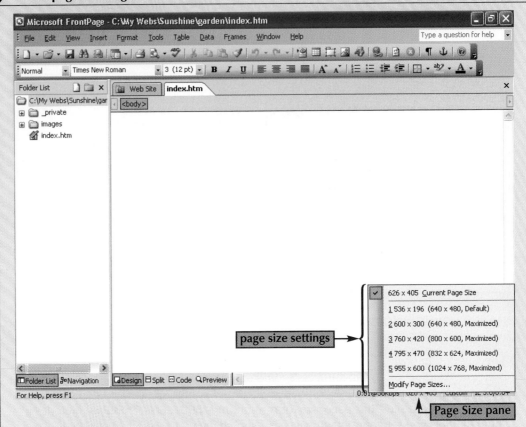

page size settings

Page Size pane

▶ **3.** Click **760 × 420** in the menu. The Page Size pane on the status bar shows that the default page size is locked at 760 × 420 pixels, which is the size allowed for a monitor with 800 × 600 resolution.

Entering Text in a Web Page

After creating a Web site, you can create its individual Web pages. FrontPage automatically created and saved the index.htm home page when you used the One Page Web Site template to create the garden Web site. The home page doesn't contain any content yet, so your first task is to add content to it. Brett wants to add the company's name and address to the site's home page. So you will be able to view more of the home page as you work, you will close the Folder List.

To close the Folder List and enter text in a Web page:

▶ **1.** Click the **Close** button ⊠ on the Folder List. Notice that the name of the home page—index.htm—appears both as a page tab at the top of the Contents pane and on the Microsoft FrontPage 2003 title bar. Because you have not yet added any content to the home page, it is blank.

▶ **2.** Type **Sunshine Landscape & Garden Center**, and then press the **Enter** key. FrontPage creates a new paragraph in the Web page. Notice that the default setting for a paragraph in a Web page is to add some white space between lines.

▶ **3.** On the new line, type **2002 Hwy 620 South**, press the **Enter** key, and then type **555-2610**. You have added the nursery's name, address, and phone number to the Web page.

Brett wants to include information that changes regularly on the home page to make that page more interesting to site visitors. He asks you to speak with Clara McShane, the company's chief landscaper, to see if she has some content you can insert for now.

Inserting a File into a Web Page

You can enter new content for a Web page by typing all the necessary text in Design view. If the content already exists in another text-based file format or in a Word, Excel, or PowerPoint file, you can insert it directly into the page instead of retyping it. When you include content from another file in a Web page, FrontPage automatically converts the new content to HTML. Being able to insert the contents of a file into a Web page allows members of a Web site development team to divide the tasks required to complete a Web page and to exchange information.

Inserting a File into a Web Page   Reference Window

- Place the insertion point where the new content should appear.
- Click Insert on the menu bar, click File, and then use the Look in list arrow to browse to the location that contains the desired file.
- Click the Files of type list arrow, and then click All Files (*.*) to display a list of all available files or click the file type for which you are searching.
- Double-click the desired file to insert its contents.

As you catch up with Clara between jobs, she tells you that she used Microsoft Word to prepare a feature that includes a checklist of information about the tasks that local gardeners should perform during the current month. She prepared the checklist for February. When the site is published, she will give you the correct checklist for the current month. You can insert her text from the Word file to save yourself some typing.

To insert a Word file into a Web page:

▶ **1.** Press the **Enter** key to position the insertion point below the phone number, click **Insert** on the menu bar, and then click **File**. The Select File dialog box opens.

▶ **2.** If necessary, click the **Look in** list arrow, change to the drive or folder that contains your Data Files, double-click the **Tutorial.01** folder to display its contents, and then double-click the **Tutorial** folder to open it.

By default, FrontPage displays only HTML files. You need to display Word files, however, to find Clara's document. Word files have a .doc file extension.

▶ **3.** Click the **Files of type** list arrow to display a list of available file types, and then click **Word 97-2003 (*.doc)** to display a list of Word files.

▶ **4.** Double-click **list.doc** to select this file, to convert its content to HTML, and to insert it into the home page. Figure 1-15 shows the home page with the new text inserted from the Word file.

Trouble? If Windows is configured to hide filename extensions, double-click the list file (without the filename extension).

Trouble? If a Microsoft FrontPage dialog box opens and informs you that it can't import the specified format because it is not currently installed, insert your Microsoft FrontPage 2003 CD into the correct drive, and then click the Yes button. If you do not have this CD, ask your instructor or technical support person for help, or simply type the text shown in Figure 1-15.

Figure 1-15 — **Home page with new content**

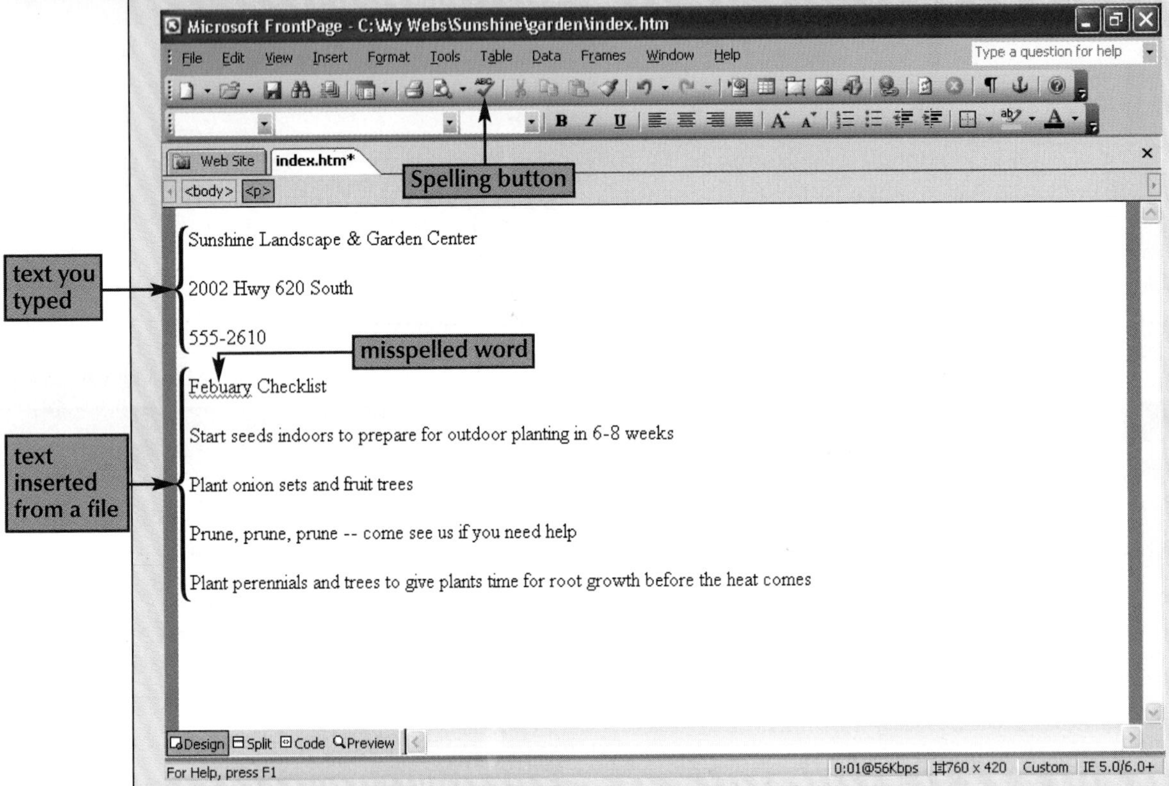

After creating the content of a Web page, you tell Brett that it's a good idea to check the document for spelling errors.

Spell Checking a Web Page

Brett asks you about the wavy red line below the word "Febuary" in the content he inserted from Clara's file. You tell him that this line indicates a word that the dictionary doesn't recognize. To correct a single misspelled word, you can right-click it and then select the correctly spelled word from the menu that opens. To check the spelling in the entire Web page, you tell Brett that he can use the spell check feature.

Reference Window

Spell Checking a Web Page

- Click the Spelling button on the Standard toolbar to open the Spelling dialog box.
- As potentially misspelled words are highlighted in the Spelling dialog box, either click the correct suggestion and then click the Change button, click the Ignore button to accept the original spelling, or type the correct word in the Change To text box and then click the Change button.
- To ignore all instances of a word or to change the spelling of all instances of a misspelled word, click the Ignore All button or the Change All button, respectively.
- When the spell check feature is complete, click the OK button to close the message box.

To check the spelling in a Web page:

▶ **1.** Click the **Spelling** button 🔡 on the Standard toolbar. The word "Febuary" is selected in the Web page and the Spelling dialog box opens with the word "Febuary" displayed in the Not in Dictionary box. See Figure 1-16.

Spelling dialog box ◀ **Figure 1-16**

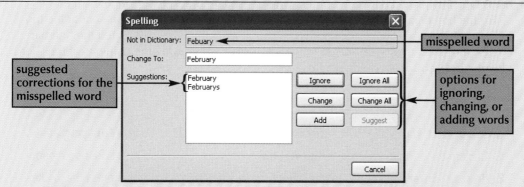

Trouble? If a different word appears in the Not in Dictionary box, you may have typed another word incorrectly. Use the information in the following paragraph to ignore or change the word as appropriate.

Trouble? If you do not encounter any misspelled words in your Web page, then the word "Febuary" is in your dictionary. Click the OK button to close the Spelling dialog box, and then edit the word to change it to "February."

You can click one of the suggested corrections in the Suggestions list box to change the spelling of the selected word, and then click the Change button. Alternatively, you can type a new spelling in the Change To text box, and then click the Change button. If the selected word is spelled correctly, click the Ignore button. You can also click the Change All or Ignore All button to avoid checking the spelling of the same word again. If you want to add a word to FrontPage's dictionary, click the Add button; normally, you should add only those words to the dictionary that you will type often, such as your name.

▶ **2.** Click **February** in the Suggestions list box, and then click the **Change** button.

▶ **3.** If necessary, correct any other misspellings that appear in the Spelling dialog box. When you are finished, click the **OK** button in the message box that opens to tell you that the spell check is complete.

After completing the spell check, you remind Brett that he cannot rely on the spell check feature to catch all of the errors in a document, and that he needs to read everything to make sure that it is grammatically correct before finalizing it.

Adding a Link Bar

Based on Brett's plan for the entire Web site, you know that you need to create the hyperlinks on the home page that will let visitors open other pages in the Web site. Even though you haven't created these pages yet, you can add the text for the hyperlinks as placeholders until you are ready to create the actual pages and the links to them. The feature in a Web page that contains hyperlinks that open other pages in the Web site is called a **link bar**. One way to create a link bar is to type the text you want to use and then format that text as hyperlinks to open other Web pages. Another type of link bar is a link bar component, which is a group of hyperlinks that FrontPage creates and manages for you. Because you have not created any other pages in the Web site yet, you will just type the text to use as the links that appear on the home page.

When you create a link bar using text that you type, you can separate the entries in the link bar using one of several options. One popular way to separate entries is to use characters, such as a vertical bar (|) or square brackets ([ ]), as the separators. A single vertical bar is typically placed between entries, whereas square brackets surround each entry.

For the home page of the garden Web site, you decide to place the link bar at the top of the page and use square brackets as the separators. Brett already created the link bar entries and saved them in a Word document. Instead of inserting the contents of the Word file into the Web page, you decide to show him how to copy the text and paste it into the Web page.

To copy text from a Word document and paste it into a Web page:

1. Click to the left of the word **Sunshine** at the beginning of the first line of the home page.

2. Press the **Enter** key to insert a line before the first paragraph, and then press the ↑ key. The insertion point moves to the beginning of the new line, where you will insert the text for the link bar.

3. Click the **Start** button on the taskbar, point to **All Programs**, point to **Microsoft Office**, and then click **Microsoft Office Word 2003** to start Word.

4. Click the **Open** button 🖼 on the Standard toolbar, click the **Look in** list arrow and browse to the drive and folder where your Data Files are stored, double-click the **Tutorial.01** folder to open it, double-click the **Tutorial** folder to open it, and then double-click the **link.doc** file to open it. This document contains text that you will copy and then paste into the home page.

5. Click **Edit** on the menu bar, and then click **Select All**. The text in the document is selected.

6. Click the **Copy** button 🗐 on the Standard toolbar to copy the selected text to the Windows Clipboard.

7. Click the **Close** button ⊠ on the Microsoft Word title bar to close Word. If necessary, click the **Microsoft FrontPage** program button on the taskbar to return to FrontPage.

   The insertion point appears on the first line of the home page. You will paste the text into this location.

8. Click the **Paste** button 🗐 on the Standard toolbar. The text that you copied from the Word document appears in the Web page. See Figure 1-17.

Copied text added to Web page | **Figure 1-17**

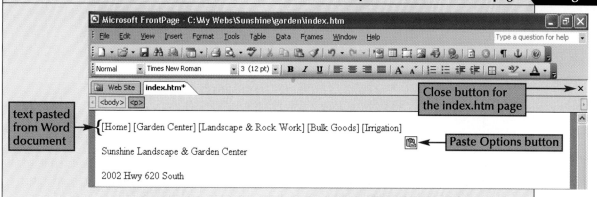

Notice the Paste Options button that appears below the pasted text. The Paste Options button is a **smart tag**, which provides choices for establishing the layout and content of pasted text in a Web page. When you paste text into a Web page, FrontPage provides up to three options related to the format of the pasted text. The first option, Use Destination Styles, removes any styles in the original document in which the text appeared and uses defined styles in the Web page in their place. The second option, Keep Source Formatting, ensures that any formatting applied to the original text is retained in the Web page. For example, if the pasted text uses specific fonts or colors, choosing this option would ensure that these characteristics carry over to the Web page. The third option, Keep Text Only, pastes just the text, without retaining any formatting. Depending on the format of the pasted text, some of these options might not appear in the list. Working with plain text gives you greater flexibility as you work in FrontPage, so you tell Brett to choose this option.

9. Click the **Paste Options** button 📋 that appears below the pasted text, and then click the **Keep Text Only** option button. Now you have plain text, without any formatting. The Paste Options button will disappear when you perform another task in the document. If you don't select an option after pasting text in a Web page, the default selection is to keep the source formatting. If you know that you want to keep the source formatting, you can ignore the Paste Options button and it will disappear when you perform another task.

Brett asks you about the asterisk that appears on the index.htm page tab. You tell him that the asterisk is a reminder that the page contains unsaved changes. Brett is finished with his work on the home page for now, so you will show him how to save it.

Saving a Web Page

Saving your work on a regular basis is important. You use the Save command on the File menu or the Save button on the Standard toolbar to save a Web page. Keep in mind that using the Save command or Save button does not create a separate version of your old Web page; instead, it replaces the old version with the new version. To retain the original file and create a new file, you must save the Web page with a different filename by using the Save As command on the File menu.

Saving a Web Page

- Click the Save button on the Standard toolbar.

or

- Click File on the menu bar, and then click Save.

Brett needs to save the home page before closing the Web site.

To save the home page:

1. Click the **Save** button 🖫 on the Standard toolbar to save the home page. Because the home page was automatically given the filename index.htm when FrontPage created it, the page is saved immediately without requesting a filename. Notice that the asterisk following the index.htm text on the page tab disappears.

Brett's work on the home page is finished, so you will show him how to close the page, the garden Web site, and FrontPage.

Closing a Web Page, a Web Site, and FrontPage

You can close a single Web page, a Web site, or FrontPage by choosing the appropriate Close command. When you close FrontPage, it automatically closes any open page. If you did not save your changes to a Web page, FrontPage will prompt you to do so before closing the page. Next, you will show Brett how to close the home page, the garden Web site, and FrontPage.

To close a Web page, a Web site, and FrontPage:

1. Click the **Close** button ⊠ for the index.htm page to close it. You have not made any changes since the last time you saved the page, so the home page closes. Because there are no other pages open in Page view, the Web site is displayed in Folders view.

   Trouble? If you changed the Web page since you last saved it, a FrontPage message box opens and asks whether you want to save the file. Click the Yes button to save your changes and to close the home page.

2. Click **File** on the menu bar, and then click **Close Site**. The garden Web site closes, but FrontPage remains open.

   Trouble? If you do not see the Close Site command on the File menu, click the double arrow that appears at the bottom of the File menu. The rest of the menu will open and display the Close Site command.

3. Click the **Close** button ⊠ on the Microsoft FrontPage 2003 title bar to close FrontPage.

Brett is pleased with his progress in creating the home page. In the next session, you will teach him how to format the home page to make it more visually interesting.

Session 1.1 Quick Check

1. What is the difference between a static Web page and a dynamic Web page?
2. List the five major tasks involved in developing a Web site.
3. What is a hyperlink?
4. What filename does FrontPage give the home page in a disk-based Web site?
5. Why should you determine and set a default page size before working on the pages in a Web site?
6. What are three ways to enter text into a Web page?
7. What is a smart tag?
8. To close a FrontPage Web site, click File on the menu bar, and then click _____.

Session 1.2

Opening a Web Site

Unlike other programs with which you might be familiar, FrontPage has two "open" options: You can open a single Web page or an entire Web site. In most cases, you will open a Web site so that you have access to all of the Web pages and files that make up the entire site. When you open a Web site, you select the folder that contains the Web site. Because of these two options, the Open button on the Standard toolbar has two options and icons. The first option, Open 📂, lets you open a specific file. The second option, Open Site 📁, lets you open a Web site. The button changes appearance based on its previous use. If you don't see the option you need, clicking the list arrow on the button lets you select either open option.

Opening a Web Site

- Click the list arrow for the Open button on the Standard toolbar.
- Click Open Site in the list.
- Click the folder that contains your Web site.
- Click the Open button.

If you have just started FrontPage, you can use the Getting Started task pane to open an existing Web site. Because you closed FrontPage at the end of the previous session, you will need to open the garden Web site to continue your work. You will open the garden Web site using the Getting Started task pane.

To start FrontPage, open the garden Web site, and open the home page:

1. Start FrontPage. A blank Web page opens in the FrontPage program window, and the Getting Started task pane opens on the right side of the screen.

   Trouble? If the Getting Started task pane does not open automatically, click View on the menu bar, and then click Task Pane.

2. In the Web Sites section of the Open section of the Getting Started task pane, click the **More** link or the **Open an existing site** link. The Open Site dialog box opens.

   Trouble? If the Open File dialog box opens, you clicked the More link or the Open link in the Pages section. Click the Cancel button and then repeat Step 2.

3. If necessary, use the **Look in** list arrow to browse to the location where you are storing your Web sites, and then click the **garden** folder. (The location used in the figures in this book is C:\My Webs\[YourName].) When you use FrontPage to create a Web site, FrontPage adds a blue dot to the folder to indicate that it stores a Web site.

4. Click the **Open** button. The Open Site dialog box closes, the Getting Started task pane closes, and the garden Web site opens in Folders view. See Figure 1-18.

Figure 1-18	Web site in Folders view

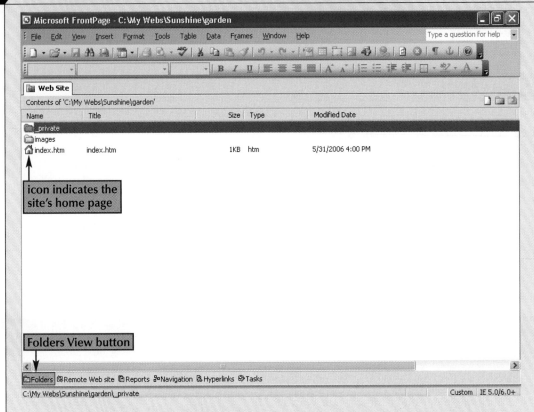

In Figure 1-18, the 🏠 icon indicates that this page is the Web site's home page. If you open the garden Web site in a browser and do not request a specific file, index.htm will open automatically. The other files in the Web site will use different page icons to indicate that they are HTML and other types of documents.

Trouble? If the Folder List opens, click its Close button to close it.

Trouble? If a different view of the Web site opens, click the Folders View button 🗀 Folders at the bottom of the Contents pane to change to Folders view.

5. Double-click **index.htm** to open the home page in Design view.

Now that the home page is open in Design view, you can start formatting the text in the page.

Formatting a Web Page

Formatting is the process of changing the appearance of text in a Web page; it does not alter the Web page's content, but it does make changes to the HTML document that creates the page. You usually work in Design view to apply formatting. You can access the FrontPage formatting options in three ways:

- Use the Format menu commands, which provide access to all formatting commands, ranging from revising paragraph organization to creating numbered lists.
- Right-click the text or an object in a Web page to open the shortcut menu, which provides quick access to many formatting commands, such as those for fonts, numbered lists, or special effects. You can use the shortcut menu commands to apply formatting to specific characters, words, text, or pictures.
- Click the buttons on the Formatting toolbar. Figure 1-19 describes the Formatting toolbar buttons and their uses in more detail.

Formatting toolbar buttons ◄ **Figure 1-19**

Button Name	Button	Function
Style list box	Normal	Lets you apply different styles, such as headings, to paragraphs in your document; contains styles compatible with HTML
Font list box	Times New Roman	Lets you apply a font to a selection; contains fonts that are available on your system
Font Size list box	3 (12 pt)	Lets you apply different font sizes to a selection; contains sizes compatible with HTML, where 1 is the smallest, 7 is the largest, and 3 is the default
Bold	**B**	Changes selected text to bold
Italic	*I*	Changes selected text to italic
Underline	U	Underlines the selected text
Align Left		Aligns the selected paragraph or object to the left
Center		Centers the selected paragraph or object
Align Right		Aligns the selected paragraph or object to the right
Justify		Justifies the selected paragraph
Increase Font Size	A	Increases the font size of the selected text to the next higher HTML level
Decrease Font Size	A	Decreases the font size of the selected text to the next lower HTML level
Numbering		Changes a list of selected items to a numbered list
Bullets		Changes a list of selected items to a bulleted list
Decrease Indent		Moves the indentation of a selected paragraph or object left by one tab stop (0.5 inch)
Increase Indent		Moves the indentation of a selected paragraph or object right by one tab stop (0.5 inch)
Borders		Adds a border to the selected text; use the list arrow to select a border option other than the one displayed on the button
Highlight		Highlights the selected text; click the list arrow to choose a highlight color other than the one displayed on the button or to choose None to remove highlighting from the selected text
Font Color	A	Changes the color of the selected text; click the list arrow to choose a text color other than the one displayed on the button

The first thing that Brett wants to do is to make the words "February Checklist" more prominent. To make this change, you will show him how to format this text as a heading.

Creating a Heading

Headings in a Web page affect paragraphs. In a Web page, a paragraph might be a single line containing one word, a single line containing multiple words, or several lines. The heading options available for a Web page are limited to those defined by HTML tags. HTML provides six levels of headings, identified as h1, h2, h3, h4, h5, and h6. The h1 tag creates the largest font; the h6 tag creates the smallest font. Figure 1-20 shows the default formatting options for the six levels of headings that you can create in a Web page.

Figure 1-20 ▶ **HTML headings**

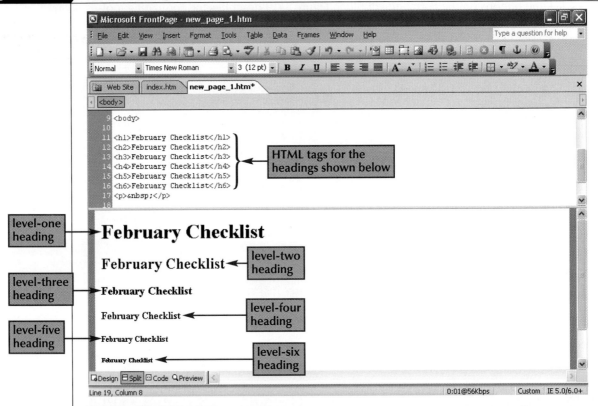

Reference Window

Creating a Heading in a Web Page

- Click anywhere in the paragraph that you want to format as a heading.
- Click the Style list arrow on the Formatting toolbar to display a list of available paragraph format styles, and then click the desired heading style.

Because the words "February Checklist" already exist in the Web page, you only need to select the paragraph that contains them and change their style from the default style, Normal, to a heading. Selecting a paragraph is different from selecting a word or all of the text in a paragraph. To select a paragraph, you only need to click in it to position the insertion point in the paragraph; you do not need to use the pointer to select all of the text in the paragraph. To make the heading prominent, you will format it using the Heading 1 style.

To change text to a heading:

1. Click anywhere in the line that contains the text "February Checklist." Notice that the QuickTag Selector toolbar shows that the HTML <p> tag, which creates a paragraph in a Web page, formats this text.

2. Point to the **<p>** tag on the QuickTag Selector toolbar, as shown in Figure 1-21.

Using the QuickTag Selector toolbar ◄ **Figure 1-21**

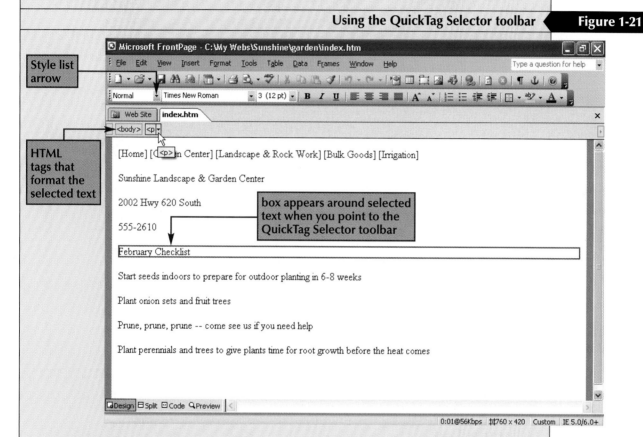

Notice that the paragraph you selected appears with a box around it. If you click the list arrow on the <p> tag, you can select from the options available for formatting paragraphs and the change you make will appear in the selected paragraph. You can use this method to make changes in a WYSIWYG (what you see is what you get) environment while at the same time seeing the HTML tags that create and format your text. For now, you will teach Brett how to use the Formatting toolbar to make his changes.

3. Click the **Style** list arrow on the Formatting toolbar to display the list of available paragraph styles. These styles correspond to the HTML tags that you can use to define the various paragraphs in a Web page.

4. Click **Heading 1** to apply this style to the heading. Because headings format entire paragraphs, all of the text in the current paragraph changes to the Heading 1 style, which is 24 points and bold.

   Brett wants to format the link bar using a heading. You tell him he can change this text to the Heading 2 style to emphasize it.

5. Click anywhere in the link bar at the top of the page (beginning with "[Home]") to select it.

6. Click the **Style** list arrow on the Formatting toolbar, and then click **Heading 2**. The paragraph changes to the Heading 2 style, which is 18 points and bold.

   Brett thinks that the text in the link bar is too large and wants to reduce its size.

7. Click the **Style** list arrow on the Formatting toolbar, and then click **Heading 3**. The paragraph changes to the Heading 3 style, which is 14 points and bold. The home page now contains two headings. See Figure 1-22.

| Figure 1-22 | Home page with headings |

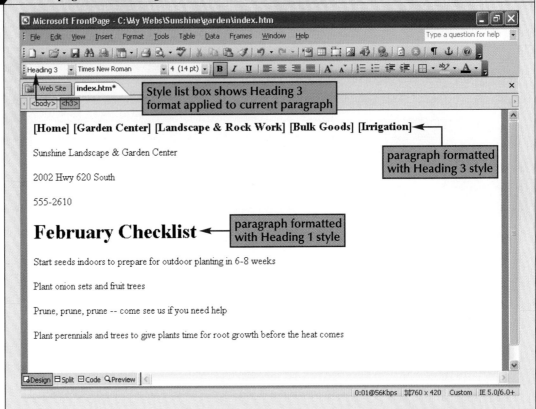

Aligning Text

Like a word-processing program, you can use FrontPage to justify, left-align, center, or right-align paragraphs in a Web page. When you type text in a Web page, the default alignment is set to left. You can use the alignment buttons on the Formatting toolbar to change text alignment.

| Reference Window | **Aligning a Paragraph in a Web Page** |

- Click in the paragraph you want to align.
- Click one of the alignment buttons on the Formatting toolbar to apply the desired alignment.

or

- Right-click the paragraph to open the shortcut menu, click Paragraph, click the Alignment list arrow, click the desired alignment, and then click the OK button.

Brett wants to center the paragraph that contains the link bar and the heading that contains the words "February Checklist."

To center a paragraph in a Web page:

1. With the insertion point positioned in the paragraph that contains the link bar at the top of the page, click the **Center** button ▤ on the Formatting toolbar to center the paragraph.

2. Click anywhere in the paragraph that contains the words "February Checklist."

3. Click ▤ to center the paragraph. See Figure 1-23.

Home page with aligned paragraphs | **Figure 1-23**

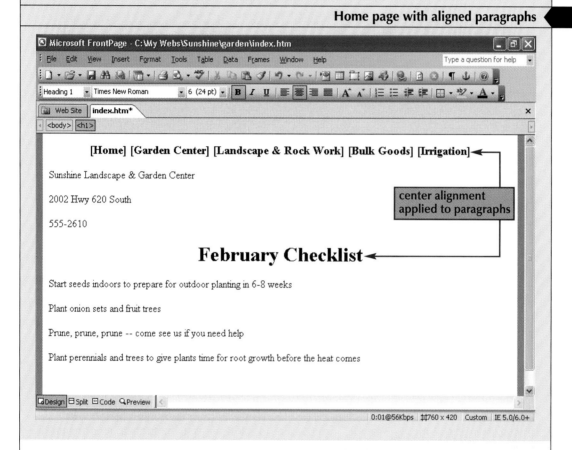

Using Fonts

A **font** is a design for a set of letters, numbers, and symbols distinguished by their typeface, point size, and style. When you select fonts to use in your Web pages, you need to keep several things in mind. First, a font is a group of characters that is installed on your computer. When you install a program, such as FrontPage, on your computer, the program might install fonts with it. Or, you can install fonts on your computer by downloading them from Web sites or from standalone programs that install fonts. Thus, the fonts you have on your computer are ones that you have installed, which might not match the fonts another user has on his or her computer. Because the user's browser can display only fonts that are installed on the user's computer, you have to be careful about which fonts you use in your Web pages. If you format text using a font that a site visitor doesn't have on his or her computer, the user's browser will substitute another font in its place. Sometimes, the browser might select a font that's close to the one you used in your Web page; other times, the font might be quite different in appearance or, even worse, it might be a collection of symbols (like the Wingdings font). The safest fonts to use in a Web page are Times New Roman and Arial, because most computers have these fonts. Other fonts that are commonly installed on computers are Verdana, Georgia, Comic Sans, Trebuchet MS, Impact, Arial Black, and Courier New. Figure 1-24 shows some sample text using each of these fonts.

Figure 1-24 **Commonly installed fonts**

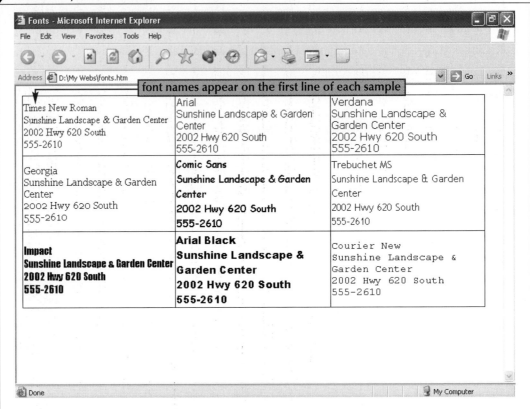

The second thing to keep in mind when selecting a font is that different fonts convey different messages. In most business correspondence, Times New Roman is a frequently chosen font because it is easy to read and has a professional appearance. Receiving an official letter from the CEO of a company that was written in the Comic Sans font, which has a more casual and playful appearance, wouldn't convey the same level of professionalism as a letter written in the Times New Roman font. Likewise, if that letter was written in the Arial Black font, it might be hard to read. In addition to using fonts that your site visitors are likely to have on their computers, you should choose fonts based on the mood you want to create in your pages. If your site is formal, choose Times New Roman. If your site is developed for parents and children, use a more playful font like Comic Sans. If you want an easy-to-read, informal font, use Arial.

For almost any font you use, you can create characters in different sizes and styles. The sizes of fonts are limited to those supported by HTML. Fonts with size 1 are the smallest (8 points), and fonts with size 7 are the largest (36 points). You can also create different styles of text in your Web pages. The default font is called regular; other styles are italic, bold, and bold italic. Some fonts, like Arial Black, already have a bold appearance.

Brett wants to include a copyright notice at the bottom of the home page so it is clear that the Web page belongs to the Sunshine Landscape & Garden Center. You will apply a different font and italics to the text to distinguish it from other text in the page.

To enter and format text:

1. Press **Ctrl + End** to move to the bottom of the home page.

2. Type **Copyright 2006 Sunshine Landscape & Garden Center**.

3. Press **Shift + Enter** to advance to a new line without starting a new paragraph and without inserting a blank line between paragraphs. When you press the Enter key, you create a new paragraph, which has white space above and below it. Pressing Shift + Enter creates a new line in the current paragraph (using the HTML <br> tag), which does not create any additional white space.

    Notice that a dotted line appears near the text you typed. This line tells you that visitors viewing the page with a browser set to 800 × 600 pixels will need to scroll down the page to see the text. In other words, the dotted line represents the number of lines and pixels that visitors will see in one window, based on the page size setting you selected. If your Web page includes content outside the dotted line, visitors can use the scroll bars for their browser to view it.

4. Type **All rights reserved.**

    Now that you've entered the copyright information, you will format it in a different font.

5. Use the pointer to select the two lines that you just typed.

6. Click the **Font** list arrow on the Formatting toolbar. The fonts that are installed on your computer appear in a scrollable list. Notice that the font name appears in the font's face so it is easy to preview the font's appearance. Because you want to ensure that all browsers will render the font correctly, you ask Brett to format the text using the Arial font.

7. Click **Arial** in the list. The Font list box closes and the text changes to the Arial font.

8. With the two lines of text still selected, click the **Italic** button I on the Formatting toolbar, and then click anywhere in the selected text to deselect it. The completed copyright information now appears as Arial, italic font, as shown in Figure 1-25.

New font and italics applied to copyright text   **Figure 1-25**

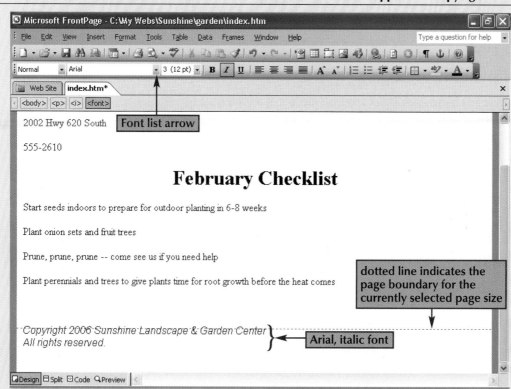

Font list arrow

dotted line indicates the page boundary for the currently selected page size

Arial, italic font

Inserting Special Characters

You can insert special characters, such as the copyright symbol (©), in the text of a Web page just as you can in other types of documents. In FrontPage, you insert special characters using the Symbol dialog box. Brett wants to add a copyright symbol after the word "Copyright."

To insert a special character:

1. Click to the left of the number **2** in the year 2006. You will place the copyright symbol here.

2. Click **Insert** on the menu bar, and then click **Symbol** to open the Symbol dialog box. The copyright symbol, ©, might appear in the list of recently used symbols or you might need to scroll the complete list of symbols to locate it.

3. Find the © symbol and click it. If you do not see the © symbol in the Recently used symbols list, scroll down to the seventh row of symbols, and then click the © symbol (ninth character from the left).

4. With the © symbol selected, click the **Insert** button, and then click the **Close** button. The Symbol dialog box closes and the copyright symbol appears to the left of 2006.

5. Press the **spacebar** to insert a space between the © symbol and 2006.

    When you insert a symbol into a Web page, it's a good idea to change the symbol's font to the same font used in the text in which it appears because the symbol might be inserted from a different font or character set. The text in which the copyright symbol appears is formatted with the Arial font, so you'll change the copyright symbol's font to Arial.

6. Select the first line (which begins with the word "Copyright"), click the **Font** list arrow on the Formatting toolbar, and then click **Arial**. The copyright symbol is formatted using the Arial font.

Changing Font Size

You can change the size of text that appears in a Web page by selecting the desired text and then using the Font Size list arrow or the Increase Font Size and Decrease Font Size buttons on the Formatting toolbar. Just like headings, font sizes are limited to ones supported by HTML. Font size 1 is the smallest, and font size 7 is the largest. However, unlike headings, font changes affect only selected text, and not entire paragraphs. When designing a Web page, you often will need to experiment with font sizes to find the best one for your purposes.

Brett wants to de-emphasize the copyright information, so you need to show him how to change the size of this text so that it is smaller than other text in the page.

To change font size:

1. Use the pointer to select both lines of the copyright information, click the **Decrease Font Size** button A on the Formatting toolbar, and then click anywhere in the selected text to deselect it. The font size is reduced to 10 points, which is the equivalent of HTML font size 2. See Figure 1-26. Notice that the Font Size list box on the Formatting toolbar now displays "2 (10 pt)" to reflect the new size.

Reduced font size for the copyright information ◄ **Figure 1-26**

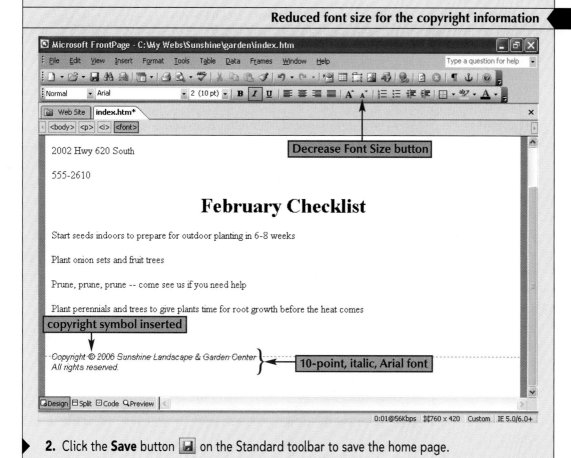

2. Click the **Save** button on the Standard toolbar to save the home page.

Changing Font Color

Although FrontPage lets you select any standard color or create your own custom color, some colors are considered to be "Web safe." If you create a custom color in a Web page using a monitor with high resolution and 16.7 million colors (32-bit color), you might be surprised when viewing the page on a lower-resolution monitor that is set for 256 colors—the colors might look dithered (speckled), washed out (faded), or completely different. Computers with different operating systems (Macintosh, Windows 95/98/Me/2000/NT/XP, and so on) use different color palettes. A color that you create on a Macintosh computer might look different—or even terrible—when viewed on a computer running Windows Me. Although the color palettes of different operating systems are different, they do have 216 colors in common. These colors are called **Web-safe colors** because a browser, regardless of the operating system on which it is running, will display these colors consistently. The Student Online Companion page for Tutorial 1 includes links to sites that identify these colors. FrontPage identifies the 216 Web-safe colors in the More Colors dialog box. If you want to make sure that the color you select will appear consistently for all of your Web site's visitors, select a color from this dialog box.

In HTML, there are 16 colors that are specified using their names. These colors are aqua, black, blue, fuschia, gray, green, lime, maroon, navy, olive, purple, red, silver, teal, white, and yellow. If you want to use shades of these colors or other colors, you must specify the amount of red, green, and blue (abbreviated **RGB**) in the mix that creates the desired color. In HTML, colors are written as a pound sign (#) followed by two characters each to represent the amount of red, green, and blue in the color. For example, the RGB value #008000 specifies the color green. The digits in the RGB value are expressed in

hexadecimal, which is a numbering system that uses 16 characters (0 through f) to represent values in a base-16 numbering system. For example, the RGB value of #008000 combines 00 amounts of red, 80 amounts of green, and 00 amounts of blue to produce the color green. All colors are created through combinations of red, green, and blue.

Brett wants to call attention to the center's name so it will stand out better on the home page. To accomplish this goal, he decides to format this information as bold and change its color to a pleasing shade of blue. To make sure that this color is the same for all of the site's visitors, you will show him how to select it from the Web-safe color palette.

To change font color:

1. Press **Ctrl + Home** to scroll to the top of the home page.
2. Select the text **Sunshine Landscape & Garden Center**, which appears below the link bar.
3. Click the **Bold** button B on the Formatting toolbar to change this text to bold.
4. Click the **list arrow** for the Font Color button A ▾ on the Formatting toolbar to open the color palette, and then click **More Colors** to open the More Colors dialog box shown in Figure 1-27.

Figure 1-27	More Colors dialog box

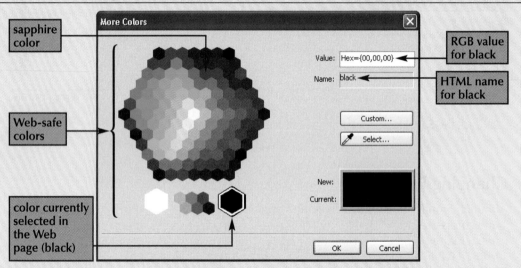

The color palette shown in the More Colors dialog box includes only the Web-safe colors. Any color you select from this palette will appear consistently in any browser that displays it. As you select colors in the palette, the value for the selected color appears in the Value text box. For colors that you can specify by name, such as black or navy, the HTML color name will also appear in the Name text box. For example, the color black is selected. In the More Colors dialog box, its value is Hex={00,00,00} and its HTML name is "black."

If you need to create a different color, clicking the Custom button in the More Colors dialog box opens the Color dialog box, where you can specify colors using RGB values or by clicking the desired color in a color spectrum. Because it is considered good Web design to use the Web-safe colors, you will choose one from the color palette in the More Colors dialog box.

5. Click the **sapphire** color (third row, fourth color tile from the right) to select it. The value in the Value text box should be Hex={00,66,FF}.
6. Click the **OK** button to close the More Colors dialog box and apply the sapphire color to the selected text.
7. Click anywhere in the Web page to deselect the text.

Using the Format Painter

Brett wants to change the center's address and phone number to match formatting he applied to the name. You tell him that he could select the address and phone number, change their text style to bold, and then change their color to sapphire. An easier way to achieve this goal, however, is to use the Format Painter. The **Format Painter** lets you copy the format from existing formatted text and paste it to new text.

To use the Format Painter:

1. Click anywhere in the text **Sunshine Landscape & Garden Center** to select it.

   If you click the Format Painter button once, you can copy the format of the selected text and apply it once to any other text. If you double-click the Format Painter button, you can continue to apply the format to additional locations until you click the button again to turn it off. Brett needs to copy the format and apply it twice, so he will double-click the Format Painter button.

2. Double-click the **Format Painter** button ⬦ on the Standard toolbar to set the button to apply the format more than once.

3. Use the pointer, which changes to a ⬦ shape, to select the address. The text is selected and changes to bold, sapphire text.

4. Repeat Step 3 to change the phone number on the next line to bold, sapphire text.

5. Click ⬦ to turn off the Format Painter, and then click the selected text to deselect it.

6. Save the home page.

Before finishing your work for the day, you want to show Brett how to view the Web page in a browser and how to print it.

Previewing a Web Page

Working in Design view lets you see a Web page as you create it, but this view also includes dotted lines and other formatting to indicate the page size and other features. If you want to see how the page will appear in a Web browser, you can examine it in one of two ways. The first way is to click the Show Preview View button at the bottom of the Contents pane to change to Preview view. Using the Show Preview View button lets you look at the Web page without actually opening it in a browser. In most cases, the appearance of your Web page in Preview view will be the same as or very similar to the way it looks in Design view. The second way is to open the page in a browser. When you click the list arrow for the Preview button on the Standard toolbar, you can choose a Web browser from a list of installed browsers on your computer to open the page. Once you select a browser from the list, you can click the Preview button on the Standard toolbar to preview pages using the Web browser you selected because it becomes your default Web browser.

You tell Brett that browsers can display fonts and other Web page elements differently, so it's a good idea to check your Web pages in one or more Web browsers periodically as you work on them to verify that your pages are rendered correctly in different situations. As you add other features (such as hyperlinks) to your Web pages, you should confirm that they work correctly by testing them in the browser.

Previewing a Web Page

- Click the Show Preview View button at the bottom of the Contents pane.
- Click the Show Design View button at the bottom of the Contents pane to return to Design view.

or

- Click the list arrow for the Preview button on the Standard toolbar, and then select the desired browser from the list that opens.
- Close the browser to return to FrontPage.

So that Brett can use both methods to preview the home page, you'll have him open it in Preview view, and then use the Preview button to open it in a Web browser.

To preview the Web page:

1. Click the **Show Preview View** button [Preview] at the bottom of the Contents pane. The home page opens in Preview view.

2. Click the **list arrow** for the Preview button [image] on the Standard toolbar. A list of installed Web browsers and page size settings opens, as shown in Figure 1-28. Your list of browsers and page size settings might differ, depending on the Web browsers installed on your computer. Clicking a browser in the list starts that browser and opens the current Web page. If you select a screen size, FrontPage will start the Web browser with the indicated screen size. If more than one browser is installed on your computer and you want to preview the Web page using multiple browsers, clicking the Preview in Multiple Browsers option starts all browsers on your computer and opens the home page in each one. You can also select a screen size using one of the Preview in Multiple Browsers options that includes a screen size (such as 640 × 480).

Figure 1-28 | **Options for previewing the Web page using a browser**

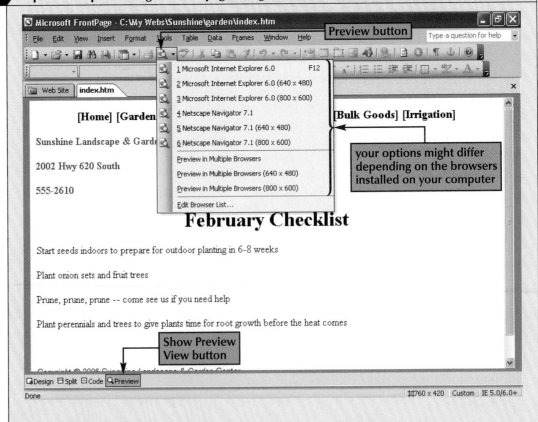

At this time, Brett wants to view the page using Internet Explorer, so he'll select that option.

3. Click the **Microsoft Internet Explorer 6.0** option in the list. FrontPage starts a maximized program window of Internet Explorer and opens the home page, as shown in Figure 1-29.

Home page in a maximized Internet Explorer window 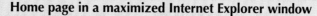 Figure 1-29

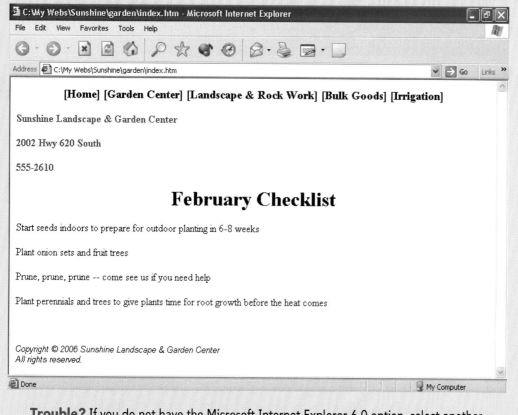

Trouble? If you do not have the Microsoft Internet Explorer 6.0 option, select another browser in the list.

4. Click the **Close** button ☒ on the browser title bar to close it. You want Brett to see how the page looks with 640 × 480 resolution, so you ask him to preview the page in Internet Explorer again, but this time at the lower resolution.

5. Click the **list arrow** for the Preview button 🔍 on the Standard toolbar, and then click **Microsoft Internet Explorer 6.0 (640 × 480)**. Internet Explorer opens again, but this time the window size is set to 640 × 480 resolution. Notice that less of the page is visible in this window. As you work on future Web pages together, you tell Brett that he will need to keep in mind that some users will view the Web pages at this resolution.

6. Click the **Close** button ☒ on the browser title bar to close it.

Closing the Web browser as you are working in FrontPage is a personal choice. You might want to leave the browser open and then use the Refresh button or the Reload button on the browser's toolbar to refresh the page. Refreshing the page loads the most recently saved version of the page in the browser window. If you leave the browser open, you can check the page's appearance in the browser window without having to click the Preview button on the Standard toolbar in FrontPage.

Printing a Web Page

Brett wants to print a copy of the home page so he can share it with other staff members and obtain their feedback. You can print a Web page in Design view using the Print/File menu when you need to change the printer to use or the number of copies to print. If you do not need to change or verify your printer's settings, clicking the Print button on the Standard toolbar prints the page. If the Web page appears in Preview view, you can print it by right-clicking the Web page, and then clicking Print on the shortcut menu that opens. After printing the page, Brett can close FrontPage.

Reference Window	**Printing a Web Page**

- With the page displayed in Design view, click File on the menu bar, and then click Print.
- If necessary, click the Name list arrow and select the printer that you will use.
- If necessary, use the options in the Print range section to print all pages, a specific page range, or a page selection.
- If necessary, use the Number of copies list arrow to select the number of copies of the page(s) to print.
- If necessary, click the Properties button and use the options in the dialog box that opens to change the settings for your printer. Click the OK button to return to the Print dialog box.
- Click the OK button.

After using the Print dialog box to select a printer and change its settings, you can click the Print button on the Standard toolbar to print Web pages in the future. You need to use the Print dialog box only when you need to select a printer or change its settings.

To print the Web page and close FrontPage:

1. Click the **Show Design View** button [Design] at the bottom of the Contents pane to return to Design view.

2. Click **File** on the menu bar, and then click **Print**. The Print dialog box opens.

3. If necessary, click the **Name** list arrow and select the printer that you will use to print your Web page, make sure that the **All** option button is selected in the Print range section, and then click the **OK** button. FrontPage prints the home page using the printer you selected.

4. Click **File** on the menu bar, and then click **Close Site**. The home page and the garden Web site close.

5. Click the **Close** button [X] on the Microsoft FrontPage 2003 title bar to close FrontPage.

In the next session, you will review with Brett some basic HTML tags and their use. Although you and Brett will use FrontPage to create and edit Web pages, it is important for FrontPage users to have a basic understanding of the HTML that creates those pages. If you want to learn more about HTML, the Student Online Companion page for Tutorial 1 includes several resources about working with HTML.

Session 1.2 Quick Check

1. Describe the three methods that you can use to access the formatting commands in Design view.
2. Which HTML heading style creates a heading with the largest font size?
3. Which HTML font size creates the largest font?
4. A set of letters, numbers, and symbols that are distinguished by their typeface, point size, and style is called a(n) _____.
5. What is a Web-safe color?
6. How would you use the Format Painter to apply the formatting of selected text to one other location in a Web page?
7. What are the two methods you can use to preview a Web page?

Session 1.3

Understanding Hypertext Markup Language

As you learned in Session 1.1, Web pages are written in Hypertext Markup Language (HTML). HTML documents use a standard group of characters, called a **character set**, that all computers recognize. In addition, each HTML document contains special tags that a Web browser interprets to display data in the desired format on a client computer. The browser interprets the tags in an HTML document to display the Web page. The tags in an HTML document specify the appearance of text in terms of its font (such as Arial or Times New Roman), its style (such as a heading or bold), or its position (such as a fixed or floating position). An HTML document also specifies the playing of media files, the placement of pictures, and the appearance of the page's background, if these elements are used. A Web browser interprets the HTML tags in a Web page to determine how to display and use these elements on the page.

The name of an HTML tag is enclosed in angle brackets (< >). Most tags are **two-sided tags**; that is, they are used in pairs that consist of an opening tag and a closing tag. The **opening tag** tells the browser to turn on a particular feature and apply it to the document content that follows this tag. The browser continues applying the feature until it encounters the **closing tag**, which tells the browser to stop applying the feature. The forward slash character (/) identifies a closing tag in the tag name. For example, the tags <body> and </body> specify the beginning and end of the body of an HTML document, respectively, and the tags <b> and </b> indicate the beginning and end of bold text, respectively.

Some tags are **one-sided tags** and require only an opening tag. With this type of tag, the browser stops applying the formatting indicated by the one-sided tag when it finishes reading the tag. The HTML <br> tag, which specifies a line break in a Web page, is an example of a one-sided tag.

Figure 1-30 lists some common HTML tags. The ellipsis (...) in the tag indicates the content that is entered by the developer, either between two-sided tags or within a one-sided tag.

Figure 1-30	Selected HTML tag descriptions

HTML Tag	Description	Use
<!-- ... -->	Creates a comment, which is not displayed in the Web page	Identifies the HTML document's content, creator, and other documentation
<a> ... </a>	Defines a hyperlink or an anchor	Indicates an internal or external hyperlink and the file or location that will open
<b> ... </b>	Changes text to bold	
<bgsound src=...>	Specifies a background sound	Indicates the filename containing the sound
<body> ... </body>	Encloses the body of the HTML document	
 	Creates a line break	
<dd> ... </dd>	Specifies a definition within a glossary list	Provides a heading line for a defined term
<dl> ... </dl>	Specifies a definition or glossary list	
<dt> ... </dt>	Specifies a defined term within a glossary list	Provides the font size and indentation information for a defined term
<em> ... </em>	Emphasizes text, usually with italic	
<h1> ... </h1> <h2> ... </h2> <h3> ... </h3> <h4> ... </h4> <h5> ... </h5> <h6> ... </h6>	Specifies a heading and its level	Indicates the format of a heading (h1 has the largest size; h6 has the smallest size)
<head> ... </head>	Encloses the head section of the HTML document	Contains meta tags and the page's title, which appears in the browser's title bar
<hr>	Inserts a horizontal line across the page	Provides a visual break for sections of a page
<html> ... </html>	Encloses the entire HTML document	Identifies the file as one that contains HTML tags
<i> ... </i>	Changes text to italic	
<img> ... </img>	Specifies the appearance of a picture in a page	Inserts a picture file into the HTML document
<li> ... </li>	Specifies an individual element in a bulleted or numbered list	
<ol> ... </ol>	Specifies an ordered list of elements	Creates numbered elements in a list
<p> ... </p>	Divides text into paragraphs separated by blank lines	
<strong> ... </strong>	Strongly emphasizes text, usually with bold	
<table> ... </table>	Creates a table	Organizes data in a row-and-column table arrangement
<td> ... </td>	Defines the data contained in a table's cells	
<th> ... </th>	Creates a row of headings in a table	
<title> ... </title>	Defines the text that appears in the Web browser's title bar	Creates the Web page's title
<tr> ... </tr>	Indicates a row in a table	
<ul> ... </ul>	Specifies an unordered list of elements	Creates bulleted elements in a list

Just as important as the tags themselves is the order of their placement. Tags often appear within each other; this is called a **nested tag**. The browser first processes the tag on the outside, called the **outside tag**; it then processes the tag on the inside, called the **inside tag**. When nesting tags, you must close the inside tag before closing the outside tag. When you create a nested list—for example, a bulleted list within a numbered list—FrontPage handles the opening and closing of each pair of tags automatically. You need to be concerned with nesting the tags only if you decide to make changes directly to your HTML document, which is not the recommended approach when using FrontPage. However, it is helpful to understand how a browser applies different formats to a single code segment.

Many HTML tags require one or more **attributes**, or **properties**, that specify additional information about the tag. When you changed the color of the center's address in the home page, you used an attribute to identify the color for the selected text. Attributes appear within the brackets that enclose the tag.

Even though HTML uses a standard character set to ensure that documents can be easily transferred and viewed by many different types of computers, not all Web browsers will interpret these tags and display the requested Web page in exactly the same way. For example, text that is formatted as bold might be displayed as bold text by one browser and as blue text by another browser. Even with this limitation, the use of HTML in storing, transferring, and viewing HTML documents among the many different computers that are connected to the Internet is the key element in providing a standard method for displaying information.

Viewing the HTML Document That Creates a Web Page

By viewing the HTML document for a Web page, you can see how a particular feature has been implemented using HTML tags. In this book, you will create and edit Web pages using FrontPage. You will also study the HTML document that FrontPage creates to gain a better understanding of how HTML works. Some Web page developers find it easier to make changes directly to the HTML document, even when they are working in FrontPage. You can examine a Web page's HTML document by using FrontPage or a Web browser.

Viewing an HTML Document Using FrontPage

The work you have done in FrontPage so far has been in Design or Preview view. There are two other Page views that let you see the HTML document you have created. You can use Split view to see the HTML document and your Web page at the same time, or you can use Code view to examine only the HTML document that creates your Web page. A nice feature of Split view is that it lets you work in the HTML document and view your changes in the Web page at the same time. Because you think it's important for Brett to understand the HTML that creates the home page, you ask him to examine the HTML document and then to make changes to it to see the results in the Web page.

To examine a Web page in Code view:

1. Start FrontPage, open the **garden** Web site from the location where you are storing your Web sites, and then open the **index.htm** page in Design view. If necessary, close the Folder List.

2. Click the **Show Code View** button ⊡ Code at the bottom of the Contents pane to display the HTML document that creates the Web page, as shown in Figure 1-31. Notice that the text you entered in the Web page and the HTML tag names are black, HTML properties are red, and the values for HTML properties are blue. For example, the tag that formats the text "555-2610" as sapphire text is <font color="#0066FF">. The HTML tag is *font*, the HTML property is *color*, and the HTML value for sapphire is "*#0066FF.*"

Figure 1-31	HTML document for the home page

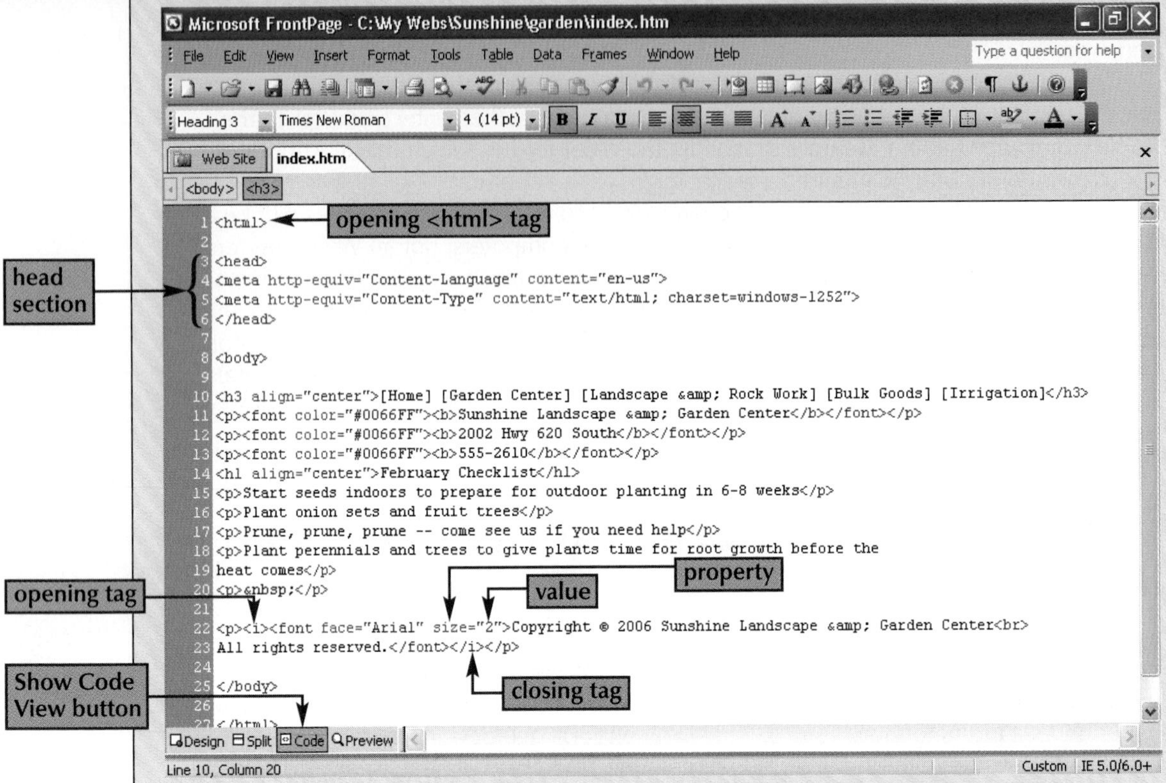

Trouble? You can customize FrontPage to display HTML tags in different ways. The colors in your HTML document might differ. In addition, you might see HTML tags and property names in all uppercase letters. Both of these differences cause no problems.

3. Inspect the HTML document and try to identify which tags provide the formatting instructions that create the home page. As you work through the tutorials in this book, you will learn about the various HTML tags that specify the appearance of the Web pages for the Sunshine Landscape & Garden Center.

4. Click the **Show Design View** button 🖵 Design to return to Design view.

Split view shows the HTML document and the Web page at the same time. When you make changes to the HTML document in Code view, pressing the F5 key updates the Web page in Design view to reflect the changes. Using Split view is an excellent way to see the results of changes to your HTML document, so you ask Brett to make a change using Split view.

To work in Split view:

1. Click the **Show Split View** button 🖵 Split. The size of the Design view window is reduced and the Code view window is added above it, as shown in Figure 1-32. Each window has its own scroll bar so you can examine the complete HTML document and Web page. Code view includes line numbers to make it easy to document and examine the HTML document.

Split view of the home page | **Figure 1-32**

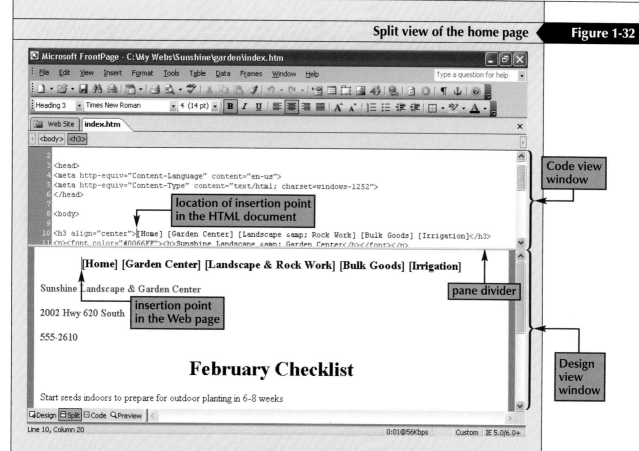

Trouble? The sizes of your Code and Design view windows might differ from what is shown in Figure 1-32. You can increase and decrease the size of the windows by positioning the ⊹ pointer on the pane divider and dragging it up or down to resize the windows.

2. In the Code view window, use the pointer to select the text **Sunshine Landscape & Garden Center**, which appears on line 11. Notice that the ampersand character (&) is written as & in the HTML document. As you select the text in the HTML document, the same text is selected in the Design view window.

   Trouble? The line numbers in your HTML document might differ depending on the way FrontPage is configured to create tags in new documents. If your line numbers are different, just make sure that you are working in the correct line of your HTML document.

3. Click the **list arrow** for the Font Color button 🅰 ⋅ on the Formatting toolbar, click the **Red** color in the menu that opens, and then click the selected text in the Design view window to deselect it. The text in the Design view window is now red, and the HTML document now shows the font color for this text as "#FF0000" for red.

4. In the Design view window, select the text **Sunshine Landscape & Garden Center**, click the **list arrow** for the Font Color button 🅰 ⋅, and then click the **Sapphire** color in the Document Colors section of the menu that opens (the ScreenTip is Hex={00,66,FF}). Click the text in the Design view window to deselect it, and then notice that the text returns to its previous color and the HTML document shows the color property for the sapphire color again.

5. On line 10 of the HTML document, change the opening tag that creates the level-three heading from <h3 to **<h4**. When you make this change, the paragraph it affects is selected in the Design view window. To update the Design view window, you need to press the F5 key.

6. Press the **F5** key and watch the selected text in the Design view window, which changes to the Heading 4 style. To complete this change, you need to update the closing HTML tag as well.

7. Change the closing </h3> tag at the end of line 10 in the Code view window to **</h4>**, and then save the page.

FrontPage includes features that make it easy to type HTML tags directly in Code view. For example, when you type an opening HTML tag, such as <h1> to create a level-one heading, FrontPage will automatically insert the required </h1> closing tag for you. However, when you change existing tags, as you did in Step 7, you need to update the opening and closing tags yourself.

8. Scroll down the Code view window and examine the HTML document that creates the rest of the home page. Notice the opening and closing tags that format the page. The body of the Web page appears within the <body> and </body> tags, and the entire HTML document is enclosed in the <html> and </html> tags. These tags are required in all HTML documents.

By making changes in one view and seeing the results of those changes in the other view, you can learn a great deal about HTML. Brett asks you about the   characters that appear in the HTML document because he cannot see these characters in the Web page. You tell him that this set of characters represents a nonbreaking space, which is created by the character set when you press the Enter key in a Web page to create the equivalent of an "empty paragraph." When you type something in the new paragraph, the text you type replaces the   characters.

Viewing an HTML Document Using Internet Explorer

You can view the HTML document that creates any Web page using a Web browser. This option is convenient when you want to inspect the HTML document for a Web page that was created by someone else and that you opened from a Web site. Next, you will view the HTML document for the home page using Internet Explorer.

To view an HTML document using Internet Explorer:

1. Click the **Preview** button on the Standard toolbar. The home page opens in the default browser for your computer.

Trouble? If you need to change your default browser, close the browser window that opened, click the list arrow for the Preview button on the Standard toolbar, and then select the browser you would like to use.

2. Click **View** on the menu bar, click **Source**, and then maximize the Notepad window, if necessary. Notepad displays the HTML document used to create the home page. When you view the HTML document in Notepad, it's a good idea to turn on the Word Wrap feature so that the lines in the HTML document won't scroll to the right and out of view.

Trouble? If you are using Netscape Navigator as your browser, click View on the menu bar, and then click Page Source to view the HTML document for the home page.

3. Click **Format** on the Notepad menu bar, and then click **Word Wrap**. The HTML document matches the one you viewed in Code view, except Notepad does not use colors to identify content, tags, properties, and values.

Trouble? If the Word Wrap command has a check mark in front of it, then the Word Wrap feature is already on. If you accidentally turned off the Word Wrap feature, repeat Step 3 to turn it back on.

Trouble? If you are using Netscape Navigator as your browser, click View on the menu bar, and then click Wrap Long Lines.

4. Click the **Close** button ☒ to close the Notepad window (or the window that opened and displayed the HTML document for the home page).

5. Click ☒ on the browser's title bar to close it.

Brett asks you about the content of line 4. You tell him that FrontPage automatically inserts tags that identify the file as an HTML document. One important tag that Brett needs to understand is the meta tag, which is important when marketing a Web site.

Using Meta Tags

A Web site can be an effective marketing tool for a company—but only if people are aware that the site exists. Most people find information on the Internet using a **search engine**, which is a Web site that automatically gathers and maintains information about sites on the Internet. Sometimes the process of getting a Web site listed with a search engine is accomplished automatically when a search engine reads the tags in your HTML document and adds your site to its index. An **index** is a database that stores information about specific Web sites. Each search engine uses a different method to index the Web, so your search results using different search engines might vary.

Most search engines gather information about Web sites by either accepting requests from Web site developers to add their sites to the search engine's index or by collecting data based on meta tags entered into the HTML document by the Web page's developer. A **meta tag** is an HTML tag that includes information about a Web page, such as the character set it uses, the name of its developer, how often the page is refreshed, and the keywords and description of the page's contents. (A developer can also use a meta tag to prevent a site from being indexed.) For example, if a user enters the search term "landscaping" in a Web search engine, Brett wants the search engine to find the home page for the Sunshine Landscape & Garden Center. To accomplish this objective, you will add a keywords meta tag with the phrase "landscaping" to the home page. To control how the search engine describes the Web site for the nursery, you'll add a description meta tag to provide the description you want the search engine to display.

In addition to their use with search engines, meta tags provide instructions for Web servers and Web browsers when transferring and interpreting data. FrontPage automatically creates a meta tag in all FrontPage-created documents with properties and values that indicate the page's default character set and content. All meta tags must appear at the beginning of the HTML document in the head section. The **head section** of an HTML document is enclosed by the <head> and </head> tags. Except for the Web page title, which also appears in the head section and is displayed by the browser in its title bar, information stored in the head section does not affect the appearance of the Web page.

Inserting a Meta Tag into a Web Page

Reference Window

- Right-click anywhere in the Web page to open the shortcut menu, click Page Properties, and then click the Custom tab.
- Click the Add button in the User variables section.
- Type the meta tag name in the Name text box, and then press the Tab key.
- Type the desired text for the meta tag in the Value text box.
- Click the OK button.
- Click the Add button, and then repeat the process to add additional meta tags as necessary.
- Click the OK button.

To promote the Web site for the Sunshine Landscape & Garden Center, Brett wants to include indexing information in the home page to increase the chances of the home page being added to the indexes of various Web search engines. You will add two meta tags—description and keywords—to the home page.

To insert meta tags in the home page:

1. Right-click anywhere in the Design view window to open the shortcut menu, click **Page Properties** to open the Page Properties dialog box, and then click the **Custom** tab.

2. In the User variables section, click the **Add** button to open the User Meta Variable dialog box.

   Trouble? If you click the Add button in the System variables section, the System Meta Variable (HTTP-EQUIV) dialog box opens instead of the User Meta Variable dialog box. Click the Cancel button, and then repeat Step 2. (Creating system variables is beyond the scope of this tutorial.)

3. Type **description** in the Name text box, and then press the **Tab** key to move the insertion point to the Value text box. You will use the description meta tag to summarize the Web site's contents.

4. With the insertion point in the Value text box, type **The Texas Hill Country's premiere full-service landscaping center, specializing in rock work, irrigation systems, and landscape design.** As you type, the text automatically scrolls across the text box. See Figure 1-33.

| Figure 1-33 | Adding meta tags to the home page |

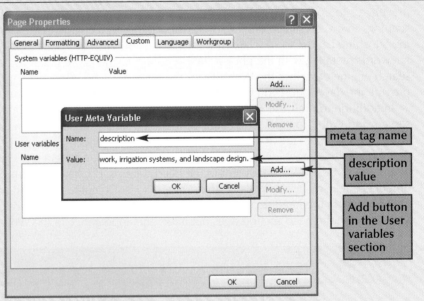

5. Click the **OK** button to return to the Page Properties dialog box. Notice that the text you just typed in the Name and Value text boxes now appears in the Name and Value columns in the User variables section.

6. Click the **Add** button in the User variables section again, type **keywords** in the Name text box, and then press the **Tab** key to advance to the Value text box. Web search engines use the keywords meta tag to catalog your Web site.

7. Type **Sunshine, Texas Hill Country, garden, gardening, flower, plant, herb, landscaping, landscape design, rock work, irrigation** in the Value text box as the desired keywords.

8. Click the **OK** button in the User Meta Variable dialog box to return to the Page Properties dialog box, and then click the **OK** button to close the Page Properties dialog box. Figure 1-34 shows the meta tags you added to the HTML document. Notice that the appearance of the Web page in the Design view window does not change.

Meta tags added to the home page | **Figure 1-34**

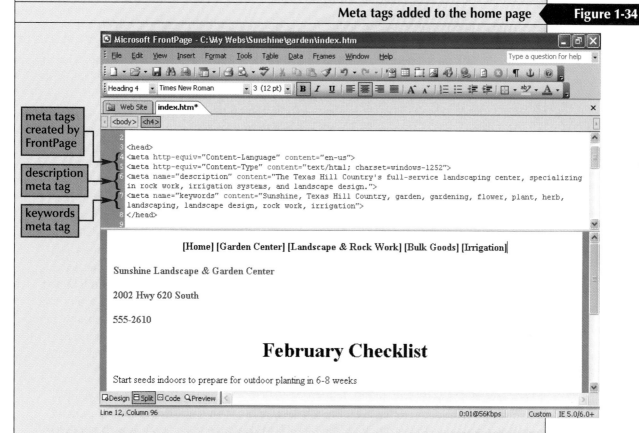

Trouble? If necessary, scroll up the Code view window so you can see the meta tags you added.

Trouble? If the meta tags scroll off the screen instead of wrapping to the next line as shown in Figure 1-34, click Tools on the menu bar, click Page Options, and then, in the Code View Options section of the General tab, click the Word wrap check box to select it. Click the OK button to close the Page Options dialog box.

9. Click the **Save** button 🖫 on the Standard toolbar to save the home page.

10. Click the **Show Design View** button ⬚Design.

As you finish working on the home page, you tell Brett that the process of adding meta tags does not ensure that a search engine will list the nursery's Web site in its results. As you continue working on the Web site, you will need to conduct some additional research to learn how to submit the nursery's site to one or more search engines to make sure that it appears in the search engine's index. The Student Online Companion page for Tutorial 1 includes resources to sites that provide information about using meta tags and getting your site indexed by the many search engines available on the Internet.

As your last task for the day, you decide to show Brett how to get Help in FrontPage, in case he is working on a task and needs additional instructions.

Getting Help in FrontPage

The FrontPage Help system provides instructions and answers common questions for FrontPage users as they do their work. In addition to the Help files that are installed with FrontPage, you can access several online resources that provide additional Help files. The primary benefit of using the online resources is that Microsoft updates these resources frequently. There are several different ways to use the Help system, so you can choose the one that you like best. The different ways of accessing Help are as follows:

- Type a question or keywords in the Type a question for help text box, which appears on the menu bar. After you type your question or keywords, press the Enter key. The Search Results task pane opens and displays a selection of topics that might help you. Clicking a topic in the Search Results task pane opens the Microsoft Office FrontPage Help window and displays the specified Help topic.
- Click the Microsoft Office FrontPage Help button on the Standard toolbar to open the FrontPage Help task pane. You can type your search keywords in the Search for text box and click the Start search button to run your search, or you can click the Table of Contents link to search for information by category. In either case, clicking a topic opens the Microsoft Office FrontPage Help window and displays your requested topic.
- Click Help on the menu bar, and then click Show the Office Assistant to display the Office Assistant, a customizable character that provides a text box into which you can ask a question. (You might need to install the Office Assistant to use it.) The default Office Assistant is a paper clip that opens in the lower-right corner of the screen. Clicking the Office Assistant opens a window in which you can type your question or keywords in the What would you like to do? text box and then click the Search button to run your search. The Search Results task pane opens and displays links to topics that might help you. Some users like to have the Office Assistant always turned on, in which case it periodically provides Help for the task on which they are currently working. If you want to turn off or hide the Office Assistant, right-click it and then click the Hide command on the shortcut menu.

Using the FrontPage Help task pane is an easy way to get Help as you are working in FrontPage. In addition to having a printed copy of the Web page, Brett wants to print the HTML document. To learn how to print the HTML document, you will show him how to use the Help system.

To use the FrontPage Help task pane to get Help:

1. Click the **Microsoft Office FrontPage Help** button 🔘 on the Standard toolbar. The FrontPage Help task pane opens and the insertion point is blinking in the Search for text box.

2. Type **How do I print an HTML document?** in the Search for text box, and then click the **Start searching** button ➡️. Figure 1-35 shows the Search Results task pane, which indicates that Help found 20 topics that might answer your question.

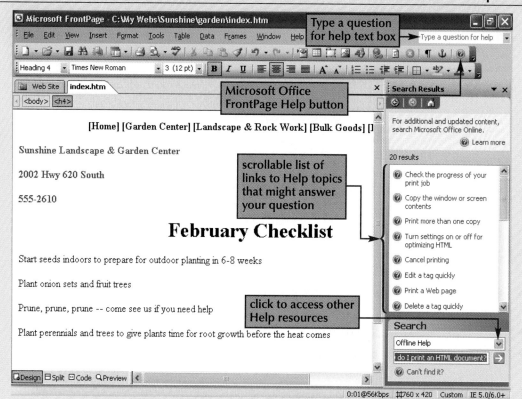

Figure 1-35 shows topics from Offline Help, which is the resource that FrontPage uses that does not require an active Internet connection. If you are connected to the Internet, your Search Results task pane might look different because it might display Help topics from Microsoft Office Online. If you don't find the help you need from the Offline Help files, you can connect to the Internet, click the list arrow in the Search panel, click Microsoft Office Online, and then click the Start searching button → to connect to Microsoft Office Online Help. The offline and online Help resources include many of the same topics; however, the online topics are updated frequently by Microsoft and might provide additional help.

Trouble? If you are connected to the Internet, your Search Results task pane might look different. To display the Offline Help topics, click the list arrow in the Search panel, click Offline Help, and then click the Start searching button →.

▶ 3. Scroll down the search results as necessary, and then click **Print a Web page**. The Microsoft Office FrontPage Help window opens. If necessary, click the **Maximize** button ▫ on the Microsoft Office FrontPage Help window title bar to maximize it. Figure 1-36 shows the Microsoft Office FrontPage Help window, which lists three topics that might answer your question. Notice the Show All link in the upper-right corner of the window. Clicking this link displays all of the information available for the topics listed. After you click the Show All link, it changes to the Hide All link, which returns the topics to the format shown in Figure 1-36.

Figure 1-36	Microsoft Office FrontPage Help window

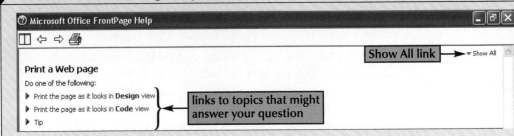

4. Click the **Print the page as it looks in Code view** link. Help displays the steps for printing the HTML document for a Web page.

5. Read the information provided for printing an HTML document, and then click the **Close** button ☒ on the Microsoft Office FrontPage Help title bar to close it.

6. Click the **Close** button ☒ on the Search Results task pane to close it.

7. Change to Code view, and then click line 2 of the HTML document and type your name as a comment (**<!-- Your Name -->**). The comment appears in a gray font.

8. Click the **Print** button ⧉ on the Standard toolbar. FrontPage prints the HTML document for the home page.

9. Save the home page, return to Design view, and then close the garden Web site.

10. Click ☒ on the Microsoft FrontPage title bar to close FrontPage.

After creating the home page and formatting its contents, Brett is excited about continuing his work on the Web site. In Tutorial 2, you will show him how to create additional pages in the Web site and how to add hyperlinks and graphics to the pages.

Review

Session 1.3 Quick Check

1. True or False: Most HTML tags are one-sided.
2. How are the <html> and </html> tags used in an HTML document?
3. Write the HTML tag to italicize the words "home page" in a Web page.
4. How do you view the HTML document that creates a Web page in FrontPage? In Internet Explorer?
5. What is a nested tag?
6. How do you update a Web page when you make changes to the HTML document while working in Split view?
7. What is a meta tag?
8. What are three ways to get Help while working in FrontPage?

Tutorial Summary

In this tutorial, you learned the five-part process for developing a Web site. You used FrontPage to create a Web site with a single Web page, entered and formatted text in a Web page, and learned about HTML. You also used the FrontPage Help system to answer a question as you completed your work in a Web site.

Because FrontPage includes an easy-to-use interface and templates for creating Web sites and Web pages, you will find that it is an easy tool to use to create your own Web sites.

Key Terms

attribute	Hypertext Markup	pixel
character set	Language (HTML)	property
client	index	QuickTag Selector toolbar
client/server architecture	index.htm	RGB
closing tag	inside tag	search engine
disk-based Web site	Internet	server-based Web site
dynamic Web page	Internet service provider	SharePoint Services
font	(ISP)	smart tag
Format Painter	link	static Web page
FrontPage Server Extensions	link bar	two-sided tag
head section	local area network (LAN)	Web folder
hexadecimal	meta tag	Web-safe color
home page	Microsoft FrontPage	Web site
host	nested tag	webmaster
HTML document	network	
hyperlink	network server	
	one-sided tag	
	opening tag	
	outside tag	

Practice the skills you learned in the tutorial using the same case scenario.

Review Assignments

There are no Data Files needed for the Review Assignments.

At a recent meeting, Brett passed around the printout he made of the new home page for the Sunshine Landscape & Garden Center. Everyone was very pleased with the content of the page. However, Brett did receive a few suggestions for changing the way text is formatted, all of which he would like to implement. You'll help him make these changes.

If necessary, start FrontPage, and then do the following:

1. Open the **garden** Web site that you created in this tutorial from the location where you are storing your Web sites. Open the home page (**index.htm**) in Design view, and if necessary, close the Folder List.
2. Select the nursery's name, address, and phone number, which appear on lines 2 through 4 of the home page, and change their alignment to center.

3. Select the link bar at the top of the home page, and then change its color to green. (*Hint:* Use the ScreenTips to find the Green tile in the Standard Colors section on the Font Color menu.)
4. Select the last two lines at the bottom of the home page (the copyright information), and then change the font to Verdana. (*Note:* If you do not have this font, select another font.)
5. Save the home page, and then preview it in Preview view. Scroll the page as necessary to see the changes you made in Design view.
6. Display the home page in Split view, and then use the Code view window to change the font color of the text in the link bar to navy. (*Hint:* Find the RGB value in the opening <font> tag that specifies the current color, and then change the value to the HTML value "navy.") Press the F5 key to update the text in the Design view window, and then save the home page.
7. Preview the home page in a Web browser, and then close the browser.
8. Use FrontPage to print the Web page and the HTML document that creates it.
9. Close the **garden** Web site, and then close FrontPage.

Apply

Apply the skills you learned in the tutorial to create a Web site for a retail business.

Case Problem 1

Data Files needed for this Case Problem: buffalo.doc, link.doc

Buffalo Trading Post Buffalo Trading Post (BTP) is a regional retail clothing business that specializes in buying, selling, and trading used clothing. The company buys its merchandise from people who take items to one of its trading post stores. Employees then sort items based on style, size, fabric, and garment condition. BTP specializes in clothing items made of natural fabric, but it also carries a limited inventory of polyester, acetate, Lycra, and other manufactured fibers in order to follow current styles and trends. BTP accepts only clothing in good condition for resale and attracts a loyal following of fashion enthusiasts and bargain hunters.

The president of the company, Nicole Beirne, hired you to lead the Web site development team. Nicole wants you to prepare a plan for BTP's Web site and create its home page. As you finished your first meeting with the Web site development team, you agreed that, in addition to the home page, the site should include five more pages with the following titles: (1) Who, (2) How, (3) What, (4) Where, and (5) Contact. Nicole asks you to begin your work by developing a Web site plan, the Web site, and the home page.

If necessary, start FrontPage, make sure you have your Data Files, and then do the following:

Explore

1. Use the information provided in the case problem description to prepare a Web site plan for the BTP Web site.

Explore

2. Prepare a preliminary sketch of the Web site that shows the desired Web pages and the expected hyperlinks from the home page.

3. Use the One Page Web Site template to create the **buffalo** Web site in the location where you are storing your Web sites.

4. Open the home page in Design view, and then make sure that the Web site's authoring settings are set to enable SharePoint Services, Browse-time Web Components, Author-time Web Components (including Navigation and Shared Borders), and VML graphics, and to support Internet Explorer versions 5.0/6.0 and later.

5. Make sure that the default page size is 800 × 600 maximized.

6. Insert into the home page the **buffalo.doc** file from the Tutorial.01\Case1 folder included with your Data Files.

7. Check the spelling in the home page and correct any misspelled words.

8. Change to Split view. In the Web page, click to the left of the sentence that begins "We also carry" and then press the Enter key, observing the change in the HTML document.

9. Return to Design view, create a new paragraph at the top of the home page, and then type "Welcome to the Buffalo Trading Post!" in the new paragraph. Center this paragraph, and then change it to the Heading 1 style.

10. Create a new paragraph above the heading you created in Step 9. Start Word, and then copy the text from the **link.doc** file in the Tutorial.01\Case1 folder included with your Data Files. Close Word, and then paste the text you copied on the new paragraph at the top of the home page. Choose the Keep Text Only option, and then change the paragraph that contains the pasted text to the Normal style.

11. Change the color of the text in the link bar to navy and its style to bold.

12. In a new paragraph at the bottom of the page, type the following text: "BTP™ is a registered trademark of Buffalo Trading Post". (*Hint:* Use the symbol set to insert the trademark character.) Change this text to 10-point, Arial font.

13. Format the text "Buffalo Trading Post" in the first sentence of the page as bold and change its color to navy. Then use the Format Painter to change other text occurrences of "Buffalo Trading Post" in the same and next paragraphs in the home page to match.

Explore

14. Create meta description and keywords tags in the home page using values that you provide.

15. Save the home page, examine it in Preview view, and then preview it in a Web browser. Use the browser to print the home page, and then close the browser.

16. Use FrontPage to print the HTML document for the home page. On the printout, circle the meta tags that you created.

17. Close the **buffalo** Web site, and then close FrontPage.

Apply

Apply the skills you learned in the tutorial to create a Web site for a restaurant.

Case Problem 2

Data Files needed for this Case Problem: grill.doc, linkbar.doc

Garden Grill Garden Grill is a growing national chain of casual, full-service restaurants. Its moderately priced menu features delicious dishes taken from various locations around the world. Garden Grill uses sophisticated consumer marketing research techniques to monitor customer satisfaction and evolving customer expectations. It strives to be a market leader in its segment by utilizing technology as a competitive advantage. Since 1976, management has used in-store computers to assist in the operation of the restaurants. The corporate office provides support seven days a week, 24 hours a day. Management believes that its information systems have positioned the chain to handle both its current needs and its future growth.

The corporate office has prepared a long-range information systems plan, which it reviews annually with all levels of management. Management's plan for the coming year includes the development of a Web site. Meghan Elliott just completed her management training at the corporate offices of Garden Grill and was assigned to work with Callan Murphy, who manages the information systems department. Last week, Callan's job responsibilities were increased to include managing the company's Web site development team. Callan wants Meghan to help him prepare the Web site design plan and create a home page for Garden Grill.

Callan and Meghan just met with the rest of the Web site development team. All agreed that, in addition to the home page, the company's Web site should include six additional pages with the following titles: (1) Company Profile, (2) Menu, (3) Franchise Info, (4) Employment, (5) Feedback, and (6) Search. Callan has asked you to assist Meghan with the design and development activities.

If necessary, start FrontPage, make sure you have your Data Files, and then do the following:

Explore

1. Use the information provided in the case problem description to prepare a Web site plan for the Garden Grill Web site.

Explore

2. Prepare a preliminary sketch of the Web site that shows the desired Web pages and the expected hyperlinks from the home page.
3. Use the One Page Web Site template to create the **grill** Web site in the location where you are storing your Web sites.
4. Open the home page in Design view, and then make sure that the Web site's authoring settings are set to enable SharePoint Services, Browse-time Web Components, Author-time Web Components (including Navigation and Shared Borders), and VML graphics, and to support Internet Explorer versions 5.0/6.0 and later.
5. Make sure that the default page size is 800 × 600 maximized.

6. Insert into the home page the **grill.doc** file from the Tutorial.01\Case2 folder included with your Data Files.

7. Check the spelling in the home page and correct any misspelled words.

8. Change to Split view. In the Web page, click to the left of the sentence that begins "Garden Grill is a premier" and then press the Enter key, observing the change in the HTML document.

9. Return to Design view, create a new paragraph at the top of the home page, and then type "Welcome to Garden Grill" in the new paragraph. Center this paragraph, change its style to Heading 3, change its font color to red, and change its font to Comic Sans MS. (*Hint:* Red is a standard color. Use the ScreenTips to locate it on the Font Color menu. The Comic Sans MS font might appear on your computer as "Comic Sans.")

10. Create a new paragraph above the heading you created in Step 9. Start Word, and then copy the text from the **linkbar.doc** file in the Tutorial.01\Case2 folder included with your Data Files. Close Word, and then paste the text you copied on the new paragraph at the top of the home page. Choose the Keep Text Only option, and then change the paragraph that contains the pasted text to the Normal style.

Explore ▶ 11. Change the font color of the text in the link bar to purple and its style to bold, and make sure its font is Times New Roman. (*Hint:* Purple is a standard color. Use the ScreenTips to locate it on the Font Color menu.)

Explore ▶ 12. In a new paragraph at the bottom of the page, insert a copyright symbol and then type a space, the current year, and the company name. Press Shift + Enter to create a new line, and then add the text "Last updated" and a date field that indicates when the page was last edited. (*Hint:* To add the date field, click Insert on the menu bar, and then click Date and Time.) Format the date with the day of the week and the full date with the month spelled out. Do not include the time.

13. Change the style of the text you created in Step 12 to italic, 10-point, Arial font.

Explore ▶ 14. Create meta description and keywords tags in the home page using values that you provide.

15. Save the home page, examine it in Preview view, and then preview it in a browser. Use the browser to print the home page, and then close the browser.

16. Use FrontPage to print the HTML document for the home page. On the printout, circle the meta tags that you created.

17. Close the **grill** Web site, and then close FrontPage.

Case Problem 3

Data Files needed for this Case Problem: link.doc, swenson.doc

Swenson Auctioneers Scott Swenson became a professional auctioneer in 1983 when he left his job at a real estate brokerage to become an approved auctioneer for the U.S. Bankruptcy Court. As an auctioneer before the Bankruptcy Court, he realized that he was very comfortable in the position of auctioneer and really enjoyed working with people in different types of businesses. After several years, he left his job and started his own firm, Swenson Auctioneers. At first, the firm handled auctions of personal estates only, but it soon expanded to handle auctions for commercial and industrial institutions, government entities, financial institutions, national retailers, law firms, manufacturers, and small businesses. As the business expanded and Scott began handling multiple auctions each month, he hired an assistant auctioneer, a marketing representative, an appraiser, an auction clerk, and a collectibles specialist. To handle the daily business of the office, Scott also hired a receptionist and a personal assistant. After 10 years, Swenson Auctioneers has grown from a small, local "mom and pop" organization to one of the leading auctioneering firms in the Midwest.

Scott wants to create a Web site for the business as part of his commitment to customer service. He thinks that the Web site can offer current and potential clients information about the types of auctions that Swenson Auctioneers handles, and provide a way for the new clients to get information about upcoming auctions that might interest them. As part of his overall vision for the Web site, Scott wants to showcase the business's past auctions and provide information about its key employees. After discussing the Web site at a recent staff meeting, Scott decides that in addition to the home page, he wants to create pages with the following titles: (1) Upcoming Auctions, (2) Auction & Appraisal Services, (3) Our Team, and (4) Mailing List. Scott has hired you to teach him how to develop and maintain his FrontPage Web site. You'll start by creating a Web site plan, the Web site, and the home page.

If necessary, start FrontPage, make sure you have your Data Files, and then do the following:

1. Use the information provided in the case problem description to prepare a Web site plan for the Swenson Auctioneers Web site.
2. Prepare a preliminary sketch of the Web site that shows the desired Web pages and the expected hyperlinks from the home page.
3. Use the One Page Web Site template to create the **swenson** Web site in the location where you are storing your Web sites.
4. Open the home page in Design view, and then make sure that the Web site's authoring settings are set to enable SharePoint Services, Browse-time Web Components, Author-time Web Components (including Navigation and Shared Borders), and VML graphics, and to support Internet Explorer versions 5.0/6.0 and later.
5. Make sure that the default page size is 800 × 600 maximized.

6. Insert into the home page the **swenson.doc** file from the Tutorial.01\Case3 folder included with your Data Files.

7. Check the spelling in the home page and correct any misspelled words.

Explore
8. Change to Split view. In the HTML document, select the text "Swenson Auctioneers" in the first sentence of the first paragraph, and then use the More Colors dialog box to change this text to the red color with the value Hex={FF,00,00}. Click anywhere in the Web page to deselect the text.

9. In the HTML document, select the text "Swenson Auctioneers" again, and then use the Bold button on the Formatting toolbar to change the text to bold, noticing the nested tag created in the HTML document. Click anywhere in the Web page to deselect the text.

10. Return to Design view, and then use the Format Painter to apply the formatting you applied in Steps 8 and 9 to the text "Swenson Auctioneers" in the second paragraph.

11. Create a new paragraph at the top of the home page. In this new paragraph, type "Swenson Auctioneers provides nationwide auction and appraisal services for a variety of industries."

12. Change the paragraph you inserted in Step 11 to the Heading 4 style.

13. Create a new paragraph above the paragraph you created in Step 11. Start Word, and then copy the text from the **link.doc** file in the Tutorial.01\Case3 folder included with your Data Files. Close Word, and then paste the text you copied into the new paragraph at the top of the home page. Choose the Keep Text Only option, and then change the paragraph that contains the pasted text to the Normal style.

Explore
14. Click anywhere in the link bar at the top of the page, change the alignment to center, and then apply a solid border around the paragraph. (*Hint:* Click the list arrow for the Borders button on the Formatting toolbar, and then use the ScreenTips to find and click the Outside Borders option in the menu that opens.)

Explore
15. In a new paragraph at the bottom of the page, insert a copyright symbol and then type a space, the current year, and the company name on the first line. Press Shift + Enter to create a new line, and then add the text "Last updated" and a date field that indicates when the page was last edited. (*Hint:* To add the date field, click Insert on the menu bar, and then click Date and Time.) Format the date with the day of the week and the full date with the month spelled out. Do not include the time.

16. Change the style of the text you created in Step 15 to bold, italic, 10-point, Arial font.

Explore
17. Create meta description and keywords tags in the home page using values that you provide.

18. Save the home page, examine it in Preview view, and then preview it in a browser. Use the browser to print the home page, and then close the browser.

19. Use FrontPage to print the HTML document for the home page. On the printout, circle the meta tags that you created.

20. Close the **swenson** Web site, and then close FrontPage.

Examine Internet Web sites that provide residential mortgage loans, and then create a Web site for an online mortgage broker.

Case Problem 4

Data File needed for this Case Problem: loan.doc

Mortgage Services, Inc. While working her way through college, Natalie Fuselier worked part-time as a teller at a small regional bank in her hometown of Baton Rouge. After she graduated from Louisiana State University with a degree in finance, she accepted a position at the bank as a loan officer. Loan officers typically specialize in commercial, consumer, or mortgage loans. Natalie was assigned to manage commercial loans, where she worked with companies seeking loans to pay for new equipment and business expansions. As part of her duties, Natalie was responsible for contacting businesses in the area and persuading them to use the bank for their loan needs. As she found new clients, Natalie would help them apply for the loan, and then she would manage the process of verifying the information provided by the business to make a decision about the business's ability to repay the loan. If the business could provide sufficient collateral to insure the loan, Natalie would approve it and then service the account over the term of the loan.

For five straight years, Natalie was the bank's top loan officer, closing millions of dollars in loans per year. Part of her success was due to her ability to develop effective working relationships with others and her enthusiasm for ensuring a smooth process for businesses. Natalie enjoyed her position but realized that working with commercial loans was cyclical and tied to the nation's economy. In an economic downturn, the number of business loans decreases. Natalie feared that her job might be tied to the needs of her clients, so she decided to leave her position to start her own company. Natalie decided to work with consumers this time. She counted on the existing relationships she had built with realtors in the area and started asking them to recommend her to provide residential home loans to their clients. As business increased, Natalie determined that a Web site would automate much of the loan application process and has hired you to help her design and create a Web site. To help her make some decisions about the kind of site to produce, she wants to examine some existing Internet Web sites that are set up to access applications from individuals.

If necessary, start FrontPage, make sure you have your Data Files, and then do the following:

1. Start your Web browser, and then open the home page for the search engine of your choice or the Google home page (**www.google.com**). Type the search expression "online mortgage application" in the search engine's text box, and then initiate the search. Examine the list of sites returned by the search engine and explore a few sites that provide applications for residential mortgages. As you explore the sites, notice features that make it easy to apply for a loan and the type of information the sites provide. (*Note:* Do not complete any on-screen forms at any of the sites that you visit.)

2. Use the information provided in the case problem description and the Web sites you explored in Step 1 to prepare a Web site plan for Natalie's Web site.
3. Prepare a preliminary sketch of the Web site that shows the desired Web pages and the expected hyperlinks from the home page. In addition to the home page, the Web site should include a minimum of the following pages: Loan Types, Application, Post Application Help, Resources, and Contact Us.

4. Use the One Page Web Site template to create the **loan** Web site in the location where you are storing your Web sites.

5. Open the home page in Design view, and then make sure that the Web site's authoring settings are set to enable SharePoint Services, Browse-time Web Components, Author-time Web Components (including Navigation and Shared Borders), and VML graphics, and to support Internet Explorer versions 5.0/6.0 and later.

6. Make sure that the default page size is 800 × 600 maximized.

7. Insert into the home page the **loan.doc** file from the Tutorial.01\Case4 folder included with your Data Files.

8. Check the spelling in the home page and correct any misspelled words.

Explore
9. Change to Split view and click the blank line between the opening <body> tag and the opening <p> tag in the HTML document. Add a level-one heading to the Web page using the text "Mortgage Services, Inc." (*Hint:* When you type the opening tag, FrontPage will insert the closing tag for you automatically.) Press the F5 key to update the Web page.

Explore
10. In the HTML document, select the text in the level-one heading that you added in Step 9, and then change its color to a blue color with the value Hex={00,00,CC} and change its alignment to center. Return to Design view.

11. Create a new paragraph above the heading. Create a centered link bar using the information you prepared in Steps 2 and 3. Format the link bar using the Normal style and a font, font style, and font color of your choice.

Explore
12. Switch to your Web browser, and then use a search engine of your choice to learn more about the different properties of the HTML meta tag. (*Hint:* Use the search expression "HTML meta tag" and follow some of the links to Web sites that provide HTML tutorials and resources.) After examining the resources you find, use the User Meta Variable dialog box to add three meta tags to the home page: description, keywords, and robots. Select appropriate values for the description and keywords properties, and set the robots value to "all."

13. Save the home page, examine it in Preview view, and then preview it in a browser. Use the browser to print the home page, and then close the browser.

14. Use FrontPage to print the HTML document for the home page. On the printout, circle the meta tags that you created.

15. Close the **loan** Web site, and then close FrontPage.

Reinforce

Computer
History
Hypermedia

The Internet:
World Wide
Web

Lab Assignments

The New Perspectives Labs are designed to help you master some of the key concepts and skills presented in this text. The steps for completing this Lab are located on the Course Technology Web site. Log on to the Internet and use your Web browser to go to the Student Online Companion for New Perspectives Office 2003 at **www.course.com/ np/office2003**. Click the Lab Assignments link, and then navigate to the assignments for this tutorial.

Computer History Hypermedia The Computer History Hypermedia Lab is an example of multimedia hypertext, or hypermedia, that contains text, pictures, and recordings that trace the origins of computers. This Lab provides you with two benefits: First, you learn how to use hypermedia links, and second, you learn about some of the events that took place as the computer age dawned.

The Internet: World Wide Web One of the most popular services on the Internet is the World Wide Web. This Lab is a Web simulator that teaches you how to use Web browser software to find information. You can use this Lab whether or not your school provides you with Internet access.

Review

Quick Check Answers

Session 1.1

1. A static Web page is one that displays information that does not change; a dynamic Web page contains data that changes on a schedule, such as stock market information.
2. defining the goal and purpose of the Web site, determining and preparing the Web site's contents, designing the Web site, building the Web site, and testing the Web site
3. a keyword, phrase, or picture in a Web page that, when clicked using a mouse, connects to related information located in the same Web page, in the same Web site, or in another Web site
4. index.htm
5. Determining a default page size lets you customize the appearance of your Web pages for the majority of your visitors. Viewing the Web site's pages at different resolutions is an important part of testing to ensure that all visitors will see your pages as you intend them to be viewed.
6. Type the text, insert the text from a file, and paste the text from an existing document.
7. A smart tag appears when you paste text in a Web page and provides options for working with that text, such as keeping the text's original formatting or only pasting the text.
8. Close Site

Session 1.2

1. Use the Format menu commands, right-click the text and use the shortcut menu commands, or use the Formatting toolbar buttons.
2. h1 (Heading 1)
3. 7
4. font
5. One of 216 colors common to all computer operating systems. A browser will display these colors consistently regardless of the computer on which the browser is installed.
6. Select the text whose format you want to copy, click the Format Painter button on the Standard toolbar once, and then select the text to which you want to copy the format with the Format Painter pointer.
7. Click the Show Preview View button at the bottom of the Contents pane, or click the Preview button list arrow on the Standard toolbar and select the browser(s) to use to open the page.

Session 1.3

1. False
2. The <html> tag identifies the beginning of the HTML document, and the </html> tag identifies the end of the HTML document.
3. <i>home page</i>
4. In FrontPage, click the Show Code View button at the bottom of the Contents pane; in Internet Explorer, click View on the menu bar, and then click Source.
5. an HTML tag that appears within another HTML tag
6. Press the F5 key.
7. an HTML tag that includes information about a Web page, such as the character set it uses, the name of its developer, how often it is refreshed, and the keywords and description of the page's contents
8. Type a question or keywords in the Type a question for help text box; click the Microsoft Office FrontPage Help button on the Standard toolbar; and click Help on the menu bar, and then click Show the Office Assistant.

Objectives

Session 2.1
- Change the background color of a Web page
- Insert a background picture into a Web page
- Save a Web site's embedded files
- Create a marquee
- Insert a picture into a Web page
- Learn about different picture file formats

Session 2.2
- Import a Web page into a Web site
- Create hyperlinks to other Web pages and to an e-mail address
- Create an image map
- Use a picture as a hyperlink

Session 2.3
- Create a thumbnail picture
- Change the characteristics of a picture
- Create an interactive button, a page transition, and animated text

Working with Graphics and Hyperlinks

Creating Graphics and Hyperlinks for the Sunshine Landscape & Garden Center Web Site

Case

Sunshine Landscape & Garden Center

The Web site for the Sunshine Landscape & Garden Center currently includes only the home page that you created in Tutorial 1. You formatted the page using different fonts and colors and added the text to use as entries in the link bar that will connect the home page to other pages that you will develop in the Web site.

Because nurseries are very colorful places, Sunshine's owner, Brett Kizer, wants to make sure that the pages in the Web site are colorful and attractive, like the nursery itself. Toward that goal, Brett hired a graphic designer to create a company logo and other graphics to include in the Web site. Brett also began taking digital pictures of the plants arriving at the nursery for use in the Garden Center page. The graphic designer also created a map with directions to the nursery for Brett to use in a Map page.

In this tutorial, you will continue enhancing the home page by adding a background color, a company logo, and some animated text. Then you will create hyperlinks to connect the home page to the Garden Center and Map pages. Finally, you will use features that create dynamic elements in Web pages, including page transitions and interactive buttons.

Student Data Files

To complete this tutorial, you will need your ending files from Tutorial 1 and the following Data Files. Additional Data Files needed to complete the end-of-tutorial exercises are listed with the Review Assignments and Case Problems.

▼ **Tutorial.02**

▽ **Tutorial folder**

back.jpg	gc_pic.gif	map_page.htm
center.htm	map.jpg	sun_logo.gif

Session 2.1

Changing the Background Color of a Web Page

The background color of a Web page can enhance its appearance and readability. If you don't specify a background color, the default background color is white. You can select any available color as the background of a Web page, but you should follow good design principles and select Web-safe colors that provide sufficient and complementary contrast with the rest of the Web page's contents. You might need to try several colors before you find one that provides the desired appearance for your Web page.

You can select a background color for a Web page using the Page Properties dialog box.

Reference Window

Setting the Background Color of a Web Page

- Click Format on the menu bar, and then click Background to open the Page Properties dialog box with the Formatting tab selected.
- In the Colors section, click the Background list arrow, and then click the desired color. If you want to use a color that is not listed, click More Colors, click a color in the color palette, and then click the OK button.
- Click the OK button to apply the new background color and close the Page Properties dialog box.

Although Brett likes the current white background of the home page, he asks you to select another color to see whether it might be more attractive.

To set the background color of the home page:

1. Start **FrontPage**, open the **garden** Web site from the location where your Web sites are stored, and then open the home page in Design view. If necessary, close the Folder List.

2. Click **Format** on the menu bar, and then click **Background** to open the Page Properties dialog box with the Formatting tab selected, as shown in Figure 2-1. In the Colors section, the background color is currently set to Automatic, which produces the default background color, white.

Background settings for the home page **Figure 2-1**

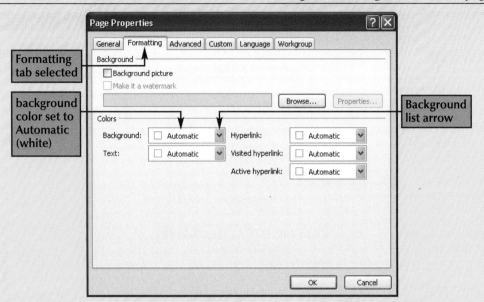

3. In the Colors section, click the **Background** list arrow. The menu includes 16 standard colors and a section named "Document Colors," which includes the colors used in the current Web page. Because you used the sapphire and navy colors in Tutorial 1 to change the font colors in the home page, these are the only two colors listed in the Document Colors section. Clicking More Colors opens the More Colors dialog box, which contains the 216 Web-safe colors.

4. Point to the **Yellow** color in the Standard Colors section. After a few seconds, a ScreenTip identifies the color as "Yellow." See Figure 2-2.

Changing the background color of the home page **Figure 2-2**

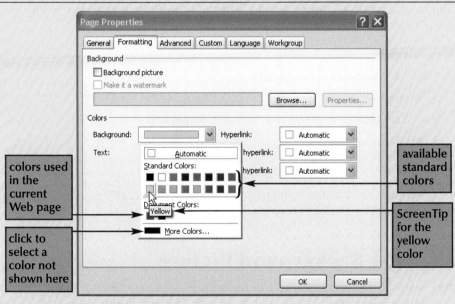

5. Click the **Yellow** color to select it, and then click the **OK** button to close the Page Properties dialog box. The background color of the home page changes to yellow. See Figure 2-3.

Figure 2-3 ▶ **Home page with yellow background color**

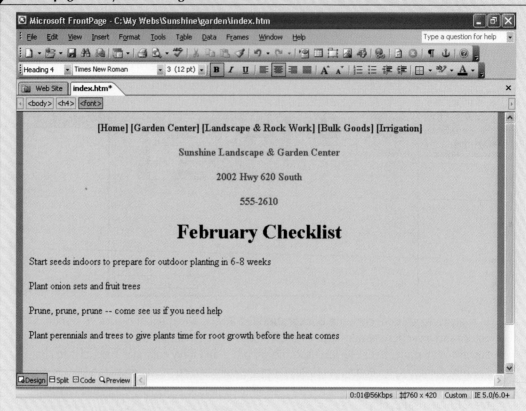

The yellow background provides a good contrast with the text in the home page, but Brett thinks that it is too bright. Instead of trying a different background color, Brett wonders how the page would look with a background picture that his graphic designer created. Before adding a background picture, you will show Brett how to change the background color back to Automatic (white).

To restore the background color:

▶ **1.** Click **Format** on the menu bar, and then click **Background**.

▶ **2.** Click the **Background** list arrow, and then click **Automatic**.

▶ **3.** Click the **OK** button. The home page appears again with the white background color.

The background color of the home page returns to its default setting, which is white. Now you can insert the background picture.

Inserting a Background Picture

A **picture** is any file that contains a graphic image, such as a logo, photograph, or computer-generated image. Almost every Web site that you visit contains pictures to enhance the site's appearance and provide visual representations of people and products. Because the Internet is a highly visible medium, many of its users have high expectations when viewing a Web site for the first time. They expect to find pictures of products and interesting graphics to enhance their use of the site. Pictures are an expected and vital part of communication; a Web site's users often perceive a Web site without pictures as having little or no value. As you work in a Web site, you will find many ways to use pictures to enhance the appearance and functionality of your pages. Even simple graphics can meet this goal. For example, the logo that Brett wants to include in the home page identifies the company's corporate logo, connecting the Web site in the virtual world to the nursery's physical location in the real world. The logo also includes the business's name, address, and phone number.

To include a picture in a Web page, it must be stored as a file. This file might be a digital picture that you purchase from a company that sells them, a digital picture that you take with a digital camera, a scanned copy of a picture that exists on paper, or a clip-art image that you find at a Web site or in the Microsoft Office Clip Art gallery. Pictures can be saved in a variety of file formats, but there are certain formats that are commonly used on the Web because they produce high-quality images with low file sizes and low download times. In most cases, the content of the graphic dictates the file type you choose for it. Three of the most popular formats for picture files are:

- **JPG** (or **JPEG**), pronounced "jay-peg," stands for **Joint Photographic Experts Group**, which is the name of the group that wrote this file standard. JPEG uses lossy compression technology to compress the file. **Lossy compression** technology eliminates redundant and unnecessary data in an image to reduce its file size, which reduces the amount of time it takes to download the file from the Web server on which it is stored and display it in the Web page. In most cases, the discarded data is invisible to the human eye. Because it supports 16 million colors, JPEG is used primarily for photographs and complex graphics.
- **GIF**, pronounced "giff" (with a hard "g"), stands for **Graphics Interchange Format**. GIF uses a **lossless compression** technology that reduces the file size of an image without any loss of data. The algorithm that compresses GIF files is owned by Unisys, which requires a licensing fee when the algorithm is used to compress GIF files. However, the licensing fee does not apply to people using GIF files in their Web pages; it only applies to companies that create programs that output GIF files. This format supports color and different screen resolutions. Because GIF files are limited to 256 colors, they are suitable for scanned images, line drawings, and simple graphics, but not photographs. In addition, GIF files can be combined to create animated images in a Web page.
- **PNG**, pronounced "ping," stands for **Portable Network Graphic**. The PNG format was created as a license-free alternative to GIF. PNG also uses lossless compression technology, but its compression algorithm produces files that are smaller than GIF files. PNG files support up to 16 million colors, but unlike GIF files, you cannot combine PNG files to create animation.

Most Web browsers will display pictures that are created using the GIF and JPEG formats. Some browsers cannot display PNG files, so this format is less popular on the Internet. The Student Online Companion page for Tutorial 2 includes resources that you can use to learn more about different graphics resources available on the Web and the picture file formats used on the Web.

A **background picture**, which appears behind the Web page content, can be almost any picture file, but some pictures work better than others. When you surf the Internet, you might find businesses that use background pictures to enhance the appearance of their Web pages. These background pictures might be a single copy or multiple small copies of a company logo, a picture or clip-art image that represents the business, or an interesting graphic, such as a three-dimensional shape or a series of lines. You can use any picture as a background in a Web page, but the primary goal of any background is to enhance the content of the Web page and ensure its readability.

Inserting a Background Picture into a Web Page

- Click Format on the menu bar, and then click Background.
- In the Background section, click the Background picture check box to select it, and then click the Browse button to open the Select Background Picture dialog box.
- Browse for and select the desired background picture file.
- Click the Open button to return to the Page Properties dialog box, and then click the OK button to insert the background picture.

Brett received a file from the graphic designer that he wants to use as the background for the home page. You'll show him how to make this change next.

To insert the background picture:

1. Click **Format** on the menu bar, and then click **Background** to open the Page Properties dialog box with the Formatting tab selected.

2. In the Background section, click the **Background picture** check box to select it, and then click the **Browse** button. The Select Background Picture dialog box opens. You will insert the background picture from your Data Files.

3. Click the **Look in** list arrow, select the drive or folder that contains your Data Files, open the **Tutorial.02** folder, and then open the **Tutorial** folder.

4. Select **back.jpg** in the list box, and then click the **Open** button. The Page Properties dialog box reappears, and the text box in the Background section shows the path to the file you selected as a background picture. See Figure 2-4.

Figure 2-4 | Background picture selected for the home page

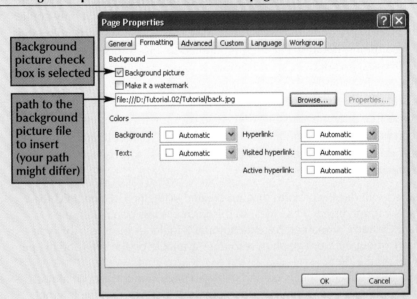

Background picture check box is selected

path to the background picture file to insert (your path might differ)

Trouble? The path to the back.jpg file on your computer might differ. Just make sure that you see "back.jpg" in the path. If you do not see "back.jpg," click the Browse button and repeat Steps 3 and 4 to select it.

5. Click the **OK** button to close the Page Properties dialog box. The background picture now appears in the home page for the Sunshine Landscape & Garden Center. Notice that the text from the page appears on top of the background picture.

Saving an Embedded File in a Web Site

When you insert a picture into a Word or other Office document, the picture is saved *with* the document. In FrontPage, however, inserting a file only adds an HTML tag in the HTML document that creates the Web page to indicate *where* the file that contains the picture is stored. Until you save the page, the reference for the background picture points to the location from which you inserted it. This location might be a removable drive, hard drive, or server. Because an HTML tag can only insert a picture from a file location into your Web page, a picture is called an **embedded file**. This embedded file does not become part of your Web site until you save it in the Web site's images folder, which most developers use to store all picture and multimedia files that are used in the Web site. Saving the embedded background picture file in your Web site ensures that all of your Web site's files are saved within the Web site itself and that they will be accessible to all users.

Reference Window

Saving a Web Page That Contains an Embedded File

- Click the Save button on the Standard toolbar. The Save Embedded Files dialog box opens.
- If necessary, click the Change Folder button, select the images folder for the current Web site, and then click the OK button.
- Click the OK button to save the Web page and the embedded file.

Before saving the file, you want to show Brett the HTML tag that inserts the background picture into the Web page. To accomplish this goal, you ask him to change to Split view.

To change to Split view and save the home page and the embedded picture file:

1. Click the **Show Split View** button ⊟Split at the bottom of the Contents pane to change to Split view, and then examine the HTML document to find the HTML tag that inserts the background picture. This tag appears below the closing </head> tag and begins <body background=. The file location, which appears in quotation marks, is the location of the back.jpg file on your computer; Figure 2-5 shows the HTML document for Brett's computer.

Figure 2-5 | Split view of the home page after inserting the background picture

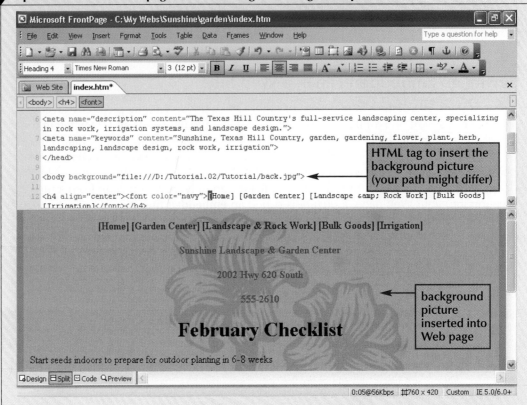

2. Click the **Save** button 🖫 on the Standard toolbar. The Save Embedded Files dialog box opens, as shown in Figure 2-6. Notice that the Save Embedded Files dialog box shows the name of the embedded file (back.jpg), the action to perform (Save), and a preview of the picture. You can use this dialog box to rename the picture, to change the folder in which to save it, or to change the action either to save or avoid saving the file in the Web site. In addition, clicking the Picture File Type button lets you change the picture's properties. For example, you might change the file from one format to another or change the quality of the image. (You will learn about changing a file's type and properties later in this tutorial.)

Figure 2-6 | Save Embedded Files dialog box

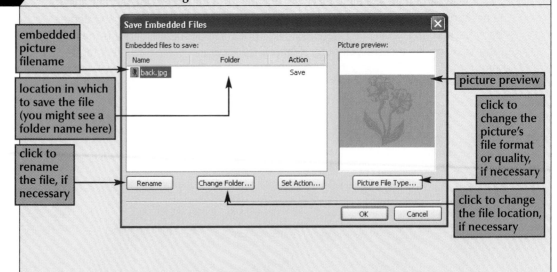

You will save the background picture file, back.jpg, in the garden Web site's images folder.

Trouble? As you use FrontPage to save Web pages with embedded files, FrontPage might select the images folder for you automatically based on your previous actions. If the images folder is already listed in the Folder column, skip to Step 5.

3. Click the **Change Folder** button. The Change Folder dialog box opens and displays the folders in the garden Web site.

4. Click the **images** folder to select it, and then click the **OK** button. The Save Embedded Files dialog box shows the folder in which to save the back.jpg file as "images/."

5. Click the **OK** button to save the back.jpg file in the garden Web site's images folder and to save the changes you made to the home page. The back.jpg file is still with your Data Files, but now it is also saved in the garden Web site. These files are independent and are not linked to each other in any way. Notice that the <body> tag in the Code view window now shows that the file is saved in the images folder of the current Web site (the garden Web folder).

6. Return to Design view, click the **Web Site** tab at the top of the Contents pane, and then double-click the **images** folder to open it. The back.jpg file is stored in the images folder.

7. Click the **index.htm** tab at the top of the Contents pane to return to the home page in Design view.

Brett likes the appearance of the home page with the background picture. He asks you about using other techniques to enhance the appearance of the home page and call attention to important specials or promotions at the nursery. You suggest using a marquee to display important text in the home page.

Using a Marquee

A **marquee** is a text box that displays a scrolling text message in a Web page. You can create a marquee by using existing text or by entering new text. Most businesses use marquees to call attention to important announcements, promotions, and other messages. You should use marquees sparingly, however, because they can easily overpower a Web page and distract users. Most browsers can animate the text in a marquee; if a browser does not support the <marquee> tag, then it will display the text in the marquee without the animation. Internet Explorer can display and animate marquee text. However, certain versions of Netscape Navigator cannot animate the text or display the text box; a person using Navigator to view a Web page that contains a marquee might see static text, or the text might scroll across the screen in a smaller text box.

Creating a Marquee in a Web Page

- Select the text in the Web page that you want to include in the marquee.
- Click the Web Component button on the Standard toolbar to open the Insert Web Component dialog box.
- If necessary, click Dynamic Effects in the Component type list, and then click Marquee in the Choose an effect list.
- Click the Finish button. The Marquee Properties dialog box opens.
- If necessary, edit the text that will appear in the marquee in the Text text box.
- In the Behavior section, click the option button to implement the desired behavior for the marquee's text.
- Specify any other desired characteristics of the marquee, such as the direction, speed, or size of the text and the background color of the text box, or accept the default settings for these characteristics.
- If necessary, click the Style button, click the Format button in the Modify Style dialog box, and then click an option in the list that opens to change the settings for the marquee's font, paragraph, border, bullets, and position. Click the OK button to close any open dialog boxes and return to the Marquee Properties dialog box.
- Click the OK button.

Brett wants to call attention to the nursery's new shipments of plants for the spring growing season, and he wants to put this notice in a marquee. Placing this text in a marquee will animate it when the user views the home page in a browser. You tell Brett that the text in a marquee should fit on one line, and that shorter phrases or sentences work better than longer ones.

To create and test the marquee:

 ▶ 1. Scroll down the home page as necessary, click the blank paragraph above the copyright information, and then type **Vegetables and perennials arrive next month!** You will use this text in the marquee.

   When you create a marquee, you need to make sure that you select only text, and not the paragraph mark at the end of the paragraph. If you select the paragraph mark, the paragraph below the marquee will move up to the same line as the marquee. To help Brett select the text correctly, you ask him to turn on the display of the nonprinting characters in the home page.

 ▶ 2. Click the **Show All** button ¶ on the Standard toolbar. Paragraph marks appear at the end of each paragraph. See Figure 2-7.

Nonprinting characters in a Web page | **Figure 2-7**

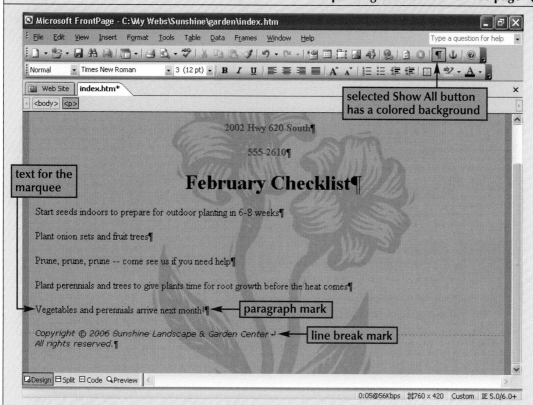

Trouble? If the Show All button has a colored background [¶], then this feature is already enabled and you do not need to click the Show All button. (Clicking the Show All button again turns this feature off.)

3. Select the text that you typed in Step 1, but not the paragraph mark at the end of the line.

4. Click the **Web Component** button [▣] on the Standard toolbar. The Insert Web Component dialog box opens.

   Trouble? If your Web site is set to support Netscape Navigator browsers, the Marquee option in the Choose an effect list will be dimmed and a message will appear in the dialog box indicating that you need to change the authoring settings for the Web site because Navigator cannot display marquees. To complete these steps, click the Cancel button in the Insert Web Component dialog box, click Tools on the menu bar, click Page Options, select the Authoring tab, click the Browsers list arrow and click Microsoft Internet Explorer only, click the Browser versions list arrow and click 5.0/6.0 browsers and later, and then click the OK button. Repeat Steps 3 and 4.

5. Make sure that **Dynamic Effects** is selected in the Component type list and **Marquee** is selected in the Choose an effect list. A description of the Marquee Web component appears in the dialog box.

6. Click the **Finish** button. The Marquee Properties dialog box opens, as shown in Figure 2-8. Notice that the text you selected in the home page appears in the Text text box. This is the text that will appear in the marquee. You can change this text if you need to do so by editing the text in the Text text box.

Figure 2-8 ▶ **Marquee Properties dialog box**

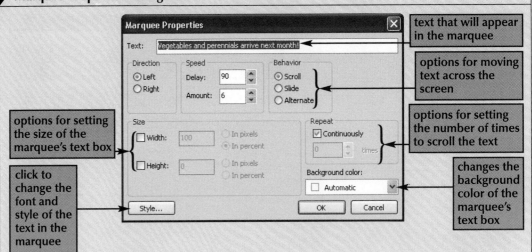

7. Click the **Alternate** option button (if necessary) in the Behavior section. Selecting this setting causes the marquee's text to move back and forth across the screen. The Scroll setting causes the text to move across the screen in only one direction, and the Slide setting causes the text to scroll across the screen and then stop.

8. In the Size section, click the **Width** check box to select it, select the value in the Width text box and type **90**, and then (if necessary) click the **In percent** option button to select that screen measurement. These settings limit the width of the marquee to 90% of the screen's width. Notice that you can set similar limits on the marquee's height or use pixels as the unit of measurement.

   Trouble? If you accidentally close the Marquee Properties dialog box, double-click the marquee text in the Web page to reopen it.

   Brett wants to use a different background color for the marquee's text box so that it will stand out in the page.

9. Click the **Background color** list arrow to open the list of available colors.

10. Click the **White** color in the Standard Colors section.

    Notice that you can change other marquee options as well. For example, selecting the Continuously check box in the Repeat section causes the marquee's text to remain animated indefinitely while the page is open. If you clear this check box, you can specify the number of times that the marquee's text will move across the screen. You can also set the text's direction of movement so that it scrolls from the left or right side of the page. You can specify delay and speed parameters in the Speed section. In the Delay text box, you can specify the amount of time, in milliseconds, that the text should wait before it begins to move. In the Amount text box, you can specify the speed at which the text should move in the marquee. The default settings for these options are acceptable, so you will close the dialog box.

11. Click the **OK** button. The Marquee Properties dialog box closes and a marquee with a white background encloses the text you typed in Step 1. No movement is shown, however. To test this feature, you must save the page and change to Preview view.

12. Click the **Save** button 🖫 on the Standard toolbar, and then click the **Show Preview View** button ⚲Preview at the bottom of the Contents pane to preview the page. If necessary, scroll down the page to see the marquee. The text moves back and forth in the white marquee.

13. Return to Design view.

The logo picture that Brett received from the graphic designer includes the nursery's name, address, and phone number. Brett wants to replace the text at the top of the home page with the new logo. Because the logo is a picture, you'll show Brett how to insert a picture into a Web page.

Inserting a Picture into a Web Page

Inserting a picture into a Web page uses the same techniques as inserting a background picture into a Web page. Just as for background pictures, a picture in a Web page might be any file format, with JPEG, GIF, and PNG being the most popular formats used on the Internet. When inserting pictures in a Web page, try to insert files with the smallest file sizes to meet your objectives. You might have a beautiful picture to include in your site, but if it takes two or three minutes for people to download it, they will quickly become frustrated when viewing your site.

Reference Window

Inserting a Picture into a Web Page

- Click the location in the page where you want to insert the picture.
- Click the Insert Picture From File button on the Standard toolbar.
- In the Picture dialog box, browse to and then select the desired file.
- Click the Insert button to insert the picture.

Brett wants to replace the text in the home page that identifies the nursery's name, address, and phone number with the logo created by the graphic designer. To make this change, he'll need to select the text and then replace it with the file that contains the logo.

To add a picture to a Web page:

1. Scroll up the home page as necessary, and then use the pointer to select the text on lines 2, 3, and 4 of the Web page, containing the nursery's name, address, and phone number, as shown in Figure 2-9. Because this text was centered, the picture that you insert in this location will also be centered.

Figure 2-9

Text to replace with a picture

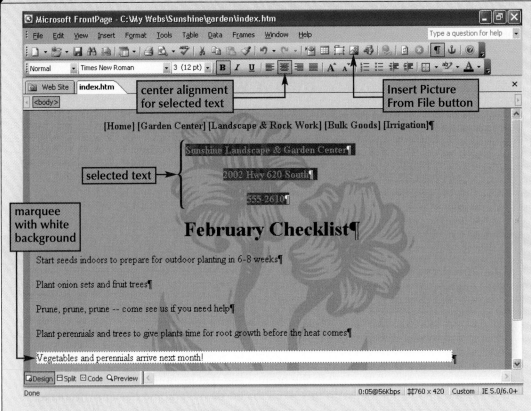

2. Click the **Insert Picture From File** button 🖾 on the Standard toolbar. The Picture dialog box opens.

3. If necessary, click the **Look in** list arrow, change to the drive or folder that contains your Data Files, and open the **Tutorial.02\Tutorial** folder to display its contents.

4. Click **sun_logo.gif** to select it, click the **Insert** button to insert the picture into the Web page, and then, if necessary, press the **Enter** key to make the picture appear on its own line.

    Trouble? If your picture is not centered, click the picture to select it, and then click the Center button ≣ on the Standard toolbar.

5. Click the picture to select it. See Figure 2-10.

Figure 2-10

Picture inserted into the home page

Notice the **sizing handles**—eight small squares around the picture—that you can use to resize the selected picture. When you are working with a picture, you can display the Pictures toolbar to gain access to common commands used for pictures. You'll display the Pictures toolbar next.

To display the Pictures toolbar:

1. Click **View** on the menu bar, and then point to **Toolbars**. The Toolbars submenu includes all of the FrontPage toolbars. A toolbar that is displayed has a check mark to the left of its name. Clicking a toolbar name either displays or hides it.

   Trouble? If the Pictures command on the Toolbars submenu has a check mark to the left of its name, this toolbar is already displayed. Skip to Step 3.

2. Click **Pictures** on the Toolbars submenu. The Pictures toolbar opens. It might appear as either a floating or docked toolbar, depending on how it was last used. Figure 2-11 shows the default setting, which is a floating toolbar. You can move a toolbar by dragging its title bar to a new location. Working with toolbars is a matter of personal preference, but to make sure that you can see all of the Web page in Design view, you'll dock toolbars at the top of the window.

Pictures toolbar ◄ **Figure 2-11**

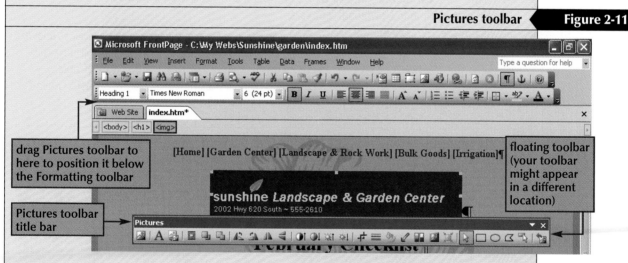

3. If your Pictures toolbar is not docked below the Formatting toolbar, click the title bar of the Pictures toolbar, and then drag it to below the Formatting toolbar. When the toolbar appears below the Formatting toolbar, release the mouse button. Now the Pictures toolbar is docked below the Formatting toolbar. When you display a toolbar in the FrontPage window, the size of the Web page decreases slightly to make room for the new toolbar. Because you see less of your Web page, it is a good practice to hide toolbars that you don't need as you complete your work.

When you start adding graphics to a Web page, it is a good idea to keep an eye on the Estimated Time to Download pane on the status bar. The speed at which you view Web pages in a browser on your computer is dependent upon the way you connect to the Internet. If you use a dial-up connection, pages will load more slowly for you than for a user with a high-speed Internet connection, such as a cable modem or Digital Subscriber Line (DSL), both of which download data very quickly. The Estimated Time to Download pane uses a download speed that you select to estimate the amount of time required to download the page and its embedded files from the Web server on which they are stored. Remember that when you use a Web browser to view a Web page, the browser uses your Internet connection to download the HTML document that creates the Web page and the embedded files that are displayed in the page. HTML documents are usually small text files, but pictures can vary in size from a few to several hundred or thousand kilobytes. Because file sizes can vary based on content, it's important to check the file sizes of pictures you include in a Web site and to use the appropriate file format to compress the files as much as possible to make them download more quickly. Some Internet Web sites and ISPs provide research data about the types of connections people make to access different servers, and some cities have a much higher percentage of high-speed connections than others. A good rule of thumb is to assume that some of your site's visitors will use dial-up connections. You'll check the options for setting the download speed next, and then make sure it is set to 56 Kbps (kilobits per second), which is a "fast" dial-up connection.

To view the Estimated Time to Download options:

1. Point to the **Estimated Time to Download** pane on the status bar so the ScreenTip "Estimated Time to Download" appears.

2. Click the **Estimated Time to Download** pane to open a list of connection speeds, as shown in Figure 2-12. The first two options, 28.8 and 56, are connection speeds for dial-up modems. DSL transfers data at a rate of approximately 256 Kbps to 512 Kbps. Cable modems transfer data at a rate of 1,000 Kbps, and T1 connections are the fastest connections, with transfers of up to 1,500 Kbps.

Figure 2-12 ▶ **Estimated Time to Download options**

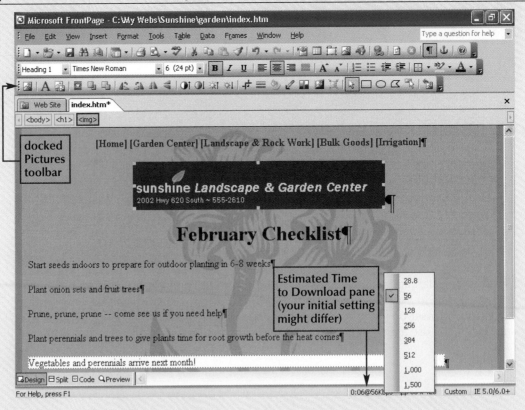

3. Click **1,000** in the Estimated Time to Download menu. The list closes and the Estimated Time to Download pane shows that the page requires 0:01, or one second, to be downloaded at 1,000 Kbps (a cable modem).

4. Click the **Estimated Time to Download** pane again, and then click **56**. The page requires 0:06, or six seconds, to be downloaded using a dial-up connection. This download time tells you that even with the simple graphics you have included, the page will take six seconds to be downloaded over a dial-up connection.

As you are working on your Web pages, it is important to consider the audience you are trying to reach and how it will access the site. For example, your preliminary planning should give you a good idea of the kind of information to include and which browsers visitors will use to access the site. When you begin using graphics in your pages, you should consider the needs of your Web site visitors who are using text-only browsers (which cannot display graphics) and visually impaired visitors using special software to read the content of Web pages. One way to enhance your Web site for this audience is to include alternative text with pictures.

Alternative text is a short phrase that identifies or describes a picture in a Web page using the HTML alt property. For example, the alternative text for the picture you just added could be "logo" or "Sunshine Landscape & Garden Center logo," which would identify the picture's function as decorative. For pictures that are used as hyperlinks, you might identify the picture's function as "Bulk Goods page hyperlink," so a user can infer its purpose in the page. This optional setting is important for two reasons. First, it identifies the picture's contents while it is being downloaded from the server. People viewing the pages with fast connections won't see the alternative text unless they point to the picture, but people viewing the page with slow connections will see the text in the place where the picture will eventually appear. Alternatively, people using browsers that cannot display pictures will see the alternative text *instead* of the picture. The second reason for adding alternative text is to identify the picture for visually impaired and other people using software that reads a Web page. Even though visually impaired users won't see the pictures in your Web pages, alternative text can tell them that the picture is included and describe its function.

When adding alternative text to a picture, be sure to include a short description and not just the picture's filename or the word "picture." Some developers use alternative text such as "decorative photo" to describe pictures that simply complement the Web page's appearance and alternative text such as "picture of Hewlett-Packard 1100A printer" for descriptions that are more important to conveying a message. This subtle difference is one to consider as you add alternative text to your pictures because it will increase the utility of your Web pages for all users.

Adding Alternative Text to a Picture

Reference Window

- Right-click the picture to open the shortcut menu, and then click Picture Properties.
- Click the General tab.
- Click the check box to the left of the Text text box to select it.
- Type the alternative text in the Text text box in the Alternative representations section, and then click the OK button.

Because he replaced the center's name, address, and phone number with the logo, Brett realizes that he deleted this important information for users who cannot view pictures. He wants to add alternative text to the picture to include this information in the Web page.

To add alternative text to a picture:

▶ 1. Right-click the picture to open the shortcut menu, and then click **Picture Properties** to open the Picture Properties dialog box.

▶ 2. Click the **General** tab.

▶ 3. Click the **check box** to the left of the Text text box to select it.

▶ 4. Click the **Text** text box in the Alternative representations section, type **Sunshine Landscape & Garden Center, 2002 Hwy 620 South, 555-2610**, and then click the **OK** button. The Picture Properties dialog box closes and the alternative text is added to the HTML document.

You can see the alternative text that you added by viewing the HTML document or by pointing to the picture in a browser.

▶ 5. Click the **Show Code View** button □ Code at the bottom of the Contents pane. The alt property includes the alternative text that you added to the picture. See Figure 2-13.

Figure 2-13	HTML document for the home page

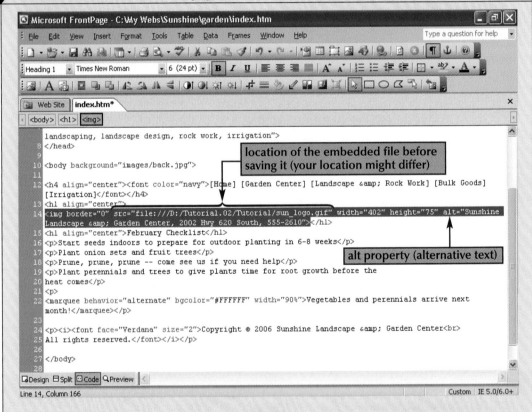

▶ 6. Click the **Show Preview View** button Q Preview at the bottom of the Contents pane to change to Preview view, and then point to the picture so the ScreenTip displays the alternative text that you added to the picture. After a few seconds, the alternative text will disappear.

▶ 7. Click the **Show Design View** button Design at the bottom of the Contents pane to return to Design view.

Brett added another picture to the Web site, so you remind him that he needs to save its file in the garden Web site's images folder.

To save the home page and the picture:

1. Click the **Save** button 🔲 on the Standard toolbar. The Save Embedded Files dialog box opens and displays the name of the new embedded file (sun_logo.gif), the folder in which to save it (images/), and the action to perform (Save). Notice that the Picture preview box shows a preview of the picture.

   Trouble? If the images folder is not selected automatically, click the Change Folder button, select the images folder in the garden Web site, and then click the OK button and continue with Step 2.

2. Click the **OK** button to save the embedded file in the garden Web site and your changes to the home page. After a few seconds, the file is saved and the Web site is updated.

Working with Pictures in Different Formats

When you are working in a photo-editing program, such as Adobe Illustrator or PhotoShop, you can edit a picture's characteristics; for example, you might change the background color or add special effects to the picture's edges. FrontPage includes tools that let you change some of a picture's characteristics to enhance its appearance in a Web page. For example, you can rotate and flip a picture to change its orientation, increase and decrease the picture's contrast and brightness, crop a picture to remove an unwanted area, change the picture to black and white or gray, or add a beveled edge. For pictures saved as GIF files, you can also change a color in the picture to transparent, which lets the background color of the Web page show through the picture.

Because the different picture formats support different features, you will find as you work on a Web site that there are effects that don't work as well or at all with some pictures. For example, if you insert a JPEG picture into a Web page and want to change its background to transparent, FrontPage will first require you to convert it to a GIF picture because JPEG pictures do not support transparency. When you convert a picture from JPEG to GIF, you are converting an image with up to 16 million colors to one limited to 256 colors. The converted GIF file might look fine in your Web page, but when you try to change the background to transparent, the image might look like the one shown in Figure 2-14.

| JPEG file converted to a GIF file with a transparent background | Figure 2-14 |

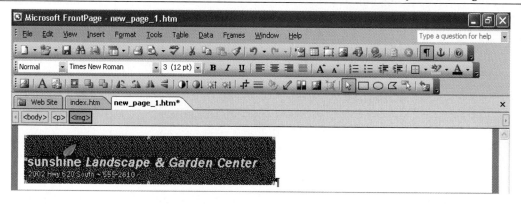

Instead of a solid background color, the conversion created different shades of the background color. The shades aren't visible to you until you convert the picture. If this problem occurs as you work in your Web pages, you will need to use a photo-editing program to change the background color to solid and change the file format to GIF. Although FrontPage has tools to convert pictures from one format to another, the pictures you use in your Web sites might make the FrontPage tools unusable. For this reason, it's important to have a graphic designer to make changes to pictures for you or for you to learn how to use a photo-editing program and make the changes yourself.

Reference Window

Converting a Picture to Another Format

- Right-click the picture to open the shortcut menu, click Picture Properties to open the Picture Properties dialog box, and then click the General tab.
- Click the Picture File Type button to open the Picture File Type dialog box.
- Click the option button to select the format to which you want to convert the picture.
- For GIF and JPEG files, use the Settings options to change the picture's settings as necessary.
- Click the OK button.

Next, you will show Brett the options for converting a picture to another format.

To examine the options for changing a picture's file type:

1. Right-click the picture to open the shortcut menu, and then click **Picture Properties**.

2. Click the **General** tab to select it.

3. Click the **Picture File Type** button. The Picture File Type dialog box opens and displays four formats for pictures, as shown in Figure 2-15. You can tell that the picture is saved as a GIF file because the GIF option button is selected. Notice that the Settings options at the bottom of the dialog box show settings that only GIF files support. Clicking the Interlaced check box causes a GIF picture to be displayed with increasing detail as it is being downloaded from the server. You also can make the background of a picture transparent, so that the background of the Web page shows through the picture, by checking the Transparent check box (when this option is enabled). Also notice that there are two options for PNG files. PNG-8 has better color support than GIF, and PNG-24 uses a lossless compression technique, resulting in a larger file size. The note for both of these formats indicates that some browsers do not support them.

Figure 2-15 ▶ **Picture File Type dialog box**

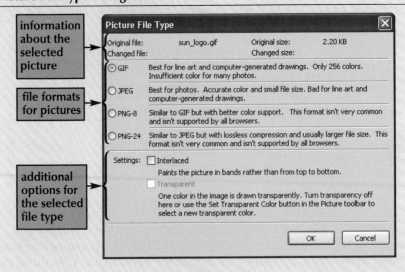

▶ **4.** Click the **JPEG** option button to select it. Notice that the information at the top of the dialog box changes to show the original filename and size and the changed filename and size. As expected, a JPEG file requires more space than a GIF file because this format includes more colors and detail. Also notice that the Settings options change to show the available settings for a JPEG file. Because the JPEG format does not support transparency or interlacing, these options are not available. For a JPEG picture, you can set the desired quality as a number from 1 to 100, with 100 being the best. In addition, you can set the number of progressive passes as a number from 0 to 100, with 100 being the most passes; the browser will then make this number of passes to display the picture before it is completely downloaded from the server.

▶ **5.** Click the **PNG-8** option button to select it. The file size increases slightly. Because there are no additional settings for PNG files, the Settings options disappear.

▶ **6.** Click the **Cancel** button to close the dialog box without making any changes, and then click the **Cancel** button to close the Picture Properties dialog box.

   When you save a picture for the first time as an embedded file in a Web site, you can click the Picture File Type button in the Save Embedded Files dialog box to change the picture's format. However, after you save the file the first time, you need to use the Picture Properties dialog box to change the file's format. For more information about editing pictures and setting their characteristics, consult FrontPage Help.

   Brett wants to see how the logo will look with a transparent background.

Changing a Color in a Picture to Transparent

One way to enhance the appearance of a picture in a Web page is to change one of the picture's colors to transparent. A transparent color will not be visible in the picture, thereby allowing the page's background to show through the picture.

Changing a Color in a Picture to Transparent   Reference Window

- Click the picture to select it.
- Click the Set Transparent Color button on the Pictures toolbar.
- Click the color in the picture that you want to make transparent.

   Brett wants to change the green background of the picture to transparent to see how it looks.

To change a color in a picture to transparent:

▶ **1.** If necessary, click the picture to select it so sizing handles appear around the picture.

▶ **2.** Click the **Set Transparent Color** button 🖉 on the Pictures toolbar.

▶ **3.** Point to the green color in the picture. The pointer changes to a 🖌 shape. See Figure 2-16.

Figure 2-16 | **Changing a color to transparent**

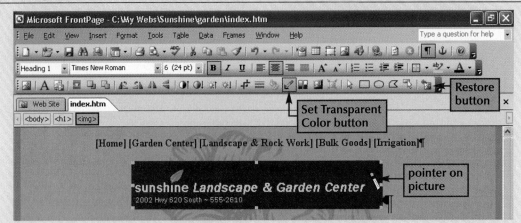

4. Make sure that the small arrow of the ✎ pointer points to the green color that you want to make transparent, and then click the green color. The green background of the picture becomes transparent, allowing the background of the Web page to show through.

   Trouble? If you change the wrong color in the picture to transparent, click the Undo button 🔄 on the Standard toolbar, and then repeat Steps 1 through 4.

   Without the background color, Brett decides that the logo isn't as attractive and wants to cancel this change. You tell him that he could click the Undo button on the Standard toolbar, but instead you will show Brett how to restore a picture to its original settings.

5. Click the **Restore** button 🔳 on the Pictures toolbar. The picture returns to its original state with the green background. Clicking the Restore button erases any changes you have made to a picture since the last time you saved it.

6. Click the **Save** button 💾 on the Standard toolbar. Even though you restored the picture, the Save Embedded Files dialog box opens with the "Overwrite" command in the Action column. This command will save the picture by overwriting the one that is saved in the images folder. If you do not want to overwrite the picture, clicking the Set Action button lets you select the option to cancel this action. You'll accept the default setting and overwrite the existing file.

7. Click the **OK** button to overwrite the picture file and save the home page.

Inserting a Horizontal Line

The last graphic that you want to show Brett is the **horizontal line**, which is frequently used for emphasis or to divide a Web page into sections. There are two ways to create horizontal lines in a Web page. The first way is to use the HTML <hr> tag (which stands for "horizontal rule"). This tag draws a line in a Web page. After inserting a horizontal line, you can change its characteristics by adjusting its length, width, and color. The second way is to insert a picture of a horizontal line, such as the one shown in Figure 2-17. When you use a picture to create a divider in a Web page, the line can be more visually interesting than the horizontal line drawn by the HTML <hr> tag. Keep in mind that using a picture does add to the overall download time for the Web page, so you need to use picture dividers carefully. You can search for picture dividers to use in your Web pages by displaying the Clip Art task pane and searching using the keyword "dividers."

Picture used as a horizontal line ◀ **Figure 2-17**

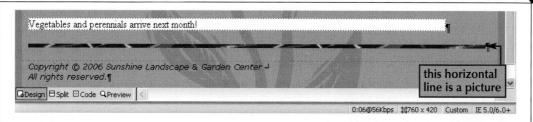

this horizontal
line is a picture

Inserting a Horizontal Line and Changing Its Properties

Reference Window

- Click at the beginning of the line directly below the location in which to insert the horizontal line.
- Click Insert on the menu bar, and then click Horizontal Line to insert a horizontal line.
- If necessary, double-click the horizontal line in the Web page, and then use the Horizontal Line Properties dialog box to change its characteristics.

To provide a visual break between the content of the home page and the copyright information at the bottom of the page, Brett wants to insert a horizontal line.

To insert a horizontal line in the home page:

1. Scroll down the home page as necessary, and then click to the left of the word **Copyright** at the bottom of the home page. The insertion point is now positioned below the location in which to insert the horizontal line.

2. Click **Insert** on the menu bar, and then click **Horizontal Line**. A horizontal line is inserted above the first line of the copyright information.

Next, Brett wants to make the line more prominent by making it shorter and wider and by changing its color.

To change horizontal line settings:

1. Double-click the **horizontal line** to select it and open the Horizontal Line Properties dialog box. See Figure 2-18.

Figure 2-18 ▶ **Horizontal Line Properties dialog box**

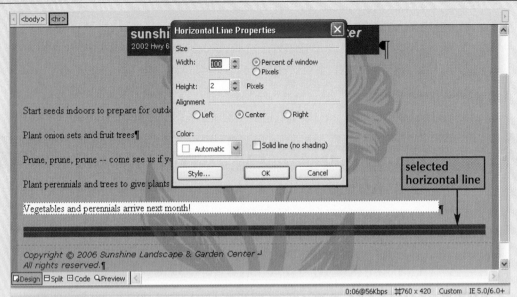

2. In the Size section, replace the selected text in the Width text box by typing **90**. The line's width will now be 90% of the screen's width.

3. Click the **Height** up arrow until the value changes to **5**. The height of the line is set to five pixels.

4. Click the **Color** list arrow, and then click the **Navy** color in the Document Colors section. The horizontal line will be the same navy color as the text in the link bar.

5. Click the **OK** button, and then click below the horizontal line to deselect it. The horizontal line appears as a centered, thicker, shorter, navy line. See Figure 2-19.

Figure 2-19 ▶ **Horizontal line with new properties**

6. Click the **Save** button 🖫 on the Standard toolbar to save the home page. Because a horizontal line is created with the HTML <hr> tag, you do not need to save it as an embedded picture file in the Web site.

7. Close the garden Web site, and then exit FrontPage.

In the next session, you will show Brett how to import a Web page into a Web site, create hyperlinks to Web pages and an e-mail address, and use pictures as hyperlinks.

Session 2.1 Quick Check

1. If you do not specify a background color for a Web page, which color appears in the background when a browser opens the page?
2. What are the three popular file formats for pictures on the Internet? What are the primary characteristics and uses of each file type?
3. True or False: All Web browsers can display marquees in a Web page.
4. Explain why it is important to use the Estimated Time to Download pane when creating Web pages.
5. What are two important uses of alternative text?
6. True or False: You can change a color in a GIF picture to transparent.
7. True or False: You can specify a horizontal line's size as a percentage of the screen's width.

Session 2.2

Importing a Web Page into a Web Site

In Tutorial 1, you learned how to copy text from a Word document and insert it into a Web page, and how to insert a Word file into a Web page. When you perform these tasks, FrontPage converts the content to HTML and adds it to the Web page. Sometimes the content you need to add to your Web site already exists as an HTML document. This content may have been created using FrontPage or another program that creates HTML files. When you want to use a Web page that exists outside of your Web site, you can import it into the Web site. When you import a Web page into a Web site, you add a copy of the file that contains the Web page to your Web site. Importing a Web page saves you time and eliminates the need to retype material.

Clara McShane, the nursery's chief landscape designer, used Notepad to create a draft of the Garden Center page for the Web site. This page will contain links to pictures of current inventory at the nursery. Instead of retyping Clara's material, you will show Brett how to import Clara's document into the garden Web site.

Importing an Existing Web Page into a Web Site

Reference Window

- If necessary, open the Web site into which to import the Web page, and then display the Folder List.
- Click the folder in the Web site into which you want to import the file.
- Click File on the menu bar, click Import, and then click the Add File button in the Import dialog box. The Add File to Import List dialog box opens.
- Use the Look in list box to browse to the desired file, click the file to select it, and then click the Open button.
- Click the OK button in the Import dialog box to import the page.

After importing a Web page into a Web site, you tell Brett that he can use it just like any other Web page created by FrontPage.

To open the garden Web site and import an existing Web page into it:

1. Make sure you have your Data Files, start **FrontPage**, open the **garden** Web site from the location where your Web sites are stored and, if necessary, display the Pictures toolbar and dock it below the Formatting toolbar.

2. If necessary, click the **Toggle Pane** button 🔲 on the Standard toolbar to display the Folder List.

   When you import a Web page into a Web site, you must select the folder into which you want to save the file. The Garden Center page will be stored in the Web site's root folder, so you will select the root folder before importing the page.

3. If necessary, click the Web site's root folder to select it.

4. Click **File** on the menu bar, and then click **Import** to open the Import dialog box.

5. Click the **Add File** button to open the Add File to Import List dialog box.

6. If necessary, click the **Look in** list arrow and change to the drive or folder that contains your Data Files, and then open the **Tutorial.02\Tutorial** folder.

7. Click **center.htm** to select this file, and then click the **Open** button. The Add File to Import List dialog box closes and the center.htm file appears in the Import dialog box. Clicking the Add Folder button lets you import a folder and all of its files into the Web site. Clicking the From Site button starts the Import Web Site Wizard, which you can use to import Web pages from a disk, network, or URL.

   Trouble? If you selected the wrong file to import, make sure that the file you selected by mistake is highlighted, click the Remove button in the Import dialog box, and then repeat Steps 5 through 7 to select the correct file.

8. Click the **OK** button. The Garden Center page, center.htm, is now in the garden Web site. See Figure 2-20.

Figure 2-20	Garden Center page imported into the garden Web site

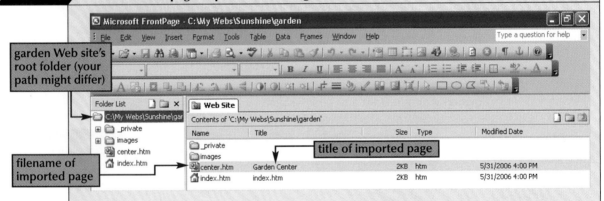

When Clara created the Garden Center page, she gave it a descriptive title, "Garden Center," using the HTML <title> </title> tags. The page's title appears in Folders view in the Title column. Brett notices that FrontPage used the title "index.htm" when it created the home page and the garden Web site. Because the title appears in the browser's title bar, "index.htm" is not a good choice. You tell Brett that he can change the title easily in Folders view.

To change a page's title in Folders view:

1. Click **index.htm** to select the file. FrontPage highlights the entire line of information about this file.

2. Click **index.htm** in the Title column to select the page title. The title is selected and FrontPage changes to editing mode by adding an insertion point.

3. With the title selected, type **Sunshine Landscape & Garden Center home page**, and then press the **Enter** key. FrontPage changes the title and selects the entire line again. If the text you entered exceeds the column width, an ellipsis (...) appears in the title. You can increase the width of the Title column to see the complete title.

4. If necessary, point to the right side of the Title column so the pointer changes to a ◀┼▶ shape, as shown in Figure 2-21.

Increasing a column's width in Folders view ◀ **Figure 2-21**

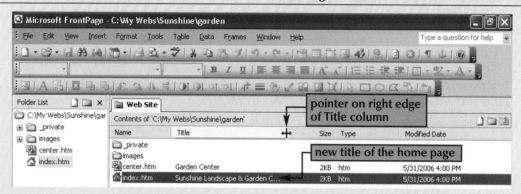

5. Double-click ◀┼▶ on the right side of the Title column. FrontPage resizes the Title column and displays the complete title. Because the width of the Title column increased, some other columns scrolled to the right of the screen. To see these columns, you would click the right arrow on the horizontal scroll bar.

Now that Brett has imported the Garden Center page into the garden Web site, he can open it just like any other Web page.

To open the imported Web page:

1. Double-click **center.htm** to open the partially completed Web page in Design view, and then close the Folder List. Notice that the Garden Center page appears with the default white background.

The first thing that Brett wants to do is link the home page and the Garden Center page to each other.

Linking to Other Web Pages

In Tutorial 1, you told Brett that a hyperlink is text or a picture in a Web page that, when clicked using a mouse, connects to related information located in the same Web page, the same Web site, or another Web site. The most common use of a hyperlink is to connect to different pages in the same Web site. When connecting Web pages with a hyperlink, the page that opens when the hyperlink is clicked is called the hyperlink's **target** or **target page**.

Creating a Hyperlink to an Existing Web Page in the Same Web Site

- Select the text or picture to use as the hyperlink.
- Click the Insert Hyperlink button on the Standard toolbar. If necessary, click the Existing File or Web Page button on the Link to bar.
- Browse to and then select the target of the hyperlink.
- Click the OK button.

Brett wants to create one hyperlink from the Garden Center page to the home page and another hyperlink from the home page to the Garden Center page to connect these pages to each other. You will show him how to use the link bar text that he created in Tutorial 1 to create the hyperlinks.

To create a hyperlink to another Web page:

1. Double-click the word **Home** in the link bar to select it. This text will become a hyperlink that opens the home page when clicked.

2. Click the **Insert Hyperlink** button on the Standard toolbar to open the Insert Hyperlink dialog box, and then, if necessary, click the **Existing File or Web Page** button on the Link to bar. See Figure 2-22.

Figure 2-22 | Insert Hyperlink dialog box

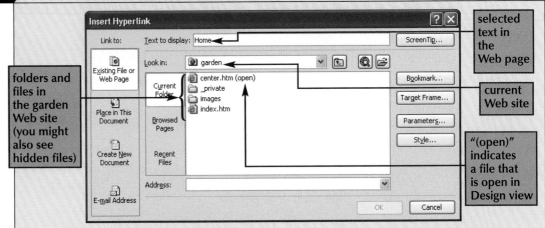

Trouble? If you see additional files and folders in the Insert Hyperlink dialog box, FrontPage might be configured to display hidden files and folders. This difference causes no problems.

The list box includes all of the folders and files in the garden Web site. The "center.htm (open)" entry indicates that this page is currently open in Design view.

Also notice that you can link to existing files in the current folder (in this case, the garden Web site), to browsed pages (pages you have opened in a Web browser), to recent files (files that you have recently opened in FrontPage), and to an e-mail address.

3. Click **index.htm** to select it as the target of the hyperlink. Notice that the Address list box now displays the filename for the selected page, index.htm.

4. Click the **OK** button to close the Insert Hyperlink dialog box and return to the center.htm page.

5. Click **Home** in the link bar to deselect the hyperlink. "Home" is now formatted as underlined text, which is the default format for a hyperlink.

6. Point to the **Home** hyperlink. The target of the hyperlink, "index.htm," appears on the status bar. The ScreenTip tells you that pressing and holding the Ctrl key and then clicking the hyperlink will open the hyperlink's target in Design view.

7. Save the center.htm page.

Brett created the hyperlink from the Garden Center page to the home page; now you will show him how to create the hyperlink from the home page to the Garden Center page. Although he could use the same method to create the return hyperlink, you decide to show Brett another method.

Creating a Hyperlink Using Drag and Drop

Drag and drop is another method you can use to create a hyperlink between pages in a Web site. By default, the title of the linked page (the target page) becomes the text for the hyperlink in the Web page that contains the hyperlink (the **source page**). Therefore, you might want to consider a title for a Web page that you can use later as the text for its hyperlink.

To use drag and drop to create a hyperlink, open the source page in Design view and then open the Folder List. Select the filename of the target page in the Folder List and drag the pointer to the location where you want to insert the hyperlink. When you release the mouse button, FrontPage creates a hyperlink using the target page's title. You can change the hyperlink's name by editing it after placing the hyperlink in the Web page.

Creating a Hyperlink Using Drag and Drop

Reference Window

- If necessary, open the source page in Design view.
- If necessary, click the Toggle Pane button on the Standard toolbar to display the Folder List.
- Drag the filename of the target page from the Folder List to the location in the source page where you want to create the hyperlink.
- Release the mouse button to create the hyperlink.

You ask Brett to create the hyperlink from the home page to the Garden Center page using drag and drop.

To create a hyperlink using drag and drop:

1. In the Garden Center page, point to the **Home** hyperlink in the link bar, press and hold the **Ctrl** key, click the **Home** hyperlink, and then release the **Ctrl** key. The home page opens in Design view.

2. Click the **Toggle Pane** button 🖼 on the Standard toolbar. The Folder List opens and displays the files and folders in the garden Web site.

3. Click **center.htm** (the target page) in the Folder List to select it, and then hold down the left mouse button as you drag the pointer from the Folder List to the home page. The pointer changes to a 🚫 shape while you are moving the file out of the Folder List; it changes to a ⬆ shape when it is in Design view. Do *not* release the mouse button yet.

4. While still holding down the mouse button, move the pointer to the left of the **G** in "Garden Center" in the link bar in the home page. See Figure 2-23.

Figure 2-23	Creating the hyperlink to the Garden Center page

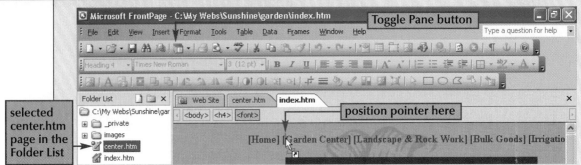

5. Release the mouse button to create the hyperlink. A Garden Center hyperlink is inserted into the link bar in the home page, using the page title from the center.htm page. See Figure 2-24. The text in the link bar now appears as "<u>Garden Center</u>Garden Center" because the page title was inserted in front of the text already present in the link bar.

Figure 2-24	Hyperlink added to the link bar

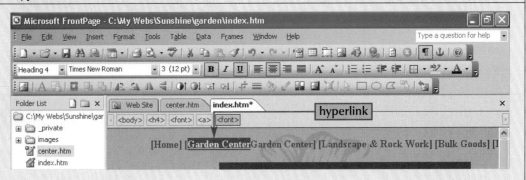

Next, remove the extra "Garden Center" text to create the desired entry in the link bar.

6. Select the **Garden Center** text that is *not* underlined in the link bar, and then press the **Delete** key to remove it. The Garden Center hyperlink (the underlined text) remains in the link bar.

7. Click 🖫 to close the Folder List.

8. Save the home page.

Now Brett can test the hyperlinks between the home page and the Garden Center page in a browser.

To test hyperlinks between Web pages in a browser:

1. Click the **Preview** button 🔍 on the Standard toolbar to open the home page in your browser. Notice that the Garden Center entry in the link bar is underlined, indicating that it is a hyperlink.

2. Point to the **Garden Center** hyperlink. The target of the hyperlink, the center.htm page, appears on the status bar to confirm that this hyperlink connects to a different Web page.

3. Click the **Garden Center** hyperlink in the link bar. The Garden Center Web page opens.

▶ **4.** Click the **Home** hyperlink in the link bar of the Garden Center Web page to reopen the home page.

▶ **5.** Close your browser and return to FrontPage.

Brett is excited about linking pages in the Web site. Next, you want to show Brett how to create a hyperlink to an e-mail address.

Creating a Hyperlink to an E-mail Address

A **mailto** is a hyperlink that contains an e-mail address. When a user clicks a mailto link in a Web page, the user's default e-mail program automatically opens and addresses a message to the address contained in the mailto. The user then can type the message and send it as usual.

When you type an e-mail address followed by a space in a Web page in Design view, FrontPage automatically creates a mailto and changes the appearance of the e-mail address to a hyperlink.

Reference Window

Creating a Mailto

- Click the location where you want to place the mailto, type the e-mail address, and then press the spacebar.

or

- Select the text to format as a mailto, and then click the Insert Hyperlink button on the Standard toolbar.
- In the Insert Hyperlink dialog box, click the E-mail Address button on the Link to bar.
- Type the target e-mail address in the E-mail address text box.
- If desired, type an optional subject in the Subject text box.
- Click the OK button.

Brett wants to format the nursery's name, which appears in the copyright information in the home page, as a mailto so visitors can click it to send an e-mail message to him. Because this text already exists, you'll need to show him how to format it as a hyperlink.

To create a mailto from existing text:

▶ **1.** If necessary, scroll to the bottom of the home page, and then select the text **Sunshine Landscape & Garden Center**.

▶ **2.** Click the **Insert Hyperlink** button 🖳 on the Standard toolbar. The Insert Hyperlink dialog box opens.

▶ **3.** Click the **E-mail Address** button 🖼 on the Link to bar to select it. The options for working with mailtos appear in the dialog box.

▶ **4.** Click the **E-mail address** text box, and then type your full e-mail address. (If you do not have an e-mail address, make one up.) As you begin typing, FrontPage adds "mailto:" to the beginning of your e-mail address.

When you create a mailto using the Insert Hyperlink dialog box, you can also specify a subject that will appear automatically in all messages sent using the mailto link. To help Brett identify messages sent from the Web site from other messages sent to him, he can add the subject "Web Site" to the mailto link. When Brett receives the messages, he will be able to determine those messages sent from the Web site by the message subject.

▶ **5.** Press the **Tab** key to move to the Subject text box, and then type **Web Site**. The mailto is complete.

▶ **6.** Click the **OK** button to close the Insert Hyperlink dialog box. The text is underlined, indicating that you created a hyperlink.

▶ **7.** Click the mailto link to deselect it, and then point to the mailto link you just created. The target of the hyperlink, which in this case is an e-mail address, appears on the status bar. Notice that the mailto contains your e-mail address, followed by a question mark and the subject you specified, "Web Site." See Figure 2-25.

Figure 2-25	Mailto link created in the home page

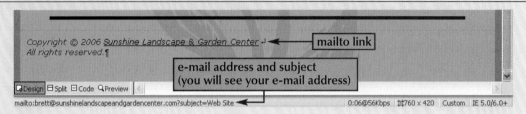

▶ **8.** Save the home page.

Brett's e-mail address is now included in the home page. Next, Brett can test this feature in a browser.

To test a mailto:

▶ **1.** Click the **Preview** button on the Standard toolbar to open the home page in the browser, and then press **Ctrl + End** to scroll to the bottom of the page.

▶ **2.** Click the **Sunshine Landscape & Garden Center** link to start your default e-mail program and to open a new message. Figure 2-26 shows the New Message window for Microsoft Outlook Express (the default e-mail program for Internet Explorer). If your computer uses an e-mail program other than Outlook Express, your e-mail window will look different. Notice that Brett's e-mail address was entered automatically in the To field, and that the subject you specified, "Web Site," appears in the Subject field.

Figure 2-26	Microsoft Outlook Express New Message window

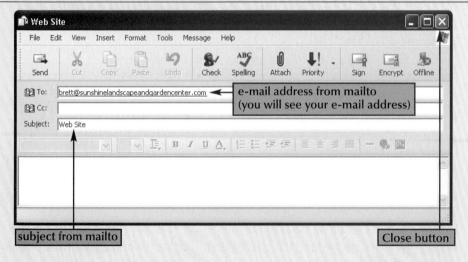

Trouble? If an Outlook Express dialog box opens and asks whether you want to specify a default e-mail program, click the No button.

Trouble? If an Internet Connection Wizard dialog box opens, click the Cancel button, and then click the Yes button to close the dialog box.

Trouble? If a Microsoft Outlook dialog box opens and indicates that no e-mail client is specified for your computer, click the OK button to continue.

Because Outlook Express started when you clicked the mailto link in the Web page, your test is complete. A Web site visitor who wants to send a message would type the message text and click the Send button to mail it. Because you are just testing the mailto to see whether it links to your e-mail program, rather than actually sending a message, you can close the New Message window.

3. Click the **Close** button ☒ on the New Message window title bar to return to the home page.

4. Click ☒ on the browser title bar to close it.

Now visitors can click the mailto link to send a message.

Using Pictures as Hyperlinks

You remind Brett that a picture can do more than enhance the appearance of a Web page. A picture can also contain a hyperlink that opens another Web page. There are two ways to use a picture as a hyperlink. The first method is to create an **image map**, which is a picture that contains one or more hotspots. A **hotspot** is an area of a picture that, when clicked, opens the hyperlink target. A hotspot can have a rectangular, circular, or polygonal shape. The second method is to format the entire picture as a hyperlink. Clicking any part of the picture opens the target of the hyperlink. You'll show Brett how to create an image map first.

Creating an Image Map

To demonstrate how to create an image map, you'll show Brett how to format the word "sunshine" in the logo in the Garden Center page as a hotspot that opens the home page.

Creating an Image Map Reference Window

- Click the picture in which to create the hotspot to select it.
- Click the button for the desired hotspot shape on the Pictures toolbar.
- Click and hold down the mouse button while you drag the pointer to specify the desired size of the hotspot on the picture, and then release the mouse button. The Insert Hyperlink dialog box opens.
- Click the button on the Link to bar to specifiy the target of the hyperlink (an existing file or Web page, a place in the document, a new document, or an e-mail address), and then specify the target of the hyperlink on the page that opens.
- Click the OK button.

Because the content is rectangular in shape, Brett needs to create the hotspot as a rectangle.

To create a rectangular hotspot:

▶ **1.** Click the **center.htm** tab at the top of the Contents pane, and then click the picture (the Sunshine logo) in the Garden Center page to select it.

▶ **2.** Click the **Rectangular Hotspot** button 🔲 on the Pictures toolbar, and then position the pointer in the upper-left corner of the picture. The pointer changes to a 𝒫 shape when it is pointing to the picture. See Figure 2-27.

Figure 2-27	Creating a hotspot

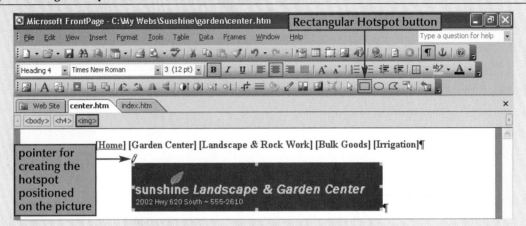

▶ **3.** Hold down the left mouse button and drag the pointer down and to the right until you have enclosed the word "sunshine" and the leaf graphic in the hotspot box. As you drag the pointer, the box that appears on the picture indicates the size and location of the hotspot.

▶ **4.** Release the mouse button. The Insert Hyperlink dialog box opens. If necessary, click the **Existing File or Web Page** button 🔳 on the Link to bar.

▶ **5.** Double-click **index.htm (open)** in the list to select the home page as the target of the hotspot. The Insert Hyperlink dialog box closes and the rectangle on the picture indicates the location of the hotspot you just created.

   Trouble? If your hotspot appears in the wrong location, press the Delete key to remove it, select the picture, and then repeat Steps 2 through 5, or use the sizing handles on the hotspot to resize it.

▶ **6.** Save the Garden Center page.

   Brett successfully created the hotspot that opens the home page. Now users of the garden Web site can click either the word "sunshine" in the logo or the word "Home" in the link bar to open the home page.

Highlighting Hotspots in a Picture

When you create a hotspot, you usually can see its shape while it is selected. Depending on the picture, however, it might be difficult to see the hotspot or hotspots it contains. By highlighting a picture's hotspots, you can see their location more clearly and confirm their placement.

Highlighting Hotspots in a Picture

- Click the picture that contains the hotspot(s) to select it.
- Click the Highlight Hotspots button on the Pictures toolbar.
- Click the Highlight Hotspots button again to turn off the highlights.

Next, you will check the location of the hotspot and verify its placement.

To highlight the hotspot:

1. Make sure that the picture is still selected, and then click the **Highlight Hotspots** button on the Pictures toolbar. The hotspot in the picture appears as a dark square in a white picture. See Figure 2-28.

Highlighting hotspots in a picture | Figure 2-28

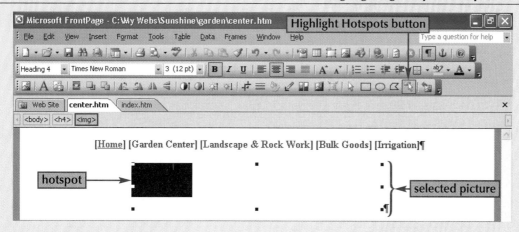

Trouble? If the hotspot is selected when you click the Highlight Hotspots button, it will appear as a solid black image, as shown in Figure 2-28. If the hotspot is not selected, it will appear as a white object with a black outline.

2. Click the **Highlight Hotspots** button to turn off the hotspot highlights, and then press **Ctrl + Home** to deselect the picture and scroll to the top of the page.

3. Point to the word "sunshine" in the picture, which is the hotspot. Notice that the filename for this hyperlink—index.htm—appears on the status bar, confirming that it is a hyperlink.

Next, Brett will test the hotspot in the browser to verify that it works correctly.

To test a hotspot in the browser:

1. Click the **Preview** button on the Standard toolbar to open the Garden Center page in a browser.

2. Point to the word "sunshine" in the picture. The pointer changes to a 🖑 shape, and the filename for the hyperlink appears on the status bar; both of these changes indicate that the word "sunshine" is a hyperlink.

3. Click the word "sunshine" in the picture to open the home page.

4. Click **Garden Center** in the link bar in the home page to return to the Garden Center page.

5. Close your browser.

The hotspot in the picture provides users with another way to return to the site's home page.

Inserting a Picture Hyperlink into a Web Page

Next, you'll show Brett how to use an entire picture as a hyperlink. The graphic designer created small pictures for each page in the Web site. You'll insert these pictures in place of the text that you created in the link bar. Brett hopes that the graphics will be more visually interesting than the text.

To insert a picture into a Web page:

1. Click the **index.htm** tab at the top of the Contents pane to switch to this page.

2. At the top of the home page, select the text **[Garden Center]**, including the brackets around the words, but not the spaces on either side of the brackets. You'll replace this selected text with a picture that has the same text.

3. Click the **Insert Picture From File** button ⊞ on the Standard toolbar. The Picture dialog box opens.

4. If necessary, open the **Tutorial.02\Tutorial** folder included with your Data Files.

5. Click the **gc_pic.gif** file to select it, and then click the **Insert** button. As shown in Figure 2-29, a picture with the text "Garden Center" replaces the text you selected in Step 2.

Figure 2-29 ▶ **Picture inserted into the home page**

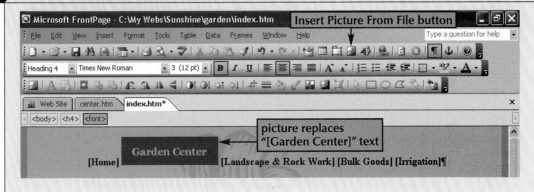

Now that Brett has inserted the picture, you can show him how to format it as a hyperlink. The target of the hyperlink will be the center.htm page in the Web site; clicking anywhere on the picture will open the Garden Center page. Formatting a picture as a hyperlink is different from creating an image map, which only uses the specified part of the picture (the hotspot) as the hyperlink.

To format the picture as a hyperlink:

1. Click the Garden Center picture to select it.
2. Click the **Insert Hyperlink** button 🖼 on the Standard toolbar. The Insert Hyperlink dialog box opens.
3. If necessary, click the **Existing File or Web Page** button 📄 on the Link to bar. The files and folders in the garden Web site appear in the dialog box. The target of the hyperlink is the center.htm page, so you'll select this page.
4. Click **center.htm (open)** in the list box, and then click the **OK** button. The picture is formatted as a hyperlink that opens the Garden Center page.
5. Save the home page and save the gc_pic.gif file in the Web site's images folder.

To test the hyperlink, you ask Brett to open the home page in a browser.

To test the picture hyperlink:

1. Click the **Preview** button 🔍 on the Standard toolbar. The home page opens in a browser.
2. Click the Garden Center picture at the top of the page. The Garden Center page opens.
3. Click the word "sunshine" in the picture on the Garden Center page. The home page opens.
4. Close your browser.

Brett likes the picture in the link bar better than the plain text. When you complete the Review Assignments at the end of this tutorial, you will replace the remaining text entries in the link bars on the home and Garden Center pages with pictures and format them as hyperlinks.

Examining HTML for a Picture Hyperlink and an Image Map

Brett is curious about the differences in the HTML document between using an entire picture as a hyperlink and using a part of a picture as a hyperlink. To explain the differences, you decide to show him the HTML documents for the home page and the Garden Center page.

To view the HTML documents and examine the picture hyperlinks:

1. With the home page displayed in Design view, click the Garden Center picture to select it, and then click the **Show Code View** button 🔲 Code at the bottom of the Contents pane. The HTML document that creates the home page opens. Figure 2-30 shows the HTML <a> </a> tags that create the hyperlink from the gc_pic.gif file to the center.htm page. Notice that the <img> tag is nested in the anchor tags.

Figure 2-30 HTML document for the home page

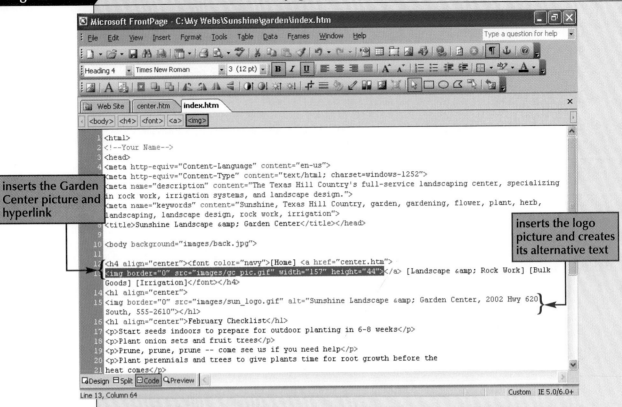

The second <img> tag in this document creates the logo at the top of the page. Notice the alt attribute, which contains the alternative text you added to this picture.

2. Click the **center.htm** tab at the top of the Contents pane, and then change to Code view for this page. Figure 2-31 shows the HTML <map> </map> tags that create the rectangular hotspot in the logo. Notice that the shape property defines the area as "rect" (for rectangle) and that the coords property defines the pixel locations for the four corners of the rectangular hotspot (your coordinates might be slightly different). The href property identifies the target of the hyperlink, index.htm, which is the home page.

HTML document for the Garden Center page | Figure 2-31

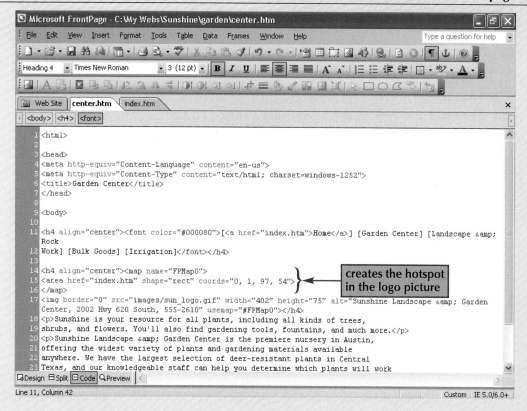

3. Return to Design view for the center.htm and index.htm pages.
4. Close the garden Web site, and then exit FrontPage.

In the next session, you'll show Brett how to create a small version of a picture that contains a hyperlink to the original picture. You'll also teach Brett how to change a picture's characteristics, create an animated button that contains a hyperlink, use a page transition, and create animated text in a Web page.

Session 2.2 Quick Check

Review

1. True or False: You can import a folder and its contents into a Web site.
2. What are three common targets of a hyperlink?
3. What is a source page? What is a target page?
4. What is a mailto, and what happens when you click one in a Web page?
5. What are the three shapes of hotspots that you can create using FrontPage?
6. What is the difference between an image map and a picture that is formatted as a hyperlink?

Session 2.3

Creating a Thumbnail Picture

So far in this book, you have included pictures in your Web pages to increase visual interest and create hyperlinks to other pages. You can use FrontPage to change a picture's appearance in other ways, as well. For example, you can create a smaller version of a picture, a picture with washed-out colors, or a picture with special edges.

A **thumbnail picture** is a small picture that contains a hyperlink to a larger version of the same picture, or to any other target, such as a Web page. Using a thumbnail picture is appropriate when some users might not need the larger version. Users who want to view the larger picture can click the thumbnail picture, which contains a hyperlink that opens the larger picture. Thumbnail pictures are commonly used in Web pages that contain catalog items, such as a clothing or shoe store. Using thumbnail pictures reduces the download time of the Web page for all users, especially for users with dial-up connections.

The hyperlink in a thumbnail picture might connect to a picture file or to a Web page that contains the picture and some text. When the thumbnail's target is a picture file (such as a GIF file), the browser opens the picture file; the user must then click the browser's Back button to return to the previous Web page. If the hyperlink opens a Web page that contains the larger picture, the page can include hyperlinks to other Web pages, just like any other Web page. When you create a thumbnail of a larger picture, FrontPage automatically creates the thumbnail picture, inserts it in place of the larger picture, and then creates a hyperlink from the thumbnail picture to the larger picture.

Reference Window

Creating a Thumbnail Picture

- If necessary, insert the full-size picture into the Web page in the desired location.
- Select the picture.
- Click the Auto Thumbnail button on the Pictures toolbar.

Brett received a picture of a map to the nursery's location from the graphic designer and has asked you to show him how to insert it into the home page. To save space in the home page and to decrease its download time, you suggest that he instead use a thumbnail of the map with a hyperlink to the full-size map.

To open the home page and create the thumbnail picture:

1. Make sure you have your Data Files, start **FrontPage**, open the **garden** Web site from the location where your Web sites are stored, open the **index.htm** page in Design view, and, if necessary, display the Pictures toolbar and dock it below the Formatting toolbar.

2. Click at the end of the marquee, press the **Enter** key to create a new paragraph, and then click the **Center** button on the Formatting toolbar to center the paragraph.

3. Click the **Insert Picture From File** button on the Standard toolbar, open the **Tutorial.02\Tutorial** folder included with your Data Files, and then double-click **map.jpg**. The picture of a map to the nursery is inserted into the home page. The picture is large, and adding it to the home page increased the download time of the home page from seven to 14 seconds (at 56 Kbps).

4. Click the map picture to select it.

5. Click the **Auto Thumbnail** button on the Pictures toolbar to create the thumbnail picture. See Figure 2-32.

Thumbnail picture added to the home page

Figure 2-32

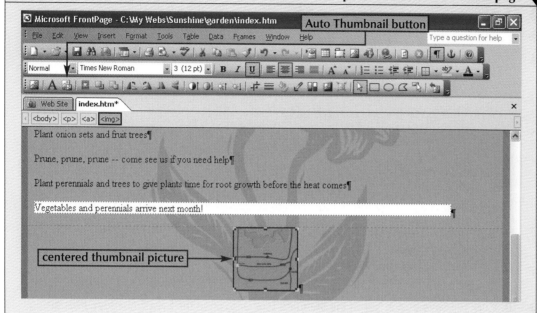

The thumbnail picture replaces the full-size picture in the home page. FrontPage created a hyperlink from the thumbnail to the map.jpg file in the Tutorial.02\Tutorial folder included with your Data Files, which is the location of the original, full-size picture from which the thumbnail was created. When you save the home page, you will need to save both pictures in the garden Web site. Before you save the pictures, however, Brett wants you to show him how to change the characteristics of the thumbnail picture.

Changing Picture Characteristics

You can use FrontPage to change many picture characteristics. For example, you can convert a picture to black and white, rotate it, change its contrast or brightness level, add a beveled edge to the picture, or wash out a picture. When you **wash out** a picture, you reduce its brightness and contrast to create a faded appearance. You can also change a picture's position; for example, you can position it in front of or behind text and other page elements.

In viewing the thumbnail picture, Brett wonders if site visitors will know to click the picture to display a larger version of the map. You tell Brett that he can add text on top of the picture to indicate its function. Because the map image is dark, it would be appropriate to wash out the colors to make the text more readable.

To change picture characteristics:

1. With the thumbnail picture still selected, click the **Color** button 🖼 on the Pictures toolbar. A menu opens, providing four options: Automatic, Grayscale, Black & White, and Wash Out. Only the Grayscale and Wash Out effects are enabled for a color picture. If you select the Grayscale option, FrontPage will convert the picture to use shades of gray instead of colors. When it is enabled, the Black & White option lets you change a picture's colors to black and white, with no shading. This option is available for pictures without any shading.

2. Click **Grayscale**. The picture changes to light and dark shades of gray instead of colors.

3. Click the ▦ button, and then click **Grayscale** to restore the colors to the thumbnail picture.

4. Click the **Rotate Left 90°** button ▥ on the Pictures toolbar. The picture flips on its left side.

5. Click the **Rotate Right 90°** button ▥ to rotate the picture 90 degrees to the right, which returns the picture to its original orientation.

6. Click the ▦ button, and then click **Wash Out**. Notice that the colors in the picture become faded, but the picture still contains colors.

7. Click the **Restore** button ▥ on the Pictures toolbar to remove the wash-out effect and restore the picture to its original state. Clicking the Restore button removes all previously applied, unsaved picture effects.

   Brett believes that the wash-out effect provides the best appearance for the thumbnail picture, so he wants to use it. He also wants to apply a new effect to the picture's edges.

8. Click the **Undo** button ▥ on the Standard toolbar to return to the thumbnail picture with the wash-out effect.

9. Click the **Bevel** button ▥ on the Pictures toolbar. Notice that the edges of the picture change to include a raised effect. The picture now has a wash-out effect and a beveled edge.

10. Click the **Save** button ▥ on the Standard toolbar to open the Save Embedded Files dialog box. You need to save the original picture file, map.jpg, and the thumbnail picture, which FrontPage automatically named map_small.jpg, in the images folder of the garden Web site. FrontPage names a thumbnail by appending "_small" to the filename of the full-size picture.

11. Make sure that the files will be saved in the garden Web site's images folder, and then click the **OK** button. The picture files are saved in the garden Web site.

Next, you'll show Brett how to add text on top of a picture so users can easily identify its function.

Adding Text on Top of a Picture

When you insert a picture that you plan to use as a hyperlink into a Web page, a good design practice is to add descriptive text on top of the picture to identify its function. You place text on a picture by selecting the picture and then using the Text button on the Pictures toolbar to add the text. To add text on a picture, the picture must be saved as a GIF file. FrontPage will convert the picture to a GIF file, if necessary, when you try to add text on it.

Adding Text on a Picture

- Click the picture to select it.
- Click the Text button on the Pictures toolbar to open a text box on top of the selected picture. If necessary, click the OK button to convert the picture to a GIF file.
- Type the desired text. If necessary, press the Enter key to start a new line, and format the text as desired.
- Click anywhere in the Web page to close the text box.

Brett wants to add text on the picture to indicate that it opens a map to the nursery. You ask him to use the Formatting toolbar to format the text so it is easy to read.

To add text on a picture:

1. If necessary, click the thumbnail picture to select it. Sizing handles appear around the edge of the picture.

2. Click the **Text** button [A] on the Pictures toolbar. Because the thumbnail is a JPEG file, a FrontPage message box opens and tells you that you'll need to convert the picture to a GIF file.

3. Click the **OK** button in the message box to convert the picture to a GIF file. A text box with eight sizing handles and an insertion point opens on top of the picture.

4. Type **Map to**, press the **Enter** key to start a new line, and then type **Sunshine**. This text will appear on top of the picture. By default, text is centered, but it looks left-aligned when you are in editing mode.

5. Click outside the picture to deselect the picture and the text box, and then click the text on the picture to select the picture and the text box. Sizing handles appear around the picture and the text box. The text isn't vertically centered on the image. You can resize a text box using a sizing handle or by dragging it to a new location. You'll move the text box up.

6. Click anywhere in the text box and hold down the left mouse button, drag the text box up so it looks like the one shown in Figure 2-33, and then release the mouse button.

Text added on thumbnail picture ◄ **Figure 2-33**

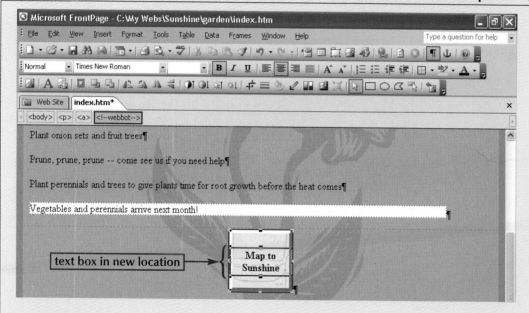

Trouble? If you click in the text box and release the left mouse button, you will change to editing mode, which displays an insertion point. If this problem occurs, repeat Steps 5 and 6.

When you add text on a picture, the text is not treated as regular text in the HTML document; the text box is coded as an image map. However, you can format the text just like any other text in a Web page. Brett wants to change the font color and style of the text to make it more prominent. After he makes this change, you'll show Brett the HTML document so he understands the difference between text in a Web page, alternative text for a picture, and an image map that contains text.

To change the font color and style of the text:

1. Click the text **Map to Sunshine**. The insertion point appears in the text and the text box changes to editing mode.

2. Use the mouse to select the text **Map to Sunshine**.

3. Click the **list arrow** for the Font Color button on the Formatting toolbar to open the color palette, and then click the **Navy** color in the Document Colors section. The text that you added on top of the thumbnail picture changes from black to navy, but you won't see this change until you deselect the text.

4. Click the **Italic** button on the Formatting toolbar to change the text to italic.

5. Click outside the picture to deselect it and the text box. The completed thumbnail picture appears in Figure 2-34.

Figure 2-34 **Completed thumbnail picture**

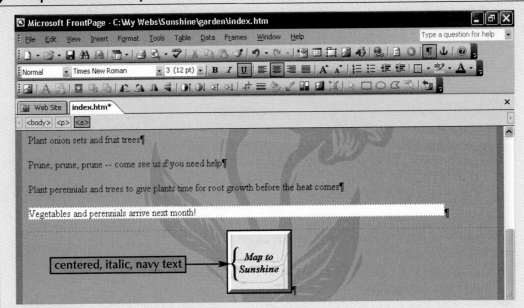

6. Save the home page. Because you converted the thumbnail to a GIF file, you need to save the map_small.gif file in the garden Web site. Make sure that the images folder is selected in the Save Embedded Files dialog box, and then click the **OK** button.

Now Brett has created a thumbnail picture, changed several of its characteristics, and added text on it. You ask him to test the thumbnail picture to make sure the hyperlink works correctly and opens the full-size map picture.

To test the thumbnail picture:

1. Click the **Preview** button on the Standard toolbar to open the home page in a browser, and then scroll to the bottom of the page (if necessary) so you can see the thumbnail picture.

2. Point to the thumbnail picture. The pointer changes to a shape. The path on the status bar indicates that this picture contains a hyperlink to the map.jpg file.

3. Click the thumbnail picture. The map.jpg file opens in your browser. The URL in the Address bar indicates that this page is a JPEG file and not an HTML document. Because you opened a picture file and not a Web page with hyperlinks, you will need to use your browser's Back button to return to the home page.

4. Click your browser's **Back** button to return to the home page, and then close your browser.

To return to the previous Web page, you had to click your browser's Back button. Some Web users might not know to do this, so you tell Brett that he will need to provide a hyperlink to return to the home page. To do so, he needs to include the full-size map picture in a Web page. You already created a Web page that contains the map picture, so Brett only needs to import that page into the garden Web site and then create the appropriate hyperlink.

To import the Web page into the garden Web site:

1. Click the **Web Site** tab on the top of the Contents pane, click the **Toggle Pane** button on the Standard toolbar to display the Folder List, and then make sure the garden Web site's root folder is selected.

2. Click **File** on the menu bar, and then click **Import** to open the Import dialog box.

3. Click the **Add File** button to open the Add File to Import List dialog box, open the **Tutorial.02\Tutorial** folder included with your Data Files, and then double-click **map_page.htm**. The map_page.htm file is listed in the Import dialog box.

4. Click the **OK** button to import the Web page into the garden Web site.

With the Web page imported into the garden Web site, you are ready to show Brett how to add the link back to the home page. First, he'll need to change the link from the thumbnail picture in the home page to the imported Map to Sunshine Landscape & Garden Center page (map_page.htm). Then he'll need to create the link from the Map page to the home page.

To change the hyperlink for the thumbnail picture:

1. Click the **index.htm** tab to switch to the home page in Design view, and then close the Folder List.

2. Right-click the thumbnail picture (not the "Map to Sunshine" text) to select it and open the shortcut menu, click **Hyperlink Properties**, and then, if necessary, click the **Existing File or Web page** button on the Link to bar. The Address text box displays the current hyperlink to the map.jpg file in the Web site's images folder.

   Trouble? If the Insert Hyperlink dialog box opens and the Address text box is empty, then you right-clicked the picture's text box. Click the Cancel button, and then repeat Step 2.

3. Click **map_page.htm** in the list box to set this page as the target of the hyperlink, and then click the **OK** button to close the Edit Hyperlink dialog box.

4. Save the home page.

After changing the target of the hyperlink, Brett needs to test the page to verify that the hyperlink from the thumbnail picture opens the correct Web page.

To test the hyperlink from the thumbnail picture:

1. Click the **Preview** button 🔍 on the Standard toolbar.

2. If necessary, scroll down the home page until you see the thumbnail picture, and then click the Map to Sunshine picture to open the Map page. The URL in the Address bar specifies the map_page.htm Web page, and not the map.jpg file. The page doesn't include a hyperlink back to the home page yet, so you will need to add one.

3. Close your browser.

4. Right-click the thumbnail picture (not the "Map to Sunshine" text) to open the shortcut menu, and then click **Follow Hyperlink**. The map_page.htm file opens in Design view.

Brett successfully created the link from the home page to the Map page. Now he needs to complete the link in the other direction—from the Map page to the home page. You tell Brett that a fun way to do this is to use an interactive button.

Creating an Interactive Button

You have already shown Brett how to create hyperlinks from text and pictures. Another way to create a hyperlink is to use an interactive button. An **interactive button** is a button that displays special effects to change its appearance depending on how the user interacts with it. When the user clicks the button, it opens the target location. You can set special effects from a list of available effects, or you can use the custom option to create a picture that changes on mouse over. **Mouse over**, or **mouse fly over**, is the act of moving the pointer over an interactive button or picture. When you point to an interactive button, the appearance of the button changes to match the mouse-over effect specified for that button.

Brett wants you to create an interactive button in the Map page that changes on mouse over and contains a hyperlink that opens the home page.

Reference Window	**Creating an Interactive Button in a Web Page**

- Click the location in the Web page to insert the interactive button.
- Click Insert on the menu bar, and then click Interactive Button. The Interactive Buttons dialog box opens.
- On the Button tab, select the type of button you want to create. Select the default text in the Text text box, and then type the text that you want to appear on the button. Finally, click the Browse button to select the target of the hyperlink.
- If desired, click the Text tab to change the default font, font style, font size, font color, and alignment of the button.
- If desired, click the Image tab to change the button's size, characteristics, background color, or transparency.
- Click the OK button.

Brett wants the interactive button to display the text "Return to Home Page," to contain a hyperlink that opens the home page, and to use coordinated colors for the interactive button's effects.

To create an interactive button:

▶ **1.** Click the blank paragraph between the logo picture and the map picture.

▶ **2.** Click **Insert** on the menu bar, and then click **Interactive Button**. The Interactive Buttons dialog box opens.

The Text text box displays the default text, "Button Text," which you will change to "Return to Home Page." Then you will preview several buttons to view their colors and effects by selecting a button in the Buttons list box and pointing to the sample button that appears in the Preview box.

▶ **3.** Select the text **Button Text** in the Text text box, and then type **Return to Home Page**. This text will appear on the button to indicate its function. As you type, notice that the sample button in the Preview box is updated, as shown in Figure 2-35.

Interactive Buttons dialog box ◀ **Figure 2-35**

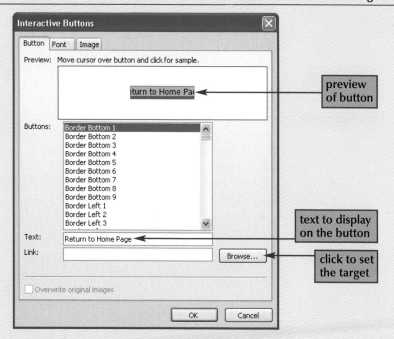

The text you entered exceeds the current button's size, so you will need to change the button's size. You change the button's size using the Image tab. However, because changing the button type returns the button to its default dimensions, you should change the button size as your last task so you don't have to resize it twice.

▶ **4.** Click a few of the button types in the Buttons list box and preview their samples. Notice that the buttons have different default shapes and color combinations.

Brett likes the Embossed Capsule 1 button because its color coordinates well with the map picture in the page.

▶ **5.** Scroll the Buttons list as necessary, and then click **Embossed Capsule 1**. (The button types are listed alphabetically.)

Next, you'll select the button's target.

▶ **6.** Click the **Browse** button. The Edit Hyperlink dialog box opens. If necessary, click the **Existing File or Web page** button 🔳 on the Link to bar.

▶ **7.** Click **index.htm (open)** in the list, and then click the **OK** button.

Next, Brett needs to change the default size of the button so all of the text that appears on it is visible. You ask him to make this change using the Image tab.

To change the interactive button's size:

▶ **1.** Click the **Image** tab. If you know the exact size in pixels for the button you want to create, you can enter those values in the Width and Height text boxes. In most cases, however, you'll need to increase or decrease the button size by viewing the changes as you make them.

▶ **2.** Click the **Width** up arrow several times and watch the sample button in the Preview box. As you click the Width up arrow, the width of the button increases. Keep clicking the **Width** up arrow until you can see all of the button text. (You will need to change the width to approximately 140 pixels to accommodate the text.) See Figure 2-36.

Figure 2-36	**Revised button size**

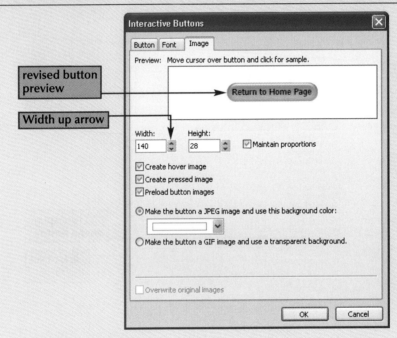

Now all of the text is visible on the button. The last change that you'll ask Brett to make is to change the button's text color. You tell him that he can set three different colors for a button's text: inactive (original), hover, or clicked (pressed).

To change the button's effects:

▶ **1.** Click the **Font** tab to display those options. The message at the top of the Font tab indicates that you can move the pointer over and click the button in the Preview box to view its behavior in the Web page.

▶ **2.** Click the **Original Font Color** list arrow, and then click the **Navy** color. When the button is inactive, the button's text will be navy.

▶ **3.** Click the **Hovered Font Color** list arrow, and then click the **Maroon** color. When you point to the button, the text color will change to maroon.

4. Click the **Pressed Font Color** list arrow, and then click the **Fuchsia** color. When you click the button, the text color will change to fuchsia. The completed Font tab appears in Figure 2-37.

button with the original font color (pointing to the button displays the hovered font color; clicking the button displays the pressed font color)

5. Point to and then click the sample button in the Preview box to view your changes. If you need to make any changes to the button, you could do so. You could also use this tab to change the font, font style, and font size of the button text.

The interactive button is complete, so Brett can close the dialog box and test the changes in a browser.

To test the interactive button:

1. Click the **OK** button to close the Interactive Buttons dialog box and to insert the button into the Map page.

2. Save the Map page, and save the button files created by FrontPage for the interactive button in the Web site's images folder. Three picture files are created to represent each state of the interactive button: original, hovered, and pressed.

3. Preview the Map page in a browser, and then point to and click the interactive button, noting the effects for each situation. When you click the interactive button, the home page opens.

4. Click the thumbnail picture to return to the Map page, and then close your browser. Your test is successful.

The interactive button provides an attractive, animated way of creating a hyperlink to another Web page. The interactive button effect helps draw the user's attention to the button for selecting the hyperlink. As with other Web page features, you should apply these effects carefully to avoid overwhelming or distracting users.

Using Dynamic HTML

Dynamic HTML (**DHTML**) gives you the ability to control the display of text and objects, such as pictures, in a Web page. When a DHTML command is applied to text or a picture, Internet Explorer (and other Web browsers that support DHTML) will animate the text or picture (or apply other effects that you specify) by executing a **script**, which is a small program that contains a set of instructions. When a Web browser encounters a Web page that contains a script, it interprets the instructions and performs a specific action. Because DHTML does not require additional information from the Web server that stores the Web page, it is very efficient and animates content without consuming network resources. Page transitions and animations are two methods of making a Web page more interesting. Brett wants to apply each of these features to enhance the Map to Sunshine Landscape & Garden Center page. However, just like any other animation, you remind Brett that too many effects in a Web page increase its download time and can be very distracting to users.

Creating a Page Transition

A **page transition** is an animated effect that you can apply to one or more Web pages in a Web site. When a user opens a page with a transition, the specified transition occurs while the page is being loaded. You can specify a closing transition for a page, as well. Although transitions are easy to apply, you should use transitions sparingly because having too many can overwhelm users and make opening and closing pages occur much more slowly than when no transitions are used.

Reference Window	**Applying a Page Transition**

- With the desired page open in Design view, click Format on the menu bar, and then click Page Transition to open the Page Transitions dialog box.
- If necessary, click the Event list arrow, and then select the desired event.
- Enter a value (in seconds) in the Duration (seconds) text box.
- Click the desired transition effect.
- Click the OK button.

Brett wants to add a transition effect to the Map page.

To add a page transition:

1. Click **Format** on the menu bar, and then click **Page Transition** to open the Page Transitions dialog box shown in Figure 2-38.

Figure 2-38	**Page Transitions dialog box**

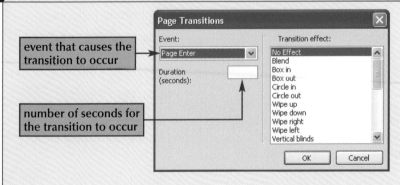

The default event is Page Enter, which means that the transition will occur when the page is opened or refreshed in the browser. Three other options are available: Page Exit, which applies the transition when the user leaves the page; Site Enter, which applies the transition when the user opens any page in the Web site; and Site Exit, which applies the transition when the user leaves the Web site.

Trouble? If the Event list box is not set to Page Enter, click the Event list arrow, and then click Page Enter.

2. Click the **Duration (seconds)** text box, and then type **5** as the number of seconds that the transition should occur.

3. In the Transition effect list box, click **Wipe right** to select that effect.

Trouble? If you do not have the Wipe right transition, select another transition effect.

4. Click the **OK** button to complete the page transition specifications. FrontPage creates a script to execute the action you selected. When a browser that can interpret the script opens the Map page, it will create the page transition.

5. Save the Map page.

In addition to page transitions, you tell Brett that he can also control the manner in which text and individual objects, such as pictures, are displayed in a Web page.

Creating Animated Text in a Web Page

Animation is an effect that causes an element to "fly" into view from a corner or side of the page or in some other eye-catching way, such as a spiraling motion. You can apply animation to either text or a picture. Animation is also created using a script that FrontPage creates.

Creating Animated Text or an Animated Picture in a Web Page	Reference Window

- Select the text or picture that you want to animate.
- Click View on the menu bar, point to Toolbars, and then click DHTML Effects to display the DHTML Effects toolbar.
- Click the On list arrow, and then select an event on which you want the effect to occur.
- Click the Apply list arrow, and then select an effect to apply.
- If it is active, click the Effect list arrow and select a direction from which to apply the effect.

Brett wants to see how the home page would look with animated text. To demonstrate this effect, you'll animate the "February Checklist" heading.

To add text animation:

1. Click the **index.htm** tab at the top of the Contents pane.

2. Scroll the page as necessary and select the text **February Checklist**. To access the commands for animating text, you'll need to display the DHTML Effects toolbar.

3. Click **View** on the menu bar, point to **Toolbars**, and then click **DHTML Effects**. The DHTML Effects toolbar opens, as either a docked or floating toolbar. If necessary, drag this toolbar and dock it below the Pictures toolbar. Then make sure that the Highlight Dynamic HTML Effects button ⊞ on the DHTML Effects toolbar has an orange background to indicate that this feature is enabled, so that DHTML elements will be highlighted in Design view, making them easier to locate.

Next, specify the effects for the selected text.

4. Click the **On** list arrow on the DHTML Effects toolbar, and then click **Page load**. This setting will apply the effect when the page is opened or refreshed in the browser.

You can specify three other effects for pictures: Click, which causes the animation to occur when the user clicks the element; Double click, which causes the animation to occur when the user double-clicks the element; and Mouse over, which causes the animation to occur on mouse over.

5. Click the **Apply** list arrow on the DHTML Effects toolbar, and then click **Fly in**. This setting will cause the selected text to fly into the page from a direction that you specify. When you select certain effects, you must also indicate the direction from which to apply the effect. You will know that you need to select a direction if the Effect list arrow becomes active.

6. Click the **Effect** list arrow on the DHTML Effects toolbar, which displays the text "< Choose Settings >" when it is active, and then click **Along corner**. See Figure 2-39. This setting indicates that the specified effect will occur from the corner of the window. Notice that the DHTML element in the Web page has a light-blue background; this background will not be visible in the browser.

Figure 2-39	Animated text added to the home page

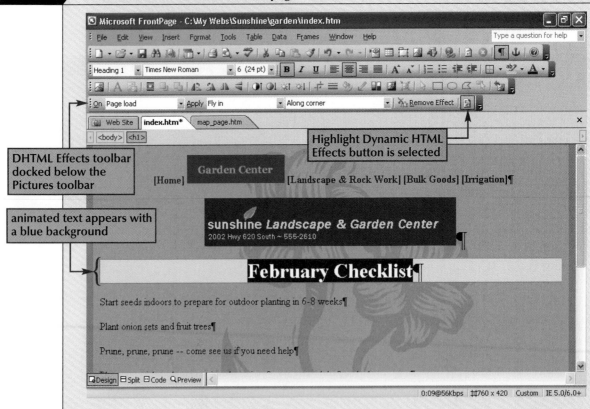

You are finished setting the text animation.

7. Save the home page.

If a browser cannot process these effects, it will ignore them and open the page anyway. To verify that these effects work correctly, you must use a browser to test the page transition and text animation.

To test the text animation and page transition:

1. Click the **Preview** button 🔍 on the Standard toolbar to open the home page in the browser. The animation occurs for the "February Checklist" text.

Trouble? If you do not see the text animation in the page, refresh the Web page.

2. Click the thumbnail picture to open the Map to Sunshine Landscape & Garden Center page. As the browser loads the page, the page transition occurs.

3. Click the interactive button. The "February Checklist" text is animated again.

4. Close your browser.

So Brett will better understand the different effects that he created in this tutorial, you'll show him the HTML document for the home page and the Map page.

Examining the HTML for Pages with Special Effects

When you created the interactive button for the Map page, FrontPage created a Java applet and inserted it into the HTML document. The page transition and text animation were implemented with Java scripts. An **applet** uses a series of parameters that specify an object's behavior. You can see this program by examining the page that contains it in Code view. Before exiting FrontPage, you ask Brett to hide the DHTML Effects and Pictures toolbars.

To view the HTML documents for the pages containing special effects:

1. Click **View** on the menu bar, point to **Toolbars**, and then click **DHTML Effects**. The DHTML Effects toolbar closes.

2. Click **View** on the menu bar, point to **Toolbars**, and then click **Pictures** to close the Pictures toolbar.

3. With the home page displayed in Design view, click the **Show Code View** button ⊡ Code to change to Code view. The HTML document for the home page appears in Figure 2-40.

Figure 2-40 | **HTML document for the home page**

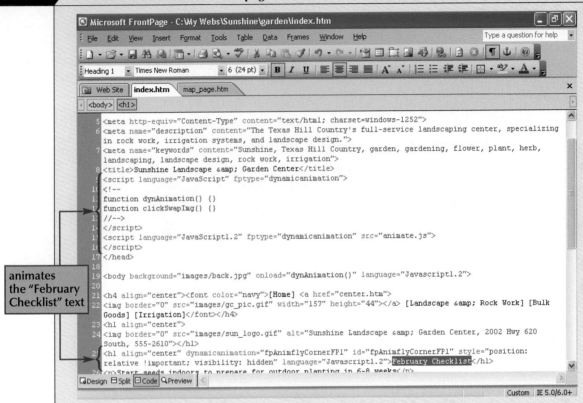

animates the "February Checklist" text

4. Return to Design view for the home page, and then click the **map_page.htm** tab and change to Code view.

5. Press **Ctrl + Home** to scroll to the top of the page. The first half of the HTML document for the Map page appears in Figure 2-41.

HTML document for the Map page | **Figure 2-41**

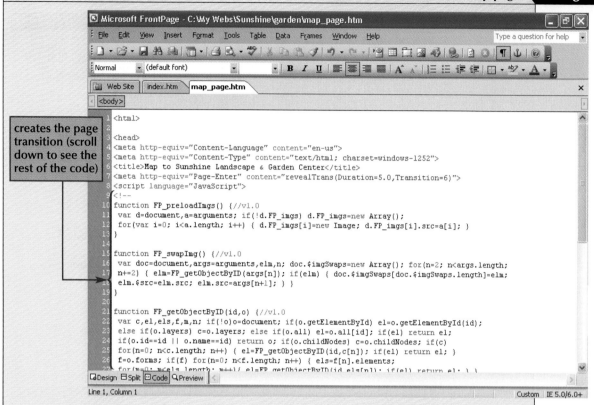

6. Press **Ctrl + End** to scroll to the bottom of the Map page, and then examine the rest of the HTML document shown in Figure 2-42.

Figure 2-42	HTML document for the rest of the Map page

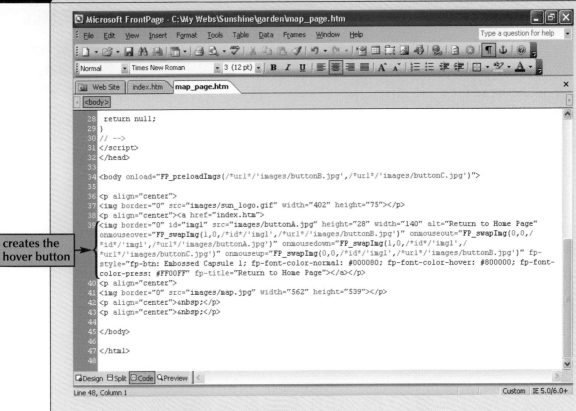

creates the hover button

7. Return to Design view for the Map page. You are finished with your work, so you can close FrontPage.

8. Close the garden Web site, and then exit FrontPage.

The Web site for the Sunshine Landscape & Garden Center now contains three pages that are linked together. In the next tutorial, you will help Brett to learn more about hyperlinks and to examine the different views of a Web site.

Session 2.3 Quick Check

1. When you create a thumbnail picture in a Web page, FrontPage automatically creates a(n) _____ to the original picture that was used to create the thumbnail.

2. List three effects that you can apply to a picture using the Pictures toolbar.

3. Describe the process for adding text on top of a picture in a Web page.

4. Moving the pointer over an interactive button is called _____.

5. True or False: An HTML tag creates an interactive button in a Web page.

6. True or False: A page transition reduces the speed at which a Web page opens and closes.

7. True or False: Animation is an effect that causes an element to "fly" into view from a designated area of the page.

Review

Tutorial Summary

In this tutorial, you learned how to add graphics to a Web site, create page transitions, and create animated text. You also learned about the different file formats of pictures and the advantages and disadvantages of each type. Finally, you learned how to create hyperlinks using text, e-mail addresses, and pictures.

As you use FrontPage to create your own Web sites, be sure to include graphics to increase the visual interest and functionality of your pages, but keep in mind that different users will see and use your site's pictures in many ways. If you use the proper file format for individual pictures, you can be sure that your pictures download as quickly as possible from the server. If you need to include pictures with large file sizes in your Web pages, try using thumbnails to leave the choice to the user as to whether to display the full picture. Finally, if you cannot reduce the file size of your picture by changing its format and it requires a significant amount of time to download, try using a corner sizing handle to reduce the size of the picture, and then click the Resample button to reduce the file size of the image. You might lose some of the image's quality by reducing the picture's size, but you can ensure that all of your site's visitors will be able to download the picture and use it.

Key Terms

alternative text	image map	page transition
animation	interactive button	picture
applet	Joint Photographic Experts	Portable Network
background picture	Group (JPEG or JPG)	Graphic (PNG)
dynamic HTML (DHTML)	lossless compression	script
embedded file	lossy compression	sizing handle
Graphics Interchange	mailto	source page
Format (GIF)	marquee	target
horizontal line	mouse fly over	target page
hotspot	mouse over	thumbnail picture
		wash out

Practice

Practice the skills you learned in the tutorial using the same case scenario.

Review Assignments

Data Files needed for the Review Assignments: bulk_pic.gif, home_pic.gif, irr_pic.gif, land_pic.gif

Brett is pleased with the progress he has made on the garden Web site. He asks you to finish changing the text in the link bar on the home page to pictures, which you will format as hyperlinks. You'll also add alternative text to these pictures.

If necessary, start FrontPage, make sure you have your Data Files, and then do the following:

1. Open the **garden** Web site from the location where your Web sites are stored, and then open the home page in Design view.
2. Select the text "[Home]" in the link bar at the top of the page, and then replace it with the **home_pic.gif** file in the Tutorial.02\Review folder included with your Data Files.

3. Repeat Step 2 to replace the text "[Landscape & Rock Work]" with the **land_pic.gif** file, the text "[Bulk Goods]" in the link bar with the **bulk_pic.gif** file, and the text "[Irrigation]" with the **irr_pic.gif** file. If necessary, delete any spaces that remain between the pictures you inserted so the pictures look like one large picture instead of five smaller pictures. Save your changes to the home page and save the pictures in the Web site's images folder.

4. Format the Landscape & Rock Work, Bulk Goods, and Irrigation pictures as hyperlinks that open new pages with the filenames **land.htm**, **bulk.htm**, and **irr.htm**, respectively, that you create in the Web site at the same time. (*Hint:* Click the Create New Document button on the Link to bar in the Insert Hyperlink dialog box for the first hyperlink, and then type the filename that you need to create in the Name of new document text box. Click the option to edit the new document later, and then click the OK button.)

5. In Folders view, change the titles of the **land.htm**, **bulk.htm**, and **irr.htm** pages that you created in Step 4 to "Landscape & Rock Work," "Bulk Goods," and "Irrigation," respectively.

6. Format the Home picture in the home page as a hyperlink that opens the home page.

7. For each picture in the link bar, create alternative text to identify the picture's function, such as "Home page hyperlink." When you are finished, save the home page.

8. Copy the picture link bar at the top of the home page by selecting it and clicking the Copy button on the Standard toolbar, and then use Ctrl + Click to open the Garden Center page. Select the text link bar at the top of the Garden Center page, and then replace it with the picture link bar you copied from the home page. (*Hint:* Do not use the Paste Options button to change the pasted pictures.) Save the Garden Center page.

9. On the home page, animate the thumbnail picture with the Page load event and the Wave animation.

10. Remove the effect that you applied to the "February Checklist" heading. (*Hint:* Click the heading to select it, and then click the Remove Effect button on the DHTML Effects toolbar.) Save the home page.

11. Preview the home page in a browser and test the hyperlinks you created in the home page and in the Garden Center page. (The new pages you added to the Web site will be blank; you will add their content in another tutorial.) When you are finished, close your browser.

12. Use FrontPage to print the HTML documents for the home page and the Garden Center page.

13. If necessary, hide the Pictures and DHTML Effects toolbars.

14. Close the **garden** Web site, and then exit FrontPage.

Case Problem 1

Data Files needed for this Case Problem: buffalo.gif, how.htm, how_logo.jpg, w_mark.gif, who.htm, who_logo.gif

Buffalo Trading Post Business at Buffalo Trading Post remains strong. Nicole Beirne and her sales staff receive approximately 50 phone calls each day from potential customers. To serve these customers better, Nicole wants to add a "How" page to the Web site that describes the company's procedures for trading and selling clothes. Nicole and the sales staff agree that one page should contain sections entitled "Frequently Asked Questions" and "How It Works" to describe the process of buying and selling clothing. They also want a "Choose To Re-Use" section that will describe Buffalo's overall commitment to reselling reusable materials. Nicole created this page and wants you to add it to the Web site. She also created a "Who" page that describes the history and philosophy of the business. After importing these pages, you will add logos and other graphics, hyperlinks, and features to enhance the overall appearance of the Web site.

If necessary, start FrontPage, make sure you have your Data Files, and then do the following:

1. Open the **buffalo** Web site from the location where your Web sites are stored, and then, if necessary, display the Folder List. (If you did not create this Web site in Tutorial 1, ask your instructor for assistance.)
2. If necessary, select the root folder of the **buffalo** Web site, and then import the **how.htm** page from the Tutorial.02\Case1 folder included with your Data Files into the Web site. After importing the page, open it in Design view, close the Folder List, and quickly examine the page contents.
3. In the centered paragraph above the link bar, insert the **how_logo.jpg** picture from the Tutorial.02\Case1 folder. Add the alternative text "How page logo" to the picture to describe its function.

Explore

4. Save the How page, use the Picture File Type dialog box to convert the JPEG picture that you added in Step 3 to a GIF picture, and then save it in the Web site's images folder.
5. Insert the **w_mark.gif** file from the Tutorial.02\Case1 folder as the background picture for the How page. Select the option to make the background picture a watermark.

Explore

6. Type your e-mail address at the bottom of the Web page in a new paragraph below the "For additional information please contact us:" text. (If you don't have an e-mail address, create one or use one provided by your instructor.) Set the message subject to "How Page." (*Hint:* After typing the mailto and pressing the spacebar, right-click the mailto link to open the shortcut menu, and then click Hyperlink Properties to open the Edit Hyperlink dialog box.)
7. Save the How page, and save the background picture file in the Web site's images folder.
8. Create a hyperlink in the link bar from the How page to the home page, and then create a hyperlink in the link bar from the home page to the How page. Click File on the menu bar, and then click Save All to save both pages.
9. Create a rectangular hotspot that encloses the "Buffalo Trading Post" text in the logo picture at the top of the How page. Set the target of the hotspot to the home page.

Explore

10. Use the What entry in the link bar of the How page to create a hyperlink to the **what.htm** page. (*Hint:* Click the Create New Document button on the Link to bar in the Insert Hyperlink dialog box, and then type the filename in the Name of new document text box. Click the option to edit the new document later, and then click the OK button.)

11. In Folders view, change the title of the **what.htm** page to "What." Then change the title of the home page to "Buffalo Trading Post."

12. Import the Who page (**who.htm**) from the Tutorial.02\Case1 folder into the **buffalo** Web site's root folder. Insert the **who_logo.gif** picture from the Tutorial.02\Case1 folder on the centered line at the top of the page. Add the alternative text "Who page logo" to the picture to describe its function. Save the picture in the Web site's images folder.

13. Create the hyperlinks between the Home, Who, How, and What pages so that each page has an active hyperlink to the other three pages. (Do not create any links in the What page, which is blank.) Save each page after creating its hyperlinks. Use a browser to test these hyperlinks, and then close your browser.

14. Change the background color of the home page to a Web-safe, light-yellow color of your choice. In a new, centered paragraph below the link bar in the home page, insert the **buffalo.gif** picture from the Tutorial.02\Case1 folder, and then change its background to transparent and add the alternative text "Buffalo Trading Post logo" to describe its function. Save the home page and save the embedded file in the Web site's images folder.

15. Change the "Welcome to the Buffalo Trading Post" heading on the home page to use an animation of your choice, and then save the home page.

Explore

16. In the How page, change the e-mail address you typed at the bottom of the page to an interactive button. (*Hint:* Select the text in the mailto link and then open the Interactive Buttons dialog box. Change the button text to your e-mail address, and then click the Browse button. On the E-mail Address tab, select your e-mail address in the Recently used e-mail addresses list (make sure that you choose the e-mail address that has the subject "How Page;" the space character will appear as "%20"), and then click the OK button). Change the button's properties to select a button type of your choice, increase the button size as necessary so it displays your complete e-mail address, and change the original, hovered, and pressed font colors to complementary colors of your choice. When you are finished, save the How page and save the embedded files in the Web site's images folder.

17. Use your browser to test the hyperlinks you created, including the interactive button. When you are finished, close your browser and the window that opens when you clicked the interactive button.

18. Use FrontPage to print the HTML documents for the home page, the How page, and the Who page.

19. If necessary, hide the Pictures and DHTML Effects toolbars.

20. Close the **buffalo** Web site, and then exit FrontPage.

Challenge

Expand the skills you learned in the tutorial by creating multiple hotspots in a single picture, copying and pasting an image map, and changing a text hyperlink to an interactive button.

Explore

Explore

Case Problem 2

Data Files needed for this Case Problem: about.htm, garden.gif, jobs.htm, link_bar.gif

Garden Grill Hiring and retaining the best possible staff is key to the continued growth of Garden Grill. Recently, Callan Murphy and Meghan Elliott met with the corporate Human Resources director to discuss the content of the planned Job Opportunities Web page. They want the page to emphasize that Garden Grill is a fun place to work and that employees are well rewarded. All agreed that the Job Opportunities page should include information about both management and staff associate positions. Meghan began developing the Job Opportunities page based on the detailed requirements from the meeting. Callan wants you to help Meghan complete the development and testing of this Web page. In addition to this work, you will import the About Us page into the site and work on enhancing the site's appearance and functionality with graphics and hyperlinks.

If necessary, start FrontPage, make sure you have your Data Files, and then do the following:

1. Open the **grill** Web site from the location where your Web sites are stored. (If you did not create this Web site in Tutorial 1, ask your instructor for assistance.)
2. In Folders view, change the title of the home page to "Garden Grill."
3. Display the Folder List, make sure the Web site's root folder is selected, and then import the **jobs.htm** page from the Tutorial.02\Case2 folder included with your Data Files into the Web site. Open the page in Design view and examine its contents.
4. In the centered paragraph at the top of the page, insert the **link_bar.gif** picture from the Tutorial.02\Case2 folder. In a new, centered paragraph below the picture you just inserted, insert the **garden.gif** file from the Tutorial.02\Case2 folder. Save the page and save the embedded files in the Web site's images folder.
5. Create two hotspots in the appropriate locations in the link bar of the Job Opportunities page so that one opens the home page and the other opens the **jobs.htm** page. Then create hotspots using the text entries in the picture link bar to open new pages that you create in the Web site as follows: Menu opens **menu.htm**; About Us opens **about.htm**; Franchise opens **fran.htm**; Feedback opens **feedback.htm**; and Search opens **search.htm**. (*Hint:* Click the Create New Document button on the Link to bar in the Insert Hyperlink dialog box, and then type the filename in the Name of new document text box. Click the option to edit the new document later, and then click the OK button.)
6. Highlight the hotspots you created and make sure that none of the hotspots overlap each other. To change the size of a hotspot, turn off the display of hotspots, click a hotspot to select it, and then use a sizing handle to change its size. Turn off the hotspot highlights, and then save the **jobs.htm** page.
7. Use Folders view to change the titles of the **menu.htm**, **about.htm**, **fran.htm**, **feedback.htm**, and **search.htm** pages to "Menu," "About Us," "Franchise Info," "Feedback," and "Search," respectively.

Explore

8. Include your e-mail address in a new paragraph at the bottom of the **jobs.htm** page below the "For additional information please contact us:" text. (If you don't have an e-mail address, create one or use one provided by your instructor.) Set the message subject to "Job Opportunities Page." (*Hint:* After typing the mailto and pressing the spacebar, right-click the mailto link to open the shortcut menu, and then click Hyperlink Properties to open the Edit Hyperlink dialog box.)

Explore

9. Save the **jobs.htm** page, and then copy the link bar picture and hotspots you created. (*Hint:* To copy the picture and the hotspots you created, click to the left of the picture, press and hold the Shift key, and then click to the right of the picture and release the Shift key. The Copy button on the Standard toolbar becomes active if you do this task correctly.) Use Ctrl + Click to open the home page, select the text link bar in the home page, and then paste the picture you copied in its place. (*Hint:* Do not use the Paste Options button to change the pasted pictures.) After pasting the picture, center it, and then point to each text entry in the link bar to make sure that you copied all of the hotspots. If you did not, copy and paste the picture again. Save the home page.

10. If necessary, display the Folder List, make sure the Web site's root folder is selected, and import the About Us page (**about.htm**) from the Tutorial.02\Case2 folder into the Web site, replacing the page that you created in Step 5. Review the page contents.

11. Replace the "Welcome to Garden Grill" heading in the home page with the **garden.gif** file from the Tutorial.02\Case2 folder. Add the alternative text "Garden Grill logo" to the picture to describe its function, and then save the home page and overwrite the embedded file in the Web site's images folder.

12. Insert a horizontal line above the copyright information on the home page. Change the line's properties so it is 95% of the window's width, five pixels high, and purple.

Explore

13. In a new paragraph above the horizontal line you inserted, insert a centered, scrolling marquee that is 95% of the window's width with the text "See the store manager for information about our new catering services!" Change the marquee's text to Arial, bold, 10-point, white font. (*Hint:* Click the Style button in the Marquee Properties dialog box, click the Format button, and then click Font to change the marquee text font color and style.) In the Marquee Properties dialog box, use the Background color list arrow to change the background color of the marquee to purple. Save the home page.

Explore

14. In the Job Opportunities page, change the e-mail address you typed at the bottom of the page to an interactive button. (*Hint:* Select the text in the mailto link and then open the Interactive Buttons dialog box. Change the button text to your e-mail address, and then click the Browse button. On the E-mail Address tab, select your e-mail address in the Recently used e-mail addresses list (make sure that you choose the e-mail address that has the subject "Job Opportunities Page;" the space character will appear as "%20"), and then click the OK button). Change the button's properties to select a button type of your choice, increase the button size as necessary so it displays your complete e-mail address, and change the original, hovered, and pressed font colors to complementary colors of your choice. When you are finished, save the page and save the embedded files in the Web site's images folder.

15. Use your browser to test the hyperlinks you created, including the interactive button. When you are finished, close your browser and the window that opened when you clicked the interactive button.
16. Use FrontPage to print the HTML documents for the home page, the About Us page, and the Job Opportunities page.
17. If necessary, hide the Pictures toolbar.
18. Close the **grill** Web site, and then exit FrontPage.

Case Problem 3

Data Files needed for this Case Problem: back.gif, mail.htm, services.htm, sw_logo.gif, team.htm, upcoming.htm

Swenson Auctioneers   Scott Swenson likes the home page that you created for the new Swenson Auctioneers Web site. In accordance with his Web site plan, Scott and his staff created the content of the four main pages in the Web site: Upcoming Auctions, Auction & Appraisal Services, Our Team, and Mailing List. Today, Scott asks you to add these pages to the Web site. Also, he wants you to add hyperlinks to these pages to connect them to each other. His graphic designer completed the Swenson Auctioneers logo, and Scott wants to include this logo in each page in the Web site. Finally, Scott asks you to make changes to create subtle, professional backgrounds and graphics in the pages to enhance their appearance and functionality.

If necessary, start FrontPage, make sure you have your Data Files, and then do the following:

1. Open the **swenson** Web site from the location where your Web sites are stored. (If you did not create this Web site in Tutorial 1, ask your instructor for assistance.)
2. Use Folders view to change the title of the home page to "Swenson Auctioneers."
3. If necessary, display the Folder List, make sure the Web site's root folder is selected, and then import the **mail.htm**, **services.htm**, **team.htm**, and **upcoming.htm** pages from the Tutorial.02\Case3 folder included with your Data Files into the Web site. (*Hint:* In the Add File to Import List dialog box, select the first file to import, press and hold the Ctrl key, click the other files to import to select them, and then release the Ctrl key and click the Open button.)
4. Open the home page in Design view, and then change the text in the link bar to hyperlinks that open the correct pages in the Web site.
5. To the left of the "Upcoming Auctions" link in the link bar, insert the **sw_logo.gif** picture from the Tutorial.02\Case3 folder. Insert two spaces between the picture and the word "Upcoming." Add the alternative text "Swenson Auctioneers logo" to the picture to describe its function.
6. Change the alignment of the paragraph that contains the picture and the link bar to left.
7. Remove the border from the link bar. (*Hint:* Click the link bar to select it, click the list arrow for the Borders button on the Formatting toolbar, and then click the No Border button.)

Apply

Apply the skills you learned in the tutorial to enhance a Web site with a picture, hyperlinks, and a background picture.

Explore

Explore

8. Format the picture you inserted in Step 5 as a hyperlink that opens the site's home page.
9. Save the home page, and save the picture in the Web site's images folder.
10. Copy the link bar in the home page (including the picture), and paste it at the top of the **mail.htm**, **services.htm**, **team.htm**, and **upcoming.htm** pages. Make sure the link bar text is formatted using the Normal style. Save each page as you complete it.
11. Add the **back.gif** file from the Tutorial.02\Case3 folder as a background picture in all five pages of the Web site. Save the picture in the Web site's images folder, and save each page as you complete it.
12. Add a horizontal line that is 100% of the window width, four pixels high, and red to the home page. Position the horizontal line above the copyright information, and then save the home page.
13. Add a page transition of your choice to the **team.htm** page, and then save the **team.htm** page.

Explore

14. At the end of the last sentence on the **services.htm** page, insert your e-mail address as a mailto by typing your address and pressing the spacebar. Then change the e-mail address you typed to an interactive button. (*Hint:* Select the text in the mailto link and then open the Interactive Buttons dialog box. Change the button text to your e-mail address, and then click the Browse button. On the E-mail Address tab, type your e-mail address in the E-mail address text box and "Web Site" in the Subject text box.) Change the button's properties to select a button type of your choice, increase the button size as necessary so it displays your complete e-mail address, and change the original, hovered, and pressed font colors to complementary colors of your choice. When you are finished, save the page and save the embedded files in the Web site's images folder.
15. Use your browser to test the hyperlinks you created, including the interactive button. When you are finished, close your browser and the window that opened when you clicked the interactive button.
16. Use FrontPage to print the HTML documents for the home page and the **team.htm** page.
17. If necessary, hide the Pictures toolbar.
18. Close the **swenson** Web site, and then exit FrontPage.

Apply

Apply the skills you learned in the tutorial to enhance the loan Web site with graphics and hyperlinks.

Case Problem 4

Data Files needed for this Case Problem: back.gif, collage.gif, loantype.htm, help.htm, repair.htm, resource.htm

Mortgage Services, Inc. After examining multiple Web sites that have the same functionality as the one that she has hired you to create, Natalie Fuselier now has a better sense of the overall content and appearance that she wants to see in the new Web site for her company, Mortgage Services, Inc. Natalie began working on the content of several pages in the Web site and has given you the HTML documents to import into the Web site. She wants you to work on linking the pages together and enhancing the site with graphics and some animation. Because Natalie deals with many clients who need credit repair services, she has decided to include a Web page for this service in the Web site. Because these applicants will have different needs than her applicants who do not need credit repair services, she asks you to format the Credit Repair Services page with a different appearance to differentiate between the different kinds of loans.

If necessary, start FrontPage, make sure you have your Data Files, and then do the following:

1. Open the **loan** Web site from the location where your Web sites are stored. (If you did not create this Web site in Tutorial 1, ask your instructor for assistance.)
2. Use Folders view to change the title of the home page to "Mortgage Services, Inc."

Explore ▶ 3. If necessary, display the Folder List, make sure the **loan** Web site's root folder is selected, and then import the **help.htm**, **loantype.htm**, **repair.htm**, and **resource.htm** pages from the Tutorial.02\Case4 folder included with your Data Files into the Web site. (*Hint:* In the Add File to Import List dialog box, select the first file to import, press and hold the Ctrl key, click the other files to import to select them, and then release the Ctrl key and click the Open button.)

Explore ▶ 4. Open the home page in Design view, and then change the text in the link bar to hyperlinks that open the correct pages in the Web site. For the Application and Contact Us entries, create new pages in the Web site with the filenames **apply.htm** and **contact.htm**. (*Hint:* Click the Create New Document button on the Link to bar in the Insert Hyperlink dialog box, and then type the filename that you need to create in the Name of new document text box. Click the option to edit the new document later, and then click the OK button.) If your link bar contains other entries, delete them.

5. In Folders view, change the titles of the **apply.htm** and **contact.htm** pages to "Application" and "Contact Us," respectively.
6. Create a hyperlink from the text "credit repair services" in the last sentence on the home page to the **repair.htm** page. Save the home page.

Explore ▶ 7. In a new, centered paragraph below the heading in the home page, insert the **collage.gif** file from the Tutorial.02\Case4 folder. Note the number of seconds required to download the home page at 56 Kbps. Then select the picture, use a corner-sizing handle to reduce the size of the picture by approximately one-half, and then click the Resample button on the Pictures toolbar to resize the picture. Note the number of seconds required to download the page after resizing the picture.

8. Add the alternative text "Decorative photograph" to the picture you added in Step 7 to describe the picture's function. Save the home page and save the embedded file in the Web site's images folder.
9. Add the **back.gif** file from the Tutorial.02\Case4 folder to the background of the home page, the **resource.htm** page, the **loantype.htm** page, and the **help.htm** page. Save each page as you complete it and save the embedded file in the Web site's images folder.
10. Change the background color of the **repair.htm** page to the light-yellow color with hex FF,FF,CC, and then save the page.

11. Format the heading "Mortgage Services, Inc." in the home page as a hyperlink that opens the home page. Then copy the link bar and the heading and paste them at the top of the **resource.htm**, **loantype.htm**, and **help.htm** pages.
12. In the **repair.htm** page, create a centered interactive button below the heading at the top of the page with the text "Return to Mortgage Services, Inc. home page." Choose a button type, colors, and other features for the button. Set the target of the interactive button to the site's home page. Save the **repair.htm** page and save the embedded files in the Web site's images folder.
13. Add a page transition of your choice to the **repair.htm** page, and then save the page.
14. Click File on the menu bar, and then click Save All to save all of the changes you have made. Use your browser to test the hyperlinks you created, including the interactive button. When you are finished, close your browser.
15. Use FrontPage to print the HTML documents for the home page and the **repair.htm** page.
16. If necessary, hide the Pictures toolbar.
17. Close the **loan** Web site, and then exit FrontPage.

Quick Check Answers

Session 2.1

1. white
2. JPEG, GIF, and PNG. A JPEG file has up to 16 million colors and is suitable for photographs. A GIF file has up to 256 colors and is suitable for scanned images, line drawings, and simple graphics. GIF files can be combined to create animated images. PNG files are similar to GIF files but can have up to 16 million colors. PNG files are smaller than GIF files but cannot be combined to create animated images. Some browsers cannot display PNG files.
3. False
4. The Estimated Time to Download pane estimates the time needed to download the page using the specified connection speed. Because some users might have dial-up connections, it is important to monitor the download time as you add graphics to a Web page to ensure that pages will load quickly for all users.
5. (1) Alternative text identifies a picture's contents while the picture is being downloaded from the server. Users who cannot see the picture will see the alternative text instead of the picture, which identifies the missing content. (2) Alternative text is used to describe a picture's contents for visually impaired users who are using software that reads a Web page.
6. True
7. True

Session 2.2

1. True
2. a Web page in the same site, a Web page in another site, or related information in the same Web page
3. A source page contains a hyperlink; a target page is the page that opens when the hyperlink in the source page is clicked.
4. A mailto is a hyperlink that contains an e-mail address. When you click a mailto link, your default e-mail program starts and opens a new message addressed to the e-mail address specified by the mailto.
5. rectangular, circular, or polygonal
6. An image map is a picture that contains one or more hotspots. Clicking a hotspot opens the target of the hyperlink. When you format a picture as a hyperlink, clicking any area of the picture opens the target.

Session 2.3

1. hyperlink
2. any three of: convert to black and white, rotate, change contrast or brightness level, add a beveled edge, and wash out colors
3. Click the picture to select it, click the Text button on the Pictures toolbar, click the OK button, if necessary, to convert the picture to a GIF file, type the desired text, and then click anywhere in the Web page to deselect the text.
4. mouse over (or mouse fly over)
5. False
6. True
7. True

New Perspectives on

Microsoft® Office FrontPage® 2003

Read This Before You Begin: Tutorials 3–6

To the Student

Data Disks

To complete the Tutorials, Review Assignments, and Case Problems in this book, you will need the starting student Data Files. Your instructor will either provide you with these Data Files or ask you to obtain them yourself.

FrontPage Tutorials 3–6 require the folders shown in the next column to complete the Tutorials, Review Assignments, and Case Problems. You will need to copy these folders from a file server, a standalone computer, or the Web to the drive and folder where you will be storing your Data Files. Your instructor will tell you which computer, drive letter, and folders contain the files you need. You can also download the files by going to www.course.com; see the inside front cover for more information on downloading the files to your working folder, or ask your instructor or technical support person for assistance.

You will need to store your Data Files on a Zip disk, hard drive, or network drive that you can access. You will also need a location in which to create and save Web sites; the default location used in this book is C:\My Webs\[YourName], where "[YourName]" is your first and last names. You cannot complete this book using floppy disks.

▼ **FrontPage**

Tutorial.03

Tutorial.04

Tutorial.05

Tutorial.06

The Data Files you work with in each tutorial build on the work you did in the previous tutorial. Thus when you begin Tutorial 3, you will use the Data Files that resulted after you completed the steps in Tutorial 2 and the Tutorial 2 Review Assignments.

Course Labs

Tutorial 3 features an interactive Course Lab to help you understand HTML concepts. There are Lab Assignments at the end of Tutorial 3 that relate to this lab. Contact your instructor or technical support person for assistance in accessing this lab.

To the Instructor

The Data Files and Course Labs are available on the Instructor Resources CD for this title. Follow the instructions in the Help file on the CD-ROM to install the programs to your network or standalone computer. See the "To the Student" section above for information on how to set up the Data Files that accompany this text. To complete the tutorials in this book, students must have a Web browser, access to a Web server with the FrontPage 2002 Server Extensions or Windows SharePoint Services installed on it, and an Internet connection. You are granted a license to copy the Data Files and Course Labs to any computer or computer network used by students who have purchased this book.

System Requirements

If you are going to work through this book using your own computer, you need:

- **Computer System** Microsoft Windows 2000 Professional or higher, Microsoft FrontPage 2003, and Microsoft Office 2003 must be installed on your computer. (The screens shown in this book use Microsoft Windows XP Professional. If your computer has Microsoft Windows 2000 Professional, your screens will look slightly different.) This book assumes a typical installation of FrontPage 2003 and Office 2003. To publish your Web sites in Tutorial 6, you also must have Internet Information Services version 5.0 or higher, Microsoft Windows 2003 Server, or access to a compatible Web server and a network connection, and the Microsoft FrontPage 2002 Server Extensions or Windows SharePoint Services installed on the Web server. You can install Internet Information Services from your Windows 2000 Professional or Windows XP Professional CD and you can download the FrontPage 2002 Server Extensions from www.msdn.com. The recommended browser for viewing Web pages is Internet Explorer 6.0 or higher.

- **Data Files** You will not be able to complete the tutorials or exercises in this book using your own computer until you have a set of Data Files.

- **Course Labs** See your instructor or technical support person to obtain the Course Lab software for use on your own computer.

www.course.com/NewPerspectives

Session 3.1
- Create bulleted, numbered, and definition lists
- Create nested lists
- Create anchors in a Web page
- Create hyperlinks to anchors

Session 3.2
- Work with advanced features of Page view
- Work with advanced features of Folders view
- Examine a Web site in Reports view
- Use Hyperlinks view to examine the hyperlinks in a Web page
- Add, sort, change, and delete tasks in Tasks view

Lab

Student Data Files

To complete this tutorial, you will need your ending files from Tutorial 2 and the following Data Files. Additional Data Files needed to complete the end-of-tutorial exercises are listed with the Review Assignments and Case Problems.

Using Lists, Anchors, and Web Site Views

Creating the Contact Sunshine Web Page

Case

Sunshine Landscape & Garden Center

In a weekly staff meeting, Brett Kizer, owner of the Sunshine Landscape & Garden Center, comments that he is pleased with the appearance and content of the Web site you are developing. The site's basic structure is now in place. The home page contains a link bar with links to the other pages in the site: Garden Center, Landscape & Rock Work, Bulk Goods, and Irrigation. In addition, the thumbnail picture that you inserted into the home page opens a page with a map that customers can use to find the center. At this point, you have added some content to the Garden Center page, but the other pages (Landscape & Rock Work, Bulk Goods, and Irrigation) are blank. As you continue developing the Web site, you will add content to these pages.

Because many grocery and discount stores in the area sell landscaping materials and plants, Brett wants to add a page to the Web site that will showcase the combined experience of the center's staff so that prospective customers will know they can trust the advice the staff gives and feel confident they are buying the best products and plants for use in their landscapes. Brett already collected biographical material from the center's senior employees and has prepared a draft of the page. Because this page contains a lot of content, Brett asks you to show him how to format information in bulleted lists and add hyperlinks that scroll to different locations in the document. You tell Brett that this type of hyperlink is easy to create, and you turn your attention to working on the new Contact Sunshine page.

▼ **Tutorial.03**

▽ **Tutorial folder**

contact.gif	land.htm	rock_sam.gif
contact.htm	land_sam.jpg	sun.gif
land.gif	rock_pic.gif	

Session 3.1

Web Pages & HTML

Creating Lists

Just like in word-processing documents, you can use different types of lists to organize content in a Web page. The basic list types are bulleted, numbered, and definition. A bullet character, such as a dot, precedes each item in a **bulleted list**. You can customize a bulleted list to use almost any graphic to enhance its appearance. A **numbered list** displays items preceded by numbers, letters, or Roman numerals. A **definition list** is used to format defined terms and their definitions. A **defined term** is the term being explained; the paragraph below the defined term contains a definition to describe the term.

When you use the tools in Design view to create these types of lists, FrontPage generates the HTML tags that create the lists. Figure 3-1 shows the basic list types and the HTML tags that create them. A bulleted list is also called an **unordered list** because items in the list are not sequentially organized. The <ul></ul> tags, which stand for "unordered list," create a bulleted list in a Web page. Notice that each item in the list is enclosed in <li></li> tags, which stand for "line item." A numbered list is also called an **ordered list** because items in the list are sequentially organized. The <ol></ol> tags, which stand for "ordered list," create a numbered list in a Web page. Items in an ordered list also are enclosed by the <li></li> tags. A definition list is different from unordered and ordered lists because it contains different tags to format the defined terms and definition items in the list. The <dt></dt> tags, which stand for "defined term," enclose the terms in the list. The <dd></dd> tags, which stand for "defined definition," enclose the definitions for each defined term in the list. The <dl></dl> tags, which stand for "definition list," enclose all of the <dt></dt> and <dd></dd> items in the list. Although FrontPage generates these tags for you automatically, it's often helpful to understand their presentation in an HTML document for those times when you need to make minor adjustments to the tags that you cannot perform using the tools in Design view.

Figure 3-1 ▶ **Basic list types**

```
                                        <body>

 •  This is a bulleted list.¶            <ul>
 •  This is a bulleted list.¶                <li>This is a bulleted list.</li>
 •  This is a bulleted list.¶                <li>This is a bulleted list.</li>
                                             <li>This is a bulleted list.</li>
                                        </ul>
 1.  This is a numbered list.¶          <ol>
 2.  This is a numbered list.¶              <li>This is a numbered list.</li>
 3.  This is a numbered list.¶              <li>This is a numbered list.</li>
                                            <li>This is a numbered list.</li>
                                        </ol>
This is a defined term in a definition list.¶   <dl>
     This is a definition in a definition list. ¶    <dt>This is a defined term in a definition list.</dt>
This is a defined term in a definition list.¶        <dd>This is a definition in a definition list. </dd>
     This is a definition in a definition list. ¶    <dt>This is a defined term in a definition list.</dt>
This is a defined term in a definition list.¶        <dd>This is a definition in a definition list. </dd>
     This is a definition in a definition list. ¶    <dt>This is a defined term in a definition list.</dt>
                                                     <dd>This is a definition in a definition list. </dd>
                                        </dl>

                                        </body>
```

Web page   HTML document

The items in a list can themselves be lists. A **nested list** is one that is contained within another list. A list that contains one or more nested lists is also called a **multi-level list** or **outline list**. Multi-level lists can use the same or different list types for each level. To create a standard outline, for example, you would nest numbered lists; each level would use the same numbered list type but a different number, letter, or Roman numeral format. In contrast, you would use different list types for each level when nesting a numbered list within a bulleted list or vice versa.

Brett finished the biographies that he wants to include in the Contact Sunshine page and has sent the page to you via e-mail. Now he wants you to import his page into the garden Web site. Then you will examine the page together and decide what types of lists would be appropriate to organize the content of the page.

To import the Contact Sunshine page into the Web site and open it in Design view:

▶ **1.** Start **FrontPage** and then open the **garden** Web site from the location where your Web sites are stored.

▶ **2.** If necessary, display the Folder List and make sure the root folder of the garden Web site is selected in the Folder List.

▶ **3.** Click **File** on the menu bar, and then click **Import**. The Import dialog box opens.

▶ **4.** Click the **Add File** button, open the **Tutorial.03\Tutorial** folder included with your Data Files, click the **contact.htm** file to select it, and then click the **Open** button. The contact.htm file appears in the Import dialog box.

▶ **5.** Click the **OK** button to import the page into the Web site.

▶ **6.** Close the Folder List and then open the **contact.htm** page in Design view. The Contact Sunshine page appears in Figure 3-2.

Contact Sunshine page ◀ **Figure 3-2**

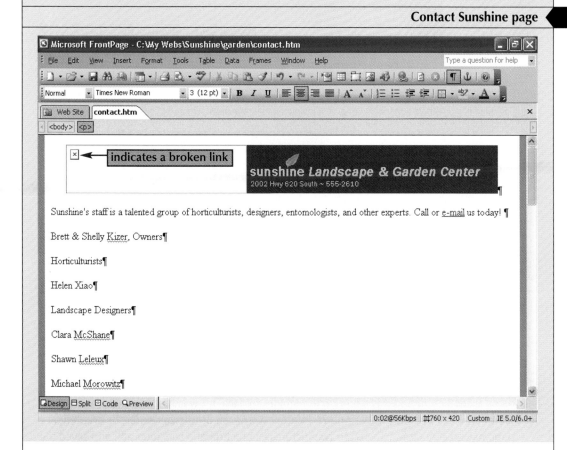

The first thing that Brett notices about the page he gave you is that the logo for the Sunshine Landscape & Garden Center appears in the upper-right corner of the page.

However, an empty box with a ☒ icon appears to the left of the logo. Brett explains that he inserted a "Contact Sunshine" logo picture in that location when he created the page on his computer. He wonders why this picture doesn't appear on your computer. You tell Brett that the Sunshine logo appears in the page because it is already stored in the Web site's images folder. However, the picture on the left, which appears as a **broken link**, is not stored in the Web site. To show Brett this problem, you decide to switch to Split view, so Brett can see the HTML document and the Web page simultaneously.

To switch to Split view and examine the broken link:

1. Click the **broken link** ☒ at the top of the page. Sizing handles appear around the missing picture.

2. Click the **Show Split View** button ⊟Split at the bottom of the Contents pane. The HTML document for the Contact Sunshine page appears in the Code view window and the Web page appears in the Design view window. Because you selected the broken link in Design view, the HTML tag for the broken link is selected in the Code view window, as shown in Figure 3-3.

Figure 3-3	Split view of the Contact Sunshine page

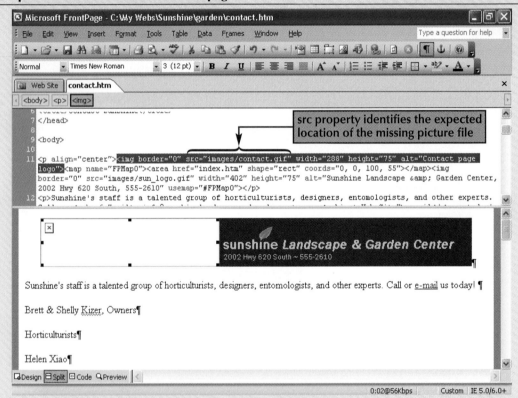

Trouble? If necessary, scroll down the HTML document in the Code view window so you can see the HTML tag for the broken link.

The <img> tag inserts a picture into a Web page; the src property identifies the location where the picture is stored. In this case, the src property indicates that the picture's file-name is contact.gif and it is stored in the images folder. This was the original location of the file when Brett created this Web page. In other words, on Brett's computer, he created a page named contact.htm, inserted two pictures (contact.gif and sun_logo.gif), and saved the picture files in the Web site's images folder. You imported the contact.htm Web page into the garden Web site on your computer, but you did not import the contact.gif file. Because FrontPage cannot locate the picture file, it appears as a broken link. When you see ☒ icons in a Web page, the picture files used in the Web page are not stored in the location indicated by the src property. When this situation occurs, you can insert the picture file into the location referenced by the src property, change the path to the picture file so it points to the correct location, or delete the picture from the page. Brett can supply the missing picture file to you so that you can import it into the Web site's images folder, which will correct the problem.

▶ **3.** Return to Design view for the Contact Sunshine page, and then display the Folder List.

▶ **4.** Click the **images** folder in the Folder List to select it. You will import the missing contact.gif file into the images folder.

▶ **5.** Click **File** on the menu bar, and then click **Import**.

▶ **6.** Click the **Add File** button, open the **Tutorial.03\Tutorial** folder included with your Data Files (if necessary), click the **contact.gif** file to select it, click the **Open** button, and then click the **OK** button. The contact.gif file is added to the Web site's images folder, and the picture now appears in the contact.htm Web page. You corrected the broken link problem.

▶ **7.** Close the Folder List, and then use the vertical scroll bar in Design view to examine the contents of the Contact Sunshine page. When you are finished viewing the page's contents, press **Ctrl + Home** to scroll to the top of the page.

After reviewing the page's contents, you decide that the information at the top of the page would benefit from being formatted differently. You suggest that the general title of each position, such as "Horticulturists" and "Landscape Designers," be formatted as a bulleted list. You also recommend formatting the names appearing below each title as a numbered list. Further down the page, each person's name and title appear on a line above a paragraph that describes his or her biography. This material would work very well in a definition list. Figure 3-4 shows the plan for the various lists you will create in the Contact Sunshine page.

Plan for the Contact Sunshine page ◀ **Figure 3-4**

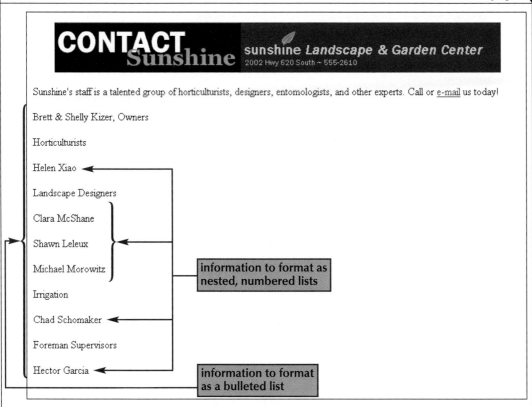

| Figure 3-4 | Plan for the Contact Sunshine page (continued) |

Brett & Shelly Kizer, Owners

Sunshine Landscape & Garden Center has been a family owned and operated business since 1976 when the Carpenters first opened their shop. In August 1998, Brett and his wife, Shelly, became part of the Sunshine family, purchasing the business from the Carpenters. Over the years Brett and Shelly have expanded the products and services available at Sunshine and they continue to offer the highest level of quality and expertise that has made Sunshine the best garden center in the area. In August 2000, when Sunshine purchased Rainmaker Irrigation Company, Brett took courses and became a licensed irrigator.

Helen Xiao, Horticulturalist

Helen wasn't born in Texas but she got here as fast as she could! Raised and educated in Columbus, Ohio, Helen holds two horticulture degrees from Ohio State University, one of our nation's best horticulture programs. She has worked in the nursery industry for 28 years and has lived in Texas since 1971. Helen is an expert in native Texas plants; she holds the TNLA certification Texas Master Certified Nursery Professional from Texas A&M. Helen also has 14 years of experience with landscape design and installation having worked for commercial and residential landscape firms across central Texas.

Clara McShane, Chief Landscape Designer ◄── defined term   definition

Clara came to Sunshine in March 2001 as sort of a "relief pitcher" to help out during the busy spring season and she hasn't left yet! Clara's passion has always been gardening, and after graduating from UT she studied plants and practiced landscape design for over 10 years. Her expertise ranges from designing the perfect entryway for a home to coordinating large-scale installations. Clara's creative abilities are also on display in our monthly newsletter as she serves as Sunshine's publicist.

Shawn Leleux, Landscape Designer

Shawn joined Sunshine in March 2000 only two years after graduating from Texas A&M University, but he has wisdom beyond his years. He earned his degree in Entomology and is Sunshine's resident expert on insects and how to treat them. Shawn comes to Sunshine from Marble Falls, Texas, where he grew up enjoying outdoor activities, including hunting, fishing, camping, and hiking. His love for nature is one of the reasons he designs and builds such beautiful and successful landscapes.

information to format as a definition list

Michael Morowitz, Landscape Designer

A landscape painter and portrait artist from McLean, Virginia, Mike was certified as a Master Gardener in 1996. He is a member of the education committee at Zilker Botanical Garden here in Austin. For several years, Mike owned a successful design business in Austin and worked with Sunshine on many projects. He officially joined Sunshine in October 2002. "I love my work because I get to dream up beautiful things and watch them become reality."

Chad Schomaker, Irrigation

Chad has been the Supervisor of RainMaker Irrigation since May 2002. He's originally from Salem, Oregon, where he worked his way through school as an Agricultural Irrigator. After moving to Texarkana in 1981, he continued to work in irrigation. He then made his way to Houston and then to Austin, where he has specialized in residential and commercial underground irrigation systems for three years. Chad has been installing landscape lighting for 13 years. In 1999, Chad earned his backflow certification and is able to conduct tests required by local municipalities.

Hector Garcia, Foreman

Hector has been with Sunshine since 1982 and he has done it all. He has worked on the maintenance crew, the landscape crew, and is now the head of the rock crew and foreman of all Sunshine crews. Hector is a real professional and a true hardscape genius. He can build patios, fountains, benches, fireplaces, walls, walkways, and columns with precision. Because of his ability to build exactly what a customer wants, even when they can't fully describe it, some customers think he can read minds!

Finally, looking ahead, you tell Brett that after you format the lists in the page, you can create hyperlinks from a person's name at the top of the page to the place in the page that describes that person. Your first task is to create the bulleted list using the titles.

Creating a Bulleted List

A bulleted list, or an unordered list, contains items that are not sequentially organized. Each item in the list begins with a bullet character; the default bullet character displayed by most Web browsers is a dot. You can create a bulleted list either by clicking the Bullets button on the Formatting toolbar before typing the items in the list, or by selecting existing text and then clicking the Bullets button.

Reference Window

Creating a Bulleted List

- Select the paragraph that will contain the first item in the bulleted list.
- Click the Bullets button on the Formatting toolbar.
- Type each item in the list, pressing the Enter key after each item.
- If necessary, press the Enter key twice to end the bulleted list.

Bulleted lists are indented by one tab stop when you first create them. You can change this indention if desired by using the Decrease Indent button 📑 or the Increase Indent button 📑 on the Formatting toolbar. To create the bulleted list, you will select all of the items at the top of the page, and then use a toolbar button. To create the nested, numbered lists, you will need to select the items individually and format them as numbered lists.

To create a bulleted list:

1. Click to the left of the word **Brett** at the top of the Contact Sunshine page, scroll down as necessary, press and hold the **Shift** key as you click to the right of the word **Garcia**, and then release the **Shift** key. You selected 11 lines in the Web page.

2. Click the **Bullets** button 📄 on the Formatting toolbar to format these lines as a bulleted list, and then scroll up the page as necessary and click the first item in the list to deselect the entire bulleted list. See Figure 3-5.

Information formatted as a bulleted list | **Figure 3-5**

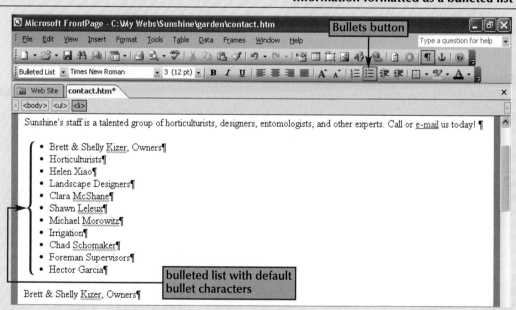

bulleted list with default bullet characters

Notice that the items in the bulleted list appear with the default bullet and that the entire list is indented by one tab stop (one-half inch). Brett asks about changing the default bullet character to a small sun that the graphic designer created for him. You can use almost any graphic as a bullet character, as long as it is sized in proportion to the text. In other words, a graphic such as the contact.gif picture wouldn't work as a bullet character, but a small graphic of an arrow would work well. When you change the default bullet character to a picture, you must store the picture in the Web site; otherwise, visitors will see a broken link icon instead of the bullets.

To change the default bullet character in the bulleted list:

1. Select all 11 lines in the bulleted list.

2. Click **Format** on the menu bar, and then click **Bullets and Numbering**. The Plain Bullets tab of the List Properties dialog box opens, as shown in Figure 3-6. The current bullet character, the dot, is selected. Notice that you can change the dot to a small, open circle or to a small, solid square by clicking these samples on the Plain Bullets tab. To change the bullet to a picture, you need to select the Picture Bullets tab.

Figure 3-6 ▶ **List Properties dialog box**

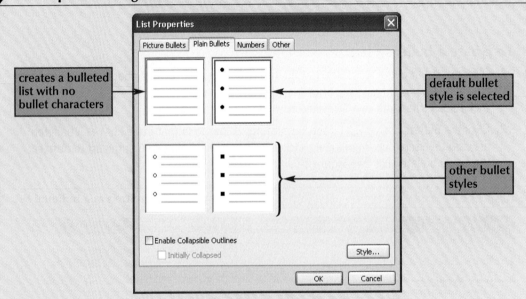

creates a bulleted list with no bullet characters

default bullet style is selected

other bullet styles

3. Click the **Picture Bullets** tab, click the **Specify picture** option button, and then click the **Browse** button. The Select Picture dialog box opens. The picture file you need to select, sun.gif, is stored in the Tutorial.03\Tutorial folder.

4. Open the **Tutorial.03\Tutorial** folder included with your Data Files, click the **sun.gif** file to select it, and then click the **Open** button. The path to the sun.gif file appears in the Specify picture text box on the Picture Bullets tab. See Figure 3-7.

Completed Picture Bullets tab ◄ **Figure 3-7**

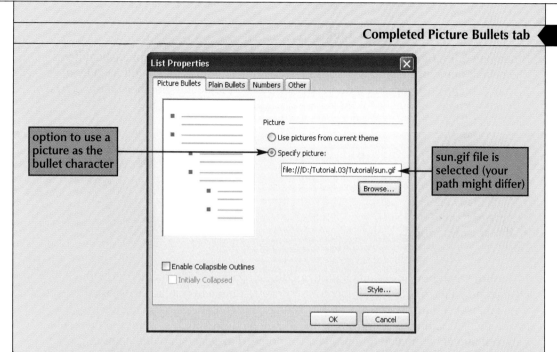

5. Click the **OK** button, and then click the first bulleted item in the list to deselect the list. The bullets are pictures, as shown in Figure 3-8.

Bulleted list with picture bullets ◄ **Figure 3-8**

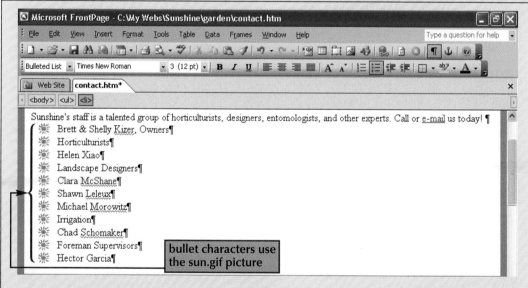

Because you inserted a picture into the Web page, you need to save the picture file in the Web site's images folder.

6. Click the **Save** button 📷 on the Standard toolbar, and then save the sun.gif picture in the Web site's images folder.

According to your plan, you need to change the bullets next to people's names to numbered lists. Before making this change, you want to show Brett how to create a numbered list.

Creating a Numbered List

A numbered list, or ordered list, contains sequentially numbered or alphabetical items. The default numbers in a numbered list are the numerals 1, 2, 3, etc., followed by a period. You can customize a numbered list to change the default numbers to uppercase or lowercase Roman numerals, or uppercase or lowercase letters.

Reference Window | **Creating a Numbered List**

- Select the paragraph that will contain the first item in the numbered list.
- Click the Numbering button on the Formatting toolbar.
- Type each item in the list, and then press the Enter key after each item.
- If necessary, press the Enter key twice to end the numbered list.

To show Brett how to create a numbered list and change its characteristics, you'll change the bulleted list to a numbered list. Because the items already exist as a bulleted list, you just need to click any item in the bulleted list and then click the Numbering button on the Formatting toolbar to change all of the items to a numbered list. If the items were not already formatted as a list, you would need to select all of the items to format in a numbered list before clicking the Numbering button.

To create a numbered list and examine its default settings:

1. Click any item in the bulleted list at the top of the page.
2. Click the **Numbering** button 📄 on the Formatting toolbar. Because the items were already formatted as a bulleted list, all of the items in the bulleted list change to a numbered list, as shown in Figure 3-9.

Figure 3-9 | **Items formatted as a numbered list**

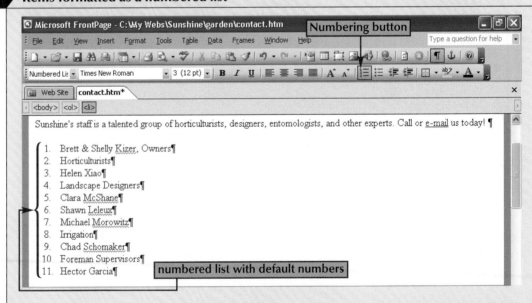

3. Click **Format** on the menu bar, click **Bullets and Numbering**, and then click the **Numbers** tab. See Figure 3-10.

Numbers tab in the List Properties dialog box | **Figure 3-10**

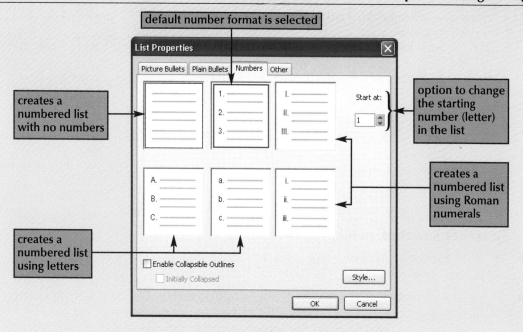

default number format is selected

creates a numbered list with no numbers

option to change the starting number (letter) in the list

creates a numbered list using Roman numerals

creates a numbered list using letters

The default number in a numbered list is a numeral, which is the currently selected item. You can format the numbered list using uppercase or lowercase Roman numerals or uppercase or lowercase letters. Notice the Start at list box, which shows that the current starting number is 1. When you need to start a numbered list with a specific number, Roman numeral, or letter, you can change the Start at value to the beginning value you need.

Because you don't want to change the items to a numbered list, you will close the List Properties dialog box without making any changes, and then you will undo the change you made.

To return the items to a bulleted list:

1. Click the **Cancel** button in the List Properties dialog box to close it.

2. Click the **Undo** button on the Standard toolbar. The numbered list returns to a bulleted list with picture bullets.

Now you can change the people's names to nested, numbered lists.

Creating a Nested, Numbered List

A nested list contains one or more items that appear within another list. You can create a nested, numbered list or a nested, bulleted list within an existing numbered or bulleted list.

Creating a Nested List

- Within a numbered or bulleted list, insert or select the list item where you want the nested list to start.
- Click the Increase Indent button on the Formatting toolbar twice to nest the first item in the list.
- If necessary, click the Numbering button or the Bullets button on the Formatting toolbar to change the list type.
- Type each item in the list, pressing the Enter key after each item. Do not press the Enter key after typing the final item in the nested list.

To format specific items in an existing list as a nested list, you need to select the items for the nested list first.

To create a nested, numbered list:

1. In the bulleted list, click anywhere in the name **Helen Xiao**. Helen is the only horticulturist currently on staff.

2. Click the **Increase Indent** button [icon] on the Formatting toolbar. The line with Helen's name changes to a normal paragraph. Notice that additional space now separates the line with Helen's name in it from the bullet that appears above her name. In addition, Helen's name no longer contains a bullet.

3. Click the [icon] button again. The line with Helen's name changes to a nested, bulleted list. If you wanted to create the nested list using the same bullet as the original list, no further action would be necessary. However, if you want to change the nested list's type from bulleted to numbered, you must click the Numbering button on the Formatting toolbar.

4. Click the **Numbering** button [icon] on the Formatting toolbar. The number 1 appears to the left of Helen's name. You created a nested, numbered list.

    Trouble? If the nested list still uses the sun.gif picture as its bullet character, you clicked the Increase Indent button only once. Click the Numbering button on the Standard toolbar again to change the list type.

5. Click anywhere in the name **Clara McShane**, and then repeat Steps 2 through 4 to format this item as a nested, numbered list.

6. Change the following names to nested, numbered lists: **Shawn Leleux**, **Michael Morowitz**, **Chad Schomaker**, and **Hector Garcia**. When you are finished, your list should look like the one shown in Figure 3-11. Notice that the list with more than one item is formatted automatically to use sequential numbers, and that the second, third, and fourth numbered lists all begin with the number 1.

Nested, numbered lists created | **Figure 3-11**

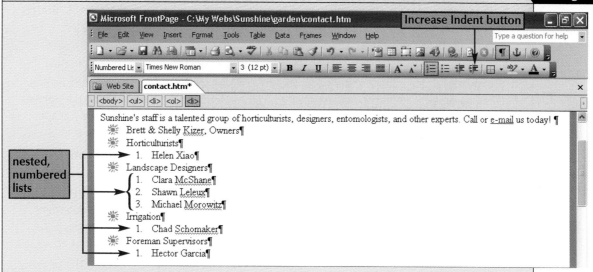

nested, numbered lists

7. Click the **Save** button 🖫 on the Standard toolbar to save your changes, and then click the **Preview** button 🔍 on the Standard toolbar to view the page in your browser. Depending on the browser you use, you might see blank lines above and below the nested lists that did not appear in Design view. You could change the HTML document to change the tags for the nested lists to eliminate the extra space, but you decide not to do so at this time. However, this situation does show the importance of testing your pages in a browser to note any changes that occur when a browser interprets the HTML document. Some differences you discover in a browser are acceptable, like this one, but others are not.

8. Close your browser.

Now you can create the definition list.

Creating a Definition List

A definition list contains defined terms and their definitions. The default organization of a definition list is for the defined term to appear on a left-aligned line by itself, and the definition for that defined term to appear in an indented paragraph below the defined term.

Reference Window

Creating a Definition List

- Select the paragraph that will contain the first item in the definition list, and then type the term you want to define.

or

- Click an item in an existing list that you want to use for the defined term.
- Click the Style list arrow on the Formatting toolbar, and then click Defined Term.
- Press the Enter key, and then type the definition for the term.
- If necessary, press the Enter key twice to end the definition list.

Brett already provided the content for the defined terms and their definitions, so you only need to change the format of this content in the Web page. You'll accomplish this task by using the Style list arrow on the Formatting toolbar.

To change existing paragraphs to a definition list:

1. If necessary, scroll down the Web page so you see the paragraph with the content "Brett & Shelly Kizer, Owners" (the one without a bullet character), and then click to the left of the word **Brett**.

2. Scroll to the bottom of the Web page, press and hold the **Shift** key as you click to the right of **minds!** at the bottom of the page, and then release the **Shift** key. The paragraphs that will become the definition list are selected. You can format all of the text using the Defined Term style or the Definition style to create the list; it doesn't matter which style you apply first. Then you need to format the individual paragraphs with the correct style.

3. Click the **Style** list arrow on the Formatting toolbar, and then click **Defined Term**. All of the selected paragraphs change to the Defined Term style.

4. Scroll up the Web page and click the paragraph below the text "Brett & Shelly Kizer, Owners" to select it. Looking at the Style list box on the Formatting toolbar, you determine that this paragraph has the Defined Term style applied to it. You need to change this paragraph to use the Definition style because it describes the defined term that appears above it.

5. Click the **Style** list arrow on the Formatting toolbar, and then click **Definition**. The selected paragraph changes to the Definition style. The default format for a paragraph with the Definition style is indented one tab stop. See Figure 3-12.

| Figure 3-12 | **Definition list created** |

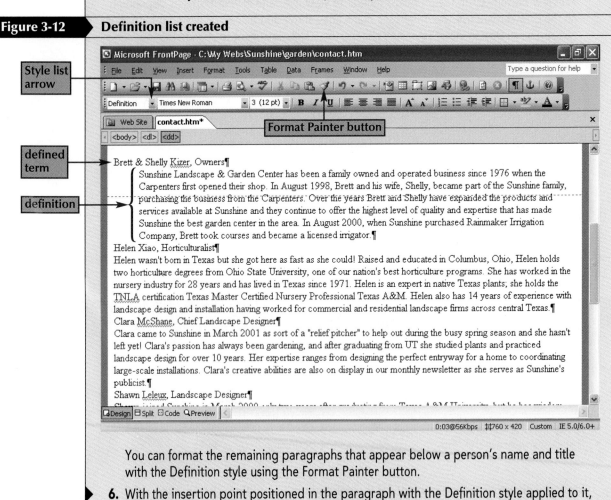

You can format the remaining paragraphs that appear below a person's name and title with the Definition style using the Format Painter button.

6. With the insertion point positioned in the paragraph with the Definition style applied to it, double-click the **Format Painter** button on the Formatting toolbar, and then scroll down the Web page as necessary and click the paragraphs that appear below a person's name and title to change them to the Definition style.

Trouble? If you change a person's name and title to the Definition style by mistake, click the Undo button 🔄 on the Standard toolbar, and then use the Style list arrow on the Formatting toolbar to change the paragraph to the Defined Term style.

▶ 7. After formatting the last paragraph in the page, click the **Format Painter** button 🖌 on the Formatting toolbar to turn off the Format Painter. Scroll to the top of the page, checking to make sure that you have formatted the page correctly.

▶ 8. Save the page.

The Contact Sunshine page now uses lists to organize its contents. Next, you will format the names at the top of the Web page as hyperlinks that jump to the section in the Web page that describe them.

Creating Anchors and Hyperlinks to Anchors

In Tutorial 2, you created hyperlinks to link the pages in the garden Web site to each other. A hyperlink consists of two parts—the text or object that is linked and a target location. For example, the home_pic.gif picture in the center.htm page is the object that is linked to the index.htm page in the Web site. Clicking the picture opens the home page. In this example, the target is another page in the Web site. You can also create hyperlinks to locations in the *same* Web page. To create links to locations in the same Web page, you need a way to identify the location of the target. In HTML, you identify a location in a Web page by creating an anchor. An **anchor** is specially marked text or an object that identifies a named location in a Web page. (In FrontPage, anchors are called **bookmarks**.) When you create a hyperlink to an anchor, the anchor becomes the target of the hyperlink. For example, if you create an anchor named "top" at the beginning of a Web page, you could also create a hyperlink from the text "Back to Top" at the bottom of the Web page that links to the "top" anchor. In this case, a user can click the "Back to Top" text, and the browser will jump to the target, which is the "top" anchor, and as a result, the user is able to scroll immediately to the top of the page. The "top" anchor isn't visible in the Web page itself; it is just a way of identifying a location in the document. You can create an anchor using text, a picture, or a location in a Web page that is not based on text or a picture.

Brett wants to format the list at the top of the Contact Sunshine page so that users can scroll to each person's biography by clicking the person's name in the list. You can place bookmarks (anchors) anywhere in a Web page to make it easier for users to navigate the page, and you can create multiple hyperlinks in a Web page to the same anchor.

When viewed in Design view, text in a bookmark appears as dashed, underlined text. A bookmark that is not based on text appears as a 🔖 icon when viewed in Design view. When you view a page with bookmarks using a browser, there is no underlining or other identification of the bookmark.

Each bookmark within a Web page must have a unique name. You can use the name that FrontPage suggests for the bookmark—which is taken from the text that you selected when you created it—or you can assign a new name. For Web sites stored on some servers, the names of bookmarks—just like filenames for Web pages—cannot contain any spaces or mixed-case filenames, and cannot exceed eight characters. For this reason, it is a good idea to use bookmark names that will work on any Web server, even if you know that the Web server on which you will eventually publish your Web site supports filenames containing spaces, mixed-case filenames, and filenames exceeding eight characters. The bookmark's name serves only to identify its location in the Web page, so using bookmark names that will work on any server does not affect the content of the Web page.

Creating a Text-Based Bookmark

The Contact Sunshine page contains content that you organized using bulleted, numbered, and definition lists. Now you need to create the bookmarks in the Web page, so when a user clicks a name at the top of the page, the browser will scroll to the bookmark you created for that link. For the names, you will create text-based bookmarks using the defined terms in the definition list.

Reference Window

Creating a Text-Based Bookmark in a Web Page

- Select the text for the bookmark.
- Click Insert on the menu bar, and then click Bookmark.
- Type a bookmark name in the Bookmark name text box, or accept the suggested name.
- Click the OK button to create the bookmark.

You'll create the first bookmark for Brett and Shelly's biography.

To create a text-based bookmark:

1. Double-click the word **Brett** in the first defined term in the Web page (not the word "Brett" in the bulleted list). The word "Brett" will become the location of the bookmark you will create. You could have also selected the entire line, "Brett & Shelly Kizer, Owners," or any combination of words on this line when creating the bookmark. The browser would still scroll to this location in the Web page.

2. Click **Insert** on the menu bar, and then click **Bookmark** to open the Bookmark dialog box. See Figure 3-13.

Figure 3-13 | **Bookmark dialog box**

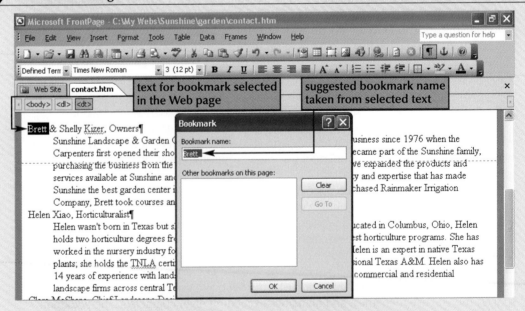

FrontPage used the text you selected to create the bookmark name. When you double-clicked the word "Brett" to select it, you selected the word "Brett" and the space that follows it. Because a bookmark cannot contain a space, FrontPage changed the space character to an underscore character. You could accept the suggested bookmark name of

"Brett_" but decide to delete the underscore character. In addition, to ensure that this bookmark is valid on any Web server, you will change it to all lowercase letters.

3. With Brett_ selected in the Bookmark name text box, type **brett** (with all lowercase letters), and then click the **OK** button. The selected word "Brett" in the Web page has a dashed underline, indicating the location of the bookmark you just created.

4. Scroll down the Web page as necessary, double-click the word **Helen** in the next defined term to select it, click **Insert** on the menu bar, and then click **Bookmark**. The Bookmark dialog box opens again, as shown in Figure 3-14. This time, notice that the brett bookmark you created appears in the Other bookmarks on this page list. As you create bookmarks in a Web page, they will appear in this dialog box. By giving the bookmarks simple names, it makes it easier for you to remember and identify where you created them in the Web page. This association will be helpful when you create hyperlinks to the bookmarks.

Bookmark created in the Web page ◄ **Figure 3-14**

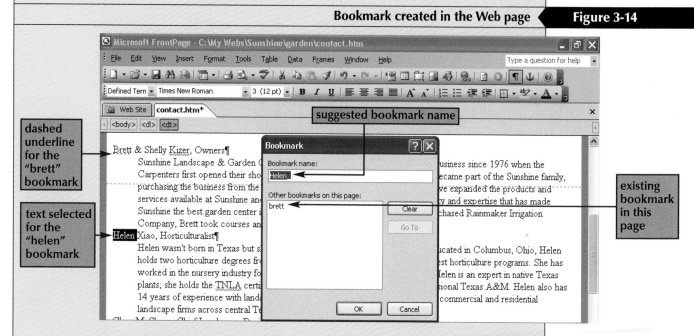

5. Type **helen** (with all lowercase letters) in the Bookmark name text box, and then click the **OK** button to create the bookmark.

6. Repeat Steps 1 through 3 to create bookmarks using the words **Clara**, **Shawn**, **Michael**, **Chad**, and **Hector** in the remaining defined terms in the Web page. For each bookmark, change the default bookmark name to the same name but with all lowercase letters and no underscore character.

7. When you have finished creating the bookmarks, scroll to the top of the page.

Your next task is to create hyperlinks from the names at the top of the page to the associated bookmark in the definition list.

Creating a Hyperlink to a Bookmark

After you format the names at the top of the page as hyperlinks, clicking a link will scroll the Web page to the bookmark. Figure 3-15 illustrates how these bookmarks will work.

Figure 3-15 **Hyperlinks and bookmarks for the Contact Sunshine page**

CONTACT Sunshine sunshine *Landscape & Garden Center*
2002 Hwy 620 South ~ 555-2610

Sunshine's staff is a talented group of horticulturists, designers, entomologists, and other experts. Call or e-mail us today!

- Brett & Shelly Kizer, Owners
- Horticulturists

  1. Helen Xiao

- Landscape Designers

  1. Clara McShane
  2. Shawn Leleux
  3. Michael Morowitz

- Irrigation

  1. Chad Schomaker

- Foreman Supervisors

  1. Hector Garcia

format as hyperlinks with targets to bookmarks

bookmarks

hyperlink will scroll the page to the bookmark

Brett & Shelly Kizer, Owners
  Sunshine Landscape & Garden Center has been a family owned and operated business since 1976 when the Carpenters first opened their shop. In August 1998, Brett and his wife, Shelly, became part of the Sunshine family, purchasing the business from the Carpenters. Over the years Brett and Shelly have expanded the products and services available at Sunshine and they continue to offer the highest level of quality and expertise that has made Sunshine the best garden center in the area. In August 2000, when Sunshine purchased Rainmaker Irrigation Company, Brett took courses and became a licensed irrigator.

Helen Xiao, Horticulturalist
  Helen wasn't born in Texas but she got here as fast as she could! Raised and educated in Columbus, Ohio, Helen holds two horticulture degrees from Ohio State University, one of our nation's best horticulture programs. She has worked in the nursery industry for 28 years and has lived in Texas since 1971. Helen is an expert in native Texas plants; she holds the TNLA certification Texas Master Certified Nursery Professional Texas A&M. Helen also has 14 years of experience with landscape design and installation having worked for commercial and residential landscape firms across central Texas.

Clara McShane, Chief Landscape Designer
  Clara came to Sunshine in March 2001 as sort of a "relief pitcher" to help out during the busy spring season and she hasn't left yet! Clara's passion has always been gardening, and after graduating from UT she studied plants and practiced landscape design for over 10 years. Her expertise ranges from designing the perfect entryway for a home to coordinating large-scale installations. Clara's creative abilities are also on display in our monthly newsletter as she serves as Sunshine's publicist.

Shawn Leleux, Landscape Designer
  Shawn joined Sunshine in March 2000 only two years after graduating from Texas A&M University, but he has wisdom beyond his years. He earned his degree in Entomology and is Sunshine's resident expert on insects and how to treat them. Shawn comes to Sunshine from Marble Falls, Texas, where he grew up enjoying outdoor activities, including hunting, fishing, camping, and hiking. His love for nature is one of the reasons he designs and builds such beautiful and successful landscapes.

Michael Morowitz, Landscape Designer
  A landscape painter and portrait artist from McLean, Virginia, Mike was certified as a Master Gardener in 1996. He is a member of the education committee at Zilker Botanical Garden here in Austin. For several years, Mike owned a successful design business in Austin and worked with Sunshine on many projects. He officially joined Sunshine in October 2002. "I love my work because I get to dream up beautiful things and watch them become reality."

Chad Schomaker, Irrigation
  Chad has been the Supervisor of RainMaker Irrigation since May 2002. He's originally from Salem, Oregon, where he worked his way through school as an Agricultural Irrigator. After moving to Texarkana in 1981, he continued to work in irrigation. He then made his way to Houston and then to Austin, where he has specialized in residential and commercial underground irrigation systems for three years. Chad has been installing landscape lighting for 13 years. In 1999, Chad earned his backflow certification and is able to conduct tests required by local municipalities.

Hector Garcia, Foreman
  Hector has been with Sunshine since 1982 and he has done it all. He has worked on the maintenance crew, the landscape crew, and is now the head of the rock crew and foreman of all Sunshine crews. Hector is a real professional and a true hardscape genius. He can build patios, fountains, benches, fireplaces, walls, walkways, and columns with precision. Because of his ability to build exactly what a customer wants, even when they can't fully describe it, some customers think he can read minds!

Creating a Hyperlink to a Bookmark

- Select the text for the hyperlink.
- Click the Insert Hyperlink button on the Standard toolbar.
- Click the Place in This Document button on the Link to bar to display the list of bookmarks created in the Web page.
- Click the desired bookmark to select it, and then click the OK button.

When you created the bookmarks, you could use one word or the entire line as the bookmark location in the document. When you create the hyperlinks, however, you must select the exact text that you want to format as a hyperlink. Now you are ready to create the hyperlinks to the bookmarks you created.

To create the hyperlinks to the bookmarks:

1. In the bulleted list at the top of the page, select the text **Brett & Shelly Kizer, Owners**. This is the text that you will format as a hyperlink.

2. Click the **Insert Hyperlink** button 🖳 on the Standard toolbar to open the Insert Hyperlink dialog box. Because you are creating a hyperlink to a location in the current document, you must display the options for working with bookmarks.

3. Click the **Place in This Document** button 🖺 on the Link to bar to display a list of bookmarks in the Contact Sunshine page. See Figure 3-16.

Selecting a bookmark as the hyperlink target | **Figure 3-16**

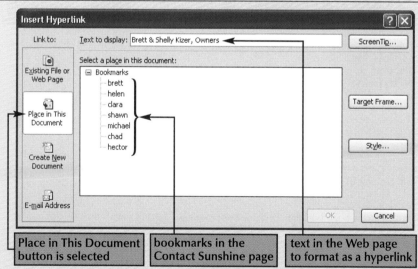

Place in This Document button is selected | bookmarks in the Contact Sunshine page | text in the Web page to format as a hyperlink

Trouble? If you do not see the bookmarks in the page, click the plus box to the left of the word "Bookmarks" in the list box.

▶ 4. Click **brett** to select it, and then click the **OK** button. The Insert Hyperlink dialog box closes, and the first item in the bulleted list is formatted as a hyperlink.

▶ 5. Click the text **Brett & Shelly Kizer, Owners** to deselect it. This text now appears with a solid underline, indicating that it is a hyperlink.

▶ 6. Point to the hyperlink you created. When you point to the hyperlink, the status bar displays the text #brett, which identifies the bookmark's location in the Web page. The pound sign (#) indicates that the target of the hyperlink is a bookmark.

▶ 7. Select the text **Helen Xiao** in the nested, numbered list, and then repeat Steps 2 through 5 using the **helen** bookmark.

▶ 8. Repeat Steps 2 through 5 to create hyperlinks using the text **Clara McShane**, **Shawn Leleux**, **Michael Morowitz**, **Chad Schomaker**, and **Hector Garcia** in the nested, numbered lists to their associated bookmarks. When you are finished, deselect any selected text. See Figure 3-17.

Figure 3-17 ▶ **Hyperlinks created using bookmarks as their targets**

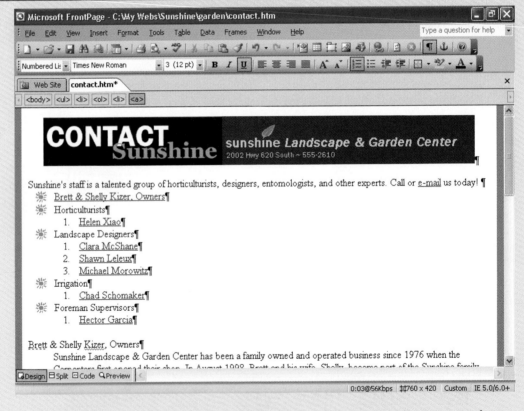

You could have named the bookmarks differently, but Brett now sees that using text from the bookmark's location has made it very easy to associate the hyperlink text with the correct bookmark in the Web page.

▶ 9. Click the **Save** button 🖫 on the Standard toolbar to save your changes.

Before continuing, you need to verify that the hyperlinks to the bookmarks work correctly. You will test the hyperlinks in a browser.

To test an internal hyperlink using a browser:

1. Click the **Preview** button on the Standard toolbar.

2. Point to the **Helen Xiao** hyperlink at the top of the page. The pointer changes to a shape.

3. Click the **Helen Xiao** hyperlink. The Web page scrolls so that the helen bookmark's location is at the top of the window. Notice that the word "Helen," which is the text for the helen bookmark, does not have a dashed underline.

4. Scroll to the top of the page, and then click the **Hector Garcia** hyperlink. Hector's biography appears at the bottom of the Web page, so you see the bottom of the Web page instead of seeing the hector bookmark at the top of the window.

5. Close your browser.

All of the bookmarks that you have created so far used text in the Web page to identify their locations. You can also use a picture to create a bookmark that works exactly like one that uses text. You create a bookmark to a picture by selecting the picture, opening the Bookmark dialog box, and giving the picture a name. Next you'll learn how to create a third type of bookmark, one that is not based on text or a picture.

Creating Nontext-Based Bookmarks

As you were testing the Contact Sunshine page, you had to scroll up the page to return to the hyperlinks. Most users expect and appreciate a "Top of Page" link that scrolls to the top of the page. As the anchor for such a link, you could create a "top" bookmark in the Contact Sunshine page using the contact.gif picture at the top of the page. However, you decide to show Brett something new—you'll create a bookmark that is based on a specific location in the page. In this case, a icon will appear in Design view to identify the bookmark's location. When you view the Web page in a browser, the icon is not visible.

You'll create a bookmark at the top of the page, and then you'll create a "Top of Page" hyperlink after each definition in the Web page that will scroll back to the top of the page.

To create a nontext-based bookmark:

1. Click the **contact.gif** picture at the top of the page, and then press the **left arrow** key ← to move the insertion point to the left of the picture. The picture should *not* be selected.

2. Click **Insert** on the menu bar, and then click **Bookmark** to open the Bookmark dialog box. Because you did not select any text, FrontPage does not suggest a name for the bookmark. When you create bookmark names, it is a good idea to select ones that describe the location in which the bookmark appears, so it is easy to recognize a bookmark in the page. When you click the "Top of Page" hyperlink in this page, the page will scroll to the bookmark. For this reason, "top" is a good bookmark name.

3. Type **top** in the Bookmark name text box as the name for this new bookmark, click the **OK** button, and then press the **End** key to deselect the bookmark icon, which has a dashed underline. See Figure 3-18.

Figure 3-18 | **Creating a bookmark that is not based on text**

"top" bookmark

Next, you will create a "Top of Page" hyperlink below the first definition in the definition list. After creating this hyperlink, you can copy and paste it below other definitions in the list so the user can scroll back to the top of the page after reading any person's biography in the page.

Creating Multiple Hyperlinks to a Bookmark

A bookmark can have many hyperlinks to it from different locations within a Web page. Regardless of which biography the user reads, he needs an easy way to return to the top of the page. You can create a single bookmark in the Web page and then create as many hyperlinks as necessary to that bookmark. When multiple hyperlinks reference a single bookmark, the bookmark has multiple hyperlinks, or multiple references, to it.

With the bookmark already created at the top of the page, you can create a hyperlink to it.

To create multiple hyperlinks to a bookmark:

1. Scroll down the Web page, and then click to the right of **irrigator.** at the end of the first definition in the definition list (the definition paragraph for Brett & Shelly).

2. Press the **Enter** key to create a new paragraph, click the **Style** list arrow on the Formatting toolbar, and then click **Normal.** The new paragraph changes to the Normal style.

3. Type **Top of Page** as the text for the new hyperlink.

4. Select the text **Top of Page**, click the **Insert Hyperlink** button 🔗 on the Standard toolbar to open the Insert Hyperlink dialog box, and then, if necessary, click the **Place in This Document** button 📄 on the Link to bar to display the list of available bookmarks.

5. Click the **top** bookmark, and then click the **OK** button. The Insert Hyperlink dialog box closes and the text "Top of Page" is formatted as a hyperlink.

6. With the Top of Page hyperlink still selected, click the **Copy** button 📋 on the Standard toolbar to copy the hyperlink to the Clipboard.

7. Scroll down the Web page, click to the right of **Texas.** at the end of the definition for Helen, press the **Enter** key to create a new paragraph, change the new paragraph to the **Normal** style, and then click the **Paste** button 📋 on the Standard toolbar. The hyperlink to the top bookmark now appears below the definition for Helen, as shown in Figure 3-19. Because you want to copy the text and its formatting, which is the default option, you can ignore the Paste Options button that might appear when you paste the text.

Hyperlinks created to bookmark target | **Figure 3-19**

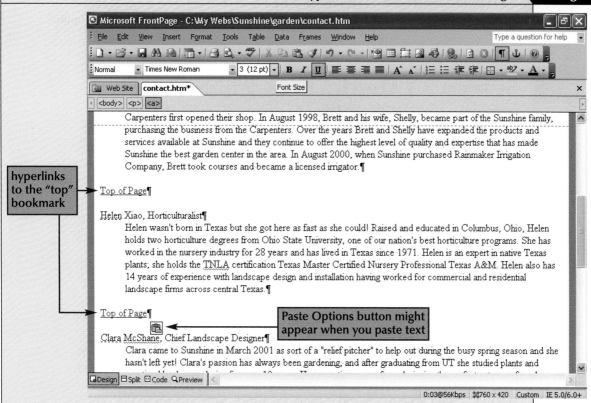

hyperlinks
to the "top"
bookmark

Paste Options button might
appear when you paste text

8. Repeat Step 7 to create Top of Page hyperlinks below the definition paragraphs for Clara, Shawn, Michael, Chad, and Hector.

9. Save the Contact Sunshine page.

Now you will use a browser to test all the hyperlinks you have created.

To test the hyperlinks in a browser:

1. Click the **Preview** button on the Standard toolbar. The Contact Sunshine page opens in a browser.

2. Test each hyperlink that you created in this session to make sure that it works correctly. Depending on your monitor and its resolution, clicking the last several hyperlinks in the bulleted list might result in the browser scrolling to the bottom of the page instead of displaying the defined term at the top of the window.

Trouble? If you have problems with a hyperlink, return to Design view and make any necessary changes. When you are finished, save the page and preview it again in a browser.

3. Close your browser.

4. Close the **garden** Web site, and then exit FrontPage.

The hyperlinks to bookmarks you created in the Contact Sunshine page work as expected. Brett is pleased with the final version of this page and feels confident that his customers will be able to use the page to learn more about the center's expert employees.

In the next session, you will show Brett how to use different Web site views to learn about the Web site's organization, reports, and hyperlinks. You will also show Brett how to use Tasks view to organize the tasks required to complete a Web site when it has multiple contributors.

Review

Session 3.1 Quick Check

1. A(n) _____ list is one that is not sequentially organized.
2. What is a nested list?
3. True or False: Press the Enter key twice to end a bulleted or numbered list.
4. What is an anchor?
5. If a bookmark is not associated with a text selection or a picture, then a(n) _____ appears in Design view to specify the bookmark's location.
6. How do you create a hyperlink to a bookmark in a Web page?
7. In a hyperlink, what does a pound sign (#) indicate?

Session 3.2

Using Web Site Views

So far in this book, you have worked in Folders view, which shows the folders and files that make up a Web site, and in Page view, which shows the content of a Web page and the HTML document that creates a Web page. FrontPage has five other views that let you create your Web pages and manage your Web sites. The seven Web site views are described in Figure 3-20. In this session, you will learn about Hyperlinks view, Reports view, and Tasks view. You will also learn more about the views in which you have been working, Page view and Folders view. In Tutorial 4, you will learn about Navigation view when you create the Web site's navigation structure to identify how pages in the Web site are related to each other. Finally, you will learn about Remote Web Site view in Tutorial 6 when you publish the garden Web site to a server.

Figure 3-20 ▶ **FrontPage Web site views**

View	Description
Page	Use to create, edit, format, and view the content of a Web page
Folders	Use to view, create, delete, copy, rename, and move folders and files in the current Web site
Remote Web Site	Use to publish a Web site to another location and to synchronize copies of the Web site stored in different locations
Reports	Use to analyze, summarize, and produce various types of reports about a Web site
Navigation	Use to create or display a Web site's navigation structure, which identifies the relationships among pages
Hyperlinks	Use to examine the hyperlinks in a Web site
Tasks	Use to maintain a list of the tasks required to complete a Web site

Page View

Most of the work you have completed thus far in the garden Web site has been in **Page view**, which is the Web site view you use to create, edit, format, and view the content of the site's Web pages. Page view has four different ways of displaying a Web page. You can work in Design view, which shows the formatted content of the Web page. Code view shows the HTML document that creates the Web page. Split view shows the HTML document and the formatted Web page at the same time, so you can see both the code that creates the content of the Web page and the appearance of the Web page simultaneously. Finally, Preview view shows the Web page as it will appear when viewed using a browser.

Because Brett has been working in Page view for some time now, you decide that he is ready to learn more about some of the settings that are important for using FrontPage to its full potential, but that might overwhelm a new FrontPage user. You decide to show him a few tricks to help him become more proficient at using FrontPage. The first thing you'll show him is how to use the Clipboard task pane.

To display the Clipboard task pane:

▶ 1. Start **FrontPage**, open the **garden** Web site from the location where your Web sites are stored, and then open the home page in Design view.

▶ 2. Click **View** on the menu bar, and then click **Task Pane**.

▶ 3. Click the **Other Task Panes** list arrow, and then click **Clipboard**.

The **Windows Clipboard** is a temporary storage area in Windows that stores items that you cut and copy from FrontPage and from other programs. The content of the Clipboard is accessible using the Clipboard task pane. If you just started Windows and FrontPage, then your Clipboard task pane is empty. If you have been working in FrontPage or another program and have copied or cut text or other objects, then you might see these objects on the Clipboard task pane. The items on the Clipboard are deleted when you click the Clear All button on the Clipboard task pane or when you turn off your computer.

While working on the Contact Sunshine page in the previous session, you used the Copy button on the Standard toolbar to copy a hyperlink, and then you used the Paste button on the Standard toolbar to paste that hyperlink in other locations in the same Web page. As you cut and copy text and graphics, they are stored on the Clipboard task pane (and on the Windows Clipboard), even if the Clipboard task pane isn't visible. Because the Clipboard task pane can store up to 24 items, it can save you a lot of time. For example, you tell Brett that the link bar and Sunshine logo need to be inserted into other Web pages. You will show him how to use the Clipboard task pane to make these changes.

To use the Clipboard task pane:

▶ 1. Position the pointer to the left of the link bar in the home page so it changes to a ⬀ shape, and then click the left margin. The link bar is selected.

▶ 2. Click the **Copy** button 🖼 on the Standard toolbar. A picture appears on the Clipboard task pane, making it easy to recall the item later. The link bar you copied is really five separate pictures, but only the Home picture is visible in the Clipboard task pane. The Home picture just reminds you what you copied; the full content of the item you copied or cut does not always appear on the Clipboard task pane.

3. Click the logo picture on the next line, and then click 🖺. The logo is copied and a reduced image of it appears on the Clipboard task pane. The Clipboard task pane lists the most recently cut or copied item at the top of the list, so the logo picture appears first in the list.

4. Click the **Web Site** tab, if necessary change to Folders view, and then open the **bulk.htm** page in Design view.

5. Click the Home picture on the Clipboard task pane. The link bar and its hotspots are pasted into the bulk.htm page. Because you pasted pictures, you can ignore the Paste Options button that might appear on your screen.

6. Click the logo picture on the Clipboard task pane. The logo is pasted into the Web page, as shown in Figure 3-21.

| Figure 3-21 | Using the Clipboard task pane |

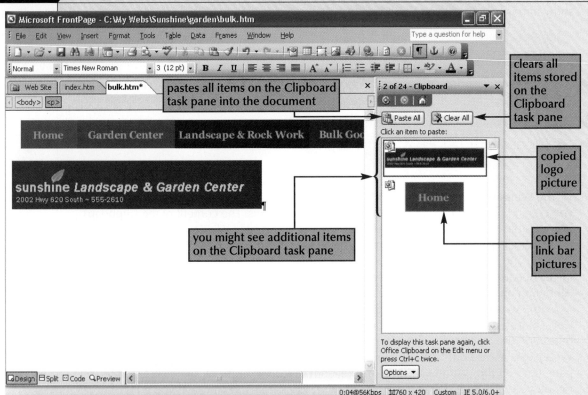

You need to center the paragraph that contains the logo picture.

7. Click the **Center** button ≡ on the Formatting toolbar.

   Trouble? If you see any blank paragraphs in the page, select and delete them.

   Trouble? If the link bar isn't centered on the page, click any picture in the link bar, and then click the Center button on the Formatting toolbar.

8. Save the bulk.htm page, and then click the **Close** button ✖ on the Clipboard task pane to close it.

The items you cut or copy from FrontPage and other programs will remain on the Clipboard task pane until you turn off your computer or delete them. If you want to paste all items on the Clipboard task pane at the same time, click the Paste All button. To clear the contents in the Clipboard task pane, click the Clear All button.

Another thing that you want to demonstrate to Brett is how to document your work in a Web page. Many developers use HTML **comments** to identify the pages on which they have worked, the date the page was last revised, and notes about the page's content or format. These comments appear in the HTML document, but not in the Web page. In FrontPage, there are two ways to add a comment to a Web page. The first way is to type the HTML comment tags (<!-- and -->) directly into the HTML document shown in Code view. The text you want to insert as a comment appears between the tags, such as <!--This document was last revised by Brett Kizer.--> This content will not appear in the Web page because the browser ignores content in comment tags.

When you insert a comment into the HTML document, you can see it only in Code view. If you want to see the comment in Design view, you can use the Comment command on the Insert menu to insert the comment. The text you type appears within the HTML comment tags in Code view, but it is also visible in Design view. However, when you view the page in a browser, the browser ignores the comment.

Inserting a Comment into a Web Page

- Click the location where you want to insert the comment.
- Click Insert on the menu bar, and then click Comment.
- In the Comment text box, type the content of your comment, and then click the OK button.

You'll show Brett how to insert a comment into the bulk.htm page so it will show up in Design view.

To insert a comment into a Web page so it appears in Design view:

1. Press the **Enter** key to create a new paragraph below the logo picture, and then click the **Align Left** button ![button] on the Formatting toolbar to left-align the paragraph.

2. Click **Insert** on the menu bar, and then click **Comment**. The Comment dialog box opens and the insertion point appears in the Comment text box.

3. Type **Clara will take the photographs to include in this page.** and then click the **OK** button. The comment appears as purple text in the Web page, as shown in Figure 3-22.

Comment added in Design view | **Figure 3-22**

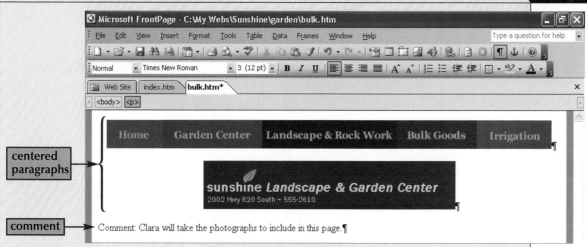

To see the HTML comment tags, you need to change to Code view.

4. Select the comment you inserted in Step 3, and then change to Code view. The comment is selected in the HTML document. Notice the HTML comment tags that enclose the comment. The bot and PREVIEW properties that FrontPage added to your comment make it visible in Design view, but a browser will ignore everything in the <!-- and --> tags.

5. Click the **Show Preview View** button Preview at the bottom of the Contents pane. The comment does not appear in Preview view.

6. Return to Design view, and then save and close the bulk.htm page.

Brett appreciates the tips you have given him for working in Page view. He asks if there are any helpful things that he needs to know about Folders view.

Folders View

You use **Folders view** to display and navigate the folders in a Web site. Clicking a folder in Folders view shows the folder's contents, along with valuable information about each file in the folder, such as its size, type, title, the name of the person who last modified it, and the date and time it was last modified. Using Folders view is very similar to using Windows Explorer to examine files. When you double-click the filename of a Web page in Folders view, that page opens in Design view.

When you first create a Web site, you must indicate the location in which to store the Web site and give it a name. By default, FrontPage creates the images folder in a Web site, in which you can store all of your site's multimedia files, and the _private folder, in which you can store files that you do not want to make accessible to Web site visitors after you publish your site. When a folder name begins with an underscore character, it is called a hidden folder. The _private folder is always visible in Folders view; depending on how FrontPage is configured, you might see other hidden folders that FrontPage creates as you work in your Web site.

You can examine and change a Web site's settings using the Site Settings dialog box. You decide to show Brett the Site Settings dialog box so he knows how to change some of the Web site's general settings, including how to change the Web site's name, check the settings of the Web site's server and the version of the FrontPage Server Extensions or SharePoint Services that are in use, delete temporary files, and display a Web site's hidden folders.

To examine a Web site's general settings:

1. Click the **Web Site** tab to change to Folders view.

2. Click **Tools** on the menu bar, and then click **Site Settings**. The Site Settings dialog box opens with the General tab selected. See Figure 3-23.

General tab of the Site Settings dialog box | Figure 3-23

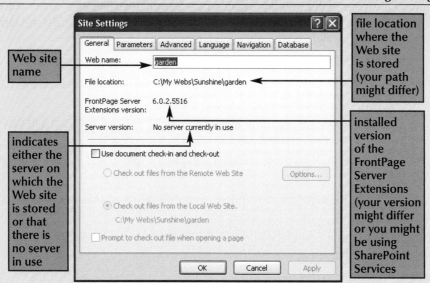

Web site name

file location where the Web site is stored (your path might differ)

indicates either the server on which the Web site is stored or that there is no server in use

installed version of the FrontPage Server Extensions (your version might differ or you might be using SharePoint Services

The Web site name, garden, appears in the Web name text box. If Brett needs to change the name of the Web site, he could type a new one in the Web name text box. FrontPage would change the name of the Web site's root folder and update the hyperlinks and pages in the Web site to use the new folder name.

You tell Brett that he will learn more about publishing a Web site in Tutorial 6, but you want to point out the information provided on the General tab about the FrontPage Server Extensions or SharePoint Services version and server version used in the current site. When you are working in a disk-based Web site, there is no server version indicated on the General tab. When you publish the Web site, the General tab will tell you the version of FrontPage Server Extensions or SharePoint Services in use and the server on which the current Web site is stored.

▶ **3.** Click the **Advanced** tab. See Figure 3-24.

Advanced tab of the Site Settings dialog box | Figure 3-24

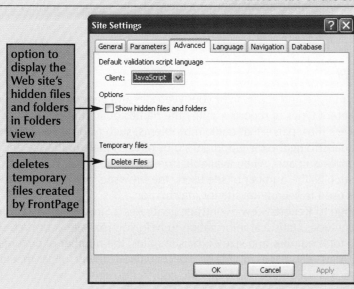

option to display the Web site's hidden files and folders in Folders view

deletes temporary files created by FrontPage

The Advanced tab lets you set the default validation script language (a feature that is beyond the scope of this tutorial). Selecting the Show hidden files and folders check box displays the Web site's hidden files and folders. The Delete Files button deletes temporary files that FrontPage has created while you are working.

4. If necessary, click the **Show hidden files and folders** check box to select it.

   Trouble? If your Show hidden files and folders check box already contains a check mark, skip Step 4.

5. Click the **Delete Files** button. FrontPage deletes the temporary files from a directory on your hard drive or server where it has been storing temporary files.

6. Click the **OK** button. A message box opens and asks if you would like to refresh the Web site.

   Trouble? If the message box doesn't open, your Web site's hidden files are already displayed. Skip Step 7.

7. Click the **Yes** button. FrontPage refreshes the Web site, and one additional folder, _overlay, which had been hidden, is now visible in Folders view.

8. Double-click the **_overlay** folder to open it. This folder stores one file that creates the text on the thumbnail picture in the home page. (You might see additional files, depending on how FrontPage is configured.)

9. Click the **Up One Level** button [icon] at the top of the Contents pane. The contents of the root folder are displayed again. Notice that there are two other buttons on the Contents pane in Folders view. The New Page button [icon] creates a new page in the current folder, and the New Folder button [icon] creates a subfolder in the current folder. You can use folders to organize the pages in your Web site to make them easier for you to locate and use.

   Trouble? If you do not see the files in the root folder, click the Refresh button [icon] on the Standard toolbar.

10. Click **Tools** on the menu bar, click **Site Settings**, click the **Advanced** tab, click the **Show hidden files and folders** check box to clear it, click the **OK** button, and then click the **Yes** button. FrontPage refreshes the Web site and hides the Web site's hidden files and folders.

Brett appreciates knowing more about changing the Web site's general settings. Next you'll show him how to use Reports view.

Reports View

Reports view lets you analyze and summarize your Web site and generate reports about your Web site. The different types of reports identify the names of, and important information about, all of the site's files; pages that contain problems, such as broken hyperlinks; workflow information describing the development status of each page in the site and the person assigned to complete it; and, when available from the server, usage information about your Web site, such as the number of site users, the browsers used to access the site, and the keywords used to search the site for information.

When you first change to Reports view, FrontPage generates a Site Summary report. The **Site Summary report** includes statistical information to help you manage your Web site, such as data about the total number and size of the site's files, the number of pictures in the site, and the number of Web pages in the site that download slowly (pages that take longer than a set number of seconds using a specific connection speed; the default setting is 30 seconds).

To change to Reports view:

1. Click the **Reports View** button 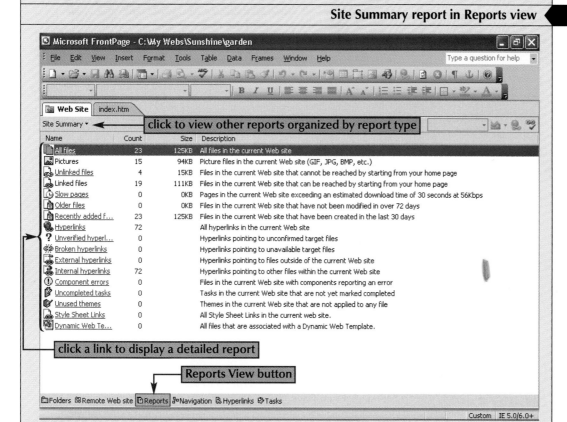 at the bottom of the Contents pane. Figure 3-25 shows a Site Summary report for the garden Web site. (The statistics in your report might look different, but you should see the same list of reports.)

Site Summary report in Reports view | **Figure 3-25**

Each hyperlink in the first column of Reports view opens another report with detailed information. For example, clicking the Unlinked files link opens a list of files in the Web site that are not linked to any other files in the Web site.

2. Click the **Unlinked files** link in the Site Summary report. Figure 3-26 shows that there are four files in the Web site that aren't linked to any other file. (Depending on how FrontPage is configured, you might see additional unlinked files.) The contact.gif file is a graphic and does not need to be linked to any other page, and you saved the map_small.jpg file as map_small.gif when you converted it to a GIF file and applied effects to it. The sun.gif file is the picture bullet that you used in the contact.htm page. All of these unlinked files are acceptable. However, seeing that the contact.htm file is not linked to any other page is a problem because site visitors will have no way to access this file. As you work in Reports view, you will find that there are some problems that you need to correct, and others that you can ignore.

Figure 3-26 ▶ **Unlinked Files report**

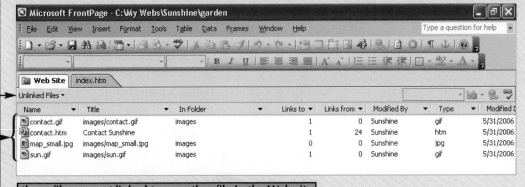

> these files are not linked to any other file in the Web site

▶ **3.** Click the **Unlinked Files** button at the top of the Contents pane, and then click **Site Summary**. The Site Summary report reappears in Reports view.

▶ **4.** Click the **All files** link in the Site Summary report. The All Files report lists each file in the garden Web site along with its title, the folder in which it is stored, its file size, its file type, the date and time it was last modified, and the person's name who last modified it.

▶ **5.** Click the **All Files** button at the top of the Contents pane, and then click **Site Summary**. The All files entry in the Site Summary report indicates that the Web site has 23 files that use 125 KB of file space. (Your file size might differ slightly.)

Brett also notices the other reports, many of which display zero as their counts. The descriptions indicate that some of the reports have specific settings, such as the Slow pages report, which lists pages that require more than 30 seconds to download at 56 Kbps, and the Older Files report, which lists pages that have not been modified in the previous 72 days. You tell Brett that these reports are customizable and decide to show him how to change their default settings.

To change time intervals for reports:

▶ **1.** Click **Tools** on the menu bar, and then click **Options**. The Options dialog box opens.

▶ **2.** Click the **Reports View** tab. As shown in Figure 3-27, you can change the settings for the reports that list recent files, older files, and slow pages. In addition, when your Web site is stored on a server, you can change the way usage data is displayed by specifying the number of months to show in the report.

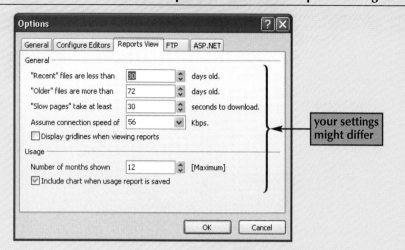

3. If necessary, change your settings to match the ones shown in Figure 3-27, and then click the **OK** button to close the Options dialog box.

You tell Brett that after the garden Web site is published on a Web server, he can learn about his site's visitors by examining the Usage reports, which are accessible by clicking the Site Summary button at the top of the Contents pane, pointing to Usage, and then clicking the desired report. (The Web server on which the site is stored must be configured to support these reports. Some ISPs provide usage data reporting other ways.) These reports include usage statistics about the number of page hits, the operating systems and browsers used to access the site, and information about the domain names of site visitors. Brett can use these reports to monitor usage of the site and to determine the popularity of different pages in the Web site.

Hyperlinks View

Hyperlinks view shows the hyperlinks that connect the pages in a Web site, along with hyperlinks to locations outside the Web site and other types of links, such as mailtos. As you develop a Web site, you can get an overview of it by using Hyperlinks view to examine the hyperlinks that connect the site's pages. You should check Hyperlinks view periodically to verify that your links are set up correctly. Because it is easier to check your site's hyperlinks after you've added only a few hyperlinks to its pages, you might prefer to check smaller parts of the Web site as you go, instead of waiting until the entire Web site has been completed. A completed Web site might contain hundreds of hyperlinks, so checking them as you create them makes it easier to confirm that they are set up as desired.

You want to show Brett how to use Hyperlinks view to examine the Web site's pages for missing hyperlinks and to see the overall structure of the Web site.

To view the Web site in Hyperlinks view:

1. Click the **Hyperlinks View** button 🔗 Hyperlinks at the bottom of the Contents pane, display the Folder List, and then click **index.htm** in the Folder List. Hyperlinks view of the home page for the garden Web site appears, as shown in Figure 3-28.

Figure 3-28 | Hyperlinks view of the home page

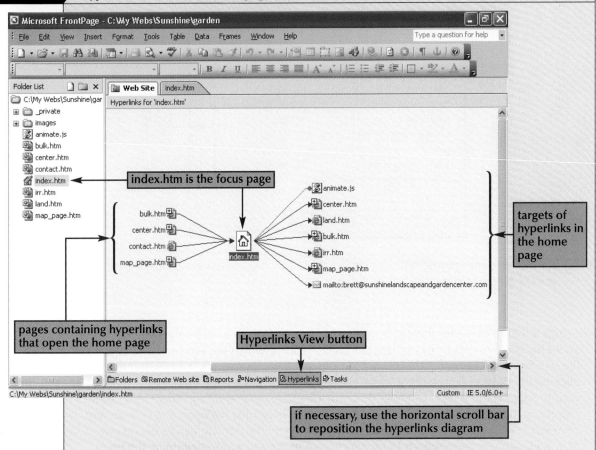

Trouble? If necessary, use the horizontal scroll bar to scroll the Contents pane to the right until the hyperlinks are centered in the window as shown in Figure 3-28.

Trouble? You can customize Hyperlinks view to display page titles instead of page file-names. Figure 3-28 shows filenames; your Hyperlinks view might display page titles. To display the page filenames, right-click an empty area in the Contents pane to open the shortcut menu, and then click Show Page Titles to turn this feature off.

The page you selected, index.htm, appears in the center of the diagram in Hyperlinks view. The selected page is called the focus page; in this case, the home page is the focus page. The links to the left of the focus page contain hyperlinks that open the focus page. In other words, the bulk.htm, center.htm, contact.htm, and map_page.htm pages contain at least one hyperlink that opens the home page. The links to the right of the focus page are targets of hyperlinks in the focus page. For example, the home page contains hyperlinks that open the center.htm, land.htm, bulk.htm, irr.htm, and map_page.htm pages. The home page also contains a link to the animate.js file, which is a JavaScript file that creates the animation for the thumbnail picture in the home page, and the mailto, which includes your e-mail address.

2. Right-click an empty area in the Contents pane to open the shortcut menu, and then click **Hyperlinks to Pictures**. Hyperlinks view of the home page now includes hyperlinks to pictures in the home page. See Figure 3-29.

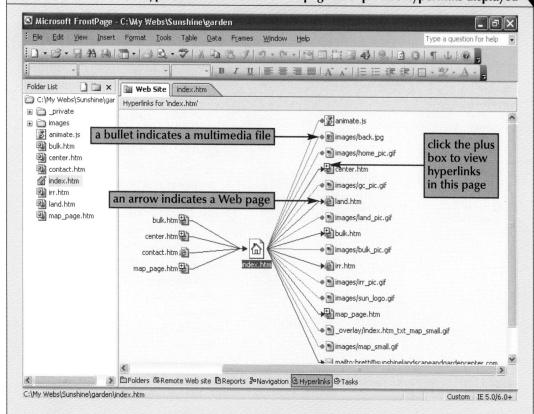

Trouble? If you see a check mark to the left of the Hyperlinks to Pictures command on the shortcut menu, this feature is already turned on and you do not need to click it.

A hyperlink that ends with an arrow indicates a hyperlink to a Web page in the Web site; a hyperlink that ends with a bullet indicates a hyperlink to a picture or other multimedia file or a script file. The animate.js file creates the animation that you applied to the thumbnail picture in the home page. The other files with bullets are pictures that appear in the home page. The envelope icon indicates a hyperlink to the mailto you created in the home page (you will see your e-mail address in the mailto).

Notice also the plus box on the upper-left corner of the center.htm icon to the right of the focus page. You can follow the hyperlinks from one document to another by expanding (showing) or contracting (hiding) the hyperlinks. Clicking the plus box expands the hyperlinks in the page; clicking the minus box collapses the hyperlinks in the page. Expanding the hyperlinks enables you to see how the pages in a Web site are connected.

To expand the hyperlinks for the center.htm page:

1. Click the **plus box** on the center.htm icon to the right of the focus page to expand this hyperlink and display the hyperlinks it contains. Figure 3-30 shows the hyperlinks in the center.htm page.

Figure 3-30 | Hyperlinks in the center.htm page

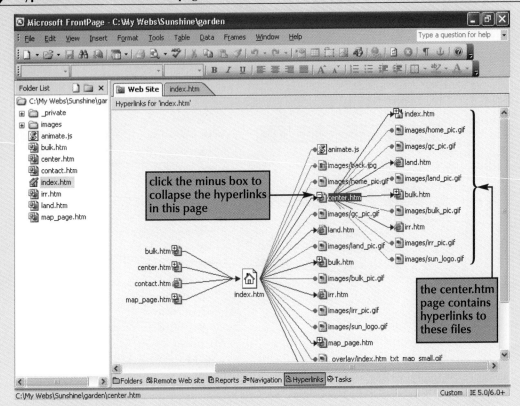

Trouble? If necessary, use the vertical and horizontal scroll bars on the Contents pane to view the expanded hyperlinks from the center.htm page.

▶ **2.** Click the **minus box** on the center.htm icon to the right of the focus page to collapse this hyperlink.

You can change the focus page in Hyperlinks view by clicking a new page in the Folder List.

To change the focus page in Hyperlinks view:

▶ **1.** Click the **center.htm** page in the Folder List. The Contents pane shows the center.htm page as the focus page of Hyperlinks view. There are two pages that contain hyperlinks that open the center.htm page, and the center.htm page contains hyperlinks that open four pages (index.htm, land.htm, bulk.htm, and irr.htm). In addition, the center.htm page contains six picture files, all indicated with bullets in Hyperlinks view.

▶ **2.** Click the **land.htm** page in the Folder List. There are three pages in the Web site that contain hyperlinks that open this page, but the land.htm page does not contain any pictures or links that open other pages. This lack of hyperlinks in the page indicates a problem in the Web site.

▶ **3.** Double-click **land.htm** in the Folder List. The land.htm page opens in Design view and is empty. You note this problem so you can correct it later.

▶ **4.** Close the land.htm page.

Displaying Repeated Hyperlinks

Some pages contain hyperlinks with the same target. When a single target of a hyperlink appears in more than one location in a Web page, it is called a **repeated hyperlink**. You can display repeated hyperlinks in Hyperlinks view. First, you'll turn off the hyperlinks to pictures so you can see the repeated links better.

To display repeated hyperlinks:

1. Click the **Web Site** tab to return to Hyperlinks view, right-click an empty area of the Contents pane to open the shortcut menu, and then click **Hyperlinks to Pictures**.

2. Click **index.htm** in the Folder List to select this page as the center focus of Hyperlinks view. If necessary, use the scroll bars to center the hyperlinks diagram in the Contents pane.

3. Right-click an empty area of the Contents pane to open the shortcut menu, and then click **Repeated Hyperlinks** to display the repeated hyperlinks for this page. Because each page listed to the right of the home page appears only once, you determine that there are no repeated hyperlinks in this page.

4. Click the **center.htm** page in the Folder List. The center.htm page becomes the focus of Hyperlinks view. As shown in Figure 3-31, there are two links to the index.htm page, indicating a repeated hyperlink.

Repeated hyperlinks in the center.htm page ◀ Figure 3-31

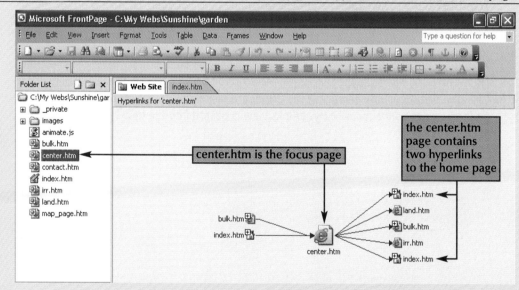

5. Double-click **center.htm** in the Folder List to open the page in Design view. There are two hyperlinks to the home page. The first one is in the link bar (the "Home" picture). The second link is the image map you created in the logo picture (using the word "sunshine").

6. Close the center.htm page.

Printing Hyperlinks View

When you are working in Hyperlinks view, the Print button is disabled. Sometimes it is helpful to have a printout of the hyperlinks for a specific page, especially if you work with a team to develop a Web site. To print Hyperlinks view, you must copy it to the Windows Clipboard, paste it into a document that you can print, and then print that document. You can paste the picture into a new document created by WordPad or Microsoft Word, but an easier way is to paste the picture into a new Web page. After pasting the picture, you can resize it to reduce its size or print it as usual. Because the pasted picture is wider than it is long, you will need to print it in landscape orientation. After printing the Web page, you can close the page without saving changes. You want to show Brett how to print Hyperlinks view before finishing your work in this view.

To copy and paste the screen in Hyperlinks view:

▶ 1. Click the **Web Site** tab to return to Hyperlinks view, click the **index.htm** page in the Folder List, and then, if necessary, use the scroll bars to center the hyperlinks diagram in the Contents pane.

▶ 2. Press the **Print Screen** key. A picture of your screen (called a screenshot) is copied to the Windows Clipboard. You will paste the picture into a new Web page.

▶ 3. Click the **Create a new normal page** button 🗎 on the Standard toolbar. A new page opens in Design view, and the Layout Tables and Cells task pane opens.

   Trouble? If the Layout Tables and Cells task pane does not open, click View on the menu bar, and then click Task Pane. Don't worry about which task pane opens; you'll change it in the next step.

▶ 4. Click the **Other Task Panes** list arrow, and then click **Clipboard**. The picture of your screen appears on the Clipboard task pane.

▶ 5. Click the picture of your screen on the Clipboard task pane. A picture of your screen with the home page as the focus of Hyperlinks view is pasted into the new Web page. See Figure 3-32.

New Web page created | **Figure 3-32**

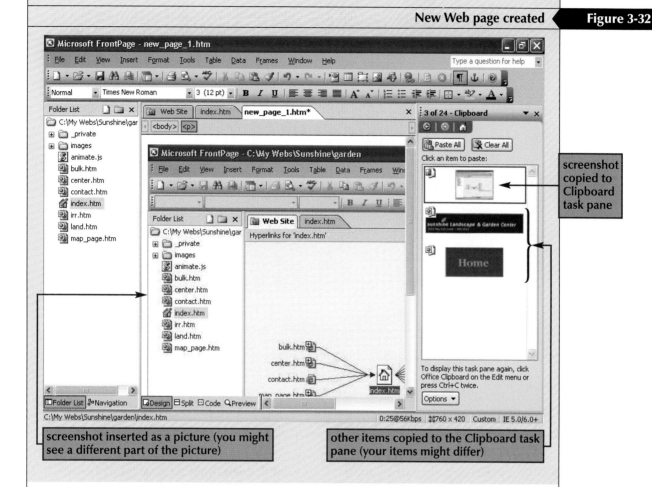

screenshot inserted as a picture (you might see a different part of the picture)

other items copied to the Clipboard task pane (your items might differ)

screenshot copied to Clipboard task pane

To make sure your screenshot prints on one page, you'll reduce the picture's size.

To reduce the picture's size and print it:

1. Close the Clipboard task pane.

2. Click the picture to select it. Sizing handles appear around the picture.

3. Point to the sizing handle in the upper-left corner of the picture so the pointer changes to a ◥ shape, and then drag the sizing handle toward the center of the picture. Release the mouse button when the pointer is about two inches from the upper-left corner of the picture. The picture looks blurry because you resized it. To correct this problem, you'll resample the picture.

4. Find the **Picture Actions** button 🖾, which should appear in the lower-right corner of your screen.

5. Click the 🖾 button, and then click the **Resample Picture To Match Size** option button. The picture is resampled and the image is clear.

6. Click **File** on the menu bar, and then click **Page Setup**. The Print Page Setup dialog box opens.

7. Click the **Options** button. The Print Setup dialog box opens and displays options unique to the printer you have installed and connected to your computer, so your Print Setup dialog box might look different from the one show in Figure 3-33. As you print Web pages using different printers, you might see different options and settings in the Print Setup dialog box.

Figure 3-33   **Print Setup dialog box**

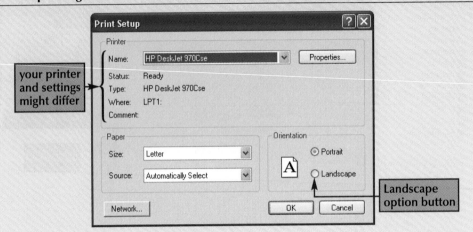

8. Click the **Landscape** option button in the Orientation section.

Trouble? If you do not see an Orientation section, click the Properties button to see if you can locate the print orientation settings. If you cannot find these settings, click the OK button to close the dialog box, then continue with Step 10.

9. Click the **OK** button to close the Print Setup dialog box, and then click the **OK** button to close the Print Page Setup dialog box.

10. Click **File** on the menu bar, and then click **Print Preview**. Make sure that the picture will print on one page. If not, click the Close button above the page (not the Close button ☒ for the new_page_1.htm page), repeat Steps 2 through 5 to reduce the size of the picture, and then preview the page again. When the picture fits on one page, click the Close button above the page.

11. Click the **Print** button 🖨 to print the page, and then if necessary click the **OK** button in the dialog box that opens.

12. Close the new page and click the **No** button to skip saving the page.

13. Close the index.htm page.

You're finished working in Hyperlinks view, so you will turn off the display of repeated hyperlinks and close the Folder List.

To turn off the display of repeated hyperlinks and close the Folder List:

1. Right-click an empty area of the Contents pane to open the shortcut menu, and then click **Repeated Hyperlinks**.

2. Click the **Close** button ☒ on the Folder List to close it.

The final Web site view that you want to demonstrate for Brett is Tasks view.

Tasks View

To manage a Web site developed by one or many people, you can use **Tasks view** to organize tasks as you work on the site. Each task can include the person assigned to complete it, the task's name and description, and an assigned priority. When a task is finished, you can mark it as completed and then archive or delete it from the Web site. When many people are collaborating to develop a new Web site, they can use Tasks view to manage the Web site's overall development.

Adding a Task to Tasks View

You can add new tasks in Tasks view or by clicking the list arrow for the Create a new normal page button on the Standard toolbar, and then clicking Task. You can add general tasks to the Web site from any view. If you want to associate a task with a specific Web page, change to Folders view and select the page you want to associate with the task or open the page in Design view, and then create the task. In Tasks view, the task will be associated with the page you selected.

Reference Window

Adding a Task to Tasks View

- In any Web site view, click the list arrow for the Create a new normal page button on the Standard toolbar, and then click Task. To associate a Web page with the task, select the Web page in Folders view or open the Web page in Design view before creating the new task.
- In the New Task dialog box, type a task name, assign the task to the appropriate person or group, type a description, and then click an option button as necessary to assign the task a priority.
- Click the OK button.

During your exploration of Hyperlinks view, you noted that the land.htm page did not contain any content. To show Brett how to create a task in the Web site, you will add a task to complete this page and assign the work to yourself. Because the land.htm page already exists in the Web site, you will associate the new task with this page.

To add a task to the Web site:

1. Click the **Folders View** button [Folders] at the bottom of the Contents pane to change to Folders view, and then click the **land.htm** page to select it.

2. Click the **list arrow** for the Create a new normal page button [□ ▾] on the Standard toolbar, and then click **Task**. The New Task dialog box opens, as shown in Figure 3-34. Notice that the land.htm page is associated with this task. The default assignment of tasks is to the user who is currently logged on. You might see your name or the logon you use for your computer in the Assigned to list box. The Created by date shows today's date and time. The default priority for all tasks is medium. The user determines the priority for a task; you might give all tasks medium priority or choose to have a system for ranking tasks as high, medium, or low priority.

Figure 3-34	New Task dialog box

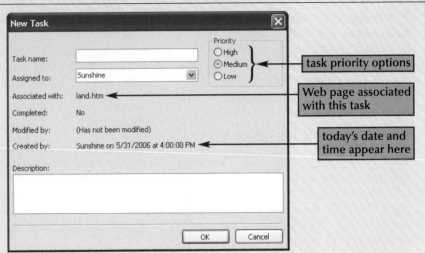

3. In the Task name text box, type **Add content to Landscape & Rock Work page**, and then press the **Tab** key.

4. If your name is selected in the Assigned to list box, press the **Tab** key to move the insertion point to the Description text box. If your name is not selected in the Assigned to list box, type your first and last names, and then press the **Tab** key.

5. Type **Talk to Clara about the content for this page.** The task has a name and description and you assigned the task to yourself.

6. Click the **High** option button in the Priority section. The task is complete.

7. Click the **OK** button. The New Task dialog box closes and the task is added to the Web site.

   Brett reminds you that the irr.htm page is also blank and that the bulk.htm page only has a link bar and the Sunshine logo. You decide to add these tasks to the Web site.

8. Select the **irr.htm** page in Folders view, and then repeat Steps 2 through 7 to add a task to the Web site with **Add content to Irrigation page** as the task name and **Talk to Chad about the content for this page.** as the description. Assign the task to yourself and give it a high priority.

9. Select the bulk.htm page in Folders view, and then repeat Steps 2 through 7 to add a task to the Web site with **Finish bulk.htm page** as the task name and **Get the file for this page from Michael.** as the description. Assign the task to yourself give it a high priority.

To see the tasks you created, you need to change to Tasks view. You can use Tasks view to sort tasks by different values and change them as necessary to update their status.

Sorting, Changing, and Deleting Tasks

If you are working on a large Web site with a team, the site might contain hundreds of tasks, so keeping it organized is important. You can sort tasks in many ways to organize their presentation. For example, you might want to sort tasks by priority, by the people assigned to complete them, or alphabetically by task name. You want to show Brett how to sort and change tasks now, while the list is still small, so he can practice this skill. In the future, Brett might rely on Tasks view to organize the work required to create and maintain the Web site.

To sort Tasks view and change a task:

1. Click the **Tasks View** button ⚙Tasks at the bottom of the Contents pane to change to Tasks view. The three tasks you added appear in the list, as shown in Figure 3-35.

Tasks added to the Web site ◄ **Figure 3-35**

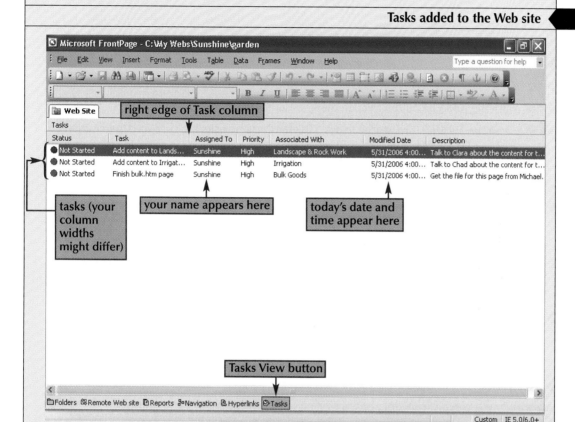

You can resize the columns in Tasks view using the pointer. You will show Brett how to resize the columns so he can read the task names better.

2. Point to the right edge of the Task column so the pointer changes to a ↔ shape, and then double-click the column. The Task column's width increases so that the longest entry is completely visible in the column. The columns to the right of the Task column scroll further to the right. You can use the horizontal scroll bar to see columns that have scrolled off the screen.

3. Click the **Task** column heading to sort the tasks alphabetically by task name.

4. Click the **Task** column heading again to sort the tasks in descending alphabetical order.

   You can double-click any task to see its details.

5. Double-click the **Finish bulk.htm page** task to open the Task Details dialog box. In this dialog box, you can change the priority of a task, its description, or the person assigned to complete it.

6. Type **Finish Bulk Goods page** in the Task name text box to provide a more descriptive name for the task.

   You could click the Start Task button to open the page associated with this task (bulk.htm) in Design view so you can begin working on the page. For now, you will simply close the Task Details dialog box.

7. Click the **OK** button. The task is updated.

Clara just sent Brett the files for the land.htm page, so he tells you that you can complete this task. You'll import the new land.htm and its picture files into the Web site, and then you can mark the task as complete. The process of completing a task can entail anything from importing a new page to updating a hyperlink in an existing page.

To complete a task:

1. Display the Folder List, and then make sure the garden Web site's root folder is selected.
2. Click **File** on the menu bar, and then click **Import** to open the Import dialog box.
3. Click the **Add File** button to open the Add File to Import List dialog box.
4. Open the **Tutorial.03\Tutorial** folder, click **land.htm** to select it, click the **Open** button, click the **OK** button, and then click the **Yes** button to overwrite the file in the Web site with the same name.

   You'll also need to import the pictures into the Web site's images folder.

5. In the Folder List, click the **images** folder to select it, and then import the **land.gif**, **land_sam.jpg**, **rock_pic.gif**, and **rock_sam.gif** files from the Tutorial.03\Tutorial folder into the images folder. (Press and hold the Ctrl key to select multiple files.)
6. Double-click **land.htm** in the Folder List to open the Landscape & Rock Work page in Design view. Use the scroll bars to examine the page contents, and then close the page and the Folder List.
7. In Tasks view, right-click the **Add content to Landscape & Rock Work page** task to open the shortcut menu, and then click **Mark Complete**. The task's status changes from Not Started to Completed, as shown in Figure 3-36.

Figure 3-36   **Completed task in Tasks view**

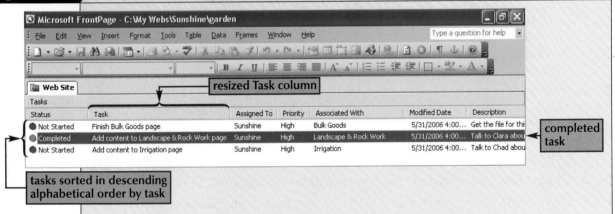

After finishing a task, you can mark it as completed. The task will remain in Tasks view after you change its status. However, if you close the Web site and then reopen it in Tasks view, you'll need to turn on the task history to see completed tasks. Because it might seem like completed tasks have disappeared, you want to show Brett how to turn on the task history. You will simulate closing the Web site by refreshing it. You also want to show Brett how to delete a task, so you will delete the completed task from the site.

To turn on task history and delete a task:

▶ 1. Click the **Refresh** button 🔃 on the Standard toolbar. Notice that the Add content to Landscape & Rock Work page task, which was marked as completed, no longer appears in Tasks view. To display completed tasks, you must show the task history.

▶ 2. Right-click an empty area in Tasks view to open the shortcut menu, and then click **Show History**. Tasks view now shows unfinished and completed tasks.

   Trouble? If the Show History command has a check mark to the left of its name on the shortcut menu, then the task history is already enabled. Click outside the shortcut menu to close it, and then continue with Step 3.

▶ 3. Right-click the **Add content to Landscape & Rock Work page** task to open the shortcut menu, and then click **Delete Task**. The Confirm Delete dialog box opens and asks you to confirm the deletion.

▶ 4. Click the **Yes** button. The task is deleted from Tasks view.

▶ 5. Right-click an empty area in Tasks view to open the shortcut menu, and then click **Show History** to turn this feature off.

▶ 6. Change to Folders view, close the **garden** Web site, and then exit FrontPage.

Brett is pleased with the Contact Sunshine page and appreciates the tour of the different views of a Web site. In the next tutorial, you will show Brett how to use Navigation view and how to create shared borders and themes in a Web site.

Session 3.2 Quick Check

Review

1. How many items can you store in the Clipboard task pane at the same time?
2. How would you change the name of the folder that stores a Web site?
3. What does an underscore character indicate when it is the first character in a folder in a Web site?
4. When you change to Reports view, what does FrontPage automatically generate?
5. What is a repeated hyperlink?
6. True or False: Click the Print button on the Standard toolbar to print Hyperlinks view.
7. How do you add a task to a Web site and associate the task with a specific Web page?
8. True or False: Marking a task as completed deletes the task from the Web site.

Tutorial Summary

Review

In this tutorial, you learned how to create bulleted, numbered, definition, and nested lists. You learned about creating anchors (bookmarks) in a Web page to increase the ease of use for that page's user. Finally, you learned about the different Web site views available in FrontPage. In Page view, you learned how to use the Clipboard task pane and how to enter comments in a Web page. In Folders view, you learned how to display a Web site's hidden files and folders and how to delete temporary files created by FrontPage. You examined a Site Summary report in Reports view and examined a few of the Web site's detailed reports. In Hyperlinks view, you learned how to examine the hyperlinks leading to and coming from a single Web page. Finally, you used Tasks view to create, change, and delete tasks.

As you work on your own Web sites in the future, you will make your Web pages easier to use if you create anchors and hyperlinks to anchors in pages that contain a lot of information. As you saw in this tutorial, creating anchors and hyperlinks to those anchors makes it easier for your site's visitors to find the content they need.

As you develop a Web site, you will do most of your work in Page view and Folders view. Some developers use Tasks view to coordinate the tasks required to complete a Web site, but others do not. Regardless of your preference, Tasks view can be an effective way of managing the many details involved in creating a Web site. You can use Hyperlinks view to see the hyperlinks in your Web pages, and you will use this view in the future when you test the Web site to identify broken links. Finally, after publishing a Web site, you can use Reports view to study the ways different users access your site. This information is both interesting and informative and should be a part of the overall maintenance of a Web site.

Key Terms

anchor	Folders view	Page view
bookmark	Hyperlinks view	repeated hyperlink
broken link	multi-level list	Reports view
bulleted list	nested list	Site Summary report
comment	numbered list	Tasks view
defined term	ordered list	unordered list
definition list	outline list	Windows Clipboard

Practice

Practice the skills you learned in the tutorial using the same case scenario.

Review Assignments

Data Files needed for the Review Assignments: bulk2.htm, bulk.gif, bulk.htm, bulk_sam.jpg, irr.htm, mlch_art.gif, mulch.jpg, soil.jpg, soil_art.gif, stne_art.gif, stone.jpg

Brett is happy with the way the garden Web site is shaping up. He is pleased that you were able to include the content for the Landscape & Rock Work page, but he is concerned about other missing content in the site's pages. He asks you to review the entire Web site and add tasks to the Web site for the remaining work, and then to complete as much of the work as possible using files that have been developed to date by the Sunshine staff.

If necessary, start FrontPage, make sure you have your Data Files, and then do the following:

1. Open the **garden** Web site from the location where your Web sites are stored, and then preview the home page in a browser. Use the browser to examine all of the pages in the Web site. As you note problems in the pages that you open, use the Windows taskbar to switch between the browser and FrontPage to add appropriate tasks in Tasks view. (You already added two of these tasks to the Web site in Session 3.2.) Assign tasks you find to yourself and give them a medium priority. If necessary, associate the task with a specific Web page.
2. When you have finished examining the Web site using your browser, close your browser and switch to Hyperlinks view. For each Web page in the site (**bulk.htm**, **center.htm**, **contact.htm**, **index.htm**, **irr.htm**, **land.htm**, and **map_page.htm**), examine the hyperlinks leading to and from the page. With the exception of the **map_page.htm** page, each page should contain links that open the other pages in the Web site. The **contact.htm** page should be accessible using a hyperlink in the home page. If you need to make any changes to these planned links, note the changes as tasks in the Web site.

3. Compare your notes to Figure 3-37, and then, if necessary, update Tasks view in your Web site to match. When you have finished, sort the tasks alphabetically by task name.

Figure 3-37

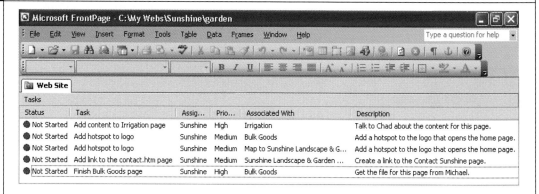

4. Display the Folder List, and then import the following pages from the Tutorial.03\Review folder included with your Data Files into the root folder of the **garden** Web site: **bulk2.htm**, **bulk.htm**, and **irr.htm**. When prompted to overwrite the **bulk.htm** and **irr.htm** files, click the Yes button.

5. Import the following files from the Tutorial.03\Review folder into the images folder of the garden Web site: **bulk.gif**, **bulk_sam.jpg**, **mlch_art.gif**, **mulch.jpg**, **soil.jpg**, **soil_art.gif**, **stne_art.gif**, and **stone.jpg**.

6. Open the home page in Design view. Select the word "us" in the third line on the page and change it to "our expert staff." Then format the "our expert staff" text as a hyperlink that opens the **contact.htm** page. Save the home page.

7. Copy the link bar in the home page and paste it at the top of the **contact.htm** page. Make sure to insert the link bar so the top bookmark remains at the top of the page. (*Hint:* Press the right arrow key to move the insertion point between the bookmark icon and the **contact.gif** file, and then insert the link bar. If necessary, delete any blank lines above the link bar.) Save the **contact.htm** page.

8. In the **bulk2.htm** page, select the broken link to the **mulch_art.gif** file, and then open the Picture Properties dialog box and display the General tab. Change the picture from **mulch_art.gif** to **mlch_art.gif**, and then save the **bulk2.htm** page.

9. Copy the logo picture in the **bulk2.htm** page, open the **map_page.htm** page, and then replace the logo picture in the **map_page.htm** page with the one you copied. Make sure that the hotspot that opens the home page appears in the pasted logo picture, and then save the **map_page.htm** page.

10. Open the **bulk.htm** page in Design view, and then verify that the logo picture in the revised **bulk.htm** page that you imported into the Web site contains a hotspot that opens the home page.

11. Open the home page in a browser, and then use the links in the Web site to open all of its pages. (*Note:* You will continue adding pages to the Web site as you complete this book. There are still some missing pages that are linked to the **land.htm** and **bulk2.htm** pages.)

12. Close your browser.

13. In Tasks view, mark the tasks you created for linking the home page and the **contact.htm** page, adding the content to the Irrigation page, and adding the hotspot to the logo picture in the **bulk.htm** and **map_page.htm** pages as complete. Print Tasks view. (*Hint:* There is no Print command in Tasks view, so you will need to print a screenshot.)

14. Change to Hyperlinks view, and set the **contact.htm** page as the focus page. If necessary, center the hyperlinks diagram in the Contents pane, and then print Hyperlinks view.

15. Close the Folder List and then change to Reports view. Change the Slow Pages report so it lists pages that take longer than 10 seconds to download at 56 Kbps, and then open the Slow Pages report and print it. (*Hint:* There is no Print command in Reports view, so you will need to print a screenshot.)

16. Close the **garden** Web site, and then close FrontPage.

Case Problem 1

There are no Data Files needed for this Case Problem.

Apply

Apply the skills you learned in the tutorial to organize the content of an existing Web page and to examine the Web site in Hyperlinks, Reports, and Tasks view.

Buffalo Trading Post Nicole Beirne, president of Buffalo Trading Post, wants you to format the How page you created in the Web site so it is easy to navigate. In reviewing the page's contents, you tell Nicole that this page, which contains answers to commonly asked questions, would be an ideal candidate for a bulleted list and a definition list. To make the page easier to scroll, you also suggest adding anchors to the page and hyperlinks to them.

Nicole also wants you to examine the Web site and create a list of its remaining tasks. Nicole knows that the content of the What page is missing and the Where page has not been added to the Web site. She will assign the creation of these pages to an associate and ask her to send the files to you later. For now, you will note these problems to ensure their future completion.

Because you have completed some of the initial design work, you tell Nicole that you will also examine the Web site in Hyperlinks view and Reports view to look for any problems that you can fix now.

If necessary, start FrontPage, and then do the following:

1. Open the **buffalo** Web site from the location where your Web sites are stored. (If you did not create this Web site in Tutorial 1 and change it in Tutorial 2, ask your instructor for assistance.)

2. Open the **who.htm** page in Design view, and then change the numbered list at the bottom of the page to a bulleted list. After creating the bulleted list, change the default bullet character from a dot to a solid square, and then save the **who.htm** page.

3. Open the **how.htm** page in Design view, and then format the first three paragraphs below the link bar as a bulleted list with solid square bullet characters.

4. Create a bookmark for each heading in the page ("How It Works," "Frequently Asked Questions," and "Choose to Re-Use") using a lowercase name of your choice that does not contain spaces or exceed eight characters. Then create a hyperlink from each item in the bulleted list to its corresponding bookmark.

5. Format the paragraphs beginning with the bold "How It Works" text and ending with the paragraph ending "per person per day." as a definition list. Format the paragraphs with the headings "How It Works," "Frequently Asked Questions," and "Choose to Re-Use" as defined terms.

6. Create a bookmark named "top" to the left of the picture at the top of the page. Below the first definition paragraph in the definition list, create a "Back to top of page" hyperlink using the top bookmark as its target. Format the paragraph containing this link with the Normal style.

7. Copy the "Back to top of page" hyperlink you created in Step 6 and paste it on a new line below each of the other definition paragraphs. (For the "Frequently Asked Questions" definition, paste the link after the last answer.) Format each paragraph containing this link with the Normal style. When you are finished, save the **how.htm** page.

8. Add a task to the Web site to get the content of the **what.htm** page from its developer and associate the task with the existing page with the same name. Assign the task to yourself, add an appropriate description and task name, and give it a medium priority.

Explore ▶

9. Add another task to the Web site to get the **where.htm** Web page from its developer and import it into the Web site. Assign the task to yourself, add an appropriate description and task name, and give it a medium priority. (*Hint:* Create the task in Tasks view to create the task without associating it with a page.)

10. Display the **how.htm** page in Hyperlinks view. If necessary, center the hyperlinks diagram in the Contents pane. Display the hyperlinks to pictures in the page, and then print Hyperlinks view.

11. Use Hyperlinks view to examine the hyperlinks in the Web site for the **index.htm**, **what.htm**, and **who.htm** pages, and then turn off the display of hyperlinks to pictures.

Explore ▶

12. Change to Reports view and then open the Broken Hyperlinks report. Use the information in this report to identify the filename of the broken hyperlink and the page in which it is located. Open the **who.htm** page in Design view, and then change the broken link to the watermark background picture from **bwmark.gif** to the **w_mark.gif** file in the Web site's images folder. When you have corrected the broken link, save the **who.htm** page, and then run another Site Summary report in Reports view.

13. Open the home page in a browser and test the hyperlinks between pages and the hyperlinks to bookmarks you created. (*Note:* You will add content to the **what.htm** page in another tutorial.) Print the **how.htm** page, and then close your browser.

14. In a new paragraph below the horizontal line at the bottom of the **who.htm** page, add a comment that you can see in Design view with the following content: "This page last updated by [Your Name]." Save and print the **who.htm** page.

15. Close the **buffalo** Web site, and then close FrontPage.

Apply

Apply the skills you learned in the tutorial to organize the content of an existing Web page and to examine the Web site in Hyperlinks, Reports, and Tasks view.

Case Problem 2

Data File needed for this Case Problem: bullet.gif

Garden Grill Meghan Elliott provided you with the content of the new Job Opportunities page, and you added this content to the jobs.htm page. As the list of new positions grows, Meghan wants to make sure that it is easy for people to scroll to the job description in which they are interested. Meghan asks you to format the Job Opportunities page to make it easier to navigate. She also wants you to examine the existing hyperlinks in the Web site to locate any pages that are not linked to other pages in the site. Meghan will use your research to coordinate her work with Callan Murphy, who will either develop missing pages or assign the work to the appropriate staff.

If necessary, start FrontPage, make sure you have your Data Files, and then do the following:

1. Open the **grill** Web site from the location where your Web sites are stored. (If you did not create this Web site in Tutorial 1 and change it in Tutorial 2, ask your instructor for assistance.)

2. Open the **jobs.htm** page in Design view and then review its contents.

3. Format the second and third paragraphs in the page (with the text "Managers" and "Staff Associates") as a bulleted list. Change the bullet character to the **bullet.gif** picture, which is stored in the Tutorial.03\Case2 folder included with your Data Files. Save the **jobs.htm** page and save the picture in the Web site's images folder.

4. Change the five paragraphs below the paragraph that begins "Garden Grill's managers are outstanding…" to a bulleted list with the **bullet.gif** picture. (*Hint:* Insert the **bullet.gif** picture from the Web site's images folder.)

5. Change the six paragraphs below the paragraph that begins "Garden Grill is one of the most…" to a bulleted list with the **bullet.gif** picture.

6. Create a bookmark for each heading in the page (the bold "Managers" and "Staff Associates" text) using a lowercase name of your choice that does not contain spaces or exceed eight characters. Then create a hyperlink from each item in the first bulleted list in the page to its corresponding bookmark.

7. Create a bookmark named "top" to the left of the picture link bar at the top of the page.

8. Format the two paragraphs beginning with the bold "Managers" heading and ending with the paragraph that ends "the following qualifications:" as a definition list. The paragraph with the bold "Managers" heading is a defined term and the paragraph below it is the definition.

Explore ▶ 9. Indent the bulleted list below the definition paragraph you created in Step 8 one additional tab stop. (*Hint:* Select the bulleted list and then use a toolbar button.)

10. Format the two paragraphs beginning with the bold "Staff Associates" heading and ending with the paragraph that ends "at a Garden Grill location near you:" as a definition list. The paragraph with the bold "Staff Associates" heading is a defined term and the paragraph below it is the definition. Indent the bulleted list below the definition paragraph by one additional tab stop.

Explore ▶ 11. Create a new paragraph below the third bulleted list, and then decrease the paragraph's indentation to zero. (*Hint:* Click at the end of the "Bartenders" item in the list, press the Enter key twice to end the bulleted list and create a new paragraph, and then use a toolbar button to change the new paragraph so it is not indented.)

12. In the new paragraph you created in Step 11, create a "Top of Page" hyperlink using the top bookmark as its target.

13. Create a "Top of Page" hyperlink to the top bookmark below the bulleted list that appears below the "Managers" heading. Save the **jobs.htm** page.

Explore ▶ 14. Display each page in the Web site as the focus page in Hyperlinks view. If a page does not contain any hyperlinks that open other pages in the Web site, add a task associated with the focus page to finish the page. Assign the task to yourself, add an appropriate description and task name, and give it a medium priority. (*Hint:* You should add four tasks to the Web site. You can add the tasks in Hyperlinks view as you examine the pages.)

Explore ▶ 15. Change to Reports view. Set the time for the Slow Pages report to 20 seconds and the connection speed to 28.8 Kbps, and then print the Site Summary report. (*Hint:* There is no Print command in Reports view, so you will need to print a screenshot.)

16. Open the home page with a browser and test the hyperlinks between pages and the hyperlinks to bookmarks you created. (*Note:* You will add content to the **menu.htm**, **fran.htm**, **feedback.htm**, and **search.htm** pages in another tutorial.) Use your browser to print the **jobs.htm** page, and then close your browser.

17. In a new paragraph at the bottom of the **jobs.htm** page, add a comment that you can see in Design view with the following content: "This page last updated by [Your Name]." Save the **jobs.htm** page, and then print the HTML document for the **jobs.htm** page.

18. Close the **grill** Web site, and then close FrontPage.

Case Problem 3

There are no Data Files needed for this Case Problem.

Swenson Auctioneers Scott Swenson, president of Swenson Auctioneers, has reviewed your progress on the Web site. He likes the background picture that you added to each Web page and the overall presentation of material. One change that he asks you to make is to organize the content of the Our Team page so it is easy to scroll to a specific person's information. You will also examine the pages in the Web site to make sure they are linked together as desired and examine the Site Summary report for the entire site.

If necessary, start FrontPage, and then do the following:

1. Open the **swenson** Web site from the location where your Web sites are stored. (If you did not create this Web site in Tutorial 1 and change it in Tutorial 2, ask your instructor for assistance.)
2. Open the **team.htm** page in Design view and examine its contents. As you conduct your examination, decide the best way to format the organization in this page so it will be easy for its users to scroll the page's contents.
3. Display the Clipboard task pane. If any items appear in the list, click the Clear All button.
4. If necessary, display the nonprinting characters in the page so you can see paragraph marks and line breaks. Use the pointer to select each person's name, but not the line break character at the end of the line on which the name appears. Do not select the person's title. After selecting each person's name, copy it to the Clipboard.
5. Scroll to the top of the page, and then create a new paragraph below the "Swenson Auctioneers takes pride…" paragraph. Click a toolbar button to start a bulleted list.
6. Use the Clipboard task pane to paste each name you copied in the Web page into the bulleted list in the order the names appear in the Web page. (Scott's name should be first, then Tucker's, etc.) Each name should appear as an item in the bulleted list.
7. Create a bookmark for each person's biography using a lowercase name of your choice that does not contain spaces or exceed eight characters. Then create a hyperlink from the person's name in the bulleted list to the person's biography.
8. After the last paragraph in each person's biography, create a new paragraph containing a link that scrolls to the Swenson logo at the top of the page. After you have finished, save the **team.htm** page.
9. Add a task to the Web site to create the form in the **mail.htm** page. Associate the task with the **mail.htm** page, assign the task to yourself, add an appropriate description and task name, and give the task a high priority.
10. Display each page in the Web site as the focus page in Hyperlinks view with the hyperlinks to pictures and page titles displayed. As you view each page, examine the hyperlinks leading to and coming from the focus page so you understand how the pages are linked. Display the **team.htm** page as the focus page, and then print Hyperlinks view. Turn off the display of page titles.
11. Change to Reports view. Set the time for the Slow Pages report to 10 seconds and the connection speed to 28.8 Kbps, and then print the Slow Pages report. (*Hint:* There is no Print command in Reports view, so you will need to print a screenshot.)
12. Open the home page with a browser, and then test the hyperlinks between pages and the hyperlinks to bookmarks you created. Use your browser to print the **team.htm** page, and then close your browser.

Explore

Explore

Explore

Explore

13. In a new paragraph at the bottom of the **team.htm** page, add a comment that you can see in Design view with the following content: "This page last updated by [Your Name]." Save the **team.htm** page, and then print the HTML document for the **team.htm** page.
14. Close the **swenson** Web site, and then close FrontPage.

Case Problem 4

Data File needed for this Case Problem: arrow.gif

Create

Explore a Web site's structure and settings by examining it in Hyperlinks view, and organize page content using lists.

Mortgage Services, Inc. Natalie Fuselier, owner of Mortgage Services, Inc., is pleased with the pages and appearance of the Web site you are creating for her. She wants to review the structure of the Web site and make improvements to some of its pages.

If necessary, start FrontPage, make sure you have your Data Files, and then do the following:

1. Open the **loan** Web site from the location where your Web sites are stored. (If you did not create this Web site in Tutorial 1 and change it in Tutorial 2, ask your instructor for assistance.)
2. Change to Hyperlinks view and then display the Folder List. Display each page in the Web site as the focus page and examine its hyperlinks. Each page in the Web site should open all of the other pages in the Web site, with the exception of the **repair.htm** page, which should be accessible from the home page and contain a hyperlink to the home page. If you find any pages that do not meet these specifications, add a task to the Web site for finishing the page. Associate the page with the task, assign the task to yourself, add an appropriate description and task name, and give it a medium priority.

Explore

3. Open the **loantype.htm** page in Design view and close the Folder List. Review the page contents and formulate a plan to organize it so a user can click a loan type at the top of the page to scroll to the description of that loan type.
4. Create a bulleted list using the loan types at the top of the page. Use the **arrow.gif** file in the Tutorial.03\Case4 folder included with your Data Files as the bullet character. Save the page and save the picture file in the Web site's images folder.

Explore

5. Create bookmarks and hyperlinks in the page according to the plan you developed in Step 3. Use lowercase bookmark names of your choice that do not contain spaces or exceed eight characters.

Explore

6. Use existing text in the page to create hyperlinks that scroll to the "Loan Types" heading near the top of the page.
7. Change each level-three heading in the Web page to the Defined Term style, and then change the paragraph below the defined term to the Definition style. (The "Back to top" text should retain the Normal style.) The text in the paragraphs formatted using the Defined Term style should be bold. When you have finished, save the **loantype.htm** page.
8. Open the **help.htm** page in Design view, and then format its contents using Figure 3-38 as a guide. (*Hint:* Use the **arrow.gif** file to format the bulleted list. The bullets in the nested lists are the default bullet character.) When you have finished, save the **help.htm** page.

Figure 3-38

[Loan Types] [Application] [Post Application Help] [Resources] [Contact Us]

Mortgage Services, Inc.

Post Application Help

▶ **What Happens After I Apply Online?**

1. You receive an e-mail message confirming receipt of your application.
2. We review your loan application and credit history.
3. We contact you and tell you how much you can borrow.
4. You send us the required documents we need to verify your loan application. This page describes the original documents necessary to start processing your loan. During processing, additional information may be required. Do not send these forms until you receive an e-mail message from us requesting you to mail them.

▶ **Please provide these documents for the Borrower and Co-Borrower:**

- **Bank Statements:** Last three months of consecutive statements on every account showing liquid funds/cash to close (include all pages of statements)
- **IRA, 401K, Stocks, Bonds, etc.:** Most recent statements showing balances for the last three months or two quarters (include all pages of statements)
- **W-2 Statements:** Past two years
- **Pay Stubs:** Consecutive pay stubs covering one complete month's salary (if paid by personal check, supply canceled checks from each company)
- **(Homeowner's) Insurance Agent:** Name, company, and phone number of agent

▶ **If you are self-employed, please provide the following information:**

- **Personal Federal Income Tax Returns:** Past two years, signed, all schedules
- **Business Federal Income Tax Returns:** Past two years, signed, all schedules
- **Business Financial Statements:** Within three months of today's date, signed
- **Business Profit/Loss Statements:** Within three months of today's date, signed

▶ **If you own income-producing property, please provide the following information:**

- **Leases:** Current copies for each leased property
- **Income/Expense/Payment:** Information for each leased property

▶ **If you are divorced, please provide the following information:**

- **Final Judgment:** Divorce and child support agreements, fully executed

We will review the documents and will approve or not approve your loan based on the information you provided and according to the conditions of the lender.

Once approved, you are ready to buy or refinance your home!

When you find a house you like, your offer will have a much better chance of being accepted because the seller knows that you have already been approved for a loan from one of over 400 recognized national or local lenders. Along with your real estate agent, we will help guide you through the rest of the home buying process until closing.

Please keep in mind that lenders do not provide the final approval for a loan until after the close of the sale. Funds are disbursed when all conditions of the mortgage approval and real estate sale have been met. Conditions include the following, among other things: verification of borrower's employment and funds for down payment, acceptable appraised value of the house, survey of property, title commitment, signatures on all closing documents, and other standard requirements involved in any real estate transaction.

9. Open the home page in a browser, and then examine all of the site's pages and check the bookmarks you created in the Loan Types page. (You will add content to the **apply.htm** and **contact.htm** pages in another tutorial.) When you have finished examining all of the pages, use your browser to print the Post Application Help and Loan Types pages, and then close your browser.

10. Close the **loan** Web site, and then close FrontPage.

Reinforce

Web Pages & HTML

Lab Assignments

The New Perspectives Labs are designed to help you master some of the key concepts and skills presented in this text. The steps for completing this Lab are located on the Course Technology Web site. Log on to the Internet and use your Web browser to go to the Student Online Companion for New Perspectives Office 2003 at **www.course.com/np/office2003**. Click the Lab Assignments link, and then navigate to the assignments for this tutorial.

Review

Quick Check Answers

Session 3.1

1. bulleted (unordered)
2. a list within another list
3. True
4. An anchor is specially marked text or an object that identifies a named location in a Web page.
5. icon
6. Create the bookmark in the page by selecting the text, picture, or location for it, clicking Insert on the menu bar, and then clicking Bookmark. Accept the default bookmark name or provide a new name, and then click the OK button. Select the text or picture in the page that will contain the hyperlink to the bookmark, click the Insert Hyperlink button on the Standard toolbar, click the Place in This Document button on the Link to bar, select the bookmark, and then click the OK button.
7. The hyperlink's target is a bookmark.

Session 3.2

1. 24
2. Click Tools on the menu bar, click Site Settings, click the General tab, type a new name in the Web name text box, and then click the OK button.
3. The folder is hidden.
4. a Site Summary report
5. more than one hyperlink in a Web page that opens the same target
6. False
7. In Folders view, select the page with which to associate the task or open the page in Design view, click the list arrow for the Create a new normal page button on the Standard toolbar, click Task, supply the required information in the New Task dialog box, and then click the OK button.
8. False

Objectives

Session 4.1

- Add pages to a Web site's navigation structure
- Create shared borders in a Web site
- Edit a shared border
- Delete, rename, and create new pages in Navigation view
- Add a link bar component and page banner to a page
- Create a custom link bar

Session 4.2

- Apply a theme to a Web site
- Customize an existing theme
- Delete a theme
- Create a new theme

Session 4.3

- Add a photo gallery to a page
- Learn about using drawings and AutoShapes
- Create a WordArt object in a page

Using Shared Borders and Themes

Updating the Content and Appearance of the Garden Web Site

Case

Sunshine Landscape & Garden Center

Brett Kizer, owner of the Sunshine Landscape & Garden Center, has been examining the garden Web site with a careful eye for detail. He wants to make sure that the Web site is colorful, professional, and reflects the atmosphere at the nursery. As he examined the site's current pages with several of the nursery's key employees, he noticed that the pages do not share a common presentation of material. Brett likes certain elements included in each page, but no one page stands out as a potential design sample. For example, he likes the background picture included with the home page, but does not like the white background in other pages. He likes the link bar and the Sunshine logo that appear in most pages, but thinks they take up too much space in the browser window. As a result, Brett decided to make some changes to the Web site, with the goal of freeing up space at the top of pages and using consistent formatting in all pages. You told Brett that these goals are very attainable and spent some time changing the pages to prepare them for the updates he requested. For the pages in the Web site, you deleted the link bar and Sunshine logo at the top of the pages, and then you deleted extra pictures and other content that were inconsistently formatted and presented. You will import these revised pages into the garden Web site and overwrite the pages with the same names.

Student Data Files

To complete this tutorial, you will need your ending files from Tutorial 3 and the following Data Files. Additional Data Files needed to complete the end-of-tutorial exercises are listed with the Review Assignments and Case Problems.

▼**Tutorial.04**

▽ Tutorial folder

bulk.htm	garden82.jpg	mulch.htm
bulk2.htm	garden98.jpg	rock.htm
center.htm	index.htm	soil.htm
contact.htm	irr.htm	stone.htm
deer.htm	land.htm	bulk_pic (folder)
garden2.htm	land2.htm	gc_pics (folder)
garden3.htm	leon.jpg	land_pic (folder)
garden4.htm	map_page.htm	rock_pic (folder)
garden57.jpg		

As you were talking with Brett, Clara McShane, the nursery's senior landscape designer, told you that she has finished some additional pages that should be linked to the Garden Center, Landscape & Rock Work, and Bulk Goods pages. She gave you these files and their embedded pictures on a disk and asked you to add them to the Web site. You told Brett that with the addition of these pages, it's more important now to use the tools in FrontPage to format the site's hyperlinks and page formatting. These tools—shared borders, link bars, and themes—are dependent upon the Web site's navigation structure, which you create in Navigation view. By maintaining these features with FrontPage, you can ensure that all pages in the Web site have a consistent look and feel, and that future updates to the Web site are reflected automatically in the site's link bars.

Session 4.1

Understanding Shared Borders and Link Bars

Up to this point, you have been creating hyperlinks to other pages in the Web site using a link bar with pictures formatted as hyperlinks and with text formatted as hyperlinks. You also added the Sunshine logo to most pages. You have completed this work manually by inserting text and pictures into each Web page in the site. Although this system has worked well, it will soon be impractical to continue inserting link bars and logos in all future pages. This effort requires time, and the possibility for error increases. For example, if you add a new page to the Web site, you would need to add a link to it in the site's existing pages to make it accessible from the home page and other pages in the Web site.

If your Web site contains many pages, you can use Navigation view to identify the way pages are related to each other in a hierarchical manner. For example, a site's home page is usually the top page in a Web site and contains links that open pages at the next level. When you create a Web site, FrontPage adds the site's home page to the navigation structure in Navigation view, but you must add the remaining pages to the navigation structure to identify their relationships. You can think of a Web site's navigation structure as an organizational chart, with the home page as an organization's president. The next level of pages would include the top-level managers, the assistants would appear at the next level, and so forth. In this context, the home page is the called a **parent page**, and the pages below the home page are **child pages** of the home page. In some cases, you will add every page in a Web site to the navigation structure; in other cases, you might exclude pages based on their content.

After you identify how pages in a Web site are related to each other, you can enable features in the Web site that use the navigation structure to enable navigation-related features. A **link bar component** is a link bar that FrontPage maintains and updates automatically, thus saving time and ensuring that the links to other pages are always consistent and accurate. In many cases, you will create a link bar component in one or more shared borders. A **shared border** is an area at the top, bottom, right, or left side of a page that contains content that appears in every page that uses it. You can set up the Web site to use one or more of these borders in a page. For example, you might use a top shared border for the company's name and a link bar component, and a bottom shared border for copyright and other information about the company. A shared border presents the same information in all Web pages that use it, so it ensures consistency in the site's pages. Because FrontPage maintains the links in a link bar component, you don't have to worry about updating the link bars in all pages in the site as you add new pages to it and delete pages from it. For a new page, you would just need to create the new page in the Web site (or import its file into the Web site), position the page in the navigation structure to identify its relationship to other pages, and activate the shared borders that you want to use in the new page. After saving your changes, FrontPage automatically makes appropriate changes to the link bar component.

After creating the navigation structure and activating the shared border(s), you add the content of a shared border to your Web site in any page that uses the border. In Design view, a dashed line indicates the boundary of a shared border in a Web page; these boundary lines are not displayed in the browser. When you edit the content of a shared border in a single Web page, your changes apply to *all* pages in the Web site that use the shared border. For example, adding a company name and logo to a top shared border in one page will cause all other pages in the Web site that use the top shared border to display the same name and logo in the same location.

Brett likes the idea of maintaining the Web site's hyperlinks with link bar components. You tell Brett that enabling the Web site's shared borders will make it easy to accommodate his request for the link bars, but first he must import the revised pages into the Web site and position them in the navigation structure in Navigation view to identify the relationships among pages in the site.

Adding Pages to the Site's Navigation Structure

After you import or create Web pages in a Web site, you must add them to the navigation structure in Navigation view to identify how they are related to each other. When you first change to Navigation view, only the site's home page will appear in the navigation structure. You can drag and drop files from the Folder List and position them in the navigation structure according to your Web site plan.

To import the revised pages into the Web site and add pages to the navigation structure:

1. Start **FrontPage** and then open the **garden** Web site from the location where your Web sites are stored.

2. Display the Folder List and make sure that the garden Web site's root folder is selected, click **File** on the menu bar, click **Import**, click the **Add File** button, open the **Tutorial.04\Tutorial** folder included with your Data Files, press and hold the **Ctrl** key, click the files **bulk.htm**, **bulk2.htm**, **center.htm**, **contact.htm**, **index.htm**, **irr.htm**, **land.htm**, and **map_page.htm**, release the **Ctrl** key, and then click the **Open** button. Eight files are listed in the Import dialog box.

3. Click the **OK** button, and then click the **Yes to All** button to overwrite the files in the Web site with the same names.

4. Change to Navigation view by clicking the **Navigation View** button 🔲 Navigation at the bottom of the Contents pane. When you first change to Navigation view, only the site's home page appears in the navigation structure. To add pages to Navigation view, you drag a file from the Folder List to the navigation structure, and then release the mouse button when the page is in the correct position. You'll add the center.htm page first.

5. Click **center.htm** in the Folder List, and then drag it to the navigation structure. Position the center.htm page below the home page, as shown in Figure 4-1.

| Figure 4-1 | Adding a page to the navigation structure |

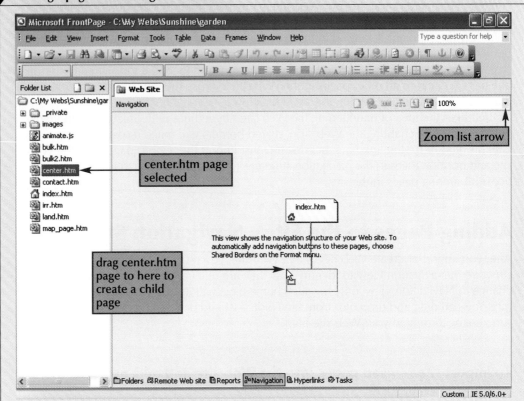

Trouble? Your home page might display part of the page title "Sunshine Landscape & Garden Center home page" instead of the filename. This difference causes no problems, because you will change this page title later.

6. When you have positioned the page as shown in Figure 4-1, release the mouse button to add it to the navigation structure. The page's title, Garden Center, appears in the page icon you added. If you need to know the filename of a page in the navigation structure, you can click it and the page's filename will appear on the status bar.

Trouble? If your page icons are larger or smaller than those shown in Figure 4-1, click the Zoom list arrow on the Contents pane, and then click 100%.

7. Repeat Steps 5 and 6 to add the **land.htm** and **irr.htm** pages as child pages of the home page and to the right of the Garden Center page, and then click anywhere in a blank area of the Contents pane to deselect the pages. See Figure 4-2.

Three child pages added to the navigation structure | **Figure 4-2**

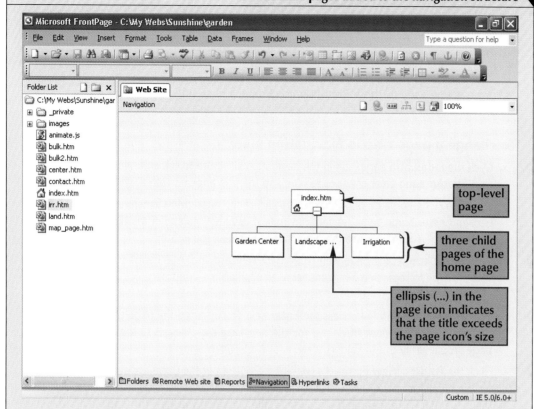

Trouble? If you drop a page in the wrong position, click the page that you need to fix and drag it into the correct position. If you drag the wrong page into the navigation structure, right-click the page icon to open the shortcut menu, click Delete, click the Remove page from the navigation structure option button, and then click the OK button.

As you add pages to the navigation structure, you'll notice that the titles for some pages exceed the size of the page icon, as is the case for the land.htm page, whose title is "Landscape & Rock Work." When the page title exceeds the size of the page icon, an ellipsis (…) appears in the page title. To see the entire title, you click it once to select it, and then again to change to editing mode.

Brett wonders why the page title for the home page is "index.htm," instead of "Sunshine Landscape & Garden Center home page," which is the page title in Folders view. You tell Brett that the page titles in Folders view and Navigation view are separate. The page title that you see in Folders view is the HTML title of the Web page, which appears in the <title> and </title> tags. The page title in Navigation view is not always the same as the HTML title; it is the page name that will appear in the site's link bars. In some cases, the HTML page title might be long to convey the page's contents; in those instances, you might not want to use the long title to identify the page in the site's link bars because it would require a lot of space.

Renaming a Page's Title in Navigation View

- Right-click the page icon in the navigation structure to open the shortcut menu, and then click Rename.
- Type the new page title, and then press the Enter key.

For now, you want to show Brett how to change a page title in Navigation view.

To change a page title in Navigation view:

1. Click the **index.htm** page icon in the navigation structure to select it. Notice that the page icon's background color changes to blue and the title appears with a white background.

   Trouble? The home page might display part of the page title "Sunshine Landscape & Garden Center home page" in your navigation structure instead of the filename "index.htm." Just make sure that you click the home page in Step 1.

2. Click **index.htm** on the page icon. The title is selected and you change to editing mode. You can type to replace the current value or position the insertion point in the selected text to make an editing correction.

3. Type **Home Page** and then press the **Enter** key. You updated the page title of the home page in Navigation view. However, you did not make any changes to the HTML title of the page. You'll verify this in Folders view.

4. Click the **Folders View** button ▣Folders at the bottom of the Contents pane. The page title for the index.htm page is still "Sunshine Landscape & Garden Center home page," which is the value that will appear in the browser's title bar when you view this page in a browser.

   Trouble? If the title of the home page changed to "Home Page" in Folders view, click the title to select it and change to editing mode, type Sunshine Landscape & Garden Center home page, and then press the Enter key.

5. Return to Navigation view.

Now you can finish adding pages to the navigation structure.

To continue adding pages to the navigation structure:

1. Click the **bulk.htm** page in the Folder List to select it, and then position it to the left of the Irrigation page in the navigation structure.

2. Position the **contact.htm** page to the left of the Bulk Goods page.

3. Position the **map_page.htm** page to the right of the Irrigation page.

4. Position the **bulk2.htm** page below the Bulk Goods page, as shown in Figure 4-3. The bulk2.htm page is now a child page of the bulk.htm page and you have finished adding pages to the navigation structure.

Completed navigation structure | **Figure 4-3**

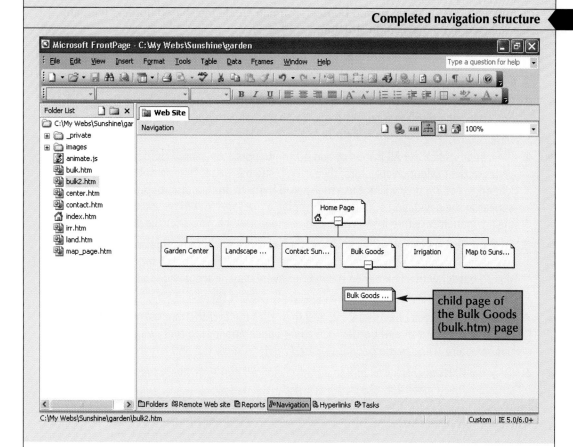

Now that you have created the navigation structure, you can create the shared borders and the link bar components.

Creating Shared Borders in a Web Site

After you position pages in the navigation structure, you can create one or more shared borders in those pages. You can create shared borders at the top, bottom, left, and right sides of the page. FrontPage automatically adds the page title to the top shared border, and provides the option to use the navigation structure to create link bar components in the top, left, and right shared borders.

Creating Shared Borders for a Web Site	Reference Window

- If necessary, position pages in the navigation structure.
- Click Format on the menu bar, and then click Shared Borders.
- Select the option button for applying the shared border to all or selected pages, select the shared border(s) to add, select the option to include navigation buttons if desired, and then click the OK button.

Your next task is to create the shared borders for the Web site. Brett wants the pages in the Web site to have three shared borders: a top shared border containing the page's title and a link bar with links to pages at the same level, the home page, and the parent page; a left shared border containing a link bar with links to child pages; and a bottom shared border with the company's copyright information. All pages appearing in the navigation structure will use the same shared borders. You can create the shared borders with any page selected in the navigation structure.

To create the shared borders:

1. Click **Format** on the menu bar, and then click **Shared Borders**. The Shared Borders dialog box opens and displays a sample page. You have not yet added any shared borders to the Web site, so no options are selected.

2. If necessary, click the **All pages** option button to apply the shared borders you select to all pages in the navigation structure; if your Web site has pages that do not appear in the navigation structure, they will not use the shared borders. In this case, pages that do not appear in the navigation structure will display a message to remind you to add the page to the navigation structure if you want it to use the shared borders for the Web site.

3. Click the **Top** check box to select it, and then click the **Include navigation buttons** check box, which becomes active after you click the Top check box. This change adds a top shared border with a link bar component to every page in the navigation structure. Notice that the sample page in the Shared Borders dialog box reflects this change.

4. Click the **Left** check box to select it, and then click the **Include navigation buttons** check box to add the left shared border with a link bar component to every page in the navigation structure. The sample page is updated again to show top and left shared borders.

5. Click the **Bottom** check box to add a bottom shared border to every page in the navigation structure. See Figure 4-4.

| Figure 4-4 | Shared Borders dialog box |

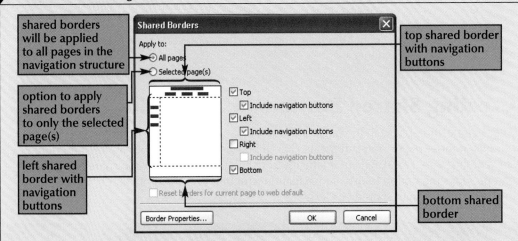

shared borders will be applied to all pages in the navigation structure

option to apply shared borders to only the selected page(s)

left shared border with navigation buttons

top shared border with navigation buttons

bottom shared border

6. Click the **Border Properties** button. The Border Properties dialog box opens. See Figure 4-5.

| Figure 4-5 | Border Properties dialog box |

option to add a background color to the selected shared border

option to add a background picture to the selected shared border

click to select a shared border

You can use the options in the Border Properties dialog box to add a background color or background picture to the different shared borders. For example, by selecting the Color check box, you can use the list box to select a background for a shared border. By selecting the Picture check box and then selecting a file, you can display a background picture in a shared border. Brett doesn't want to include these options, so he can close the Border Properties dialog box and then finish creating the shared borders.

7. Click the **Cancel** button to close the Border Properties dialog box, and then click the **OK** button to close the Shared Borders dialog box and to create the top, bottom, and left shared borders in pages you added to the navigation structure. The status bar will display some messages indicating that the Web site's shared borders are being created. This process might take a few seconds, depending on where your Web site is stored.

8. Close the Folder List.

Although FrontPage created the shared borders, you can't see them in your Web site in Navigation view. When you open any page that appears in Navigation view in Design view, however, you will see the shared borders. Next, you will open the Bulk Goods page in Design view.

To open the Bulk Goods page in Design view:

1. Double-click the **Bulk Goods** page icon (the child page of the home page, bulk.htm) to open that page in Design view. See Figure 4-6.

Shared borders in the Bulk Goods page ◄ **Figure 4-6**

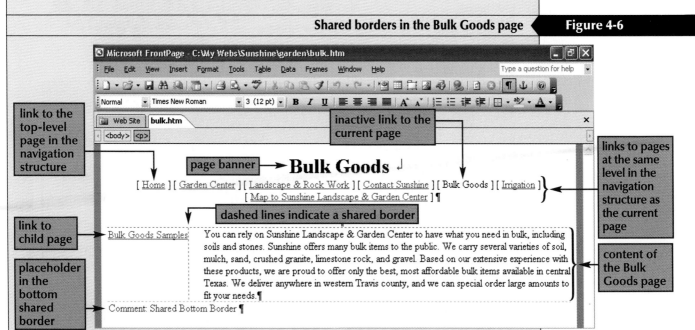

Trouble? If the Bulk Goods page does not open in Design view, repeat Step 1 and double-click the icon, not the page title.

The top shared border includes the page's title (Bulk Goods) and a link bar component that includes links to the home page and to pages at the same level in the navigation structure as the Bulk Goods page. The page title is called a **page banner**. A page banner can be text, as shown in Figure 4-6, or a picture. Its text is taken from the page's title in Navigation view. The hyperlinks below the page banner and in the left shared border appear in link bar components. The option for including the home page was automatically selected for the top shared border. When this option is selected, FrontPage inserts the link named "Home" in the link bar and creates a link to the site's top-level page.

The Bulk Goods page is currently the only child page in the Web site with its own child page, and the link to that page (Bulk Goods Samples) appears automatically in the left shared border. If a page contains no links in a border for which navigation buttons have been specified, a message in that border will indicate that you can edit the link bar's properties to display hyperlinks. The bottom shared border does not yet contain any content; the "Comment: Shared Bottom Border" text is an HTML comment that will not be displayed when the page is viewed using a browser. To add content to the bottom shared border, you would select the comment and type the new content to replace it.

The home page does not contain any links in the top shared border, as you will see next.

To examine the shared borders for the home page:

1. Click the **Web Site** tab to return to Navigation view.
2. Double-click the **Home Page** page icon to open this page in Design view. See Figure 4-7.

Figure 4-7   ▶   **Shared borders in the home page**

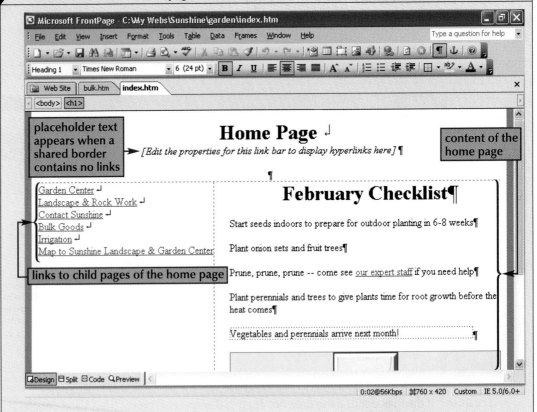

The top shared border displays the page's title and a message. The top shared border does not contain a link bar because the home page is the top-level page in the Web site and no "higher" or same-level pages exist in the navigation structure. The left shared border contains links to the child pages of the home page. The bottom shared border contains a comment.

You decide to show Brett the Web site in a browser so he can better understand how the shared borders work and see how FrontPage creates the link bars.

To test the shared borders and link bars in a browser:

▶ 1. Click the **Preview** button 🔍 on the Standard toolbar. The home page opens in a browser. The top shared border displays the page's title and the left shared border displays the links to child pages of the home page. Notice that the page title in the top shared border is "Home Page," which is this page's title in Navigation view. The browser's title bar displays the HTML title for the document, which is the same title you see in Folders view and that appears in the HTML document's <title> and </title> tags. See Figure 4-8.

Home page in a browser ◀ **Figure 4-8**

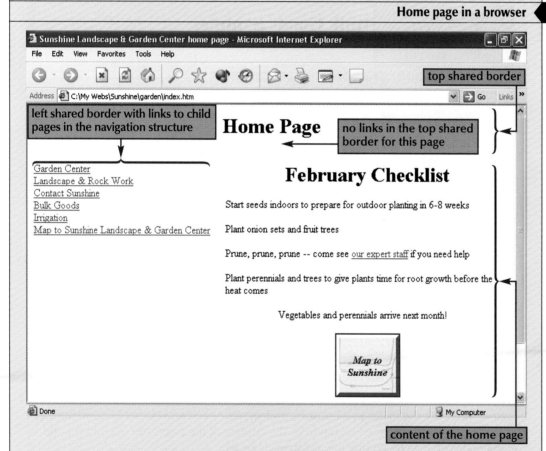

2. Click the **Garden Center** link in the left shared border to open that page. The top shared border for this page includes the page's title, plus links to the home page and to pages in the navigation structure at the same level as the Garden Center page. The left shared border is empty because the Garden Center page does not have any child pages in the navigation structure.

3. Click the **Bulk Goods** link to open that page. The top shared border includes the page's title and links to the home page and to same-level pages in the navigation structure. Because the Bulk Goods page has a child page in the navigation structure, a hyperlink to the child page, Bulk Goods Samples, appears in the left shared border.

4. Click the **Bulk Goods Samples** link to open that page. Because this page has no child pages in the navigation structure, the left shared border is empty. The top shared border includes links entitled "Home" and "Up." Clicking the Home link opens the home page. Clicking the Up link opens the parent page, which in this case is the Bulk Goods page, which is the parent of the Bulk Goods Samples page in the navigation structure. See Figure 4-9.

Figure 4-9 | **Bulk Goods Samples page in a browser**

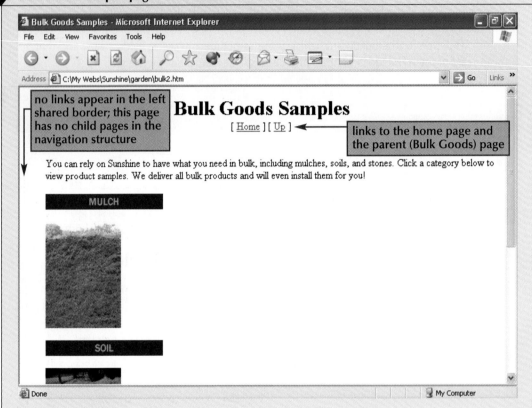

5. Click the **Up** link. The Bulk Goods page opens.

6. Close your browser.

After examining the pages in a browser, Brett wants to add a horizontal line in the top shared border to separate the link bar from the content of the page. You tell him that he can make this change by editing the top shared border.

Editing a Shared Border

After creating a shared border, you can modify it by opening any page in Design view that uses the shared border and then making the desired changes. Remember that all of the Web pages included in the navigation structure use the *same* shared borders, so any changes that you make to a shared border are automatically applied to all pages that use it. You can change the content of the shared border using the same techniques that you would use to revise any page in Design view.

Brett wants to add a horizontal line below the link bar component in the top shared border to separate the border from the page content. He also wants to add a copyright notice to the bottom shared border. You will show him how to make these changes in

Design view for the home page. He could also make these changes using any page in the Web site because all of the pages currently use the same shared borders.

To edit the top and bottom shared borders:

1. In the home page, move the pointer over the text that begins "Edit the properties" in the link bar component in the top shared border of the home page until the pointer changes to a 🖺 shape, and then click the link bar placeholder text to select it.

2. Press the **down** arrow key ↓ on the keyboard to position the insertion point on the next line, and then press the **Delete** key to remove this line.

3. Click **Insert** on the menu bar, and then click **Horizontal Line**. A horizontal line appears in the shared border below the link bar placeholder text.

   Brett wants to use the copyright information at the bottom of the home page as the content for the bottom shared border. He can cut and paste this text to move it to the bottom shared border.

4. Scroll down the home page as necessary, use the pointer to select the last two lines in the home page (beginning "Copyright" and "All," and including the paragraph mark at the end of the second line), and then click the **Cut** button 🔏 on the Standard toolbar.

5. Click the comment placeholder text in the bottom shared border to select it, press the **Enter** key, and then click the **Paste** button 🖺 on the Standard toolbar. As shown in Figure 4-10, the copyright information now appears in the bottom shared border. A blank paragraph appears above and below the pasted text.

Pasting the content of the bottom shared border ◄ **Figure 4-10**

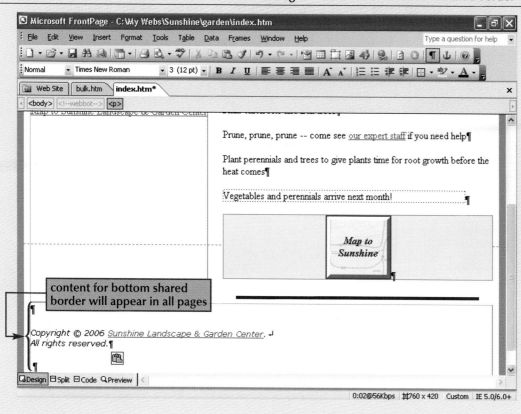

> **Trouble?** If you don't have a blank paragraph in the bottom shared border above the "Copyright" line, click at the beginning of that line, and then press the Enter key.

▶ **6.** Save the home page. FrontPage saves the home page and the changes you made to the top and bottom shared borders.

▶ **7.** Click the **bulk.htm** page tab to open the Bulk Goods page in Design view. Notice that the horizontal line appears in the top shared border for this page and the copyright information appears in the bottom shared border.

You tell Brett that he can make other types of changes to the shared borders, as well. For example, he might want to add a company logo to the top shared border or the date and time the page was last updated to the bottom shared border. To make changes to a link bar component, however, he needs to know how to use the Link Bar Properties dialog box. You want to show Brett this dialog box in case he needs to change the default settings of a link bar.

Revising a Link Bar Component

After you create a link bar component, you might need to revise it to change the hyperlinks or to change the style of the links.

To open the Link Bar Properties dialog box:

▶ **1.** Double-click the link bar component in the top shared border to open the Link Bar Properties dialog box for the link bar component in the top shared border. See Figure 4-11. Notice that most of the choices are option buttons, so only one selection is permitted.

Figure 4-11	Link Bar Properties dialog box for the link bar component in the top shared border

Figure 4-12 describes the settings on the General tab in the Link Bar Properties dialog box and provides examples of how these settings would apply to the Bulk Goods page. When you change an option in this dialog box, the sample diagram changes to reflect the new links. Make sure that you study these settings and understand how they work before continuing.

Link bar property descriptions and examples ◄ Figure 4-12

Option	Description	Example for the Bulk Goods page in the garden Web site
General tab: Select one option button and one or both check boxes.		
Parent level option button	All pages will include a link to the parent-level page.	Home link only (the parent page)
Same level option button	All pages will include links to pages at the same level as the current page.	Links to the Garden Center, Landscape & Rock Work, Contact Sunshine, Irrigation, and Map to Sunshine Landscape & Garden Center pages
Back and next option button	All pages will include links to the pages immediately to the left and right of the current page, based on page positions in the navigation structure.	Back and Next links, which open the Contact Sunshine and Irrigation pages, respectively
Child level option button	All pages will include a link to child pages of the current page, when applicable.	Link to the Bulk Goods Samples page only
Global level option button	All pages will include a link to the top-level page in the Web site.	Home link only (the top-level page in the navigation structure)
Child pages under Home option button	All pages will include links to child pages of the home page.	Links to the Garden Center, Landscape & Rock Work, Contact Sunshine, Irrigation, and Map to Sunshine Landscape & Garden Center pages
Home page check box	All pages will include a link to the home page, regardless of what other options are selected.	Home link, plus any other links included by the option button selected in the Hyperlinks to add to page section
Parent page check box	All pages will include a link to the parent-level page of the current page, regardless of which other options are selected.	Home link (which is the parent page of the Bulk Goods page), plus any other links included by the option button selected in the Hyperlinks to add to page section

To change the link bar properties:

▶ **1.** Click the **Back and next** option button to select it. The Home page and Parent page check boxes are still selected. Notice that the diagram in the dialog box shows these changes to the hyperlinks included in the link bar.

▶ **2.** Click the **Same level** option button to select it and to return to the original configuration.

▶ **3.** Click the **Style** tab. See Figure 4-13.

Figure 4-13 | **Style tab for the link bar component in the top shared border**

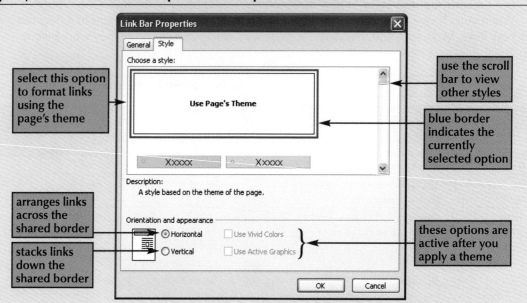

The options on the Style tab control the appearance of the links that you selected on the General tab. By scrolling the Choose a style list box, you can select a theme or text style as the basis for formatting your links. In the Orientation and appearance section, clicking the Horizontal option button arranges the hyperlinks in the link bar across the shared border; clicking the Vertical option button vertically stacks the hyperlinks in the link bar in the shared border. When you select a theme to format the hyperlinks, the Use Vivid Colors and Use Active Graphics check boxes become active so you can choose to apply these options, as well.

For now, Brett wants to keep the buttons arranged horizontally across the top shared border and to select the default style, which is to use the page's theme. You'll show him how to apply a theme to the garden Web site in the next session.

4. Make sure that the **Use Page's Theme** option and the **Horizontal** option button are selected, and then click the **OK** button. The link bar component in the top shared border does not change because you did not change any of its settings.

   You can also examine the selections in the left shared border.

5. Double-click the link bar component in the left shared border to open the Link Bar Properties dialog box for the link bar component in the left shared border. The top shared border will include a link to the home page, so you don't need to repeat that link in the left shared border.

6. Make sure that the **Child level** option button is selected and that the **Home page** and **Parent page** check boxes do not contain check marks, and then click the **Style** tab.

7. Scroll up the Choose a style list and click the **Use Page's Theme** option, make sure that the **Vertical** option button is selected, and then click the **OK** button. The Link Bar Properties dialog box for the left shared border closes. The link in the left shared border looks the same, even though you changed its style. The link's appearance will change when you apply a theme to the Web site in the next session.

8. Save the page.

These changes to the shared borders will appear in every page in the Web site that uses them. You won't see some of the changes you made, however, until you apply a theme in Session 4.2.

Making Changes in Navigation View

As you work on a Web site, you will frequently return to Navigation view to update the site. For example, as you add pages to the Web site, you'll need to add them to the navigation structure. You also can delete pages from the navigation structure or set a page so its link will not appear in a link bar. You can drag the page icons in the navigation structure to rearrange their order in the link bars.

Deleting a Page from the Navigation Structure

When examining the Web pages in a browser, Brett noticed that the link to the map_page.htm page has a very long title. As he considers the function of this page, he realizes that it does not need to be accessible from every Web page in the site; the thumbnail picture and hyperlink in the home page are sufficient. You tell Brett that he is correct to discover that some Web pages aren't part of the main structure of the Web site and don't need to appear in the navigation structure. Because the map_page.htm page is the target of a hyperlink that appears in the home page, you can choose not to make it accessible from other pages in the site. If you decide later that you want visitors to be able to open the map_page.htm page from any page in the Web site, you could add it back to the navigation structure.

You can use Navigation view to delete a page from the navigation structure only or from the navigation structure *and* the Web site. If you delete the page from the navigation structure only, then the page is deleted from any link bar components that include it, but it remains in the Web site. Deleting the page from the Web site permanently removes the page from the navigation structure, the site's link bars, and the Web site.

Reference Window

Deleting a Page in Navigation View

- Right-click the page icon in the navigation structure that you want to delete to select the page and open the shortcut menu.
- Click Delete to open the Delete Page dialog box.
- Click the Remove this page from the navigation structure option button to delete the page from only the navigation structure, or click the Delete this page from the Web option button to delete the page from the navigation structure and the Web site.
- Click the OK button.

If you need to make a page in the navigation structure temporarily unavailable through the site's link bar components, you can right-click the page icon in the navigation structure to open the shortcut menu, and then click Included in Link Bars. If you choose this option, the page icon's background color changes from yellow to gray, as shown in Figure 4-14, and the page's link is removed from the site's link bar components. To add the page back to the site's link bar components, right-click it again, and then click Include in Link Bars on the shortcut menu.

Figure 4-14 | **Omitting a page from a site's link bar components**

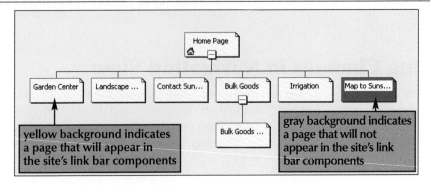

Brett wants to delete the Map to Sunshine Landscape & Garden Center page from the navigation structure, but not from the Web site.

To delete a page from the navigation structure:

▶ **1.** Return to Navigation view.

▶ **2.** Right-click the **Map to Sunshine Landscape & Garden Center** page icon to open the shortcut menu, and then click **Delete** to open the Delete Page dialog box.

▶ **3.** Click the **Remove page from the navigation structure** option button to select it (if necessary), and then click the **OK** button. The page is deleted from the navigation structure, but its file (map_page.htm) is still in the Web site.

You can also add Web pages to the navigation structure, which creates the page in the Web site and positions the page in the navigation structure at the same time.

Creating a New Page in Navigation View

Helen Xiao, Sunshine's senior horticulturist, told Brett this morning that customers frequently request a list of products that deter deer from eating landscaping materials and a list of deer-resistant plants to install. Helen asks if this would be a good page to include in the Web site, so staff members could point customers to the Web site for a complete list of anti-deer products and deer-resistant plants. Brett agrees with Helen's suggestion and asks you to show him how to create a new page in the Web site. Helen said that she would create the content for this new page and send it to Brett in a couple of days.

When you use Navigation view to create a new Web page, you add it to the navigation structure and to the Web site at the same time. Because the planned content of this new page deals with plants, Brett will add the new page as a child page of the center.htm page.

Reference Window | **Creating a New Page in Navigation View**

- Right-click the page icon that will be the parent for the new page to select it and to open the shortcut menu.
- Point to New on the shortcut menu, and then click Page.
- Right-click the page icon for the new page to open the shortcut menu, click Rename, enter the page's title, and then press the Enter key. FrontPage will create the Web page using the title you entered. To change the default filename, change to Folders view, click the filename of the new page to select it, type a new filename, and then press the Enter key.

FrontPage uses the title you entered (or the default title's filename, new_page_1.htm, if you don't enter a title) as the filename for a new Web page that you create in Navigation view. If you change the default title to one that contains spaces, FrontPage will save the filename with underscore characters in place of the spaces. You'll show Brett how to add the new page to the Web site, and then you will show him how to change its page title and filename.

To add a new page to the Web site and change its title and filename:

1. Right-click the **Garden Center** page in the navigation structure to select it and to open the shortcut menu, point to **New**, and then click **Page**. A new page with the default title of "New Page 1" and the temporary filename of new_page_1.htm is added to the navigation structure and to the Web site.

   Trouble? If your default page title includes another number, don't worry. Just make sure that a new page was created.

   Next, rename the new page.

2. Right-click the **New Page 1** page icon to open the shortcut menu, and then click **Rename**.

3. Type **Anti-Deer Products** as the page's title, and then press the **Enter** key.

4. Double-click the **Anti-Deer Products** page icon. The page opens in Design view. Notice the shared borders at the top, bottom, and left side of the page. See Figure 4-15. These are the same shared borders that you set for all pages in the Web site.

Design view of the Anti-Deer Products page | Figure 4-15

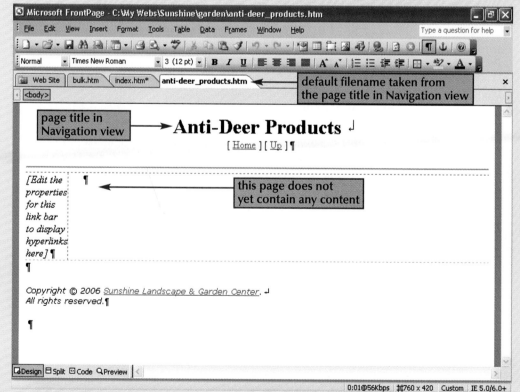

Trouble? FrontPage might assign the filename new_page_1.htm to the Anti-Deer Products page. This is not a problem; you will change the filename next.

5. Click the **Web Site** tab at the top of the Contents pane, and then change to Folders view.

6. In Folders view, right-click the filename **anti-deer_products.htm** to select it and to open the shortcut menu, click **Rename**, type **deer.htm**, and then press the **Enter** key. FrontPage updates the filename in the Web site.

   Trouble? If you see new_page_1.htm in Folders view, right-click that filename instead of anti-deer_products.htm in Step 6.

Brett reminds you that Clara finished some of the pages that are linked to the existing land.htm, center.htm, and bulk2.htm pages in the Web site. Keeping with Brett's overall vision of the Web site, Clara used photographs in the new pages to provide pictures of landscaping and rock work jobs Sunshine has completed and pictures of the different available soils, mulches, and stones. Brett will import these pages into the Web site, and then you will help him position them in the navigation structure to identify their relationships to their parent pages. You will also help him include links to these pages in the site's link bar components.

Adding New Pages to the Navigation Structure

Clara sent Brett the new Web pages and the embedded pictures they contain. Because Clara needed a way to organize the pictures, she saved them in folders. You tell Brett he can import the pages into the Web site, and then position them in Navigation view to enable the shared borders. Then he can import the folders that contain the pictures into the Web site.

To import the new pages into the Web site and position them in Navigation view:

1. Display the Folder List, and then make sure the Web site's root folder is selected in the Folder List.

2. Click **File** on the menu bar, click **Import**, click the **Add File** button, open the **Tutorial.04\Tutorial** folder included with your Data Files, press and hold the **Ctrl** key, click the files **garden2.htm**, **garden3.htm**, **garden4.htm**, **land2.htm**, **mulch.htm**, **rock.htm**, **soil.htm**, and **stone.htm**, release the **Ctrl** key, and then click the **Open** button. Eight files appear in the Import dialog box.

3. Click the **OK** button. The files are imported into the garden Web site.

4. Change to Navigation view, and then position the pages in the navigation structure as shown in Figure 4-16. Use the horizontal scroll bar as needed to display different parts of the navigation structure as you position the pages.

Imported pages positioned in the navigation structure ◄ **Figure 4-16**

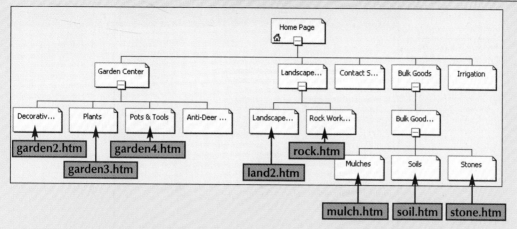

5. Double-click the **Decorative Items** page icon to open the garden2.htm page in Design view. This page and the other new pages you imported into the Web site will not use the Web site's shared borders until you activate this feature.

6. Click **Format** on the menu bar, click **Shared Borders**, click the **All pages** option button to select it, make sure the **Top**, **Left**, and **Bottom** check boxes contain check marks and that the **Include navigation buttons** check boxes contain check marks, and then click the **OK** button. Now the new pages you imported into the Web site use the Web site's existing shared borders.

Brett notices that the Decorative Items page contains broken links to the pictures that Clara inserted into the page. To correct these broken links, he must add the pictures to the Web site. Clara stored the pictures in four folders. To make it easier to identify the pictures used with the new pages, you'll show him how to import the folders into the Web site.

To import folders into the Web site:

1. In the Folder List, click the Web site's root folder to select it.

2. Click **File** on the menu bar, click **Import**, and then click the **Add Folder** button. The File Open dialog box opens.

3. Open the **Tutorial.04\Tutorial** folder included with your Data Files. Four folders appear in the list. You can't select multiple folders for importing, so you'll need to select the folders individually.

4. Click the **bulk_pic** folder to select it, and then click the **Open** button. The File Open dialog box closes and the Import dialog box reappears. Each file in the bulk_pic folder appears in the list. You can continue adding the additional folders and import everything at the same time.

5. Click the **Add Folder** button, click the **Up One Level** button 📷 in the File Open dialog box, click the **gc_pics** folder to select it, and then click the **Open** button.

6. Repeat Step 5 to select the **land_pic** and **rock_pic** folders. The Import dialog box lists all of the files you have selected. See Figure 4-17.

Figure 4-17 | **Folders and files selected for importing**

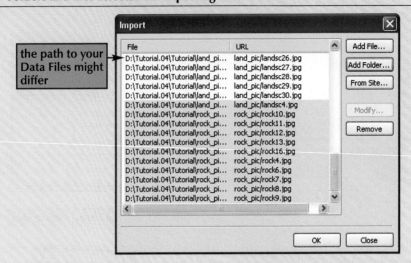

7. When you have selected all four folders, click the **OK** button in the Import dialog box. The folders and their contents are imported into the Web site and the pictures appear in the garden2.htm page.

Brett asks if he can move the folders and their contents from the Web site's root folder to the Web site's images folder without creating broken hyperlinks to the pictures. You tell Brett that using FrontPage to move files and folders automatically updates the links to the files. You'll show him how to move the folders into the Web site's images folder next.

To move the folders into the Web site's images folder:

1. Click the **Web Site** tab at the top of the Contents pane, and then change to Folders view.

2. If necessary, scroll the Folder List so you can see the Web site's root folder at the top of the list, and then scroll Folders view so you can see the bulk_pic, gc_pics, land_pic, and rock_pic folders.

3. In Folders view, click the **bulk_pic** folder to select it, press and hold the **Ctrl** key, click the **gc_pics**, **land_pic**, and **rock_pic** folders to select them, and then release the **Ctrl** key. All four folders are selected in Folders view.

4. Point to the **bulk_pic** folder, click and hold the left mouse button, and then drag the pointer to the **images** folder in the Folder List. While you are dragging the mouse, the pointer with a ⊘ shape appears. When you point to the images folder, the pointer changes to a ⬚ shape, indicating a valid operation.

5. While pointing to the **images** folder in the Folder List, release the left mouse button. FrontPage moves the selected folders into the images folder and updates the hyperlinks to these pictures.

6. Click the **garden2.htm** tab to display the page in Design view. The pictures appear in the page because FrontPage updated the path to the files.

   Trouble? Don't worry if the pictures or text appears to be cut off. They will appear correctly in a browser.

7. Close the Folder List.

You tell Brett that moving files and folders stored in a Web site using Windows Explorer or another file management program would not update the hyperlinks. Because Brett used FrontPage to move the folders and their contents, FrontPage updated all of the paths to the embedded pictures in the Web pages.

Disabling Shared Borders in a Page

Brett asks if there is a way to turn off the shared borders for one or more pages in the Web site without removing the page from the site's link bar components. You tell him that this is possible and that it's common for the content of a shared border to be inappropriate for one or more pages. You can disable one or all of the shared borders in a page using the Shared Borders dialog box.

Reference Window

Disabling Shared Borders for a Single Web Page

- Open the page in Design view.
- Click Format on the menu bar, and then click Shared Borders to open that dialog box.
- Click the Current page option button to select it.
- Click the Top, Left, Right, and Bottom check boxes, as necessary, to turn off the appropriate shared borders.
- Click the OK button.

Brett noticed that the home page does not include any links in the top shared border because it is the top-level page in the Web site and the top shared border includes only links to the top-level and same-level pages. Because the top shared border of the home page does not contain any links, Brett asks you to turn it off. He also wants to change the appearance of the home page to remove the links that appear on the left side of the page, so that the marquee and text will appear centered in the browser window. You'll turn off the left shared border to make this change.

To turn off shared borders for a single Web page:

1. Click the **index.htm** tab to display the home page, click **Format** on the menu bar, and then click **Shared Borders** to open the Shared Borders dialog box.

2. Click the **Current page** option button to select it, and then click the **Top** and **Left** check boxes to clear them. The sample diagram changes to display a page with a bottom shared border, but not top and left shared borders.

3. Click the **OK** button to close the Shared Borders dialog box and to turn off the top and left shared borders in the home page. The other Web pages in the navigation structure still use the top, left, and bottom shared borders.

4. Save the home page.

Without the shared borders, Brett notices that the home page no longer has a page title or link bar. You will show him how to add this content back to the home page by manually inserting a page banner and a link bar component.

Adding a Link Bar Component to a Page

You can add a link bar component to any Web page, not just to a shared border. Brett wants to include a link bar component in the home page with links to its child pages in the Web site. When you include a link bar component in a Web page, you can use a different arrangement of hyperlinks than what is available in the shared borders. FrontPage will use the information in the navigation structure to create the link bar in the home page, just as it does for the link bar in the site's shared borders.

To add a link bar component to the home page:

1. Press **Ctrl + Home** to scroll to the top of the home page, press the **Enter** key, and then press the **up** arrow key ↑ to move the insertion point to the new paragraph you created. Before inserting the link bar component, you'll change the style of the new paragraph to Normal.

2. Click the **Style** list arrow on the Formatting toolbar, and then click **Normal**.

3. Click **Insert** on the menu bar, and then click **Navigation**. The Insert Web Component dialog box opens, with the Link Bars component type selected. You can choose from three styles of link bars: a bar with custom links to pages in the current Web site or to pages in other Web sites, a bar with Back and Next links to pages in the current site, or a bar based on the arrangement of pages in the navigation structure. You'll choose the third option so the hyperlinks match the appearance and content of other link bars in the Web site.

4. In the Choose a bar type list box, click **Bar based on navigation structure**, and then click the **Next** button. The second dialog box opens, in which you choose a style for the link bar.

5. Make sure that the **Use Page's Theme** option is selected, and then click the **Next** button. The third dialog box opens, in which you select an option for the arrangement of the hyperlinks. You'll use the horizontal option, which is the default.

6. Make sure that the page with horizontal links is selected (the page on the left), and then click the **Finish** button. The Link Bar Properties dialog box shows that the default setting is for the link bar to contain links to child-level pages.

7. Click the **OK** button. The link bar component is inserted at the top of the page. See Figure 4-18.

Link bar component added to the home page ◄ **Figure 4-18**

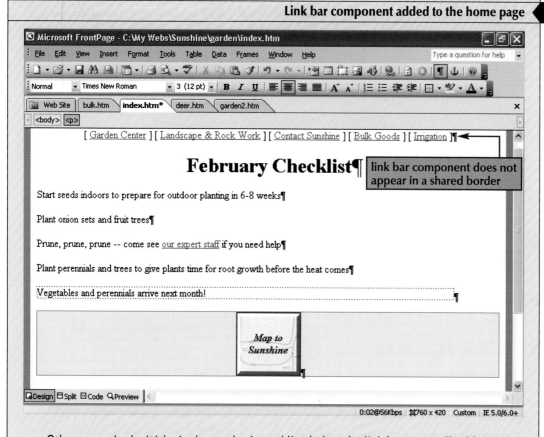

Other pages in the Web site have a horizontal line below the link bar, so you'll add one to the home page to match this style.

8. With the insertion point positioned to the right of the link bar component, click **Insert** on the menu bar, and then click **Horizontal Line**. A horizontal line is inserted below the link bar.

9. Save the home page.

You added a link bar component to the home page that is separate from the link bar component that appears in the top shared border of other Web pages in the site. When Brett adds new pages to the Web site, FrontPage will update this link bar automatically to include hyperlinks to the new pages after you add those pages to the navigation structure.

When he turned off the top shared border for this page, Brett removed the title from the top of the page. Brett wants the home page to include a title, but not a shared border. You explain that you can add a page banner to identify a page's content.

Adding a Page Banner to a Page

A page banner is a text or picture object that usually appears at the top of each page in a Web site. You can add a page banner to any page, but the page must appear in the navigation structure to use this feature.

Creating a Page Banner

- If necessary, position the page in the site's navigation structure.
- Click the location in the Web page where you want the banner to appear.
- Click Insert on the menu bar, and then click Page Banner.
- Select the Picture or Text option button to indicate the type of banner to create.
- Edit the text in the Page banner text text box as necessary.
- Click the OK button.

The home page is already positioned in the navigation structure, so you won't need to perform this step.

To add a page banner to the home page:

1. Press **Ctrl + Home** to move the insertion point to the top of the page, press the **Enter** key to create a new paragraph, and then press the **up** arrow key ↑ to move the insertion point to the new paragraph. You will add the page banner here.

2. Click **Insert** on the menu bar, and then click **Page Banner**. The Page Banner Properties dialog box opens. See Figure 4-19.

Figure 4-19   **Page Banner Properties dialog box**

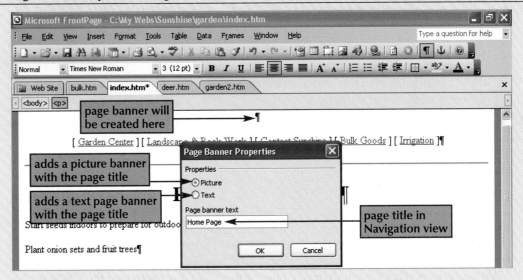

Brett notices that you can change the page title in this dialog box. He asks you to change the title of this page to "Sunshine Landscape & Garden Center." You will change the page title in the Page Banner Properties dialog box.

3. Make sure that the **Picture** option button is selected, select the text in the Page banner text text box, type **Sunshine Landscape & Garden Center**, and then click the **OK** button to insert the page banner into the page. FrontPage automatically updates the page title in Navigation view.

4. Save the home page. The page banner, Sunshine Landscape & Garden Center, appears at the top of the Web page. Brett asks why the page banner is displayed as regular text instead of as a picture. You explain that you could use the Formatting toolbar to change the appearance of the text in the page banner, but an easier way is to apply a theme that automatically formats the entire page—including the page banner—using predefined pictures and fonts. You'll show Brett how to apply a theme in the next session.

5. Preview the home page in a browser, and then follow some of the links in the Web site's pages to examine the new pages you added to the Web site and the link bars created by FrontPage. As you examine the pages, notice that the link bar components display links based on the configuration of pages in the navigation structure. For example, the bulk.htm page contains links in the top shared border to the home page and to Web pages at the same level in the navigation structure. The left shared border contains a link to its child page, bulk2.htm. When you click the Bulk Goods Samples link, the bulk2.htm page opens. Because this page contains child pages in the navigation structure, links to these child pages appear in the left shared border. To return to the parent page (bulk.htm), click the Up link in the top shared border. The link to the site's home page is named "Home," even though you changed the title of the home page in Navigation view. The default setting for the link bar component is to use a "Home" link, even if you change the title of the home page.

6. When you have finished examining the pages in the Web site and understand how the link bar components work, close your browser.

Brett is satisfied with the current content and appearance of the Web site. However, he asks if there is a way to include a link to the page that contains a map to the nursery in the link bar of the home page. He deleted this page from the navigation structure because he doesn't want it to appear as a link in the site's shared borders. You tell Brett that this request can be met by creating a custom link bar.

Creating a Custom Link Bar

When you inserted the link bar component into the home page, the Insert Web Component dialog box included three options for the bar type: Bar with custom links, Bar with back and next links, and Bar based on navigation structure. You created the link bar component in the home page using the third option so the links would match the pages in the Web site's navigation structure. Sometimes you might need to include a link to one or more pages in a Web site, but you don't want to include these links in all pages in the navigation structure. This situation is the one Brett has described: He wants to include a link to the Map page in the link bar component in the home page, but he does not want this link to appear in any other pages positioned in the navigation structure. To add the Map link to the link bar component in the home page, you tell Brett that he needs to create a custom link bar to replace the link bar based on the navigation structure that currently appears in the home page.

There are two ways to create a custom link bar. The first way is to position the insertion point where you want to insert the custom link bar, and then to insert a link bar based on custom links using the Insert Web Component dialog box. When you choose this method, you add the custom link bar to the Web site and Web page at the same time, and use the Link Bar Properties dialog box to select the links to include in the custom link bar. When you choose this method, the links use filenames unless you change them by editing the text to display in the link.

If you know you want to use page titles as your link names, you can create the custom link bar in Navigation view. You can still change the link names by renaming the page icons that appear in the custom link bar navigation structure. This method takes a little less time because you can drag and drop pages into the custom link bar's navigation structure instead of selecting pages individually.

Creating a Custom Link Bar in Navigation View

- Change to Navigation view, and, if necessary, display the Folder List.
- Make sure that no page icon is selected in the navigation structure, and then click the New Custom Link Bar button on the Contents pane.
- Right-click the New Link Bar page icon to select it and to open the shortcut menu, type a name for the custom link bar, and then press the Enter key.
- Drag the filename of the first page you want to include in the custom link bar from the Folder List and position it in the custom link bar navigation structure. Repeat this step to include the appropriate pages in the custom link bar.
- Open the page in which to display the custom link bar, position the insertion point where you want to insert it, click Insert on the menu bar, and then click Navigation. Select the Bar with custom links option in the Choose a bar type list, click the Next button, choose the desired bar style, click the Next button, choose the desired orientation, and then click the Finish button.
- In the Link Bar Properties dialog box, click the Choose existing list arrow and select the custom link bar to use in the page. (If your Web site has only one custom link bar, then the one you created will be selected automatically.)
- Use the Add link, Remove link, and Modify link buttons to add new links and delete or modify existing links. To move a link's position in the link bar, select it and then click the Move up or Move down buttons to position it in the desired location.
- Click the OK button.

You'll show Brett how to create a custom link bar in Navigation view. The custom link bar will include the same links as the one currently in the home page plus a new link to the Map page.

To create a custom link bar:

1. Switch to Navigation view, and then, if necessary, display the Folder List.

2. Click any blank area in the Contents pane to deselect any selected page icons, and then click the **New Custom Link Bar** button [icon] on the Contents pane. A New Link Bar page icon is added to the Contents pane. See Figure 4-20.

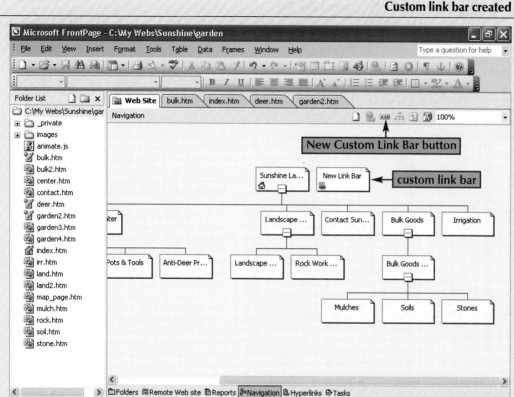

Trouble? If you cannot see the New Link Bar page icon, use the horizontal scroll bar to scroll the Contents pane to the left.

Trouble? If your New Link Bar page icon appears within the navigation structure for the Web site, then a page icon was selected when you created the custom link bar. Right-click the New Link Bar page icon to select it and open the shortcut menu, click Delete, and then repeat Step 2.

To add links, you drag files from the Folder List and position them below the New Link Bar page icon.

▶ **3.** Drag the **center.htm** file from the Folder List and position it as a child page of the New Link Bar page icon. Release the mouse button to add the Garden Center page to the custom link bar.

▶ **4.** Repeat Step 3 to add the **land.htm**, **contact.htm**, **bulk.htm**, **irr.htm**, and **map_page.htm** pages to the right of the Garden Center page icon in the navigation structure for the custom link bar. Figure 4-21 shows the navigation structure for the custom link bar.

Figure 4-21 | Navigation structure for the custom link bar

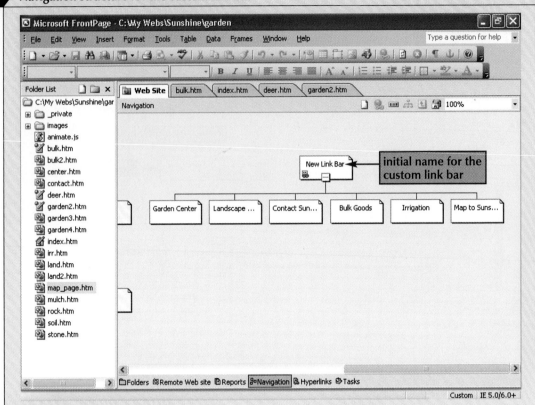

Trouble? If you cannot see the navigation structure for the custom link bar, scroll the Contents pane to the left.

When you create a custom link bar, FrontPage assigns it the name "New Link Bar." You can name the custom link bar using this suggested name or you can give it a name that describes the links it contains or the page in which you plan to use it. You suggest changing the name of the link bar to "Home Page" so Brett remembers the page in which this custom link bar will appear. Even though you created the link bar for a specific page, you can use it in other pages in the Web site. You can also create additional custom link bars to use in other pages of the Web site.

After renaming the custom link bar, you'll insert it into the home page.

To rename the custom link bar and insert it into the home page:

1. Right-click the **New Link Bar** page icon to select it and to open the shortcut menu, and then click **Rename**.

2. Type **Home Page** to identify the new link bar, and then press the **Enter** key. The name of the custom link bar changes to "Home Page."

3. Click the **index.htm** tab to change to the home page in Design view.

4. Click the **link bar component** to select it, and then press the **Delete** key. You deleted the existing link bar component, which was based on the Web site's navigation structure. You will replace it with the custom link bar component you just created.

5. Click **Insert** on the menu bar, and then click **Navigation**. The Insert Web Component dialog box opens, with the Link Bars component type selected and the Bar with custom links bar type selected.

6. Click the **Next** button, make sure the **Use Page's theme** option is selected, click the **Next** button, make sure the horizontal option is selected, and then click the **Finish** button. The Link Bar Properties dialog box opens. Because the Home Page custom link bar is the only custom link bar in the Web site, it is selected in the Choose existing list box. The links that appear in the custom link bar appear in the Links list box. See Figure 4-22.

Link Bar Properties dialog box for the custom link bar ◀ **Figure 4-22**

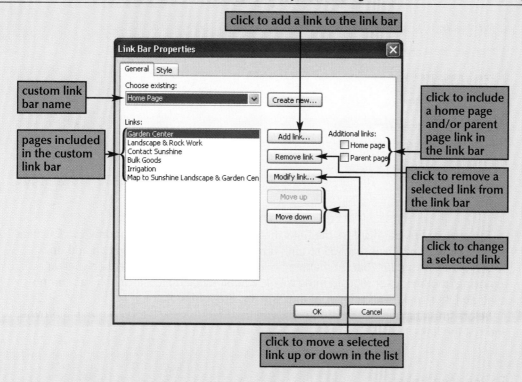

At this point, you could make changes to the custom link bar, but these settings are correct, so you can just insert it into the home page.

7. Click the **OK** button, close the Folder List, and then save the home page. Figure 4-23 shows the custom link bar in the home page.

Figure 4-23 **Custom link bar added to the home page**

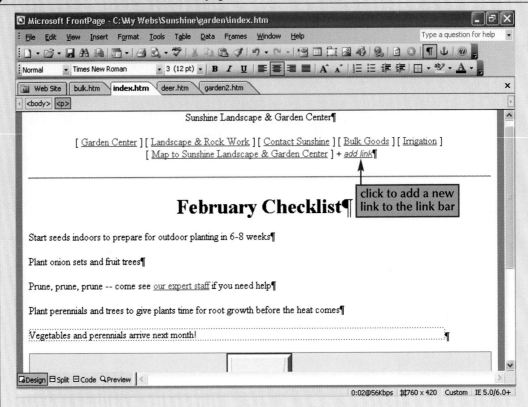

The custom link bar displays the links that Brett specified in Navigation view. Clicking the "add link" link opens the Add to Link Bar dialog box, in which you can add new pages to the custom link bar. To make other changes to the custom link bar, such as removing, modifying, or repositioning a link, double-click the custom link bar component, and then make the changes in the Link Bar Properties dialog box.

Before finishing your work for the day, you ask Brett to view the Web site in a browser and test the links.

To test the links:

1. Click the **Preview** button on the Standard toolbar. The home page opens in your browser.

2. Use the links that you created to navigate the pages in the Web site. When you are finished, close your browser.

3. Close the garden Web site and FrontPage.

Now Brett can be sure that people can find the map to the nursery. In the next session, you will show him how to apply a theme to the Web site to change the overall appearance of pages in the site.

Session 4.1 Quick Check

1. What is the main reason for positioning pages in the navigation structure in Navigation view?
2. Where can you create shared borders in a Web page? Which shared borders can contain optional link bar components?
3. True or False: Renaming a Web page in Navigation view updates the HTML title of the page.
4. True or False: You can add shared borders to a Web page that does not appear in the Web site's navigation structure.
5. True or False: Editing a shared border in a Web page updates the shared border for all Web pages that use that shared border.
6. When you delete a page from the navigation structure, which two options are available?
7. How do you turn off a shared border for a page?
8. True or False: You can insert a link bar component into a Web page even if that page does not use a Web site's shared borders.

Session 4.2

Applying a Theme to a Web Site

By creating shared borders, link bar components, and page banners in the garden Web site, you have made the pages easy to identify and navigate. Brett wants you to focus now on the appearance of the Web site's pages to make them visually interesting and professional, reflecting the atmosphere of the nursery itself. Brett's first suggestion is to add a background picture and change the format of text that appears in each page in the Web site to create this visual interest. However, you tell Brett that an easier way of applying the same formatting to all pages in a Web site is to apply a theme to its pages.

A **theme** is a collection of design elements—bullets, backgrounds, table borders, fonts, and pictures—that you can apply to an entire Web site or to only one or more specific Web pages. A Web site with a theme applied to it has a consistent appearance because the formatting applied by the theme is the same in every page. Everything in the page—from its bullets to its background picture—is professionally designed to fit together. When you insert new bullets, horizontal lines, page banners, link bars, and other features into a page that uses a theme, these features are formatted automatically by the theme. Also, if you add a new page to a Web site that has a theme applied to it, the new page will use the same theme automatically. FrontPage includes many themes with styles ranging from conservative to flashy; you can visit the Microsoft Web site to download and install additional themes. When you apply a theme, you can change it to use vivid colors, active graphics, or a background picture. You can even modify a theme to customize it for your needs.

Reference Window	**Applying a Theme to a Web Site**

- In Design view, Folders view, or Navigation view, click Format on the menu bar, and then click Theme.
- Scroll the themes in the Theme task pane to find one of interest. If a page is open in Design view, clicking the theme temporarily applies the theme to the page.
- If desired, select the options for Vivid colors, Active graphics, and a Background picture in the Theme task pane.
- When you locate an appropriate theme, click the list arrow that appears when you point to the desired theme. To apply the theme to the entire Web site, click Apply as default theme in the menu. To apply the theme to the currently selected page(s) in Folders, Navigation, or Design view, click Apply to selected page(s) in the menu.
- Click the Yes button to apply the theme.

You can use the Theme task pane to preview the themes installed on your computer. Brett wants to find one that has easy-to-read text and complementary colors that he can apply to the entire Web site. Because Brett wants to preview the theme before applying it to the entire Web site, you'll ask him to open the home page in Design view. You tell Brett, however, that he can preview the theme with any page in Design view.

To apply a theme to a Web site:

1. Start **FrontPage**, open the **garden** Web site from the location where your Web sites are stored, and then open the home page **(index.htm)** in Design view.

2. Click **Format** on the menu bar, and then click **Theme**. The Theme task pane opens, as shown in Figure 4-24.

Figure 4-24	**Theme task pane**

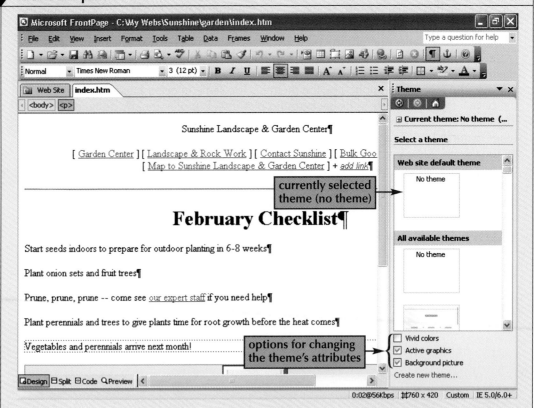

The first entry in the Select a theme section shows the Web site's current default theme, which is "No theme" because you have not applied a theme yet. After you apply a theme to the Web site, the theme you select will appear in this location. You might see a Recently used themes section below the Web site default theme section, which displays previews of themes that you (or other users) have recently applied to other Web sites or pages. This list changes as you use FrontPage. If you scroll the Select a theme list, the All available themes section shows the themes installed on your computer; this list will vary depending on whether you have installed other themes from the FrontPage 2003 CD or from the Microsoft Web site. As you scroll the list, you'll see the previews and names of the themes available on your computer.

3. Scroll down the Select a theme list so you see the "All available themes" heading. The first option, No theme, deletes a previously applied theme. The remaining entries are the available themes on your computer, displayed in alphabetical order by theme name.

4. Click the first theme (but not the No theme theme) in your list of available themes. (The default first theme is "Afternoon.") As shown in Figure 4-25, the home page is formatted using the elements of the Afternoon theme (or the theme that you clicked in the Theme task pane). Notice that the theme uses different fonts and a background picture. The link bar component now uses buttons for the hyperlinks, instead of plain text. The page banner is formatted according to the theme, which simply changes the font of the text.

Afternoon theme temporarily applied to the home page ◄ **Figure 4-25**

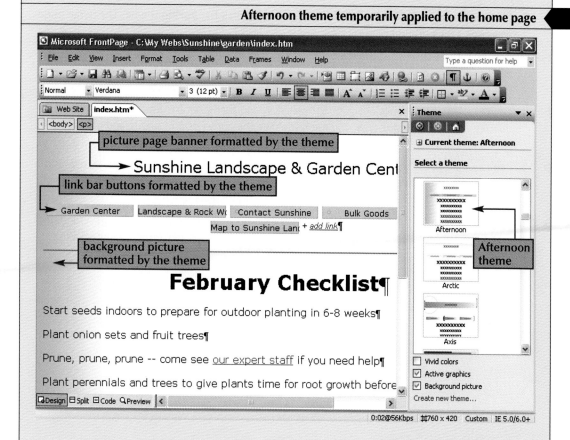

5. Scroll down the themes in the Select a theme list and click some of the themes in the list. Notice that the theme's name might indicate its contents. For example, the Checkers theme displays a checkerboard in the page.

   Trouble? Depending on your installation of FrontPage and other Microsoft Office programs, you might see a different list of themes than those identified in the text. If you don't have a specified theme, select another theme.

6. Scroll down the list of available themes until you see Spring, and then click **Spring** to preview this theme for the home page. Brett likes this theme.

   You can change a theme to use vivid colors, active graphics, and a background picture. As you select these features, you can update the preview of the theme to see their effect.

7. If necessary, clear the **Vivid colors**, **Active graphics**, and **Background picture** check boxes, and then click the **Spring** theme again. The home page now uses a white background instead of a background picture. The options for active graphics and vivid colors are disabled. When you enable active graphics for a theme, certain theme elements, such as the buttons in the link bar, will change their appearance on mouse over. For most themes, the vivid color set is a collection of brighter, more intense colors. You may have previewed some sample themes in Step 5 that use dark background colors. In some cases, you might like the theme but not the background picture. You can disable the background picture by clearing its check box.

8. Click the **Background picture** check box, and then click the **Spring** theme. The home page now uses a background picture.

9. Click the **Vivid colors** check box to select it, and then click the **Spring** theme. For some themes, like the Spring theme, there might not be a noticeable difference between the regular and vivid color sets. For other themes, the change is more obvious.

10. Click the **Active graphics** check box to select it, and then click the **Spring** theme. For some themes, like the Spring theme, you might not see the active graphics until you preview the page in a browser.

11. Point to the **Spring** theme to display a list arrow on its right side, click the **list arrow**, and then click **Apply as default theme**. A message box opens and indicates that this action will permanently replace some of the existing formatting information.

12. Click the **Yes** button to apply the theme to the pages in the garden Web site. Several messages are displayed on the status bar while this action is being performed; Figure 4-26 shows the home page after applying the theme. The style of the headings, page banner, background, and link bar component has changed to match the theme.

Spring theme applied to the home page | **Figure 4-26**

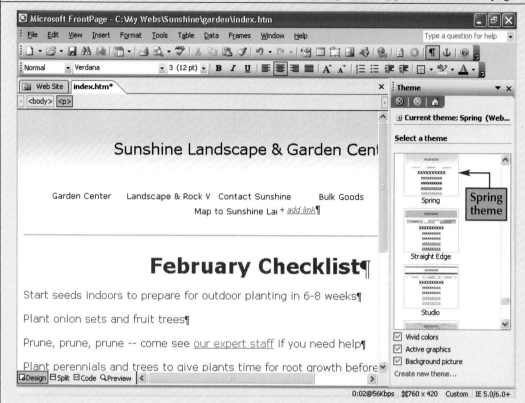

Trouble? It might take several minutes to apply the theme if your Web site is saved on a server or a removable disk. If you are storing your Web site on a hard drive, themes are applied and saved quickly.

Next, you ask Brett to open the home page in a browser and test the link bar component.

To view the page in a browser and test the link bar:

1. Close the Theme task pane, and then preview the home page in a browser. Click the **Yes** button when prompted to save your changes.

2. Point to the **Garden Center** button in the link bar. The button's appearance changes to add a background color. This animation occurs because you chose the active graphics option when you applied the theme.

3. Click the **Garden Center** button in the link bar to open that page. See Figure 4-27. The link bars in the top and left shared borders, the page banner, and the horizontal line are formatted by the theme. You selected these settings when you created the link bar in the top and left shared borders and the page banner. The Garden Center button in the top shared border has a background color; for this theme, the background color on a button indicates that it is the currently displayed page. If you point to the Garden Center button, you'll notice that it is not a hyperlink; FrontPage disables hyperlinks to the current page in a link bar component. The other buttons in the link bar are active hyperlinks. As Brett examines the Garden Center page, he notices that the link to the Landscape & Rock Work page is incomplete; part of the "W" and the rest of the word "Work" are missing.

Figure 4-27 | **Garden Center page with Spring theme applied**

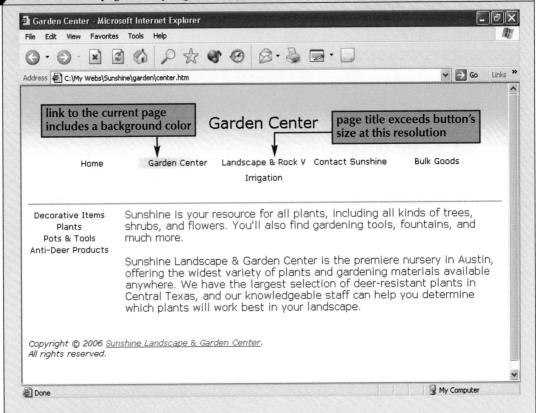

Trouble? If your monitor displays more than 800 × 600 pixels, your link bar might appear on a single line. This difference is not a problem.

4. Use the link bars to examine the pages in the Web site and note how the theme formats the pages. When you are finished, close your browser.

Brett likes the Spring theme but wants to make a couple of changes and asks you how to make them. You tell him that it's easy to customize an existing theme.

Customizing an Existing Theme

After selecting a theme, you might want to make some changes to it. For the Spring theme, you have already noticed that the font the theme applies to the buttons in the link bar components is too large to display the full page titles. You could change the names of pages in Navigation view to decrease their size and make them fit. Another solution is to customize the theme to use a smaller font size for the buttons. You can also customize a theme by changing the colors, graphics, and fonts it uses.

Reference Window

Customizing an Existing Theme

- Click Format on the menu bar, and then click Theme to open the Theme task pane.
- Point to the theme that you want to customize, and then click the list arrow that appears.
- Click Customize in the menu that opens. The Customize Theme dialog box opens.
- Click the Colors button to customize the colors used in the theme, click the Graphics button to customize pictures and other graphic elements used in the theme, or click the Text button to customize the fonts and font styles of text elements used in the theme.
- When you have finished customizing the desired theme elements, click the Save button, type a name for the custom theme, click the OK button, and then click the Yes button.

When you customize a theme, all pages that use the theme will display the changes. In addition, the theme is saved on your hard drive so you can use it to format future Web sites.

To customize the Spring theme:

1. Click **Format** on the menu bar, and then click **Theme**. The Theme task pane opens.

2. Scroll to the top of the Select a theme list. Notice that the Theme task pane now identifies the default theme for the Web site as Spring.

3. Point to the **Spring** theme in the Web site default theme section of the Theme task pane, click the **list arrow** that appears, and then click **Customize** in the menu that opens. The Customize Theme dialog box opens, as shown in Figure 4-28. The "What would you like to modify?" section of the dialog box includes buttons that let you change the theme's colors, graphics, and text.

Customize Theme dialog box | **Figure 4-28**

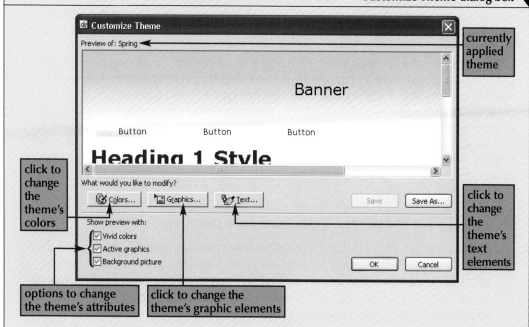

As you work with themes and customize them, you'll become more familiar with which button to click to change the theme's various features. The Colors button opens a dialog box in which you can change the color scheme used in the pages. The **color scheme** is the coordinated collection of colors used in the page's fonts, headings, background, and other elements. You can also change the intensity of the color scheme to make colors lighter or darker. Finally, you can apply custom colors to specific elements, such as the background color, the Heading 1 text, and horizontal lines.

Clicking the Graphics button lets you change the pictures used in specific graphics, such as a background picture, a page banner, or the different buttons used in the link bar components. For graphics that include fonts, such as a page banner or a button in a link bar component, you can also change the style, size, horizontal alignment, vertical alignment, and font of the button. There are several types of buttons used in a theme. The horizontal navigation buttons appear horizontally across the page in a link bar component, usually in the top shared border. The vertical navigation buttons appear vertically down a page in a link bar component, usually in the left or right shared border. The quick back, quick home, quick next, and quick up buttons include the words "Back," "Home," and "Up" in a link bar; these buttons appear when you have set a link bar to display links to the back and next pages, to the home page, and to the parent page. The bullet list buttons are the bullet characters in a bulleted list. When you set a page banner to display a picture, the picture is created using the banner picture for the theme. Finally, the global navigation buttons are buttons used in the theme but not in any of the preceding categories. If you specify the use of active graphics in a theme, you will see three pictures used for some graphic elements to represent samples of the button, the selected button (after it is clicked), and the hovered button (the button on mouse over).

The Text button lets you change the font and text styles of paragraphs formatted using the Normal, Heading 1, Heading 2, Heading 3, Heading 4, Heading 5, and Heading 6 styles. Paragraphs formatted with the Normal style are collectively called body text; paragraphs formatted with any of the heading styles are collectively called headings.

When you create a custom theme, you use the Save button in the Customize Theme dialog box to save the theme with a new name. After you create a custom theme, it is stored on your computer so you can use it to format other Web sites or Web pages. After applying a custom theme to a Web site, the files that create the theme are stored in the Web site itself in the _themes folder. After you apply a custom theme, you can delete it from the Theme task pane to remove the theme's files from your computer, but the Web site that uses the theme will still have the files that create it. You can save a custom theme using the default name, which is "Copy of" plus the original theme name, or you can change the default name to one that is easier to associate with the Web site that uses it.

Brett wants to customize the existing Spring theme to reduce the font size used in the buttons in the top shared border. To make this change, you will need to show him how customize the theme's graphics.

To customize a theme's graphics and save the theme:

1. In the Customize Theme dialog box, click the **Graphics** button. As shown in Figure 4-29, a new Customize Theme dialog box opens and displays an Item list arrow, which lets you select the graphic to customize; a Picture tab, which lets you browse for a new picture for the selected item; a Font tab, which lets you change the font used in the selected item; and a Preview box, which displays a sample page with the changes you apply.

Changing the theme's graphic elements ◀ **Figure 4-29**

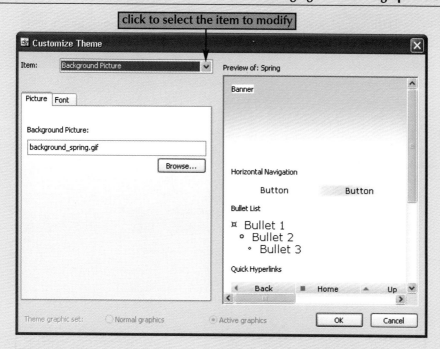

click to select the item to modify

2. Click the **Item** list arrow, and then click **Horizontal Navigation**. Because you enabled active graphics for this theme, there are three pictures for creating the horizontal navigation buttons: one for the button, one for the selected (clicked) button, and one for the hovered button. You can change any of these pictures using the Browse button. If you change the theme to use normal graphics, the hovered picture will be disabled, and depending on the theme you applied, the buttons might change.

3. Click the **Font** tab. The Font tab shows the font, font style, font size, horizontal alignment, and vertical alignment for text that appears on the horizontal navigation buttons. You need to make the text smaller, so you will change the font size.

4. Click the **Size** list arrow, and then click **1 (8 pt)**. Notice that the preview changes to show horizontal buttons with 8-point text. See Figure 4-30.

| Figure 4-30 | Changing the font used on the horizontal navigation buttons |

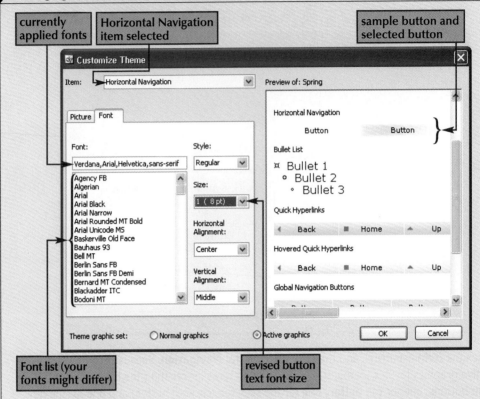

currently applied fonts

Horizontal Navigation item selected

sample button and selected button

Font list (your fonts might differ)

revised button text font size

To make the buttons in the top and left shared borders match, you'll make this same change to the vertical navigation buttons.

▶ **5.** Click the **Item** list arrow, and then click **Vertical Navigation**. The current settings for the vertical navigation buttons appear on the Font tab and the preview scrolls automatically to display the sample vertical navigation buttons.

▶ **6.** Click the **Size** list arrow, and then click **1 (8 pt)**. The preview shows the revised font for the vertical navigation buttons.

▶ **7.** Click the **OK** button. For now, you do not need to make any other changes to the custom theme. You'll save the theme using the Web site name so it's easy to identify it later.

▶ **8.** Click the **Save** button. The Save Theme dialog box opens and displays the default theme title, Copy of Spring.

Trouble? If another user already created a Copy of Spring theme, your initial theme name will differ. This difference causes no problems.

▶ **9.** Type **Garden Web Site** in the Save Theme dialog box, and then click the **OK** button.

Trouble? If another user already created the Garden Web Site theme, add your initials to the theme or a number to save it with a unique name.

▶ **10.** Click the **OK** button to close the Customize Theme dialog box, and then click the **Yes** button to apply your changes as the new default theme for the Web site. After a few moments, the Garden Web Site theme is applied to every page in the Web site.

▶ **11.** Save the home page, and then preview it in a browser and examine the revised theme.

Brett notices that the reduced font size only partially corrected the problem with the link for the Landscape & Rock Work page. In addition, he notices that the link for the Map to Sunshine Landscape & Garden Center page also has some dropped text. You tell him that you could apply another theme to the Web site, or customize the theme's buttons to find ones that have more space. Because you've already tried reducing the font size, you decide to fix this problem by renaming the affected pages in Navigation view. Because there are two link bars (the link bar created from the navigation structure and the custom link bar for the home page) in the garden Web site, you will need to change the page title for the land.htm page twice.

To change page titles in Navigation view:

1. Close your browser.

2. Change to Navigation view and close the Theme task pane.

3. Right-click the **land.htm** page icon in the navigation structure to select it and open the shortcut menu, click **Rename**, type **Landscape/Rock Work**, and then press the **Enter** key.

   Trouble? If you are unsure of which page icon is the land.htm page, click the page icons and look at the path on the status bar until you see the land.htm page.

4. Scroll the navigation structure so you can see the navigation structure for the custom link bar, right-click the **land.htm** page icon to select it and to open the shortcut menu, click **Rename**, type **Landscape/Rock Work**, and then press the **Enter** key.

   Next, you'll rename the page title for the map_page.htm page. This page icon appears only in the navigation structure for the custom link bar.

5. Right-click the **Map to Sunshine Landscape & Garden Center** page icon in the custom link bar navigation structure to select it and to open the shortcut menu, click **Rename**, type **Map to Sunshine**, and then press the **Enter** key.

6. Click the home page icon in the navigation structure (not in the custom link bar), and then click the **Preview** button 🔍 on the Standard toolbar. The home page opens in a browser. If necessary, refresh the page in the browser to display the revised titles for the Landscape/Rock Work and Map to Sunshine buttons. Now the page titles fit on the buttons. See Figure 4-31.

Figure 4-31 ▶ **Home page with revised theme**

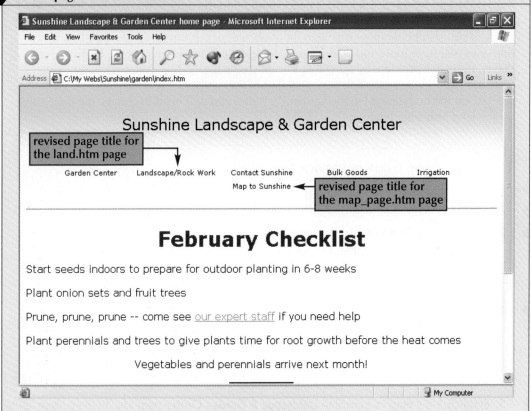

7. Click the **Garden Center** link in the top shared border.

Brett likes the changes to the link bars. Now he asks you to show him how to customize the theme again to left-align the links in the left shared border.

To change text alignment in a custom theme:

▶ **1.** Close your browser.

▶ **2.** Click **Format** on the menu bar, and then click **Theme** to open the Theme task pane.

▶ **3.** Point to the **Garden Web Site** theme in the Web site default theme section of the Theme task pane, click the **list arrow** that appears, and then click **Customize**. The Customize Theme dialog box opens.

▶ **4.** Click the **Graphics** button.

▶ **5.** Click the **Item** list arrow, and then click **Vertical Navigation**.

▶ **6.** Click the **Font** tab.

▶ **7.** Click the **Horizontal Alignment** list arrow, and then click **Left**. The sample buttons in the theme preview change to use a left alignment.

▶ **8.** Click the **OK** button, click the **Save** button to save your changes to the custom theme, click the **OK** button to close the Customize Theme dialog box, and then click the **Yes** button to apply the theme to the entire Web site.

9. Click the **Garden Center** page icon in the navigation structure, and then preview it in a browser. The links in the left shared border are left-aligned. See Figure 4-32.

Garden Center page with revised theme ◄ **Figure 4-32**

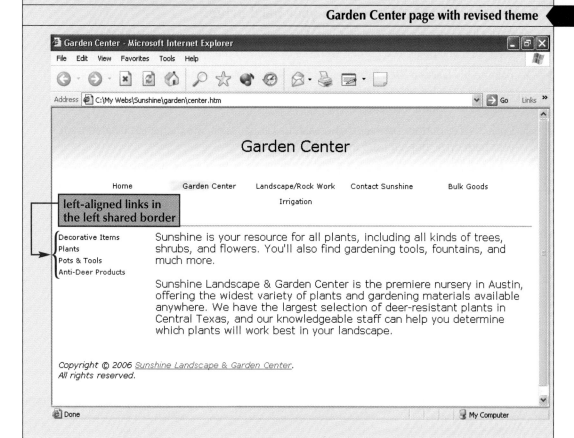

10. Close your browser.

Brett likes the revised theme. Because Brett is concerned about file management on his computer, he asks you how to remove the custom theme from his computer.

Deleting a Custom Theme From Your Hard Drive

After you create a theme, you can delete it from your hard drive to save disk space. After you apply a custom theme to a Web site, you can delete it from your hard drive after closing the Web site; the files for the theme will continue to be stored in the Web site that uses the custom theme.

Deleting a Custom Theme From Your Hard Drive

Reference Window

- If necessary, close all open Web sites in FrontPage.
- Click Format on the menu bar, and then click Theme to open the Theme task pane.
- Locate and click the custom theme in the All available themes section that you want to delete.
- Click Delete in the menu that opens.
- Click the Yes button in the message box that opens.

Brett wants to delete the theme from his computer.

To delete a custom theme from your hard drive:

1. Click **File** on the menu bar, click **Close Site**, and then, if necessary, click the **Yes** button to save the home page. The garden Web site closes, and the Theme task pane remains open.
2. Point to the **Garden Web Site** theme in the All available themes section of the Theme task pane, click the **list arrow** that appears, and then click **Delete**. A message box opens and asks you to confirm the deletion.
3. Click the **Yes** button. The files that create the Garden Web Site theme are deleted from your hard drive, but not from the garden Web site.

Brett really likes the customized theme that he created, but he also likes the background picture that he used in the first version of the home page. He asks if there is a way to create a new theme that uses a background picture, fonts, and colors that he selects. You tell him that FrontPage does include an option to create a new theme and decide to show it to him next.

Creating a New Theme

When you create a new theme, you can customize any or all of a theme's elements. If you choose not to customize a theme element, such as a heading or the way a followed hyperlink appears, then FrontPage applies the default formatting to it.

Reference Window	**Creating a New Theme**

- In the Theme task pane, click the Create new theme link.
- Use the Colors, Graphics, and Text buttons to apply the desired formatting to different elements of the theme.
- Click the Save button and provide a name for the new theme, and then click the OK button.
- Click the OK button to close the Customize Theme dialog box.

Brett wants you to show him how to create a new theme using the back.jpg file as the background picture. He also wants to select a color scheme and specific fonts.

To create a new theme:

1. Click **File** on the menu bar, point to **Recent Sites**, and then click the **garden** Web site.
2. At the bottom of the Theme task pane, click the **Create new theme** link. The Customize Theme dialog box opens. This is the same dialog box that you use to customize an existing theme. Notice that the preview name is "New Theme" and that the default formatting is applied to the elements shown in the preview. See Figure 4-33.

theme being customized is a new theme

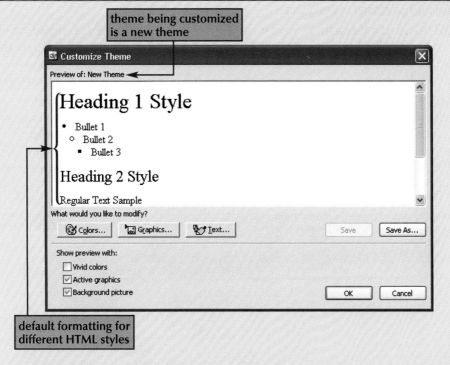

default formatting for different HTML styles

The first thing Brett wants to do is select a color scheme.

3. Click the **Colors** button. The Color Schemes tab displays the names and sample colors of the color schemes available on your computer. When you click a color scheme, a preview of it using text samples representing different styles of text appears in the Preview box.

4. Make sure that the **Normal colors** option button is selected in the Theme color set section, scroll down the color schemes list, click **Spiral**, and then scroll down the Preview box to view the samples of the colors used in this color scheme.

5. Click the **OK** button, and then click the **Graphics** button. "Background Picture" is the selected item in the Item list box.

6. Click the **Browse** button on the Picture tab, open the **images** folder of the garden Web site (if necessary), and then double-click **back.jpg**. The theme now uses the back.jpg picture, and a preview of this background picture appears in the Preview box.

7. Click the **OK** button, click the **Save** button, type **Custom Garden** in the Save Theme dialog box, click the **OK** button to close the Save Theme dialog box, and then click the **OK** button to close the Customize Theme dialog box.

The Custom Garden theme Brett created is now available for use just like any other theme, and it appears in the All available themes section of the Theme task pane. Brett wants to preview the theme he created before applying it to the entire Web site.

To preview the new theme:

▶ **1.** Open the home page in Design view.

▶ **2.** Scroll the Select a theme list so you can see the Custom Garden theme you created, point to the **Custom Garden** theme, click the **list arrow** that appears, and then click **Apply to selected page(s)**. The Custom Garden theme is applied to the home page, as shown in Figure 4-34. This theme uses the back.jpg picture and colors from the Spiral color scheme.

Trouble? If you do not see the colors from the Spiral color theme, point to the Custom Garden theme in the All available themes section of the Theme task pane, click the list arrow that appears, and then click Customize. Click the Colors button, select the Spiral color scheme, click the Normal colors option button, and then click the OK button. Click the Save button, click the OK button to close the Customize Theme dialog box, and then repeat Step 2.

Figure 4-34 ▶ **Custom Garden theme applied to the home page**

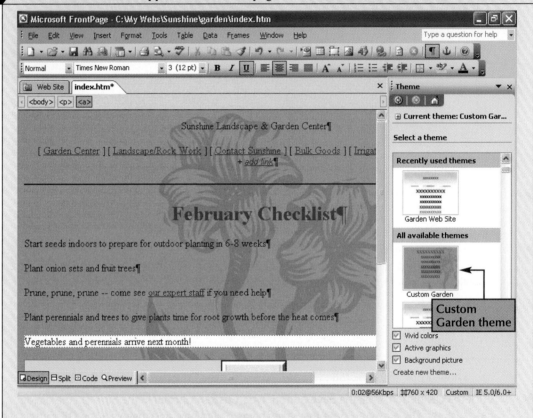

Brett realizes that creating a new theme requires a lot more effort than just applying a background picture and selecting a color scheme. He sees that he will need to create buttons to use in the link bar component and a picture to use in the page banner. Brett wants to check with his graphic designer to inquire about creating custom graphics to use in this new theme. You also suggest browsing one of the many free clip-art sites on the Internet to see if Brett can find graphics that he can use. Because Brett isn't prepared to finish this work today, he wants to restore the Garden Web Site theme. Instead of just reapplying the Garden Web Site theme to the home page, you want to show Brett how to remove a theme from a page first so he knows how to do this.

Removing a Theme From a Page

To remove a theme from a page, you just apply the "No theme" theme to it, which removes the link to the files that create the theme. You can also remove a theme from an entire Web site.

Removing a Theme From a Page or Web Site

- To remove a theme from a Web page, open the page in Design view, open the Theme task pane, point to the No theme theme in the All available themes section, click the list arrow that appears, and then click Apply to selected page(s).
- To remove a theme from a Web site, open the Theme task pane, point to the No theme theme in the All available themes section, click the list arrow that appears, click Apply as default theme, and then click the Yes button.

First, you'll show Brett how to remove the Custom Garden theme from the home page.

To remove a theme from a Web page:

▶ 1. If necessary, scroll the Select a theme list so you can see the No theme theme in the All available themes section.

▶ 2. Point to the **No theme** theme, click the **list arrow** that appears, and then click **Apply to selected page(s)**. The Custom Garden theme is removed from the home page.

   Now you can reapply the Garden Web Site theme.

▶ 3. Scroll up the Select a theme list until you see the Garden Web Site theme, point to the **Garden Web Site** theme, click the **list arrow** that appears, and then click **Apply to selected page(s)**. The home page is formatted using the Garden Web Site theme.

▶ 4. Save the home page.

▶ 5. Close the Theme task pane, the garden Web site, and FrontPage.

Brett likes the changes that he made to the Web site. The customized theme is not only attractive, but it also helps to unify the Web site's pages with a consistent, professional appearance. In the next session, you'll show Brett another way to present pictures and art in a Web page.

Session 4.2 Quick Check

1. What is a theme?
2. True or False: You can temporarily apply a theme to a page by opening the page in Design view, and then clicking the theme to apply.
3. In a theme, what changes when you select the Vivid colors option?
4. True or False: When you customize a theme, the files for the customized theme are saved in the Web site and on your computer's hard drive.
5. What are three categories of elements that you can customize in a theme?
6. True or False: You can apply a custom theme to only a single Web site.

Session 4.3

Creating a Photo Gallery in a Page

In Tutorial 2, you learned how to insert pictures into a Web page and change their characteristics, and how to create thumbnail pictures with hyperlinks that open larger pictures and Web pages. You can insert pictures into any Web page and position them using the alignment and formatting tools in FrontPage. In some cases, however, you might want to present a group of thumbnail pictures that, when clicked, display a larger version of the same picture. A **photo gallery** lets you add pictures with captions and descriptions to your Web pages. The advantage of using a photo gallery is that you can create and format the captions, descriptions, and thumbnail pictures automatically. After creating a photo gallery, you can change its properties by revising the captions and descriptions or by adding and deleting pictures. A photo gallery is an excellent way to organize photos and descriptions of their contents.

Reference Window	**Creating a Photo Gallery in a Page**

- Click the desired location in which to add the photo gallery.
- Click Insert on the menu bar, point to Picture, and then click New Photo Gallery.
- Click the Add button, click Pictures from Files, and then browse to and double-click a picture file to include in the photo gallery.
- Click in the Caption text box, and then type the photo's caption.
- Press the Tab key, and then type the photo's description.
- If necessary, click the Override and use custom font formatting option button to enable the options to format the caption and description using the Formatting toolbar options in the dialog box.
- Add more photos and their captions and descriptions to the photo gallery as necessary.
- Click the Layout tab, and then select a layout for the photo gallery.
- When you are finished adding photos, click the OK button.

Helen Xiao, Sunshine's senior horticulturist, contacted Brett this morning to tell him that she has been working on the content of the Anti-Deer Products page. So far, she has some content describing the anti-deer products available for purchase at the nursery. Because many people believe that deer-resistant plants are less colorful than plants that are not deer-resistant, she suggests including pictures of beautiful, flowering, deer-resistant plants that are in season at the nursery, but she's not sure how to incorporate this content. She has some descriptions and photos that she can send to you. You tell Helen and Brett that this content is an excellent candidate for a photo gallery. You'll begin by importing Helen's files into the Web site, and then you'll create the photo gallery.

To import the files into the Web site:

1. Start **FrontPage**, and then open the **garden** Web site from the location where your Web sites are stored. You'll import Helen's files into the root folder, and then you'll move the pictures into the Web site's images folder.

2. Display the Folder List (if necessary), make sure the garden Web site's root folder is selected, click **File** on the menu bar, click **Import**, click the **Add File** button, open the **Tutorial.04\Tutorial** folder included with your Data Files, press and hold the **Ctrl** key, click **deer.htm** and **leon.jpg**, release the **Ctrl** key, and then click the **Open** button. Two files are selected to import into the Web site.

3. Click the **OK** button. When the Confirm Save dialog box opens, click the **Yes** button to overwrite the existing deer.htm page in the Web site.

4. In the Contents pane, select the file **leon.jpg**, and then drag it to the **images** folder in the Folder List. When the pointer changes to a ⬚ shape, release the mouse button.

5. Close the Folder List, and then open the **deer.htm** page in Design view and examine its contents. The first thing you should notice is that the page does not use the Web site's theme. You can apply the theme using the Theme task pane.

6. Click **Format** on the menu bar, click **Theme**, point to the **Garden Web Site** theme in the Web site default theme section, click the **list arrow** that appears, and then click **Apply to selected page(s)**. The page is formatted using the Garden Web Site theme.

To add the shared borders to this page, you need to open the Shared Borders dialog box.

7. Click **Format** on the menu bar, click **Shared Borders**, make sure that the **Current page** option button is selected, and then click the **OK** button. Because you already positioned this page in the navigation structure, the shared borders contain links to other pages in the Web site.

8. Close the Theme task pane.

With Helen's page and pictures imported into the Web site, you can create the photo gallery. You'll create the photo gallery at the bottom of the page. As the nursery gets new stock, you can add new pictures to the photo gallery.

To create the photo gallery:

1. Press **Ctrl + End** to scroll to the bottom of the deer.htm page, and then press the **Enter** key to start a new paragraph.

2. Click **Insert** on the menu bar, point to **Picture**, and then click **New Photo Gallery**. The Photo Gallery Properties dialog box opens. The pictures that you will add to the photo gallery are saved with your Data Files.

3. Click the **Add** button, and then click **Pictures from Files**. The File Open dialog box opens. Open the **Tutorial.04\Tutorial** folder included with your Data Files, and then double-click **garden57.jpg**. The picture's filename and a preview appear in the dialog box. See Figure 4-35.

Figure 4-35 ▶ **Photo Gallery Properties dialog box**

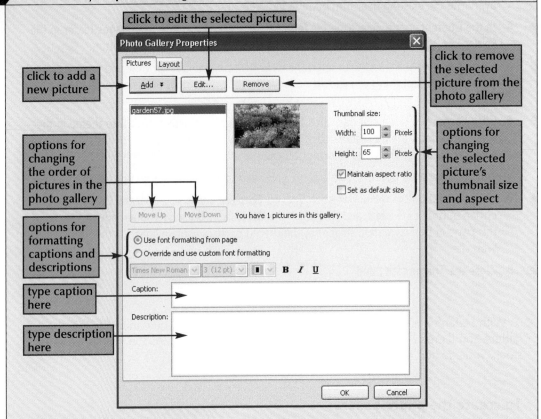

The next step is to add the caption and description for this photo. Notice the two option buttons in the middle of the dialog box. If you want the caption and description to use the same formatting as other text in the page, click the Use font formatting from page option button. If you want to format the caption and description using the formatting options in the dialog box, click the Override and use custom font formatting option button.

Because the deer.htm page uses a theme, you will not use custom formatting, which will ensure that the photo gallery has the same font style as other text in the page.

▶ 4. Click the **Caption** text box, and then type **Mexican Bush Sage**.

▶ 5. Press the **Tab** key to move to the Description text box, and then type **Sages are very drought-tolerant and deer-resistant plants. They need good drainage and full sun, and come in a variety of colors.**

▶ 6. Repeat Steps 3 through 5 to add the **garden82.jpg** picture to the photo gallery with the caption **Salvia Greggii** and the description **This plant comes in many colors and blooms from spring to the first freeze. Very drought-tolerant and the deer don't like it!**

▶ 7. Repeat Steps 3 through 5 to add the **garden98.jpg** picture to the photo gallery with the caption **Black-eyed Susan** and the description **This self-seeding perennial thrives in most soil types, loves full sun, and blooms all summer.**

▶ 8. Click the **OK** button. FrontPage creates the photo gallery in the deer.htm page. (Scroll down the page as necessary to see the photo gallery.) See Figure 4-36.

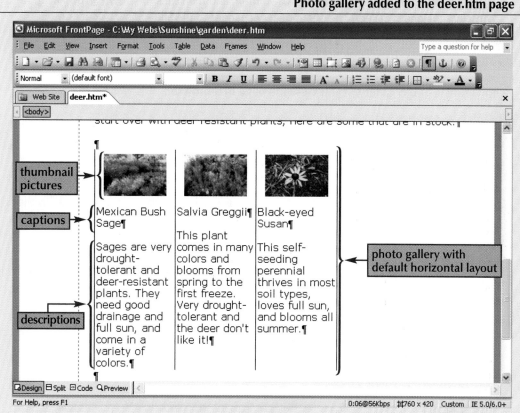

When you create a photo gallery, the default style is the horizontal layout, which arranges thumbnails of the pictures you selected into rows, with their captions and descriptions positioned below the pictures. Clicking a thumbnail picture opens the full-size version of the picture. There are three other layouts that you can use for a photo gallery. Brett wants to see the other layouts, so you need to open the Photo Gallery Properties dialog box again.

To change the photo gallery's layout:

1. Double-click the photo gallery to open the Photo Gallery Properties dialog box, and then click the **Layout** tab. The Layout tab contains options for arranging the pictures in the photo gallery. The default, Horizontal Layout, displays each picture, its caption, and its description in a row format. You can change the number of pictures to display in each row by changing the value in the Number of pictures per row box. The default value is to display five pictures in each row.

2. Click the **Montage Layout** option. This layout arranges pictures as a collage. When you point to a picture in the collage, its caption appears. This layout does not support descriptions.

3. Click the **Slide Show** option. This layout arranges the pictures in a scrollable format, with the selected image being displayed in its full size with a description below it.

4. Click the **Vertical Layout** option. This layout displays pictures in columns with their captions and descriptions.

   Brett likes the Slide Show layout, so you will select that one.

5. Click the **Slide Show** option, click the **OK** button, and then click the **down** arrow key ↓ to deselect the photo gallery. The photo gallery changes to the Slide Show layout.

6. Save the deer.htm page and save the pictures in the Web site's images folder.

To view the photo gallery, you'll view the page in a browser.

To view the photo gallery in a browser:

1. Click the **Preview** button 🔍 on the Standard toolbar, and then scroll down the page so you can see the entire photo gallery.

2. Point to the first thumbnail picture on the left. The ScreenTip, "Mexican Bush Sage," is the picture's caption. The full-size picture and its caption and description appear below the thumbnail pictures.

3. Click the middle thumbnail picture (with the ScreenTip "Salvia Greggii"). The Slide Show changes to display the full-size picture, caption, and description for this Salvia Greggii picture. See Figure 4-37.

Figure 4-37 ▶ **Photo gallery with Slide Show layout**

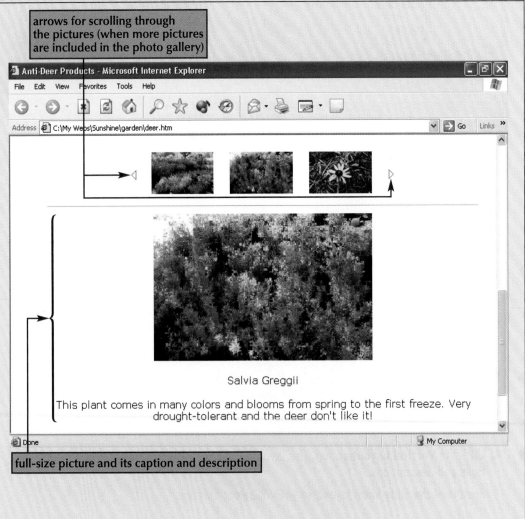

arrows for scrolling through the pictures (when more pictures are included in the photo gallery)

full-size picture and its caption and description

4. Click the third thumbnail picture to display it in the photo gallery.

5. Close your browser.

As you look at the completed photo gallery in the deer.htm page, Brett wonders if you can insert a heading to showcase this new feature. You suggest that instead of using a heading and plain text, you can use WordArt to create an interesting graphic from normal text.

Using Drawings, AutoShapes, and WordArt in a Page

Sometimes the content of your Web pages requires you to draw objects, such as arrows and callouts, or shapes, such as hearts or smiling faces. In other cases, you might want to format text in a special way by controlling its color, font, and appearance. In these cases, you can insert a drawing, AutoShape, or WordArt in the page.

A **drawing** is a canvas object that contains other objects, such as text boxes and arrows. For example, you might use a drawing object to create the simple diagram shown in Figure 4-38 on the home page to call attention to the nursery's sale on deer-resistant plants. If you have used the drawing tools in another program, such as Microsoft Paint, Word, or PowerPoint, you'll find that the tools in FrontPage work the same way.

Canvas object displayed by a browser ◀ **Figure 4-38**

To insert a drawing into a Web page, click Insert on the menu bar, point to Picture, and then click New Drawing. A canvas object opens in the Web page, along with the Drawing and Drawing Canvas toolbars. You use the buttons on the Drawing toolbar to draw lines, change colors, and add text boxes. Clicking the Fit, Expand, or Scale Drawing buttons on the Drawing Canvas toolbar lets you control the size of the canvas object. Figure 4-39 shows the Drawing toolbar, the Drawing Canvas toolbar, and the drawing object shown in Figure 4-38 in FrontPage.

| Figure 4-39 | Canvas object in FrontPage |

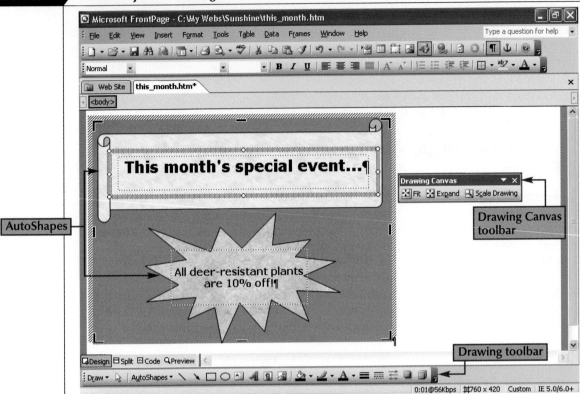

An **AutoShape** is a predesigned shape, such as an arrow, bracket, square, circle, banner, star, or callout. Figure 4-39 includes two AutoShapes—a horizontal scroll at the top of the canvas and an explosion 1 star at the bottom. You insert an AutoShape in a canvas by clicking the AutoShapes button on the Drawing toolbar to open a menu with several AutoShape categories. Pointing to the Lines AutoShape category, for example, opens a palette of line styles that you can use to draw a line. After clicking a line style, you use the pointer to draw a line in a Web page. FrontPage then automatically generates the HTML tags required to position and draw the object. You can also insert an AutoShape into a Web page (without the canvas) by clicking Insert on the menu bar, pointing to Picture, and then clicking AutoShapes. The AutoShapes toolbar then opens and provides buttons for accessing the same AutoShape styles available on the Drawing toolbar.

WordArt is a text object to which you can apply a font, font size, and special effects. When creating a WordArt object in a Web page, you can either select existing text or insert new text. In either case, when you create a WordArt object, you can select the style, font, font size, and font style for your text. After creating the WordArt object, you can use the WordArt toolbar to change its attributes or double-click the object to edit the text.

Creating a WordArt Object in a Page

- If necessary, select the existing text that you will format as a WordArt object.
- Click Insert on the menu bar, point to Picture, and then click WordArt. The WordArt Gallery dialog box opens.
- Click the WordArt style to use for your text, and then click the OK button. The Edit WordArt Text dialog box opens.
- Select the font, font size, and font style for your text. If necessary, type or edit the text for the WordArt object in the Text text box.
- Click the OK button.
- Use the WordArt toolbar to change the color, shape, letter height, direction, alignment, or character spacing of the WordArt object, if desired.
- Use the sizing handles on the WordArt object to resize the WordArt object, if desired.

Brett wants to use a WordArt object to add visual interest to the deer.htm page.

To create a WordArt object:

▶ **1.** Scroll up the page as necessary, insert a blank paragraph above the photo gallery, and then, if necessary, position the insertion point on the new line.

▶ **2.** Click **Insert** on the menu bar, point to **Picture**, and then click **WordArt**. The WordArt Gallery dialog box opens and shows the WordArt styles that you can apply to text. See Figure 4-40.

WordArt Gallery dialog box ◀ **Figure 4-40**

▶ **3.** Click the first style in the second row, and then click the **OK** button. The Edit WordArt Text dialog box opens. You use this dialog box to specify the font, font size, and font style for your WordArt object. Notice that default text "Your Text Here" appears in the Text text box. If you select text before creating the WordArt object, the text you selected will appear in the Text text box. In either case, you can edit or type the text to include in the WordArt object.

▶ **4.** Type **This week's featured deer-resistant plants are on sale!** to replace the default text in the WordArt object.

When you create a WordArt object, the default font is Arial Black and default font size is 36 points. The WordArt text is formatted using italics because you selected a WordArt style that uses italics. The font size is large for the amount of text you entered, so you'll reduce it.

▶ 5. Click the **Size** list arrow, and then scroll up and click **14**. The text changes to use the new specifications.

▶ 6. Click the **OK** button. The WordArt object appears in the Web page and is selected, and the WordArt toolbar opens. See Figure 4-41.

Figure 4-41 | **WordArt object added to the deer.htm page**

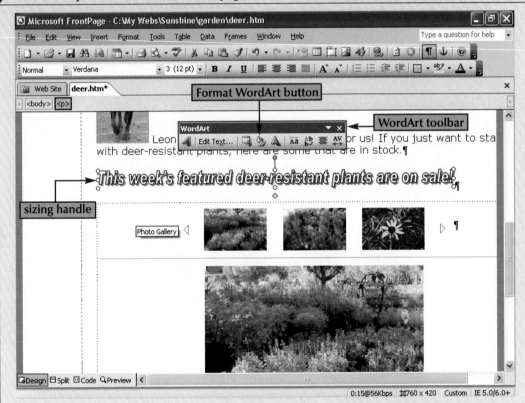

Trouble? If the WordArt toolbar blocks the WordArt object in the Web page, drag it to another location or dock it below the Formatting toolbar.

When a WordArt object is selected, the WordArt toolbar appears. The buttons on the WordArt toolbar let you change the WordArt text and the style, color, shape, letter height, direction, alignment, and character spacing of the letters in the WordArt object. There are two options for changing the alignment of a WordArt object. The first option is to align the WordArt text within the WordArt object. The second option is to align the WordArt object on the Web page. Brett likes the WordArt object but suggests that you change its color and center it on the page.

To change a WordArt object:

1. With the WordArt object selected, click the **Center** button ▤ on the Formatting toolbar. The WordArt object is centered on the page.

2. Click the **Format WordArt** button 🦋 on the WordArt toolbar. The Format WordArt dialog box opens. See Figure 4-42.

Format WordArt dialog box ◄ | **Figure 4-42**

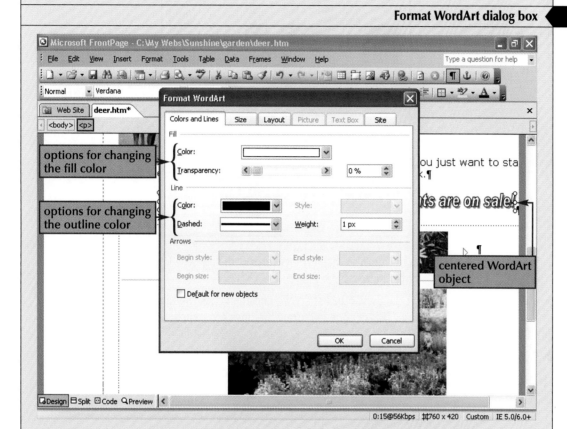

You can use the Colors and Lines tab in this dialog box to control the color, style, and weight of the lines and the fill color of the letters in the WordArt object. The Size tab lets you control the size, rotation, and scale of a WordArt object. The Layout tab lets you control the positioning style of the WordArt object. Usually, you can accept the default options on the Size and Layout tabs.

Instead of filling the WordArt object with a color, you want to show Brett how to fill the object with a pattern or a texture.

3. In the Fill section, click the **Color** list arrow, and then click **Fill Effects**. The Fill Effects dialog box opens. You can fill a WordArt object with a gradient color by applying a pattern of shading of one or more colors, a texture, a pattern, or a picture that you select. You'll apply a texture.

4. Click the **Texture** tab, and then click the last texture in the third row. After clicking the texture, its name (Bouquet) appears below the samples. See Figure 4-43.

Figure 4-43   **Fill Effects dialog box**

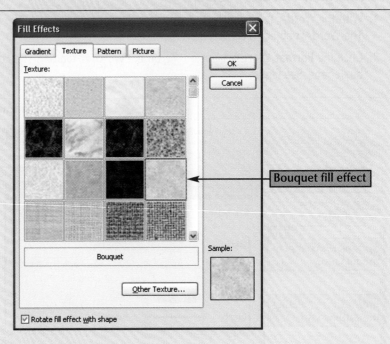

5. Click the **OK** button to return to the Format WordArt dialog box. The texture you selected appears in the Color list box.

6. In the Line section, click the **Color** list arrow, and then click the **Light Blue** color (the sixth color in the third row). This change will draw the lines around each letter using a light-blue color.

7. Click the **OK** button, and then click an empty area in the Web page to deselect the WordArt object. The WordArt object now has a textured fill and a light-blue border. See Figure 4-44.

Completed WordArt object | **Figure 4-44**

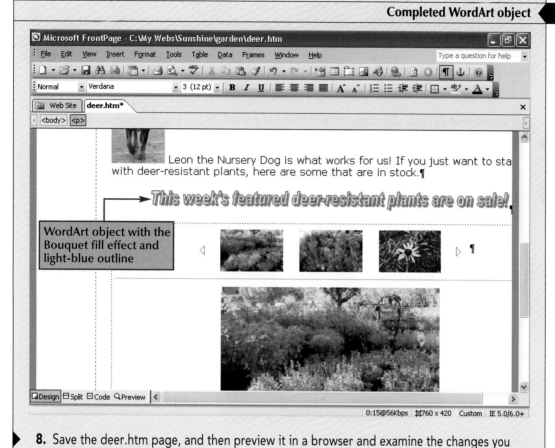

8. Save the deer.htm page, and then preview it in a browser and examine the changes you made in this page.

9. Close your browser.

You have added several new elements to the deer.htm page, and you want to show Brett the HTML tags and scripts that FrontPage created to implement them.

Examining the HTML Document for the deer.htm Page

FrontPage stores the files needed to support the photo gallery in the Web site's photogallery folder. FrontPage stores most of the files that it uses to create the interactive buttons and animations, shared borders, link bars, and themes in the Web site's hidden folders and files. The _borders and _themes folders are the primary folders in which the theme's shared border and theme files are stored. FrontPage does not display hidden folders in Folders view unless you configure it to do so by clicking Tools on the menu bar, clicking Site Settings, clicking the Advanced tab, and then selecting the Show hidden files and folders check box. After closing the Site Settings dialog box and refreshing the Web site, you can see the Web site's hidden files and folders in Folders view.

Shared borders and themes are implemented in FrontPage using meta tags (which were described in Tutorial 2). When you enable a Web site to use a theme and shared borders, FrontPage adds meta tags to the affected pages. FrontPage then uses these meta tags to display the theme and shared borders by using the files that are stored in the Web site's hidden _themes and _borders folders.

The banners and link bars were created using FrontPage Web components, which are identified in each page's HTML document with a comment tag (<!-- ... -->). If a Web browser cannot process a component, it will ignore the instructions in the comment tags. When you use Code view to examine an HTML document that contains a component, FrontPage displays the component in a different color to distinguish it.

To view the HTML document for themes and FrontPage components:

► **1.** Change to Code view, and then press **Ctrl + End** to scroll to the bottom of the document. Figure 4-45 shows the HTML that creates the WordArt object and the photo gallery.

Figure 4-45	HTML document for the deer.htm page

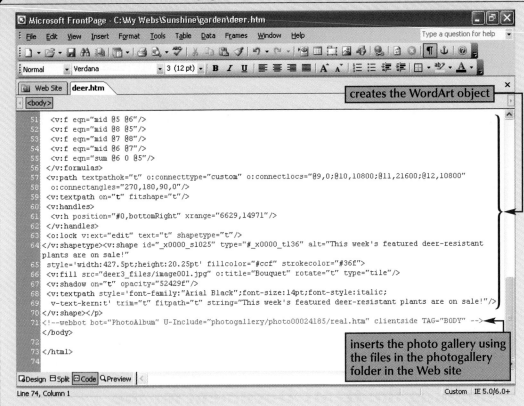

► **2.** Scroll to the top of the page. There are two meta tags at the beginning of the document that identify the theme and the borders to include in this page.

► **3.** Change to Design view, close the garden Web site, and then close FrontPage.

Helen and Brett like the Anti-Deer Products page and are certain that it will be a useful page in the Web site. In Tutorial 5, you will show Brett how to create tables and frames pages in a Web site.

Review

Session 4.3 Quick Check

1. True or False: When you create a caption in the photo gallery, you have the option of applying custom formatting to the text.
2. How do pictures in a photo gallery appear on the page when you apply the montage layout to the photo gallery?
3. Which photo gallery layout does not support captions?
4. The files that create a photo gallery in a Web site are stored in the site's _____ folder.
5. What is a drawing?
6. Arrows, callouts, and special graphics such as a heart shape are examples of _____.
7. True or False: WordArt creates a picture from text using characteristics that you specify.

Review

Tutorial Summary

In this tutorial, you learned how to use features in a Web site that are dependent upon the organization of pages in Navigation view. After positioning existing pages in the navigation structure, you learned how to create shared borders in a Web site and how to change the default presentation of links in the site's link bar components. You also learned how to turn off a shared border in a Web page and how to replace the content formerly supplied by the shared border. You also made changes in Navigation view to maintain the Web site, including removing a page from the site's link bar components, renaming a page, adding and deleting pages, and moving pages to reposition them. Finally, you learned how to create a custom link bar in a Web site to add links based on a separate navigation structure in Navigation view.

You also practiced formatting pages using preexisting, customized, and new themes. As you develop Web sites in the future, you can use existing themes and create your own themes to streamline the process of formatting your site's pages.

Finally, you inserted a photo gallery and a WordArt object in a page to organize pictures related to a single topic and to create visual interest using normal text. These features are easy to implement and enhance the appearance and utility of your Web site.

Key Terms

AutoShape	link bar component	shared border
child page	page banner	theme
color scheme	parent page	WordArt
drawing	photo gallery	

Practice

Practice the skills you learned in the tutorial using the same case scenario.

Review Assignments

Data File needed for these Review Assignments: garden99.jpg

Brett wants to make a few changes to the Web site. First, he wants to change the font used in the page banner of the Garden Web Site theme. Next, in the Anti-Deer Products page, he wants to add another plant to the photo gallery and change the WordArt object text to indicate that the featured plants are 10% off. Finally, he wants to create two child pages of the Irrigation page—one each for residential and commercial systems. Because Chad

Schomaker, supervisor of the irrigation work at Sunshine, has not yet completed these new pages, Brett wants to add them to the navigation structure but not to the site's link bars.

If necessary, start FrontPage, make sure you have your Data Files, and then do the following:

1. Open the **garden** Web site from the location where your Web sites are stored, and then open the **deer.htm** page in Design view.

2. Scroll down the **deer.htm** page, and then double-click the WordArt object. Change the text in the WordArt object to "This week's featured deer-resistant plants are 10% off!" Change the font to Verdana, the font size to 16, and the font style to bold. Close the dialog box.

3. Click the WordArt Gallery button on the WordArt toolbar, and then change the WordArt style to the first style in the first row.

4. Click the Format WordArt button on the WordArt toolbar, and then set the fill effect to a two-color, diagonal-up gradient. In the Colors section, click the Two colors option button. Click the Color 1 list arrow, and then select the Yellow color. Select Light Orange as the second color, and then click the Diagonal up option button in the Shading styles section. Click the OK button, and then set the line color to Orange.

5. Double-click the photo gallery in the **deer.htm** page, and then add the **garden99.jpg** picture from the Tutorial.04\Review folder included with your Data Files to the photo gallery. Use the caption "Mexican Butterfly Weed" and the description "This plant blooms from spring to fall. The deer don't like it, but the butterflies and hummingbirds do!"

6. Use the Move Up button to change the order of the pictures so the **garden99.jpg** picture is first in the list. Save the **deer.htm** page and save the new picture in the Web site's images folder.

7. Open the Theme task pane, and then customize the Garden Web Site theme to use a bold, 24-point, Tahoma font for the page banner. Save the revised Garden Web Site theme, and then apply it to all pages in the Web site. Save and close the **deer.htm** page.

8. Click the Garden Web Site theme in the All available themes section of the Theme task pane, click the Vivid colors check box on the Theme task pane to clear it, click the Garden Web Site theme again, and then apply the Garden Web Site theme to all pages in the Web site. (*Hint:* Do not use the Garden Web Site theme in the Web site default theme section of the Theme task pane; your changes will not be updated.) Close the Theme task pane

9. In Navigation view, create two new child pages of the Irrigation page in the navigation structure titled Residential Systems and Commercial Systems. Change to Folders view and rename these pages **res_sys.htm** and **comm_sys.htm**, respectively.

10. Return to Navigation view, and then set the pages you created in Step 9 so they will not appear in the site's link bar components.

11. Open the **irr.htm** page in Design view and confirm that links to the child pages do not appear in the left shared border, and then close the **irr.htm** page.

12. Open the home page in Design view, and then click the add link link on the custom link bar. Add the **deer.htm** page to the link bar. In the Add to Link Bar dialog box, change the Text to display to "Anti-Deer Products." Save the home page, and then preview it in a browser. Use the link bars in the site's pages to navigate the Web site. Print the Anti-Deer Products page and then close your browser.

13. In Navigation view, make sure that the Folder List is turned off, use the Zoom list arrow to change this setting to 50%, and then print Navigation view.

14. Close the **garden** Web site, and then close FrontPage.

Challenge

Expand on the skills you learned in this tutorial to customize a theme in a new way, add a picture to a shared border, and create your own WordArt object.

Case Problem 1

Data File needed for this Case Problem: bullet.gif

Buffalo Trading Post Nicole Beirne realizes that as business at Buffalo Trading Post (BTP) continues to grow, she will be adding more Web pages to the company's Web site. Nicole wants to make sure that it is easy to update the site when new pages are added. She asks you to change the existing link bars to ones generated by FrontPage, which will be updated automatically when new pages are added to the site. Also, she wants you to add a theme to the pages so they will have a consistent appearance.

If necessary, start FrontPage, make sure you have your Data Files, and then do the following:

1. Open the **buffalo** Web site from the location where your Web sites are stored. (If you did not create this Web site in Tutorial 1 and change it in Tutorials 2 and 3, ask your instructor for assistance.)

2. Change to Navigation view, and then add the existing pages as follows. The home page should be the top-level page; and the What, How, and Who pages should be child pages of the home page. If necessary, change the title of the home page to "Buffalo Trading Post."

3. Add three new pages to the navigation structure as child pages of the What page: Accessories, Women's Clothing, and Children's Clothing. After adding these pages to the navigation structure, change to Folders view and change their filenames to **acc.htm**, **women.htm**, and **child.htm**, respectively. Return to Navigation view and print it.

4. Open the home page in Design view, and then add a bottom shared border to all the pages in the Web site.

5. Select the paragraph at the bottom of the home page (it begins with the text "BTP™ is"). Cut this paragraph from the page, select the comment placeholder text that appears in the bottom shared border, and then paste the paragraph into the bottom shared border. If necessary, delete any blank lines that appear in the bottom shared border.

6. Position the insertion point to the left of the "B" in "BTP" in the bottom shared border, and then insert a horizontal line.

Explore

7. Change the background color of the bottom shared border to white. (*Hint:* Use the Border Properties dialog box to make this change.) Save the home page.

8. Apply the Poetic theme to the entire Web site. (If you do not have this theme, select another theme.) The theme should use vivid colors, active graphics, and a background picture. Save the home page, and then preview it in a browser to observe the formatting applied by the theme. When you have finished examining the home page, close your browser.

Explore

9. Customize the Web site's default theme to make the following changes. First, change the list bullet 1 picture to the **bullet.gif** file in the Tutorial.04\Case1 folder included with your Data Files. Next, change the font of the horizontal and vertical navigation buttons to Arial Black. Save the customized theme as Buffalo Web Site, apply the Buffalo Web Site theme to all pages in the Web site, and then save the home page.

10. Delete the user-defined link bar, the **buffalo.gif** picture, and any blank paragraphs that remain at the top of the home page; open the **who.htm** page and then delete the user-defined link bar, the **who_logo.gif** picture, and any blank paragraphs that remain at the top of the page; and then open the **how.htm** page and delete the user-defined link bar and the **how_logo.gif** picture. In the **how.htm** page, move the top bookmark to the left of the "How It Works" text in the bulleted list, and then delete any blank paragraphs that appear above the bulleted list. Save all of these pages by clicking File on the menu bar, and then clicking Save All.

Explore

11. Apply top and left shared borders to the entire Web site. Include navigation buttons in both borders.

12. Open the home page, and then display the DHTML Effects toolbar. Select the animated text ("Welcome to the Buffalo Trading Post!"), and then click the Remove Effect button on the DHTML Effects toolbar. Close the DHTML Effects toolbar.

13. With the "Welcome to the Buffalo Trading Post!" heading selected, change it to a WordArt object that uses a style of your choice and a 24-point font. Center the WordArt object in the Web page and make sure that it appears on its own line. Change the WordArt object's color to plum and experiment with different formatting options to make the WordArt object easy to read and visually interesting. When you have finished, save the home page.

14. Turn off the top and left shared borders in the home page only. At the top of the page, insert a picture page banner with the text "Buffalo Trading Post." On the next line, insert a horizontal link bar based on the Web site's navigation structure with links to child-level pages formatted using the site's theme. Save the home page.

Explore

15. Click to the left of the "B" in "BTP" in the bottom shared border, and then insert the **buffalo.gif** picture from the Web site's images folder. Save the home page.

16. Open the home page in a browser and use the link bars to navigate the site's pages. Use your browser to print the home page, and then close your browser.

17. Close the **buffalo** Web site and then close FrontPage.

Create

Create a Web site's navigation structure and a new page in the Web site.

Case Problem 2

Data Files needed for this Case Problem: italy.gif, mexico.gif, and us.gif

Garden Grill   Meghan Elliott and Callan Murphy want to include Garden Grill's menu in the Web site so patrons can browse it before coming to the restaurant. They anticipate including pages that feature entrees, sandwiches, appetizers, and desserts. These pages aren't ready yet, but Meghan and Callan want you to add them to the Web site now so they are part of the site's navigation structure. Meghan and Callan also want to promote the new "Today's Special" feature at Garden Grill. They also want to include the daily special on the Web site and ask you to create a new specials page. In addition to promoting the daily special, Meghan and Callan also want to include suggested dishes from Italy, Mexico, and America. After creating this content, they want you to format the Web site using a theme and link bars to ensure that the site is visually appealing and easy to navigate.

If necessary, start FrontPage, make sure you have your Data Files, and then do the following:

1. Open the **grill** Web site from the location where your Web sites are stored. (If you did not create this Web site in Tutorial 1 and change it in Tutorials 2 and 3, ask your instructor for assistance.)

Explore

2. Change to Navigation view and create the navigation structure shown in Figure 4-46. In Folders view, change the filenames for the Appetizers and Sandwiches pages to **app.htm** and **sand.htm**, respectively.

Figure 4-46

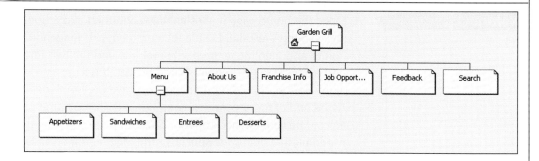

3. In Folders view, right-click any blank area in the Contents pane, point to New, and then click Blank Page. Change the filename of the new page to **specials.htm**, and then change the page title to Specials.

Explore

4. Open the Specials page in Design view, and then create the content shown in Figure 4-47. The pictures are saved in the Tutorial.04\Case2 folder included with your Data Files. When you are finished, save the page and save the pictures in the Web site's images folder.

Figure 4-47

Today's Special

Extra Hot Chili

Try a bowl of our home-baked chili with cheddar cheese. This dish is not for folks who can't take the heat! Served with a bottomless glass of iced tea for only $3.95.

And may we suggest...

...something from Italy?	**...something from Mexico?**	**...something from America?**
Who can resist our 16-layer lasagna with three different cheeses? Served with our garden side salad and your choice of dressing, and our famous garlic bread.	If you're in the mood for something spicy, try our roasted chicken enchiladas with green chili sauce. Served with Spanish rice and your choice of refried or charro beans.	Try our delicious chicken fried steak with country gravy and your choice of golden french fries or mashed potatoes. Served with a garden side salad and your choice of dressing.

Explore

5. Change to Navigation view, and then create a custom link bar named **Specials** that includes links to the site's home page and the Menu page. In a new centered paragraph at the top of the **specials.htm** page that is formatted with the Normal style,

insert the Specials custom link bar. Choose the options to arrange the buttons horizontally and to format them using the Web site's theme. Save the **specials.htm** page.

6. Open the home page in Design view, and then add a bottom shared border to all pages in the Web site. Delete the comment text placeholder in the bottom shared border and then move the horizontal line and the two lines at the bottom of the home page into the bottom shared border. If necessary, delete any blank paragraphs in the bottom shared border, and then save the home page.

7. At the end of the second paragraph of text on the home page, add the following sentence: "Be sure to check out our Specials page!" Format the word "Specials" as a hyperlink that opens the **specials.htm** page, and then save the home page.

8. Add the Watermark theme to the entire Web site. Be sure to select the options to use vivid colors, active graphics, and a background picture.

9. Save the home page, and then preview it in a browser. Use the links to navigate the site, use your browser to print the **specials.htm** page, and then close your browser.

10. Close the **grill** Web site and then close FrontPage.

Case Problem 3

Data Files needed for this Case Problem: benecr.jpg, buggy.jpg, conf.jpg, couches.jpg, manu.jpg, pic2.jpg, retail.jpg, sndcrf.jpg, sw.gif

Swenson Auctioneers   Scott Swenson wants to begin working on defining the categories of auctions conducted by Swenson Auctioneers. He has some pictures that he wants you to insert into the Web site in an organized way. You suggest arranging the pictures in a photo gallery, and Scott agrees with your idea. You also want to streamline the Web site's appearance by creating a new theme that uses the existing background picture in the Web pages. By defining the background picture, fonts, and bullet characters with a theme, you can save some time by applying the theme to new pages instead of formatting these elements individually.

If necessary, start FrontPage, make sure you have your Data Files, and then do the following:

1. Open the **swenson** Web site from the location where your Web sites are stored. (If you did not create this Web site in Tutorial 1 and change it in Tutorials 2 and 3, ask your instructor for assistance.)

2. Position the site's existing pages in the navigation structure as follows. The home page is the top-level page in the Web site, and the **upcoming.htm**, **services.htm**, **team.htm**, and **mail.htm** pages are child pages of the home page.

3. Create a new theme named Swenson Web Site as follows:

a. For the background picture, use the **back.gif** file stored in the Web site's images folder.

b. Use the **sw.gif** file in the Tutorial.04\Case3 folder included with your Data Files as the List Bullet 1 picture.

c. Change the body text font to Arial.

d. Change the Heading 1, Heading 2, and Heading 3 font to Arial Black.

e. Change the color scheme to Street Writing.

f. Select the options for active graphics and a background picture.

4. Save the Swenson Web Site theme, and then apply it as the default theme to all pages in the Web site. (*Hint:* After creating the theme, you must apply it as the default theme from the All available themes section of the Theme task pane.)

5. Open the **services.htm** page in Design view, and then format the four paragraphs below the paragraph that begins "As skilled marketing specialists" as a bulleted list, observing the bullet characters added by the Swenson Web Site theme. Save the **services.htm** page.

Explore

6. Open the **upcoming.htm** page in Design view, and then scroll to the bottom of the page. In a new, centered paragraph, insert a WordArt object with the text "Auction Categories" and format it using a WordArt style of your choice and 24-point Arial Black font. Change the WordArt object's color fill color to red and the line color to black.

Explore

7. In a new centered paragraph below the WordArt object you created in Step 6, insert the following pictures and captions into a photo gallery as follows. Format each caption using bold text, and arrange the pictures in a Slide Show format. (*Hint:* You can add multiple pictures to the photo gallery at the same time by selecting them in the File Open dialog box, and then clicking Open. You need to set the caption to bold only once. You won't insert any descriptions.) All pictures are saved in the Tutorial.04\Case3 folder included with your Data Files.
    a. **conf.jpg**: Business Equipment & Computers
    b. **manu.jpg**: Manufacturing & Heavy Equipment
    c. **couches.jpg**: Furniture, Art, & Rugs
    d. **sndcrf.jpg**: Sound & Lighting
    e. **pic2.jpg**: Special Use
    f. **retail.jpg**: Retail FF&E
    g. **buggy.jpg**: Estates & Antiques
    h. **benecr.jpg**: Benefit Auctions
8. Save the **upcoming.htm** page and save the pictures in the Web site's images folder.
9. Preview the home page in a browser, and then print the **upcoming.htm** page with the Estates & Antiques picture displayed. (*Hint:* Click the arrow to scroll the thumbnail pictures.) Close your browser.
10. Close the **swenson** Web site and then close FrontPage.

Case Problem 4

Challenge

Customize a theme for a Web site.

There are no Data Files needed for this Case Problem.

Mortgage Services, Inc. Natalie Fuselier wants to reformat the Web site's pages to ensure that they have a consistent appearance and hyperlinks to other pages in the Web site. She asks you to make some changes to accomplish these tasks. Because she wants to distinguish the Credit Repair Services page as being separate from the rest of the site, she asks you to format this page differently.

If necessary, start FrontPage, and then do the following:

1. Open the **loan** Web site from the location where your Web sites are stored. (If you did not create this Web site in Tutorial 1 and change it in Tutorials 2 and 3, ask your instructor for assistance.)
2. Position the site's existing pages in the navigation structure as follows. The home page is the top-level page in the Web site, and the **repair.htm**, **loantype.htm**, **apply.htm**, **help.htm**, **resource.htm**, and **contact.htm** pages are child pages of the home page.

Explore

3. Set the **repair.htm** page so it is not included in the site's link bars.
4. Open the home page in Design view, and then delete the user-defined link bar, the Mortgage Services, Inc. heading, and any blank paragraphs at the top of the page. Delete these same items from the **loantype.htm**, **help.htm**, and **resource.htm** pages. Click File on the menu bar, and then click Save All to save your changes.

5. Apply the Profile theme to all pages in the Web site, and then customize the Profile theme as follows:
   a. Change the body text to Times New Roman.
   b. Change the font used in the page banner to Arial Black.
   c. Change the font and style of the horizontal navigation buttons and the vertical navigation buttons to 8-point, bold, and Arial.
   d. Save the theme using the name Loan Web Site, and then apply it to all pages in the Web site.
6. Open the **repair.htm** page in Design view, remove the theme from this page only, and then save the page.
7. Create top and left shared borders for all pages in the Web site and select the options to include navigation buttons in both shared borders.

8. In the **repair.htm** page, remove the top and left shared borders for this page only. Replace the Heading 1 paragraph at the top of the page with a picture page banner. Apply the Blends theme to the **repair.htm** page only. Select the options for vivid colors, active graphics, and a background picture. Save the **repair.htm** page and close the Theme task pane.
9. Preview the home page in a browser, and then print the home page and the **repair.htm** page. Close your browser.
10. Close the **loan** Web site and then close FrontPage.

Quick Check Answers

Session 4.1

1. to identify the relationships between pages so you can create link bar components and page banners in a Web site
2. You can create shared borders at the top, bottom, left, and right. The top, left, and right shared borders can include link bar components.
3. False
4. False
5. True
6. You can delete the page from the navigation structure only (which removes the link for the page from the site's link bars), or you can delete the page from the navigation structure and the Web site.
7. Open the page in Design view, click Format on the menu bar, click Shared Borders, click the Current page option button, clear the check box for the shared border(s) to remove, and then click the OK button.
8. True

Session 4.2

1. A theme is a collection of design elements such as bullets, backgrounds, table borders, fonts, and pictures that you can apply to a Web site or one or more Web pages.
2. True
3. The theme's color scheme changes to use a brighter, more intense set of colors.
4. True
5. colors, graphics, and text
6. False

Session 4.3

1. True
2. The pictures appear as a collage.
3. All of the photo gallery layouts support captions.
4. photogallery
5. a canvas object that contains objects such as text boxes and arrows
6. AutoShapes
7. True

Objectives

Session 5.1
- Create a table in a Web page
- Align a table and its cells
- Enter data in a table
- Insert, delete, resize, merge, and split cells
- Add a caption to a table
- Apply a Table AutoFormat

Session 5.2
- Create a frames page
- Create hyperlinks in a frames page and specify their targets
- Examine and change a frame's properties
- Change a frame's target
- Add a new frame to a frames page
- Print a frames page

Creating Tables and Frames

Revising the Bulk Goods Samples and Irrigation Pages and Creating the Lawn Care Page

Case

Sunshine Landscape & Garden Center

Brett Kizer, owner of the Sunshine Landscape & Garden Center, compliments you this morning on the Web site. He really likes the theme that you applied to the site's pages and the consistency of the navigation features provided by the link bar components in the pages' shared borders. Brett is eager to finish the Web site and make it available to his customers.

As you review the site's content with Brett in your regular weekly meeting, you suggest a different arrangement of content in the existing Bulk Goods Samples page. Currently, this page includes pictures that you intend to link to child pages of the Bulk Goods Samples page. However, as you view the page with Brett, you tell him that a table might provide a better way to organize the pictures. Brett is surprised that you would suggest using a table in this manner, because he doesn't think that drawing lines around the pictures would look very good. You tell Brett that tables are used very frequently in Web pages as a way of controlling the position of objects, including pictures and text. When used as a layout tool, a table usually includes invisible borders so that the table is transparent to the user. Because most browsers interpret the HTML tags that create and format tables consistently, a table is an important Web design tool.

Student Data Files

To complete this tutorial, you will need your ending files from Tutorial 4 and the following Data Files. Additional Data Files needed to complete the end-of-tutorial exercises are listed with the Review Assignments and Case Problems.

▼ Tutorial.05

▽ Tutorial folder

    irr folder

    lawn.htm

As you are talking with Brett, Helen Xiao, Sunshine's horticulturist, mentions that many customers have been seeking help in solving problems with their lawns. She started a Web page that will provide answers to common questions and asks if you can finish it for her. After looking at the information Helen plans to provide in this page, you tell Brett that this page is an excellent candidate for a traditional table with gridlines to identify each cell.

Earlier in the Web site development process, Chad Schomaker, Sunshine's irrigation specialist, had asked you to add two pages to the Web site—one each for residential and commercial customers. After creating the content he wants to include in the Web site, Chad decides that he doesn't have enough content to justify having different pages for different kinds of customers. He shows you the content he completed and you tell him and Brett that this content is well suited for a frames page. You'll create a frames page to display Chad's pages in the Web site.

Session 5.1

Understanding Tables

You are probably already familiar with the process of creating tables in Microsoft Word documents. In FrontPage, just as in Word, a **table** consists of one or more rows of cells that organize and arrange data. A **cell** is the smallest component of a table. You can place text or a picture in a table cell. You can also create a **nested table**, which is a table within a table cell.

If your Web site development plan includes a Web page with a table, you should sketch out the desired appearance of the table before you create it using FrontPage. Sketching a table first helps you plan how many rows and columns you will need. Although you can add or delete columns after creating the table, it is easier to create the table correctly from the start.

The steps you take to create a table using FrontPage are similar to those you would use to create a table with Word. To create a table quickly, you can use the Insert Table button; clicking that toolbar button displays the **Insert Table button grid**, a miniature table with four rows and five columns that you can use to specify the table's size. If your table is relatively small (fewer than four rows by five columns), you can click a cell in the grid to specify the desired table size. If your table is larger than four rows by five columns, you can drag the last cell in the grid to enlarge it to the desired table size; when you release the mouse button, FrontPage creates the desired table using the default settings for tables.

After creating a table, you can change its default properties, such as the size of the border, the cell padding, the cell spacing, and the table width. A **border** is a line that surrounds each cell and the entire table. **Cell padding** is the distance between the contents of a cell and the edge of the cell, measured in pixels. Increasing the cell padding adds space around the data in a cell. **Cell spacing** is the distance between table cells, also measured in pixels. Increasing the cell spacing adds space around the individual cells in a table.

You can specify the table width as a percentage of the width of the browser window or as a fixed width in pixels. Remember that a variety of computers and monitors will display your Web pages. For this reason, most developers set widths for their tables as a percentage of the screen's width (such as 85%), or as a fixed measurement (such as 620 pixels). You should specify these types of settings to ensure that all users of your Web pages will be able to view your tables correctly regardless of their particular monitors, computers, or Web browsers. A good rule of thumb for setting a table's width is to use a percentage for tables that contain mostly text and to use pixels when you need tight control over the placement of objects that have a fixed size, such as pictures.

Figure 5-1 shows a sketch of the table you will create in the Bulk Goods Samples page. The words "mulch," "soil," and "stone" are pictures that will include hyperlinks to open the mulch.htm, soil.htm, and stone.htm pages in the Web site. The pictures below each of these hyperlinks represent a sample of the medium (mulch, soil, and stone). Because the pictures have fixed sizes, you'll create the table by setting the width in pixels to ensure that the pictures appear as desired.

Sketch of the table for the bulk2.htm page | **Figure 5-1**

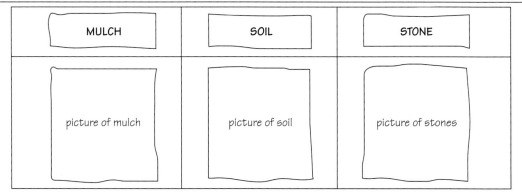

In addition to being able to create tables in a Web page, you can base the design of an entire Web page on a table. When a table is used to design a Web page, FrontPage calls it a layout table. A **layout table** is a framework that holds a page's contents. A **layout cell** is a region in a layout table that displays text, pictures, and other features in your Web page. For example, the layout table might include a cell at the top of a page to display a company's name and logo, cells that give the appearance of columns in the page, and a cell across the bottom of a page to display copyright information. FrontPage includes several templates that provide different visual appearances for a Web page. Layout table templates and options for changing them appear in the Layout Tables and Cells task pane. In this session, you'll learn about tables that appear as objects in a Web page, and not about tables that are used to design (lay out) an entire Web page's structure.

Creating a Table Using the Insert Table Button

After sketching the table, you are ready to create the new table in the desired location in the Web page.

Creating a Table in a Web Page

Reference Window

- Click the location in the Web page where you want to insert the table.
- Click the Insert Table button on the Standard toolbar to open the Insert Table button grid, click the grid cell that represents the desired table size or drag the last cell in the Insert Table button grid to expand the grid to the desired table size, and then release the mouse button.

or

- Click Table on the menu bar, point to Insert, and then click Table. In the Insert Table dialog box, specify the number of rows and columns in the Size section, and then click the OK button.

You'll show Brett how to use the Insert Table button on the Standard toolbar to make the changes to the bulk2.htm page.

To insert the table:

1. Start **FrontPage**, open the **garden** Web site from the location where your Web sites are stored, open the **bulk2.htm** page in Design view, and then if necessary click the **Show All** button ¶ on the Standard toolbar to display the nonprinting characters.

   The pictures in the page will function as hyperlinks to the Mulches, Soils, and Stones pages, duplicating the hyperlinks in the left shared border, so you'll turn off the left shared border for this page only before creating the table.

2. Click **Format** on the menu bar, and then click **Shared Borders**. The Shared Borders dialog box opens.

3. Click the **Current page** option button (if necessary), click the **Left** check box to clear it, and then click the **OK** button. The left shared border is removed from the page.

4. Click at the end of the paragraph at the top of the page (which ends "...install them for you!"), and then press the **Enter** key to create a new paragraph. You will insert the table here.

5. Click the **Insert Table** button 🔲 on the Standard toolbar to open the Insert Table button grid. You might notice that it is the same Insert Table button grid that Word uses.

6. Point to the third cell in the second row, as shown in Figure 5-2. Clicking this cell will create a table with two rows and three columns.

Figure 5-2	Insert Table button grid

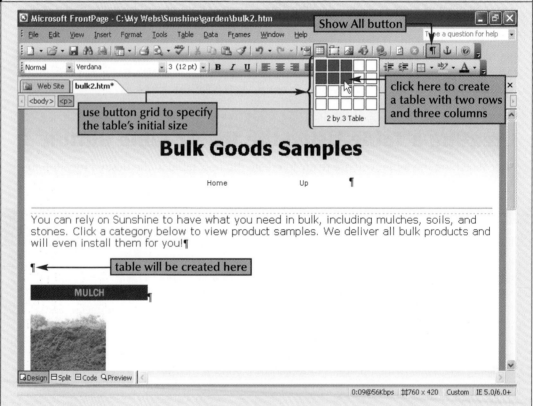

7. Click the third cell in the second row. The Insert Table button grid closes and a table with two rows and three columns is created in the Web page. The Table menu includes commands for working with tables. Displaying the Tables toolbar provides easy access to these same commands.

Trouble? If you clicked the wrong cell in the Insert Table button grid, click the Undo button on the Standard toolbar, and then repeat Steps 5 through 7.

8. Click **View** on the menu bar, point to **Toolbars**, and then click **Tables**. If necessary, drag the title bar of the Tables toolbar and dock it below the Formatting toolbar, as shown in Figure 5-3.

Table created in page ◄ **Figure 5-3**

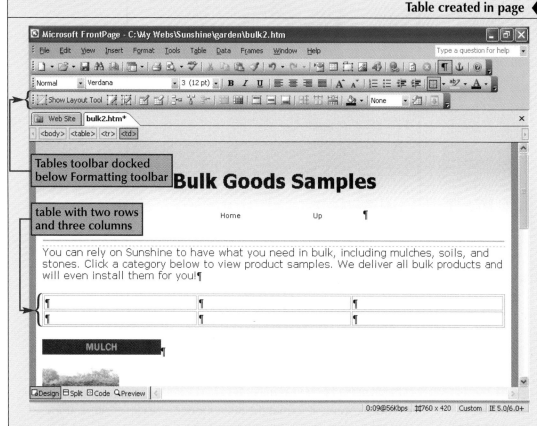

When you first create a table, FrontPage applies the default table settings to it. You can view these default settings by examining the Table Properties dialog box.

9. Right-click anywhere in the table to open the shortcut menu, and then click **Table Properties** to open the Table Properties dialog box. This dialog box lets you examine and specify the table's properties and characteristics. See Figure 5-4.

Figure 5-4 ▶ **Table Properties dialog box**

options for changing the table's alignment and width

options for changing cell spacing and padding

option for changing the border size between cells

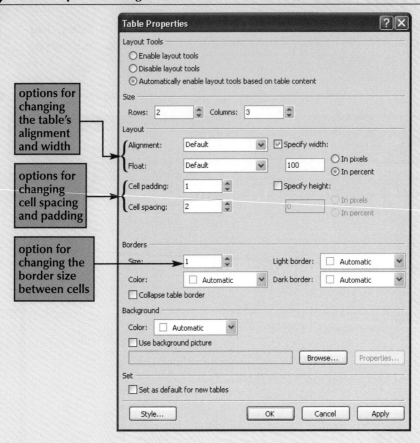

Your sketch of the table (see Figure 5-1) indicates a center alignment for the pictures in the cells and invisible borders. You will format the table for these design specifications next. In addition, because the table contains pictures with fixed sizes, you will set the table's width to 640 pixels to make sure that the pictures are always visible without scrolling the page horizontally, regardless of the user's monitor size and resolution. The minimum resolution for most monitors is 640 × 480 pixels.

To format the table:

1. Make sure that the **Specify width** check box in the Layout section contains a check mark, select the current value in the Specify width text box and type **640**, and then click the **In pixels** option button. This setting specifies that your table will be 640 pixels wide regardless of the monitor and resolution at which it is viewed. Selecting 640 pixels as the width ensures that people viewing the page with a monitor that displays 640 × 480 pixels will see the pictures without having to scroll the page horizontally. For people viewing the page using monitors with higher resolutions, the table will look narrower on the page.

2. In the Layout section, click the **Cell padding up arrow** as necessary to change the cell padding to **4**, and then click the **Cell spacing up arrow** as necessary to change the cell spacing to **3**. These settings will increase the spacing between and around cells in the table, which will make the table's contents easier to read.

3. In the Borders section, click the **Size down arrow** to change the border size to **0**. The border size is measured in pixels; a size of 0 indicates an invisible border, and a size of 1 indicates a thin border.

There are two types of borders in a table: the border that encloses the table and the borders that enclose each cell. You can turn off the display of cell borders by adding a check mark to the Collapse table border check box. Because you have selected a border value of 0, you won't need to select the Collapse table border check box because all borders will be invisible.

4. Click the **OK** button. The Table Properties dialog box closes, and the new properties are applied to the table. Notice that a dashed outline, which identifies the position of the table and its cells, indicates the borders. The browser will not display these outlines.

When you click a cell in a table, the options on the Tables toolbar become active. Figure 5-5 describes the tools available on the Tables toolbar. You'll use some of these buttons as you create tables in the Web site.

Tables toolbar buttons and their descriptions | **Figure 5-5**

Button Name	Button	Function
Show Layout Tool	Show Layout Tool	Turns on the layout tools for cells and tables
Draw Layout Table		Lets you draw a new layout table using the pointer, which changes to a ∥ shape
Draw Layout Cell		Lets you draw a new layout cell in a layout table using the pointer, which changes to a ∥ shape
Draw Table		Lets you draw a new table or modify an existing table using the pointer, which changes to a ∥ shape, to draw lines to indicate rows and columns
Eraser		Lets you use the pointer, which changes to a ⬙ shape, to merge cells
Insert Rows		Inserts a new row above the selected row
Insert Columns		Inserts a new column to the left of the selected column
Delete Cells		Deletes the selected cells
Merge Cells		Merges the selected cells into one larger cell
Split Cells		Splits the selected cell into two or more cells
Align Top		Vertically aligns the data in the selected cells at the top of the cells
Center Vertically		Vertically centers the data in the selected cells
Align Bottom		Vertically aligns the data in the selected cells at the bottom of the cells
Distribute Rows Evenly		Changes the height of the selected rows to equal measurements
Distribute Columns Evenly		Changes the width of the selected columns to equal measurements
AutoFit to Contents		Increases or decreases the size of selected columns in the table to best fit the data they contain
Fill Color		Lets you change the background color of the selected cells to a standard or custom color
Table AutoFormat Combo	None	Lets you apply a Table AutoFormat to an existing table by selecting the desired Table AutoFormat from a list
Table AutoFormat		Opens the Table AutoFormat dialog box, where you can select and apply a Table AutoFormat and special formats to an existing table
Fill Down (or Fill Right)	(or)	Copies data from the topmost (or leftmost) cell in a range of selected cells and pastes it into the range of selected cells

You inserted the table in the correct location in the page, but Brett thinks that the table would look better if it were centered.

Aligning a Table

A table's alignment in a Web page differs from the alignment of data in a table's cells. A table can have only one alignment, whereas each cell in a table can have a different alignment. The alignment of a table and the alignment of a table's cells are specified using different HTML tags. To specify a different alignment for a table, you need to change the table's properties.

Reference Window | **Aligning a Table in a Web Page**

- Right-click anywhere in the table to open the shortcut menu, and then click Table Properties.
- In the Table Properties dialog box, click the Alignment list arrow in the Layout section, click the desired alignment, and then click the OK button.

The table that you inserted in the Bulk Goods Samples Web page is left-aligned, which is the default alignment. Brett wants this table to be centered to give it a more balanced appearance when viewed in a browser. He asks you to center the table next.

To align a table in a Web page:

1. Right-click anywhere in the table to open the shortcut menu, and then click **Table Properties** to open that dialog box.

2. In the Layout section, click the **Alignment** list arrow, and then click **Center**. Selecting this option will center the table (but not the data in the table's cells) in the page.

3. Click the **OK** button. The Table Properties dialog box closes and the table's alignment changes to centered. See Figure 5-6.

Figure 5-6 | **Centered table**

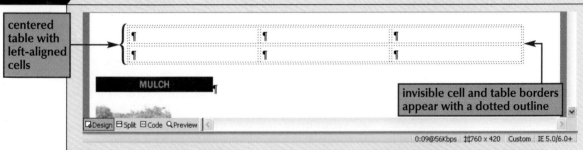

centered table with left-aligned cells

invisible cell and table borders appear with a dotted outline

MULCH

Design | Split | Code | Preview

0:09@56Kbps | 760 x 420 | Custom | IE 5.0/6.0+

Moving Existing Data into a Table

The table that you created will contain the pictures that already exist in the Web page. You can drag the pictures into the correct cells to position them in the table. Using a table to position graphics is common on the Web because it provides good control over the positioning of objects in a Web page.

To drag existing items and position them in a table:

1. Click the picture with the word "mulch" on it to select it. Sizing handles appear around the picture.

2. Drag the picture to the first cell in the first row of the table. When the insertion point appears in the table as shown in Figure 5-7, release the mouse button. The picture now appears in the first cell of the table. The width of the first column increases after you position the first picture. This problem will correct itself after you insert all of the pictures into the table.

Moving a picture into a cell | **Figure 5-7**

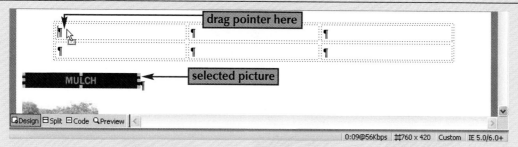

3. Drag the picture of bulk mulch from below the table and position it in the first cell in the second row.

4. Drag the picture with the word "soil" on it and its sample photo to the cells in the second column of the table.

5. Drag the picture with the word "stone" on it and its sample photo to the cells in the third column of the table.

6. Select the paragraphs below the table (but not a paragraph in the bottom shared border), and then press the **Delete** key. Figure 5-8 shows the table, which now contains six pictures. Notice that the heights of the two rows in the table were adjusted automatically to store the content they contain.

Figure 5-8 ▶ **Pictures moved into cells**

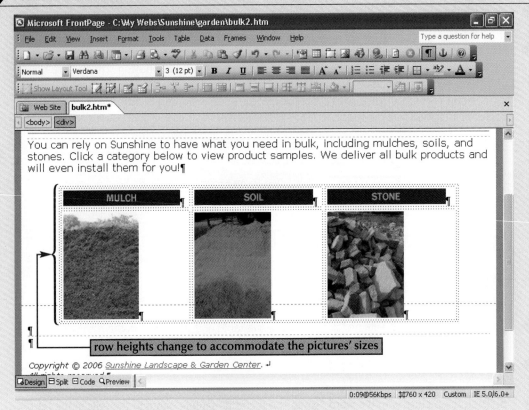

row heights change to accommodate the pictures' sizes

Although the table is centered in the Web page, the pictures are left-aligned within their cells. You can change the cell alignment by using the alignment buttons on the Formatting toolbar, or by opening the Cell Properties dialog box. Because the Cell Properties dialog box contains additional options for working with table cells, you want to show Brett its settings.

Aligning Cells in a Table

In addition to the horizontal alignment of left, right, center, and justified, you can select a vertical alignment of top, middle, baseline, or bottom for cells. These two alignments—horizontal and vertical—are specified using different HTML tags. Middle is the default vertical alignment, and left is the default horizontal alignment. Figure 5-9 shows the different horizontal and vertical alignments you can select for cells.

Vertical and horizontal cell alignments ◄ **Figure 5-9**

Align Top Vertical Alignment		Left Horizontal Alignment
Center Vertically (Middle) Alignment		Center Horizontal Alignment
Align Bottom Vertical Alignment		Right Horizontal Alignment
Baseline Vertical Alignment (cells in the same row are vertically aligned so the first text line in each cell has a common baseline)	This is a line of text. This is a line of text.	This cell uses the Justify horizontal alignment and the baseline vertical alignment. Notice that the lines are aligned on the right and left sides of the cell, similar to how articles appear in newspaper or magazine publications.
No baseline alignment	This is a line of text. This is a line of text.	This is a line of text. This is a line of text. Notice that the lines of text in this row are not vertically aligned in the cells.

You align cell contents by selecting the cells and specifying the desired alignment. You can align cells as a group or individually. Unlike a table, which can have only one alignment, the cells in a table can have different alignments to present data in the best manner. In some cases, cell alignment is a matter of personal preference—you might want to center data to make it look better. Numeric values, especially for currency, are usually right-aligned because this is a common practice in accounting. Vertically aligning data is also a matter of personal preference—you can select the vertical alignment that best presents your data.

Because your plan specifies that all cells in the table will have a center alignment, you could select the entire table and change the alignment once. However, you want to show Brett how to select cells, groups of cells, columns, and rows in a table first, so he can use these skills as he works with tables.

To select and align cells in a table:

► **1.** Move the pointer to the left border of the first row in the table so that it changes to a ➡ shape, and then click the left border to select the first row of the table. See Figure 5-10.

Figure 5-10 ▶ **Selecting a row**

top of first column

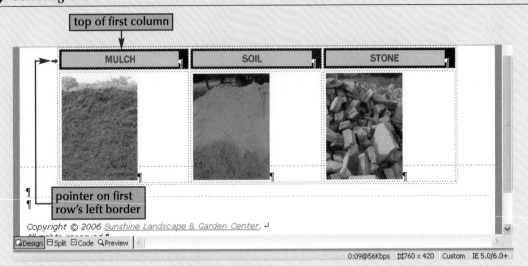

pointer on first row's left border

2. Hold down the **Ctrl** key, click ➡ on the border for the second row, and then release the **Ctrl** key. Now the first and second rows are selected.

   You can select sequential columns and rows in one step by dragging the pointer over the rows or columns you want to select. You'll practice this next by selecting the columns.

3. Click the first cell in the first row to deselect the rows, point to the top of the first column of the table so the pointer changes to a ⬇ shape, and then click and hold the left mouse button and drag the ⬇ pointer to the top of the third column. When all three columns are selected, release the mouse button. It doesn't matter which method you use to select all cells in a table; you can accomplish the same task by selecting all of the rows or all of the columns.

4. With all cells selected, right-click any selected cell to open the shortcut menu, and then click **Cell Properties**. The Cell Properties dialog box opens for the group of cells that you selected. See Figure 5-11.

Figure 5-11 ▶ **Cell Properties dialog box**

horizontal alignment option

vertical alignment option

options for changing the border size and colors

options for adding a background color or picture

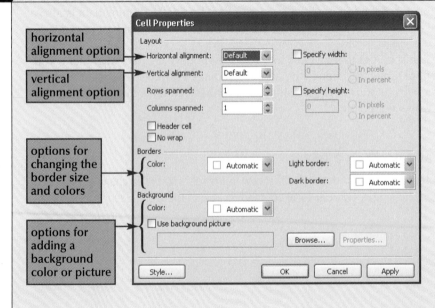

5. Click the **Horizontal alignment** list arrow in the Layout section, and then click **Center**. The data in the selected cells will be centered horizontally.

6. Click the **Vertical alignment** list arrow in the Layout section, and then click **Middle**. The data in the selected cells will use the middle alignment.

   Notice that you can change other values for selected cells, as well. For example, the Borders section includes options to change the color of individual cell borders. The Background section includes options that let you specify a background color or picture to use in individual cells.

7. Click the **OK** button, and then click any cell to deselect the cells. The data in the selected cells changes to a center horizontal alignment and a middle vertical alignment. See Figure 5-12.

Table with revised cell alignments **Figure 5-12**

cells are horizontally and vertically centered

Next, Brett asks if you can format the picture with the word "mulch" on it to open the mulch.htm page.

To format a picture in a cell as a hyperlink:

1. Click the picture with the word "mulch" on it to select it.

2. Click the **Insert Hyperlink** button 🖳 on the Standard toolbar. The Insert Hyperlink dialog box opens.

3. Make sure that the **Existing File or Web Page** button 🖼 is selected, scroll down the list of files, click **mulch.htm**, and then click the **OK** button. Now the picture is a hyperlink that will open the mulch.htm Web page. (When you complete the Review Assignments at the end of this tutorial, you will finish creating the hyperlinks for this page.)

4. Save the bulk2.htm page, and then preview it in a browser. Figure 5-13 shows the Bulk Goods Samples page. The cells in the table are center-aligned and the borders of the table and cells are hidden. The table is centered in the Web page and its width is 640 pixels.

Figure 5-13 Completed Bulk Goods Samples page

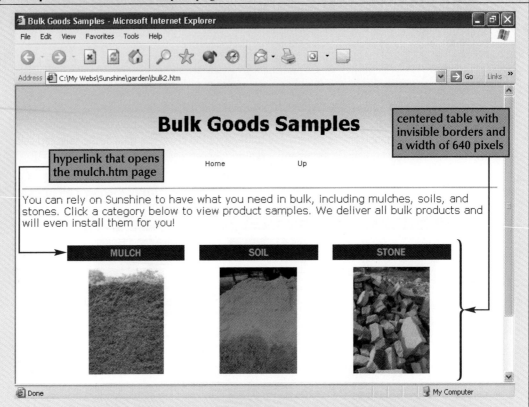

Trouble? If your monitor's resolution is more than 800 × 600 pixels, your table will be the same size but will look much narrower on the page. If your monitor's resolution is 640 × 480 pixels, your table will fill the width of the page.

5. Click the picture with the word "mulch" on it. The Mulches page opens.

6. Close your browser.

Brett likes the new appearance of the Bulk Goods Samples page and now sees how tables are used to organize Web page content. Helen Xiao stops by and mentions that she finished her draft of the new page in the Web site that will feature information about lawn care and common lawn problems. She already sent you a draft of this page via e-mail and asks you to import it into the Web site. You'll need to apply the theme and shared borders to this page, and then add the page to the Web site's navigation structure as a child page of the Garden Center page.

To import the page, apply the theme and shared borders, and add the page to the navigation structure:

1. Display the Folder List, make sure the Web site's root folder is selected, click **File** on the menu bar, click **Import**, click the **Add File** button, open the **Tutorial.05\Tutorial** folder included with your Data Files, double-click the **lawn.htm** file, and then click the **OK** button. The lawn.htm page is added to the Web site.

2. Scroll down the list of files in the Folder List, double-click the **lawn.htm** page to open it in Design view, and then close the Folder List.

3. Click **Format** on the menu bar, and then click **Theme**. The Theme task pane opens.

4. Point to the **Garden Web Site** theme in the Web site default theme section, click the **list arrow** that appears, and then click **Apply to selected page(s)**. The page is formatted by the theme.

5. Close the Theme task pane.

6. Click **Format** on the menu bar, and then click **Shared Borders**. The Shared Borders dialog box opens.

7. Make sure the **Current page** option button is selected, make sure the **Top**, **Left**, and **Bottom** check boxes contain check marks, and then click the **OK** button. Top, left, and bottom shared borders are added to the page. You need to add this page to the navigation structure, however, for these features to be displayed correctly.

8. Click the **Web Site** tab, change to Navigation view, and then display the Folder List.

9. Drag the **lawn.htm** page from the Folder List and position it in the navigation structure as a child page of the Garden Center page and to the right of the Anti-Deer Products page, as shown in Figure 5-14.

| Imported lawn.htm page added to the navigation structure | Figure 5-14 |

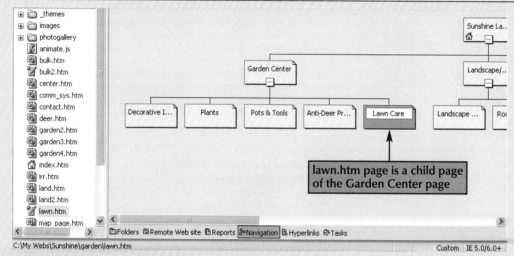

10. Close the Folder List, click the **lawn.htm** tab, and then save the lawn.htm page. The Lawn Care page now has a theme and shared borders. See Figure 5-15.

   Trouble? If a Confirm Save dialog box opens, click the Yes button.

Figure 5-15   Lawn Care page in Design view

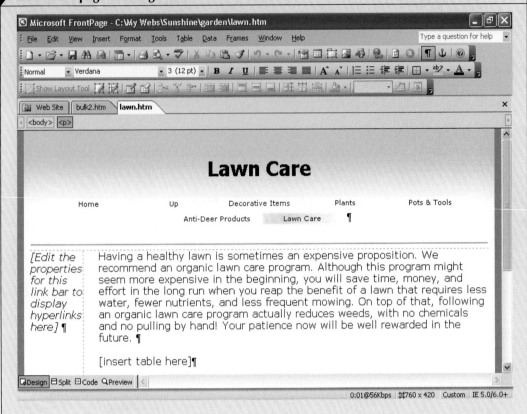

Helen typed placeholders in the page to indicate where she wants you to insert the tables. The first table you'll create is one that presents common lawn problems and their solutions. Helen's sketch of the table appears in Figure 5-16.

Sketch of the table with common lawn care problems and solutions | **Figure 5-16**

Problem	Occurrence	Symptoms	Treatment
Brown patch	Fall or late spring	Circular areas with brown centers and a yellow to light green outer edge.	Aerate lawn, improve drainage and soil fertility, and apply bacteria that will protect the roots from the fungus.
Take all patch	Summer	Soil disease that is similar in appearance to brown patch, but occurs in the heat of the summer.	Remove thatch buildup, and improve drainage and soil fertility.
Chinch bugs	Summer	Yellow grass that has been watered properly.	Apply insecticides such as pyrethrums or soap sprays until gone.
Grub worms	Summer	Brown grass with no roots that has been watered properly.	Apply beneficial nematodes to control infestation.
Fire ants	Anytime, especially after a rain	Dirt mounds appearing in the turf.	Treat mounds immediately with an approved pesticide.

Creating a Table Using the Insert Table Command

With Helen's sketch in hand, you can create the table. You already showed Brett how to use the Insert Table button on the Standard toolbar to create a table. When you use the Insert Table button grid, you can create a table with the default settings for new tables very quickly. After you create a table, you can use the Table Properties dialog box to make any necessary adjustments to the table's appearance. If you know that the table you want to create will require changes to the default characteristics, you can use the Table menu to create the table and change its characteristics at the same time.

Helen's table has six rows and four columns. To make the appearance of this table consistent with the one you already created in the Bulk Goods Samples page, you'll set the table's alignment to center, the cell padding to 4, and the cell spacing to 3. However, this table requires a border to look like a traditional table. You will use a border size of 2 with the default colors supplied by the Garden Web Site theme you applied to the Web site and a left cell alignment. In addition, because Helen's table contains mostly text, you'll set its width as a percentage of the browser window's width.

To create the table using the Insert Table command:

▶ 1. Scroll down the lawn.htm page, and then select the text **[insert table here]** that appears immediately above the bottom shared border. You will insert the table in this location.

▶ 2. Click **Table** on the menu bar, point to **Insert**, and then click **Table**. The Insert Table dialog box opens, as shown in Figure 5-17. This dialog box is similar to the Table Properties dialog box that you used to change the properties of the table in the Bulk Goods Samples page.

Figure 5-17 Insert Table dialog box

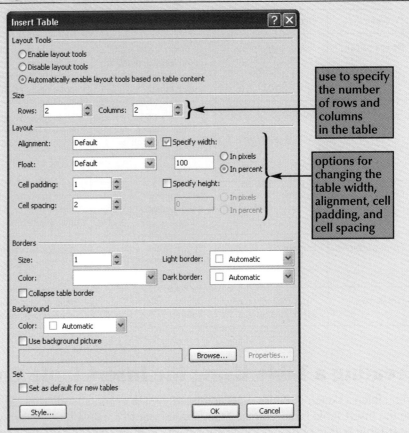

use to specify the number of rows and columns in the table

options for changing the table width, alignment, cell padding, and cell spacing

3. Select the value in the Rows list box, type **6**, press the **Tab** key to select the value in the Columns list box, and then type **4**. These settings create a table with six rows and four columns.

4. Click the **Alignment** list arrow in the Layout section, and then click **Center**. This setting will center the table in the Web page.

5. Make sure that the **Specify width** check box contains a check mark, select the value in the text box that appears below the Specify width check box, type **95**, and then make sure the **In percent** option button is selected.

6. Select the value in the Cell padding list box, type **4**, press the **Tab** key to select the value in the Cell spacing list box, and then type **3**. These settings will increase the spacing between and around cells in the table, which will make the table's contents easier to read.

7. Select the value in the Size list box in the Borders section, and then type **2**. Increasing the table's border size creates a thicker border.

8. Click the **OK** button. The Insert Table dialog box closes and a table with the characteristics you specified appears in the Web page. If necessary, scroll down the Web page so you can see the complete table, as shown in Figure 5-18.

Table created in page ◀ **Figure 5-18**

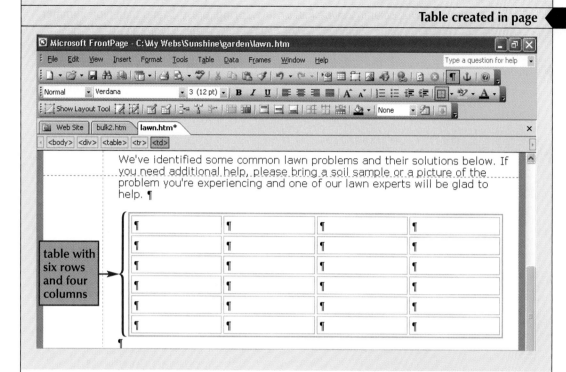

With the table created, you can use Helen's sketch to add data to its cells.

Entering Data in a Table

Entering data in a table in a Web page is similar to entering table data in a Word document or in an Excel worksheet. You position the insertion point by clicking a cell and then type the data. You move the insertion point into another cell by clicking the cell or by pressing the appropriate arrow keys or the Tab key to move to the desired cell.

When your table contains repetitive data, you can type the data once and then use the Fill Down or Fill Right buttons on the Tables toolbar to copy and paste one value into adjacent cells. You'll begin by adding the text for the column headings, which appear in the first row of the table.

To enter data in a table:

▶ **1.** Click the cell in row 1, column 1, and then type **Problem**. As you type, the width of the first column increases.

   Trouble? If you aren't sure where to enter the column heading in the table, refer to the sketch shown in Figure 5-16.

▶ **2.** Press the **Tab** key to move to the cell in row 1, column 2, and then type **Occurrence**.

▶ **3.** Press the **Tab** key, type **Symptoms**, press the **Tab** key, type **Treatment**, and then press the **Tab** key again. The first row contains data, and the insertion point moves to the first cell in the second row.

▶ **4.** Type **Brown patch**, press the **down** arrow key ↓, type **Take all patch**, press ↓, and then type the following values in the remaining cells in the first column: **Chinch bugs**, **Grub worms**, and **Fire ants**.

5. Click the cell in row 2, column 2, type **Fall or late spring**, press ↓, and then type **Summer**. Instead of typing the value "Summer" in the cells in rows 4 and 5, you can use the Fill Down button to copy the value in row 3 into rows 4 and 5.

6. Use the pointer to select the cells in rows 3, 4, and 5 of column 2, as shown in Figure 5-19. Notice that the Fill Down button on the Tables toolbar becomes active when you select cells in a column. You can also copy cells to the right of a cell; when you select cells to the right, the Fill Right button on the Tables toolbar becomes active.

| Figure 5-19 | Cells selected to fill down |

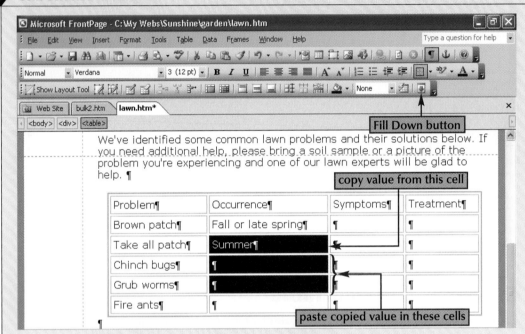

7. Click the **Fill Down** button on the Tables toolbar. The value "Summer" is entered in the selected cells.

8. Click the last cell in the second column, and then type **Anytime, especially after a rain**.

9. Use Figure 5-20 to enter the data in the rest of the table. Press the **Tab** key after typing the data in a cell to move to the next cell. Do not press the Tab key after typing the data in the last cell in the table or you will create a new row.

Problem	Occurrence	Symptoms	Treatment
Brown patch	Fall or late spring	Circular areas with brown centers and a yellow to light green outer edge.	Aerate lawn, improve drainage and soil fertility, and apply bacteria that will protect the roots from the fungus.
Take all patch	Summer	Soil disease that is similar in appearance to brown patch, but occurs in the heat of the summer.	Remove thatch buildup, and improve drainage and soil fertility.
Chinch bugs	Summer	Yellow grass that has been watered properly.	Apply insecticides such as pyrethrums or soap sprays until gone.
Grub worms	Summer	Brown grass with no roots that has been watered properly.	Apply beneficial nematodes to control infestation.
Fire ants	Anytime, especially after a rain	Dirt mounds appearing in the turf.	Treat mounds immediately with an approved pesticide.

Trouble? Don't worry if the lines in your table wrap differently than those shown in Figure 5-20. The appearance of data depends on many variables, including your monitor's resolution.

10. Save the lawn.htm page.

Helen likes the table's appearance, but wants to add a column to the table that identifies the cause of the problem. To make this change, you'll need to add a column to the table. She also wants to create a row at the top of the table that identifies the nursery's name when the table is printed. To make this change, you'll need to add a row at the top of the table.

Inserting Columns and Rows in a Table

After creating a table, you can insert additional rows and columns as needed, either before or after entering data in the table's cells.

| **Inserting a Column in a Table**

- Click any cell in the column to the left of which you want to insert the new column, and then click the Insert Columns button on the Tables toolbar.

or

- Click a cell adjacent to where you want to insert the new column, click Table on the menu bar, point to Insert, and then click Rows or Columns to open the Insert Rows or Columns dialog box.
- Click the Columns option button, and then enter the number of columns to insert in the Number of columns text box.
- Click the Left of selection option button to insert the new column(s) to the left of the currently selected column, or click the Right of selection option button to insert the new column(s) to the right of the currently selected column.
- Click the OK button.

You'll start by adding a new column to the table. Helen wants the new column to appear between the Symptoms and Treatment columns.

To insert a column in the table:

1. Click the last cell in the first row, which contains the value "Treatment." When you insert the new column, it will appear to the left of the selected column.

2. Click the **Insert Columns** button on the Tables toolbar. A new column is added to the left of the Treatment column. The new column's width is very narrow. When you begin typing data in it, its width will increase automatically.

3. Use Figure 5-21 to add the content to the cells in the new column you added.

Data entered into the Causes column ◀ **Figure 5-21**

Problem	Occurrence	Symptoms	Causes	Treatment
Brown patch	Fall or late spring	Circular areas with brown centers and a yellow to light green outer edge.	Poor drainage, soil compression, and overwatering.	Aerate lawn, improve drainage and soil fertility, and apply bacteria that will protect the roots from the fungus.
Take all patch	Summer	Soil disease that is similar in appearance to brown patch, but occurs in the heat of the summer.	Imbalanced soil fertility, excessive herbicide use, and overwatering.	Remove thatch buildup, and improve drainage and soil fertility.
Chinch bugs	Summer	Yellow grass that has been watered properly.	Infestation by adult chinch bugs.	Apply insecticides such as pyrethrums or soap sprays until gone.
Grub worms	Summer	Brown grass with no roots that has been watered properly.	Infestation by grub worm larvae.	Apply beneficial nematodes to control infestation.
Fire ants	Anytime, especially after a rain	Dirt mounds appearing in the turf.	Infestation by a fire ant colony.	Treat mounds immediately with an approved pesticide.

▶ **4.** Save the page.

You insert a row using a similar procedure.

Inserting a Row in a Table   Reference Window

- Click any cell in the row above which you want to insert the new row, and then click the Insert Rows button on the Tables toolbar.

or

- Click a cell adjacent to where you want to insert the new row, click Table on the menu bar, point to Insert, and then click Rows or Columns to open the Insert Rows or Columns dialog box.
- Click the Rows option button, and then enter the number of rows to insert in the Number of rows text box.
- Click the Above selection option button to insert the new row(s) above the currently selected row, or click the Below selection option button to insert the new row(s) below the currently selected row.
- Click the OK button.

Helen asks you to insert the new row at the top of the table.

To insert a row in a table:

▶ 1. Click any cell in the first row. When you insert the new row, it will appear above the first row.

▶ 2. Click the **Insert Rows** button 🔲 on the Tables toolbar. A new row is inserted, as shown in Figure 5-22.

Figure 5-22   Table with new row added

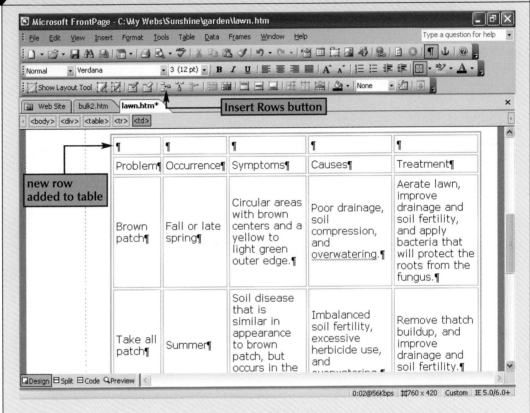

Helen asks if you can format the cells in the new row so there are no gridlines between the individual cells. You tell her that you can do this by merging the five cells in the first row to become a single cell.

Merging Table Cells

You can arrange a group of selected cells to span a row or column by merging them into a single cell. When you **merge** a group of cells, the resulting cell spans multiple columns or rows.

Merging Table Cells

- Select the cells to be merged, and then click the Merge Cells button on the Tables toolbar.
or
- Click the Eraser button on the Tables toolbar, and then use the pointer to erase the cell border that separates the cells to be merged.

You'll show Helen two methods for merging cells so she sees how to use each one. First, you'll merge the first two cells in the first row using a toolbar button, and then you'll use the pointer to erase the borders between the third, fourth, and fifth cells in the first row.

To merge cells:

▶ **1.** Click the cell in row 1, column 1, press and hold the **Shift** key, click the cell in row 1, column 2, and then release the mouse button and the **Shift** key to select cells 1 and 2 in row 1. See Figure 5-23.

Merging cells in a table ◀ **Figure 5-23**

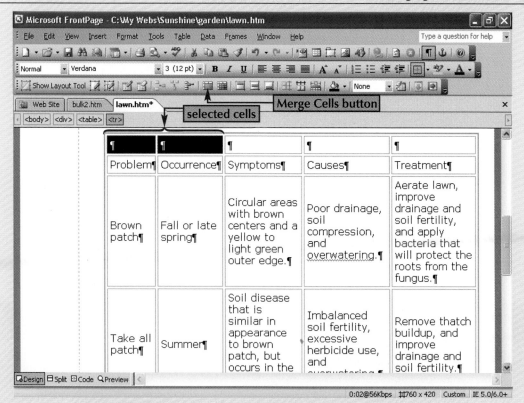

▶ **2.** Click the **Merge Cells** button 🖾 on the Tables toolbar, and then click the cell to the right of the selected merged cell to deselect the merged cell. The cells that were in columns 1 and 2 are joined to become a single cell.

Now, you want to show Helen how to use the Eraser.

▶ **3.** Click the **Eraser** button 🖾 on the Tables toolbar to select this tool. The pointer changes to a ⬦ shape when you move it over the Web page.

4. With the ✐ pointer positioned over the first cell in the first row (the merged cell), click and hold the mouse button, and then drag the pointer across the right border of the merged cell. The border turns red, as shown in Figure 5-24.

Figure 5-24 ▶ **Merging cells using the pointer**

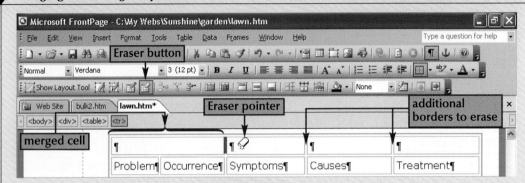

5. Release the mouse button to erase the cell border.

  Trouble? If you erase the wrong border, click the Undo button 🔄 on the Standard toolbar to undo your change, and then repeat Steps 4 and 5.

6. Repeat Steps 4 and 5 to erase the borders between the remaining cells in the first row. Now the first row contains a single cell.

7. Click 🖾 on the Tables toolbar to turn off the Eraser.

8. Click the **Center** button 🖹 on the Formatting toolbar, and then type **Sunshine Landscape & Garden Center** in the merged cell.

Helen wants to add another merged cell to the table to display the text, "Come see us if you're having problems with your lawn!" You tell her that you can split the first row into two rows, instead of adding another row and merging its cells.

Splitting Table Cells

When you **split** a cell, you are dividing a selected cell or group of cells into two or more rows or columns.

Reference Window | **Splitting Table Cells**

- Use the pointer to select the cell(s) to split.
- Click the Split Cells button on the Tables toolbar.
- In the Split Cells dialog box, click the Split into columns or Split into rows option button.
- Use the Number of columns or Number of rows list box to indicate the number of columns or rows to split.
- Click the OK button.

You'll split the cell in row 1 into two rows.

To split a cell:

1. Make sure the insertion point is positioned in the cell in the first row (the merged cell).

2. Click the **Split Cells** button ▦ on the Tables toolbar. The Split Cells dialog box opens. See Figure 5-25.

Split Cells dialog box | **Figure 5-25**

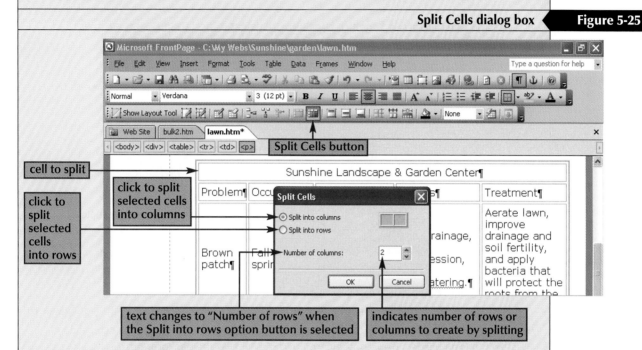

Split Cells button

cell to split

click to split selected cells into columns

click to split selected cells into rows

text changes to "Number of rows" when the Split into rows option button is selected

indicates number of rows or columns to create by splitting

3. Click the **Split into rows** option button, make sure that **2** appears in the Number of rows list box, and then click the **OK** button. The Split Cells dialog box closes, and the table now contains a new row.

4. Click in the new row, click the **Center** button ▤ on the Formatting toolbar, and then type **Come see us if you're having problems with your lawn!** Figure 5-26 shows the revised table.

Revised table | **Figure 5-26**

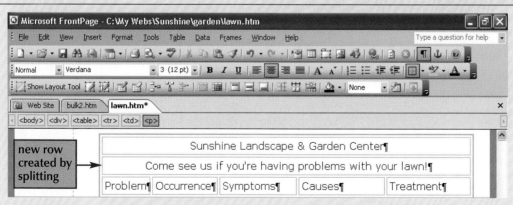

new row created by splitting

Helen likes the table's new organization. She asks if you can format the cell in the second row with a background color so its message stands out better.

Reference Window

Changing the Background Color or Picture in a Table or Cell

- Right-click anywhere in the table to open the shortcut menu, click Table Properties to change the background color of the table or click Cell Properties to change the background color of a selected cell, and then click the Color list arrow in the Background section to select a background color.

or
- Click the Use background picture check box to select it, and then click the Browse button to select a file to use as the table's background picture.

To add the message to the cell in the second row, you'll select the cell and open the Cell Properties dialog box.

To change the background color of a cell:

1. Right-click the cell in row 2 to select it and open the shortcut menu, and then click **Cell Properties**. The Cell Properties dialog box opens.

2. In the Background section, click the **Color** list arrow, and then click the fourth color in the Theme Colors section. This color has the ScreenTip RGB(EB,B6,6C).

   Trouble? If you do not have the color specified in Step 2, select any light color in the color palette.

   You'll change the border color for the selected cell, as well.

3. In the Borders section, click the **Color** list arrow, and then click the same color you selected in Step 2. By changing the border color to match the background color, the cell will look like it has no borders because they are the same color as the background.

4. Click the **OK** button. The Cell Properties dialog box closes and the cell in the second row has a background color. Because you formatted this cell's border using the same color as the background, the border seems to disappear. See Figure 5-27.

| Figure 5-27 | Background color added to cell |

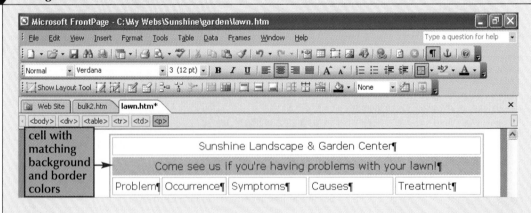

5. Save the page.

Helen likes the table's overall appearance but decides that the data in the Occurrence column isn't very usable. She asks you to delete this column from the table.

Deleting Cells from a Table

Even when you sketch a table before inserting it in a Web page, sometimes you might need to add or delete cells, including entire rows and columns, to create the right table for your data. The process of deleting cells is straightforward. First, you select the cell, row, or column that you want to delete or drag the pointer over a group of cells to select them. If you need to select additional cells, rows, or columns at the same time, press and hold the Shift key while you select them. These selection methods are similar to how you would select table cells in Word. After selecting the cells, click the Delete Cells button on the Tables toolbar.

Reference Window

Deleting Cells from a Table

- Select a single cell, group of cells, row, or column.
- Click the Delete Cells button on the Tables toolbar.

Helen's request is to delete the cells in the Occurrence column. You'll select these cells and then delete them.

To delete cells from a table:

1. Click the cell in row 3, column 2 (which contains the word "Occurrence").

2. Scroll down the table as necessary so you can see the last row, press and hold the **Shift** key, click the second cell in the last row of the table (which contains the phrase "Anytime, especially after a rain"), and then release the **Shift** key. Six cells in the second column of the table are selected.

3. Click the **Delete Cells** button [🔳] on the Tables toolbar. The selected cells are deleted from the table.

After deleting the cells, Helen asks if you can resize the columns in the table. There are two methods for resizing rows and columns. The first method uses the pointer and the second method uses a toolbar button.

Resizing Rows and Columns

When you enter data in a cell, FrontPage automatically increases the size of the cell and the column in which it appears to accommodate the text that you entered. You can also manually resize a table's rows and columns to affect the overall appearance of your table.

The easiest way to resize a column is to use the pointer—you drag the column's right border to the left to decrease the column's width, or drag the column's right border to the right to increase the column's width. You can also use the pointer to drag the bottom border of a row up to decrease the row's height or down to increase its height.

Resizing a Row or Column in a Table Using the Mouse

- Select the row or column that you want to resize.
- For a row, drag the bottom border down to increase the row's height, or drag the bottom border up to decrease the row's height.

or

- For a column, drag the right border to the left to decrease the column's width, or drag the right border to the right to increase the column's width.

You'll start by resizing the first column to make it slightly wider.

To resize a column using the mouse:

1. Select the first column in the table by clicking the first cell in the third row, scrolling down to the first cell in the last row, pressing and holding the **Shift** key, clicking the first cell in the last row, and then releasing the **Shift** key.

2. Position the pointer on the right border of the selected column so it changes to a ↔ shape, and then click and hold down the mouse button as you drag the right border of the selected column to the right. When the dotted vertical line is positioned as shown in Figure 5-28, release the mouse button.

Figure 5-28 ▶ | **Changing a column's width**

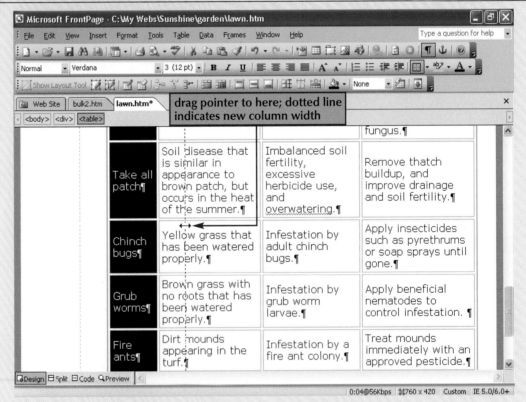

Trouble? If you do not see the dotted vertical line, drag the pointer to approximately the same location shown in Figure 5-28 and then release the mouse button.

3. Click the cell in row 3, column 1, to deselect the first column.

As you resized the first column, the width of the second column in the table decreased. You can select the second, third, and fourth columns as a group and use the Distribute Columns Evenly button on the Tables toolbar to change them to have equal widths, which is called distributing the columns evenly.

To distribute the columns evenly:

1. Click the cell in row 3, column 2, scroll down to the last row, press and hold the **Shift** key, click the cell in the last row and last column (row 8, column 4), and then release the **Shift** key. The cells are selected.

2. Click the **Distribute Columns Evenly** button ⊞ on the Tables toolbar. The cells in the second, third, and fourth columns have equal widths.

3. Click the cell in row 1 to deselect the selected cells.

   When you distribute the columns evenly, FrontPage changes the width setting of the table to pixels. If you want to accept this change, you don't need to do anything. However, if you want to use a percentage as the table width, you need to reset the width property.

4. Right-click any cell in the table to open the shortcut menu, and then click **Table Properties**. The Table Properties dialog box opens. Notice that the Specify width setting changed to use pixels.

5. Select the value in the Specify width text box, type **95**, click the **In percent** option button, and then click the **OK** button. The table width is set to a percentage, but the table looks the same.

You can select rows and use the Distribute Rows Evenly button on the Tables toolbar to change the heights of a group of selected rows to the same measurement as well.

To help identify the table in the Web page, you suggest adding a table caption to it.

Adding a Table Caption

A **table caption** is a title that appears either above or below a table. It can contain one or more lines of text. Although the table caption appears to be a part of the table, it actually resides outside of the table's border and is created by a separate HTML tag. When you insert a caption, its default location is above the table. You can relocate the caption by clicking the Caption Properties command on the table's shortcut menu.

Adding a Table Caption

Reference Window

- Click anywhere in the table to select it.
- Click Table on the menu bar, point to Insert, and then click Caption.
- Type the caption at the location of the insertion point.

Because this page will contain two tables, Helen agrees that adding a caption to the tables will help clarify their functions. She asks you to add the caption above the table.

To add a table caption:

1. Click **Table** on the menu bar, point to **Insert**, and then click **Caption**. A new line appears above the table, and the insertion point moves to the new line. This new line is the table's caption. Although the caption *looks* like a paragraph in Design view, it is formatted as an HTML caption and not as a new paragraph.

2. Type **Common Lawn Problems and Solutions**.

3. Select the **Common Lawn Problems and Solutions** caption, and then click the **Bold** button **B** on the Formatting toolbar to change the caption to bold text.

4. Click anywhere in the caption to deselect it.

After adding a caption to a table, you can change its properties. For example, you might want to display the caption on two lines, or place one or more blank lines between the caption and the table. You can press Shift + Enter to create a new line in a caption. Another way to change an existing caption's properties is to use the settings in the Caption Properties dialog box.

Helen wants to see how the caption would look below the table.

To change caption properties:

1. Right-click the **Common Lawn Problems and Solutions** caption to open the shortcut menu, and then click **Caption Properties** to open that dialog box. See Figure 5-29.

Figure 5-29	Caption Properties dialog box

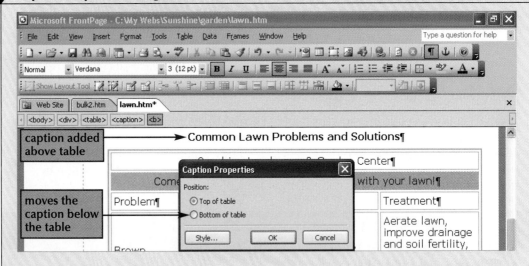

2. Click the **Bottom of table** option button, and then click the **OK** button. Now the caption appears below the table. (You might need to scroll down the table to see the caption below it.)

Helen prefers the caption above the table, so you will undo this action.

3. Click the **Undo** button 🔄 on the Standard toolbar. The caption appears above the table again.

4. Save the lawn.htm page.

Helen likes the appearance and content of the table. Before finishing it, you want to show her how to apply a Table AutoFormat to the table.

Applying a Table AutoFormat

After you create a table, you might decide to use the Table Properties and Cell Properties dialog boxes to enhance its appearance with a background color and complementary cell and table border colors. You can also format your table with a **Table AutoFormat**, which is a predefined combination of colors, colored borders, and other special effects that enhance a table's appearance. A Table AutoFormat might be simple, colorful, classic, or three-dimensional. After applying an AutoFormat, you can use the Table Properties and Cell Properties dialog boxes to change the AutoFormat to customize your table's appearance even further.

Reference Window

Applying a Table AutoFormat

- Click anywhere in the table to select it, click the list arrow for the Table AutoFormat Combo button on the Tables toolbar, and then select an AutoFormat in the list.

or

- Click anywhere in the table to select it, and then click the Table AutoFormat button on the Tables toolbar. The Table AutoFormat dialog box opens.
- Select an AutoFormat in the Formats list.
- If necessary, change the options in the Formats to apply and Apply special formats sections.
- Click the OK button.

Helen is curious to see how a Table AutoFormat might change the table's appearance. You will show her several samples to see if she likes any of them.

To apply a Table AutoFormat to the table:

1. Click any cell in the table to select the table, click the **list arrow** for the Table AutoFormat Combo button `None ▾` on the Tables toolbar, and then click **Simple 3**. As shown in Figure 5-30, the table's format changes to use the styles created by the Simple 3 Table AutoFormat.

Figure 5-30	Simple 3 Table AutoFormat applied to table

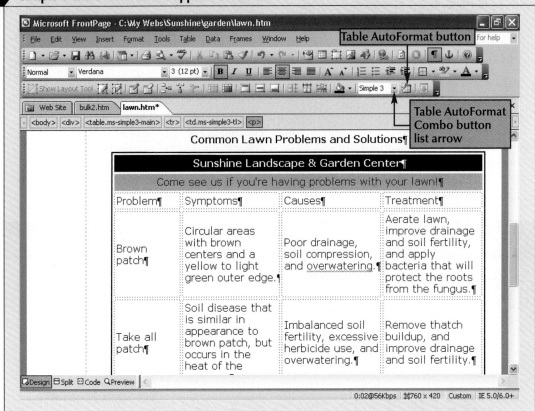

You could continue clicking the Table AutoFormat Combo button list arrow and selecting different formats. However, an easier way to find a suitable Table AutoFormat is to use the Table AutoFormat dialog box.

▶ 2. Click the **Table AutoFormat** button 🔲 on the Tables toolbar. The Table AutoFormat dialog box opens. See Figure 5-31.

Figure 5-31	Table AutoFormat dialog box

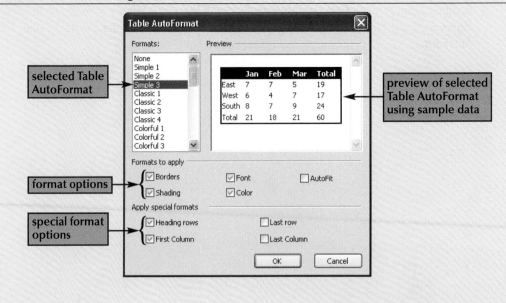

The Simple 3 format is selected, and a preview of its appearance is shown in the Preview box. Notice that you can also use this dialog box to control which formats are applied to your table. For example, deselecting a check box in the Formats to apply section omits those elements from the AutoFormat. In addition, you might want to apply or deselect special formats in your tables. A heading row is the first row in a table; it usually contains column headings. The table's first column usually contains row headings. You can also apply special formats to the last row and last column in a table when these table elements require special formatting.

Helen wants to see whether any of the AutoFormats are more appealing than the Simple 3 format that you applied.

3. Click **Classic 3** in the Formats list. The Preview box shows the appearance for the Classic 3 format. This format's dark background might make the page difficult to read. In addition, the AutoFormat's color scheme doesn't match well with the current colors in the Garden Web Site theme.

4. Scroll down the Formats list and click **3D Effects 2**. This format uses a background color with a raised effect to distinguish alternating rows in the table.

5. Scroll up the Formats list and click **Colorful 2**. This AutoFormat complements the colors in the Garden Web Site theme, so Helen asks you to apply it.

6. Click the **OK** button. The table now uses the styles from the Colorful 2 Table AutoFormat. See Figure 5-32.

Colorful 2 Table AutoFormat applied to table ◄ | **Figure 5-32**

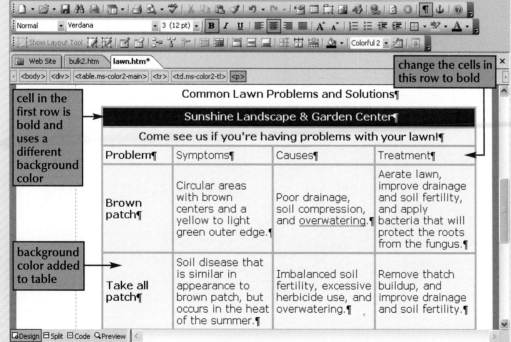

The AutoFormat changed the first cell in each row to bold. In addition, the background color from the Table AutoFormat replaced the one you created in the cell in the second row. To improve on this style, you'll manually change the column headings, which appear in the third row, to bold.

▶ 7. Select the third row in the table, and then click the **Bold** button **B** on the Formatting toolbar. The column headings are now bold.

▶ 8. Save the page.

Now that you've completed the table, you can view it in a browser.

To view the table in a browser:

▶ 1. Click the **Preview** button 🔍 on the Standard toolbar. If necessary, scroll down the page to see the table. Notice the appearance of the caption and the formatting applied by the Table AutoFormat.

▶ 2. Close your browser.

Helen wants to make one final change to the table. She asks you to change the vertical alignment of the cells in rows 4 through 8 so that the text in each cell starts at the top of the cell instead of being vertically centered in the cell.

To align cells vertically on the top:

▶ 1. Use the pointer to select rows 4 through 8.

▶ 2. Click the **Align Top** button 🔲 on the Tables toolbar. The selected cells are aligned vertically at the top of the cells.

▶ 3. Save the lawn.htm page, and then preview it in your browser. Figure 5-33 shows the completed table.

Completed table ◀ **Figure 5-33**

Common Lawn Problems and Solutions			
Sunshine Landscape & Garden Center			
Come see us if you're having problems with your lawn!			
Problem	**Symptoms**	**Causes**	**Treatment**
Brown patch	Circular areas with brown centers and a yellow to light green outer edge.	Poor drainage, soil compression, and overwatering.	Aerate lawn, improve drainage and soil fertility, and apply bacteria that will protect the roots from the fungus.
Take all patch	Soil disease that is similar in appearance to brown patch, but occurs in the heat of the summer.	Imbalanced soil fertility, excessive herbicide use, and overwatering.	Remove thatch buildup, and improve drainage and soil fertility.
Chinch bugs	Yellow grass that has been watered properly.	Infestation by adult chinch bugs.	Apply insecticides such as pyrethrums or soap sprays until gone.
Grub worms	Brown grass with no roots that has been watered properly.	Infestation by grub worm larvae.	Apply beneficial nematodes to control infestation.
Fire ants	Dirt mounds appearing in the turf.	Infestation by a fire ant colony.	Treat mounds immediately with an approved pesticide.

bold column headings

cells aligned vertically at the top

Trouble? If you are viewing the table at 1024 × 768 resolution or higher, the spacing in your cells might differ. This difference causes no problems.

4. Close your browser.

If you are more comfortable creating a table using a spreadsheet program (such as Excel) or a word processor (such as Word), you can create a table in another program and then insert the file in the Web page. FrontPage will recognize the table and convert its content and format to HTML tags. The HTML document that FrontPage produces for a table originally created in another program is almost the same, and you can use the tools in FrontPage to edit the inserted table as if you had originally created it using FrontPage.

Viewing HTML Tags for a Table

When you create a table in a Web page, whether using FrontPage or another program, you create a complex HTML document. For example, the <table> and </table> tags specify the beginning and end of the table. The <tr> and </tr> (table row) tags indicate the beginning and end of one row in the table, whereas individual <td> and </td> (table data) tags indicate the beginning and end of each cell. FrontPage generates a separate line for each cell in a table. The <div> tag and center attribute center the table in the page.

So that you can gain a better understanding of the HTML tags that FrontPage used to create the table, you will view the HTML document for the bulk2.htm and lawn.htm pages.

To view the HTML documents that produce tables:

▸ **1.** Click the **bulk2.htm** tab to display the Bulk Goods Samples page.

▸ **2.** Change to Code view, and then if necessary, press **Ctrl + End** to scroll to the bottom of the HTML document. Figure 5-34 shows the HTML document that creates the bulk2.htm page. The <div align="center"> tag centers the table on the page. The <td align="center"> tag centers the data in an individual cell. The <tr> and </tr> tags indicate a single row in the table. Notice that the width for this table is set to 640 pixels.

Figure 5-34	HTML document for the bulk2.htm page

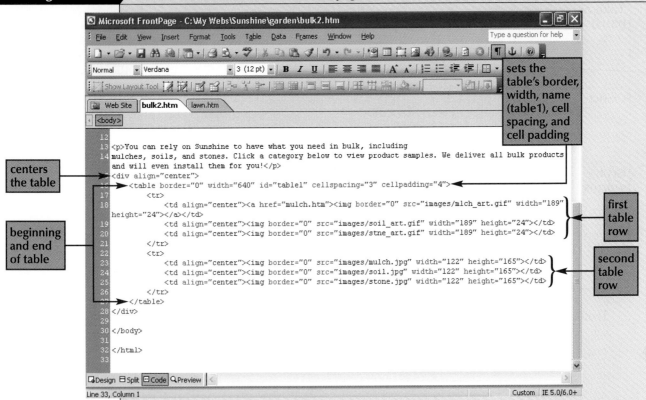

▸ **3.** Change to Design view, and then close the bulk2.htm page.

▸ **4.** In the lawn.htm page, click anywhere in the page to deselect the selected cells, change to Code view, and then scroll the HTML document so the <div align="center"> tag is at the top of the window, as shown in Figure 5-35. Notice the <caption> and </caption> tags, which format the table's caption. This table is also centered in the page, as indicated by the <div align="center"> tag. The opening <table> tag contains properties that format the table's border size, width in the browser window, cell spacing, cell padding, name, and the Table AutoFormat. The colspan property merges the cells in the first row. The other properties in the <td> tags were inserted by the Table AutoFormat and affect the table's appearance.

HTML document for the lawn.htm page | Figure 5-35

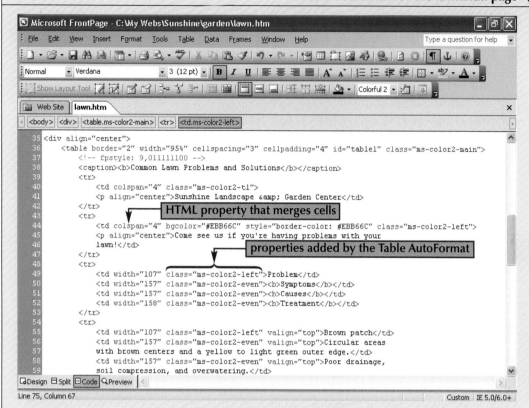

5. Press **Ctrl + End**. Notice the width property in the <td> tags, which indicates the widths of the cells in pixels. These widths represent the column widths you indicated when you resized the first column using the pointer and the remaining columns using the Distribute Columns Evenly button.

Trouble? The widths of the second, third, and fourth columns might not be exactly equal; their measurements might vary by one or two pixels. This difference does not cause any problems.

6. Change to Design view.

7. Click **View** on the menu bar, point to **Toolbars**, and then click **Tables** to hide the Tables toolbar.

8. Close the garden Web site, and then close FrontPage.

Brett and Helen now understand how to use and create tables in a Web page. In the next session, you will create a page with frames in the Web site.

Session 5.1 Quick Check

1. What is the smallest component of a table?
2. When should you create a table in a Web page using a percentage of the window size? When should you create a table in a Web page using a fixed number of pixels?
3. _____ is the distance between the contents of a cell and its edges.
4. True or False: If you select a table cell and then click the Align Left button on the Formatting toolbar, you will left-align the selected cell's contents.
5. True or False: Clicking the Center button on the Formatting toolbar will center a table in a Web page.
6. When you insert a row in a table using the Tables toolbar, the new row appears _____ the currently selected row.
7. Describe two ways to merge two adjacent cells into a single cell.
8. The default location for a table's caption is _____ the table.

Session 5.2

Understanding Frames

A **frames page**, or a **frameset**, is a single Web page divided into two or more windows, each of which can contain a separate, scrollable page. It is important to understand that the frames page itself does not contain any content—it contains only the empty frames.

You use a frames page when you want the contents of one frame in the browser window to remain unchanged while the contents of other frames change. For example, one frame might display a set of hyperlinks, while a second frame displays the target pages of the hyperlinks.

Chad Schomaker wants to replace the existing Irrigation page in the Web site with a frames page. His vision of the new Irrigation page is one that lends itself very well to a frames page with three frames. He wants a page at the top of the frames page that contains navigation links to other pages in the garden Web site, and a page on the left side of the frames page that contains links to topics related to irrigation; the pages for those related irrigation topics would open in the third, or main, frame. A frames page itself is just a set of empty frames; its HTML tags specify each frame's name and size.

After planning the content of the new Irrigation page, Chad created several pages. The first page, banner.htm, is the page that will appear at the top of the frames page. The second page, contents.htm, is the page that will appear on the left side of the frames page. The pages war.htm, request.htm, faq.htm, and intro.htm will open in the main frame of the frames page. Chad saved these pages in a folder. You'll import this folder into the Web site, and then you'll create the frames page and set its pages to open in the correct frames.

When you open a frames page in a browser, the browser first opens the frames page, then it opens the pages that are specified to load into the individual frames. If the frames page contains three frames, your browser is really opening *four* separate Web pages—the frames page and one page in each of the three frames. Figure 5-36 shows the RainMaker Irrigation page that you will create and describes how it works.

RainMaker Irrigation frames page | Figure 5-36

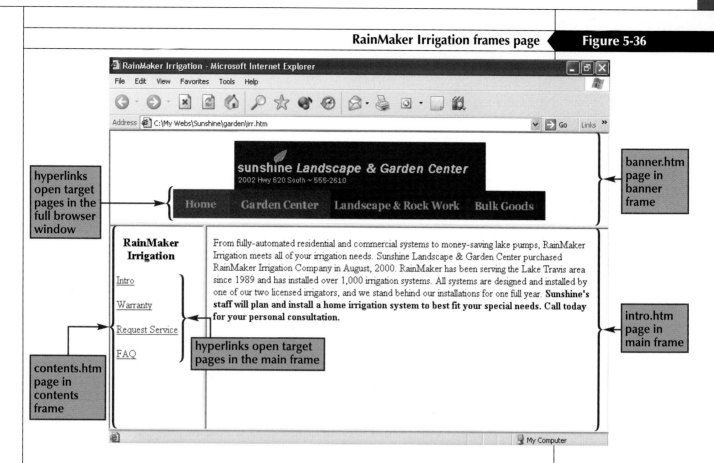

Frames provide Web site developers with a way to display two or more Web pages at once. An advantage of displaying multiple Web pages simultaneously is that the navigation links can be always visible, making it easier to navigate the site. Using a frames page has some disadvantages as well. Some browsers cannot display Web pages that contain frames, which means that some visitors to your Web site might not see the frames page with the different Web pages. Therefore, you should use frames only when you are certain that your Web site's users will be able to display them. Another concern when using a frames page is that the page displayed in the main frame appears in a smaller window than when it is displayed in the full browser window. If the page in the main frame contains a lot of text, users will need to scroll the page frequently to read its contents, which might be distracting.

Creating a Frames Page

FrontPage includes many frames page templates that you can use to create a frameset; Figure 5-36 shows just one example of a frames page that you can create. A **frames page template** is a Web page that contains the specifications for the individual locations and sizes of the frames in a frames page. When you create a frames page using a template, FrontPage assigns a default name to each frame. You can resize any of the frames in a frames page and change other frame properties after creating them.

Figure 5-37 shows the plan for the new RainMaker Irrigation page. The irr.htm page is the frames page, banner.htm contains links that open other pages in the garden Web site, contents.htm contains links that open in the main frame, and intro.htm is one of the pages that will open in the main frame.

Figure 5-37 ▷ **Sketch of the frames page**

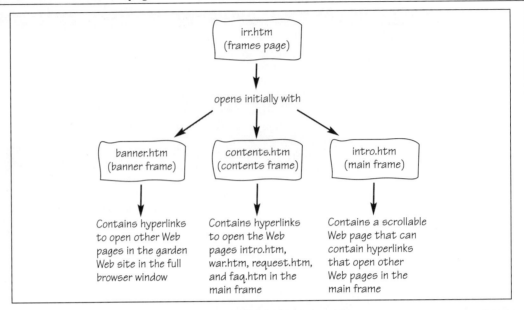

Creating a Frames Page

- Click File on the menu bar, and then click New.
- In the New page section of the New task pane, click More page templates.
- In the Page Templates dialog box, click the Frames Pages tab.
- Click a template to see its preview and description.
- Double-click a template icon to close the Page Templates dialog box and to create the new frames page.

You will create the new RainMaker Irrigation page using a frames page template.

To create a frames page:

▶ 1. Start **FrontPage**, and then open the **garden** Web site from the location where your Web sites are stored.

▶ 2. Click **File** on the menu bar, and then click **New**. The New task pane opens.

▶ 3. In the New page section of the New task pane, click **More page templates**. The Page Templates dialog box opens.

▶ 4. Click the **Frames Pages** tab to display a list of available frames page templates.

You can preview a template to see its description and appearance before using it.

▶ 5. If necessary, click the **Banner and Contents** icon. A preview and description of the selected template appear on the right side of the Page Templates dialog box. See Figure 5-38.

Page Templates dialog box ◄ **Figure 5-38**

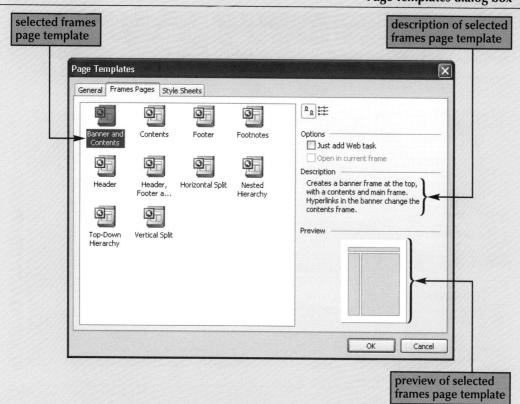

selected frames
page template

description of selected
frames page template

preview of selected
frames page template

▶ **6.** Select other templates and examine their previews and descriptions.

Chad's description of the page he wants you to create most closely matches the Banner and Contents template. This template has a banner frame, a contents frame, and a main frame.

▶ **7.** Double-click the **Banner and Contents** icon to close the Page Templates dialog box and the New task pane and to create the frames page, which opens in Design view with the filename new_page_1.htm. (Your page might use a different number in the filename.) See Figure 5-39.

| Figure 5-39 | New frames page in Design view |

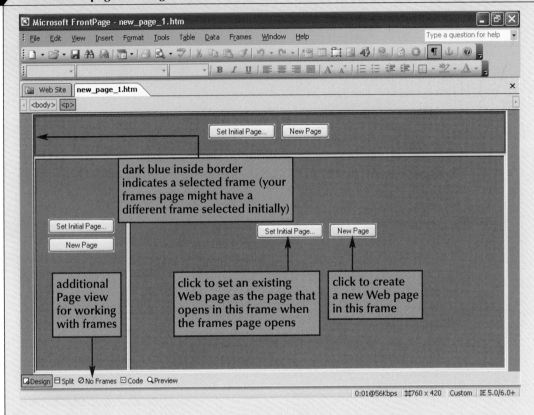

Before beginning your work, you'll save the frames page using the filename irr.htm. Because a page with this filename already exists in the Web site, you'll overwrite the existing file.

▶ **8.** Click the **Save** button 🖫 on the Standard toolbar. The Save As dialog box opens. See Figure 5-40.

| Figure 5-40 | Save As dialog box |

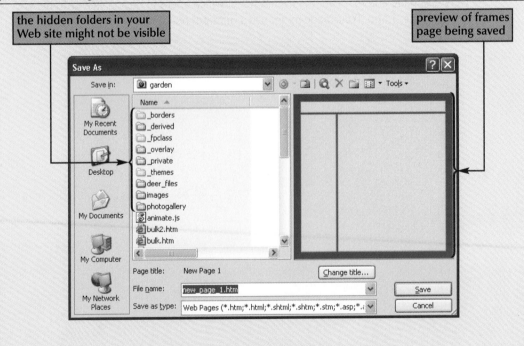

Notice that the Save As dialog box shows a preview of the frames page that you will save. The frames page contains three frames, as indicated by the thin borders. The frames page itself appears with a dark border. If you had created new pages in any of the frames, you would need to save those pages now, as well.

9. Type **irr.htm** as the filename, click the **Change title** button to open the Set Page Title dialog box, type **RainMaker Irrigation** in the Page title text box, click the **OK** button, make sure that the Save in list box displays the garden folder, and then click the **Save** button in the Save As dialog box.

   A message box opens, asking if you want to replace the existing irr.htm file in the Web site.

10. Click the **Yes** button to replace the existing page. The frames page is saved in the Web site using the filename irr.htm. When a browser displays the frames page, the title "RainMaker Irrigation" will appear in its title bar. The titles of pages displayed in the other frames will not appear anywhere in the browser. For this reason, you should create a title that is a description of all of the pages displayed by the frames page, because that title will appear the entire time the frames page is open.

Examining the HTML Document for a Frames Page

The RainMaker Irrigation page that you just created is a Web page with no content except for three empty frames named banner, contents, and main that the Banner and Contents frames page template created. Notice that one new button—No Frames—appears at the bottom of the Contents pane. This button appears when a frames page is open in Design view. A **No Frames page** provides instructions for browsers that cannot display frames.

You want to show Chad the HTML document for a frames page so he sees how the pages in the individual frames are added to the frames page.

To examine the HTML document for a No Frames page and a frames page:

1. Click the **Show No Frames View** button ⊘ No Frames at the bottom of the Contents pane. A new page opens in Show No Frames view and completely replaces the frames page. This page contains the text, "This page uses frames, but your browser doesn't support them." FrontPage created this page automatically with your frames page. If a Web browser that cannot display frames tries to open the irr.htm page, which contains frames, this page will open in its place. You explain to Chad that he could change the content of this page to include hyperlinks to pages that would otherwise be available in the frames page. Because you expect the Web site users to have current releases of browsers that support frames, you will not modify this page.

2. Click the **Show Code View** button ⊡ Code at the bottom of the Contents pane. The HTML document for the irr.htm frames page appears in this view. See Figure 5-41. Notice that the <frame> tags and the name properties identify the three frames created by the Banner and Contents frames page template: banner, contents, and main. Also notice that the title of the page, as specified by the <title> and </title> tags, is RainMaker Irrigation.

| Figure 5-41 | HTML document for the frames page |

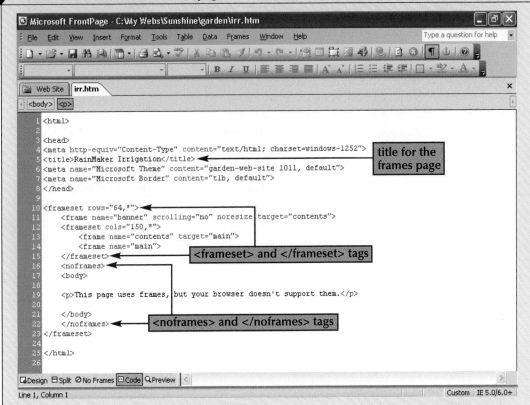

3. Click the **Show Design View** button at the bottom of the Contents pane to return to Design view for the frames page.

Your next task is to set the page that opens in each frame when a browser opens the irr.htm page. You already created these pages, so you just need to import them into the Web site.

Importing Web Pages for Use in a Frames Page

Before you can set Chad's pages to open in the RainMaker Irrigation frames page, you must import them into the Web site. Chad stored these pages in a folder, so you'll import the folder and its contents into the site to keep the pages used in the frames page organized in a single location.

To import pages for a frames page:

1. Display the Folder List, make sure the Web site's root folder is selected, click **File** on the menu bar, and then click **Import** to open the Import dialog box.

2. Click the **Add Folder** button to open the File Open dialog box. If necessary, open the **Tutorial.05\Tutorial** folder included with your Data Files, and then click the **irr** folder to select it.

3. Click the **Open** button. The Import dialog box displays six files in the irr folder.

4. Click the **OK** button to import the folder and its files into the Web site.

5. Close the Folder List.

The pages that will open in the RainMaker Irrigation page are now saved in the Web site.

Setting Initial Pages for Frames

The frames page displays three frames, each containing a Set Initial Page button and a New Page button. Clicking the Set Initial Page button lets you specify an existing Web page (from the current Web site or from another location) as the page that opens in the selected frame. Clicking the New Page button lets you create a new blank page in the Web site and open it in the frame so you can enter its content. Creating a new page for use in any of the frames in the frames page is the same as creating a new Web page in Design view—the only difference is that you are creating and editing the new page in a frame. Because you imported the Web pages that will be used with the frames page, they already exist in the Web site.

To set the initial pages for a frames page:

▶ 1. Click the **Set Initial Page** button in the banner frame. The banner frame is selected and the Insert Hyperlink dialog box opens. When you set the page, you are really creating a hyperlink to it.

   Trouble? If you accidentally click the New Page button in a frame, you will create a new page. To remove it, click Frames on the menu bar, click Frame Properties, delete the text in the Initial page text box, and then click the OK button.

▶ 2. Double-click the **irr** folder to open it, and then double-click **banner.htm**. The Insert Hyperlink dialog box closes and the banner.htm page opens in the banner frame. Notice that you cannot see all of the page's content. You will fix this problem later.

   Trouble? If you accidentally set the wrong page to open in a frame, right-click in the frame to select it and to open the shortcut menu, click Frame Properties, click the Browse button to the right of the Initial page text box to browse for and select the correct file, click the OK button, and then click the OK button again.

▶ 3. Click the **Set Initial Page** button in the contents frame, and then double-click the **contents.htm** page to set it to open in the contents frame on the left side of the frames page.

▶ 4. Click the **Set Initial Page** button in the main frame, and then double-click the **intro.htm** page to set it to open in the main frame on the right side of the frames page. You have now specified the pages to open in each frame when the browser opens the frames page. See Figure 5-42.

Figure 5-42
Initial pages set for the frames page

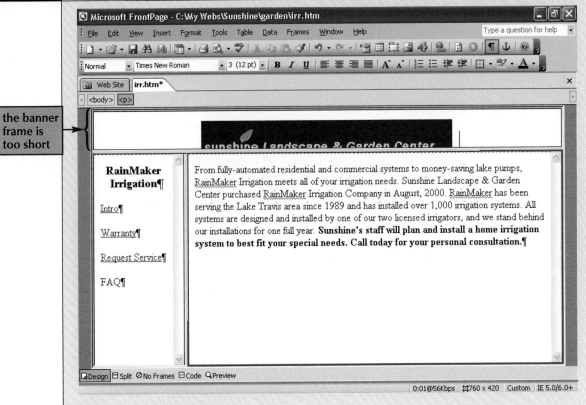

the banner frame is too short

Editing the Frames in a Frames Page

The first problem you noticed is that the banner.htm page does not fit in the frame created by the Banner and Contents frames page. You could open the banner.htm page in Design view and change its contents to fit in the frame. A simpler method, however, is to increase the size of the banner frame so the existing banner.htm page will fit in it. After creating a frames page, you can use the pointer to resize any of the individual frames. Keep in mind, however, that resizing one frame resizes the other frames in the frames page, so make your adjustments carefully.

To edit the frames:

▶ 1. Click the banner frame to select it. A dark blue border appears inside the banner frame to indicate that it is selected.

▶ 2. Move the pointer to the bottom frame border of the banner frame so that the pointer changes to a ↕ shape.

▶ 3. Click and hold the mouse button on the bottom border of the banner frame, drag the frame border down about one inch, and then release the mouse button. Figure 5-43 shows the revised height of the banner frame. Notice that the size of the contents and main frames is reduced to accommodate the larger size of the banner frame.

Frames page with resized banner frame | **Figure 5-43**

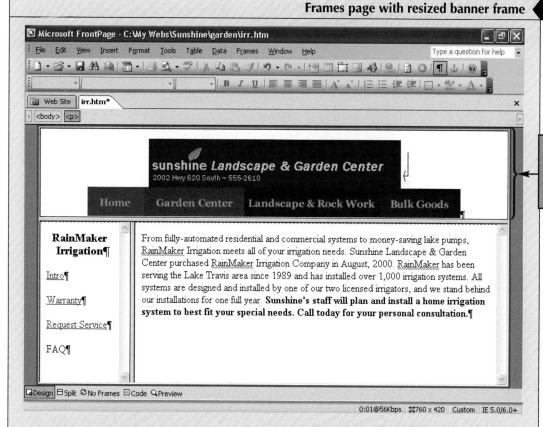

When you changed the size of the banner frame, you changed the HTML document that contains information about the frames. When you display a frames page in Design view, clicking the Save button saves the changes that you made to the pages in the frameset and to the frameset itself.

▸ **4.** Click the **Save** button 🔲 on the Standard toolbar to save the frames page with these initial page settings.

Now that you have updated and saved the pages that open in the frames page, you can work on specifying how pages will open in the frames page.

Creating a Hyperlink in a Frame

A **target frame** is the designated frame in a frames page in which a Web page opens. For example, the target frame for the Warranty page is the main frame of the frames page. When you imported the contents.htm page, it contained the hyperlinks, including their target frames, for the Intro, Warranty, and Request Service pages. You'll format the "FAQ" text as a hyperlink that opens the faq.htm page in the main frame of the RainMaker Irrigation page.

To specify the target frame for a page:

▸ **1.** In the contents frame, select **FAQ** as the text for the hyperlink, and then click the **Insert Hyperlink** button 🖎 on the Standard toolbar to open the Insert Hyperlink dialog box.

▸ **2.** Click **faq.htm** to select the FAQ page.

3. Click the **Target Frame** button. The Target Frame dialog box opens. See Figure 5-44.

Figure 5-44 Target Frame dialog box

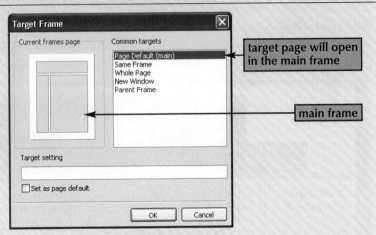

The Common targets list box identifies the available target locations in which to open a page. The Current frames page section identifies the frames in the current page. Clicking a frame in the Current frames page section sets that frame as the target location of the hyperlink. You want the faq.htm page to open in the main frame, so you'll select the main frame.

4. Click the main frame (see Figure 5-44) in the Current frames page section. Notice that the Target setting text box displays the "main" location. This is the same as the "Page Default (main)" setting in the Common targets list box. The default target for hyperlinks in the contents frame is the main frame, so this target was set correctly by the Banner and Contents frames page template.

5. Click the **OK** button to close the Target Frame dialog box, and then click the **OK** button to close the Insert Hyperlink dialog box.

6. Click **FAQ** in the contents frame to deselect it. The "FAQ" text now appears as a hyperlink.

7. Click the **Save** button 🔲 on the Standard toolbar to save the changes you made to the contents.htm page.

Examining a Frame's Properties

After creating a frames page, you can verify that the pages will open in the correct frames by opening the page in a browser and testing them, or by checking the values in the Frame Properties dialog box. You want to show Chad how to verify a frame's properties.

To examine a frame's properties:

1. Right-click the main frame to select it and open the shortcut menu, and then click **Frame Properties**. The Frame Properties dialog box opens. See Figure 5-45.

Frame Properties dialog box ◄ **Figure 5-45**

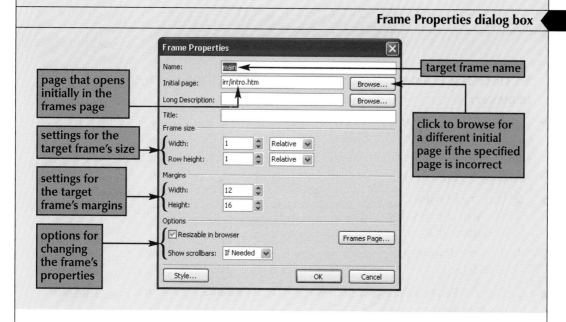

Figure 5-46 describes the changes that you can make to a selected frame using this dialog box.

Options in the Frame Properties dialog box and their descriptions ◄ **Figure 5-46**

Option	Description
Name	The name of the selected frame in the frames page.
Initial page	The filename of the page that opens in the named frame when the frames page is opened in a browser. Click the Browse button to change or set the page that opens initially.
Long Description	The optional filename of the page that contains a description of the page used in the frame. Usually you use a long description when you need to provide a long explanation of something in the frame in a separate file.
Title	The optional short description of a page that identifies its use or function. The title is usually added for users who are visually impaired or people using text-only browsers; it appears as a ScreenTip when you move the pointer over the frame in a browser that supports the title property.
Width (Frame size section)	The frame's width. Use the list box to specify the frame's width relative to other frames, to set the width as a percentage of the browser window's size, or to set the width as a fixed number of pixels. The default width is 1 with relative sizing.
Row height (Frame size section)	The frame's height. Use the list box to specify the frame's height relative to other frames, to set the height as a percentage of the browser window's size, or to set the height as a fixed number of pixels. The default height is 1 with relative sizing.
Width (Margins section)	The frame's margin width (in pixels), which indicates the amount of left and right space to indent the content in the frame from the inside frame border.
Height (Margins section)	The frame's margin height (in pixels), which indicates the amount of top and bottom space to indent the content in the frame from the inside frame border.
Resizable in browser check box	Select this check box to let users resize the current frame using a Web browser. Clear this check box to prevent users from resizing the frame.
Frames Page button	Opens the Page Properties dialog box with the Frames tab selected so that you can change the spacing between frames or turn the display of frame borders on or off.
Show scrollbars list box	Lets you specify whether to display scroll bars as needed for longer pages or to always or never display scroll bars.
Style button	Lets you change the style of the frames in the page; this topic is beyond the scope of this tutorial.

After checking the frame properties and changing them as necessary, you can close the dialog box and test the frames in a browser.

To close the Frame Properties dialog box and test the frames page in a browser:

▶ 1. Verify that the Name text box displays the value "main" and that the Initial page text box has the value "irr/intro.htm." These settings indicate that the intro.htm page will open in the main frame when the browser loads the irr.htm frames page.

▶ 2. Click the **OK** button to close the Frame Properties dialog box.

▶ 3. Click the **Preview** button 🖳 on the Standard toolbar, and then click the **Yes** button to save your changes. The RainMaker Irrigation page opens in the browser and displays the Web pages that you specified in each frame.

▶ 4. Click the **Warranty** hyperlink in the contents frame. The Warranty page opens in the main frame.

▶ 5. Click the **Request Service** hyperlink in the contents frame. The Request Service page opens in the main frame.

▶ 6. Click the **FAQ** hyperlink in the contents frame. The FAQ page opens in the main frame. If your monitor is set to 800 × 600 (or lower) resolution, a scroll bar appears on the right side of the main frame because the FAQ page exceeds the frame's size, as shown in Figure 5-47. The browser added the scroll bar so you can view the rest of this page's contents.

| Figure 5-47 | Frames page after clicking the FAQ hyperlink |

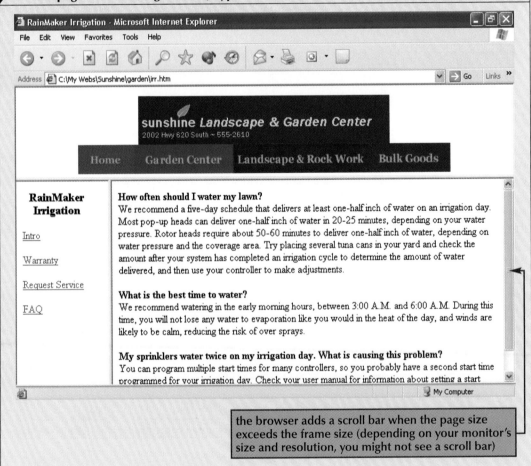

the browser adds a scroll bar when the page size exceeds the frame size (depending on your monitor's size and resolution, you might not see a scroll bar)

7. Click the **Garden Center** hyperlink in the link bar in the banner frame. Because this hyperlink is set to open the center.htm page in a full browser window, the frames page closes and the center.htm page opens.

8. Click the **Irrigation** link to return to the frames page, and then click the **Home** link in the banner frame.

   The home page for the garden Web site, which should open in the full browser window, opens in the contents frame. This indicates that a problem exists with the target for this hyperlink. See Figure 5-48.

Frames page after clicking the Home hyperlink ◄ **Figure 5-48**

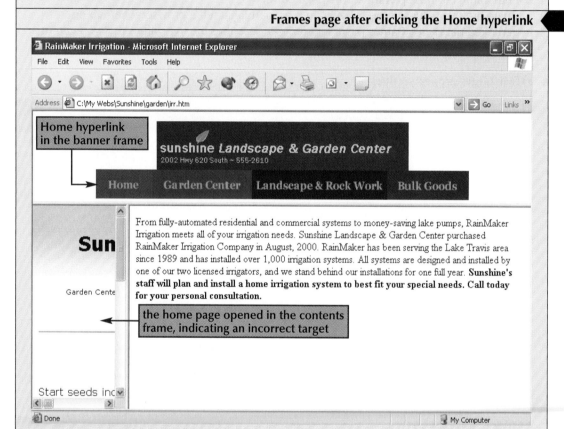

9. Click the **Landscape & Rock Work** hyperlink in the banner frame. The Landscape/Rock Work page replaces the entire RainMaker Irrigation page and opens in the full browser window. This action is the one that you want to occur when any page is opened from the link bar in the banner frame.

10. Click the **Irrigation** hyperlink in the link bar. The RainMaker Irrigation page opens and replaces the Landscape/Rock Work page in the browser window.

11. Close your browser.

When you clicked the link to the home page in the link bar in the banner frame, the page did not completely replace the frames page. Instead, the home page opened in the contents frame. You need to change the target frame for the home page by modifying its hyperlink in the link bar in the banner.htm page so that the frames page will close before the home page opens. In other words, the target of the hyperlink should open in the full browser window without any frames.

Changing a Frame's Target

When you use a FrontPage frames page template to create a frames page, the navigation between frames is already set up for you. For example, the Banner and Contents frames page template specifies that pages opened using hyperlinks in the contents frame will open in the main frame. For the irr.htm frames page, you imported the pages that open in each frame into the Web site, instead of creating them as new pages from within the frames page. Sometimes you might need to change the target frame for a hyperlink. For example, your testing in the previous section revealed that the Home hyperlink in the banner frame did not open the home page correctly.

There are five values of the HTML target property that tell a browser where to open hyperlinked pages in a frames page. Figure 5-49 describes the five values that you can use to specify target frames.

Figure 5-49	HTML target property values

HTML Value	Predefined Frame Name	Description
frame name	Page Default (*frame name*)	The target of the hyperlink is the *frame name* frame in the frames page. The *frame name* varies based on the frames page template you used to create the frames page.
_self	Same Frame	The target of the hyperlink opens in the same frame as the page containing the hyperlink.
_top	Whole Page	The target of the hyperlink replaces the frames page and opens in the full browser window.
_blank	New Window	The target of the hyperlink opens in a new window. A new window means that a second instance of the browser starts and opens the page. Use this option to open a page that is related to the frames page's contents, but is not part of the frames page. For example, a page that contains information about eye discomfort might include a hyperlink that opens a page related to diseases of the eye in a new browser window.
_parent	Parent Frame	The target of the hyperlink opens a page that replaces the entire frameset that defines the frame containing the hyperlink.

The default target frame for a hyperlink is Page Default (*frame name*), where *frame name* is the name of the frame in which the page will open. For example, if you create a hyperlink in a page that appears in the contents frame, the default target frame for the hyperlinked page would be Page Default (main). If you do not specify a predefined frame name when creating a hyperlink, the target of the hyperlink will open in the main frame.

When Chad created the link bar in the banner.htm page, he specified the _top target frame for every hyperlink except for the Home hyperlink. In your testing, you confirmed this problem: The home page opened in the contents frame, whereas the other hyperlinks in the banner frame correctly opened their targets in the full browser window. You need to change the target frame of a hyperlink.

To change the target frame of a hyperlink and test it in the browser:

1. Right-click the **Home** picture in the banner frame to open the shortcut menu, and then click **Hyperlink Properties** to open the Edit Hyperlink dialog box. Notice that the Target Frame section at the bottom of the dialog box identifies the target of the Home hyperlink as "contents," which is the contents frame. This target is incorrect.

2. Click the **Target Frame** button to open the Target Frame dialog box. The current target frame, Page Default (contents), appears in the Common targets list box, and the Target setting text box contains the value "contents." You need to change the target frame so that the home page opens in the full browser window, replacing the entire frames page. To do so, you must specify the Whole Page (_top) target setting.

3. Click **Whole Page** in the Common targets list box. FrontPage adds the HTML equivalent, _top, to the Target setting text box. See Figure 5-50.

Changing the frame target ◄ **Figure 5-50**

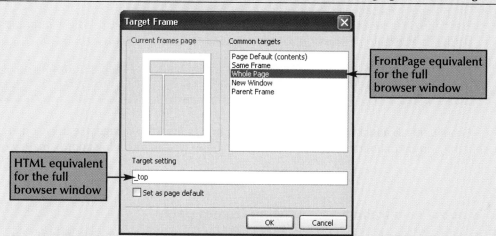

4. Click the **OK** button to close the Target Frame dialog box and return to the Edit Hyperlink dialog box. Notice that the Target Frame section now displays the correct target frame, _top.

5. Click the **OK** button to close the Edit Hyperlink dialog box, and then click the **Save** button 🔲 on the Standard toolbar to save your changes.

   Trouble? If a Picture Actions button appears in the banner frame, click it, click the Resample Picture To Match Size option button, save the page, and then choose the option to overwrite the home_pic.gif file in the Web site's images folder.

6. Click the **Preview** button 🔍 on the Standard toolbar to open the revised frames page in the browser.

   Now test the page again to make sure that it works correctly.

7. Click the **Home** hyperlink in the banner frame. The home page replaces the entire frames page in the browser.

8. Click the **Irrigation** link. The frames page opens. Your test is successful.

9. Close your browser.

Usually, you will need to change a target frame only when it is set incorrectly. Creating hyperlinks that open pages in frames can be a complicated chore, so it is important to test your frames pages thoroughly to ensure that all of the hyperlinked pages open correctly.

You can also use Hyperlinks view to examine all of the hyperlinks to and from a frames page, and use Reports view to search for broken links.

Adding a New Frame to an Existing Frames Page

After creating a frames page, you can add a new frame to it by dividing an existing frame into two separate frames. To divide one existing frame into two frames, press and hold the Ctrl key while dragging the border of the existing frame that you want to divide to create a new frame. After adding the new frame, you can specify a Web page to open in the new frame by using the same procedure you followed for creating other pages in the frames page.

Reference Window

Adding a New Frame to an Existing Frames Page

- Open the frames page in Design view.
- Press and hold the Ctrl key, and then click and hold the mouse button as you drag the border of an existing frame that you want to split to the desired location.
- Release the mouse button and the Ctrl key.
- Use the Set Initial Page button to specify an existing page to open in the new frame, or use the New Page button to create a new page.

Chad wants to add a sales slogan in a new frame in the frames page. He asks you to split the current main frame into two frames, with the new frame being approximately one inch high.

To add a new frame to an existing frames page:

1. Click the main frame to select it. A dark blue border appears around the inside of the main frame.

2. Press and hold the **Ctrl** key, point to the bottom border of the main frame so the pointer changes to a $\updownarrow$ shape, click and hold the mouse button as you drag the border up about one inch, and then release the mouse button and the **Ctrl** key. A new frame is created, containing the Set Initial Page and New Page buttons. See Figure 5-51.

New frame created by splitting the main frame ◄ **Figure 5-51**

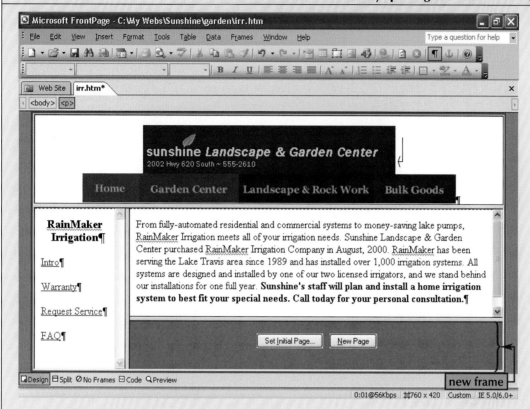

You could add the sales slogan to the new frame, but as Chad looks at the entire frames page, he realizes that the main frame is now too small to display its content effectively. He asks you to restore the main frame to its original size.

► **3.** Click the new frame to select it, click **Frames** on the menu bar, and then click **Delete Frame**. The new frame is deleted and the main frame returns to its original size.

► **4.** Save the page.

FrontPage lets you divide existing frames within a frames page easily and quickly to provide the best presentation for your Web pages. Nevertheless, you must exercise care to avoid making a frame too small to be useful.

Printing a Frames Page

Printing a frames page is not as straightforward as printing a Web page that does not contain frames. In FrontPage, you can print the individual Web pages that appear in each frame in a frames page, but you cannot print the frames page itself. For example, if you select the outer border for the frames page in Design view, the Print button on the Standard toolbar and the Print command on the File menu become disabled. If you select an individual frame in the frames page, you can use either of these methods to print the page that appears in that frame.

When you view a frames page in the browser, you have more options for printing a frames page. If you click File on the menu bar and then click Print, you can use the Print dialog box to select what to print. Figure 5-52 shows the Print dialog box in Internet Explorer.

Figure 5-52 ▶ **Print dialog box (Internet Explorer)**

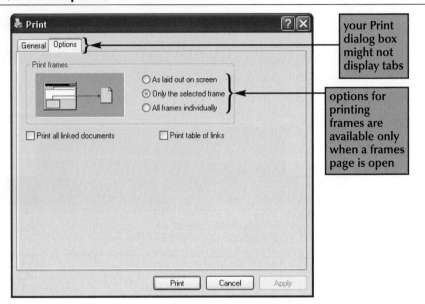

your Print
dialog box
might not
display tabs

options for
printing
frames are
available only
when a frames
page is open

When a frames page is open in the browser, the Print frames section displays three options:

- The "As laid out on screen" option prints the frames page as it appears on the screen. In other words, this option prints the full content of the pages that you see in the browser window.
- The "Only the selected frame" option prints the active frame.
- The "All frames individually" option prints the full content of each page in the frames page on a separate sheet of paper.

Chad wants you to print the frames page, not just the individual pages contained within the frames page.

To print the frames page:

▶ 1. Click the **Preview** button 🔍 on the Standard toolbar to open the RainMaker Irrigation page in the browser.

▶ 2. Click **File** on the menu bar, and then click **Print**. The Print dialog box opens. If necessary, click the **Options** tab to display those settings.

Trouble? If you are using Netscape Navigator version 6.x or lower, you must click each frame to select it, and then click the Print button on the toolbar to print each frame's contents individually. These versions of Navigator do not have an option to print a frames page. Skip to Step 4 after printing each of the three frames.

Trouble? If you are using Netscape Navigator version 7.x or higher, the Print Frames section of the Print dialog box contains the options for printing a frames page.

▶ 3. Click the **As laid out on screen** option button in the Print frames section, and then click the **Print** button (or the **OK** button). Internet Explorer prints the contents of the frames page as it appears on the screen.

▶ 4. Close your browser.

Viewing HTML Tags for a Frames Page

When you viewed the HTML document for the frames page earlier in this session, you saw only the HTML tags that created the frames page. Now you want to show Chad the HTML document for the frames page again, so he can see the HTML tags that FrontPage created to open the Web pages in the frames page. The <frameset> and </frameset> tags indicate the beginning and end of the frameset and specify each frame in the frames page. Within the <frame> tag, the src property indicates the filename for the target page, and the name property identifies the name of the frame in which to display the target page. The rows and columns properties of the <frameset> tag indicate the layout of the frames as a percentage of the size of the page when it is displayed in the browser. The Student Online Companion page for Tutorial 5 includes links that you can follow to learn more about HTML tags that create frames pages.

To view the HTML document for a frames page:

1. Click the **Show Code View** button [Code] at the bottom of the Contents pane to display the HTML document for the irr.htm page. See Figure 5-53. For each frame in the frames page, the HTML document specifies the frame's name (frame name), the page to open initially (src), and the size of the frame (frameset cols).

HTML document for the frames page ◄ **Figure 5-53**

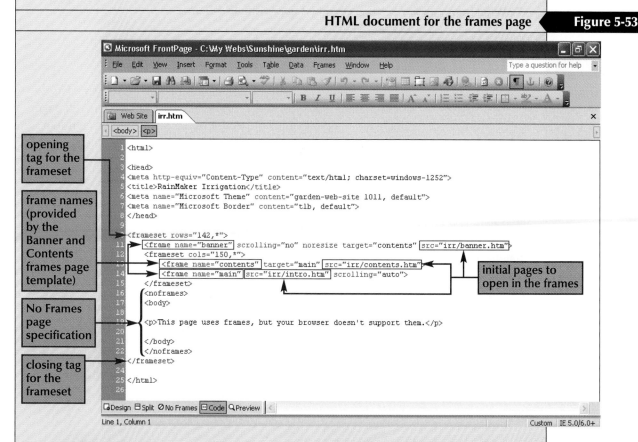

Trouble? The value you see for the rows property in the <frameset> tag might differ, depending on how you resized the banner frame in the steps. This difference causes no problems.

2. Return to Design view.

3. Close the garden Web site, and then close FrontPage.

The frames page is complete and it effectively organizes the content Chad requested. You will complete the second table for Helen's Lawn Care page in the Review Assignments. In the next tutorial, you will create forms that let visitors provide feedback and search the Web site for specific text, and then you will publish the Web site to a server.

Review

Session 5.2 Quick Check

1. True or False: A frames page does not contain any content; it contains only the specifications that define the empty frames.
2. A frames page that displays two frames will display _____ Web pages when it is opened in a browser.
3. True or False: You can use a frames page without hesitation because all browsers can display frames.
4. Click the _____ button in Design view to examine the HTML document that creates a frames page.
5. Click the _____ button in an empty frame to specify an existing Web page to open when the browser loads the frames page.
6. Which predefined frame name causes the browser to remove all loaded frames pages before displaying the target of a selected hyperlink?
7. What information does the <frame> tag provide in a frameset?

Review

Tutorial Summary

In this tutorial, you learned how to use tables to organize information in two ways. First, you learned how to position pictures in a table to control their appearance in a Web page. Then you saw how to create a traditional table with gridlines that delineate the cells in a table. Tables are an important Web design tool because all browsers interpret the HTML tags that create tables consistently, thus providing a way to align content in a Web page so it always looks the way you intend it to.

You also learned how to create a frames page in this tutorial. The use of frames in a Web site is a frequent topic of debate between Web developers. Some Web developers avoid using frames because of the possibility that some Web site visitors will not have recent versions of browsers that can display them. However, many Web developers like using frames as a way of controlling Web site content. Much like tables, frames provide a consistent way to organize the content of your Web site. If you develop a Web site using frames, you can display all of your pages in frames, or just a subset of pages as you did in the garden Web site. However, be sure to check your frames pages carefully to make sure that the hyperlinks open their targets in the correct frames. If you use a frames page template to create a frames page, FrontPage will manage the hyperlink targets for you. If you add or remove a frame from the frames page created by a template, however, be sure to test your page thoroughly to make sure that the pages open in the frames as you intend them to.

Key Terms

border	frameset	No Frames page
cell	Insert Table button grid	split
cell padding	layout cell	table
cell spacing	layout table	Table AutoFormat
frames page	merge	table caption
frames page template	nested table	target frame

Practice

Practice the skills you learned in the tutorial using the same case scenario.

Review Assignments

Data Files needed for these Review Assignments: sun1.gif, tips.doc

To finish your work for today, you will need to format the remaining pictures in the table in the Bulk Goods Samples page and create the second table in the Lawn Care page. Finally, Chad wants to add a new page to the RainMaker Irrigation page, so you'll add this page to the Web site and create a hyperlink to it in the contents frame that will open the page in the main frame.

If necessary, start FrontPage, make sure you have your Data Files, and then do the following:

1. Open the **garden** Web site from the location where your Web sites are stored.
2. Open the **bulk2.htm** page in Design view. Format the pictures with the words "soil" and "stone" on them as hyperlinks that open the **soil.htm** and **stone.htm** pages, respectively.
3. Add a light yellow background color (Hex={FF,FF,CC}) to the table in the **bulk2.htm** page. Save and close the **bulk2.htm** page.
4. Open the Lawn Care page (**lawn.htm**) in Design view. Select the caption and the entire table, and then change the font size to 10 points. (*Hint:* Use the pointer to select the caption and the table.)
5. Select the text "[insert table here]" in the page, and then create the table shown in Figure 5-54. Use the same properties for the new table (alignment, size, cell padding, Table AutoFormat, font size, font style, and so on) that you used for the Common Lawn Problems and Solutions table that appears in the same page. Resize the first column in the table you are creating to match the width of the first column in the other table in the page. Change the second, third, and fourth columns to distribute them evenly, and then reset the table's width to 95%.

Figure 5-54

Sunshine Landscape & Garden Center			
The best landscape is an organic one!			
	Spring	Summer	Fall/Winter
Mowing	Mow every one to two weeks as necessary.	Mow every two weeks.	Mow every two to four weeks.
Fertilizing	Top-dress lawn with compost, and then in three to four weeks, apply an organic fertilizer (8-2-4).	Spray once a week with liquid seaweed.	Top-dress lawn with compost, and continue foliar feeding with liquid seaweed.
Watering	Water deeply when there is no rainfall.	Water deeply, in the morning or late evening, every five days.	Water deeply when there is no rainfall and before a freeze.
Other	Apply corn gluten to turf grasses to kill pre-emergent weeds.	Apply a soil activator to energize soil.	Prune oak trees and protect new plants from freezes.

6. Click the cell in column 1, row 3, of the table you created in Step 5, and then insert the **sun1.gif** picture from the Tutorial.05\Review folder included with your Data Files. Save the page and save the picture in the Web site's images folder.

7. Add the caption "Organic Lawn Care Program Recommendations" to the table you created in Step 5. After creating the caption, change its format to bold and 10 points.

8. Save the **lawn.htm** page, preview it using a browser, and then print it. Close your browser, and then close the **lawn.htm** page.

9. Open the **irr.htm** page in Design view. In the contents frame, add a new "Tips" hyperlink below the FAQ hyperlink. When you create the hyperlink, click the Create New Document button on the Link to bar in the Insert Hyperlink dialog box. Type **tips.htm** in the Name of new document text box, set the target frame so the **tips.htm** page opens in the main frame, and then click the Edit the new document now option button.

10. Remove the theme and shared borders from the **tips.htm** page only.

11. Insert the **tips.doc** file from the Tutorial.05\Review folder into the **tips.htm** page, and then save and close the page.

12. Open the RainMaker Irrigation page in a browser and test all the hyperlinks in the banner and contents frames. If necessary, return to FrontPage and correct any problems that you discover.

13. Use your browser to print the frames page with the **tips.htm** page displayed in the main frame. (If you cannot print the frames page with your browser, print each page displayed in the frames page individually.) Close your browser.

14. Close the **garden** Web site, and then close FrontPage.

Create

Create a frames page in a Web site, create a table in a Web page, and experiment with viewing a table at different screen resolutions to understand more about setting table widths.

Case Problem 1

There are no new Data Files needed for this Case Problem.

Buffalo Trading Post Retail-clothing customers usually want to know which items are the current best-sellers. Nicole Beirne, owner of Buffalo Trading Post, has decided that a list of the current top-selling items would be a great addition to the Web site. As you discuss this concept with Nicole and several sales associates, you conclude that there are three main areas of interest: women's clothing, children's clothing, and accessories. You already added these pages to the Web site, but now you want to use them in a frames page. Because the pages will not require the Web site's shared borders, you'll need to turn off the shared borders in these pages. Nicole is eager to see the new What page in the Web site.

If necessary, start FrontPage, and then do the following:

1. Open the **buffalo** Web site from the location where your Web sites are stored. (If you did not create this Web site in Tutorial 1 and change it in Tutorials 2 through 4, ask your instructor for assistance.)
2. In Folders view, select the **acc.htm**, **child.htm**, and **women.htm** pages, and then turn off the shared borders for these selected pages only. (*Hint:* To select multiple files, click the first file, press and hold the Ctrl key, select the remaining files, and then release the Ctrl key.)
3. Use the Banner and Contents frames page template to create a new frames page with the filename **what.htm** and the title What. Replace the existing **what.htm** file in the Web site that you created in Tutorial 2.

Explore ▶

4. Create a new Web page in the banner frame with the filename **banner.htm** and the title Banner. In this new page, create a table that will contain the entries for the link bar. Your table should contain one row and five cells. Type the following text in the five cells: Home, How, Who, Where, and Contact. For the Home, How, and Who links, create hyperlinks to the appropriate pages in the Web site. Make sure to set the targets to open pages in the whole browser window.
5. Create two new Web pages in the site. The first page's filename is **where.htm** and its title is Where. The second page's filename is **contact.htm** and its title is Contact. Change to Navigation view, and then add the **where.htm** and **contact.htm** pages as child pages of the home page and to the right of the Who page.
6. In the **banner.htm** page in the frames page, format the Where and Contact text as hyperlinks that open the **where.htm** and **contact.htm** pages in the whole browser window.
7. Select the cells in the table in the banner frame, distribute the columns evenly, and then change the alignment of the data in the cells to centered. Change the table's properties so it is centered on the page.

Explore ▶

8. Apply the Classic 1 Table AutoFormat to the table in the banner frame. Turn off the features that apply special formatting to the heading rows and the first column.
9. Change the properties of the table in the banner frame so it is 640 pixels wide, and then save the **banner.htm** page.

Explore ▶

10. Create a new page in the contents frame with the filename **contents.htm** and the title Contents. Following your plan for the frames page, type Women's Clothing, Children's Clothing, and Accessories on separate lines in the **contents.htm** page, and then format these entries as hyperlinks that open the correct pages in the main frame.

Explore ▶

11. Design a table that you will use to present the different top-selling items lists. The table should contain the item's category (such as "Shoes"), the item's description (such as "Sneakers and dress shoes"), and the item's price range (such as "$15 - $50").

12. Set the **women.htm** page to open initially in the main frame, add a centered heading with the Heading 2 style at the top of the page with the text "Top Women's Clothing Items," and then follow the plan you created in Step 11 to create the first table. Add the headings and five rows of data that you make up to the table, and then save it.

13. If necessary, resize the columns in your table so they best fit the data they contain. For example, the column that holds the item descriptions should be wider than the columns that hold the item names and price ranges.

14. Change the properties of the table in the **women.htm** page so it is centered in the page and 500 pixels wide, and then save it.

Explore

15. Apply the Classic 1 Table AutoFormat to the table in the **women.htm** page, and turn off the feature to apply special formatting to the first column. After applying the Table AutoFormat, change the background color of the cells in the first row to the light-yellow color in the Theme Colors section (this color is RGB(FF,FF,CC); if you do not see this color, select another light-yellow or beige color). Save your changes.

16. With the insertion point in the main frame, press Ctrl + A to select the page's content, click the Copy button on the Standard toolbar, and then use Ctrl + Click to open the **child.htm** page in the main frame. (*Hint:* Use the hyperlink in the contents frame. If you formatted this hyperlink with the correct target in Step 10, it will open in the main frame. If the page does not open in the main frame, correct the hyperlink's target, save your changes, and then resume the steps.)

17. Paste the content you copied into the **child.htm** page, and then edit the heading and table content to reflect the top-selling items in the children's clothing category.

18. Open the **acc.htm** page in the main frame, paste the table into this page, and then edit it to reflect the top-selling items in the accessories category. (Accessories are purses, jewelry, scarves, sunglasses, hats, etc.)

Explore

19. Reduce the width of the contents frame to 115 pixels. (*Hint:* Click in the contents frame, and then use the Frame Properties dialog box.)

Explore

20. Save your changes, and then open the frames page in a browser at 640 × 480 resolution and verify that clicking each hyperlink results in the appropriate action. If you encounter any problems during testing, return to FrontPage and correct them. Then use the browser to print the frames page as it appears in the browser with the Accessories page displayed in the main frame. (If you cannot print the frames page with your browser, print each page displayed in the frames page individually.) Close the browser, and then open the frames page in a browser at 800 × 600 resolution. What differences do you find between your testing at different resolutions? Why did these differences occur? Write your response and submit it to your instructor with your completed work.

21. Close your browser, the **buffalo** Web site, and FrontPage.

Case Problem 2

Apply

Apply the skills you learned in the tutorial to create a frames page in a Web site and use tables to organize pages that open in the main frame.

There are no new Data Files needed for this Case Problem.

Garden Grill Meghan Elliott and Callan Murphy just returned from a meeting with Hazel Scherer, who runs the marketing department at Garden Grill. During the meeting, Hazel asked if they could add a new page to the Web site to highlight the restaurant's weekly menu specials. As Hazel described the content she wants you to add, Meghan decided to replace the existing menu.htm page in the Web site with a frames page that will open four pages in its main frame to list specials in four menu categories: appetizers, sandwiches, entrees, and desserts. Hazel also thinks that a table would be the best way to organize the entries in each menu; she asks you to develop prototypes of these Web pages so she can approve them.

If necessary, start FrontPage, and then do the following:

1. Open the **grill** Web site from the location where your Web sites are stored. (If you did not create this Web site in Tutorial 1 and change it in Tutorials 2 through 4, ask your instructor for assistance.)

Explore

2. In Folders view, select the **app.htm**, **desserts.htm**, **entrees.htm**, and **sand.htm** pages, and then turn off the bottom shared border for these selected pages only. (*Hint:* To select multiple files, click the first file, press and hold the Ctrl key, select the remaining files, and then release the Ctrl key.)

3. Use the Contents frames page template to create a frames page. Save the page with the filename **menu.htm** and the title Menu, and overwrite the existing page in the Web site with the same name.

4. Sketch the design and contents of the table that will contain the menu items. The table should include at least three menu choices and columns for each item's name, description, and price.

Explore

5. Create a new page in the contents frame (the frame on the left) with the filename **contents.htm** and title Contents. The Contents page should include hyperlinks to the home page and to each menu page, with the main frame being the target for each of the four menu category pages. Set the target for the hyperlink to the home page so it opens in the full browser window.

6. Set the **app.htm** as the page that opens initially in the main frame.

7. Follow the plan you designed in Step 4 and create the table in the **app.htm** page. Insert a minimum of three menu items using data that you make up. Add a new first row to the table, which contains one merged cell that spans the three columns in the table. Center this merged cell, and then type "Appetizers." Set the table so it 100% of the browser's window width and uses a collapsed table border. Set the cell padding and cell spacing properties to 2. Apply a Table AutoFormat of your choice to the table. Be sure that the Table AutoFormat's colors complement the colors provided by the page's theme, and, if necessary, format the column headings and row headings in bold. With the exception of the first row, set the vertical alignment of cells to top and the horizontal alignment of cells to left. When you are finished, save the page.

Explore

8. With the insertion point in the main frame, press Ctrl + A to select the page's content, click the Copy button on the Standard toolbar, and then use Ctrl + Click to open the **sand.htm** page in the main frame. (*Hint:* Use the hyperlink in the contents frame. If you formatted this hyperlink with the correct target in Step 5, it will open in the main frame. If the page does not open in the main frame, correct the hyperlink's target, save your changes, and then resume the steps.)

9. Paste the content you copied into the **sand.htm** page, and then edit the table content to reflect menu items in the Sandwich category. Save the page.

10. Repeat Step 9 to complete the tables in the **entrees.htm** and **desserts.htm** pages. Save each page as you finish it.

Explore

11. Create a new frame in the Menu page by splitting the contents frame. Drag the bottom border of the contents frame up approximately two inches to create the new frame. Next, create a new Web page in the new frame with the filename **contact.htm** and the title Contact Us. In the new frame, type "Didn't find your favorites? Specials change each week!" If the text you typed doesn't fit in the frame, increase the size of the new frame to best fit the text. Save your changes.

12. Test the frames page in a browser. If you see a scroll bar in the frame that you added to the frames page in Step 11, return to FrontPage and increase the height of the new frame, save the page, and then refresh the frames page in the browser. Use the browser to print the frames page as it appears in the browser with the Desserts page displayed in the main frame. (If you cannot print the frames page with your browser, print each page displayed in the frames page individually.) Close your browser.

13. Use FrontPage to print the HTML document for the frames page.

14. Close the **grill** Web site, and then close FrontPage.

Apply

Use the skills you learned in the tutorial to create a frames page and expand your knowledge of working with tables by converting existing text into a table.

Case Problem 3

Data Files needed for this Case Problem: frame folder, scott.jpg, tucker.jpg

Swenson Auctioneers Scott Swenson knows that part of the reason for his company's success is the excellent word-of-mouth advertising he receives from satisfied customers when they recommend Swenson Auctioneers to their colleagues and friends. In times of economic downturns, Scott realizes that conducting an auction can be a very stressful time for a client who has lost his business. Auctions are equally stressful when they are held to sell off the estate of a loved one who has passed away. Scott has received many positive comments from former and current clients and he wants to showcase these comments on the Web site. Scott has already contacted the people who have submitted these comments and has obtained their written permission to use their remarks in the Web site. Scott asks you to add a page to the Web site that is accessible through a hyperlink on the home page. As you review the content for this page, you recommend presenting it in a frames page. Scott likes this idea and asks you to make it happen.

Scott also wants to add his picture and Tucker Griffin's picture to the Our Team page. You agree to make this change, as well, and recommend putting the pictures in a table to control their position in the page.

If necessary, start FrontPage, make sure you have your Data Files, and then do the following:

1. Open the **swenson** Web site from the location where your Web sites are stored. (If you did not create this Web site in Tutorial 1 and change it in Tutorials 2 through 4, ask your instructor for assistance.)

2. Use the New task pane to create a new Web page using the Contents frames page template. Save the frames page using the filename **clients.htm** and the title Client Comments.

3. Open the home page in Design view, select the word "clients" in the second sentence of the paragraph that begins "Established…", and then format this word as a hyperlink that opens the **clients.htm** page. Save the home page.

Explore

4. In the contents frame (the frame on the left) of the frames page, create a new page using the filename **contents.htm** and the title Contents. In the **contents.htm** page, insert the **sw_logo.gif** file from the **swenson** Web site's images folder. Format this picture as a hyperlink that opens the home page in the whole browser window. Add the alternative text "Return to Swenson Auctioneers Home Page" to the picture. Center the picture in the page, and then save the page.

Explore

5. Increase the width of the contents frame to 30%. (*Hint:* Select the contents frame, and then change the unit of measurement in the Frame size section of the Frame Properties dialog box.)

6. Import the **frame** folder and its contents from the Tutorial.05\Case3 folder included with your Data Files into the root folder of the **swenson** Web site. This folder contains eight files that you will use in the frames page. After importing this folder, open it in Folders view, select all eight files, and then apply the Swenson Web Site theme to them.

7. Set the **bus.htm** page in the **frame** folder to open initially in the main frame when the browser loads the frames page. Then add the following items to the **contents.htm** page, making sure the entries are centered and appear on separate lines: Business Equipment & Computers; Manufacturing & Heavy Equipment; Furniture, Art, & Rugs; Sound & Lighting; Special Use; Real Estate; Estates & Antiques; and Benefit Auctions. For each entry in the **contents.htm** page, create a hyperlink that opens the related page in the main frame. (The pages that these links should open are, respectively: **bus.htm, manu.htm, furn.htm, sound.htm, special.htm, real.htm, estate.htm**, and **benefit.htm**. These files are stored in the **frame** folder of the Web site.)

8. Save the **clients.htm** page, and then preview it in a browser. Test the hyperlinks that you created, including the hyperlink to open the home page and the hyperlink in the home page to open the Client Comments page. If necessary, return to FrontPage to make any corrections, resave the page, and then test it again. When you are finished, display the Sound & Lighting page in the main frame and then print the frames page. (If you cannot print the frames page with your browser, print each page displayed in the frames page individually.) Close your browser.

Explore

9. Open the **team.htm** page in Design view, and then scroll down to the bio for Scott. Scott told you that in his picture, he is facing to the left, so you will position the picture on the right side of the page so it appears that he is "looking" at the content. Select the four paragraphs below Scott's name (but not the hyperlink that scrolls to the top of the page or his name and position), and then convert this text to a table. (*Hint:* Click Table on the menu bar, point to Convert, and then click Text to Table. In the Convert Text To Table dialog box, click the None (text in single cell) option button, and then click the OK button.) The four paragraphs now appear in a table with one cell.

10. Insert a new column to the right of the single cell that you just created. In the new cell that you created, insert the **scott.jpg** file from the Tutorial.05\Case3 folder.

11. Set the table's properties so it is has a width of 100% and invisible table borders.

Explore

12. Tucker's picture shows him looking to the right, so you will insert his picture to the left of the paragraph that appears below his name and position. Select the paragraph below Tucker's name and position, convert it to a table, and then insert a column to the left of the single cell you created and insert the **tucker.jpg** picture from the Tutorial.05\Case3 folder. Set the table's properties so it has a width of 100% and invisible table borders.

13. Change the cells that contain pictures in both tables you created to the top vertical alignment.

14. Save the **team.htm** page and save the pictures in the Web site's images folder. Preview the **team.htm** page in a browser, print it, and then close your browser.

15. Close the **swenson** Web site, and then close FrontPage.

Create

Create a frames page in a Web site.

Case Problem 4

Data Files needed for this Case Problem: resource folder

Mortgage Services, Inc. As part of her Web site plan, Natalie Fuselier wants to include a page in the Web site for Mortgage Services, Inc. that provides resources for people who are moving into the area. She plans to include lists of homeowner's insurance agents, moving companies, utilities, and other helpful numbers that might assist her clients. A draft of this page appears in the current Web site, but Natalie wants you to improve it by adding the links and organizing the content so it is easy to use. She gives you the sketch shown in Figure 5-55 and asks you to make this change to the Web site. After you create the page, Natalie will begin working on compiling the links and other information to add to these new pages.

Figure 5-55

If necessary, start FrontPage, make sure you have your Data Files, and then do the following:

1. Open the **loan** Web site from the location where your Web sites are stored. (If you did not create this Web site in Tutorial 1 and change it in Tutorials 2 through 4, ask your instructor for assistance.)

2. Examine the sketch shown in Figure 5-55, and then create a new frames page in the Web site using the Contents frames page template. Save the frames page as **resource.htm** and with the title Resources, replacing the existing file in the Web site with the same name.

Explore

3. Make the following changes to the **resource.htm** frames page:

   a. Split the main frame (on the right) to create a new "top" frame. In this frame, create a new page with the filename **top.htm** and the title Top. Type and format the text shown in Figure 5-55 in the top frame. Format the word "here" as a hyperlink that opens the home page in the full browser window. If necessary, resize the height of the new frame so you can see all of the text you typed.

   b. Split the frame on the left to create a new frame at the top that is the same height as the top frame you created in the previous step. Create a new page using the filename **corner.htm** and the title Corner. Do not add any content to the page in the corner frame.

   c. Select the contents frame, and then open the Frame Properties dialog box. Click the Frames Page button and turn off the display of the frame's borders. Close the dialog boxes, save your changes, and then view the frames page in Preview view, noticing the effect created by creating the corner frame and turning off the frame's borders. (The background picture appears only in the corner and top frames because you haven't added any pages to the contents and main frames yet.)

   d. Change to Code view for the frames page. Inspect the HTML document and notice the default names assigned to the two new frames you created in the frames page. Edit the HTML tag for the frame that contains the corner.htm page to change its name property to "corner." (Make sure to enclose this value in quotation marks.) Then find the HTML tag that creates the frame that contains the top.htm page and change its name property to "top." Return to Design view, and then save your changes.

   e. Import the **resource** folder and its contents from the Tutorial.05\Case4 folder included with your Data Files into the **loan** Web site's root folder. After importing the folder into the Web site, open it in Folders view, select the six files it contains, and then apply the Loan Web Site theme to the selected pages.

   f. In the contents frame of the frames page, create a new page using the filename **contents.htm** and the title Contents. Type the text shown in Figure 5-55 in the **contents.htm** page, and then format each item as a hyperlink that opens the related page in the main frame. The pages to open in the main frame are stored in the **resource** folder in the Web site. (*Note:* These pages contain headings, but no content.)

   g. Set the **insure.htm** page to open initially in the main frame.

   h. Save the frames page.

4. Preview the frames page in a browser, and then test the links that you created, including the link to the home page. Use the Resources link in the home page to return to the frames page. Display the Schools page in the main frame of the frames page, and then use the browser to print it. (If you cannot print the frames page with your browser, print each page displayed in the frames page individually.) Close your browser.

5. In FrontPage, display the HTML document for the frames page, and then print it.

6. Close the **loan** Web site, and then close FrontPage.

Quick Check Answers

Session 5.1

1. a cell
2. Use a percentage for tables that contain mostly text; use pixels when you need tight control over the placement of objects that have a fixed size, such as pictures.
3. cell padding
4. True
5. False
6. above
7. Select the cells, and then click the Merge Cells button; or click the Eraser button, and then use the pointer to erase the border between the cells to merge.
8. above

Session 5.2

1. True
2. three
3. False
4. Show Code View
5. Set Initial Page
6. _top (Whole Page)
7. the frame's name, the target frame, and the initial page to load in the frame

Objectives

Session 6.1
- Create a Web page using a template
- Change the properties of a search component
- Add a form component to a Web page
- Add form fields to a form and set their properties

Session 6.2
- Validate a form field
- Use a form handler
- Open an Office document from a Web site

Session 6.3
- Publish a Web site
- Process Web pages on a server
- Create a hit counter in a Web page
- Synchronize local and remote Web sites
- Recalculate and verify hyperlinks in a Web site
- Set permissions for a Web site

Publishing a Web Site

Creating Web Pages with Components and Processing Pages on a Server

Case

Sunshine Landscape & Garden Center

In this morning's staff meeting, you spent some time presenting the Web site to the senior staff at Sunshine Landscape & Garden Center. Almost everyone has contributed content to the site and is pleased with its overall content, appearance, and organization.

As you review the pages with Sunshine's owner, Brett Kizer, you suggest adding two new pages to the site. The first page would let Web site visitors search the entire site for content based on one or more keywords that they enter in a text box. This page would let visitors find the content they need without having to navigate the entire site looking for it. Brett agrees that this page would be useful and asks you to proceed with its creation.

The second page would contain a form that a visitor can use to submit a question or a request. In talking with staff members at the nursery, you found that many customers have expressed interest in using the Web site to request a consultation about landscaping or rock work installations and to ask questions about plants and lawn care. When the new site is published, you think that this functionality will be a nice way to promote the nursery's goal of increased customer service. Brett likes this idea and sees potential for it in the future to generate lists of customers and their requests for service and installations. He asks you to create this page in the Web site, as well.

After creating these two new pages and testing the Web site, you will publish the Web site to a server where you can test the site again and make it ready for its final destination on the Web server Brett selected to host it. After publishing the Web site, it will be accessible to Internet visitors.

Student Data Files

To complete this tutorial, you will need your ending files from Tutorial 5 and the following Data Files. Additional Data Files needed to complete the end-of-tutorial exercises are listed with the Review Assignments and Case Problems.

▼ **Tutorial.06**

▽ Tutorial folder

    form.doc

    requests.htm

Creating a Page That Searches a Web Site

So far in this book, you have created pages in a Web site using a template. Some of those pages were based on the Normal Page template, which creates a blank Web page. In Tutorial 5, you used templates to create frames pages. FrontPage includes many templates that create Web pages with sample formatting and text. For example, if you need to create a Web page into which users will enter personal information, you might create your page using the Guest Book template, which includes features and sample text that are commonly found in a printed guest book. When you use a template to create a new Web page that contains sample content, you can edit it just like any other Web page. Figure 6-1 describes the general templates that you can use to create Web pages.

Figure 6-1 ▶ **General template Web pages and wizards and their descriptions**

Name	Description
Normal Page	Creates a blank Web page
Bibliography	Creates a page with references to printed or electronic works
Confirmation Form	Creates a page that confirms the receipt of information from a user of a form, discussion, or registration page
Feedback Form	Creates a page that collects data entered by a user, such as comments and personal information
Form Page Wizard	A wizard that creates a page containing a form with fields to collect information
Frequently Asked Questions	Creates a page with popular questions about a topic and their answers
Guest Book	Creates a page into which visitors to a Web site can enter comments and other information
Photo Gallery	Creates a page that contains a photo gallery with pictures, captions, and descriptions that you supply
Search Page	Creates a page that accepts keywords entered by a user and then returns a list of hyperlinks to pages with matching entries
Table of Contents	Creates a page that contains a list of hyperlinks to every page in the current Web site
User Registration	Creates a page that visitors can use to register for a restricted-access Web site

After meeting with the nursery's senior staff, your first task is to add a page to the Web site that searches the entire site using one or more keywords entered by the user. The Search Page template creates content for you and adds the necessary functionality to the page to search the site, so you'll base the new page on the Search Page template.

To create the Search page using a template:

▶ 1. Start **FrontPage**, and then open the **garden** Web site from the location where your Web sites are stored.

▶ 2. Click the **list arrow** on the Create a new normal page button 🗋 ▾ on the Standard toolbar, and then click **Page**. The Page Templates dialog box opens with the General tab selected.

▶ 3. Click the **Search Page** icon to select it. See Figure 6-2. The description and preview indicate that this page will provide the capability for searching the entire Web site.

Page Templates dialog box ◀ **Figure 6-2**

templates (your list might differ)   Search Page template description

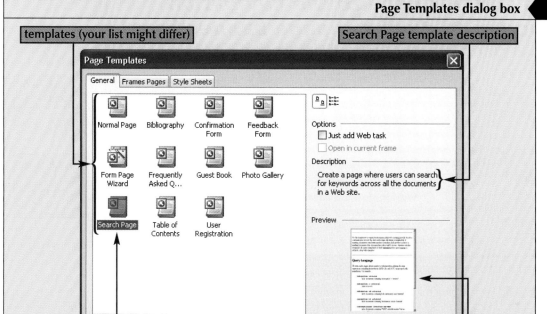

selected Search Page template   preview of the selected template

▶ 4. Click the **OK** button to create a new Web page based on the Search Page template. The new page opens in Design view, as shown in Figure 6-3. Because you have not yet added this page to the navigation structure in Navigation view, the page displays placeholder text for the page banner and link bar.

Figure 6-3   **New page created using the Search Page template**

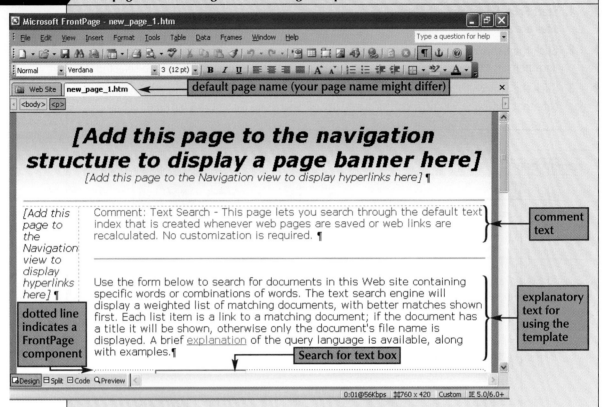

5. Scroll down the page and examine its contents. The page contains a comment at the top of the page, text that describes how to use the page, a Web component that contains a Search for text box and the Start Search and Reset buttons, and an "explanation" hyperlink that links to a Query Language section with details about using the page. The bottom of the page contains a "Back to Top" hyperlink to a bookmark at the top of the page and a footer with sample copyright information.

6. Press **Ctrl + Home** to scroll to the top of the page.

The overall design and content of the new page is similar to the page that you want to develop for the garden Web site. In reviewing the content provided by the template, you decide to make some minor changes. You will remove the comment from the top of the page, add the page to the navigation structure to display the page banner and link bar in the top shared border, and then save the page with an appropriate filename and a descriptive title.

To revise a Web page created with a template:

1. At the top of the page, point to the purple "Comment: Text Search - This page..." text at the top of the page. The pointer changes to a 🖱 shape, which identifies the location of a Web component. The comment includes text you can see in Design view, but not in a Web browser.

2. Right-click the purple comment text to select it and open the shortcut menu, and then click **Cut**. The comment is deleted, and a blank line appears above the horizontal line at the top of the page.

3. Right-click the horizontal line that appears below the comment you just deleted (but not the horizontal line that appears in the top shared border), and then click **Cut** on the shortcut menu.

4. Click the **Save** button on the Standard toolbar, type **search.htm** in the File name text box, click the **Change title** button, type **Search** in the Page title text box, click the **OK** button to close the Set Page Title dialog box, and then click the **Save** button to close the Save As dialog box. The new Web page now has the filename search.htm and an appropriate title.

5. Click the **Web Site** tab at the top of the Contents pane, change to Navigation view, and, if necessary, display the Folder List.

6. If necessary, scroll the navigation structure so you can see the yellow Irrigation page in the navigation structure (but not the white Irrigation page in the custom link bar navigation structure).

7. If necessary, scroll down the Folder List so you can see the search.htm page, and then drag the **search.htm** page from the Folder List and position it as a child page of the home page and to the right of the Irrigation page. See Figure 6-4.

Search page added to the navigation structure ◄ **Figure 6-4**

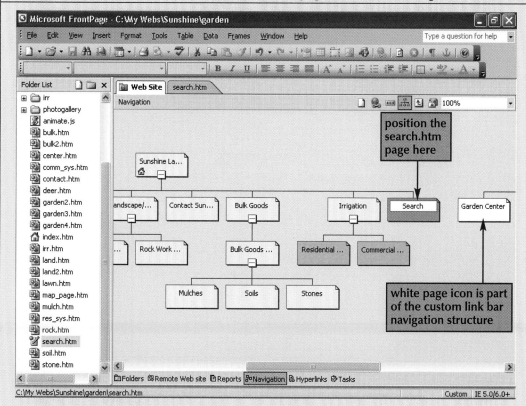

You also need to add the Search page to the custom link bar that appears in the home page.

8. Scroll the navigation structure so you can see the custom link bar navigation structure (with the white page icons), and then drag the **search.htm** page from the Folder List and position it to the right of the Anti-Deer Products page.

9. Double-click **search.htm** in the Folder List to open the page in Design view. The page now displays a page banner and a link bar in the top shared border.

10. Save the search.htm page and close the Folder List.

Changing the Search Component's Properties

When you created the Search page from the template, FrontPage automatically included a search component in it that searches the Web site using keywords entered by the user. You can also add a search component to an existing page by clicking the Web Component button on the Standard toolbar, clicking the Web Search Component type, and then following the instructions in the dialog boxes. Regardless of how you create the search component, you can change its properties as necessary. The first change you decide to make is to increase the size of the text box into which users will type keywords.

To change the properties of the search component:

▶ **1.** If necessary, scroll down the Search page so you can see the Search for text box and the Start Search and Reset buttons, and then point anywhere in the dotted-line box that contains these objects so the pointer changes to a 📑 shape.

▶ **2.** Right-click anywhere in the search component to open the shortcut menu, and then click **Search Form Properties** to open the Search Form Properties dialog box. See Figure 6-5.

Figure 6-5 ▶ **Search Form Properties dialog box**

The Search Form Properties tab includes options for changing the defaults for the label and width of the text box as well as the labels for the two buttons that are created by the page's template. (A label for a button is the text that appears on the button to identify its function.) You can accept these defaults or change them, when necessary, to match your requirements. You will change the width of the Search for text box so it will display more characters.

▶ **3.** Select the value in the Width in characters text box, and then type **25** to increase the size of the Search for text box. The other default settings are acceptable, so you can close the dialog box.

▶ **4.** Click the **OK** button to close the dialog box and return to the Search page, and then click anywhere in the paragraph above the search component to deselect it. The size of the Search for text box has increased to 25 characters.

The Search Page template added a horizontal line and sample copyright information at the bottom of the page. Because copyright information already appears in the bottom shared border of the Web site, you can delete the duplicate text added by the template. Because other pages in the Web site do not have a horizontal line at the bottom of the page, you'll also delete the horizontal line.

5. Press **Ctrl + End** to scroll to the bottom of the Search page, and then select the horizontal line and the three lines of text below it. (The first line of the footer you will delete is "Author information goes here.")

6. Press the **Delete** key to delete the selected items.

7. Save the search.htm page.

You can also insert a search component in a Web page that searches the Internet using keywords entered by the user. FrontPage also provides other components that you can use to create a link to a map at Expedia.com; to display stock market information; and to display business, living, travel, news, sports, and technology headlines, as well as weather forecasts from MSNBC. All of these components are available in the Insert Web Component dialog box.

Brett thinks that it would be a nice addition to the Web site to provide a component that searches the Internet, so if his customers don't find what they are looking for in the garden Web site, they can search other sites.

To insert a component that searches the Web:

1. Scroll up the Web page until the "Query Language" heading appears at the top of the Contents pane, and then click to the left of the letter "Q" in Query Language.

2. Click the **Web Component** button [🗔] on the Standard toolbar. The Insert Web Component dialog box opens.

3. Scroll down the list of Component types, and then click **MSN Components**. The two MSN components—Search the Web with MSN and Stock quote—appear in the Choose a MSN component list box. See Figure 6-6.

Insert Web Component dialog box ◄ **Figure 6-6**

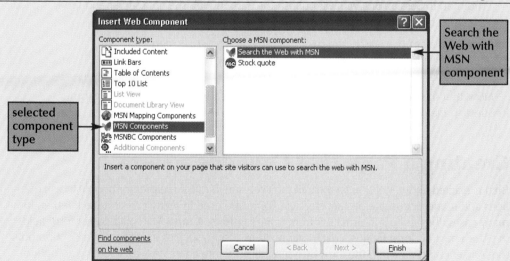

4. Make sure that the **Search the Web with MSN** component is selected, and then click the **Finish** button. A Search the Web with MSN component is inserted in the Web page. See Figure 6-7. The MSN logo appears as a broken link because this picture is not stored in the Web site.

Figure 6-7 ▶ **Search the Web with MSN component added to search.htm page**

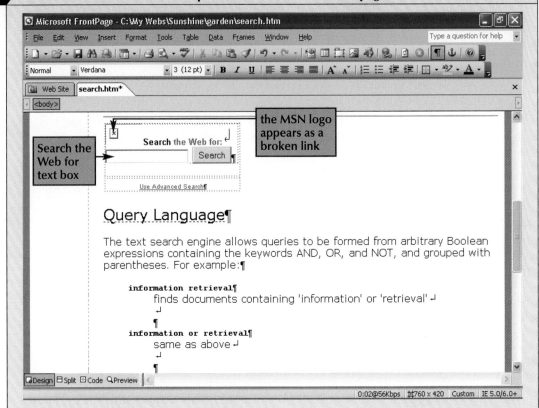

Trouble? If a Dial-up Connection dialog box opens, click the Close button to close it. You do not need an Internet connection to complete these steps.

The Search page now contains a component that will let users enter keywords to search the Internet. In Session 6.3, you will publish the garden Web site on a server and use this page to search both the site and the Internet.

5. Save and close the search.htm page, and then change to Folders view.

Now that the Search page is complete, you are ready to work on the Customer Requests page, which will contain a form.

Creating a Page That Contains a Form

Brett is excited about including a form in the Web site to make it easier for people to ask questions and request consultations and service. Forms are used in many ways on the Internet. In many cases, they collect information from a site's visitors. A **form** is a collection of form fields in a Web page. A **form field** is a data-entry field in a form, such as a text box or an option button. A user enters data into the form by typing directly into a text box, by selecting an option button or a check box, or by selecting a value from a drop-down menu. After completing the form, the user submits it to the server, where a form handler processes it. A **form handler** is a program that collects and processes the form's data in a predetermined manner. For example, you might select a form handler to save the form's data in an HTML file, or to send the form's data to an e-mail address, or both. FrontPage includes many form handlers to process common requests. If you are an experienced programmer, you can also design your own form handler and use it to process forms you create with FrontPage.

During your meeting with Sunshine's senior staff, you formulated a plan for the form that you need to create. The form will provide a text box into which customers can type a question; a section that lets the customer request a consultation or service; and a section in which the customer can enter his or her name, e-mail address, daytime phone number, and a communication preference (e-mail or phone). Brett asks if there is also a way to ask customers for the number of visits they have made to the nursery so he can determine whether new or existing customers are using the site. You tell Brett that this information is easy to collect and add it to your sketch of the form, which appears in Figure 6-8.

Sketch of the Customer Requests page ◄ **Figure 6-8**

Customer Requests

Home   Garden Center   Landscape/Rock Work   Contact Sunshine   Customer Requests
Bulk Goods   Irrigation   Search

Please use this page to ask a question or to request a consultation for rock work, landscaping, or irrigation (including service). A member of the Sunshine staff will respond to your request within 24 hours. If you cannot use your browser to send a form, click here to open a Word document that contains this form, and then complete the form by hand and mail it to the address shown.

Please complete the appropriate sections below, and then click the Submit Form button to send your request. Thank you for choosing Sunshine Landscape & Garden Center. We appreciate your business!

If you have a question about landscaping, irrigation, maintaining your landscape, or other concerns, please enter your question in the text box below:

If you need to request a free consultation or request irrigation service, please select the type of work you need (you can select more than one option):
☐ Rock Work
☐ Landscaping
☐ Irrigation Installation
☐ Irrigation Service
☐ Other

Please select the option that best describes your location: Lakeway ▾

Name:
E-Mail Address:
Daytime Phone:
Best way to reach you: ○ E-mail ○ Phone

How many times have you visited Sunshine Landscape & Garden Center?

Submit Form   Clear Form

You tell Brett that there are two ways to create a form. First, you can use the **Form Page Wizard**, which asks questions about the type of form that you want to create and lets you select the form's options to create a Web page containing the form with the fields you specified. To use this option, double-click the Form Page Wizard icon in the Page Templates dialog box. You can use this method when you want to create a standard type of form, such as a form that contains billing and shipping addresses or information about products, such as quantity ordered.

The second option is to insert a form component in an existing or new Web page. The form component appears as a box with a dotted outline in Design view. You use the Form command on the Insert menu to insert the form's fields into the form. After adding a form field, you can accept its default settings or change its properties.

Regardless of how you create the form, you edit it the same way as any other Web page. For example, if you click to the left of a form field and start typing the text to serve as its label, the form field moves to the right to make room for the text. Pressing the Enter key to the left of a form field inserts a new paragraph, which causes the form field to appear at the beginning of the next line. You can cut or copy form fields to the Clipboard and paste them into another location in the form or into another form. Although a single Web page can contain more than one form, the most common approach is to create a single form in a Web page. You will create one form in the Customer Requests page.

In addition to creating a sketch of the form's appearance, it is also a good idea to determine ahead of time any rules that you want to impose on the form's use and users. For example, do you want to permit multiple selections in drop-down boxes and check box groups? Do you want to create a default selection for an option button or check box? How many characters do you want to display at one time in a text box? Do you want to limit the amount of text a user can type in a text box? Do you want any default text to appear in a text box? Do you need to validate any entered values, to force users to enter a value in a text box, or to restrict the content entered in a text box to integers or letters? To help Brett understand how to develop the form, you prepared the document shown in Figure 6-9 to list the criteria you want to impose on the form. You'll teach Brett more about the questions to ask when designing a form as you work with him to develop the form in the Customer Requests page.

| Figure 6-9 | Form design criteria for the Customer Requests page |

Form Design Criteria
- The text area should be 80 characters wide and five lines high, with no initial value.
- The check box group should not contain a default selection. The results file should include the value "Yes" to indicate a selected check box.
- The drop-down box should have a height of 1 and allow only one selection. The choices are Lakeway, Dripping Springs, Austin, Lago Vista, West Lake Hills, and Other. The default selection is Lakeway. The Other selection should include a text box for the user to enter a location not in the list.
- The text boxes for the user's name, e-mail address, and daytime phone number should be 35 characters wide.
- The option button group should include two option buttons, with neither option button being selected initially.
- The text box to record the number of visits to the nursery should permit only integers from 0 to 100. This field must contain a value when the user submits the form to the server.

After meeting with Brett, you created a Web page based on the Normal Page template and entered most of the text in the page according to the sketch shown in Figure 6-8. You will import this page into the Web site, turn on the shared borders for the page, and then create the form component and form fields.

To import the page into the Web site and turn on the shared borders:

1. Display the Folder List, and then make sure the garden Web site's root folder is selected.

2. Click **File** on the menu bar, and then click **Import**. The Import dialog box opens.

3. Click the **Add File** button to open the Add File to Import List dialog box, open the **Tutorial.06\Tutorial** folder included with your Data Files, and then double-click **requests.htm**. The path to the requests.htm file included with your Data Files appears in the Import dialog box.

4. Click the **OK** button to import the requests.htm page into the garden Web site.

5. If necessary, scroll down the files in the Folder List, and then double-click **requests.htm** to open the Customer Requests page in Design view. You need to add this page to the navigation structure and to the custom link bar navigation structure, turn on the shared borders, and add the theme to the page.

6. Click the **Web Site** tab, change to Navigation view, and then position the **requests.htm** page in the navigation structure between the Contact Sunshine and Bulk Goods pages.

7. Scroll the navigation structure, and then position the **requests.htm** page in the custom link bar navigation structure between the Contact Sunshine and Bulk Goods pages.

8. Close the Folder List, and then click the **requests.htm** tab.

9. Click **Format** on the menu bar, click **Shared Borders**, make sure the **Current page** option button is selected, make sure that the **Top**, **Left**, and **Bottom** check boxes are selected, and then click the **OK** button. The top, left, and bottom shared borders appear in the requests.htm page.

10. Click **Format** on the menu bar, click **Theme**, point to the **Garden Web Site** theme in the Theme task pane, click the **list arrow** that appears, and then click **Apply to selected page(s)**. The Garden Web Site theme is applied to the requests.htm page. Now the page has the same appearance and navigation options as other pages in the Web site.

11. Close the Theme task pane, and then save the requests.htm page.

With the page imported into the Web site and the shared borders and theme added to the page, you are ready to add a form component. Then you will insert the form fields in the form component and modify their properties to match the criteria you specified in Figure 6-9.

Adding a Form Component to a Web Page

Before adding a form field to the Web page, you must add the form component that will contain the form's fields. The form component is required because it identifies the region of the page that the server will process. If you use the Form Page Wizard to create your Web page, FrontPage adds the form component to the page automatically. The Customer Requests page does not yet contain a form component. When you add a form component to a page, FrontPage creates the form component and inserts the Submit and Reset buttons automatically.

Creating a Form Component and Adding a Form Field

- Position the insertion point where you want to insert the form.
- Click Insert on the menu bar, point to Form, and then click Form.
- Place the insertion point inside the form component where the first form field should appear.
- Click Insert on the menu bar, point to Form, and then click the desired form field to add to the form.
- Double-click a form field object to open the form field's Properties dialog box.
- Enter the appropriate values for the form field's properties.
- Click the OK button.

Because the Customer Requests page already contains content, you will insert the form component in the page, and then cut the content from the page and paste it into the form component. The form handler on the server will process only form fields that are contained within a form component.

To insert a form component in the Customer Requests page:

1. Click to the left of the word "If" in the third paragraph to position the insertion point there. This line of text is the first one that will appear within the form.

2. Click **Insert** on the menu bar, point to **Form**, and then click **Form**. FrontPage inserts a form component above the paragraph that begins with the word "If." The insertion point moves automatically to the left of the Submit button in the form component. Notice that a dotted line identifies the form component.

   You will cut the text from the page and paste it into the form component.

3. Click to the left of the word "If," scroll to the bottom of the page, press and hold the **Shift** key, click to the right of the last line in the page (which ends "...Sunshine Landscape & Garden Center?"), and then release the **Shift** key. The text that you will cut is selected.

4. Click the **Cut** button 🔏 on the Standard toolbar to cut the selected text from the page.

5. Click to the left of the Submit button, but inside the form component, to place the insertion point there. You will paste the text that you just cut here.

   Trouble? If you see selection handles around the Submit button, then you selected the button instead of the space between the form component and the Submit button. Press the left arrow key ← to deselect the Submit button and to position the insertion point to its left.

6. Click the **Paste** button 📋 on the Standard toolbar to paste the text into the form component, and then save the page. The form component now contains the text. See Figure 6-10.

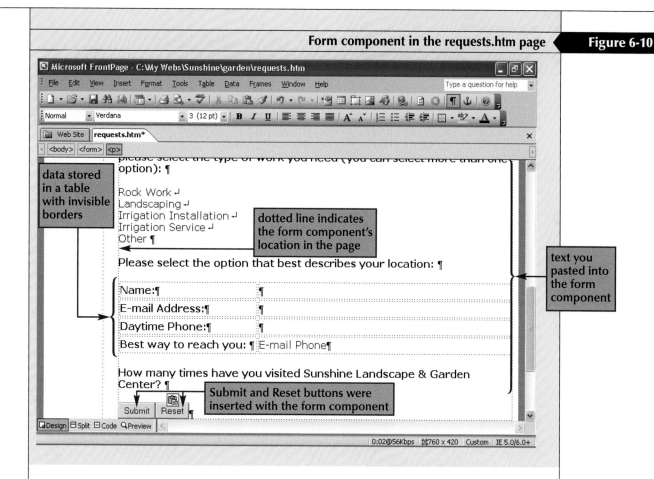

Now you can start adding fields to the form according to the sketch shown in Figure 6-8.

Adding Option Buttons to a Form

Option buttons (also called **radio buttons**) are usually arranged in groups in a form. An **option button group name** identifies a set of related option buttons. Within a group of option buttons, only one button can be selected at a time—selecting an option button automatically deselects any other selected option button. You create labels for option buttons by typing the appropriate text next to the button. For example, a form might have a section with the group name "Age" that contains corresponding option buttons with the labels "Under 25," "25-40," "41-65," and "Over 65." Option buttons are appropriate when only a few choices are available, such as when specifying age groups. A form can contain more than one option button group as long as the different option button groups use different option button group names.

The first option button you add to a form will be selected automatically when you open the form in a browser, unless you change its properties. The first option button in an option button group is usually the most common response, and selecting it automatically saves users some time so they won't need to select it if it is their choice. You can also design an option button group so that no single option button is selected, thereby forcing the form's user to make a selection.

When you create option button groups in a form, consider the following design suggestions:

- Use option buttons when you want to limit the user to selecting one of a few related and mutually exclusive choices.
- The minimum number of option buttons in a group is two, and the recommended maximum is seven.

- Clearly label each option button in a group so that users can easily determine the appropriate option button to select.
- Use a heading or text to identify the group name for the option buttons.

The sketch shown in Figure 6-8 shows an option button group for customers to use to indicate their communication preferences. You'll insert the first option button to the left of the "E-mail" response, and then you'll insert the second option button to the left of the "Phone" response.

To add an option button to a form:

1. If necessary, scroll the page so you can see the "Best way to reach you:" text. The content is organized in a table with invisible borders to control its appearance. Tables are frequently used as design tools to control the layout of text and other objects. You'll insert the first option button in the cell in row 4, column 2.

2. Click to the left of the word "E-mail" in the cell in row 4, column 2, to position the insertion point where you will insert the first option button.

3. Click **Insert** on the menu bar, point to **Form**, and then click **Option Button** to insert the first option button in the form to the left of the "E-mail" response. Notice that the option button is selected, as indicated by the black dot that appears within the white circle. See Figure 6-11.

Figure 6-11	Option button form field inserted in the form

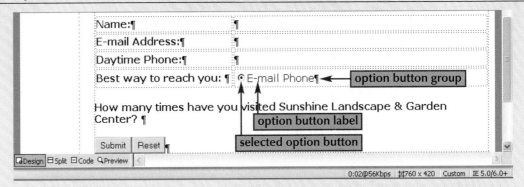

Trouble? If you insert the option button in the wrong location or insert the wrong form field, click the Undo button on the Standard toolbar to remove the form field, and then repeat the steps to insert the correct form field. You can also delete a form field by selecting it and pressing the Delete key.

You'll insert the second option button to the left of the "Phone" response.

4. Click to the left of the word "Phone" to position the insertion point, and then repeat Step 3 to insert the option button for this selection. Notice that this second option button does not appear selected, as indicated by the solid white circle.

5. Save the page.

The E-mail and Phone option buttons now belong to a group. Within this group, the user can select only one option button.

After placing a form field in the form, you can change its properties to match your needs better. For example, FrontPage assigned the group name R1 to the option button group, the value V1 to the E-mail option button, and the value V2 to the Phone option button. If you add more option buttons to this form, FrontPage will add them to the R1 group and assign sequential values to them (V3, V4, etc.). You could accept these default values for the group and button names, but you will modify the current option button properties to change the group name to CommunicationPreference and the button names to match their responses. Using more meaningful names will make the responses easier to examine and locate in the file that stores the form's results. Before changing the properties of the option buttons, you tell Brett that names for groups and form fields cannot contain spaces.

To change option button properties:

1. Double-click the **option button** to the left of the E-mail label to select it and to open the Option Button Properties dialog box. You will change the group name and the value name for the option button.

2. With the value selected in the Group name text box, type **CommunicationPreference**, press the **Tab** key to select the value in the Value text box, and then type **Email**. Now the option button group is named CommunicationPreference, and the first option button in the group is named Email. See Figure 6-12. In the Initial state section, the Selected option button is selected, indicating that the E-mail option button is the default selection.

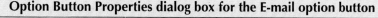

Option Button Properties dialog box for the E-mail option button | **Figure 6-12**

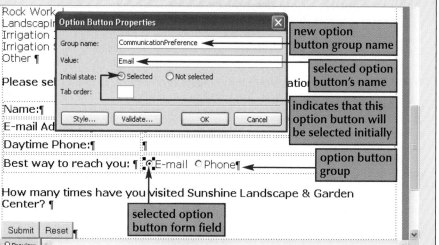

Because you want to force the user to make a choice, you'll change the initial state of the E-mail option button so it is not selected.

3. Click the **Not selected** option button to select it, and then click the **OK** button to close the dialog box. The E-mail option button changes from selected to not selected. The other changes you made appear only in the HTML document for this page.

   Trouble? If a message box opens and tells you that the name is not valid, click the OK button to continue and make sure that "CommunicationPreference" in the Group name text box does not contain a space. Click the OK button to close the dialog box.

   Next, you will change the properties of the Phone option button. When editing the properties of option buttons, make sure that the option buttons in a group have the same group name. If you change the group name for one option button, but not for another, the server will treat the option buttons as being in two groups instead of one. This problem can lead to inaccurate data because the user would be able to select an option button in each group, which might not be the action that you want.

4. Double-click the **option button** to the left of the Phone label to open the Option Button Properties dialog box for this option button.

5. With the value in the Group name text box selected, type **CommunicationPreference**, press the **Tab** key, type **Phone**, make sure the **Not selected** option button is selected, and then click the **OK** button.

6. Save the page.

Next, you will add another type of form field—a drop-down box.

Adding a Drop-Down Box to a Form

Option buttons are useful when you want a user to select a response from only a few choices. When you want to present several choices in a single form field, a **drop-down box** (also called a **drop-down menu**) is an appropriate choice because it saves space by organizing choices in an expandable list. The user displays the list by clicking a list arrow and then selects the desired choice by clicking it in the list. Although you can set a drop-down box to accept multiple selections, it is more common to limit the user to selecting only one choice in a drop-down box.

When you create drop-down boxes in a form, consider the following design suggestions:

- Use a drop-down box when you want the user to select a choice from a list.
- Drop-down boxes should contain a minimum of three choices.
- Arrange items in the list so that the most commonly selected entries appear first, or arrange items in ascending order alphabetically, numerically, or chronologically.
- The default selection in a drop-down box should be either the most used choice or the first choice in the list.

The sketch shown in Figure 6-8 includes a drop-down box located to the right of the "Please select the option that best describes your location:" text. Brett wants the customer to indicate the city or area in which he or she lives. These choices are Lakeway, Dripping Springs, Austin, Lago Vista, West Lake Hills, and Other.

To add a drop-down box to a form:

1. Scroll the form as necessary so you can see the "Please select the option that best describes your location:" text, click anywhere in the word "location," and then press the **End** key to position the insertion point in the correct location for the drop-down box. Make sure that one space appears between the colon and the insertion point.

2. Click **Insert** on the menu bar, point to **Form**, and then click **Drop-Down Box**.

FrontPage creates a drop-down box that is two characters wide. To make the drop-down box match your sketch, you will change the default settings to increase the width of the drop-down box, insert the list items, and change the default form field names.

To add choices to a drop-down box and change its properties:

1. Double-click the **drop-down box** to select it and to open the Drop-Down Box Properties dialog box. FrontPage automatically assigned the name D1 to the drop-down box. The dialog box shows that there are no choices in the list, that it has a height of one line, and that multiple selections are not permitted. You will rename the drop-down box, and then you will create the choices that will appear in the list.

2. In the Name text box, select **D1**, and then type **Location**. The drop-down box form field now has the name Location.

3. Click the **Add** button to open the Add Choice dialog box. You use this dialog box to create entries in the list. First, you will supply the item's name, or choice, which is how the item will appear in the list. Then you will supply the item's value, which is the name of the list item that will appear in the results file. Finally, you will indicate whether the item is selected or not selected in the drop-down box.

4. Type **Lakeway** in the Choice text box, and then click the **Specify Value** check box to select it. FrontPage automatically adds the value "Lakeway" to the Specify Value text box to match the choice that you entered. This value will appear in the form results file to indicate the user's choice.

   Because Brett anticipates that most of his customers live in Lakeway, where the nursery is located, he wants to program this choice as the default so it will be selected when the page opens.

5. Click the **Selected** option button in the Initial state section. See Figure 6-13. The first choice is complete.

Completed Add Choice dialog box for the Lakeway choice ◀ **Figure 6-13**

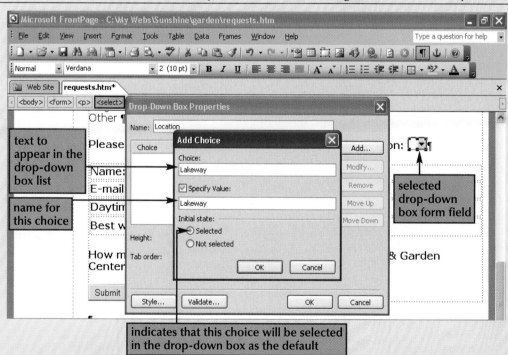

6. Click the **OK** button. The Add Choice dialog box closes and you return to the Drop-Down Box Properties dialog box, which now displays the Lakeway choice.

▶ 7. Click the **Add** button, and then type **Dripping Springs** in the Choice text box. Notice that the Specify Value text box includes a space. Because some Web servers won't process the space character, you'll need to remove it.

▶ 8. Click the **Specify Value** check box to select it. The text box below the Specify Value check box becomes active so you can edit the value. You can edit the value to make it shorter or to change it to any permissible value. In this case, you will remove the space between words.

▶ 9. Click to the left of the letter "S" in "Springs" in the Specify Value text box, press the **Backspace** key to delete the space, and then make sure the **Not selected** option button is selected. See Figure 6-14.

Figure 6-14	Add Choice dialog box for the Dripping Springs choice

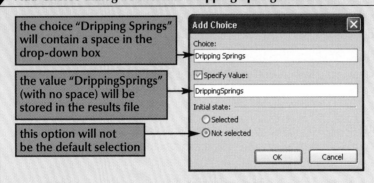

the choice "Dripping Springs" will contain a space in the drop-down box

the value "DrippingSprings" (with no space) will be stored in the results file

this option will not be the default selection

▶ 10. Click the **OK** button.

▶ 11. Add the following choices to the Location drop-down box:

Choice	Selected	Value
Austin	No	Austin
Lago Vista	No	LagoVista
West Lake Hills	No	WestLakeHills
Other	No	Other

Figure 6-15 shows the completed Drop-Down Box Properties dialog box.

Figure 6-15	Completed Drop-Down Box Properties dialog box

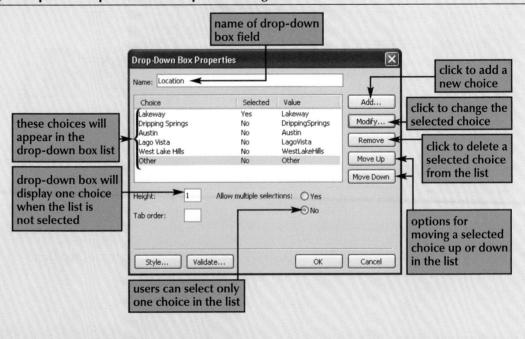

name of drop-down box field

click to add a new choice

click to change the selected choice

these choices will appear in the drop-down box list

click to delete a selected choice from the list

drop-down box will display one choice when the list is not selected

options for moving a selected choice up or down in the list

users can select only one choice in the list

12. Click the **OK** button to close the Drop-Down Box Properties dialog box. The drop-down box appears in the form. The drop-down box is wide enough to display the longest choice in the list (Dripping Springs), and the default choice (Lakeway) appears in the list box.

Trouble? Don't worry if the drop-down box appears on the next line. It will be displayed correctly in a browser.

If you click the list arrow on the drop-down box in Design view, you will select the form field instead of displaying the list. To see the list, you must open the page in a browser or Preview view and then click the list arrow. You will test all of the form fields in the browser after completing the form.

Your sketch includes several text boxes that collect information about the user. You'll show Brett how to add these form fields next.

Adding a Text Box to a Form

When you need a user to supply limited information in a form field that is unique or uncommon, such as a phone number or an e-mail address, you can use a text box to collect the data. A **text box** accepts typed information that you can limit to some maximum number of characters. Even though it will accept more characters than it can display, the text box itself might display a predetermined number of characters; in this case, the text scrolls to the left as the user types in the text box. You can also use a text box form field to permit users to enter a password, in which case the password appears as a series of dots or asterisks to conceal it while it is being typed.

When you create text boxes in a form, consider the following design suggestions:

- Use a text box when you want the user to enter unique or uncommon information that is limited to a single line.
- A text box can be set to limit the number of characters that a user can enter and see at one time.
- A text box can be used as a password field.

In addition to being unique, a user's name and e-mail address usually are short, making them suitable candidates for text box form fields.

To add a text box to a form:

1. Click the cell in row 1, column 2, of the table.

2. Click **Insert** on the menu bar, point to **Form**, and then click **Textbox**. FrontPage places a text box form field in the cell. By default, when you insert a text box in a form, it is 20 characters wide.

3. Press the **down** arrow key ↓ to move the insertion point to the cell in row 2, column 2, and then repeat Step 2 to insert a text box.

4. Repeat Step 3 and insert a text box in row 3, column 2.

5. Save the page.

To make it easier for visitors to enter their name and e-mail address in the appropriate text boxes, you can change the default width of the text boxes to display more characters. This change ensures that most people will be able to see their complete information in the text boxes without needing to scroll the text. Although a phone number will fit in the default text box, you'll increase its width to make the text boxes the same size.

To change the properties of a text box:

1. Double-click the **text box** in the cell in row 1, column 2, to open the Text Box Properties dialog box. FrontPage assigned the name T1 to the text box. If you want a default value to appear in the text box when the form is opened in the browser, you can set it by entering a value in the Initial value text box. You can also change the width of the text box (using a measurement indicating the maximum number of characters that will be displayed in the text box at one time), change the text box to accept a password, or change the order in which the user selects text boxes in the form when pressing the Tab key.

   You'll rename the text box to "Name" to describe its function. You will also increase the text box width from the default of 20 characters to 35 characters.

2. Type **Name** in the Name text box, press the **Tab** key twice to select the value in the Width in characters text box, and then type **35** to set the text box width to 35 characters. See Figure 6-16.

Figure 6-16	**Completed Text Box Properties dialog box**

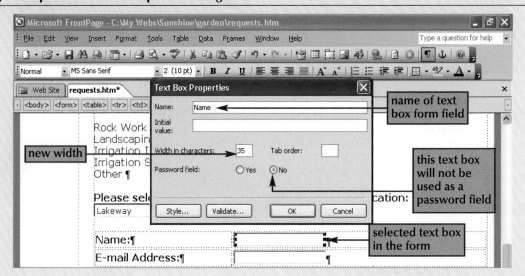

3. Click the **OK** button. The width of the Name text box increases to 35 characters.

4. Repeat Steps 1 through 3 to set the text box in the cell in row 2, column 2, to the name **Email** and a width of **35** characters.

5. Repeat Steps 1 through 3 to set the text box in the cell in row 3, column 2, to the name **Phone** and a width of **35** characters.

6. Save the page.

Text boxes are appropriate for collecting a limited amount of data, such as a name, address, or phone number. When you need to accept unique passages of longer text, such as a description of a problem or an open-ended comment, you can use a text area form field.

Adding a Text Area to a Form

A **text area** (also called a **scrolling text box**) has the same basic characteristics as a text box, except that it displays multiple lines of text and cannot be used as a password field. A text area is an effective form field when asking a user to provide comments or feedback.

When you create a text area in a form, consider the following design suggestions:

- Use a text area when you want a user to supply information that might include more than one line.
- A text area can be set to display multiple lines of text entered by the user. The size of the text area should be large enough to display several lines of text at a time.

Your sketch of the page (see Figure 6-8) includes one text area form field that allows users to enter multiple lines of text. You will add this form field next.

To add a text area to a form:

1. Scroll up the page so you can see the paragraph that begins "If you have a question," and then click the blank paragraph below it. You will insert the text area here.

2. Click **Insert** on the menu bar, point to **Form**, and then click **Text Area**. FrontPage inserts a text area in the form.

The default settings format the text area so it is 20 characters wide and two lines high. Your sketch shows a text area that nearly spans the width of the page and displays five lines. You'll need to change the properties of the text area to make these changes.

To change the properties of a text area:

1. Double-click the **text area** to open the TextArea Box Properties dialog box. FrontPage automatically assigned the name S1 to the text area. Notice that you can specify an initial value for the text area; if you leave this text box empty, then the text area will be empty when the Web page that contains it is opened in a browser. You can also set the properties for a text area to change its width and the number of lines of text displayed in the box. If the user enters more text than can be displayed in the text area, the form field will scroll the lines automatically.

   You will change the default name to be more descriptive of the text area, and then you will change the size of the text area.

2. With the value selected in the Name text box, type **Comments**, press the **Tab** key twice to move to the Width in characters text box, type **80**, press the **Tab** key twice to move to the Number of lines text box, and then type **5**. See Figure 6-17.

Figure 6-17   Completed TextArea Box Properties dialog box

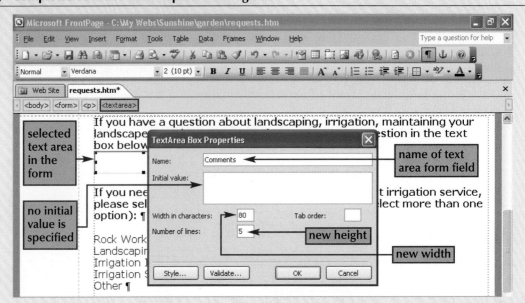

3. Click the **OK** button. The text area is displayed with the new properties—it is five lines high and 80 characters wide.

4. Save the page.

5. Close the garden Web site, and then close FrontPage.

In the next session, you will finish the Customer Requests page by adding additional form fields to it and creating rules that verify and validate the form fields so they will accept the correct data from users. You will test the Search and Customer Requests pages after you publish the Web site in Session 6.3.

Review

Session 6.1 Quick Check

1. What are the two types of search components you can insert in a Web page?
2. True or False: You can insert components in a Web page to display weather and stock market information.
3. What is a form field?
4. Before adding a form field to a Web page, you must first create a(n) _____ in the Web page that will contain the form field.
5. What is a form handler?
6. What are two important things that you should do when planning to use a form in a Web page?
7. True or False: You can use a text box form field to enter passwords.
8. You are designing a Web page for a Canadian company that includes a list of the Canadian provinces. Which form field would you use to collect the data, which properties would you assign to the form field, and which option would be the default selection? Defend your selections.

Session 6.2

Validating a Form Field

The text boxes and text area that you added to the Customer Requests page in Session 6.1 accept unique information entered by a user. In some situations, you might want to validate the information that a user enters into these form fields. For example, if you ask a user to enter a product number into a text box and all product numbers contain four digits, you might set the properties of the text box so that it must contain four digits. By ensuring that the user enters four digits, you can reduce data-entry errors.

Validation is the process of checking the information entered by a user into one or more form fields to verify that the information is acceptable and valid. If the data entered by a user fails the validation test, then the user must change it before the browser will send the form to the server for processing. You specify data validation criteria using the form field's Properties dialog box.

The sketch of the Customer Requests page (see Figure 6-8) includes a text box that lets users enter the number of times that they have visited the Sunshine Landscape & Garden Center. Although you could retain the initial properties of this text box so that a user could enter anything or nothing in it, you tell Brett that it would be helpful to restrict entries in this text box to only positive, whole numbers (or **integers**). In other words, a user shouldn't be able to enter a negative number, a number containing a decimal, or letters in this form field. You tell Brett that it would also be helpful to restrict the value a user can enter to numbers from 0 to 100. This restriction would prevent a user from accidentally entering an unreasonable number of visits, such as 1,000, as a response. To ensure that users will not inadvertently skip this form field, you also tell Brett that you can validate this form field so that it must contain an acceptable value. In other words, users cannot submit the form if this form field is empty or contains an invalid response.

To create the text box and change its properties:

1. Start **FrontPage**, and then open the **garden** Web site from the location where your Web sites are stored.

2. Double-click **requests.htm** in the Contents pane to open the Customer Requests page in Design view.

3. Press **Ctrl + End**, click anywhere in the word "Center" in the "How many times have you visited Sunshine Landscape & Garden Center?" text, and then press the **End** key. Now the insertion point is positioned in the correct location for the text box.

4. Click **Insert** on the menu bar, point to **Form**, and then click **Textbox**. A text box is added to the form. You will change the form field's name to "Visits" and decrease its width to three characters.

   Trouble? Don't worry if the text box appears on the next line. It will be displayed correctly in a browser.

5. Double-click the **text box** that you created in Step 4 to open the Text Box Properties dialog box, type **Visits** in the Name text box, press the **Tab** key twice to move to the Width in characters text box, type **3**, and then click the **OK** button. The dialog box closes and the text box is displayed with the new width.

Next, you will set the validation criteria for the Visits text box.

To validate a text box in a form:

▶ **1.** Double-click the **Visits text box** to open the Text Box Properties dialog box, and then click the **Validate** button. The Text Box Validation dialog box opens. Currently, there are no validation criteria placed on the data entered into the Visits text box, as indicated by the "No Constraints" setting in the Data type list box.

▶ **2.** Click the **Data type** list arrow. You can select Text, Integer, or Number as the data type to validate. You want to make sure that this form field accepts whole numbers, so you will select Integer as the data type.

▶ **3.** Click **Integer** to specify that data type. The settings in the Numeric format section become active.

▶ **4.** In the Numeric format section, click the **None** option button in the Grouping category, because the data should not contain a comma or a period. You can use this option to display a number with a decimal point or a comma, such as 4.5 or 10,000.

▶ **5.** In the Data length section, click the **Required** check box to select it, press the **Tab** key to move to the Min length text box, type **1**, press the **Tab** key to move to the Max length text box, and then type **3**. You specified 1 as the minimum number of digits and 3 as the maximum number of digits that a user can enter into this form field. Selecting the Required check box means that the user must enter a value—even zero—into this form field before the server will accept the form for processing.

▶ **6.** In the Data value section, click the **Field must be** check box to select it, click the **Field must be** list arrow, click **Greater than or equal to** (if necessary), press the **Tab** key to move to the Value text box, and then type **0** (the number zero—not the capital letter "O"). These settings specify that an entry in the Visits text box must be greater than or equal to zero.

▶ **7.** In the Data value section, click the **And must be** check box to select it, click the **And must be** list arrow, click **Less than or equal to** (if necessary), press the **Tab** key to move to the Value text box, and then type **100**. These settings specify that the integer must be less than or equal to 100. See Figure 6-18.

Completed Text Box Validation dialog box | **Figure 6-18**

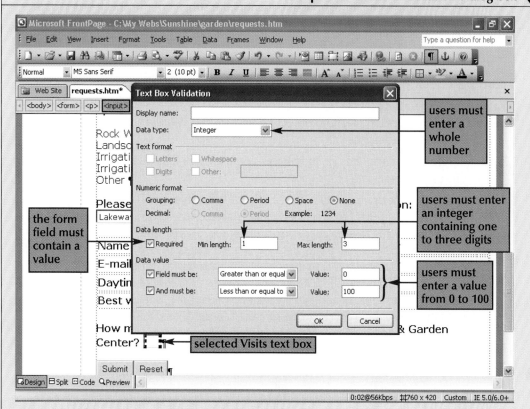

8. Click the **OK** button to close the Text Box Validation dialog box, and then click the **OK** button to close the Text Box Properties dialog box.

9. Save the page.

Now users must enter an integer from 0 to 100 in the Visits text box before the browser will send the form to the server. The final task is to add check boxes so users can request a free consultation or request irrigation service.

Adding a Check Box to a Form

You can use a **check box** by itself to collect a yes/no response to a question, or you can use check boxes in a group to let users answer yes or no for several options. Unlike option button groups, selecting one check box in a check box group does not automatically deselect another check box in the same check box group. Also, you can set the properties for each check box so that it is selected or not selected when the form opens in the browser.

When you create check boxes in a form, consider the following design suggestions:

- Use check boxes when you want a user to select from a group of one or more independent and nonexclusive choices.
- Set the default selection to the most frequently occurring selection.

- Clearly label each check box in a group.
- When necessary, use a heading or text to identify the subject of the check box group.

  Based on your sketch in Figure 6-8, you will add five check boxes to the form.

To add a check box to a form and change its properties:

▶ 1. Scroll up the form as necessary so you can see the list that begins with the "Rock Work" entry, and then click to the left of the "R" in "Rock Work." You will add a check box to the left of the text that describes it.

▶ 2. Click **Insert** on the menu bar, point to **Form**, and then click **Checkbox**. FrontPage inserts a check box at the beginning of the line.

▶ 3. Double-click the **check box** to open the Check Box Properties dialog box. Although the check box will belong to a group of check boxes based on their related topics, usually you provide a unique name to each check box in the group. This strategy is different from how you name option buttons in a group. Because the user can click zero, one, several, or all of the check boxes, you need a way to identify which check box(es) the user selected. By giving this check box the name "RockWork," you know that the check box is the one with the label with the same name. In addition, the default value, "ON," indicates the value to store in the results file when the check box is selected. You can accept this default value or change it to "Yes" or "True" to indicate a positive response. Brett asks you to change the value to "Yes," so he can easily determine if the check box was selected.

▶ 4. Type **RockWork** in the Name text box, press the **Tab** key to move to the Value text box, and then type **Yes**. In the Initial state section, the Not checked option button is selected, indicating that this check box will not contain a check mark when the page is opened in a Web browser. See Figure 6-19. Because you don't want to include a default selection, this setting is correct.

Figure 6-19	Completed Check Box Properties dialog box

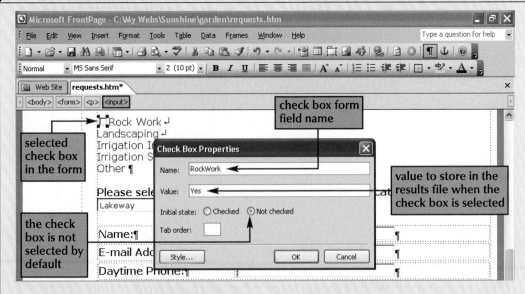

▶ 5. Click the **OK** button to close the Check Box Properties dialog box. The check box form field looks the same—changing the Name property did not affect this form field's appearance. Your changes only affected the way the server will process this form field.

You could continue inserting check boxes for the four other choices, but you want to show Brett how to copy and paste form fields to insert them into a form. After inserting the form fields, you'll need to change only the Name property for each check box to finish your work on the check boxes.

To copy and paste the check boxes:

▶ 1. If necessary, click the **RockWork** check box to select it. Sizing handles appear around the check box.

▶ 2. Click the **Copy** button on the Standard toolbar to copy the check box to the Clipboard.

▶ 3. Press the **down** arrow key ↓ , press the **Home** key to move the insertion point to the beginning of the line, and then click the **Paste** button on the Standard toolbar. A check box with the name "RockWork0" and a value of "Yes" is inserted.

▶ 4. Repeat Step 3 to paste a check box at the beginning of the lines with the following text: Irrigation Installation, Irrigation Service, and Other.

When you pasted the four copies of the check boxes, FrontPage renamed them using the name of the original check box ("RockWork") plus a digit. You will rename each check box to match its label.

▶ 5. Double-click the check box to the left of the "Landscaping" text to open its Check Box Properties dialog box, type **Landscaping** in the Name text box, and then click the **OK** button.

▶ 6. Double-click the check box to the left of the "Irrigation Installation" text to open its Check Box Properties dialog box, type **IrrigationInstallation** in the Name text box, and then click the **OK** button.

▶ 7. Double-click the check box to the left of the "Irrigation Service" text to open its Check Box Properties dialog box, type **IrrigationService** in the Name text box, and then click the **OK** button.

▶ 8. Double-click the check box to the left of the "Other" text to open its Check Box Properties dialog box, type **Other** in the Name text box, and then click the **OK** button.

Now each check box in the page has a unique name. When the user selects a check box, the value "Yes" will appear in the results file.

▶ 9. Save the page.

You have finished adding all of the form fields that collect data from the user. To finish this form, you need to supply the user with a way of sending the Web page to the server for processing.

Working With Push Buttons

Push buttons (also called **command buttons**) are used to submit a form to the server, to clear a form's fields, or to perform specific functions programmed by the developer. You can create three types of push buttons in a form; each type implements a different processing action. You use a **Submit push button** to let a user submit a form to the server for processing. Clicking a **Reset push button** clears any previously entered data from the form. Clicking a **Normal push button** initiates a user-defined script (an advanced Web page feature that is beyond the scope of this tutorial). When you create a form, FrontPage automatically creates and programs the Submit and Reset push buttons for you. By default, the Submit push button is associated with the FrontPage form handler that processes the form results on the Web server. Because these two buttons are automatically included in the form, you can either accept their default values or edit them to suit your needs better. If you add a new push button to a form, FrontPage automatically creates a Normal push button with the value "Button." You must change the properties of the new button to change its name and function.

To match the sketch shown in Figure 6-8, you will need to change the label for the Submit push button to "Submit Form" and the label for the Reset push button to "Clear Form."

To change the properties of the Submit push button:

▶ **1.** Scroll down the page as necessary, and then double-click the **Submit push button** to open the Push Button Properties dialog box.

▶ **2.** Type **Submit** in the Name text box, press the **Tab** key to move to the Value/label text box, press the **End** key, press the **spacebar**, and then type **Form**. In the Button type section, the Submit option button is selected, indicating that this button submits the form's data to the Web server. See Figure 6-20.

Figure 6-20	Completed Push Button Properties dialog box

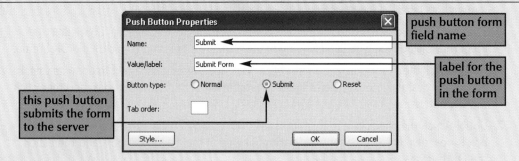

▶ **3.** Click the **OK** button to close the Push Button Properties dialog box. The Submit button now displays the label "Submit Form." FrontPage automatically resizes the push button to accommodate the new label.

Next, you will change the default settings for the Reset push button to change its name to "Clear" and its label to "Clear Form."

To change the properties of the Reset push button:

▶ **1.** Double-click the **Reset push button** to open the Push Button Properties dialog box.

▶ **2.** Type **Clear** in the Name text box, press the **Tab** key to move to the Value/label text box, and then type **Clear Form**. The Reset option button is selected in the Button type section, indicating that this button resets the values in the form's fields to their default settings.

▶ **3.** Click the **OK** button to close the Push Button Properties dialog box. The Reset push button now displays the label "Clear Form."

▶ **4.** Save the page.

You have finished placing all of the form fields that collect data in the form and provided a means for the user to submit the form to the server for processing. When a form is submitted to the server, you must tell the server how to process it by specifying a form handler.

Using a Form Handler

A form handler is a program on a Web server that communicates with a browser to process form data received from the browser. You select a form handler based on how you want to process the data collected in your form. For the Customer Requests page, you will use the FrontPage Save Results form handler, which collects form data and can save that data in a variety of file formats.

The **Save Results form handler** collects data from a browser and stores it in a specified format on the server. You have the option of sending the results to a file, to an e-mail address, or to a database. The data entered by the user in the form, or the **form results**, is stored on the server in a format that you specify. The two most popular methods of storing form results are as a text file, with one line for each form that was submitted to the server, or as an HTML file, with a line for each form field name and its value (known as a **field name-data value pair**). In the text file method, the first entry, or row, contains the names of the form fields from which the data was obtained. In the HTML file method, each form field name is included as a field name-data value pair, with the name being repeated with the data from each form submission. When using either of these methods to store form results, most developers will set the results file to add the form results at the end of the file for each form submitted to the server.

In addition to storing the results in a file on the server, you can send the results to an e-mail address. To send the form results to an e-mail address, the server must be configured to send e-mail messages. Normally, the Web site's administrator, or webmaster, configures the server for this type of processing. Check with your instructor or technical support person to determine whether your FrontPage installation and server are enabled to send a form's results to an e-mail address.

Regardless of how you choose to store your form results, you can also collect optional information, such as the date on which the form was submitted and the Internet Protocol (IP) address of the user. In most cases, the results files are saved in the Web site's _private folder so they are inaccessible to the site's visitors.

You want to show Brett how to use the Save Results form handler to specify the processing method for the data collected by the Customer Requests page.

To configure the Save Results form handler:

 1. Right-click anywhere in the form component to open the shortcut menu, and then click **Form Properties**. The Form Properties dialog box opens. See Figure 6-21.

Form Properties dialog box   **Figure 6-21**

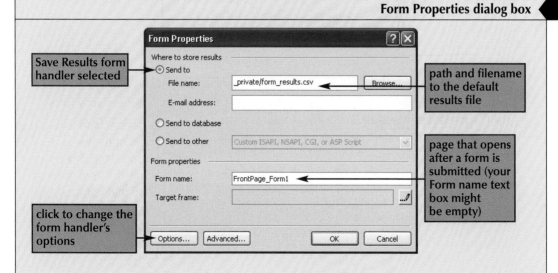

Trouble? If the Send to option button is dimmed in the Form Properties dialog box, click the Cancel button to close the dialog box. Click Tools on the menu bar, click Page Options, click the Authoring tab, and then make sure that all check boxes except Generator and ProgID tags and Downlevel image file are selected in the FrontPage and SharePoint technologies section, that Microsoft Internet Explorer only is selected in the Browsers list box, and that 5.0/6.0 browsers and later is selected in the Browser versions list box. Click the OK button, and then repeat Step 1.

The settings in this dialog box let you accept or change the default filename in which to store your results file and the optional e-mail address to which to send the results from each form submission. You can also send your form results to a database or to a location defined by a script. You use the Form properties section to supply the filename that will serve as your confirmation page. (You will learn more about confirmation pages in Session 6.3.) To change the options for any of these settings, click the Options button.

Brett wants to configure the form results to be stored in a text file and sent to an e-mail address at the nursery. You will show Brett how to configure these settings next.

2. Click the **Options** button to open the Saving Results dialog box. See Figure 6-22. The default file format listed near the top of the dialog box is "Text database using comma as a separator." This option uses a comma to separate the data entered by the user into each form field. This format, which is known as **comma-delimited text** or **comma-separated values**, is a popular choice for storing data because many different programs can read and use it.

Figure 6-22 **File Results tab of the Saving Results dialog box**

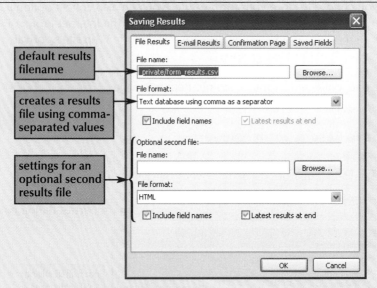

default results filename

creates a results file using comma-separated values

settings for an optional second results file

Trouble? If the File format list box at the top of the dialog box is not set correctly, click the File format list arrow, and then click Text database using comma as a separator.

The default location in which to store the results file is the _private folder of the Web site, and FrontPage suggests the filename form_results.csv to collect the form's data. (The .csv filename extension is the one for comma-separated values.) You'll change the form name to simplify it, and you will save it in the Web site's _private folder to ensure that it is protected from unauthorized access.

▶ **3.** Edit the value in the File name text box at the top of the dialog box so it is **_private/results.csv**.

▶ **4.** Make sure that the **Include field names** check box contains a check mark, and then click the **E-mail Results** tab.

▶ **5.** Type **brett@sunshinelandscapeandgardencenter.com** in the E-mail address to receive results text box, click the **Subject line** text box, and then type **Customer Requests Web Page**. When a user submits a form to the server, the server will save the form results in the results.csv file on the server. In addition, the server will send a copy of the form results to the e-mail address you entered. By entering text in the Subject line text box, you identified the source of the message for the recipient of the e-mail message. All messages containing form results and sent to this e-mail address will have the subject "Customer Requests Web Page" so Brett can easily identify the source of the message. See Figure 6-23.

E-mail Results tab ◀ | **Figure 6-23**

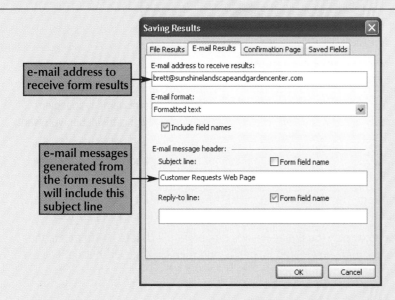

▶ **6.** Click the **Saved Fields** tab to display those settings. The Form fields to save list box displays the form fields you created in the Customer Requests page. The form fields are easy to distinguish because you gave them meaningful names, instead of accepting the default names of V1, S1, and so on.

▶ **7.** In the Additional information to save section, click the **Remote computer name** check box to select it. This setting will save the user's IP address in the results file with the field name "Remote Name." See Figure 6-24.

Figure 6-24 ▶ Saved Fields tab

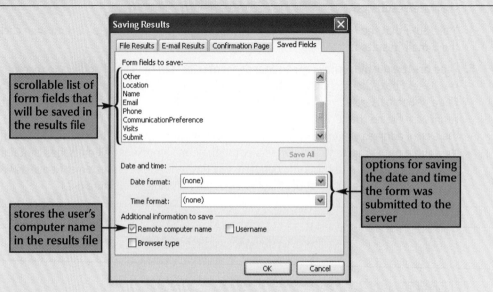

8. Click the **OK** button to return to the Form Properties dialog box, and then, if necessary, delete any text that appears in the Form name text box. When no form name is specified, FrontPage automatically generates a default confirmation page, which is the action you want.

9. Click the **OK** button. A Microsoft FrontPage message box opens, indicating that you are creating the form in a disk-based Web site that cannot be configured to send e-mail messages. For now, you will delete the e-mail address.

   Trouble? If the message box doesn't open, open the Form Properties dialog box, delete the text in the E-mail address text box, click the OK button, and then skip Step 10.

10. Click the **Yes** button to display the E-mail Results tab, press the **Delete** key to delete the selected e-mail address that you entered in Step 5, and then click the **OK** button. The dialog boxes close and you return to the form.

11. Save the page.

Now that you have identified the form handler and specified the file in which the results will be stored on the server, you need to test the form.

Testing a Form on the Client

Unlike other Web pages, you should test a page that contains a form on the client *and* on the server. When testing the form on a client, you test each form field by entering data into it. For example, you can enter text in text boxes or use drop-down boxes to ensure that they display the choices you need. Also, you can clear all data from the form and then reenter it. Any form fields that use data validation, such as the Visits text box, require a server for verification. Therefore, you cannot test form fields that are validated until you can submit the form to a server for processing.

At this point in the development of the form, you want to show Brett how to test it on the client. Your test of the form will include reviewing the layout of form fields in the form and testing their operation. You will finish testing the form in Session 6.3 after publishing the Web site on a server.

To test a form on the client:

▶ 1. Click the **Preview** button 🔍 on the Standard toolbar, and then, if necessary, click the **OK** button in the message box that reminds you that some form elements won't work in a disk-based Web site. The Customer Requests page opens in the browser.

▶ 2. Scroll down the page until you see the form fields, click the text area, and then type **At what time of year do you recommend planting trees?**

▶ 3. Scroll down the page, and then click the **Rock Work** and **Irrigation Service** check boxes. Brett wants to provide a way for users to indicate the consultation or service they require, so he asks you to include a text box to the right of the Other check box. You'll add this text box when you complete the Review Assignments.

▶ 4. Click the **Please select the option that best describes your location** list arrow, and then look at the choices in the list. The blue background for the Lakeway choice indicates that this is the default selection. To select another choice, the user would need to click it.

▶ 5. Click **West Lake Hills** in the list. The menu closes and your selection appears in the drop-down box.

▶ 6. Click the **Name** text box, type your first and last names separated by a space, press the **Tab** key to move to the E-mail Address text box, type your e-mail address, press the **Tab** key, and then type your phone number.

▶ 7. Click the **E-mail** option button, and then click the **Phone** option button. Notice that you can select only one option button in the option button group.

▶ 8. Click the **Visits** text box, and then type **2000**. Because you set this form field to accept values from one to three characters, you cannot type the third zero in the number 2000.

▶ 9. Select the value **200** in the Visits text box, and then type **7**.

▶ 10. Click the **Submit Form** button. The FrontPage Run-Time Component Page opens to advise you that a server is required for the page to function correctly. You will test the page using a server later in this tutorial.

▶ 11. Click your browser's **Back** button to return to the Customer Requests page, and then click the **Clear Form** button. The data you entered is deleted from the form; this action does not require a server. Your test of the form on the client is successful.

▶ 12. Close your browser.

Although the browser performs data validation, a server is required to generate the error message that appears when the Visits text box contains an invalid entry. Even though the form appears to work correctly, you remind Brett that he needs to test this page again after publishing the Web site to a server to ensure that this page does work correctly.

Opening an Office Document from a Web Site

Brett is happy with the form and thinks that it will expedite the process of scheduling and coordinating customer requests for consultations and service. As you consider the form's use, you tell Brett that you want to make sure that people who cannot submit forms to the server—for whatever reason—will still be able to use the form to communicate with the nursery. You could ask users to use a browser to print the Customer Requests page and complete the form, but users could not indicate their location because they cannot use a drop-down box on a paper form. A better option is to save the form in another format that the user can access and print. One popular format on the Web is Portable Document Format (PDF) from Adobe Corporation. To save a document as a PDF file, the Web developer uses a program called

Adobe Acrobat to convert it to PDF. To read the PDF document, the user must install a program on his or her computer called Adobe Reader, which is a free downloadable program from Adobe. After installing the Adobe Reader program, the user's browser will start the Reader automatically when the user clicks a link to a PDF file. Because the Reader is free, easy to download, and installs automatically, PDF is a popular format on the Web for providing documents created in other programs, such as Word, Excel, and PowerPoint, because it eliminates the problem of the user not having the required program on his or her system to read the file. Brett will investigate the possibility of using PDF files in the future, but he does not have Adobe Acrobat at this time. As an alternative, you tell him that another option is to save the form as a Word document and change some of the form fields to make them easier to complete by hand. Saving documents using Word is a good second choice, because many users have Word or a compatible program (such as WordPerfect or WordPad) installed on their systems that can open Word documents.

After converting the form to a Word document, you are ready to show Brett how to create a link to the document and to open it from the Web site. First, you will import the Word document you created into the Web site.

To import the Word document into the garden Web site:

1. Display the Folder List, and then make sure the Web site's root folder is selected.
2. Click **File** on the menu bar, click **Import**, click the **Add File** button, open the **Tutorial.06\Tutorial** folder included with your Data Files, double-click **form.doc**, and then click the **OK** button in the Import dialog box to import the file.
3. Scroll down the Folder List and double-click **form.doc**. Microsoft Word starts and opens the document.

   Trouble? If a Security Warning dialog box opens and asks you to enable macros, ask your instructor or technical support person for help. If you are working on your own computer, click the Enable Macros button.

   Trouble? If Microsoft Word does not open, your installation of FrontPage might not be configured to open Office documents in the program that created them. If necessary, close the program that opened. In FrontPage, click Tools on the menu bar, click Options, and then click the Configure Editors tab. Select the Open web pages in the Office application that created them check box, and then click the OK button. Then repeat Step 3. If Word still doesn't open, it might not be installed on your computer; ask your instructor or technical support person for help.
4. Scroll down the Word document, noticing the changes to the form fields to make it easier to complete the form by hand.
5. Close Word.
6. Close the Folder List.

Next, you will create the hyperlink to the Word document.

To create a hyperlink to a Word document:

1. Scroll to the top of the Customer Requests page, and then double-click the word **here** in the third sentence of the first paragraph.
2. Click the **Insert Hyperlink** button on the Standard toolbar to open the Insert Hyperlink dialog box, scroll down the list of files in the garden Web site, and then click **form.doc**.

   As you learned in Tutorial 5, you can set hyperlinks to open in different frames in a frames page. You can also set other hyperlinks to open in different locations, even when they are not part of a frames page. For example, there are some links that you might want to open in their own browser window, such as when linking to a different Web site. This way, the user can examine the Web site that opens without closing your Web site. You can do the same thing with documents. You'll show Brett how to set a hyperlink to open in a new browser window using the New Window target.

3. Click the **Target Frame** button. The Target Frame dialog box opens, as shown in Figure 6-25. Because you are not working in a frames page, the notation "(none)" appears in the Current frames page section of the dialog box. The Common targets section lists the same targets you can set for frames.

Target Frame dialog box | Figure 6-25

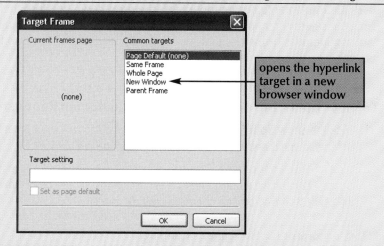

opens the hyperlink target in a new browser window

4. Click **New Window** in the Common targets list box. The HTML equivalent (_blank) appears in the Target setting text box. This setting will open the target of the hyperlink in a new browser window.

5. Click the **OK** button in the Target Frame dialog box. Notice that the Target Frame section of the Insert Hyperlink dialog box shows that this hyperlink uses the _blank target.

6. Click the **OK** button to close the Insert Hyperlink dialog box. The "here" text now contains a link to the Word document.

7. Click the **here** hyperlink to deselect it, and then save the page.

To test the here hyperlink, you need to open the Customer Requests page in a browser.

To test the hyperlink:

1. Click the **Preview** button 🔍 on the Standard toolbar.

2. Click the **here** hyperlink in the first paragraph. A new browser window opens as a result of the _blank target you set. The Word document opens and the browser's menu bar changes to include commands for working with Word documents. The user would print the document, complete it using a pen or pencil, and then take or mail it to the nursery.

   Trouble? If a File Download dialog box opens, click the Open button.

3. Close the window that displays the form.doc file.

4. Close the window that displays the Customer Requests Web page.

In Session 6.3, you will publish the Web site to a server and then test the Customer Requests and Search pages again. Before finishing your work, you want to show Brett the HTML document that FrontPage created for the Customer Requests page.

Viewing the HTML Tags That Create a Form

Creating a form in a Web page results in a complex HTML document. All of the form fields are nested within the <form> and </form> tags that specify the beginning and end of the form in the Web page. The post value of the method property specifies that the data in the form will be processed by or posted to the server. The webbot property specifies the values for the Save Results form handler. The option button, text box, and check box form fields are implemented using input tags. The drop-down box form field is implemented using the select tag, and the text area form field is implemented using the textarea tag. Each tag includes properties that specify the appearance of the form field in the form and its settings.

To view the HTML document for the Customer Requests page:

1. Click the **Show Split View** button ⊟ Split at the bottom of the Contents pane to view the HTML document and the Customer Requests page in Split view.

2. Scroll the Web page in the Design view window and click anywhere in the paragraph that begins "If you have a question about landscaping." Figure 6-26 shows the <form> tag and the properties that process the form on the server.

| Figure 6-26 | HTML document for the requests.htm page |

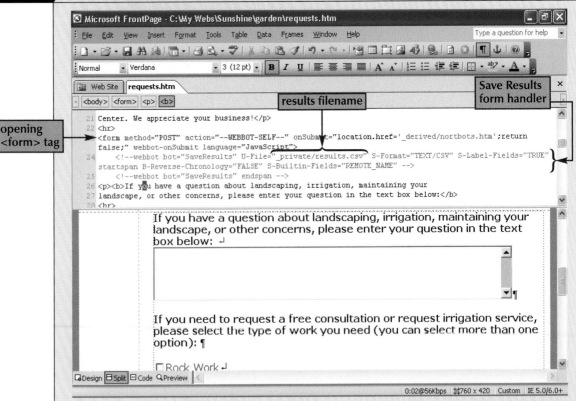

3. Scroll down the Web page in the Design view window as necessary, and then click the **text area**. The HTML textarea tag is selected in the Code view window.

4. Scroll down the Web page in the Design view window, and then click the **Other** check box. Notice that the <input> tag includes the type property "checkbox," which creates a check box in the page. The name property for each check box identifies the check box using its label in the Web page. The value property is set to "Yes," which is the value that will appear in the results file when a user selects the check box.

5. Scroll down the Web page in the Design view window, click the **drop-down box**, and then scroll down the HTML document so you can see the selected HTML <select> and </select> tags. See Figure 6-27. The <option> tags create the choices in the drop-down box. Because you specified a value to store for each choice in the list, the value property includes the name of each option.

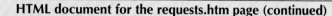 **HTML document for the requests.htm page (continued)** **Figure 6-27**

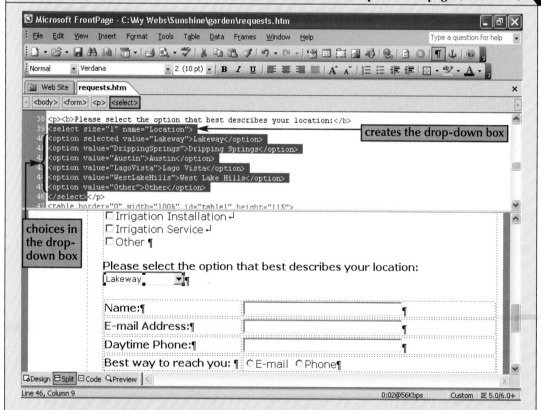

6. Scroll down the Web page in the Design view window, and then click the **Email** text box. Notice that the <input> tag includes the type, name, and size properties, which create a text box named "Email" with a width of 35 characters.

7. Scroll down the Web page in the Design view window, and then click the **E-mail** option button. An <input> tag creates the option button. Notice that its type is "radio," its value is "Email," and it belongs to an option button group named "CommunicationPreference."

▶ 8. Scroll down the Web page in the Design view window, and then click the **Visits** text box. Notice that the <input> tag includes the type, name, size, and maxlength properties. These properties create a text box with the name "Visits" that has a width of three characters. The maxlength property restricts the number of characters a user can enter into this text box to three. The HTML comment tag that appears above the <input> tag includes instructions for validating this text box so that it must contain an integer value in the range 0 to 100.

▶ 9. Click the **Submit Form** button, and then click the **Clear Form** button, noticing the HTML tags that create these form fields.

▶ 10. Return to Design view, save the requests.htm page, close the garden Web site, and then close FrontPage.

In Session 6.3, you will publish the garden Web site to a server and test the Web site. You will also enhance the Web site by adding features that require a server for processing.

Review

Session 6.2 Quick Check

1. What is validation as it relates to a form?
2. To ensure that users will enter data into a form field, click the _____ check box in the form field's Validation dialog box.
3. Name and describe three validation criteria that you can set for a form field that will contain integers.
4. Name and describe the three types of push buttons that you can create in a form.
5. The name and value of a form field in a results file is known as a(n) _____.
6. A Web site's administrator is called the _____.
7. The choices in a drop-down box list are specified by the HTML _____ tag.

Session 6.3

Using a Web Server

To function as a Web server, a computer must have special software that works with the computer's operating system to receive and execute requests for Web pages. The steps in this tutorial use **Microsoft Internet Information Services (IIS)** version 5.1, which is installed with Windows XP Professional. (You cannot install IIS using the Windows XP Home Edition, which is the operating system installed on many home computers.) The default setting starts IIS when you boot your computer. You can also start it from the Windows Control Panel.

To access a site stored on IIS, you do not need to use the "www" prefix or the server type suffix in the URL; instead, you use the computer name or the default name of **localhost**. Most Web developers use a local Web server such as IIS to develop and test a Web site before publishing it on a server and making the site available to Internet users. Because the specifications for using a local Web server vary from one computer to another, it is important to work with your instructor or technical support person to determine the correct configuration for your computer. Your instructor will note any differences that you might encounter as you complete the steps in this session.

Figure 6-28 illustrates the differences between using a disk-based Web site and using a server-based Web site to access your Web pages. In a disk-based Web site, the Web browser opens each Web page by obtaining it directly from the file stored on a disk. In a server-based Web site, also called a remote Web site, the Web browser uses the TCP/IP network protocol to send the request for a Web page to the server. The server then obtains a copy of the file stored on a disk and sends it back to the browser by way of the TCP/IP network connection, and the browser subsequently opens the file. Thus, with a local Web server, the TCP/IP network software uses the same network processing to obtain the requested files as if it were connecting to a Web server.

File transfer comparison of a disk-based and server-based Web site ◄ **Figure 6-28**

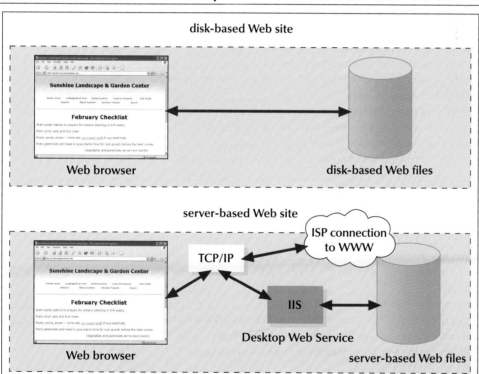

Before you can publish a Web site to a server, you need to know the proper method to transmit the files, the URL of the server, your user name and password, and any rules enforced by the server. To help you publish your Web sites, use Figure 6-29 to organize your work.

Figure 6-29 ▶ **What you need to know before publishing a Web site**

What You Need to Know Before Publishing a Web Site

In most cases, you should learn the answers to the following questions during the planning and development phases of the Web site. Your instructor or lab administrator can help you answer these questions. If you are working from home, you can use the resources on the Student Online Companion page for Tutorial 6 to learn more about publishing Web sites to your computer.

If you are publishing the Web site to a local Web server, such as IIS:

Is Windows 2000 or XP Professional and IIS installed and running on your computer?_____

What is your server's name?_____

Do you need to log on to the server and, if so, what is your logon and password? _____

Do you have permission to publish and maintain a Web site on the server? _____

Are the FrontPage 2002 Server Extensions or SharePoint Services installed on the server?_____

How will you transfer files to the server (from FrontPage, via an FTP site, etc.)? _____

Additional comments about publishing to IIS for your computer or lab:

_____

_____

_____

_____

If you are publishing the Web site to an ISP:

Have you established an account with the ISP? _____

What logon and password did the ISP provide you with for accessing your Web site?_____

What is the URL of your Web site? _____

Do you have permission to publish and maintain a Web site on the server?_____

Have you enabled the FrontPage 2002 Server Extensions or SharePoint Services on the server?___

How will you transfer files to the server (from FrontPage, via an FTP site, etc.)?_____

Additional comments about publishing to the ISP you selected:

_____

_____

_____

_____

If you are publishing the Web site to a network server:

What logon and password did the network administrator provide you with for accessing your Web site?_____

What is the URL of your Web site? _____

Do you have permission to publish and maintain a Web site on the server? _____

How will you transfer files to the server (from FrontPage, via an FTP site, etc.)? _____

Additional comments about publishing to your network server:

_____

_____

_____

_____

This morning, you installed and configured IIS and the FrontPage 2002 Server Extensions on Brett's computer. You used the default name for the Web server, "localhost," for Brett's computer (your computer's name might be different). You will test IIS to make sure that it is installed and operating correctly and that you can access it using your Web browser. Your instructor or technical support person will inform you of any differences that you might encounter in the lab. These steps assume a default installation of IIS or a compatible Web server and a default URL of http://localhost to access it. In addition, the FrontPage 2002 Server Extensions or SharePoint Services must be installed and configured on the Web server to which you will publish your Web sites. (*Note:* There are no FrontPage 2003 Server Extensions.)

To test IIS:

1. Start your Web browser. You do not need an Internet connection to complete these steps.

2. Select the URL in the browser's address field, type **http://localhost** (or the name or IP address provided by your instructor), and then press the **Enter** key. If IIS (or the Web server you accessed) is installed and running, the windows shown in Figure 6-30 will open. Depending on your browser's settings, the windows might open restored (as shown in Figure 6-30) or maximized, with one window on top of the other.

Checking the IIS installation ◄ **Figure 6-30**

IIS documentation window (your page might differ)

window containing the default IIS home page (your page might differ)

Trouble? If your browser displays a page telling you that it cannot find the page, click the Start button on the taskbar, click Control Panel, double-click the Administrative Tools icon, and then double-click the Component Services icon. (If you do not see the Component Services icon, but you do see a Personal Web Manager icon, ask your instructor or technical support person for help. If you do not see either icon, IIS might not be installed.) In the Component Services dialog box, click Services in the left pane, scroll down the services in the right pane, and then click IIS Admin in the right pane. If you see a link to Start the service, click the Start link, and then close the Component Services dialog box. If you do not see a Start link, IIS is already running and you can close the dialog box. Close the Control Panel.

Trouble? If a "Web page unavailable while offline" message box opens after you press the Enter key, click the Connect button to connect to your computer's server. You do not need to connect to your ISP, however.

Trouble? If you receive an error message or no response from the server, you might need to start, install, or configure the server. Ask your instructor or technical support person for help.

3. Close all open browser windows.

You need to move the folders and files from your disk-based Web site to the server so that you can test the garden Web site. To move the folders and files, you will publish the Web site to IIS or another server designated by your instructor.

Publishing a Web Site

You publish a Web site by copying the Web site's folders and files to your computer's server or to a Web server that is connected to the Internet. When you publish a Web site to IIS, the default server-based folder containing all server-based Web sites is C:\Inetpub\wwwroot; any Web sites that are published to IIS are stored as subfolders, or subsites, in this path.

Note: You will need to know how your computer is organized before publishing your Web site to ensure that the server is running the FrontPage 2002 Server Extensions or SharePoint Services. Your instructor will inform you of any differences that you might encounter in the lab.

Reference Window	**Publishing a Web Site to Your Computer's Server**

- Open the Web site in FrontPage, and then change to Remote Web Site view.
- Click the Remote Web Site Properties button on the Contents pane to open the Remote Web Site Properties dialog box.
- Click the option button in the Remote Web server type section to select the type of server you are using.
- Click the Remote Web site location list box, and then type http://localhost/ (or your server's name) and the name of the folder in which to store the Web site's files and folders.
- Click the OK button.

You can publish a disk-based Web site to a server using the same or a different Web site name. Before publishing a Web site, check with the server's administrator to find out if you need to use any special naming conventions, such as using only lowercase letters or omitting spaces in Web folder names and filenames. Even though a disk-based Web site and a server-based Web site can have the same name, you access pages in a disk-based Web site using a path to a folder or a drive. To access pages in a server-based Web site, you use the Hypertext Transfer Protocol (HTTP), the server name (in this case, localhost), and the name of the Web site, as in http://localhost/garden.

When publishing a Web site, you also need to determine the best way to transfer the files. FrontPage includes four methods for publishing files depending on the type of server to which you are publishing. If the remote Web server you selected to host your Web site supports the FrontPage 2002 Server Extensions or SharePoint Services, you choose the FrontPage or SharePoint Services option. If the remote Web server supports **Distributed Authoring and Versioning (DAV)**, which is an extension of the HTTP protocol that is used to transfer files over the Internet, select the WebDAV choice. If the remote Web server supports **File Transfer Protocol (FTP)**, an Internet protocol for transferring files between computers connected to the Internet, select the FTP option. Finally, if you are publishing the Web site to a folder on your computer or on a network, choose the File System option. This book assumes that you will publish the garden Web site to IIS or a compatible Web server running the FrontPage 2002 Server Extensions or SharePoint Services. However, you can publish the garden Web site using one of the other methods if required to do so by your instructor or your ISP.

When you publish a Web site to IIS, the site is added as a subfolder in the C:\Inetpub\wwwroot folder on your hard drive. If you are publishing changes to an existing server-based Web site, you can click the Publish Site button on the Standard toolbar and FrontPage will automatically publish the changes to the correct Web site on the server without reopening the Publish Remote Web Site Properties dialog box.

You'll show Brett how to publish the garden Web site to his computer's Web server using the FrontPage 2002 Server Extensions.

Note: You must be able to publish files to complete the steps in Session 6.3. If you cannot access IIS or a compatible Web server, read Session 6.3 without completing the steps at the computer so you will know how to publish a Web site. If your instructor asks you to publish the garden Web site to a location other than IIS, follow the instructions provided by your instructor to complete this section.

To publish a disk-based Web site to IIS:

1. Start **FrontPage**, and then open the **garden** Web site from the location where your Web sites are stored.

2. Click the **Remote Web Site View** button [Remote Web site] at the bottom of the Contents pane to change to Remote Web Site view. Because you haven't published the garden Web site to a server, this view is empty except for a message that tells you to click the Remote Web Site Properties button to set up a remote Web site.

3. Click the **Remote Web Site Properties** button on the Contents pane. The Remote Web Site Properties dialog box opens. See Figure 6-31.

Remote Web Site Properties dialog box ◀ **Figure 6-31**

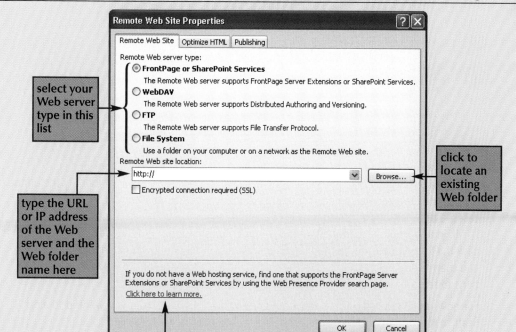

4. Make sure that the **FrontPage or SharePoint Services** option button is selected in the Remote Web server type section.

Trouble? If your ISP or instructor asks you to select a different method for publishing the Web site, choose the appropriate option button in Step 4.

You will enter the remote Web site location by typing the path to IIS or your server.

5. Select any text in the Remote Web site location list box (if necessary), and then type **http://localhost/garden**.

Trouble? If your instructor provides you with a different path or computer name, or an IP address for publishing your Web site, use that path or computer name instead of the one provided in Step 5.

6. Click the **Optimize HTML** tab. See Figure 6-32.

Figure 6-32	Optimize HTML tab

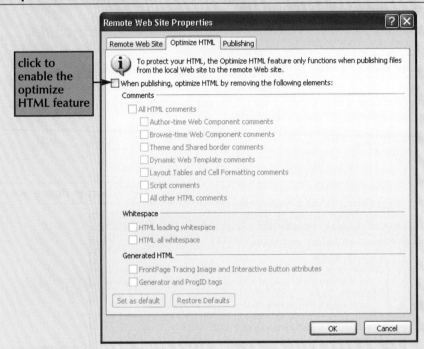

Optimizing the HTML for a Web site removes some nonstandard HTML tags and space characters that FrontPage may have inserted in your pages. These tags might identify the editor that created the page as being FrontPage or identify you as the author of the page. In most cases, a browser ignores these tags if it cannot interpret them. If you want to optimize the HTML in all of the pages in the Web site before publishing them to the Web server, you can click the When publishing, optimize HTML by removing the following elements check box, and then select the check boxes in the Comments, Whitespace, and Generated HTML sections to remove nonstandard tags and spaces from pages in your Web site.

For now, you'll publish the pages without optimizing the HTML, but you wanted to alert Brett to this option.

7. Click the **Publishing** tab. See Figure 6-33. You can change the default settings to publish either all pages or only those pages that contain changes. The advantage of publishing only changed pages is that it will speed up the publishing process. You can specify which method to use to determine a changed page: by comparing the source and destination Web sites, or by comparing the date and time that pages in the source Web site were last saved. You can publish any subsites in your Web site at the same time by selecting the Include subsites check box. Because your Web site does not include a subsite, you don't need to select this option. Finally, by selecting the Log changes during publish check box, FrontPage will create a log file when publishing the Web site. If there are errors during the publishing process, this log file can help you identify them.

Publishing tab ◀ **Figure 6-33**

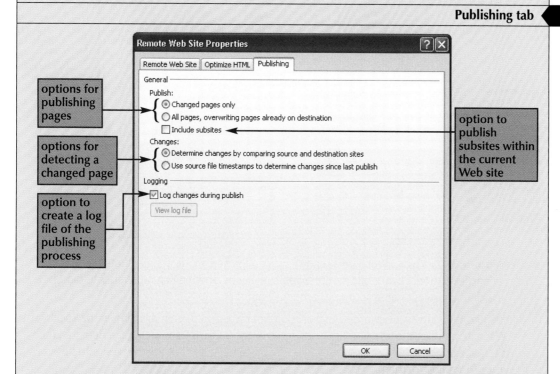

options for publishing pages

options for detecting a changed page

option to create a log file of the publishing process

option to publish subsites within the current Web site

8. Make sure that the **Changed pages only** option button is selected, that the **Determine changes by comparing source and destination sites** option button is selected, and that the **Log changes during publish** check box contains a check mark, and then click the **OK** button.

A Microsoft Office FrontPage message box opens, indicating that a Web site does not exist at the location you specified. You need to create the Web folder, so you'll click the Yes button.

9. Click the **Yes** button. Remote Web Site view now shows the folders and files in the disk-based garden Web site on the left and the remote garden Web site on the right. Because you have not yet published the garden Web site, the Remote Web site pane is empty, except for the _private and images folders that FrontPage created when you clicked the Yes button to create the Web site on the server. See Figure 6-34.

Figure 6-34 | **Remote Web Site view**

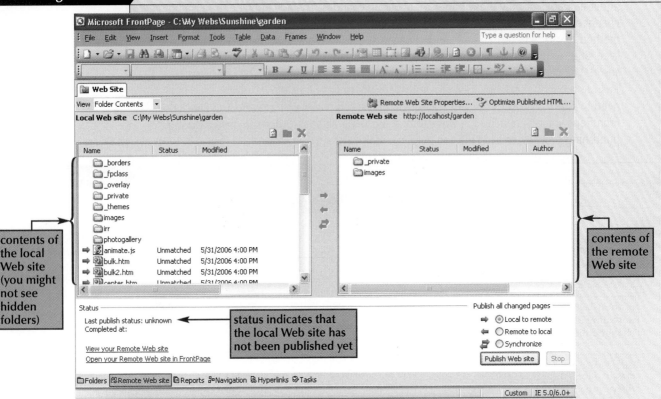

Trouble? If a garden Web site already exists on the server, click the Remote Web Site Properties button, change the Remote Web site location on the Remote Web Site tab to "garden" plus your name, and then continue with the steps.

Remote Web Site view identifies the location from which you are publishing in the Local Web site pane on the left and the location to which you are publishing in the Remote Web site pane on the right. In this case, you are publishing your disk-based Web site to IIS (http://localhost/garden).

Remote Web Site view also lists all of the folders and files in your Web site in the Local Web site pane. Each file has a status of "Unmatched" and an arrow to the left of the filename. If you had set any page so that it would not be published, the status would be "Don't publish" and a red "X" would appear instead of the arrow next to the filename. (You can set a page so that it is not published by right-clicking the filename and then clicking Don't Publish on the shortcut menu.)

The Publish all changed pages section in Remote Web Site view shows three options for publishing the Web site to the remote Web server. The first option, Local to remote, publishes the disk-based Web site to the remote Web site. This option is the one that publishes the Web site from a computer to a server. The second option, Remote to local, publishes the remote Web site to the local disk. You usually use this option to create a backup copy of the remote Web site on a local drive, such as your computer's hard drive or a removable disk. Regularly backing up your remote Web site to a hard drive or other disk is a good way to prevent data loss in the event of a problem with the Web server. The third option, Synchronize, updates the local and remote Web sites so they are identical. You can use this option when you need to update a local and remote site so they contain the same content and files. Usually you use this option when you and other users have made changes to both copies of the Web site and need to merge those changes. If there are conflicts between files on the local and remote systems during the publishing process, a Conflict dialog box opens and asks you to choose to ignore the conflict, overwrite the file with the new version (using the date), or cancel publishing the Web site.

Because you are publishing the garden Web site for the first time, you'll need to select the default option, which is to publish the local Web site to the remote Web server.

To publish the local Web site to the remote server:

1. Make sure that the **Local to remote** option button is selected, and then click the **Publish Web site** button. The Status section shows the publishing status of the Web site as FrontPage publishes the files from the local Web site to the remote Web server. When publishing is complete, the Status section displays the message "Last publish status: successful" and the date and time publishing was completed, as shown in Figure 6-35.

Successful publication of the Web site ◄ **Figure 6-35**

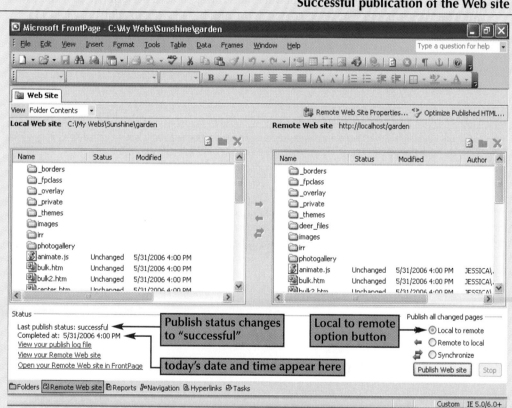

The Remote Web site pane shows the files and folders that were published to the server. If FrontPage is configured to hide the local Web site's hidden folders, you will see more folders in the Remote Web site pane than in the Local Web site pane because the Remote Web site pane shows all of the site's folders, including the hidden folders, such as _borders, which contains the files that create the Web site's shared borders, and _themes, which stores the files that create the Garden Web Site theme.

The Status section includes three hyperlinks for viewing your publish log file, viewing your remote Web site (in a browser), and opening your remote Web site in FrontPage. You'll show Brett how to work with these options next.

To view the publish log file and the remote Web site:

1. In the Status section, click **View your publish log file**. The publish log file opens in a browser and shows the actions FrontPage took to publish the Web site. As you scroll down the page, you'll see that it created each folder in and copied each file to the remote Web site. The last entries show that the navigation structure was copied and that publishing was finished. If FrontPage encountered any errors during the publishing process, these errors would appear in the publish log file.

2. Close your browser.

3. In the Status section, click the **View your Remote Web site** link. The home page for the remote Web site opens in a browser, as shown in Figure 6-36. Notice that the URL for the page is the remote Web site, http://localhost/garden (your path might differ if you published your Web site to another location). The HTTP protocol in the URL indicates that your Web browser is communicating with a server to process requests, instead of opening files directly from your computer's hard drive. The server is opening the files from the C:\Inetpub\wwwroot\garden folder on your hard drive. You can perform the same activities using this server-based Web as you did with the disk-based Web. In addition, when you open a server-based Web in FrontPage, you can edit pages, update hyperlinks, and perform other tasks, just as you did in the disk-based Web. The main difference between the two Web sites is that the server-based Web will process several key elements of the Web site, including the form that you created earlier in this tutorial.

Figure 6-36	Home page of the remote Web site

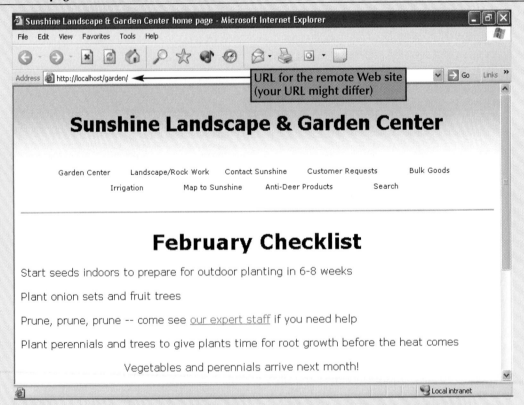

4. Follow the links on the home page to examine the pages in the remote Web site, and then close your browser.

Publishing Changes to Pages in a Web Site

As you and Brett examine the pages in the garden Web site, you notice that the marquee on the home page is set to scroll its message indefinitely. You think that this feature would be better if it scrolled twice, instead of continuously, so it doesn't become a distraction. You can make this change in the disk-based Web site and then publish the change to the remote Web server. You explain to Brett that you could also make the change in the remote Web site, but most developers make changes in the local site and then publish them. This strategy has two advantages. First, when you publish a site, you publish all of the site's changes at once, which minimizes the problems that users might encounter if they are viewing your pages as you work on them. Second, having two copies of the Web site—one on a local drive and another on the remote Web server—ensures that you can recover your files in the event of a problem.

Publishing Changes to a Server-Based Web Site

Reference Window

- In Design view, open the Web page that you need to edit, make the changes, and then save the page.
- Edit and save other Web pages, as necessary.
- Click the Publish Site button on the Standard toolbar.

You'll make the change in the home page, save the home page, and then publish the Web site.

To make a change in the home page and publish the Web site's changes:

1. Change to Folders view. The disk-based garden Web site is still open in FrontPage, as indicated by the path in the title bar.

2. Double-click **index.htm** in the Contents pane to open the home page in Design view.

3. Scroll down the page as necessary, and then double-click the marquee. (The marquee contains the text "Vegetables and perennials arrive next month!") The Marquee Properties dialog box opens.

4. In the Repeat section, click the **Continuously** check box to clear it. A "1" appears in the list box in the Repeat section. This number indicates the number of times the marquee will scroll across the page before it stops.

5. Click the **up** arrow on the list box in the Repeat section to change the value to **2**, and then click the **OK** button. This change will cause the marquee to scroll across the screen twice and then stop.

6. Save the home page, and then close it. You need to publish the Web site again to make the same change in the remote Web site.

7. Click the **Publish Site** button 🔲 on the Standard toolbar. Because you have already published this Web site, you do not have to specify a location to which to publish it. You also previously set FrontPage to publish only those pages with changes, so only the index.htm page and any other pages that changed as a result of the update you made to the index.htm page will be copied to the server. The Web site appears in Remote Web Site view and the Status section shows the publishing process. When publishing is complete, the Last publish status changes to "successful."

8. Click the **View your Remote Web site** link to open the home page of the remote Web site in a browser. The marquee scrolls across the screen twice and then stops.

Processing Web Pages on a Server

In Sessions 6.1 and 6.2, you added the Search and Customer Requests pages to the Web site. You tested these pages in the disk-based Web site but your testing served primarily to confirm that the pages appeared as desired. For the Search page, you included a component to search the site using keywords entered by the user and a second component to search the Internet using keywords entered by the user. For the Customer Requests page, you inserted a form and form fields in the page to collect data, and set the form to send its results to a file in the Web site. You tested both pages, but were limited to testing individual form fields to make sure that they contained the desired choices. Now that you have published the Web site, you tell Brett that he can test these pages by entering keywords in the search components and submitting a form to the server. Even if your Web site performs perfectly when you test it on your local drive or local server, after publishing a Web site you must resume testing again to ensure that all of the site's features work correctly.

After a server processes a Web page that contains a form, it usually sends a confirmation page to the browser that sent the page. A **confirmation page** is a Web page that contains a copy of the data entered by the user and often is used for verification purposes. FrontPage can return a default confirmation page or you can create, save, and specify a custom confirmation page. When you specify a custom confirmation page, FrontPage automatically inserts the data entered by the user in the correct locations in the confirmation page and then sends it to the browser.

Next, you will test the Search and Customer Requests pages to make sure that the server processes them correctly.

To test the Search page in a browser:

1. Click the **Search** hyperlink in the link bar in the home page. The Search page opens in the browser. The page's URL references the page in the remote Web site. The link to the MSN logo picture is broken because this picture file is not stored in the Web site.

   Trouble? If a Dial-up Connection dialog box opens, click the Close button. You do not need an Internet connection to complete these steps.

   Trouble? If you published your Web site to Windows 2003 Server using Windows SharePoint Services, the search page will not return the search results because this feature is not supported with this server configuration. Read the remaining steps so you will understand how a search component works, but do not complete them at the computer.

2. Click the **Search for** text box, type **lawn**, and then click the **Start Search** button. If necessary, scroll down the page so the Search for text box is at the top of the window. The server processes your search request and returns a new Web page with two documents that match your request and contain the word "lawn." Depending on your computer's speed, the new page might appear so quickly that you won't notice it. The Search page that is displayed in the browser is the page that the server generated to contain your search results. See Figure 6-37.

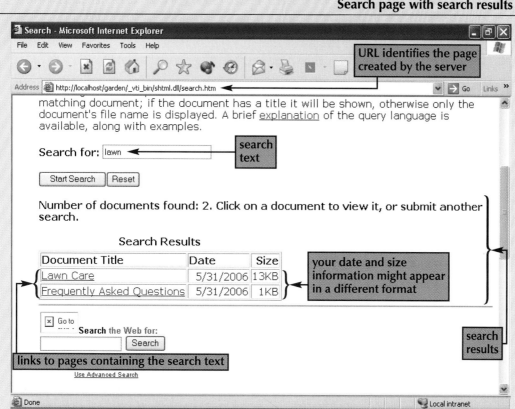

Trouble? If a page opens with the message "Service is not running" and you published the garden Web site to IIS, you will need to start the Indexing Service. Click the Start button on the taskbar, and then click Control Panel. Double-click the Administrative Tools icon, double-click the Component Services icon, and then click Services (Local) in the pane on the left. Scroll down the list of services on the right and double-click Indexing Service. Click the Startup type list arrow, and then click Automatic. Click the Start button in the Service status section. Click the OK button, close the Component Services window, close the Administrative Tools window, and then close the Control Panel. Click your browser's Back button to return to the Search page (search.htm), click the Reset button, and then repeat Step 2.

Trouble? If you published the garden Web site to IIS, it might take several minutes for the server to index the pages you just published. If you see the message "No documents found. Please try again." in the search results, click your browser's Back button to return to the Search page (search.htm), wait a few minutes for the indexing service to index the site, and then repeat Step 2.

Trouble? If an Internet Explorer dialog box opens and says that you are sending information to the local intranet, click the Yes button to continue.

3. If necessary, scroll down the Search page so you can see the search results. The server generated this revised version of the search.htm page. The Search Results table contains two entries that are formatted as hyperlinks. The Lawn Care and Frequently Asked Questions pages contain the word "lawn." Pages identified in the search results are hyperlinks that you can click to open those pages.

4. Click the **Lawn Care** hyperlink in the Search Results table. The Lawn Care Web page opens.

5. Click your browser's **Back** button to return to the search results, and then click the **Frequently Asked Questions** link. This page is part of the Irrigation frames page.

   Trouble? If a message tells you the page has expired, refresh the page.

6. Click your browser's **Back** button to return to the search results, and then press **Ctrl + Home** to scroll to the top of the page.

Now you can test the Customer Requests page, which contains the form that must be processed by a server.

To test the Customer Requests page:

1. Click the **Customer Requests** link to open the Customer Requests page.

2. Scroll down the page, click the text area, and then type **This is a test.**

3. Click the **Rock Work** and **Irrigation Service** check boxes in the check box group.

4. Click the drop-down list arrow, and then click **Lago Vista**.

5. Click the **Name** text box, type **Brett Kizer**, press the **Tab** key to move to the E-mail Address text box, type **brett@sunshinelandscapeandgardencenter.com**, press the **Tab** key to move to the Daytime Phone text box, and then type **555-2610**.

6. Click the **Phone** option button in the option button group.

7. Click the **Visits** text box, and then type **155**.

8. Click the **Submit Form** button. The Form Validation Error page opens and asks you to enter a value greater than or equal to zero and less than or equal to 100 in the Visits field. See Figure 6-38.

Figure 6-38 ▶ **Form Validation Error page**

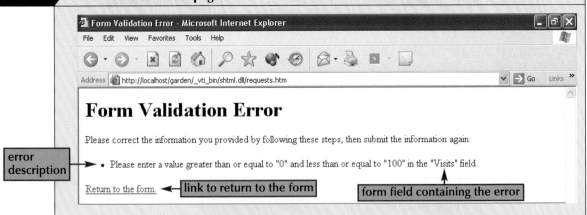

Trouble? If a dialog box opens instead of the page shown in Figure 6-38, click the OK button, and then skip clicking the Back button in Step 9.

Trouble? If an AutoComplete dialog box opens, click the No button.

9. Click your browser's **Back** button, select **155** in the Visits text box, type **15**, and then click the **Submit Form** button. The Form Confirmation page opens with a copy of the data you entered into the form. The server generated this page automatically. See Figure 6-39. Notice that the check boxes you selected contain the value "Yes." Check boxes that you did not select do not contain a value. When you clicked the Phone option button in the CommunicationPreference option button group, the value "Phone" was entered as the result.

Form Confirmation page | **Figure 6-39**

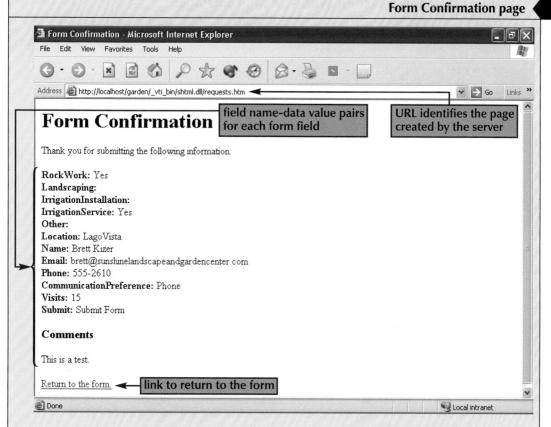

10. Click the **Return to the form** link at the bottom of the confirmation page to return to the Customer Requests Web page. Clicking the Return to the form link clears all of the form's fields and resets the form so it is ready to be completed again. Your test of the form is successful. The page correctly accepts your input, produces a confirmation page, and resets the form.

When the confirmation page was sent to your browser, the form's results were also written to the results.csv file that you specified when you created the form. You stored this file in the _private folder of the remote Web site.

Examining a Form Results File

When you set the Save Results form handler to store the form's results, you specified a comma-delimited text file format. In a comma-delimited text file, the name of each form field appears in the first line of the file. The form results from each new form submission are added as a new line at the end of the file. Unless you submitted your form more than once, the results file contains only two lines—one containing the form field names and another containing the form results from your form submission. You can examine the contents of the results file on the server at any time.

You want to show Brett how to view this file to increase his understanding of how the data submitted to the server is stored. You'll show him how to open the remote Web site in FrontPage.

To open the remote garden Web site in FrontPage:

▶ **1.** Close your browser.

In Remote Web Site view, you can click the Open your Remote Web site in FrontPage link to open the remote Web site in FrontPage. You explain to Brett that he can click this link *after* publishing a Web site to open the remote Web site on the server. However, this option is available only when the disk-based Web site is open. You want to show Brett how to open the remote Web site without first opening the disk-based Web site, so you ask him to close the disk-based Web site first.

▶ **2.** Click **File** on the menu bar, and then click **Close Site**. The disk-based garden Web site closes.

▶ **3.** Click the **list arrow** for the Open button 📂▾ on the Standard toolbar, and then click **Open Site** in the list. The Open Site dialog box opens. You need to access the folder on your computer that contains server-based Web sites.

▶ **4.** Click the **My Network Places** button in the Look in column, click the **garden on localhost** folder to select it, and then click the **Open** button.

Trouble? If you see localhost or your server's name in the list box, double-click it to open it, click the garden folder to select it, and then click the Open button.

Trouble? If you don't see a garden on localhost folder or a localhost folder, type http://localhost (or the address for the root folder of your Web server) in the Site name text box, and then click the Open button. A new FrontPage window opens and lists the Web sites stored on the server. Double-click the garden Web site to open it, and then close the FrontPage window that displays the contents of the server.

▶ **5.** Change to Folders view (if necessary). If you published your Web site to IIS, the default path to the Web site will appear in the FrontPage title bar as http://localhost/garden.

Now that the server-based Web site is open, you can examine the results file.

To examine the results file:

▶ **1.** Double-click the **_private** folder, and then double-click **results.csv** in the Contents pane. The results.csv file opens and shows the field names on line 1 and the results of the form you submitted on line 2. Each value in quotation marks represents the value for one form field in the form. Notice that the last entry is Remote Name on line 1 and 127.0.0.1 on line 2. This form field collects the IP address of the user who submitted the form, which you specified when you configured the form's handler and the data to collect. The value 127.0.0.1 is the default IP address for IIS. See Figure 6-40.

Figure 6-40 ▶ **Form results file**

> **2.** Click the **Close** button ⊠ to close the results.csv file.
>
> **3.** Click the **Up One Level** button on the Contents pane to return to the root folder of the garden Web site.

You have verified that the form's results were collected correctly and stored in the results.csv file in the _private folder of the remote garden Web site. You tell Brett that it is important to continue testing the pages in the Web site to ensure that everything is working correctly. Brett also wants to add some new features to the Web site. The first feature he wants to add is a counter that displays the number of times the home page has been accessed.

Using a Hit Counter

To fulfill Brett's request, you tell him that he will need to add a hit counter to the Web site. A **hit counter** is a component that counts the number of times a page in a Web site has been opened or refreshed using a Web browser. Usually a hit counter appears in the Web site's home page, although you can create hit counters in other pages, as well. A hit counter requires a server for processing, so you can test it only in a server-based Web site. In Web sites that do not use the FrontPage 2002 Server Extensions or SharePoint Services, you must write a program to add the functionality to a hit counter. However, if your Web site uses the FrontPage 2002 Server Extensions or SharePoint Services, you can insert a hit counter in a Web page, and FrontPage will generate the program to provide its functionality automatically. You can accept the default settings for the hit counter or change the counter style and other properties if desired. The counter style is implemented using a default or custom-designed GIF picture that contains the digits zero through nine.

Creating a Hit Counter in a Web Page

Reference Window

- Click the location in the page where you want to insert the hit counter.
- Click the Web Component button on the Standard toolbar.
- In the Component type list box, click Hit Counter.
- In the Choose a counter style list box, click the desired hit counter style, and then click the Finish button.
- In the Hit Counter Properties dialog box, set the options to reset the counter or to display a fixed number of digits as needed.
- Click the OK button.

Brett wants to insert a hit counter in the home page. Most Web developers start the counter with the number 1000 to make it look like the site is active, so you suggest doing the same. You'll also set the counter to display six digits to allow for future expansion.

To create a hit counter in the home page:

> **1.** Double-click **index.htm** in the Contents pane to open the home page in Design view. You will insert the hit counter between the marquee and the map picture.
>
> **2.** Scroll down the page, click the marquee, press the **End** key, press the **Enter** key to create a new paragraph, and then click the **Center** button on the Formatting toolbar to center the new paragraph.
>
> **3.** Click the **Bold** button B on the Formatting toolbar, type **You are visitor number** as the text that precedes the hit counter, and then press the **spacebar**.

▶ **4.** Click the **Web Component** button 🖳 on the Standard toolbar, and then in the Component type list box click **Hit Counter**. The Choose a counter style list box displays five styles of hit counters.

▶ **5.** Click the fourth hit counter style in the Choose a counter style list box, and then click the **Finish** button. The Hit Counter Properties dialog box opens. See Figure 6-41.

| **Figure 6-41** | Hit Counter Properties dialog box |

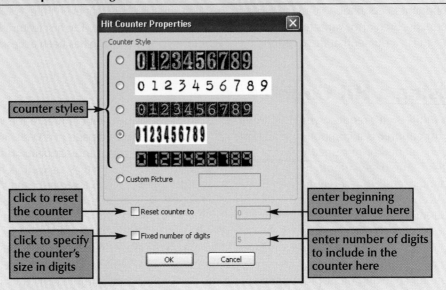

6. Click the **Reset counter to** check box to select it, press the **Tab** key to move to its text box, and then type **1000**. The hit counter will start at 1000, instead of zero. Starting the hit counter at a number other than zero or one is a common practice on the Internet.

▶ **7.** Click the **Fixed number of digits** check box to select it, press the **Tab** key to move to its text box, and then type **6**. The counter will display six digits.

▶ **8.** Click the **OK** button to close the Hit Counter Properties dialog box and to insert the hit counter. A picture of the hit counter appears in the page as a placeholder to indicate the hit counter's location.

Next, complete the rest of the sentence that contains the hit counter.

▶ **9.** Press the **spacebar**, and then type **to our Web site.** as the text that follows the hit counter.

▶ **10.** Save the home page.

You'll need to open the home page of the remote Web site in a browser to test the hit counter.

To test the hit counter:

▶ **1.** Click the **Preview** button 🔍 on the Standard toolbar to open the home page in a browser.

▶ **2.** If necessary, scroll down the home page to see the hit counter. You are the first visitor to the Web site. Because you set the hit counter to start with the value 1000, you are visitor number 1001.

3. Click the **Refresh** button 🔲 on the toolbar to refresh the page. Now you are visitor number 1002. Each time the page is opened or refreshed, the number in the hit counter increases by one. See Figure 6-42.

Hit counter after loading and refreshing the home page ◄ **Figure 6-42**

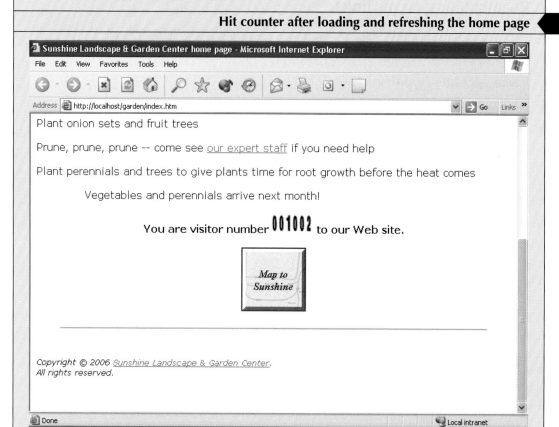

4. Close your browser.

The hit counter will count the number of times the home page has been opened. Because refreshing the page also increases the number in the counter, the counter does not indicate the exact number of visitors to a Web page, but it's a good estimate.

Recalculating and Verifying Hyperlinks

When you are working on a Web site, it is a good idea to recalculate the hyperlinks contained in it periodically. **Recalculating hyperlinks** is the process of updating the display of all views of the Web site in which you are working, including updating the text index created by a FrontPage search component (when one is used), deleting files for unused themes, and reporting any broken hyperlinks. You can recalculate the hyperlinks in a disk-based or server-based Web site. When it recalculates the hyperlinks in a server-based Web site, FrontPage updates the index that it maintains for the search component as well.

Verifying hyperlinks is the process of checking all of the hyperlinks in a Web site to identify any internal or external broken hyperlinks. An **external hyperlink** is a hyperlink to a location that is not in the current Web site, such as a hyperlink to a URL on a different Web server. Any broken hyperlinks will be listed in Reports view so you can repair them.

You can recalculate and verify hyperlinks to detect and repair broken hyperlinks. One of the primary differences between these two commands relates to how broken hyperlinks are displayed. Both commands list broken hyperlinks, but verifying hyperlinks provides a report of all broken hyperlinks (both internal and external). Both commands also provide information that is useful in locating and correcting hyperlink problems.

Recalculating Hyperlinks

First, you want to show Brett how to recalculate the hyperlinks in the remote garden Web site.

To recalculate hyperlinks:

▶ 1. Close the home page.

▶ 2. Click **Tools** on the menu bar, and then click **Recalculate Hyperlinks**. The Recalculate Hyperlinks dialog box opens and describes the actions that will occur after clicking the Yes button. See Figure 6-43.

Figure 6-43	Recalculate Hyperlinks dialog box

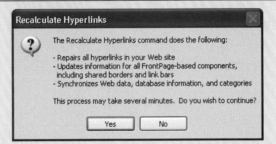

▶ 3. Read the information in the dialog box, and then click the **Yes** button. The "Updating hyperlinks and text indices..." message appears on the status bar. After a few seconds, FrontPage refreshes the files in Folders view. FrontPage also deletes any unnecessary files in the garden Web site.

The hyperlinks have been recalculated, and their display has been updated to reflect any changes. After recalculating the hyperlinks, you should verify them.

Verifying Hyperlinks

When you recalculated the hyperlinks for the garden Web site, FrontPage deleted any unnecessary files from the Web site and refreshed the Web site views. To identify broken links in a Web site, you need to switch to Reports view and verify the site's hyperlinks. When you verify hyperlinks, FrontPage checks each Web page for missing or broken hyperlinks and then displays a report of its findings.

You want to show Brett how to verify the site's hyperlinks so he can identify and correct any problems.

To verify hyperlinks:

▶ 1. Change to Reports view.

▶ 2. Click the **Verifies hyperlinks in the current web** button 🗹 on the Contents pane. The Verify Hyperlinks dialog box opens.

▶ 3. Click the **Verify all hyperlinks** option button, and then click the **Start** button. The Broken Hyperlinks report lists several broken links in the current Web site. See Figure 6-44. (Your list of broken hyperlinks might differ, which is not a problem.)

Trouble? If a Dial-up Connection dialog box opens, click the Close button.

4. Right-click the **http://www.msn.com** broken hyperlink to open the shortcut menu, and then click **Edit Page**. The search.htm page opens in Design view.

5. Scroll down the page as necessary so you can see the search components. The broken link to the picture is selected.

6. Press the **Delete** key to delete the selected broken link, and then save and close the search.htm page.

7. Click the button, and then click the **Start** button to verify the site's hyperlinks again. This time, the report shows two broken hyperlinks in the contact.htm and requests.htm pages (your broken links might differ). You'll fix these broken links when you complete the Review Assignments at the end of this tutorial.

Because you made your changes in the remote garden Web site, the local Web site is now out of date. To update the local site, you can open the local Web site in FrontPage and synchronize it with the remote Web site.

To synchronize the local and remote Web sites:

1. Close the remote Web site by clicking **File** on the menu bar, and then clicking **Close Site**.

2. Click **File** on the menu bar, point to **Recent Sites**, and then select the disk-based garden Web site to open it in FrontPage.

3. Change to Remote Web Site view.

4. Click the **Synchronize** option button in the Publish all changed pages section, and then click the **Publish Web site** button. FrontPage updates the local Web site with the changes you made in the remote Web site.

5. In the Local Web site pane, scroll down the file list as necessary and select **index.htm**, and then click the **Preview** button on the Standard toolbar. The home page of the local Web site opens in a browser. Scroll down the page and notice that the page now contains the hit counter. The synchronize action updated the local Web site with this change that you made in the remote Web site. However, because the hit counter works only in a server-based Web site, a broken link to the hit counter is displayed rather than a number.

6. Close your browser.

Recalculating and verifying hyperlinks has helped you isolate several broken hyperlinks, and possibly other problems in your Web site. After fixing any problems that you find, it is a good idea to recalculate and verify the hyperlinks again, so you can check the changes that you made.

The last thing that you want to review with Brett is how to secure a Web site.

Setting Permissions for a Web Site

Permissions allow a Web site developer to control who can browse, author, or administer a Web site after it has been published. (You cannot set permissions in a disk-based Web site.) When the Web server is properly configured for using permissions, you can use FrontPage to administer the permissions for a Web site or a subsite. Three types of permissions exist: browsing, authoring, and administering. **Browsing permissions** authorize a user to browse (open) all of the pages in a Web site, including hidden files, but the user cannot make changes to the pages. **Authoring permissions** allow a user to browse and change a site's pages by opening them in Design view. Finally, **administering permissions** allow a user to browse and change a site's pages and to set other user permissions. For example, if you do not want a user to be able to change the content of a Web site, you would set that user's permission to browsing. Permissions are hierarchical; for example, a user with administering permissions also has authoring and browsing permissions, whereas authoring permissions give a user browsing permissions but not administering permissions.

When you run IIS on a Windows NT or a Windows 2000/XP computer, users and groups are set up and maintained in Windows and cannot be created in FrontPage. In this case, the system administrator determines which users and groups can set security for Web sites that reside on that server. You will be able to set permissions for a Web site only if you have the necessary permissions to do so for the client or network on which the IIS server resides.

If the server allows permissions and the settings have not been changed, the permissions established for the root Web site are inherited by all other Web sites. The garden Web site that you published to the server is a subsite in the FrontPage root Web, which is C:\Inetput\wwwroot. Thus, any permissions that were set for the root Web also apply to the garden Web site that you published. You can change the permissions for a subsite at any time; in fact, one advantage of creating a subsite is to protect it independently of the root Web site by establishing appropriate permissions for different users.

Reference Window | Setting Permissions for a Web Site

- Open the server-based Web site in FrontPage.
- Click Tools on the menu bar, point to Server, and then click Administration Home. The Administration page opens in a browser.
- Click the Change subweb permissions link.
- Choose the Use unique permissions for this Web site option button, and then click the Submit button.
- Click the Administration link at the top of the page.
- Click the Change anonymous access settings link, use the page that opens to turn anonymous access off or on and to assign users to a role (Administrator, Advanced author, Author, Contributor, or Browser), and then click the Submit button.
- Click the Manage users link, and then click the Add a user link. Use the Configure Web User page to add a user and to select a role for the user, and then click the Add User button.
- Close the browser.

Because Brett is the administrator of the Web site, he needs to assign himself administering permissions. Brett will probably want to assign permissions to other users, such as the senior staff at the nursery, so they can make changes to pages in the Web site that represent their departments or specialties. Before setting up users, you will need to show Brett how to change the Web site to use permissions that are separate from the root Web site.

To change the garden Web site to use unique permissions:

▶ 1. Click **File** on the menu bar, and then click **Close Site**. The disk-based garden Web site closes.

▶ 2. Click **File** on the menu bar, point to **Recent Sites**, and then click the remote garden Web site.

▶ 3. Click **Tools** on the menu bar, point to **Server**, and then click **Administration Home**. The Administration page opens in a browser. Figure 6-45 shows the page in Internet Explorer. The IIS server used in these steps has the FrontPage 2002 Server Extensions installed on it. If your Web site is published on a server that uses SharePoint Services or another version of the FrontPage Server Extensions, your page will look different.

Administration page for the garden Web site ◀ **Figure 6-45**

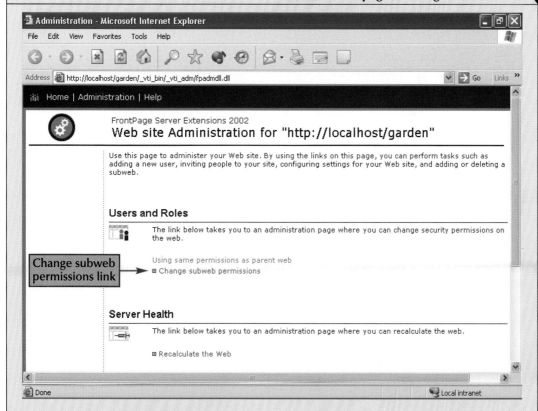

▶ 4. Click the **Change subweb permissions** link. The Edit Permissions page opens. There are two options for setting the permissions in a Web site. You can choose to use the same permissions as the parent (root) Web site, or use unique permissions for the current Web site. Brett wants to set the permissions for the current Web site.

5. Click the **Use unique permissions for this Web site** option button, and then click the **Submit** button. An Operation Results page opens while this change is being made on the server, and then the Edit Permissions page opens again.

6. Click the **Administration** link at the top of the page. The Administration page opens. As shown in Figure 6-46, the Users and Roles section has changed to reflect the fact that this Web site will have unique permissions.

Figure 6-46	Administration page after enabling the Web site for unique permissions

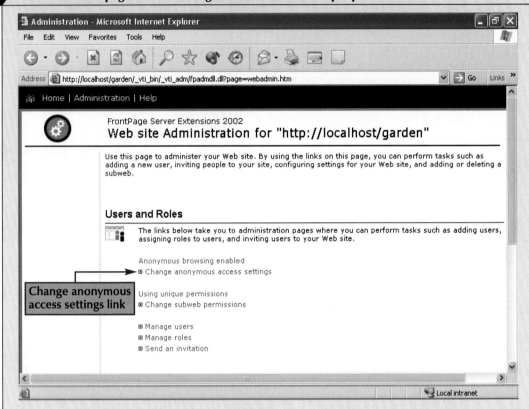

7. Click the **Change anonymous access settings** link. The Anonymous Access page opens. The default setting permits anonymous access for users with the Browser role. You tell Brett that this setting is acceptable for now. In the future, as he assigns different roles to other users, he might change the role of anonymous access to give users more authority to make changes to the Web site.

8. Click the **Cancel** button.

Brett wants to set himself as an administrator of the Web site. You'll show him how to make this change next.

To assign administering permissions to a user:

▶ **1.** On the Administration page, click the **Manage users** link. The User Management page opens, as shown in Figure 6-47. You use this page to add new users, remove existing users, or assign users new permissions. The User Management page on your computer might differ if users have been assigned permissions already.

User Management page | Figure 6-47

2. Click the **Add a user** link. The Configure Web User page opens. The insertion point is blinking in the User name text box.

3. Make sure that the **Add a new user with the following information** option button is selected, and then type **Brett Kizer** in the User name text box.

4. Press the **Tab** key, and then type **sunshine** as the password. As you type the password, dots or asterisks will appear instead of the letters you are typing to protect the password from being seen by others.

5. Press the **Tab** key, and then type **sunshine** to confirm the password. See Figure 6-48.

Figure 6-48 Adding a user

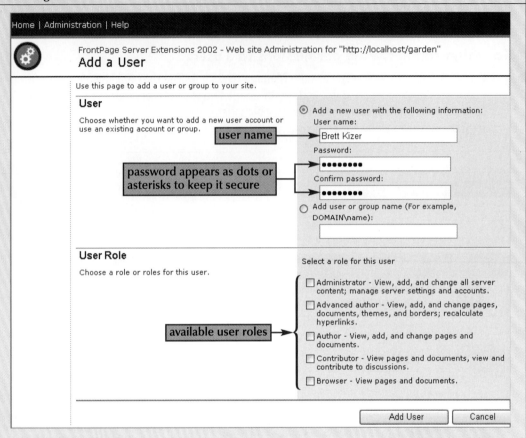

6. If necessary, scroll down to the User Role section. In this section, you select a role for the user you entered in the User section. Each role provides the user with different levels of permission for working in and changing the Web site.

7. Click the **Administrator** check box to select it, and then click the **Add User** button. On the User Management page, Brett now appears as a user with Administrator permissions.

You also want to show Brett how to change a user's permissions and how to remove a user.

To change a user's permissions and remove a user:

1. On the User Management page, click the **Brett Kizer** link but not the check box to the left of the user Brett Kizer. The Edit User Role Membership page opens. To change the role for this user, you would check the new role in the User Role section, and then click the Submit button.

Trouble? The user Brett Kizer might be preceded by a computer name and a backslash, such as DEFAULT\Brett Kizer. Just make sure that you click the link for Brett.

2. Click the **Cancel** button. You return to the User Management page.

3. Click the **check box** to the left of the Brett Kizer user, and then click the **Remove selected user(s) from all roles** link. A message box opens to confirm your intent to delete the user.

4. Click the **OK** button. The user Brett Kizer is removed from the site's list of users.

  5. Close your browser.

  6. Close the garden Web site, and then close FrontPage.

Going Live

Going live is the process of publishing your Web site on a Web server to make it accessible to other users. In this tutorial, you published a disk-based Web site to a server and tested it to ensure that its features work as expected. Before publishing a Web site on a Web server, most commercial Web site developers also test the Web site using different Web browsers, screen resolutions, and connection speeds to confirm that the Web site works consistently for the many ways in which people will access it. After thoroughly testing the site, the developer or administrator publishes it on the designated Web server.

You published the garden Web site to the server on your computer. After thorough testing and analysis, you will be ready to publish the Web site to the Web server that Brett selected to host it. You would use the Remote Web Site Properties button in Remote Web Site view to enter the information for the Web server Brett selected. To publish the site to a Web server, you need the URL for the Web server and the user name and password provided by the ISP. In addition, you must have permission to publish and maintain a Web site. In most cases, when you purchase a domain name and space on a Web server, the ISP will send you an e-mail message with your user name, password, and other important information about publishing your Web site. If the ISP hosts FrontPage Web sites, you might need to read the documentation to determine how to enable the FrontPage 2002 Server Extensions for your site. In most cases, you just need to submit a request to enable the Web site to use the FrontPage 2002 Server Extensions.

Generally, an individual designated as the administrator manages a Web server. The administrator is responsible for the overall management of the server, including the management of user access to it. The administrator determines how and where a Web site will be located on the server based on the procedures that have been established for the Web server by the company or ISP that owns and operates the server. The procedures for publishing a Web site on a Web server vary; check with your site's administrator for more information about publishing a Web site.

Acceptable Use Policies

Most companies and ISPs maintain an **acceptable use policy** (**AUP**). An AUP typically consists of a published or online document that an ISP or company creates to indicate the acceptable activities permitted on the Web server. For example, an AUP for an educational institution might prohibit users from using the network to engage in commercial activities, or an AUP for an ISP might prohibit users from creating Web sites on the network that include objectionable material. It is the responsibility of the Web server's administrator to verify that the Web site will meet these standards.

FrontPage 2002 Server Extensions and SharePoint Services

In this tutorial, you learned that the FrontPage 2002 Server Extensions or SharePoint Services must be installed and properly configured before certain features of the garden Web site, such as the hit counter and form processing, will work correctly. Some ISPs do not accept Web sites with FrontPage 2002 Server Extensions because the extensions can compromise the security of the Web server on which they reside. Before creating your Web site, it is important to identify any restrictions imposed by the operator of the Web server on which your Web site will ultimately reside. You might learn that the ISP will not accept Web sites with FrontPage 2002 Server Extensions or SharePoint Services. In this case, you can either search for another ISP to host your Web site or set your installation of FrontPage to disable features that are not supported by the ISP. If you must disable features that the ISP does not support, create the Web site as usual but, before creating any of its pages, click Tools on the menu bar, click Page Options, and then click the Compatibility tab. You can use this tab to disable features that use the FrontPage 2002 Server Extensions, SharePoint Services, and other elements, as necessary.

Fortunately, most ISPs have a technical support staff available to answer questions about publishing a Web site. Your best course of action is to find and communicate with an ISP before creating your Web site to gather information about the ISP's AUP and policy for accepting FrontPage Web sites. In most cases, the ISP can provide alternative means for creating pages in the event that the server cannot accept server extensions.

Now that you and Brett have finished the Web site, you are confident that Brett will be able to add new pages to it, update the site to make changes, and assign users different roles to help maintain the site.

Review

Session 6.3 Quick Check

1. The default name of the Web server for Windows XP is _____.
2. What is the default directory in which FrontPage publishes Web sites?
3. What are the four types of remote servers to which you can publish a FrontPage Web site?
4. What are the three options for publishing a Web site?
5. What is a confirmation page?
6. What is a comma-delimited text file?
7. What is a hit counter?
8. What happens when you recalculate the hyperlinks in a Web site?
9. What happens when you verify the hyperlinks in a Web site?

Review

Tutorial Summary

In this tutorial, you learned how to create a search component and a form in a Web page. You also learned how to use different form fields to collect different kinds of data and how to validate a form field to reduce data-entry errors and to ensure that the correct data is collected. You used a form handler to process a form on a server and viewed the form results file stored on the server. Finally, you learned how to publish a Web site from a local drive to a Web server, how to make changes in a remote Web site, and how to synchronize copies of a Web site.

As you develop Web sites in the future, you'll find other uses for forms. Forms can collect all kinds of data, from recording a visitor's name and address information to processing requests for service and collecting questions from customers. When you publish a Web site, be sure to test your forms thoroughly to ensure that they are easy to use and collect the intended data. You should also experiment with the different ways to store form data to find the one that best suits your needs. When deciding on a file format for your form results, make sure to plan ahead. For example, if you know that you will be creating a mailing list from data collected by a form, part of your testing should make sure that the data is easily imported into the program you intend to use to generate the mailing list.

When publishing a Web site, be sure to update the local site and then publish it to the remote Web server. This method ensures that you always have a local copy of the Web site that you can publish again in the case of a problem on the server.

Key Terms

acceptable use policy (AUP)
administering permission
authoring permission
browsing permission
check box
comma-delimited text
comma-separated value
command button
confirmation page
Distributed Authoring and
 Versioning (DAV)
drop-down box
drop-down menu
external hyperlink

field name-data value pair
File Transfer Protocol (FTP)
form
form field
form handler
Form Page Wizard
form results
going live
hit counter
integer
localhost
Microsoft Internet
 Information Services (IIS)
Normal push button

option button
option button group name
permission
push button
radio button
recalculating hyperlinks
Reset push button
Save Results form handler
scrolling text box
Submit push button
text area
text box
validation
verifying hyperlinks

Review Assignments

There are no new Data Files needed for these Review Assignments.

Before preparing the garden Web site for publication on a Web server and making it available to Internet visitors, Brett asks you to test the pages again and to make any necessary adjustments.

If necessary, start FrontPage, and then do the following:

1. Use My Network Places to open the **garden** Web site that you published to the server.
2. Open the Search page (**search.htm**) in Design view. Double-click the search component to open the Search Form Properties dialog box, and then make the following changes:
   a. Change the label for input to "Search the Sunshine Web Site for:".
   b. Change the label for the Start Search button to "Search the Sunshine Web Site."
   c. Change the information displayed in the search results to display the score (closeness of match) only.
3. Make the following changes to the Search the Web with MSN component:
   a. Change the text that identifies the text box to "Search the Internet for:".
   b. Change the properties of the text box so its name is "InternetSearch" and its width is 25 characters.
   c. Use the pointer to increase the width of the table in which the Search the Web with MSN component is stored so it is the same width as the search component that appears above it.
   d. Change the text in the component to the default 12-point font. (*Hint:* Select the text in the component, and the click (default font) in the font list.)
   e. Change the label for the Search push button to "Search the Internet" and change its name to "Search."
   f. Left-align the Use Advanced Search hyperlink.
   g. Delete the period that appears between the text box and the push button.
4. Save the **search.htm** page, and then close it.

5. Open the Customer Requests page (**requests.htm**) in Design view. To the right of the Other check box label, add a text box with the name "Other" and a width of 35 characters.

6. Add a new choice to the Location drop-down box. The choice name is "Round Rock," the value to store in the results file is "RoundRock," and the initial state is not selected. After adding this new choice, move it so it appears between the West Lake Hills and Other choices. Save the **requests.htm** page.

7. In Folders view, open the _private folder of the server-based Web site. Right-click the **results.csv** file to open the shortcut menu, point to Open With, and then click Microsoft Office Excel. The form results data is displayed in the worksheet using the form field names as the column headings. Resize each column to its best fit, and then print the worksheet in landscape orientation. Close Excel without saving your changes.

8. Recalculate and verify all hyperlinks in the Web site. There is a broken link in the **contact.htm** page. Right-click this broken link to open the shortcut menu, and then click Edit Page. The Contact Sunshine page opens in Design view with the broken hyperlink selected. Determine the cause of the problem and fix the broken link. (*Hint:* Read the paragraph in which the broken hyperlink appears for more information. The hyperlink's text and target both need to point to the page in the Web site that contains the form.) When you are finished, save and close the **contact.htm** page, and then recalculate and verify all hyperlinks again. Right-click any page in Reports view to open the shortcut menu, and then click Copy Report. Start Word or WordPad, and then click the Paste button on the Standard toolbar to paste the report into a new document. Click the Print button to print the report. Close Word or WordPad without saving your changes.

9. Close the server-based **garden** Web site, open the disk-based **garden** Web site, and then synchronize the remote and local Web sites. When the publishing process is complete, open the remote Web site in a browser. Thoroughly test the Web site by opening each link and examining each page. Use the Search page to conduct a search of the Web site using the keyword "deer," and then print the search results. Then use the Search the Web with MSN component to perform an Internet search using any keywords of interest. (*Note:* You must be connected to the Internet to use the Search the Web with MSN component.) Use your browser's Back button to return to the **garden** Web site.

10. Use the Customer Requests page to submit one form to the server. Print the confirmation page returned by the server.

11. Close your browser, close the **garden** Web site, and then close FrontPage.

Case Problem 1

Create

Create a page that searches a Web site and a page that contains a form. Then publish the Web site to a server and thoroughly test it.

There are no new Data Files needed for this Case Problem.

Buffalo Trading Post Many Buffalo Trading Post customers have told a sales associate that they would like to use the Web site to request more information and to add their names to a mailing list. During a recent Web site development meeting, the company's sales associates encouraged Nicole Beirne to develop a Contact Web page for customers. They agreed that the page's design should include a way for customers to add their names and addresses to the company's mailing list. Customers should also be able to send comments about items they would like to buy or sell using the categories of women's clothing, children's clothing, and accessories. The sales associates also were interested in finding out how many times a customer had visited a retail store. Nicole organized the ideas from the meeting and then met with you to review the Contact page requirements. Nicole asks you to make these enhancements to the Web site before publishing it to a server.

If necessary, start FrontPage, and then do the following:

1. Open the **buffalo** Web site from the location where your Web sites are stored. (If you did not create this Web site in Tutorial 1 and change it in Tutorials 2 through 5, ask your instructor for assistance.)

Explore

2. Open the **contact.htm** page in Design view, and then use the information supplied in the Case Problem description and Figure 6-49 to create the form. Define any necessary validation criteria to ensure that data is input correctly. Save the results collected by this form as comma-delimited text in the **contact.csv** file in the **_private** folder of the Web site. Do not save any additional fields, or the date and time the form was submitted to the server. When you are finished, save the **contact.htm** page.

Figure 6-49

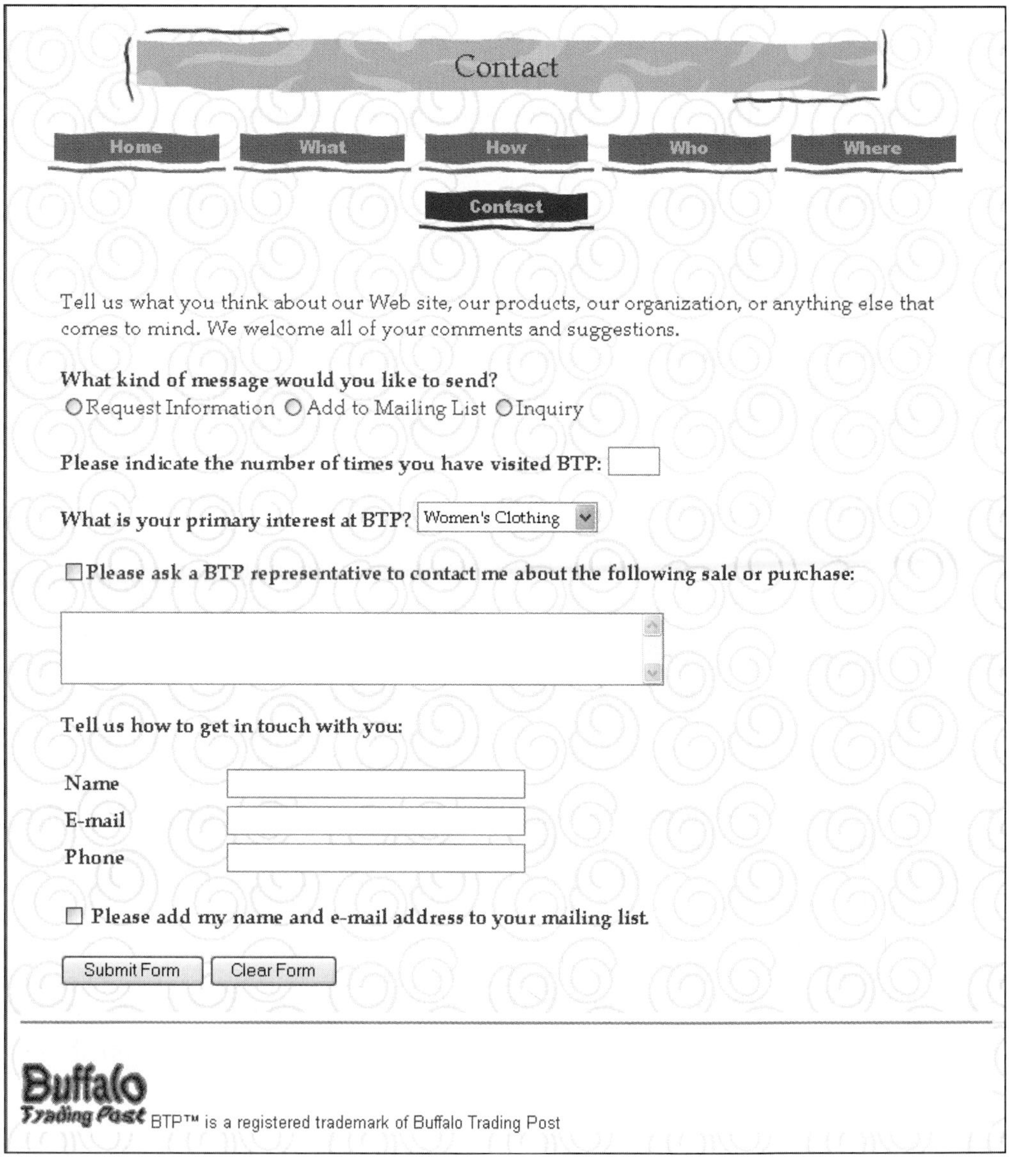

Contact

Home   What   How   Who   Where

Contact

Tell us what you think about our Web site, our products, our organization, or anything else that comes to mind. We welcome all of your comments and suggestions.

What kind of message would you like to send?
○ Request Information ○ Add to Mailing List ○ Inquiry

Please indicate the number of times you have visited BTP: [ ]

What is your primary interest at BTP? [Women's Clothing ▾]

☐ **Please ask a BTP representative to contact me about the following sale or purchase:**

[   ]

Tell us how to get in touch with you:

Name [   ]
E-mail [   ]
Phone [   ]

☐ Please add my name and e-mail address to your mailing list.

[Submit Form] [Clear Form]

Buffalo Trading Post BTP™ is a registered trademark of Buffalo Trading Post

Explore

3. Use FrontPage to print the HTML document for the **contact.htm** page. On the print-out, circle the tags that implement the FrontPage Save Results form handler. Close the **contact.htm** page.

4. Use a page template to create a page that searches the **buffalo** Web site. Delete the paragraph with the comment text and the horizontal line that appear at the top of the page, and then delete the copyright information and horizontal line that appear at the bottom of the page. Save the page using the filename **search.htm** and the title "Search." Add the **search.htm** page to Navigation view as a child page of the home page, positioning it to the right of the Contact page.

5. Publish the local **buffalo** Web site to the server using the same Web site name, and then use the hyperlink created by FrontPage to open the remote Web site in a browser. Test the Contact Web page that you created by completing the form, and then print the confirmation page that you receive from the server. Close your browser.

Explore

6. Use the Confirmation Form page template to create a new page in the disk-based **buffalo** Web site that confirms data submitted by the Contact page. After creating the page, do the following:

   a. Delete the paragraph with the comment and the horizontal line at the top of the page.

   b. Change the form field in the "Dear" line to match the form field name that you used for the text box that collects the user's name. (*Hint:* Double-click the field to open the Confirmation Field Properties dialog box, and then type the name of the text box. If you cannot remember the name you assigned to this field, open the **contact.htm** page in Design view to confirm it.)

   c. Change the first sentence in the first paragraph to "Thank you for your message."

   d. Change the form fields for the E-mail and Telephone lines to the form field names you used in the **contact.htm** page, and then delete the line containing the reference to a fax number.

   e. Save the page using the filename **confirm.htm** and the title "Confirmation" in the **_private** folder of the Web site.

   f. Return to the Contact Web page, and then open the Form Properties dialog box. Click the Options button, and then click the Confirmation Page tab. Type **_private/confirm.htm** in the URL of confirmation page (optional) text box to use the new Confirmation page with the form. Save the Contact page.

7. Open the **where.htm** page in Design view, and then type the following in the page: "For the location of the Buffalo Trading Post nearest you, please call 1-888-BUFFALO." Save the **where.htm** page.

8. Publish the local Web site to the server. After the publishing process is complete, open the remote Web site in a browser. Thoroughly test the Web site by opening each link and examining each page. Use the Search page to conduct a search of the Web site using the keywords "mailing list," and then print the search results.

9. Use the Contact page to submit one form to the server. Print the confirmation page returned by the server, and then close your browser.

10. Close the disk-based **buffalo** Web site in FrontPage, and then open the remote **buffalo** Web site. Recalculate and verify all hyperlinks in the site. Right-click any page in Reports view to open the shortcut menu, and then click Copy Report. Start Word or WordPad, and then click the Paste button on the Standard toolbar to paste the report into a new document. Click the Print button to print the report. Close Word or WordPad without saving your changes.

11. Change the **buffalo** Web site to use unique permissions.

12. Add yourself as a user with administrator permissions for the **buffalo** Web site by providing a user name and password of your choice. Use your browser to print the Manage Users page after adding yourself as a user.
13. Remove yourself from the Manage Users page, and then close your browser.
14. Close the **buffalo** Web site, and then close FrontPage.

Case Problem 2

Create

Create a page that searches a Web site and a page that contains a form. Then publish the Web site to a server and thoroughly test it.

There are no new Data Files needed for this Case Problem.

Garden Grill Meghan Elliott and Callan Murphy are pleased with your progress on the Garden Grill Web site. Their next priority is creating the Feedback and Search Web pages. After a meeting with the company's marketing department, Meghan wants to create a new Web page to gather customer information and feedback about diners' eating habits and their impressions about the restaurant's menu, prices, service, and Web site. Meghan asks you to make these enhancements to the Web site before publishing it to a server.

If necessary, start FrontPage, and then do the following:

1. Open the **grill** Web site from the location where your Web sites are stored. (If you did not create this Web site in Tutorial 1 and change it in Tutorials 2 through 5, ask your instructor for assistance.)
2. Use a page template to create a page that searches the **grill** Web site. Save the page using the filename **search.htm** and the title "Search," replacing the page in the Web site with the same name. Delete the paragraph with the comment text and the horizontal line that appear at the top of the page, and then delete the copyright information and horizontal line that appear at the bottom of the page. Open the **about.htm** page in Design view, copy the link bar graphic and page title ("About Us") from the top of the page, and then paste this information at the top of the **search.htm** page. Change the heading you pasted to "Search," and then save the page.

Explore

3. Open the **feedback.htm** page in Design view, and then paste the information you copied in Step 2 at the top of the page and change the heading you pasted to "Feedback." Use the information supplied in the Case Problem description and Figure 6-50 to create the form. Define any necessary validation criteria to ensure that data is input correctly. Save the results collected by this form as comma-delimited text in the **feedback.csv** file in the **_private** folder of the Web site. The choices for the drop-down box are Web Site, Food, Menu, Prices, Employees, and Other. When you are finished, save the **feedback.htm** page.

Figure 6-50

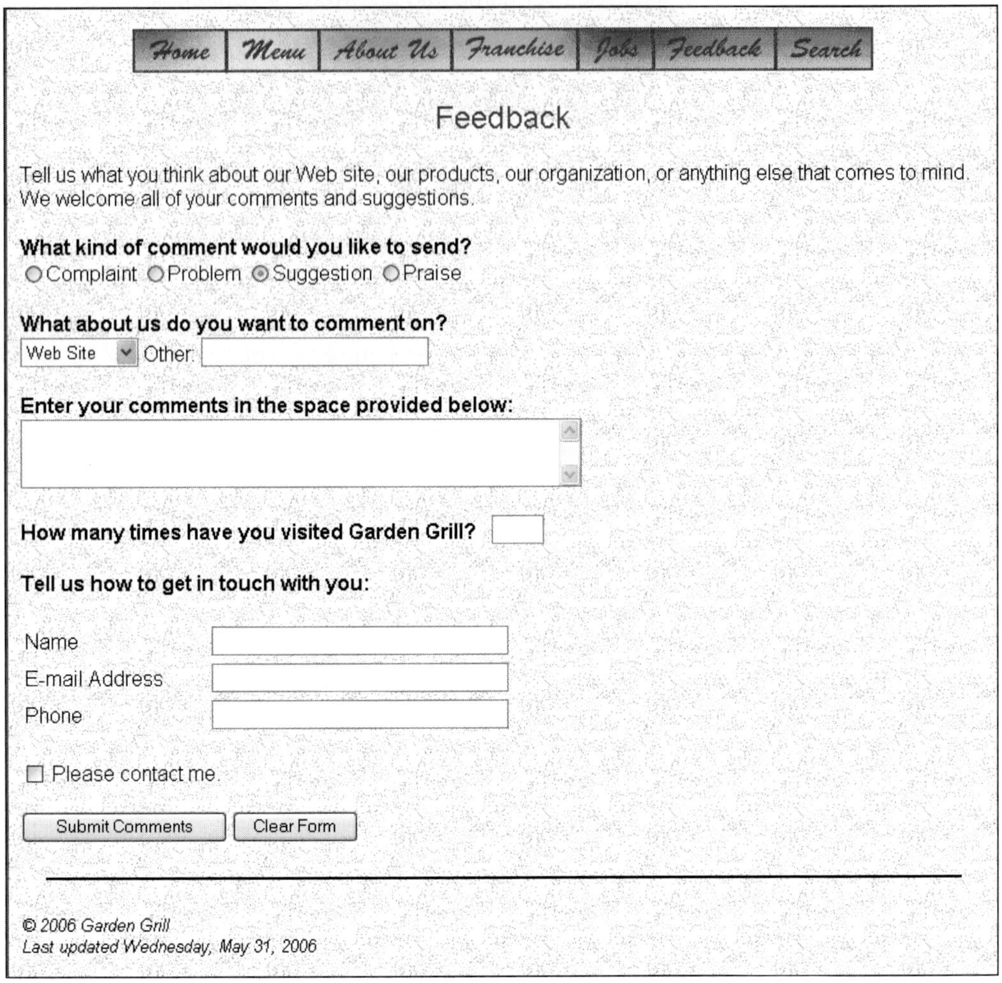

Home | Menu | About Us | Franchise | Jobs | Feedback | Search

Feedback

Tell us what you think about our Web site, our products, our organization, or anything else that comes to mind. We welcome all of your comments and suggestions.

What kind of comment would you like to send?
○ Complaint ○ Problem ◉ Suggestion ○ Praise

What about us do you want to comment on?
[Web Site ▼] Other: [   ]

Enter your comments in the space provided below:
[   ]

How many times have you visited Garden Grill? [   ]

Tell us how to get in touch with you:

Name [   ]
E-mail Address [   ]
Phone [   ]

☐ Please contact me.

[Submit Comments] [Clear Form]

© 2006 Garden Grill
Last updated Wednesday, May 31, 2006

Explore

4. Use FrontPage to print the HTML document for the **feedback.htm** page. On the print-out, circle the tags that implement the FrontPage Save Results form handler, the drop-down box, and the text boxes.

5. Publish the local **grill** Web site to the server using the same Web site name, and then use the hyperlink created by FrontPage to open the remote Web site in a browser. Test the Feedback Web page that you created by completing the form, and then print the confirmation page that you receive from the server. Close your browser.

Explore

6. Use the Confirmation Form page template to create a new page in the disk-based **grill** Web site that confirms data submitted by the Feedback page. After creating the page, do the following:
   a. Delete the paragraph with the comment and the horizontal line at the top of the page.
   b. Change the form field in the "Dear" line to match the form field name that you used for the text box that collects the user's name. (*Hint:* Double-click the field to open the Confirmation Field Properties dialog box and then type the name of the text box. If you cannot remember the name you assigned to this field, open the **feedback.htm** page in Design view to confirm it.)
   c. Change the first sentence in the first paragraph to "Thank you for your message."

d. Change the form fields for the E-mail and Telephone lines to the form field names you used in the **feedback.htm** page, and then delete the line containing the reference to a fax number.

e. Save the page using the filename **confirm.htm** and the title "Confirmation" in the **_private** folder of the Web site.

f. Return to the Feedback Web page, and then open the Form Properties dialog box. Click the Options button, and then click the Confirmation Page tab. Type **_private/confirm.htm** in the URL of confirmation page (optional) text box to use the new Confirmation page with the form. Save the Feedback page.

7. Open the Franchise Info page (**fran.htm**) in Design view. Paste the link bar and heading from the **about.htm** page at the top of the **fran.htm** page, and then change the heading to "Franchise Information." In a new left-aligned paragraph below the heading, type "If you are interested in opening a Garden Grill restaurant in your area, please call Katy Ricke at 1-800-555-4921 to discuss startup costs and franchise licensing." Save the **fran.htm** page.

8. Publish the local Web site to the server. (If a Conflicts dialog box opens, click the Overwrite Remote Files button.) After the publishing process is complete, open the remote Web site in a browser. Thoroughly test the Web site by opening each link and examining each page. Use the Search page to conduct a search of the Web site using the keyword "management," and then print the search results.

9. Use the Feedback page to submit one form to the server. Print the confirmation page returned by the server, and then close your browser.

Explore

10. Modify the form in the Feedback Web page in the disk-based Web site so that the Save Results form handler also stores the results in an HTML file named **feedback.htm** in the **_private** folder of the Web site. (*Hint:* Specify the second results file using the Options button in the Form Properties dialog box.) Publish your changes, and then use a browser to test the Feedback Web page using data that you create. Enter data for two different users. Close the browser, and then use FrontPage to print the **feedback.htm** page that contains the form results. (*Hint:* Open the **feedback.htm** page stored on the server.)

11. Recalculate and verify all the hyperlinks in the server-based **grill** Web site. Right-click any page in Reports view to open the shortcut menu, and then click Copy Report. Start Word or WordPad, and then click the Paste button on the Standard toolbar to paste the report into a new document. Click the Print button to print the report. Close Word or WordPad without saving your changes.

12. Change the **grill** Web site to use unique permissions.
13. Add yourself as a user with administrator permissions for the **grill** Web site by providing a user name and password of your choice. Use your browser to print the Manage Users page after adding yourself as a user.
14. Remove yourself from the Manage Users page, and then close your browser.
15. Close the **grill** Web site, and then close FrontPage.

Create

Create a form in a Web page to collect data to be used in print and electronic mailing lists. Then publish the Web site to a server and thoroughly test it.

Case Problem 3

There are no new Data Files needed for this Case Problem.

Swenson Auctioneers Scott Swenson is eager for you to finish the Swenson Auctioneers Web site so he can start giving the URL to his clients. The last task you need to complete is to finish the Mailing List page by adding a form that will collect a person's name, address, e-mail address, and phone number so the Web site can add this information to a mailing list. Scott will use this data to mail print advertisements and e-mail messages to clients who wish to receive information about upcoming auctions. Scott also wants to ask visitors to his site a few questions so he can better understand the kinds of auctions in which they are interested. After creating the form and thoroughly testing the Web site, you will publish it to a server.

If necessary, start FrontPage, and then do the following:

1. Open the **swenson** Web site from the location where your Web sites are stored. (If you did not create this Web site in Tutorial 1 and change it in Tutorials 2 through 5, ask your instructor for assistance.)
2. Open the **mail.htm** page in Design view, and then create the form shown in Figure 6-51. The choices for the drop-down box are Internet, Direct Mail, Newspaper, Trade Magazine, Word of Mouth, and Other. None of the form fields require validation. Save the results collected by this form as comma-delimited text in the **maillist.csv** file in the **_private** folder of the Web site. When you are finished, save the **mail.htm** page.

Figure 6-51

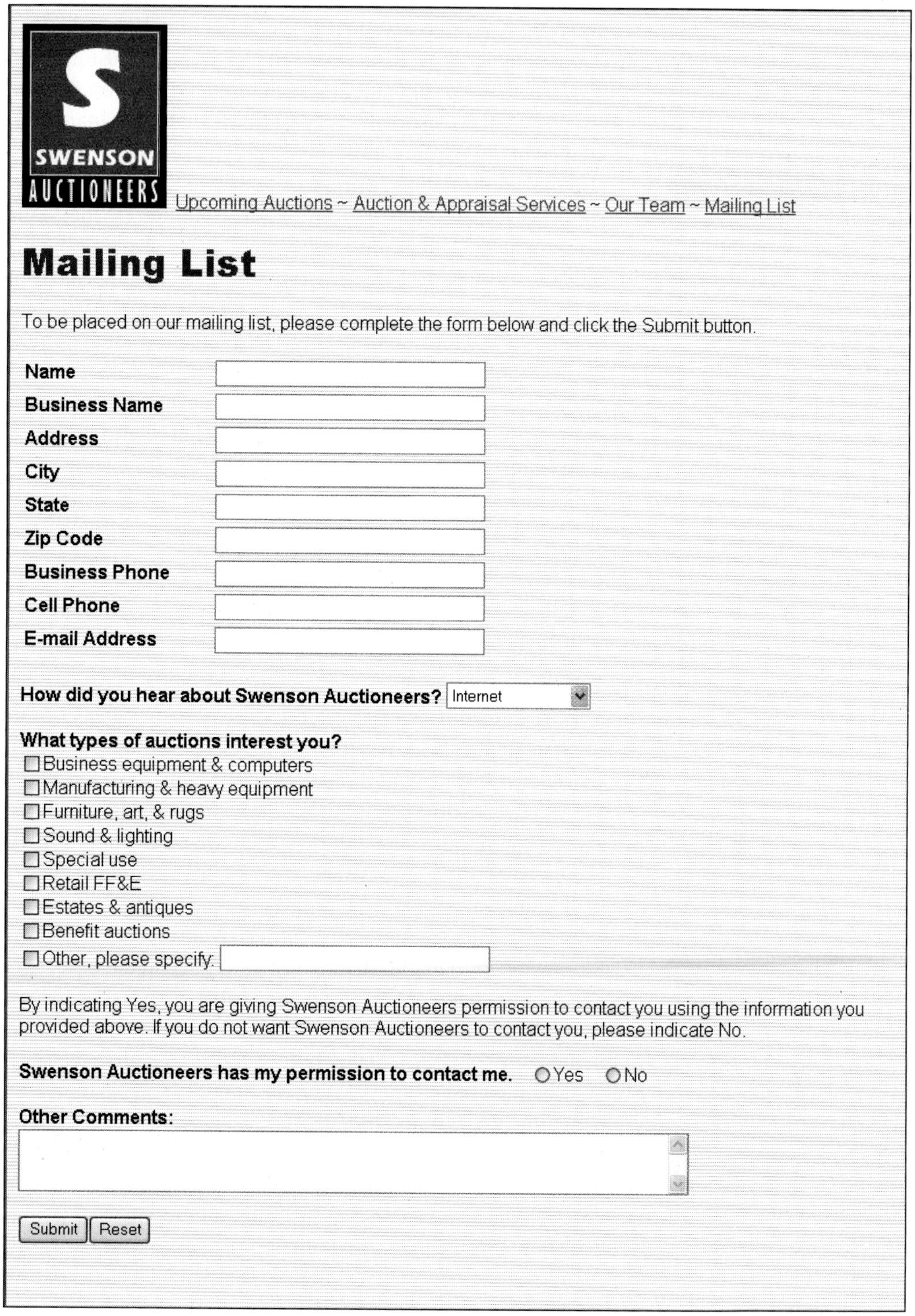

Upcoming Auctions ~ Auction & Appraisal Services ~ Our Team ~ Mailing List

Mailing List

To be placed on our mailing list, please complete the form below and click the Submit button.

Name

Business Name

Address

City

State

Zip Code

Business Phone

Cell Phone

E-mail Address

How did you hear about Swenson Auctioneers? Internet

What types of auctions interest you?
- [ ] Business equipment & computers
- [ ] Manufacturing & heavy equipment
- [ ] Furniture, art, & rugs
- [ ] Sound & lighting
- [ ] Special use
- [ ] Retail FF&E
- [ ] Estates & antiques
- [ ] Benefit auctions
- [ ] Other, please specify:

By indicating Yes, you are giving Swenson Auctioneers permission to contact you using the information you provided above. If you do not want Swenson Auctioneers to contact you, please indicate No.

Swenson Auctioneers has my permission to contact me. ○Yes ○No

Other Comments:

Submit Reset

Explore

3. Use FrontPage to print the HTML document for the **mail.htm** page. On the printout, circle the tags that implement the FrontPage Save Results form handler, the drop-down box, and the text boxes. Close the **mail.htm** page.

4. Publish the local **swenson** Web site to the server using the same Web site name, and then use the hyperlink created by FrontPage to open the remote Web site in a browser. Test the Mailing List Web page that you created by completing the form, and then print the confirmation page that you receive from the server. Close your browser.

Explore

5. Use the Confirmation Form page template to create a new page in the disk-based **swenson** Web site that confirms data submitted by the Mailing List page. After creating the page, do the following:
   a. Delete the paragraph with the comment and the horizontal line at the top of the page.
   b. Change the form field in the "Dear" line to match the form field name that you used for the text box that collects the user's name. (*Hint:* Double-click the field to open the Confirmation Field Properties dialog box and then type the name of the text box. If you cannot remember the name you assigned to this field, open the **mail.htm** page in Design view to confirm it.)
   c. Change the first sentence in the first paragraph to "Thank you for your message."
   d. Change the form fields for the E-mail and Telephone lines to the form field names you used in the **mail.htm** page. (Use the form field for the business phone.) Delete the line containing the reference to a fax number.
   e. Save the page using the filename **confirm.htm** and the title "Confirmation" in the **_private** folder of the Web site.
   f. Return to the Mailing List Web page, and then open the Form Properties dialog box. Click the Options button, and then click the Confirmation Page tab. Type **_private/confirm.htm** in the URL of confirmation page (optional) text box to use the new Confirmation page with the form. Save the Mailing List page.

6. Publish the local Web site to the server. (If a Conflicts dialog box opens, click the Overwrite Remote Files button.) After the publishing process is complete, open the remote Web site in a browser. Thoroughly test the Web site by opening each link and examining each page. Use the Mailing List page to submit one form to the server. Print the confirmation page returned by the server, and then close your browser.

Explore

7. Modify the form in the Mailing List Web page in the disk-based Web site so that the Save Results form handler also stores the results in an HTML file named **form.htm** in the **_private** folder of the Web site. (*Hint:* Specify the second results file using the Options button in the Form Properties dialog box.) Publish your changes, and then use a browser to test the Mailing List Web page using data that you create. Enter data for two different users. Close the browser, and then use FrontPage to print the **form.htm** page that contains the form results. (*Hint:* Open the **form.htm** page stored on the server.)

8. Recalculate and verify all hyperlinks in the remote **swenson** Web site. Right-click any page in Reports view to open the shortcut menu, and then click Copy Report. Start Word or WordPad, and then click the Paste button on the Standard toolbar to paste the report into a new document. Click the Print button to print the report. Close Word or WordPad without saving your changes.

9. Change the **swenson** Web site to use unique permissions.

10. Add yourself as a user with administrator permissions for the **swenson** Web site by providing a user name and password of your choice. Use your browser to print the Manage Users page after adding yourself as a user.

11. Remove yourself from the Manage Users page, and then close your browser.

12. Close the **swenson** Web site, and then close FrontPage.

Create

Create a form in a Web page that serves as a loan application and a page that searches a Web site. Then publish the Web site to a server and thoroughly test it.

Case Problem 4

Data File needed for this Case Problem: apply.doc

Mortgage Services, Inc. Natalie Fuselier is pleased with the appearance and content of the Web site for her company, Mortgage Services, Inc. An important part of the Web site is the loan application form that she needs you to create in the Application page. Natalie will use this data to begin the loan process for a client. Because the range of Internet experience varies among her clients, Natalie wants to ensure that the form is easy to complete for both inexperienced and Web-savvy clients. She wants to provide a way to complete the form for those clients who are uncomfortable submitting sensitive personal information over the Internet. Natalie also wants to create a new page that searches the Web site.

If necessary, start FrontPage, make sure you have your Data Files, and then do the following:

1. Open the **loan** Web site from the location where your Web sites are stored. (If you did not create this Web site in Tutorial 1 and change it in Tutorials 2 through 5, ask your instructor for assistance.)
2. Use a page template to create a page that searches the **loan** Web site. Delete the paragraph with the comment text and the horizontal line that appear at the top of the page, and then delete the copyright information and horizontal line that appear at the bottom of the page. Save the page using the filename **search.htm** and the title "Search." Add the **search.htm** page to Navigation view as a child page of the home page, positioning it to the right of the Contact Us page.

Explore

3. Delete the **contact.htm** page from the navigation structure and from the Web site. (*Hint:* Right-click the Contact Us page icon to open the shortcut menu, and then click Delete.)

Explore

4. Open the **apply.htm** page in Design view, and then use the information supplied in the Case Problem description and Figure 6-52 to create the form.

Figure 6-52

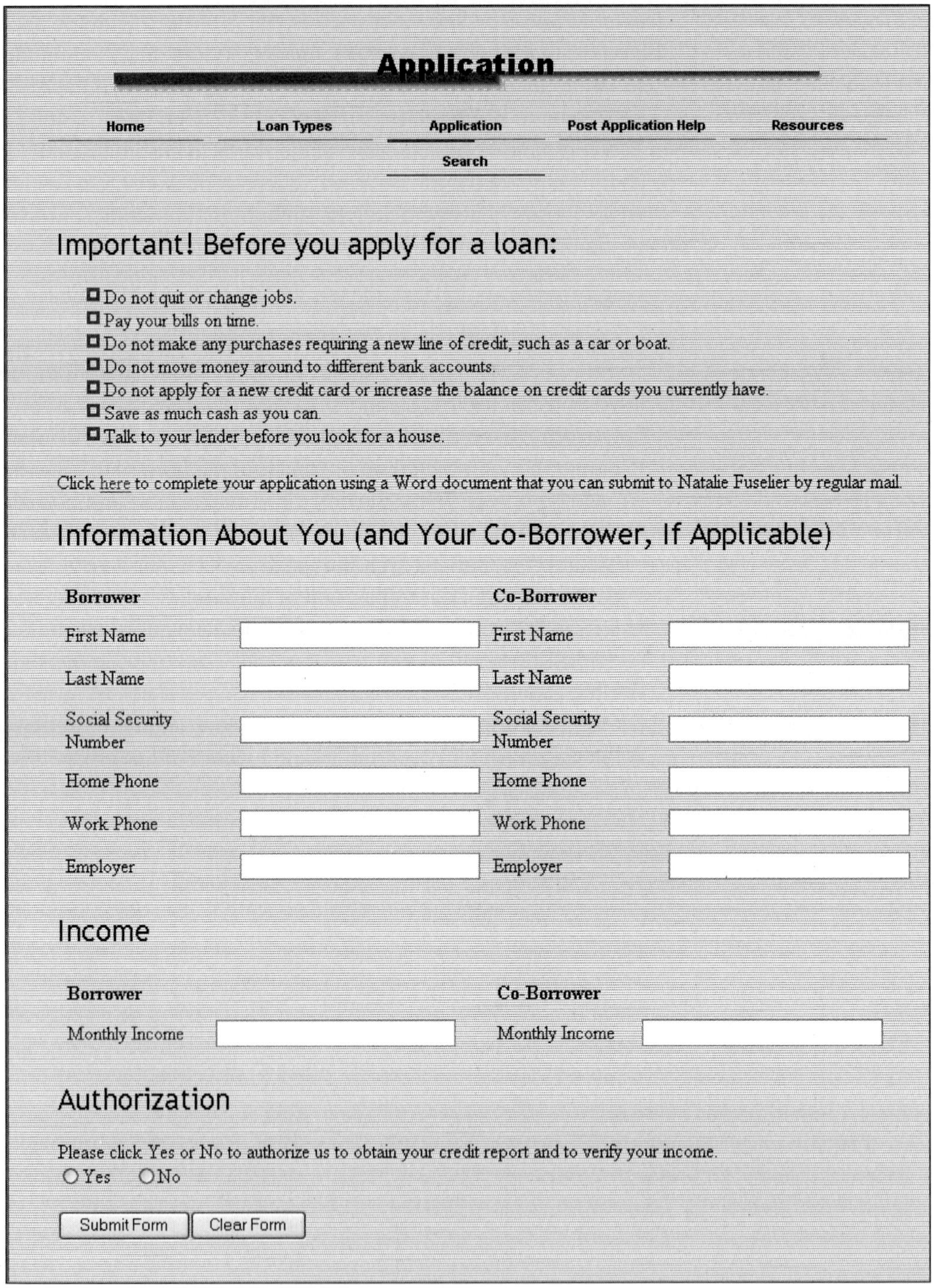

Application

Home	Loan Types	Application	Post Application Help	Resources

Search

Important! Before you apply for a loan:

- Do not quit or change jobs.
- Pay your bills on time.
- Do not make any purchases requiring a new line of credit, such as a car or boat.
- Do not move money around to different bank accounts.
- Do not apply for a new credit card or increase the balance on credit cards you currently have.
- Save as much cash as you can.
- Talk to your lender before you look for a house.

Click here to complete your application using a Word document that you can submit to Natalie Fuselier by regular mail.

Information About You (and Your Co-Borrower, If Applicable)

Borrower		**Co-Borrower**	
First Name		First Name	
Last Name		Last Name	
Social Security Number		Social Security Number	
Home Phone		Home Phone	
Work Phone		Work Phone	
Employer		Employer	

Income

Borrower		**Co-Borrower**	
Monthly Income		Monthly Income	

Authorization

Please click Yes or No to authorize us to obtain your credit report and to verify your income.

○ Yes   ○ No

[Submit Form] [Clear Form]

Define the following validation criteria in the form:

a. The borrower's first name, last name, Social Security number, and home phone number are required fields, but there are no constraints on the data a user can enter into these fields.

b. The borrower's monthly income is a required field.

5. Save the results collected by the form using the formatted text within HTML file format and the filename **form.htm** in the **_private** folder of the Web site. Save an optional file using the formatted text file format and the filename **form.txt** in the **_private** folder of the Web site. For both results files, make sure that the option to include field names is selected.

6. Import the **apply.doc** file from the Tutorial.06\Case4 folder included with your Data Files into the root folder of the **loan** Web site. Then change the word "here" in the first paragraph of the **apply.htm** page to a link that opens the **apply.doc** file in a new browser window. When you are finished, save the **apply.htm** page.

Explore ▶ 7. Use FrontPage to print the HTML document for the **apply.htm** page. On the printout, circle the tags that implement the validation you applied in Step 4. Close the **apply.htm** page.

8. Publish the local **loan** Web site to the server using the same Web site name, and then use the hyperlink created by FrontPage to open the remote Web site in a browser. Test the Application Web page that you created by completing the form (type your first and last names in the form, but enter fictitious data for the remaining fields). Print the confirmation page that you receive from the server, and then close your browser.

Explore ▶ 9. Use the Confirmation Form page template to create a new page in the disk-based **loan** Web site that confirms data submitted by the Application page. After creating the page, do the following:

a. Delete the paragraph with the comment and the horizontal line at the top of the page.

b. Change the form field in the "Dear" line to match the form field name that you used for the text box that collects the borrower's first name. (*Hint:* Double-click the field to open the Confirmation Field Properties dialog box and then type the name of the text box. If you cannot remember the name you assigned to this field, open the **apply.htm** page in Design view to confirm it.)

c. Delete the paragraphs between the salutation ("Dear") and the closing ("Sincerely"). Then type the following as a new first paragraph: "Thank you for your loan application. We will contact you in one to two business days to review your loan." Change the line below the word "Sincerely" to "Loan Services, Inc."

d. Remove the top and left shared borders from the confirmation page.

e. Save the page using the filename **confirm.htm** and the title "Application Received" in the **_private** folder of the Web site.

f. Return to the Application Web page, and then open the Form Properties dialog box. Click the Options button, and then click the Confirmation Page tab. Type **_private/confirm.htm** in the URL of confirmation page (optional) text box to use the new Application Received page with the form. Save the Application page.

10. Publish the local Web site to the server. After the publishing process is complete, open the remote Web site in a browser. Thoroughly test the Web site by opening each link and examining each page. Use the Search page to conduct a search of the Web site using the keyword "FHA," and then print the search results.

11. Use the Application page to submit one form to the server (type your first and last names in the form, but enter fictitious data for the remaining fields). Print the confirmation page returned by the server, and then close your browser.

12. Close the disk-based **loan** Web site, and then open the remote **loan** Web site in FrontPage. Recalculate and verify all hyperlinks in the site. Right-click any page in Reports view to open the shortcut menu, and then click Copy Report. Start Word or WordPad, and then click the Paste button on the Standard toolbar to paste the report into a new document. Click the Print button to print the report. Close Word or WordPad without saving your changes.
13. Change the **loan** Web site to use unique permissions.
14. Add yourself as a user with administrator permissions for the **loan** Web site by providing a user name and password of your choice. Use your browser to print the Manage Users page after adding yourself as a user.
15. Remove yourself from the Manage Users page, and then close your browser.
16. Close the **loan** Web site, and then close FrontPage.

Review

Quick Check Answers

Session 6.1

1. the search component, which searches a Web site using keywords entered by the user; and the Search the Web with MSN component, which searches the Internet using keywords entered by the user
2. True
3. a data-entry field in a form, such as a text box or an option button
4. form component
5. a program that collects and processes a form's data in a predetermined manner
6. First, you should sketch the form's appearance and determine the types of form fields to use to collect the data you need. Then you should identify any rules that you want to impose on the form's users.
7. True
8. Use a drop-down box with the name "Province" and assign each value in the list a name that is equivalent to the province's name. Using a drop-down box gives the user several mutually exclusive choices. The default selection should be the most populated province or the province that is closest to the company's location.

Session 6.2

1. the process of checking the information entered by a user into one or more form fields to verify that the information is acceptable and valid in an attempt to reduce data-entry errors
2. Required
3. grouping, which edits the value to insert a comma or decimal point; data length, which specifies the minimum and maximum number of integers that the form field can contain; and data value, which lets you specify that the entered value must be greater than, equal to, less than, or in a certain range based on a predetermined value
4. Submit, which lets a user send the form to the server for processing; Reset, which clears the form's fields of any previously entered data; and Normal, which initiates a user-defined script
5. field name-data value pair
6. webmaster
7. <option>

Session 6.3

1. localhost
2. C:\Inetpub\wwwroot\
3. servers that support the following: FrontPage Server Extensions or SharePoint Services, Distributed Authoring and Versioning, File Transfer Protocol, and File System
4. publishing the local site to the remote server, publishing the remote site to the local server or drive, and synchronizing the local and remote Web sites
5. a Web page that contains a copy of the data entered by the user and often is used for verification purposes
6. a file that contains form results where the results from each form field are separated by commas
7. a component that counts the number of times a page in a Web site has been opened or refreshed using a Web browser
8. FrontPage updates the display of all views of the Web site, updates the text index created by a search component (when one is used), deletes files for unused themes, and reports broken hyperlinks.
9. FrontPage checks all of the hyperlinks in the Web site to identify any internal or external broken hyperlinks.

New Perspectives on

Microsoft® Office FrontPage® 2003

Read This Before You Begin: Tutorials 7–9

To the Student

Data Disks

To complete the Tutorials, Review Assignments, Case Problems, and Additional Case Problems in this book, you will need the starting student Data Files. Your instructor will either provide you with these Data Files or ask you to obtain them yourself.

FrontPage Tutorials 7–9 and the Additional Case Problems require the folders shown in the next column to complete the Tutorials, Review Assignments, Case Problems, and Additional Case Problems. You will need to copy these folders from a file server, a standalone computer, or the Web to the drive and folder where you will be storing your Data Files. Your instructor will tell you which computer, drive letter, and folders contain the files you need. You can also download the files by going to www.course.com; see the inside front cover for more information on downloading the files to your working folder, or ask your instructor or technical support person for assistance.

You will need to store your Data Files on a Zip disk, hard drive, or network drive that you can access. You will also need a location in which to create and save Web sites; the default location used in this book is http://localhost/[Web site name]. You cannot complete this book using floppy disks.

▼ **FrontPage**
> Tutorial.07
> Tutorial.08
> Tutorial.09
> AddCase1
> AddCase2
> AddCase3

The Data Files you work with in each tutorial build on the work you did in the previous tutorial. Thus when you begin Tutorial 7, you will use the Data Files that resulted after you completed the steps in Tutorial 6 and the Tutorial 6 Review Assignments.

Course Labs

Tutorials 8 and 9 feature two interactive Course Labs to help you understand database and spreadsheet concepts. There are Lab Assignments at the end of Tutorials 8 and 9 that relate to these labs. Contact your instructor or technical support person for assistance in accessing this lab.

To the Instructor

The Data Files and Course Labs are available on the Instructor Resources CD for this title. Follow the instructions in the Help file on the CD-ROM to install the programs to your network or standalone computer. See the "To the Student" section above for information on how to set up the Data Files that accompany this text. To complete the tutorials in this book, students must have a Web browser, access to a Web server with the FrontPage 2002 Server Extensions or Windows SharePoint Services installed on it, and an Internet connection.

You are granted a license to copy the Data Files and Course Labs to any computer or computer network used by students who have purchased this book.

System Requirements

If you are going to work through this book using your own computer, you need:

• **Computer System** Microsoft Windows 2000 Professional or higher, Microsoft Office FrontPage 2003, and Microsoft Office 2003 must be installed on your computer. (The screens shown in this book use Microsoft Windows XP Professional. If your computer has Microsoft Windows 2000 Professional, your screens will look slightly different.) This book assumes a typical installation of FrontPage 2003 and Office 2003. To publish your Web sites, you also must have Internet Information Services version 5.0 or higher, Microsoft Windows 2003 Server, or access to a compatible Web server and a network connection, and the Microsoft FrontPage 2002 Server Extensions or Windows SharePoint Services installed on the Web server. You can install Internet Information Services from your Windows 2000 Professional or Windows XP Professional CD and you can download the FrontPage 2002 Server Extensions from www.msdn.com. The recommended browser for viewing Web pages is Internet Explorer 6.0 or higher.

• **Data Files** You will not be able to complete the tutorials or exercises in this book using your own computer until you have a set of Data Files.

• **Course Labs** See your instructor or technical support person to obtain the Course Lab software for use on your own computer.

www.course.com/NewPerspectives

Objectives

Session 7.1
- Use source control to manage access to a Web site
- Create a shared template
- Assign Web pages to categories
- Create a site map

Session 7.2
- Create a Dynamic Web Template
- Attach pages to a Dynamic Web Template
- Update a Dynamic Web Template
- Update pages attached to a Dynamic Web Template
- Detach a Dynamic Web Template from a Web page

Creating and Using Templates in a Web Site

Creating Shared Templates and Dynamic Web Templates

Case

Sunshine Landscape & Garden Center

Now that the Web site for the Sunshine Landscape & Garden Center has been published to a local Web server, you can add additional functionality and features to the site that require a server to process. In your morning meeting with the senior staff members at the nursery and its owner, Brett Kizer, you discussed several ways to enhance the site, many of which came from ideas from the nursery's employees, who interact regularly with the nursery's many residential and commercial customers. Because the Web site is now stored on the nursery's local area network, its files are accessible to more users. The first thing you want to implement is a feature that prevents two authors from working on the same Web page at the same time; that way, an author can check out a page and save his changes without worrying about another author working on the page at the same time.

Another suggestion from the senior staff that you'll implement now is to create a master document that shows visitors to the Web site the overall framework and hierarchy of the site's pages. Many Web sites use this type of feature to provide an easy way for visitors to find the content they need without having to navigate through the pages in the site.

Student Data Files

To complete this tutorial, you will need your ending files from Tutorial 6 and the following Data Files. Additional Data Files needed to complete the end-of-tutorial exercises are listed with the Review Assignments and Case Problems.

▼**Tutorial.07**

▽ Tutorial folder

anarule.gif	nabkgnd.jpg	site_map.htm
faq.htm	plant.htm	start.htm
hibiscus.htm	sage.htm	sun_logo.gif
intro.htm		

Next, Brett's vision of the Web site includes two important features. First, he wants to include detailed information about the different plants and trees at the nursery to help people plan their landscapes before coming to the nursery. He wants all of these "plant" pages to have the same general content and appearance. You tell Brett that it's easy to create a template in the Web site with the basic content and design that he wants these pages to have. An author who needs to add a new page to the Web site with information about a plant or tree would use the template to create the new page.

As the number of pages with information about specific plants and trees increases, Brett tells you that he might want to change their appearance so they are consistently formatted but different from other pages in the Web site. You tell Brett that this future enhancement is easy to accommodate and suggest storing all pages related to plants and trees in a separate folder in the Web site so it's easy to locate them. You'll also show Brett how to use a Dynamic Web Template to format these pages.

Session 7.1

Using Source Control to Manage Multiple Authors

Because the Web site is stored on the nursery's local area network, you tell Brett that it's possible for him to be working on a Web page on his computer at the same time that you or another authorized user is working on the same page on another computer. This situation is one that can be problematic because it would be possible for both authors to lose their changes to the page if they try to save it at the same time. Alternatively, Brett might be working on the home page, during which time Clara opens the same page in FrontPage. Both authors are working on the original copy of the home page. While Clara is making her changes, Brett might save his version of the page, unaware of the fact that Clara is also working on it. When Brett saves the page, he sees that his changes were made. However, when Clara saves her version of the page, she overwrites Brett's changes and they are lost; Clara's version of the page remains on the server. Because more than one person will contribute to the work required to complete the pages, you need a way to ensure that only one author can work on a specific page at a time.

Fortunately, FrontPage has a built-in feature for Web sites that are enabled with FrontPage 2002 Server Extensions or SharePoint Services to prevent this situation from occurring. **Source control** prevents multiple authors from working on the same page at the same time. Multiple authors can view a page simultaneously, but only *one* author can edit the page and subsequently save the page at any one time.

Normally, a Web site that is being developed by multiple authors is stored on an intranet, making it accessible to everyone with access to the site. If you enable the Web site to use source control, when an author uses FrontPage to check out a page to edit it, other authors can open the page, but they cannot edit it. When a page is checked out to the current author, a check mark appears to the left of the page's filename in Folders view and in the Folder List. Other authors will see a padlock icon, which indicates that the page is in use. Pages with neither a check mark nor a padlock are available for editing.

Enabling and Using Source Control for a Web Site

- Close all open pages in the Web site that you are going to enable with source control.
- In Folders view, click Tools on the menu bar, and then click Site Settings.
- If necessary, click the General tab.
- Click the Use document check-in and check-out check box to select it.
- Click the OK button, and then click the Yes button.
- To check out a page, double-click it in Folders view, and then click the Yes button. Edit and save the page as usual.
- To check in a page, close it. In Folders view, right-click the filename to open the shortcut menu, and then click Check In.
- To cancel all changes (including saved changes) you made in a checked out Web page, right-click the filename in Folders view, click Undo Check-Out on the shortcut menu, and then click the Yes button.

Brett agrees that source control is a needed feature for the garden Web site and asks you to enable it and show him how it works. First, however, you must open the garden Web site from the server.

To open the garden Web site from the server:

1. Start **FrontPage**, click **File** on the menu bar, and then click **Open Site**. The Open Site dialog box opens. You need to access the folder on your computer that contains server-based Web sites.

2. Click the **My Network Places** button, and then click the **garden on localhost** folder to select it.

   Trouble? If you see localhost or your server's name in the list box, double-click it to open it, and then click the garden folder to select it.

   Trouble? If you don't see a garden on localhost folder or a localhost folder, type http://localhost (or the address for the root folder of your Web server) in the Site name text box, and then click the Open button. A new FrontPage window opens and lists the Web sites stored on the server. Double-click the garden Web site to open it, close the FrontPage window that displays the contents of the localhost folder, make sure the Web site appears in Folders view, and then skip Step 3.

   Trouble? The steps in this tutorial are written for users who are running Windows 2000/XP Professional and Microsoft Internet Information Services (IIS). To complete this tutorial, your Web sites must be stored on IIS or a compatible Web server that is running the FrontPage 2002 Server Extensions or SharePoint Services. If you are uncertain about the configuration of your Web server, ask your instructor or technical support person for help.

3. Click the **Open** button, and then change to Folders view (if necessary). FrontPage opens the garden Web site from the server. If you published your Web site to IIS, the default path to the Web site will appear in the FrontPage title bar as http://localhost/garden.

   Trouble? If you see a disk location, such as C:\Inetpub\wwwroot\garden, in the FrontPage title bar, you opened the disk-based Web site instead of the server-based Web site. Click File on the menu bar, click Close Site, and then repeat Steps 1 through 3 to open the Web site stored on the server. If you use the disk-based Web site to complete this tutorial, your Web site will not work correctly.

Now that the garden Web site is open in FrontPage, you can enable it to use source control. Before enabling source control, you must close any open Web pages. Because you just opened the site, all Web pages are closed.

To enable source control for the garden Web site:

1. Click **Tools** on the menu bar, click **Site Settings**, and then make sure that the **General** tab is selected.

2. Click the **Use document check-in and check-out** check box to select it. When you select this check box, some or all of the options below it on the General tab become active, depending on where your Web site is stored.

3. If necessary, click the **Check out files from the Local Web Site** option button to select it, click the **Prompt to check out file when opening a page** check box so it contains a check mark, and then click the **OK** button. A dialog box opens and tells you that you have changed the source control for this Web site and that FrontPage must recalculate the Web site to proceed.

4. Click the **Yes** button. The dialog box closes. After a few moments, the Web site is refreshed and enabled with source control. To make room for the check marks and padlocks that appear when pages are checked out, the listing of files and folders in the Web site moves slightly to the right. See Figure 7-1. Any new pages added to the Web site will also use source control.

Figure 7-1	Web site enabled with source control

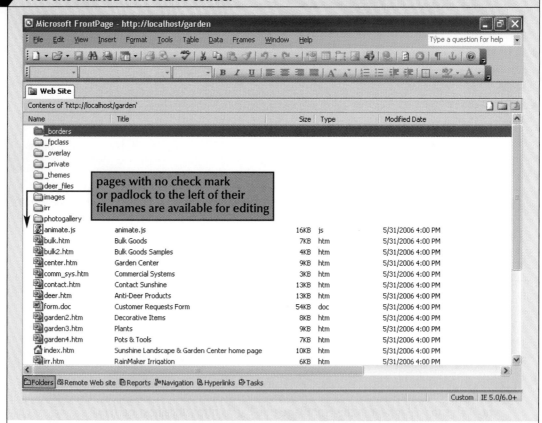

The empty space to the left of the filenames indicates that the pages are not in use by you or any other author. To check out a page so that you can edit it, double-click it. Brett wants to update the marquee in the home page, so you'll check out the page, make Brett's changes and save them, and then check in the page.

To check out a Web page:

▶ **1.** Double-click **index.htm** in the Contents pane. A message box tells you that this page uses source control. See Figure 7-2.

Message box that opens when you open a page under source control ◀ **Figure 7-2**

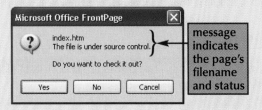

▶ **2.** Click the **Yes** button to check out the page. The home page opens in Design view.

▶ **3.** Scroll down the page as necessary, and then double-click the marquee (which contains the text, "Vegetables and perennials arrive next month!"). The Marquee Properties dialog box opens.

▶ **4.** With the text selected in the Text text box, type **Vegetables and perennials are here!**, and then click the **OK** button.

Brett also wants to center the marquee.

▶ **5.** With the marquee selected, click the **Center** button 🔳 on the Formatting toolbar.

▶ **6.** Click the **Save** button 🔲 on the Standard toolbar.

▶ **7.** Click the **Web Site** tab at the top of the Contents pane to switch to Folders view. As shown in Figure 7-3, a green check mark appears to the left of the index.htm page, indicating that this page is in use. If another author uses FrontPage to open the garden Web site right now, that person would see a padlock icon 🔒 to the left of the page's filename, indicating that the file is locked.

Checked-out page in Folders view ◀ **Figure 7-3**

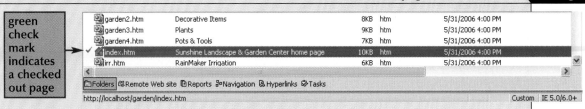

Next, you will close the page and check it in.

To check in a Web page:

▶ **1.** Click the **index.htm** tab at the top of the Contents pane to return to the home page in Design view.

▶ **2.** Click the **Close** button ⊠ on the Contents pane to close the page. You closed the page, but it is still checked out to you. If you closed the Web site now without checking in the page, the page would remain locked and no other author could edit it.

3. Right-click **index.htm** in the Contents pane to open the shortcut menu.

Figure 7-4 shows the options for checking in a page. The first option, Check In, lets you check in the page and accept all of the changes that you made in that page. The second option, Undo Check Out, lets you check in the page and discard all of the changes that you made—even those changes that you saved. Both of these options will release the lock on the page so that other authors can check out the page for editing.

| Figure 7-4 | Checking in a Web page |

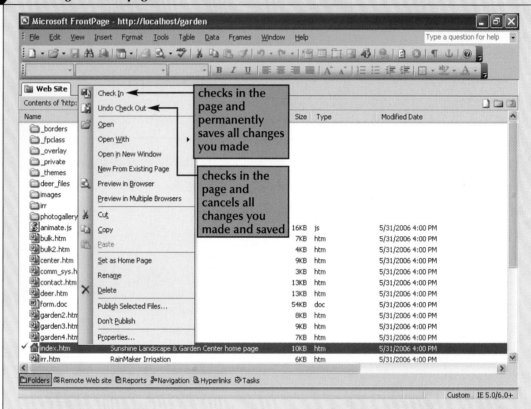

4. Click **Check In**. FrontPage checks in the page, releases the lock, and removes the green check mark to the left of the filename. Now other authors can check out and subsequently edit the page.

Usually, a site's administrator is the only person who can enable and disable source control for a Web site. When you are using IIS on a client, however, you can usually enable source control without obtaining permission.

Now Brett wants to begin work on creating pages for each plant and tree that the nursery sells. Because multiple people will work on the creation of these pages, he wants to make sure that all pages have the same content. You tell Brett that his vision for these pages is easily accomplished by creating a page template that authors can use to create the new Web pages.

Creating a Shared Template

You have learned that FrontPage includes a variety of templates, such as Normal Page, Confirmation Form, and Search Page, that you can use to create new Web pages. You can also create your own template and save it in the Web site so that other authors can use it to create new pages. When you create a template and make it available to other authors, the template is called a **shared template**. Shared template files are always saved on the drive on which FrontPage is installed. In addition, you can select the option to save the shared template file in the Web site in which you created it. Because the shared template file is stored with the FrontPage installation, it is available in other Web sites you create. Storing the shared template file in the Web site in which you created it makes it possible to move the shared template file to another Web server or computer if you publish the Web site to another location.

The template that Brett wants you to create will contain a page banner with the name of the plant or tree; a link bar in the top shared border with links to the site's home page and child-level pages of the home page; a link bar in the left shared border with links to child-level pages of the current page; information about the plant or tree, in a bulleted list format; a photo of the plant or tree; and the nursery's copyright information at the bottom of the page. Brett already started work on this page and asks you to finish it. You will import this page into the garden Web site, open it in Design view, make some changes to it, and then save it as a shared template.

To import the page into the Web site:

▶ 1. If necessary, display the Folder List and make sure that the root folder of the garden Web site is selected.

▶ 2. Click **File** on the menu bar, click **Import**, click the **Add File** button, click the **Look in** list arrow, change to the drive or folder that contains your Data Files, open the **Tutorial.07\Tutorial** folder, double-click **plant.htm**, and then click the **OK** button to import the plant.htm page into the Web site. The plant.htm page is automatically enabled with source control.

▶ 3. Scroll down the list of files in the Folder List as necessary, double-click **plant.htm**, and then click the **Yes** button to check out the page and open it in Design view.

▶ 4. Close the Folder List. The plant.htm page appears in Design view, as shown in Figure 7-5. Brett organized the content of the template in a table. The "[insert picture here]" text reminds the author to insert a picture in the first column. Brett also added HTML tags to this page so it would use the site's theme and shared borders. To include hyperlinks in the shared borders, you would need to add the page to the Web site's navigation structure. However, because you are using this page as a shared template, you won't add it to Navigation view. The placeholders that appear in the page will remind authors who use this template to create new Web pages for specific plants and trees to add those new pages to Navigation view.

Figure 7-5

Design view for the plant.htm page

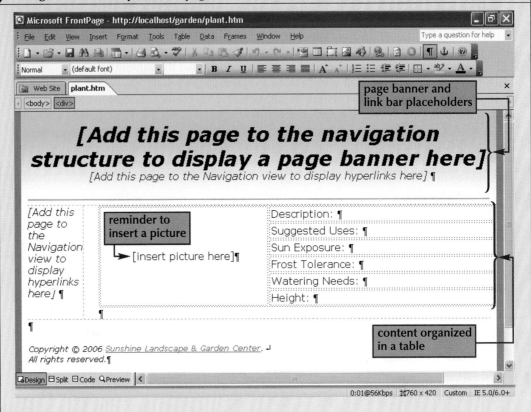

Now you can save the page as a shared template.

Reference Window

Saving a Shared Template

- Create or open the page that you want to save as a template. If necessary, make any changes that you want to appear in the template.
- Click File on the menu bar, and then click Save As.
- Click the Save as type list arrow, and then click FrontPage Template.
- Enter the template's filename in the File name text box.
- Click the Save button to open the Save As Template dialog box.
- Enter the template's title in the Title text box. Use a title that other authors will easily recognize because the template will be labeled with that title in the Page Templates dialog box.
- Enter an optional description of the template in the Description text box. When the template is selected, this description will appear in the Description section of the Page Templates dialog box.
- To store the template in the current Web site, click the Save Template in Current Web site check box to select it.
- Click the OK button.

You will save the shared template in the garden Web site so it will always be available in the Web site, regardless of where the garden Web site is stored.

To save the shared template:

1. Click **File** on the menu bar, and then click **Save As**. The Save As dialog box opens.

2. Click the **Save as type** list arrow, scroll down the list of file types, and then click **FrontPage Template**.

3. Make sure **plant.tem** (or **plant**) appears in the File name text box, and then click the **Save** button. The Save As Template dialog box opens. FrontPage automatically enters the title and name of the template in the Save As Template dialog box for you, based on the filename you used in the Save As dialog box. You can change these values in the Save As Template dialog box or accept them.

4. Make sure that **Plant** appears in the Title text box and that **plant** appears in the Name text box. The title will identify the template's name in the Page Templates dialog box. This title differs from the value in the Name text box, which is the filename of the template.

5. Select the text in the Description text box, and then type **Creates a new page in the Web site to describe a plant or tree**.

6. Click the **Save Template in Current Web site** check box to select it. See Figure 7-6.

Completed Save As Template dialog box   **Figure 7-6**

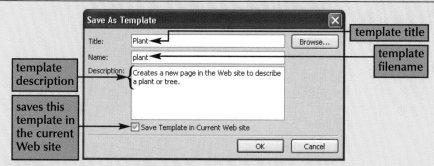

7. Click the **OK** button. Because this page uses pictures from the Web site's theme, the Save Embedded Files dialog box opens and asks you to save the pictures. You'll change the action to prevent FrontPage from saving these files. When an author uses the template to create a new Web page, these pictures will already exist in the Web site so it isn't necessary to save them with the template.

   Trouble? If another user has already created the Plant template on your computer, click the Yes button when asked to replace the file. If you don't see this option, click the Cancel button, and then rename the Plant template to "Plant1" and continue.

8. Click the **Set Action** button, click the **Don't Save this file. Use the current file on disk.** option button to select it, and then click the **OK** button. The action for each picture file changes to "Don't Save."

9. Click the **OK** button. The Save Embedded Files dialog box closes. FrontPage creates the template in two places: in a hidden folder named _sharedtemplates in the garden Web site and in a folder named using the template's filename plus "_t" (in this case, "plant_t") on the drive where FrontPage user information is saved (the default folder is Documents and Settings*user name*\Application Data\Microsoft\FrontPage\Pages\). The next time you open the Page Templates dialog box, you will see the Plant template in the list.

10. Click the **Close** button ⊠ on the Contents pane to close the plant.htm page. Because source control is enabled for this page, you must check it in.

11. Right-click **plant.htm** in the Contents pane to open the shortcut menu, and then click **Check In**.

You can verify that you created the template correctly by using it to create a new Web page.

To use the Plant template to create a new Web page:

1. Click **File** on the menu bar, and then click **New**. The New task pane opens.

2. In the New page section of the New task pane, click **More page templates**. The Page Templates dialog box opens. If this is the first shared template you have created, the "My Templates" tab is added to the Page Templates dialog box. To see the templates that you have created, you need to click the My Templates tab.

3. Click the **My Templates** tab. The Plant template appears in the list, as shown in Figure 7-7. If necessary, click the **Plant** template to select it. A preview of the page the template creates and its description appear in the dialog box.

Figure 7-7 Page Templates dialog box

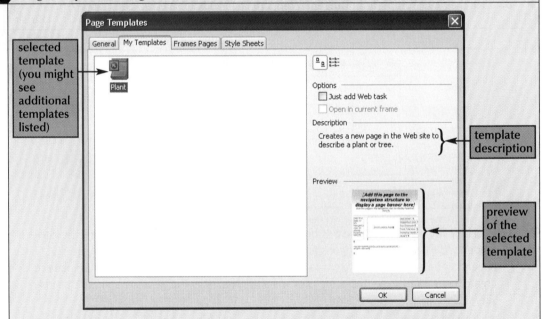

selected template (you might see additional templates listed)

template description

preview of the selected template

Trouble? If you or another user has created other shared templates, their page icons will appear on the My Templates tab.

4. Click the **OK** button. A new page named new_page_1.htm is created using the Plant template.

   An author would replace the "[insert picture here]" text with a picture, add the appropriate content to the page, save the page with an appropriate title and filename, and then position the page in the Web site's navigation structure to add the page to the Web site's link bars. You don't need to save this page, so you will close it without saving changes.

5. Click the **Close** button ☒ on the Contents pane to close the page without saving it.

Now when the nursery's staff adds new pages for plants and trees to the Web site, they can use the template to create a new page, which will ensure consistency among the pages.

The next thing that you want to show Brett is a way to organize the site's pages to make it easier for site visitors to find the content they need.

Creating a Site Map

If you have surfed the Web, you may have noticed that some Web sites include a hyperlink to a site map. A **site map** is a list of hyperlinks that shows how the pages in the site are related to one another or organizes them in some other meaningful way. In a small Web site, the site map might contain a list of hyperlinks to individual pages. In a large Web site, the site map might contain hyperlinks to subcategories and to other Web pages. Figure 7-8 shows a portion of the site map for the U.S. Food and Drug Administration's Web site. In this site map, the hyperlinks are organized into categories, such as "About FDA" and "Publications." If you need to locate specific information at this Web site, using the Site Map page might make it easier to find than trying to use the site's search feature or by browsing its pages. Although many Web sites include site maps, many visitors don't know about this very important feature.

Site Map Web page ◄ **Figure 7-8**

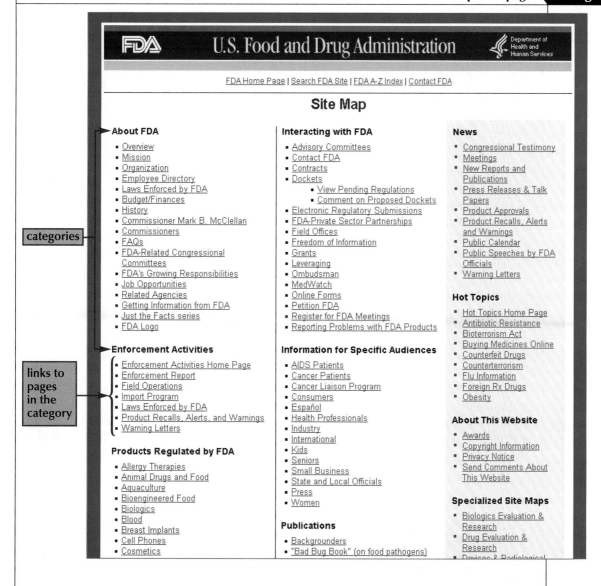

Assigning Web Pages to Categories

Before you can create a site map Web page, you must decide how to organize the pages in the Web site. Brett wants to group pages in the same way that items are physically arranged at the nursery. For example, plants are organized by type, pots and containers are arranged together, and supplies such as fertilizers and pest control products are arranged on shelves. You can create **categories** to identify logical groupings of Web pages, and then assign specific Web pages to those categories. You can then use the FrontPage table of contents component to tell FrontPage how to organize the hyperlinks to those Web pages within the site map. FrontPage supplies a variety of predefined categories, but you can also create your own categories. You can delete the default categories or categories that you do not use.

When you assign a page to a category, you can also assign the page to a particular member of the Web site development team and specify a review status for it. A **review status** is a way to select the type of review or approval that the page needs before being considered final. For example, if the page contains legal material that requires verification by an attorney, you might select the "Legal Review" category.

Reference Window	**Creating Categories and Assigning Pages to Them**

- Right-click any Web page filename in the Contents pane in Folders view to open the shortcut menu, and then click Properties.
- Click the Workgroup tab, and then click the Categories button.
- In the Master Category List dialog box, type the name of a new category in the New category text box, and then press the Enter key or click the Add button. Repeat this process as many times as necessary to add the remaining categories for the entire Web site.
- Click the OK button.
- Click the check box for the appropriate category for the page that you selected. (The selected page's name appears in the title bar of the Properties dialog box.)
- If necessary, click the Assigned to list arrow and select the team member to whom the page is assigned, or click the Names button to enter a new name.
- If necessary, click the Review status list arrow and select a review status for the page, or click the Statuses button to enter a new status.
- Click the OK button in the Properties dialog box to close it.
- To assign other Web pages to categories, right-click the page's filename in Folders view to open the shortcut menu, click Properties, click the Workgroup tab, and then click the check box for the appropriate category in the Available categories list box.
- Click the OK button.

After talking with Brett and other staff members at the nursery, you decide to create the following categories in the Web site: Plants, Bulk, Irrigation, Consumer Education, Landscaping, and Garden Supplies. After creating these categories in the Web site, you will use them to assign some of the site's existing Web pages to categories. Then you will use the table of contents component to create the site map.

To create the categories:

1. Right-click **bulk.htm** in the Contents pane to open the shortcut menu, and then click **Properties**. The bulk.htm Properties dialog box opens.

2. Click the **Workgroup** tab. See Figure 7-9. FrontPage contains several default categories that appear in the Available categories list box. You could select one of these default categories, but you and Brett decided to create new categories for this Web site. To make it easier to assign pages in the garden Web site to categories, you will delete the default categories.

When you add or delete categories, your changes apply only to the current Web site and do not affect the default categories supplied by FrontPage in other Web sites.

Workgroup tab for the bulk.htm page ◀ Figure 7-9

title bar includes the filename of the selected page

scrollable list of default categories (your list might differ)

option for assigning this page to a team member

option to exclude publishing this page with the Web site

creates new categories or deletes existing categories

option for assigning this page to a review or approval method

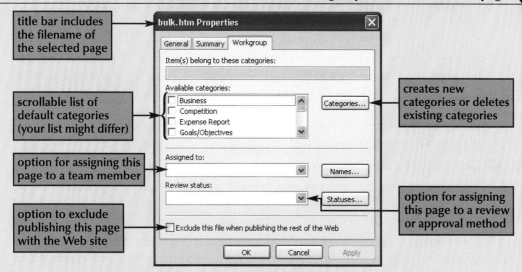

Trouble? If your Properties dialog box does not contain a Workgroup tab, then the FrontPage 2002 Server Extensions or SharePoint Services are not installed and properly configured on the server. Ask your instructor or technical support person for help.

▶ **3.** Click the **Categories** button. The Master Category List dialog box opens and displays the list of default categories.

▶ **4.** Click **Business** in the list box, and then click the **Remove** button. The Business category is deleted from the list, and the Competition category is selected. To delete the remaining categories, you can click the Remove button until all categories are deleted from the list box.

▶ **5.** Click the **Remove** button 11 times (or as many times as necessary) to remove the remaining categories from the list box.

▶ **6.** Click the New category text box, type **Plants**, and then press the **Enter** key. The Plants category is added to the list. See Figure 7-10.

Master Category List dialog box ◀ Figure 7-10

Plants category added to the Web site

resets the categories list to the default settings

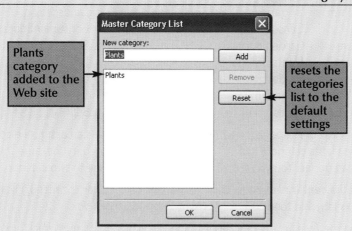

To add the next category, simply type its name and then press the Enter key.

▶ 7. Type **Bulk** and then press the **Enter** key. The Bulk category is added to the list.

▶ 8. Repeat Step 7 to add the following categories to the list: **Irrigation** and **Consumer Education**. Notice that as you add categories to the list, they are arranged in alphabetical order.

▶ 9. Repeat Step 7 to add the **Landscaping** and **Garden Supplies** categories to the list. After pressing the Enter key for the Garden Supplies category, click the **OK** button. A message box opens and tells you that categories are shared across a Web site and removing one or more categories will remove them from any pages that use them. Because you have not previously assigned any pages in the Web site to categories, it is safe to remove them. If you remove a category to which you have assigned pages, however, you would need to reassign Web pages assigned to that category to another category.

▶ 10. Click the **Yes** button. You return to the Properties dialog box for the bulk.htm file.

Before closing the dialog box, you need to assign the bulk.htm page to a category. You will not assign this page to any member of the Web site development team, nor will you select a review status.

▶ 11. Click the **Bulk** check box in the Available categories list box to select it, and then click the **OK** button. The Properties dialog box closes, and the bulk.htm page is now assigned to the Bulk category.

Now that you have created the categories, you can assign the other pages in the Web site to the appropriate categories. It isn't necessary to assign every page in the Web site to a category when you are creating a site map.

To assign pages to categories:

▶ 1. Right-click **bulk2.htm** in the Contents pane to open the shortcut menu, click **Properties**, and then click the **Workgroup** tab.

▶ 2. Click the **Bulk** check box in the Available categories list, and then click the **OK** button. The bulk2.htm page is now assigned to the Bulk category.

▶ 3. Repeat Steps 1 and 2 to assign the following pages in the Web site to the specified categories:

Page	Category	Page	Category
comm_sys.htm	Irrigation	land2.htm	Landscaping
deer.htm	Consumer Education	lawn.htm	Consumer Education
garden2.htm	Garden Supplies	mulch.htm	Bulk
garden3.htm	Plants	res_sys.htm	Irrigation
garden4.htm	Garden Supplies	rock.htm	Landscaping
irr.htm	Irrigation	soil.htm	Bulk
land.htm	Landscaping	stone.htm	Bulk

As you finish assigning pages to categories, Brett asks if you can assign the center.htm page to the Plants category and to the Garden Supplies category, because this page fits into both categories. You will show him how to assign a page to two categories next.

▶ 4. Right-click the **center.htm** page, click **Properties** on the shortcut menu, click the **Workgroup** tab, and then click the **Garden Supplies** check box.

▶ 5. Scroll down the Available categories list, and then click the **Plants** check box. Now the center.htm page has two categories—Garden Supplies and Plants.

6. Click the **OK** button. The Properties dialog box closes. Most of the pages in the garden Web site have been assigned to categories that you created. Some pages do not fit into your categories, so they will remain uncategorized for now. However, in the future, you can create new categories and assign pages to them as necessary.

If you need to delete a category assignment for a page, reopen the Properties dialog box for that page, click the Workgroup tab, and then clear the check box for that category. You can use Reports view to view the categories assigned to pages in the Web site to verify that you categorized them correctly.

To run a Categories report:

1. Click the **Reports View** button 📄 Reports at the bottom of the Contents pane.

2. Click the **Site Summary** button at the top of the Contents pane, point to **Workflow**, and then click **Categories**. The Categories report appears in Reports view and displays all of the files in the Web site, as shown in Figure 7-11. You can sort the list using any of the column headings, just as you would sort the Tasks list.

Categories report in Reports view | **Figure 7-11**

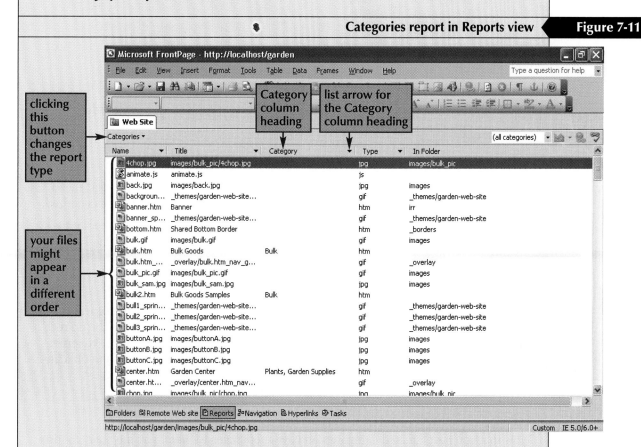

Trouble? If another user has previously filtered the Categories report, your files might appear in a different order. If a list arrow on any column heading is blue (instead of black), click the list arrow, and then click (All) at the top of the menu that appears to remove the filter.

3. Click the **list arrow** for the Category column heading, and then scroll down the list and click **(NonBlanks)** to display only those pages in the Web site that are assigned to a category.

4. If necessary, click the **Category** column heading (but not the list arrow) to sort the items alphabetically by category. Figure 7-12 shows the pages in the Web site that have been assigned to categories, sorted alphabetically by category name.

Figure 7-12 **Sorted Categories report**

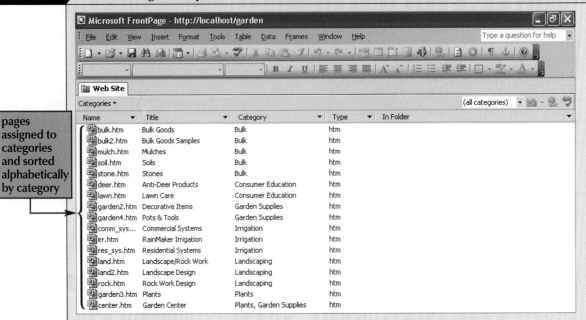

pages assigned to categories and sorted alphabetically by category

Trouble? If the entries in the Category column are alphabetized in reverse order, click the Category column heading again to resort them.

5. Click the **list arrow** for the Category column heading, and then click **(Blanks)**. The files in the Web site that have not been assigned to categories are listed.

6. Click the **list arrow** for the Type column heading, and then click **htm**. The report shows only those Web pages in the site (with .htm filename extensions) that are not categorized.

7. Click the **list arrow** for the Type column heading, click **(All)**, click the **list arrow** for the Category column heading, and then click **(All)**. The filters are removed from the Type and Category columns.

As you work in a Web site that includes a site map, the Categories report provides a way for you to check the pages to make sure that you have assigned them to the correct categories. If you need to change the category of a page, you can reopen the Properties dialog box for that page, click the Workgroup tab, clear the check box from the old category, and then click the check box for the new category.

Using the Table of Contents Component

Now that you have created categories and assigned pages to them, you are ready to insert the FrontPage table of contents component into a site map page. When you add new Web pages to the Web site, you can assign them to categories, creating new categories as necessary. FrontPage will automatically update the site map Web page and display the new Web pages in the appropriate categories.

Creating a Site Map

- Create or open the page that will contain the categories in Design view. If necessary, enter text and format the page.
- Click the Web Component button on the Standard toolbar, click Table of Contents in the Component type list box, and then click Based on Page Category in the Choose a table of contents list box.
- Click the Finish button.
- Click the check box for the appropriate category in the Choose categories to list files by list box.
- If necessary, click the check boxes to include the date on which the file was last modified and/or comments to the file.
- Click the OK button.
- Repeat the steps to add more table of contents components to the page as necessary.

Brett created the basic structure for the Site Map page. You'll import this page into the Web site and add it to the site's navigation structure. Then you can add the categories to the page.

To add categories to the Site Map page:

1. Change to Folders view, display the Folder List (if necessary), and then make sure the root folder of the garden Web site is selected.

2. Click **File** on the menu bar, click **Import**, click the **Add File** button, open the **Tutorial.07\Tutorial** folder, double-click **site_map.htm**, and then click the **OK** button. The site_map.htm page is imported into the Web site.

   You need to add the Site Map page to the navigation structure for the Web site and to the custom link bar that appears in the home page.

3. Change to Navigation view, scroll the navigation structure so you can see the Search page icon, scroll down the files in the Folder List (if necessary), then drag the site_map.htm page from the Folder List and position it to the left of the Search page icon in the navigation structure.

4. Scroll the Contents pane to the left so you can see the Search page icon in the custom link bar navigation structure, and then drag the site_map.htm page from the Folder List and position it to the left of the Search page icon in the custom link bar navigation structure.

5. Double-click **site_map.htm** in the Folder List, click the **Yes** button to check it out, and then close the Folder List. The Site Map page opens in Design view, as shown in Figure 7-13. Brett already specified that this page would include the Garden Web Site theme and the top, left, and bottom shared borders, so by adding this page to Navigation view, you activated these features in the page. Brett already created bookmarks to each category and inserted a blank paragraph below each category heading. You will insert the table of contents component for each category in the blank paragraph below its heading.

Figure 7-13 | Site Map page in Design view

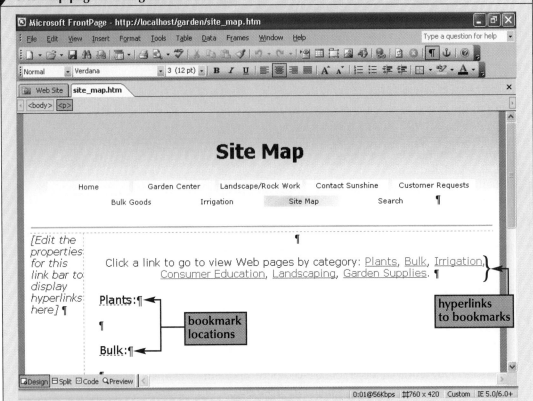

6. Click the blank paragraph below the Plants heading, click the **Web Component** button on the Standard toolbar, click **Table of Contents** in the Component type list box, click **Based on Page Category** in the Choose a table of contents list box, and then click the **Finish** button. The Categories Properties dialog box opens.

   Trouble? If the Based on Page Category component is not available, then your server does not have the FrontPage 2002 Server Extensions or SharePoint Services installed. Ask your instructor or technical support person for help.

7. Scroll down the list of available categories, click the **Plants** check box to select it, and then click the **OK** button. The Site Map page now displays three "Page in Category" placeholders below the Plants heading. The table of contents component always displays three placeholders, but these placeholders do not represent the actual number of Web pages that are currently in the category. To see the Web pages in this category, you must open the page in a browser.

   Trouble? If you do not see the three "Page in Category" placeholders, then you did not click the Plants check box. Repeat Steps 6 and 7.

8. Repeat Steps 6 and 7 to insert the appropriate table of contents component below each heading in the page.

9. Click the **Save** button on the Standard toolbar, and then click the **Preview** button on the Standard toolbar. Figure 7-14 shows the Site Map page in a browser. The table of contents component added hyperlinks to the pages in each category below the headings that Brett created. Clicking a hyperlink below a heading opens the target page.

Site Map page in a browser | Figure 7-14

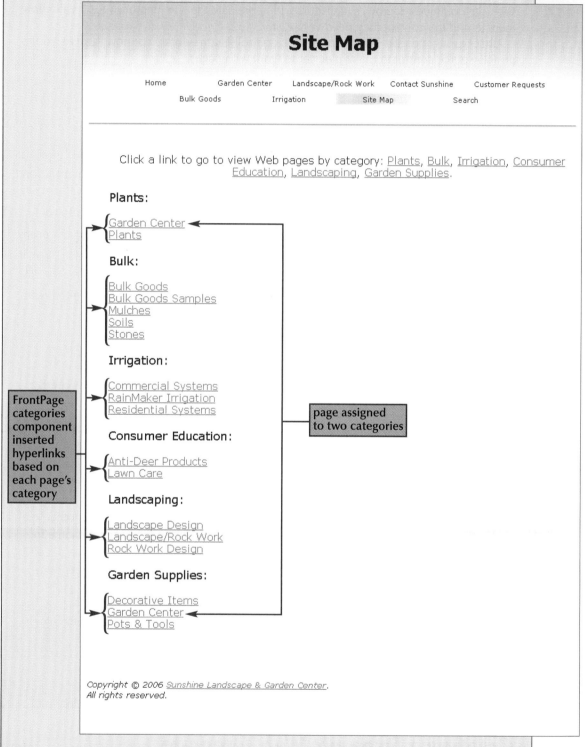

10. Close your browser.

As you add new pages to the Web site and assign them to categories, the table of contents components will update the Site Map page automatically to keep it current. As the Web site continues to grow, site visitors will appreciate the site map because it will allow them to find the content they need very easily.

Brett has a good idea of how the source control feature works. For now, he asks you to disable source control to make it easier to work with pages.

To disable source control in the Web site:

▶ 1. Click the **Close** button ☒ on the Contents pane to close the site_map.htm page.

   Trouble? If necessary, close any other Web pages.

▶ 2. Change to Folders view, right-click the **site_map.htm** page to open the shortcut menu, and then click **Check In**.

   Trouble? If necessary, check in any other Web pages that you might have checked out.

▶ 3. Click **Tools** on the menu bar, and then click **Site Settings**. The Site Settings dialog box opens.

▶ 4. Click the **Use document check-in and check-out** check box to remove the check mark from it, and then click the **OK** button. A message box opens and asks you to recalculate the Web site.

▶ 5. Click the **Yes** button. After a few moments, the Web site is refreshed and source control is disabled from the Web site.

▶ 6. Close the garden Web site, and then close FrontPage.

In the next session, you will work on Brett's request to use different formatting in the pages that describe plants and trees.

Review

Session 7.1 Quick Check

1. Suppose that you are the only person creating a Web site on your computer's server. Would you enable source control for that Web site? Why or why not?
2. When a Web page that is enabled with source control is checked out to another author, you will see a(n) _____ icon to the left of the page's filename in Folders view and in the Folder List on your computer.
3. How do you check in a Web page that is enabled with source control and permanently save the changes that you made in the page?
4. Where are shared templates stored?
5. Why must you create categories for Web pages and assign the site's pages to categories before creating a site map?
6. Which component adds categories to a Web page?

Session 7.2

Creating a Dynamic Web Template

Right now the Plant template uses the Garden Web Site theme and the garden Web site's shared borders to format its appearance and hyperlinks. Brett has expressed an interest in formatting the pages with plant and tree descriptions with a separate design. You tell him that creating these pages in a separate folder and then creating another template to format their appearance would make it easy to change the pages periodically to reflect the different seasons of the year. For example, he might format the pages featuring plants available in the spring with bright pastel colors and pages featuring plants available in the fall with earth tones.

As you have created pages in the garden Web site, you have used a variety of techniques to format them. You learned how to use the tools on the Formatting toolbar to format text and how to add a background color and background picture to a page. You also learned how to use themes to format one or all of the pages in a site with the same design. Using a theme is an easy way to format pages because all changes are automatically applied to pages that use the theme. Changing the theme is easy—you just select a new one in the Theme task pane and apply it as the new default theme for the Web site. You can use any of the themes installed with FrontPage or purchase one from any of several vendors that create themes that you can use in your Web sites. In either case, FrontPage saves the files necessary to create the theme's elements, such as horizontal lines, page banners, different types of navigation buttons, and other graphics that you might use in your pages, in a hidden folder named _themes. Although a theme can format your pages quickly and efficiently, FrontPage stores all of the theme's files—even for elements that you aren't using—in the Web site. These files require additional space on the server and increase the overall size of the Web site.

The shared template (plant.tem) that you created in the garden Web site includes some placeholder text that an author can select and replace with content that belongs in the page. For example, an author creating a page for Mexican Bush Sage would select the "[insert picture here]" text in the page and replace it with a picture of the plant. Then the author would add the content in the appropriate places in the page to add this plant's description, sun exposure and watering needs, and other information about the plant. The other placeholders in the page remind the author to add the page to the Web site's navigation structure to add hyperlinks to the page's shared borders. The tags in the shared template automatically format the page using the Web site's theme. This shared template will work well to ensure that all pages created with the Plant template will include the same content, but only as long as the author doesn't make any changes to the page. In other words, an author could change the page's theme, change the properties of the link bar in the top or left shared borders, or disable the shared borders for the page. Because Brett wants these pages to be formatted consistently *and* have the same content, you need a way to "lock" part of the template to prevent authors from accessing it. You cannot lock areas in a Web page created by a page template, but you can do so by attaching a Dynamic Web Template to the Web page created by the page template. A **Dynamic Web Template** is a file saved with the extension .dwt that lets you create editable regions in a Web page. Figure 7-15 shows a Web page that is formatted by a Dynamic Web Template.

Figure 7-15	Web page formatted by a Dynamic Web Template

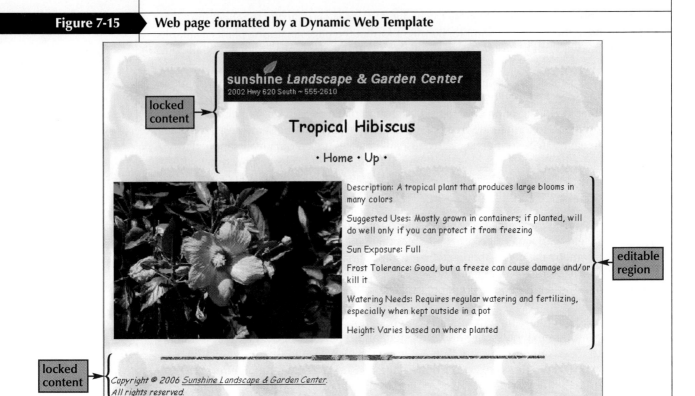

In Figure 7-15, the Sunshine logo picture, the page banner, and the link bar at the top of the page, and the horizontal line picture and copyright information at the bottom of the page are locked; users of this page cannot delete or change the logo or change the properties of the components that insert the page banner and link bar. The content in the body of the page, which includes the plant's picture and description, appears in an editable region of the page. **Editable regions** are areas in the Dynamic Web Template that are given standardized names to identify them. In this case, the editable region is called the body region because it includes the body section of the Web page. The Dynamic Web Template includes formatting instructions to insert the background picture and format text using the Comic Sans MS font. Figure 7-16 shows the HTML document for the Web page shown in Figure 7-15.

HTML document for a page attached to a Dynamic Web Template ◄ **Figure 7-16**

```
<html>

<!-- #BeginTemplate "plant.dwt" -->            ◄ identifies the Dynamic Web Template

<head>
<meta http-equiv="Content-Type" content="text/html; charset=windows-1252">
<!-- #BeginEditable "doctitle" -->              [beginning and end of doctitle editable region]

<title>Tropical Hibiscus</title>               ◄ editable region
<!-- #EndEditable -->
</head>

<body background="../images/nabkgnd.jpg">

<p align="center">
<img border="0" src="../images/sun_logo.gif" width="402" height="75"></p>
<p align="center">
<b><font face="Comic Sans MS" size="5">
<!--webbot bot="Navigation" S-Type="banner" S-Orientation="horizontal" S-
Rendering="graphics" --></font></b></p>                [locked region]
<p align="center">
<font size="4" face="Comic Sans MS">
<!--webbot bot="Navigation" S-Orientation="horizontal" S-Rendering="html" S-Bar="MoreDots" S-Btn-
Nml="&lt;A HREF=&quot;#URL#&quot; TARGET=&quot;#TARGET#&quot; STYLE=&quot;{text-decoration: none;}&quot;
&gt;#LABEL#&lt;/A&gt;" S-Btn-Sel="#LABEL#" S-Btn-Sep=" &amp;bull; " S-Bar-
Pfx="&amp;bull; " S-Bar-Sfx=" &amp;bull;" S-Type="children" B-Include-Home="TRUE" B-
Include-Up="TRUE" --></font></p>
<font face="Comic Sans MS" size="2"><!-- #BeginEditable "body" -->    ◄ beginning of body editable region
<div>

    <table border="0" width="760" id="table1" cellpadding="3">
        <tr>
            <td rowspan="6" valign="top">
            <p align="center">
            <img border="0" src="../images/gc_pics/garden97.jpg" width="359" height="238"></td>
            <td width="478" valign="top"><font size="2">Description: A tropical
            plant that produces large blooms in many colors</font></td>
        </tr>
        <tr>
            <td width="478" valign="top"><font size="2">Suggested Uses: Mostly grown in containers; if
            planted, will do
            well only if you can protect it from freezing</font></td>
        </tr>
        <tr>
            <td width="478" valign="top"><font size="2">Sun Exposure: Full</font></td>
        </tr>
        <tr>
            <td width="478" valign="top"><font size="2">Frost Tolerance: Good, but a freeze can cause
damage
            and/or kill it</font></td>
        </tr>
        <tr>
            <td width="478" valign="top"><font size="2">Watering Needs: Requires regular watering and
            fertilizing, especially when kept outside in a pot</font></td>
        </tr>
        <tr>
            <td width="478" valign="top"><font size="2">Height: Varies based on where planted</font></td>
        </tr>
    </table>
</div>
<!-- #EndEditable -->                          ◄ end of body editable region
<p align="center"><i>
<img border="0" src="../images/anarule.gif" width="600" height="10"></p>
<p><i>Copyright © 2006
<a href="mailto:brett@sunshinelandscapeandgardencenter.com?subject=Web Site">    [locked region]
Sunshine Landscape &amp; Garden Center</a>.<br>
All rights reserved.</i></p>
<p align="center"> </p>
</font>
</body><!-- #EndTemplate -->                   ◄ end of Dynamic Web Template

</html>
```

In Figure 7-16, the instructions provided by the Dynamic Web Template appear in HTML comment tags (<!-- and -->) and with yellow highlighting. The different editable regions of the document appear with <!-- #Begin Editable --> and <!-- #End Editable --> comments. These tags identify the parts of the HTML document that the user can edit. For example, the <title> and </title> tags appear in the doctitle editable region of the page, which means that the user can change the page's title. However, the HTML tags that insert the Sunshine logo picture, change the font, add the background picture, and create the page banner and link bar do not appear within an editable region, which means that these properties are locked. The second editable region in the page is named body and includes the table that contains the plant's picture and description. Because these tags appear within the body editable region, the user can make changes to this information. This format is fine for Brett's purposes, but you tell him that you could also create other editable regions in the page to prevent authors from changing the default text. In other words, you could create an editable region named "description" so that authors could type the plant's description, but they could not change the "Description:" text in the template.

Figure 7-17 shows the Dynamic Web Template that was attached to the Web page shown in Figure 7-15. Notice that the body editable region is identified with a marker and an orange box. The doctitle editable region doesn't show up in Design view because it affects only the head section of the HTML document. The content that does not appear within an editable region is locked for users who apply the Dynamic Web Template to a regular Web page. However, these areas are editable when you open the Dynamic Web Template in Design view.

Figure 7-17	Dynamic Web Template in Design view

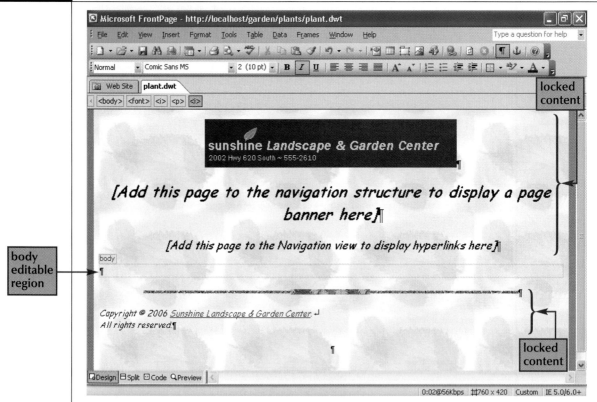

Figure 7-18 shows a Web page in Design view that uses the Dynamic Web Template. When you move the pointer over a locked area, it changes to a ⊘ shape. The author can edit content only in editable regions. In this page, the only visible editable region is the body editable region. To identify this page as being attached to a Dynamic Web Template, FrontPage inserts the template's filename in the upper-right corner of the page. This reference does not appear in the page when it is viewed with a browser.

Web page in Design view that has been attached to a Dynamic Web Template ◄ Figure 7-18

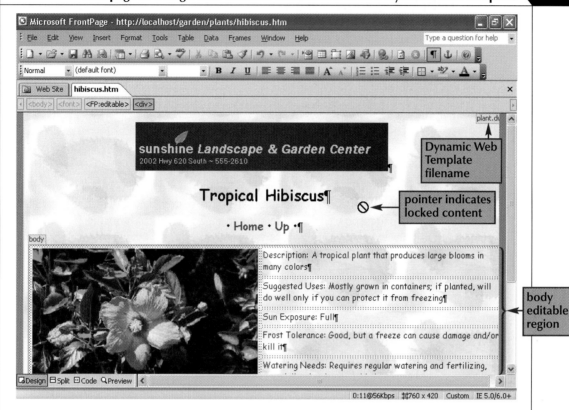

Brett wants to learn how Dynamic Web Templates work to see if he can use one to format the pages that describe plants and trees. You explain to Brett that a Dynamic Web Template cannot use shared borders like a shared template can, so if he wants to use a Dynamic Web Template to format the pages created by the Plant shared template, you would need to change the Plant shared template to delete the shared borders. For now, however, you'll just show Brett the basic steps he needs to know so he can create the Dynamic Web Template, attach it to an existing Web page, and make changes to the Dynamic Web Template and update the attached Web page automatically. Brett created two new pages for two different plants. He also created a page to organize the links to the pages with descriptions of plants and trees. You will create a new folder in the Web site and then import these files into the folder.

To create a new folder in the Web site and import pages into it:

► 1. Start **FrontPage**, and then use My Network Places to open the **garden** Web site from your Web server.

Trouble? Make sure that you see the path to the server-based Web site (such as http://localhost/garden) in the FrontPage title bar before continuing. If you see a disk location, such as C:\Inetpub\wwwroot\garden, in the FrontPage title bar, you opened the disk-based Web site instead of the server-based Web site. Click File on the menu bar, click Close Site, and then repeat Step 1 to open the Web site stored on the server. If you use the disk-based Web site to complete this tutorial, your Web site will not work correctly.

► 2. Display the Folder List (if necessary), right-click the Web site's root folder to open the shortcut menu, point to **New**, and then click **Folder**. Creating a new folder in a Web site is not the same as creating a subsite. A folder is just a regular Windows folder in which you can store files and other folders. A subsite is created to store a Web site.

▶ 3. Type **plants** as the name of the new folder, and then press the **Enter** key.

▶ 4. With the plants folder selected in the Folder List, click **File** on the menu bar, click **Import**, click the **Add File** button, open the **Tutorial.07\Tutorial** folder included with your Data Files, click the **hibiscus.htm** file, press and hold the **Ctrl** key, click the **sage.htm** file, click the **start.htm** file, and then release the **Ctrl** key. Three files are selected.

▶ 5. Click the **Open** button, and then click the **OK** button. The files are imported into the plant folder of the Web site.

Before continuing, you'll position these pages in Navigation view to add them to the site's navigation structure.

▶ 6. Change to Navigation view, if necessary, click the **plants** folder in the Folder List to open it, and then position the **start.htm** page as a child of the Garden Center page and to the left of the Decorative Items page.

▶ 7. Position the **hibiscus.htm** and **sage.htm** pages as child pages of the Plants & Trees page. Because the Garden Center page already appears in the custom link bar navigation structure for the home page, you won't need to add these pages to the custom link bar navigation structure.

▶ 8. Open the **start.htm** page in Design view, and then close the Folder List. The Plants & Trees page opens in Design view and is formatted using the Web site's default theme.

Before you show Brett how to create the Dynamic Web Template, you need to create a new Web page in the site and remove the shared borders and theme from it. Instead of using the menu commands to accomplish these tasks, you'll show Brett how to remove the tags from the HTML document that insert these features.

To create a new Web page and remove the shared borders and theme:

▶ 1. Click the **Create a new normal page** button 🗋 on the Standard toolbar. If the Layout Tables and Cells task pane opens, click its **Close** button ☒ to close it. The new page uses the Web site's theme and shared borders. Because you don't want to include these features in the Dynamic Web Template, you'll disable them.

▶ 2. Click the **Show Code View** button 🔲 Code at the bottom of the Contents pane. The HTML document for the new page appears in Code view, as shown in Figure 7-19.

Figure 7-19 ▶ **Code view for the new page**

3. Select the **<meta name="Microsoft Theme" content="garden-web-site 1011, default">** tag in the head section of the HTML document. This tag includes information about the theme.

   Trouble? If you applied a different theme to the Web site, your meta tag will differ. Make sure that you select the meta tag that has the name value "Microsoft Theme."

   Trouble? Depending on how FrontPage is configured, you might see additional meta tags in your page. This difference causes no problems.

4. Press the **Delete** key. The HTML tag is deleted from the HTML document and the theme is removed from the Web page. 1

5. Select the **<meta name="Microsoft Border" content="tlb, default">** tag, and then press **Delete**. The HTML tag is deleted from the HTML document and the shared borders are removed from the page.

6. Return to Design view. The Web page no longer includes shared borders or uses the Web site's default theme.

Now you can show Brett how to save the page as a Dynamic Web Template.

Saving a Dynamic Web Template

Reference Window

- Open a new Web page in Design view.
- Click File on the menu bar, and then click Save As.
- Type the desired filename for the Dynamic Web Template in the File name text box.
- Click the Save as type list arrow, and then click Dynamic Web Template.
- Click the Save button.

To create a Dynamic Web Template, you begin by creating a normal Web page in Design view. You have already completed this step.

To create a Dynamic Web Template:

1. Click **File** on the menu bar, and then click **Save As**. The Save As dialog box opens.

2. If necessary, double-click the **plants** folder to open it. You will save the Dynamic Web Template in this folder so the Dynamic Web Template and pages that are attached to it are stored in one place in the Web site.

3. Select the text in the File name text box, and then type **plant**.

4. Click the **Save as type** list arrow, and then click **Dynamic Web Template**. If Windows is configured to show filename extensions, the filename of the new page changes from plant to plant.dwt. The .dwt filename extension indicates a Dynamic Web Template.

5. Click the **Save** button.

Now you can add content to the Dynamic Web Template. First, you'll show Brett how to add the locked content. Adding the locked content first makes it easier to isolate the editable regions, which you will create last.

To add locked content to a Dynamic Web Template:

▶ 1. Click the **Center** button 🔲 on the Formatting toolbar, click the **Insert Picture From File** button 🔲 on the Standard toolbar, open the **images** folder of the garden Web site, scroll down and click the **sun_logo.gif** file, and then click the **Insert** button. The Sunshine logo picture appears in the page in a centered paragraph.

   Trouble? If your Web site is stored on IIS, the path to your garden Web site is http://localhost/garden. If you cannot find the folder that stores your Web site, the sun_logo.gif file is also stored in the Tutorial.07\Tutorial folder included with your Data Files.

▶ 2. Press the **Enter** key, click **Insert** on the menu bar, click **Page Banner**, make sure that the **Picture** option button is selected, and then click the **OK** button. A placeholder for the picture page banner appears in the page.

▶ 3. Press the **Enter** key, click **Insert** on the menu bar, click **Navigation**, click the **Bar based on navigation structure** bar type, click the **Next** button, scroll down the list of bar styles and click the **More Dots** style (the description is "An HTML style where each link is surrounded by dots."), click the **Next** button, make sure that the **Horizontal** orientation is selected, and then click the **Finish** button. The Link Bar Properties dialog box opens. You want to include links to child-level pages, the home page, and the parent page in these pages, so you'll select these options.

▶ 4. Click the **Child level** option button (if necessary), click the **Home page** and **Parent page** check boxes to add check marks to them, and then click the **OK** button. A placeholder for the link bar appears in the page.

▶ 5. Press the **Enter** key two times to create two blank paragraphs in the page. You'll copy the copyright information from the home page and paste it into the second blank paragraph.

▶ 6. Click the **Web Site** tab at the top of the Contents pane, change to Folders view, if necessary, click the **Up One Level** button 🔲 on the Contents pane to return to the root folder, and then double-click **index.htm** to open the home page in Design view.

▶ 7. Scroll to the bottom of the home page, select the two lines of text in the bottom shared border (beginning with the words "Copyright" and "All"), click the **Copy** button 🔲 on the Standard toolbar, and then close the home page.

   Trouble? If a dialog box opens and asks you to save the home page, click the No button.

▶ 8. Make sure the insertion point appears in the second blank paragraph at the bottom of the Dynamic Web Template, click the **Align Left** button 🔲 on the Fomatting toolbar, and then click the **Paste** button 🔲 on the Standard toolbar. The copyright information is pasted into the page.

▶ 9. Click the **Save** button 🔲 on the Standard toolbar to save your changes.

   Trouble? If the Save Embedded files dialog box opens, make sure that the sun_logo.gif file will be saved in the garden Web site's images folder, and then click the OK button. If "Overwrite" appears in the Action column, click the OK button to continue.

The picture, components, and text that you entered into the Dynamic Web Template are locked because you have not created them in editable regions. Next, you will change the blank paragraph in the middle of the page to an editable region named body.

Creating an Editable Region in a Dynamic Web Template

- Select the area in the Dynamic Web Template that you want to convert to an editable region.
- Click Format on the menu bar, point to Dynamic Web Template, and then click Manage Editable Regions.
- In the Region name text box, type a name for the editable region.
- Click the Add button, and then click the Close button.

The editable region that you will create will be named "body" because it is in the body section of the page. Other editable regions that you can create might have names such as doctitle, special, or keywords to represent content in different sections of the Dynamic Web Template. You can also create multiple body editable regions in a Dynamic Web Template, such as body1, body2, and body3, when you need to create more than one editable region in the body section of the Dynamic Web Template.

To create an editable region in a Dynamic Web Template:

1. Move the pointer to the left margin to the left of the blank paragraph in the middle of the page as shown in Figure 7-20 so it changes to a ⌐ shape, click to select the paragraph, and then click the **Align Left** button 📄 on the Formatting toolbar. The paragraph is selected and left-aligned.

Creating the body editable region ◀ **Figure 7-20**

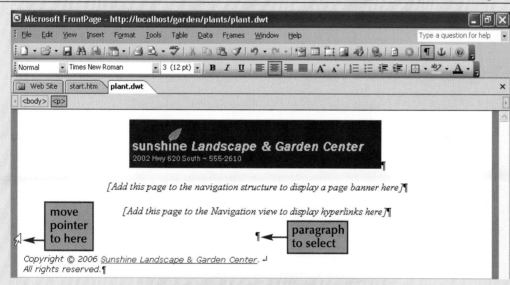

Trouble? If necessary, click the Show All button ¶ on the Standard toolbar to turn on the display of nonprinting characters.

2. Click **Format** on the menu bar, point to **Dynamic Web Template**, and then click **Manage Editable Regions**. The Editable Regions dialog box opens, as shown in Figure 7-21.

Figure 7-21 ▶ **Editable Regions dialog box**

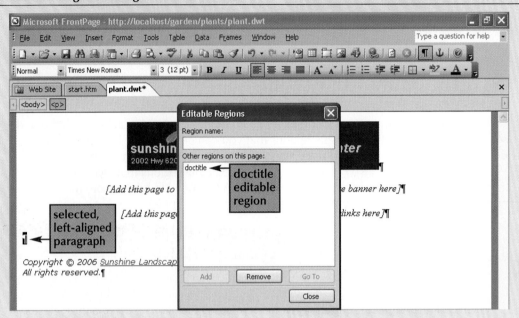

The doctitle editable region was added automatically to the Dynamic Web Template when you saved it. If you needed to lock the document's title, you could select the doctitle editable region and then click the Remove button. However, because you want authors to be able to change the page's title, you will keep the doctitle editable region.

▶ 3. In the Region name text box, type **body**, and then click the **Add** button. The body region is added to the list of editable regions.

▶ 4. Click the **Close** button. The Editable Regions dialog box closes and the body editable region appears in the Dynamic Web Template in an orange box with the word "(body)" above it. See Figure 7-22.

Figure 7-22 ▶ **Body editable region added to Dynamic Web Template**

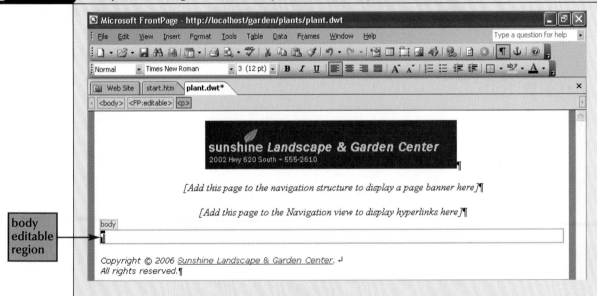

This is the only editable region you'll create, so you can save the Dynamic Web Template.

▶ **5.** Click the **Save** button 🖫 on the Standard toolbar, and then close the plant.dwt page. The start.htm page is still open in Design view.

You can attach the Dynamic Web Template to the start.htm page by using the Format menu.

Attaching a Dynamic Web Template to a Web Page

- Open the page to which you want to attach the Dynamic Web Template in Design view. If you want to attach the Dynamic Web Template to multiple pages, select them in Folders view.
- Click Format on the menu bar, point to Dynamic Web Template, and then click Attach Dynamic Web Template.
- Browse to and select the Dynamic Web Template that you want to attach to the page(s).
- In the Choose Editable Regions for Content dialog box, identify the sections of each page that you will convert to the editable regions in the Dynamic Web Template.
- Click the OK button. If you are attaching more than one page to the Dynamic Web Template, continue this step until you have identified the sections to convert in each page to attach.
- Click the Close button in the message box that opens (if necessary).

Because the start.htm page uses shared borders and a theme, when you attach the Dynamic Web Template to this page, FrontPage will automatically delete these elements from the start.htm page because the Dynamic Web Template does not support them.

To attach a Dynamic Web Template to a Web page:

▶ **1.** With the start.htm page open in Design view, click **Format** on the menu bar, point to **Dynamic Web Template**, and then click **Attach Dynamic Web Template**. The Attach Dynamic Web Template dialog box opens.

Trouble? If the Attach Dynamic Web Template command is dimmed, press the Esc key twice to close the open menus, close the plant.dwt.page, and then repeat Step 1.

▶ **2.** If necessary, open the **plants** folder in the garden Web site, and then double-click **plant.dwt**. The Choose Editable Regions for Content dialog box opens, as shown in Figure 7-23. Before attaching a template, you have to identify the regions of the page that correspond to the regions in the template. In this case, you'll match the body section of the template to the body section in the Web page (both of which are identified by the HTML <body> and </body> tags). In some cases, you might need to identify more than one region.

| Figure 7-23 | Choose Editable Regions for Content dialog box |

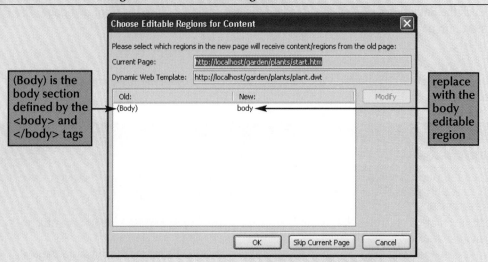

3. Click **(Body)** in the list box. If you were attaching the Dynamic Web Template to several pages, you might need to choose the editable regions for each one. The Skip Current Page button lets you skip a page when you are attaching the Dynamic Web Template to a group of pages.

4. Click the **OK** button, and then click the **Close** button in the message box (if necessary). The Dynamic Web Template formats the start.htm page. See Figure 7-24.

| Figure 7-24 | Web page formatted by Dynamic Web Template |

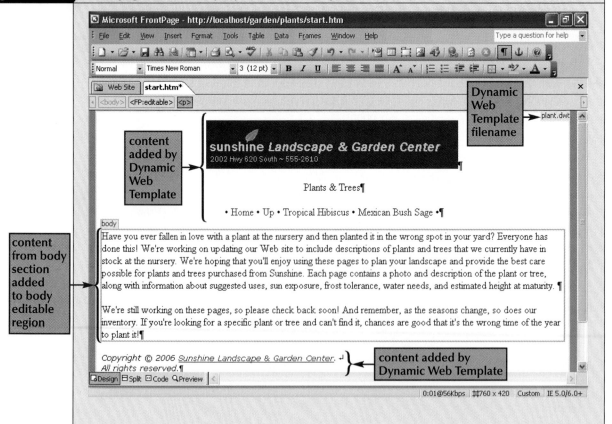

The Dynamic Web Template changed the appearance of the page by removing the shared borders and theme and inserting the logo, page banner, link bar, and copyright information. In addition, the text in the body tags of the start.htm page now appears within the body editable region defined by the template.

5. Move your pointer over the logo picture, page banner, and link bar at the top of the page, and then over the copyright information at the bottom of the page. The pointer changes to a ⊘ shape because this content is not in an editable region defined by the Dynamic Web Template.

6. Move your pointer over the body region. The pointer changes to a Ⅰ shape, indicating that you can change this text.

7. Save the start.htm page.

Now the Dynamic Web Template is attached to the start.htm page. You want to show Brett how to change the Dynamic Web Template and update the pages that are attached to it, so he knows how to make changes to the Dynamic Web Template in the future and how to update pages in the site.

Updating a Dynamic Web Template and Pages Attached to It

Reference Window

- If the attached page is open in Design view when you save the Dynamic Web Template, click the Yes button in the message box that opens and asks if you want to update the file. If a message box opens and indicates the number of updated files, click the Close button.

or

- If the attached page is closed, open it in Design view, click Format on the menu bar, point to Dynamic Web Template, and then click Update Selected Page. If necessary, click the Close button to close the message box that indicates that the file was updated.
- Save the attached page.

Brett wants to add a background picture to the Dynamic Web Template and a horizontal line picture above the copyright information. He gave you the picture files to create these elements.

To update a Dynamic Web Template and pages attached to it:

1. Open the **plant.dwt** file in Design view.

2. Click to the left of the word "Copyright" near the bottom of the page, click the **Insert Picture From File** button 🖾 on the Standard toolbar, open the **Tutorial.07\Tutorial** folder included with your Data Files, and then double-click **anarule.gif**. A horizontal line picture appears in the page.

3. Press the **Enter** key, click the horizontal line picture to select it, and then click the **Center** button 🢒 on the Formatting toolbar. The picture is centered and the copyright information appears in a paragraph below it. When you attach the Dynamic Web Template to another Web page, the picture will be locked because it does not appear within an editable region of the Dynamic Web Template.

4. Click **Format** on the menu bar, click **Background**, click the **Background picture** check box to select it, and then click the **Browse** button. The Select Background Picture dialog box opens.

5. Open the **Tutorial.07\Tutorial** folder, double-click **nabkgnd.jpg**, and then click the **OK** button. The background picture appears in the Dynamic Web Template, as shown in Figure 7-25.

Figure 7-25 **Background picture and horizontal line picture added to Dynamic Web Template**

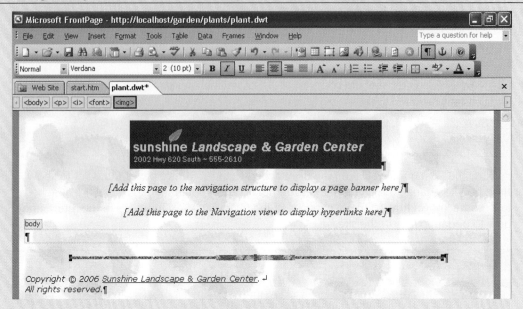

6. Save the Dynamic Web Template, and save the two pictures you inserted in the Web site's images folder. A message box opens and indicates that there is one file attached to the Dynamic Web Template you are saving. See Figure 7-26.

Figure 7-26 **Message box that opens when you save a Dynamic Web Template that is attached to other pages**

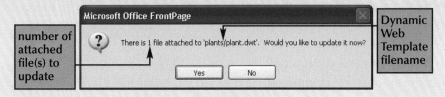

7. Click the **Yes** button. A message box might open and tell you that one file was updated. If this message box opens, click the **Close** button.

8. Click the **start.htm** tab at the top of the Contents pane. This page now includes the background picture and horizontal line picture you inserted into the Dynamic Web Template. If you move the pointer around the Web page, you can identify the regions that are locked.

9. Save the start.htm page.

Brett wants to change the font and increase the font size of the page banner and link bar to make these features more prominent. You'll show him how to do this next by making the changes in the Dynamic Web Template.

To change the font and font size in the Dynamic Web Template:

1. Click the **plant.dwt** tab at the top of the Contents pane, and then click the page banner placeholder, which appears below the Sunshine logo picture.

2. Click the **Font** list arrow on the Formatting toolbar, and then scroll down the list as necessary and click **Comic Sans MS**.

3. Click the **Font Size** list arrow on the Formatting toolbar, and then click **5 (18 pt)**.

4. With the page banner still selected, click the **Bold** button **B** on the Formatting toolbar. The page banner is formatted with 18-point, bold, Comic Sans MS font.

5. Click the link bar placeholder, and then change it to 14-point, Comic Sans MS font.

6. Save the Dynamic Web Template, click the **Yes** button to update the start.htm page that is attached to it, and then if necessary click the **Close** button to close the message box.

7. Click the **start.htm** tab at the top of the Contents pane, and then save the start.htm page. As shown in Figure 7-27, the start.htm page includes the changes you made to the page banner and link bar using the Dynamic Web Template.

Changes from Dynamic Web Template made in start.htm page Figure 7-27

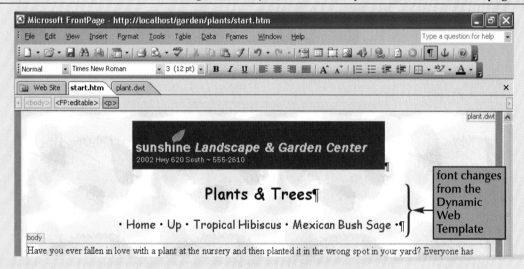

Brett also wants to change the font in the body region to Comic Sans MS. You tell him that he has to make one adjustment in the HTML document to make this change.

To change the body font in a Dynamic Web Template:

1. Click the **plant.dwt** tab at the Contents pane, and then select the paragraph mark in the body editable region of the Dynamic Web Template. To change the font in the body editable region, you need to add the HTML <font> and </font> tags to the Dynamic Web Template. You'll make this change in Code view.

2. Change to Code view for the Dynamic Web Template. The paragraph you selected in the Dynamic Web Template is selected in the HTML document, as shown in Figure 7-28. (Your selected text might be different.)

| Figure 7-28 | Code view for the Dynamic Web Template |

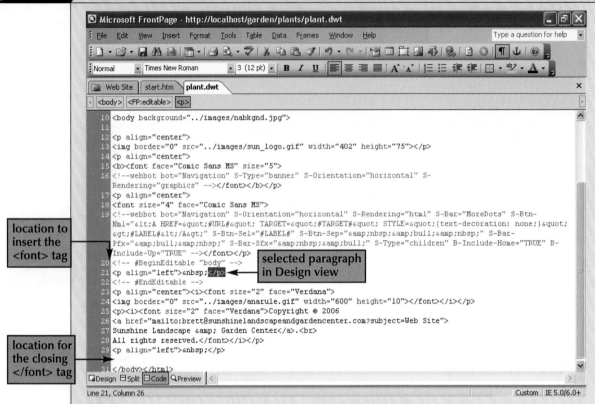

location to insert the <font> tag

selected paragraph in Design view

location for the closing </font> tag

Trouble? If necessary, scroll down the HTML document so you can see the selected </p> tag.

To change the font used in the body editable region of pages attached to the Dynamic Web Template, you need to include the opening <font> tag before the beginning comment tag for the body editable region.

 3. Click to the left of the < in the <!-- #BeginEditable "body" --> tag (see Figure 7-28), and then type **<font face="Comic Sans MS" size="2">**. FrontPage adds the closing </font> tag for you. You'll need to move this tag to appear above the closing </body> tag for the Web page.

 4. Select the **</font>** tag, click the **Cut** button on the Standard toolbar, click above (or to the left of) the </body> tag, and then click the **Paste** button on the Standard toolbar.

The copyright information that you copied from the home page includes <font> and </font> tags that format this text using a 10-point Verdana font. To make this text use the font you specified for the body of the page, you need to delete these tags.

 5. Locate and select the **<font size="2" face="Verdana">** tag, and then press the **Delete** key.

 6. Locate and select the **</font>** tag, which appears after the text "All rights reserved," and then press the **Delete** key.

 7. Save the Dynamic Web Template, click the **Yes** button to update the start.htm page, and then if necessary click the **Close** button to close the message box.

 8. Click the **start.htm** tab, save the page, and then preview it in a browser. The body text in this page now uses the fonts from the Dynamic Web Template, as shown in Figure 7-29.

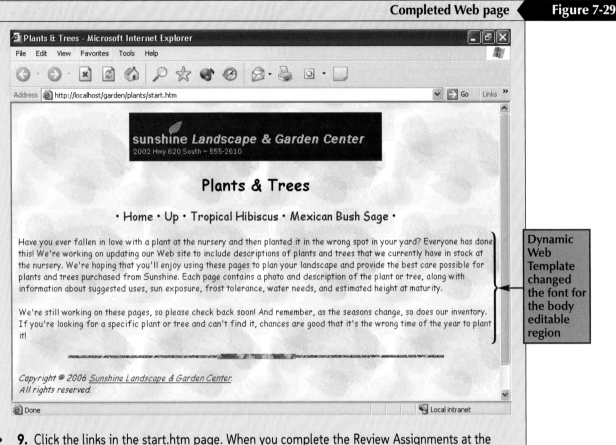

Dynamic Web Template changed the font for the body editable region

9. Click the links in the start.htm page. When you complete the Review Assignments at the end of this tutorial, you will attach the Dynamic Web Template to the hibiscus.htm and sage.htm pages, which will add links to these pages and format them using the information in the Dynamic Web Template.

10. Close your browser.

11. Close the start.htm and plant.dwt pages.

Brett likes the way the start.htm page looks. He asks you how to attach the Dynamic Web Template to additional Web pages. To show him how to do this, you will attach the Dynamic Web Template to two pages that you used in the RainMaker Irrigation frames page because these pages do not use the Web site's shared borders or themes.

To attach the Dynamic Web Template to selected pages:

1. In Folders view, open the **irr** folder, and then select the files **faq.htm** and **intro.htm**.

2. Click **Format** on the menu bar, point to **Dynamic Web Template**, and then click **Attach Dynamic Web Template**. The Attach Dynamic Web Template dialog box opens.

3. Open the **plants** folder, and then double-click **plant.dwt**. The Choose Editable Regions for Content dialog box opens.

4. Click **(Body)** in the list box, and then click the **OK** button. If a message box opens and indicates the number of files that were updated, click the **Close** button.

5. Open the faq.htm page in Design view. The Dynamic Web Template formats the page, as shown in Figure 7-30.

Figure 7-30 **Dynamic Web Template attached to faq.htm page**

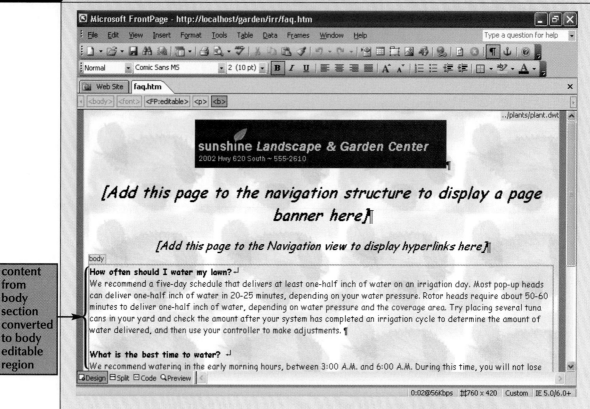

content from body section converted to body editable region

6. Close the faq.htm page, and then open the intro.htm page. The Dynamic Web Template also formats this page.

You also tell Brett that he needs to know how to detach the Dynamic Web Template from Web pages, so you will demonstrate this process for him.

When you attach a Dynamic Web Template to a Web page, the tags from the Dynamic Web Template are added to the Web page to which it is attached. When you detach the Dynamic Web Template from the attached Web page, the tags from the Dynamic Web Template are still included in the attached page, but the locked regions of the page are removed.

To detach a page from a Dynamic Web Template:

1. Click **Format** on the menu bar, point to **Dynamic Web Template**, and then click **Detach from Dynamic Web Template**. If a message box opens and indicates the number of updated files, click the **Close** button.

2. Click the **Show Code View** button ⊡Code at the bottom of the Contents pane to change to Code view. The tags that created the editable regions are gone, but the tags from the Dynamic Web Template are still in the HTML document. See Figure 7-31.

Code view for the intro.htm page after detaching it from the Dynamic Web Template ◄ **Figure 7-31**

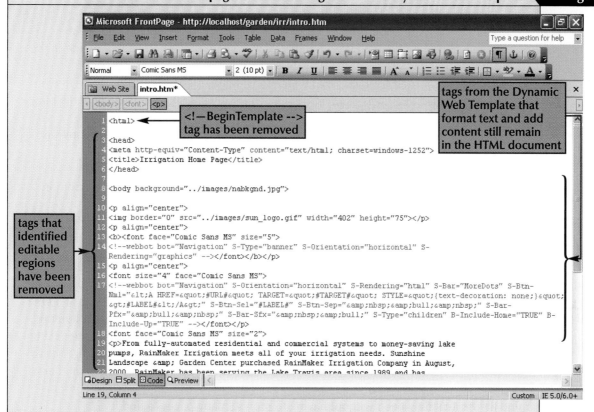

3. Save and close the intro.htm page.

4. Open the faq.htm page in Design view, click **Format** on the menu bar, point to **Dynamic Web Template**, and then click **Detach from Dynamic Web Template**. If necessary, click the **Close** button to close the message box.

5. Save and close the faq.htm page.

To restore the intro.htm and faq.htm pages to their original formatting, you'll import copies of these files into the irr folder.

6. Click **File** on the menu bar, click **Import**, click the **Add File** button, if necessary open the **Tutorial.07\Tutorial** folder, select the files **faq.htm** and **intro.htm**, click the **Open** button, and then click the **OK** button.

7. Click the **Yes to All** button to overwrite the files in the Web site with the ones you are importing.

8. Close the garden Web site, and then close FrontPage.

The Student Online Companion page for Tutorial 7 includes links that you can follow to learn more about Dynamic Web Templates and other templates that you can use to format Web pages in FrontPage. Some companies provide samples of templates that you can purchase for a small fee and use to design your Web sites. These templates are easy to install and can save you some time when developing a new Web site.

In the next tutorial, you will create Web pages that store and display information in an Access database.

Review

Session 7.2 Quick Check

1. What is a Dynamic Web Template?
2. How is a Dynamic Web Template different from a shared template?
3. True or False: A Dynamic Web Template can contain only one editable region in the body section.
4. True or False: The HTML tags that define the editable regions of a Web page that has been attached to a Dynamic Web Template are <BeginEditable> and <EndEditable>.
5. True or False: A Dynamic Web Template cannot contain shared borders.
6. Which editable region does FrontPage create automatically when you save a Web page as a Dynamic Web Template?
7. In which editable region does the Web page's title appear?
8. What happens to a Web page when you detach a Dynamic Web Template from it?

Review

Tutorial Summary

In this tutorial, you learned how to manage a Web site's pages when multiple authors are involved in the Web site's development. By enabling source control for a Web site, you can ensure that only one author can check out and save changes to a Web page at a time. You also learned how to create a shared template in a Web site. When multiple authors are working on a Web site's development, new pages developed from a shared template help guarantee consistent content in a Web site. You also assigned pages to categories so you could generate a site map, which is a page with hyperlinks to pages based on their content. Site maps are important tools in large Web sites because they help site visitors find the content they need without having to browse many pages to find it.

Finally, you created a Dynamic Web Template that formats content in a Web page that is attached to it and lets the developer control which text and other objects in a Web page will be editable and which will be locked. Dynamic Web Templates can give the developer additional control over the content of Web pages by preventing accidental deletions and changes to important content.

Key Terms

category	review status	site map
Dynamic Web Template	shared template	source control
editable region		

Practice

Practice the skills you learned in the tutorial using the same case scenario.

Review Assignments

Data File needed for these Review Assignments: garden79.jpg

Brett wants you to enhance the garden Web site by making several changes. First, he wants to change the Dynamic Web Template to add a horizontal line picture between the locked area at the top of the page and the body editable region. After making that change, he wants you to attach the Dynamic Web Template to the pages that feature Tropical Hibiscus and Mexican Bush Sage. Brett also wants you to add a new page to the Web site for Snapdragons using the shared template you created and saved in the Web site.

After reviewing the current Site Map page, Brett wants to add a new category to the Web site that will include hyperlinks to the pages in the Web site that include its contact information and a map to its location. He also wants you to add the pages that feature plants to the Plants category so they will show up as hyperlinks in the site map.

If necessary, start FrontPage, make sure you have your Data Files, and then do the following:

1. Use My Network Places to open the **garden** Web site from your Web server.
2. In Folders view, open the **plants** folder to display its contents, select the **hibiscus.htm** and **sage.htm** files, and then attach the **plant.dwt** Dynamic Web Template to the selected files. In the Choose Editable Regions for Content dialog box, convert the body section of these Web pages to the body editable region, and then update both pages.
3. Open the **plant.dwt** Dynamic Web Template in Design view. Copy the horizontal line picture near the bottom of the page, and then paste it in a new, centered paragraph above the body editable region.
4. Select the copyright information at the bottom of the Dynamic Web Template, remove the italics, and then change the font size to 8 points. Save the Dynamic Web Template, and then close it.
5. Open the **sage.htm** page in Design view, and then update the page to use the changes you saved in the Dynamic Web Template. Save the **sage.htm** page.
6. Update the **hibiscus.htm** page and then save your changes.
7. Use the Plant shared template to create a new Web page. Save the new page in the Web site's **plants** folder using the filename **snap.htm** and the title "Snapdragons."
8. Import the **garden79.jpg** file from the Tutorial.07\Review folder included with your Data Files into the Web site's **images** folder.
9. In Design view for the Snapdragons page, select the "[insert picture here]" text and replace it with the **garden79.jpg** picture saved in the Web site's **images** folder.
10. Remove the shared borders and theme from the **snap.htm** page, and then save it.
11. Attach the **plant.dwt** Dynamic Web Template to the **snap.htm** page, converting the existing body section to the body editable region. Select the text in the right column of the table, and then change it to 10 points. Use Figure 7-32 to add the new content to this page.

Figure 7-32

Description: A flowering plant available in many different colors and sizes

Suggested Uses: In the garden as a border and in large, deep containers

Sun Exposure: Full sun to part shade

Frost Tolerance: None

Watering Needs: Water on a regular basis

Height: Depending on the variety, snapdragons can be small, dense, bushy plants or grow up to 24" in height

12. Save the **snap.htm** page, and then add it to the Web site's navigation structure as a child page of the Plants & Trees page. Position the **snap.htm** page to the right of the Mexican Bush Sage page.
13. Preview the **snap.htm** page in a browser, print it, and then close your browser.
14. Open the Site Map page (**site_map.htm**) in Design view. Insert the text "Contact Sunshine" and a comma and a space to the left of the Plants hyperlink in the first paragraph. Add a new level-three heading above the Plants heading with the text

"Contact Sunshine:". Create a bookmark named contact using the heading you just created, and then create a hyperlink from the "Contact Sunshine" text in the first paragraph to the contact bookmark. Save the **site_map.htm** page.

15. Change to Folders view, and then right-click the **contact.htm** page. Use the Properties dialog box to create a new category named Contact in the Web site, and then assign the **contact.htm** page to the Contact category.

16. Add the **map_page.htm** page to the Contact category.

17. Add the **snap.htm**, **hibiscus.htm**, and **sage.htm** pages to the Plants category.

18. In the **site_map.htm** page, create a new, normal paragraph below the Contact Sunshine heading, and then insert a table of contents component to display links to pages in the Contact category. Save the **site_map.htm** page, preview the page in a browser, test the hyperlink and bookmark you created, and then print the page.

19. Close your browser, close the **garden** Web site, and then close FrontPage.

Create

Create a shared template for creating new pages, and create a Dynamic Web Template to format pages in a Web site.

Case Problem 1

Data File needed for this Case Problem: back.gif

Buffalo Trading Post In a recent staff meeting, Nicole Beirne learned that the "What" page in the Web site, which is a frames page featuring the top-selling accessories, children's clothing, and women's clothing items, has been a popular destination for Web site visitors. Nicole wants to expand this page to include additional lists of top-selling items, including men's clothing items and men's accessories. She wants to make sure that the pages in the frames page are consistently formatted and she asks you to get to work in making these changes.

If necessary, start FrontPage, make sure you have your Data Files, and then do the following:

1. Use My Network Places to open the **buffalo** Web site from your Web server. (If you did not create this Web site in Tutorial 1 and update it in Tutorials 2 through 6, ask your instructor for assistance.)

2. Create new, normal page, remove the shared borders and theme from the page, and then save it as a Dynamic Web Template in the Web site's root folder using the filename **frame.dwt**.

3. Insert the **back.gif** picture from the Tutorial.07\Case1 folder included with your Data Files as a background picture in the Dynamic Web Template.

4. Create a body editable region in the Dynamic Web Template. Save the Dynamic Web Template and save the **back.gif** file in the Web site's **images** folder, and then close the Dynamic Web Template.

5. In Folders view, select the files **acc.htm**, **banner.htm**, **child.htm**, **contents.htm**, and **women.htm**, and then remove the theme and shared borders from these selected pages.

6. With the **acc.htm**, **banner.htm**, **child.htm**, **contents.htm**, and **women.htm** files still selected in Folders view, attach the **frame.dwt** Dynamic Web Template to the selected files. In the Choose Editable Regions for Content dialog box, convert the body section of these Web pages to the body editable region.

7. Open the **women.htm** page in Design view, click Edit on the menu bar, click Select All to select the heading and table in this page, and then copy the selected content to the Clipboard.

8. In Design view, create a new, normal Web page, change to Code view, and then remove the meta tags that insert the theme and shared borders from the Web site. Return to Design view.

9. In a new, centered paragraph in the Web page, paste the content you copied from the **women.htm** page into the new page.

Explore

10. Remove the specific information for the top women's clothing items so you can save this page as a shared template in the Web site. For example, change the heading from "Top Women's Clothing Items" to "Top ###" or something similar so another author will know to update the title. The table should use the same column headings but the columns that describe individual items in a category should be blank.

11. Save the Web page as a shared template in the current Web site using the filename **top.tem**, the title "Top," and the description "Adds a new "Top" page to the what.htm frames page." Close the **top.htm** page and the **women.htm** page.

Explore

12. Use the New task pane and the Top shared template to create a new page in the Web site that includes the top clothing items for men. Remove the shared borders and theme from the new page, add content that you make up, and then save the page using the filename **men.htm** and the title "Men's Clothing."

13. Attach the **frame.dwt** Dynamic Web Template to the **men.htm** page, and then save the **men.htm** page.

14. Open the **what.htm** page, and then create a link to the **men.htm** page in the contents frame below the existing "Women's Clothing" link. Set the target so the page opens in the correct frame, and then save your changes.

15. Preview the **what.htm** page in a browser, and then use the links in the contents frame to test the pages you formatted using the Dynamic Web Template. Print the frames page with the **men.htm** page displayed in the main frame, and then close your browser.

16. Open the **women.htm** page in Code view, type your name on line 2 of the HTML document, and then print the HTML document. Close the **women.htm** page without saving changes.

17. Close the **buffalo** Web site, and then close FrontPage.

Case Problem 2

Apply

Use the skills you learned in this tutorial to add a site map to a Web site.

Data Files needed for this Case Problem: angel.htm, p_angel.jpg, p_pasta.jpg, p_pie.jpg, p_puddng.jpg, pasta.htm, pecan.htm, and pudding.htm

Garden Grill Meghan Elliott and Callan Murphy want to add several new pages to the Web site. Each page features a new menu item offered at the restaurant and includes a picture and a description. After adding these pages, they want you to create a site map to make it easier for the Web site's visitors to locate the new pages.

If necessary, start FrontPage, make sure you have your Data Files, and then do the following:

1. Use My Network Places to open the **grill** Web site from your Web server. (If you did not create this Web site in Tutorial 1 and update it in Tutorials 2 through 6, ask your instructor for assistance).

2. Import the files **angel.htm**, **pasta.htm**, **pecan.htm**, and **pudding.htm** and from the Tutorial.07\Case2 folder included with your Data Files into the root folder of the **grill** Web site. With these files selected in Folders view, apply the Web site's default theme to the pages.

3. Import the files **p_angel.jpg**, **p_pasta.jpg**, **p_pie.jpg**, and **p_puddng.jpg** from the Tutorial.07\Case2 folder into the **images** folder of the **grill** Web site.

4. Delete the default categories from the Web site, and then create the following categories in the Web site: Appetizers, Desserts, Entrees, Specials, Sandwiches, and New Menu Items.

5. Assign the pages you imported in Step 2 to the New Menu Items category and also to the appropriate category for the featured food item. Add the **menu.htm** page to the Appetizers, Desserts, Entrees, and Sandwiches categories, and then add the **specials.htm** page to the Specials category.

6. Run a Categories report and filter the report so that it lists only those Web pages with assigned categories. Sort the list alphabetically by filename. Print a screenshot of the Categories report.

7. Add a new, normal page to the Web site with the filename **site_map.htm** and the title "Menu Categories." After saving the page, add it to the Web site's navigation structure as a child page of the home page. Position the page to the right of the Franchise Info page icon in the Web site's navigation structure, and also to the right of the Menu page icon in the custom link bar navigation structure. Add the **angel.htm**, **pasta.htm**, **pecan.htm**, and **pudding.htm** pages as child pages of the Menu Categories page in the Web site's navigation structure. (You do not need to add these pages to the custom link bar navigation structure.)

Explore ▶

8. Open the **contents.htm** page in Design view, and then create a "Menu Categories" hyperlink in a new paragraph below the "Home" hyperlink that opens the **site_map.htm** page without the frames. Save and close the **contents.htm** page.

Explore ▶

9. Insert the Specials custom link bar in a new, centered paragraph below the page banner in the following pages: **angel.htm**, **pasta.htm**, **pecan.htm**, and **pudding.htm**. Save and close these pages.

Explore ▶

10. Create the content of the Menu Categories page (**site_map.htm**) using the categories you created in Step 4. Use any design that you like, but make sure that the page includes a centered page banner, a centered link bar with links to same-level pages and to the home page, and that the new menu items appear at the top of the page. Use a FrontPage component to list the pages based on their categories. When you are finished, save the page, preview it in a browser, and then print it.

11. Browse the pages in the Web site to make sure that the hyperlinks you created work correctly, and if necessary, make any corrections in FrontPage. Open the Pasta Salad page in the browser, and then print that page.

12. Close your browser, the **grill** Web site, and FrontPage.

Case Problem 3

Create

Create a Dynamic Web Template and attach it to existing Web pages to change their appearance and content.

There are no new Data Files needed for this Case Problem.

Swenson Auctioneers Scott Swenson is very pleased with the appearance of the Swenson Auctioneers Web site. He has been referring clients to the site and they have commented very positively about its appearance and content. One change that Scott would like to make is to eliminate the Client Comments frames page and replace its content with regular Web pages. Instead of making this change by opening and saving every Web page affected by this change, you decide to create a Dynamic Web Template with formatting instructions and navigation options and attach it to the pages that are displayed in the main frame.

If necessary, start FrontPage, and then do the following:

1. Use My Network Places to open the **swenson** Web site from your Web server. (If you did not create this Web site in Tutorial 1 and update it in Tutorials 2 through 6, ask your instructor for assistance.)

2. Open the **clients.htm** frames page in Design view, and reacquaint yourself with the page's contents.

3. Create a new, normal Web page in Design view, and then remove the meta tag that adds the Web site's default theme to the page.

4. Save the Web page as a Dynamic Web Template in the Web site's root folder using the filename **client.dwt**.

5. Copy the Swenson Auctioneers logo picture in the contents frame of the frames page, and then paste it at the top of the Dynamic Web Template. Close the frames page.

Explore

Explore

6. In Navigation view, create a new custom link bar. Add the eight files in the **frame** folder to the custom link bar, positioning the pages alphabetically from left to right by their filenames. Change the name of the custom link bar to "DWT."

7. Insert the DWT custom link bar in a new paragraph below the Swenson Auctioneers logo in the Dynamic Web Template. Choose the option to add the home page as a link in the custom link bar. After inserting the custom link bar, select it and change it to 10-point, Arial font.

8. Create a new paragraph below the custom link bar, and then select and convert that paragraph to a body editable region.

9. Open the home page in Design view, and then select the horizontal line and copyright information at the bottom of the page. Copy this content to the Clipboard, close the home page, and then paste this information at the bottom of the Dynamic Web Template (below the body editable region).

10. Insert the **back.gif** file from the Web site's **images** folder as a background picture in the Dynamic Web Template. Save the Dynamic Web Template, and then close it. (If necessary, overwrite the **sw_logo.gif** file in the Web site's **images** folder.)

11. In Folders view, open the **frame** folder of the Web site, select all eight files in this folder, and then remove the theme from the selected files.

12. With the files in the **frame** folder still selected, attach the **client.dwt** Dynamic Web Template to the selected files. In the Choose Editable Regions for Content dialog box, convert the body section of these Web pages to the body editable region.

13. Open the home page in Design view, and then change the target of the clients hyperlink in the second paragraph to open the **benefit.htm** page in the Web site's **frame** folder.

14. Save the home page, and then preview it in a browser. Click the clients link and use the custom link bar to navigate the pages that contain the client comments. Use your browser to print the Sound & Lighting page, and then close your browser.

15. Type your name on line 2 of the Dynamic Web Template in Code view, and then print the HTML document. Close the Dynamic Web Template without saving changes.

16. Close the **swenson** Web site, and then close FrontPage.

Create

Create and use a Dynamic Web Template to format pages in a Web site.

Case Problem 4

Data Files needed for this Case Problem: Default.htm, special.htm, back1.gif, logo.gif, and divider.gif

Mortgage Services, Inc. Natalie Fuselier has been processing a lot of loan applications recently from applicants who are in need of credit repair services. The Credit Repair Services page in the loan Web site has some basic information for applicants about credit repair. However, Natalie wants to expand the information she provides as she hires people at Mortgage Services, Inc. who are experienced in helping consumers with debt consolidation and other procedures that help restore a person's credit. Natalie wants to delete the current page in the Web site and start developing pages for the Credit Repair Services department. She wants the pages for the Credit Repair Services department to have a different appearance from other pages in the Web site, so she asks you to create a new design for these pages.

If necessary, start FrontPage, make sure you have your Data Files, and then do the following:

1. Use My Network Places to open the **loan** Web site from your Web server. (If you did not create this Web site in Tutorial 1 and update it in Tutorials 2 through 6, ask your instructor for assistance.)

Explore

2. Change to Hyperlinks view, and then select the **repair.htm** page as the focus page. Use Hyperlinks view to identify any pages in the Web site that include a link to the **repair.htm** page in them, and then delete any links that you find and save the page in which the link to this page appeared.

3. In Folders view, use the shortcut menu to delete the **repair.htm** page from the Web site.

4. If necessary, display the Folder List, right-click the Web site's root folder, and then create a new folder named **credit** in the **loan** Web site.

5. Import the **Default.htm** and **special.htm** files from the Tutorial.07\Case4 folder included with your Data Files into the **credit** folder. Open these pages in Design view and examine their contents, and then close the pages.

6. Create a new, normal Web page in Design view, remove the shared borders and theme from the new page, and then save it as a Dynamic Web Template in the **credit** folder using the filename **credit.dwt**.

Explore

7. Use the following guidelines and Figure 7-33 to create the Dynamic Web Template.

Figure 7-33

Mortgage Services, Inc.

[Add this page to the navigation structure to display a page banner here]

[Add this page to the Navigation view to display hyperlinks here]

body

Copyright Mortgage Services, Inc.
All rights reserved.

a. The background picture, horizontal line picture, and picture logo file are saved as **back1.gif**, **divider.gif**, and **logo.gif**, respectively, in the Tutorial.07\Case4 folder.

b. The page banner is 24-point, navy, bold, Trebuchet MS font.

c. The link bar is based on the Web site's navigation structure and includes links to child-level pages and to the home page. The text in the link bar is 10-point, Trebuchet MS font.

d. Change the text in the body editable region and the copyright information text to Trebuchet MS font by adding the correct font tag to the HTML document.

e. Save the Dynamic Web Template, save the picture files in the Web site's **images** folder, and then close the Dynamic Web Template.

8. Attach the **credit.dwt** Dynamic Web Template to the **Default.htm** and **special.htm** pages in the **credit** folder. In the Choose Editable Regions for Content dialog box, convert the body section of these Web pages to the body editable region, and then open the **Default.htm** and **special.htm** pages in Design view and examine their content and appearance.

9. Add the **Default.htm** and **special.htm** pages to the Web site's navigation structure. Position the **Default.htm** page to the right of the Search page icon, and position the **special.htm** page as a child of the Credit Repair Services page.
10. Delete the horizontal line picture that appears above the body editable region in the Dynamic Web Template, and replace it with a horizontal line that spans 100% of the browser window's width, is 5 pixels high, and navy in color. If necessary, delete any blank paragraphs that appear between the horizontal line and the body editable region.
11. Change the navigation options in the link bar in the Dynamic Web Template to include a link to the parent page.
12. Update the pages attached to the Dynamic Web Template and save them.
13. Preview the Credit Repair Services page in a browser, and then print it.
14. Use your browser to navigate the Web site, and then close your browser.
15. In Code view for the Dynamic Web Template, type your name on line 2, print the HTML document, and then close the Dynamic Web Template without saving your changes.
16. Close the **loan** Web site, and then close FrontPage.

Review

Quick Check Answers

Session 7.1

1. If you are the only person working on a Web site, then you do not need to enable source control for the site, because no other author will be checking out and editing pages.
2. padlock
3. Close and save the page, right-click the filename in the Contents pane of Folders view, and then click Check In on the shortcut menu.
4. in the Web site in which they were created (if you choose the Save Template in Current Web site check box when you save the template), and on the drive on which your FrontPage program is stored
5. FrontPage uses the categories to insert hyperlinks to appropriate pages in the correct location in the Web page that contains the FrontPage table of contents component (the site map).
6. table of contents

Session 7.2

1. A Dynamic Web Template is a file that has been saved with the .dwt filename extension, and that contains locked content, formatting instructions, and editable regions. When you attach a Dynamic Web Template to a Web page, the locked content is added to the Web page, the formatting instructions format the existing content, and content saved in different sections of the Web page is converted to editable regions.
2. A shared template is a template file that you can use to create a new Web page. The content in the shared template is added to the new Web page. A Dynamic Web Template is a file that you create and save, and then attach to one or more Web pages. The content and formatting from the Dynamic Web Template are added to the existing content in the Web page(s) to which you attach it.
3. False
4. False
5. True

6. doctitle

7. doctitle

8. When you detach a Web page from a Dynamic Web Template, the HTML tags that create the editable regions are removed from the Web page's HTML document. Content added by the Dynamic Web Template and formatting instructions for specific HTML tags remain in the Web page.

Objectives

Session 8.1
- Start Access and open and examine a database
- Create a database connection to a Web site
- Verify a database connection and set a Web site to run scripts
- Insert a Database Results region in a Web page
- Use a Web page to search a database

Session 8.2
- Create a form that sends data to an Access database
- Create and use a data access page

Lab

Databases

Student Data Files

To complete this tutorial, you will need your ending files from Tutorial 7 and the following Data Files. Additional Data Files needed to complete the end-of-tutorial exercises are listed with the Review Assignments and Case Problems.

Integrating a Database with a FrontPage Web Site

Using Web Pages to View and Store Data in an Access Database

Case

Sunshine Landscape & Garden Center

Brett Kizer is pleased with your progress in developing the garden Web site. After you completed your work on the shared template and Dynamic Web Template, Brett asked you to publish the Web site to the server he selected to host it. After just one week, the site has had medium traffic for its size, mostly due to the center's staff promoting the site from the nursery. Customer reaction to the Web site has been very positive so far, and Brett looks forward to working with you on the site's continuing development.

The Customer Requests page in the Web site, which lets Web site visitors ask a question or request landscaping, rock work, or irrigation services, has generated 20 new customers for Sunshine. When you first created the Customer Requests page, you set the form it contains to store the form's results in a comma-separated values file on the server. In this file, each form sent to the server is stored as a single line. Brett has decided that it's difficult to review the information contained in this format because it isn't easy to read the data or sort it in a meaningful way. Brett asks if you can improve the format so the data is stored in a way that will be

▼ **Tutorial.08**
▽ **Tutorial folder**

guest.mdb   guestbk.asp   requests.mdb

easy to read and sort. You tell Brett that continuing to store the form's results in a comma-separated values file is fine, but that he also needs to store the form's results in a database to get the options he has requested. Because Brett already has Microsoft Office Access 2003 installed on the computers at the nursery, you will use this database program to create a database to store the data submitted from the Customer Requests Web page.

To make it easy for Brett to view, sort, print, update, add, and delete records in the database, you will also create Web pages that display the data and accept user updates.

Session 8.1

Databases

Understanding Databases

A **database**, or a **relational database**, is a collection of related **tables** that store data about an object. Each table is made up of fields and records. A **field** is a single characteristic of an object. The set of fields in a table related to one particular object makes up a **record**. For example, Sunshine Landscape & Garden Center currently maintains a database of items for sale at the nursery. This database contains two tables that store the product description, characteristics, cost, and selling price of each item. The Product table contains the fields ProductID, Name, Description, and Distributor. The Price table contains the fields ProductID, Cost, and RetailPrice.

The tables in a single database can be linked together—or *related*—using a common field. A **common field** appears in two or more tables in the database. For example, the Product and Price tables are linked together using a common field that identifies each item's product number (ProductID). Figure 8-1 shows the Product and Price tables and indicates how they are related.

Figure 8-1 | **Related tables in a database**

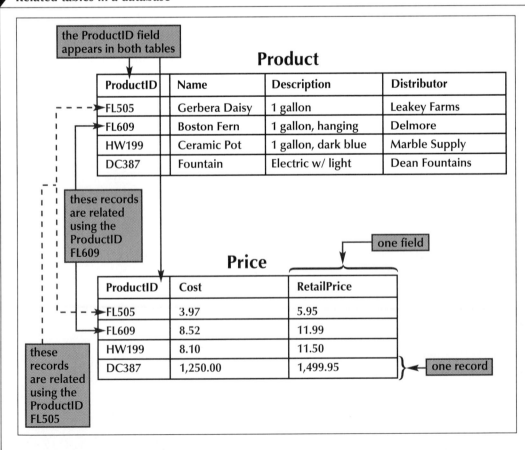

Microsoft Office Access 2003, or simply **Access**, is a relational database management program that lets you create and maintain a database. A database named requests will store the data collected by the form in the Customer Requests Web page. The requests database contains one table, named Customer Requests, which includes one field for each field in the form. You already added the 20 records stored in the comma-separated values file on the Web server into the Customer Requests table in the database. First you will open the database and examine the contents of the Customer Requests table, and then you will set the form in the Customer Requests Web page to store its results in the database.

Starting Access and Opening an Existing Database

After explaining some basic database concepts with Brett, you want to show him the database you created so he can become familiar with its content and organization.

Starting Access and Opening an Existing Database

Reference Window

- Click the Start button on the taskbar, point to All Programs, point to Microsoft Office, and then click Microsoft Office Access 2003.
- Click the Open button on the Database toolbar to open the Open dialog box.
- Click the Look in list arrow, navigate to the drive or folder that contains the database, and then double-click the database filename to open it.
- If a Security Warning dialog box opens, click the Open button.

The requests database is saved in the Tutorial.08\Tutorial folder included with your Data Files.

To start Access and open the requests database:

1. Click the **Start** button on the taskbar, point to **All Programs**, point to **Microsoft Office**, and then click **Microsoft Office Access 2003**. The Access 2003 start-up screen opens for a moment, and then the Microsoft Access program window opens.

2. Click the **Open** button 🗁 on the Database toolbar. The Open dialog box opens.

3. Click the **Look in** list arrow, navigate to the drive and folder that contains your Data Files, open the **Tutorial.08\Tutorial** folder, and then double-click **requests.mdb**. The requests database opens in the Access program window.

   Trouble? If a dialog box opens with a message about installing the Microsoft Jet Service Pack, ask your instructor or technical support person for assistance. You must have the appropriate Service Pack installed in order to open and work with Access databases safely.

   Trouble? If a dialog box opens and warns you that the requests database may not be safe, click the Open button. Your security level is set to Medium, which is the security setting that lets you choose whether to open a database that contains macros, VBA, or certain types of queries. The requests database does not contain objects that will harm your computer, so you can safely open the database.

Trouble? If a dialog box opens and warns you that Access can't open the requests database due to security restrictions, click the OK button, click Tools on the menu bar, point to Macro, click Security, click the Medium option button, click the OK button, restart your computer if you're requested to do so, and then repeat Steps 1 through 3. Your security level was set to High, which is the security setting that lets you open a database that contains macros, VBA, or certain types of queries only from trusted sources. Because the requests database does not contain objects that will harm your computer, you need to change the security setting to Medium before you can open the requests database.

> 4. Click the **Maximize** button 🔲 on the Database window.

> 5. If necessary, click the **Tables** object in the Database window to display the tables list. See Figure 8-2.

Figure 8-2	Database window for the requests database

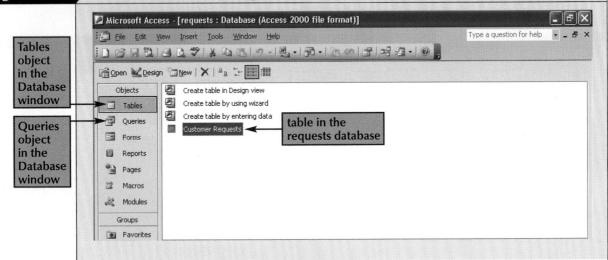

The requests database contains one table named Customer Requests. Your design for the Customer Requests table appears in Figure 8-3.

Customer Requests table design in the requests database ◄ **Figure 8-3**

Field Name	Data Type	Field Size	Description
CustomerID	AutoNumber	Long Integer	An Access AutoNumber field adds the CustomerID. CustomerIDs are assigned sequentially as new records are added to the table.
Name	Text	35	The customer's name.
Email	Text	35	The customer's e-mail address.
Phone	Text	35	The customer's telephone number.
CommunicationPreference	Text	10	The customer's indicated communication preference (e-mail or phone).
RockWork	Text	10	The value "Yes" indicates that the customer checked the Rock Work check box; no value indicates the customer did not check this check box.
Landscaping	Text	10	The value "Yes" indicates that the customer checked the Landscaping check box; no value indicates the customer did not check this check box.
IrrigationInstallation	Text	10	The value "Yes" indicates that the customer checked the Irrigation Installation check box; no value indicates the customer did not check this check box.
IrrigationService	Text	10	The value "Yes" indicates that the customer checked the Irrigation Service check box; no value indicates the customer did not check this check box.
Other	Text	10	The value "Yes" indicates that the customer checked the Other check box; no value indicates the customer did not check this check box.
Other1	Text	35	The text entered by a customer into a text box to request a service not listed on the form.
Location	Text	35	The customer's location (Lakeway, Dripping Springs, Austin, Lago Vista, West Lake Hills, Round Rock, or Other).
Visits	Number	Integer	The number entered into the Visits text box by a customer to indicate the number of times he or she has visited the nursery.
Comments	Memo	(not applicable)	A question or comment a customer entered into the Comments text area.

The requests database also contains one query named Customer. A **query** is a database object that displays data to answer a question. For example, you might ask the question, "Which records in the Customer Requests table request irrigation service?" When you run this query, Access selects the records that answer your question. The Customer query, as you will see, lists all of the Customer Requests table records in the order in which they were entered into the table.

Next, you will examine the Customer Requests table and the Customer query objects.

To open the table and query:

► 1. Double-click **Customer Requests** in the tables list. The Customer Requests table opens in Table Datasheet view, also called the Table window. Notice that some of the fields scroll to the right. You can use the horizontal scroll bar to view these fields. See Figure 8-4. The Customer Requests table contains 20 records, each of which has a unique CustomerID field value. The field that uniquely identifies each table record is called a **primary key**. The primary key of the Customer Requests table is the CustomerID field, which is an AutoNumber field whose value was assigned by Access.

Figure 8-4 | **Customer Requests table in Table Datasheet view**

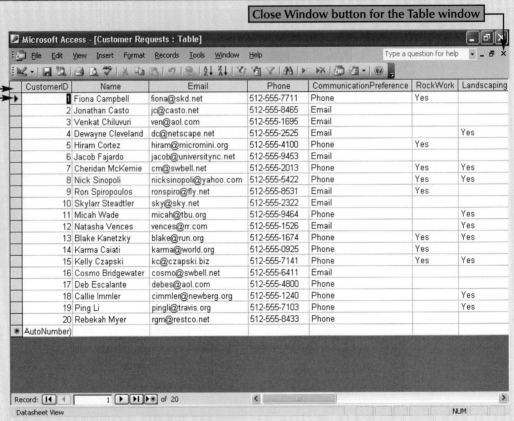

field names (column headings)

current record indicator

Close Window button for the Table window

CustomerID	Name	Email	Phone	CommunicationPreference	RockWork	Landscaping
1	Fiona Campbell	fiona@skd.net	512-555-7711	Phone	Yes	
2	Jonathan Casto	jc@casto.net	512-555-8465	Email		
3	Venkat Chiluvuri	ven@aol.com	512-555-1695	Email		
4	Dewayne Cleveland	dc@netscape.net	512-555-2525	Email		Yes
5	Hiram Cortez	hiram@micromini.org	512-555-4100	Phone	Yes	
6	Jacob Fajardo	jacob@universitync.net	512-555-9453	Email		
7	Cheridan McKemie	cm@swbell.net	512-555-2013	Phone	Yes	Yes
8	Nick Sinopoli	nicksinopoli@yahoo.com	512-555-5422	Phone	Yes	Yes
9	Ron Spiropoulos	ronspiro@fly.net	512-555-8531	Email	Yes	
10	Skylarr Steadtler	sky@sky.net	512-555-2322	Email		
11	Micah Wade	micah@tbu.org	512-555-9464	Phone		Yes
12	Natasha Vences	vences@rr.com	512-555-1526	Email		Yes
13	Blake Kanetzky	blake@run.org	512-555-1674	Phone	Yes	Yes
14	Karma Caiati	karma@world.org	512-555-0925	Phone	Yes	
15	Kelly Czapski	kc@czapski.biz	512-555-7141	Phone	Yes	Yes
16	Cosmo Bridgewater	cosmo@swbell.net	512-555-6411	Email		
17	Deb Escalante	debes@aol.com	512-555-4800	Phone		
18	Callie Immler	cimmler@newberg.org	512-555-1240	Phone		Yes
19	Ping Li	pingli@travis.org	512-555-7103	Phone		Yes
20	Rebekah Myer	rgm@restco.net	512-555-8433	Phone		
(AutoNumber)						

Record: 1 of 20

Datasheet View | NUM

▶ 2. Click the **Close Window** button ☒ on the menu bar to close the Table window. The Database window for the requests database is displayed again.

▶ 3. Click the **Queries** object in the Database window to display the queries list, and then double-click **Customer** in the queries list to open the query in Query Datasheet view, also called the Query window. This query displays all records in the Customer Requests table in the order in which they were entered. The CustomerID values do not appear in the query results because the CustomerID field is not included in the query design. See Figure 8-5.

Customer query in Query Datasheet view   Figure 8-5

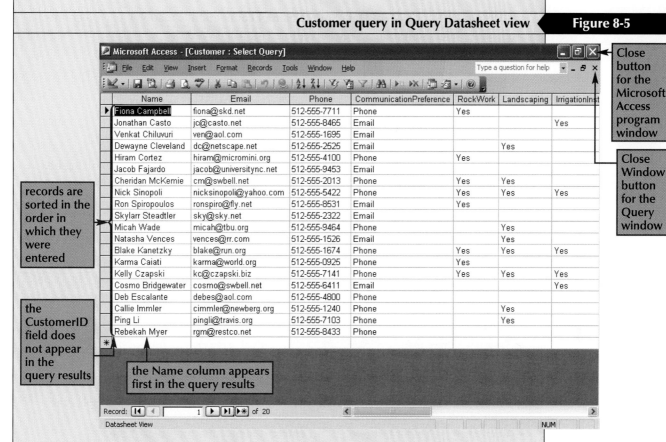

4. Click the **Close Window** button [×] on the menu bar to close the Query window.

5. Click the **Close** button [×] on the Access title bar to close both the requests database and Access.

Now that you have examined the requests database, you can begin the process of importing it into the garden Web site so you can create Web pages that are connected to the database.

Creating a Database Connection

You can import an existing database into a Web site by copying the database file in Windows Explorer and then pasting it into the open Web site in Folders view. This method is an easy way to integrate an existing database into a Web site because FrontPage creates the database connection for you. By creating a connection between a Web site and an Access database, you can display and query database data using a Web page. A **database connection** specifies the name, location, and type of database that you want to access. You can make four kinds of database connections between a FrontPage Web site and an Access database:

• A **file-based connection** is made when you copy and paste (import) an Access database into a FrontPage Web site. FrontPage creates the database connection automatically when you import a database into it.

- A **System DSN** (or **System Data Source Name**) **connection** is made when you connect a database that is stored on a Web server to a FrontPage Web site.
- A **network connection** is made to a database server, which is a server that is dedicated to managing a database. Microsoft SQL Server is one example of a database server. (Database servers are beyond the scope of this tutorial.)
- A **custom connection** is one in which you use a file that contains the commands to define the necessary connection information between the database and the FrontPage Web site. (Creating a custom connection is beyond the scope of this tutorial.)

When you paste a database into a Web site, the Add Database Connection dialog box opens and requests a connection name for the database. After you provide a connection name and click the Yes button to continue, a Microsoft FrontPage dialog box opens and asks where to store your database files. When you import a database, FrontPage automatically creates a folder named **fpdb** (for FrontPage database) and configures it so that it is inaccessible to visitors of your published Web site.

| Reference Window | **Importing an Access Database into a Web Site** |

- Click the Start button on the taskbar, point to All Programs, point to Accessories, and then click Windows Explorer.
- Browse to the database that you want to import into the Web site, right-click it to open the shortcut menu, and then click Copy.
- Close Windows Explorer.
- Start FrontPage and then open the Web site in Folders view. If necessary, display the Folder List.
- Right-click the Folder List to open the shortcut menu, and then click Paste.
- Enter the database connection name, click the Yes button, and then click the Yes button again.

Brett asks you to import the requests database into the garden Web site. First, you will copy the requests database. Then you will start FrontPage, open the garden Web site, and paste the database into it.

To import an existing database into a Web site:

1. Click the **Start** button on the taskbar, point to **All Programs**, point to **Accessories**, and then click **Windows Explorer**. Windows Explorer opens and displays the files and folders on your computer.

2. Open the drive and folder that contains your Data Files.

3. Open the **Tutorial.08\Tutorial** folder to display its contents.

4. Right-click **requests.mdb** (or **requests** if Windows is configured to hide filename extensions) to open its shortcut menu, and then click **Copy**. A copy of the requests database is stored on the Windows Clipboard. You will close Windows Explorer before starting FrontPage.

5. Click the **Close** button ☒ on the Windows Explorer title bar to close it.

6. Start FrontPage, open the **garden** Web site from the server, and then if necessary, change to Folders view and display the Folder List.

   Trouble? Make sure that you see the path to the server-based Web site (such as http://localhost/garden) in the FrontPage title bar before continuing. If you see a disk location, such as C:\Inetpub\wwwroot\garden, in the FrontPage title bar, you opened the disk-based Web site instead of the server-based Web site. Click File on the menu bar, click

Close Site, and then repeat Step 6 to open the Web site stored on the server. If you use the disk-based Web site to complete this tutorial, your Web site will not work correctly.

7. Right-click the Web site's root folder in the Folder List (the default folder is http://localhost/garden) to open the shortcut menu, and then click **Paste**. The Importing Files dialog box opens, and then the Add Database Connection dialog box opens on top of it. See Figure 8-6. You use the Add Database Connection dialog box to provide a name for the database connection. The URL for the database is its Windows filename. You can use the same connection name and URL for a database, although you need not do so.

Add Database Connection dialog box   Figure 8-6

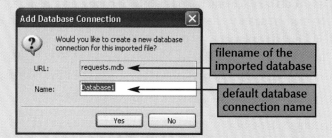

filename of the imported database

default database connection name

8. Type **Requests** in the Name text box, and then click the **Yes** button. The Importing Files dialog box becomes visible again, and the status bar indicates that FrontPage is creating the fpdb folder in which to store the database file. After a few seconds, a dialog box opens and asks whether you want to store your database file in the fpdb folder.

Trouble? If a Microsoft FrontPage dialog box opens and tells you that the database name must be unique, then a database connection named Requests already exists in your Web site. Click the OK button, change the database connection name to Requests1 (or to another name that is not in use), and then click the Yes button to continue.

9. Click the **Yes** button. After a few seconds, the Importing Files dialog box closes. The fpdb folder that FrontPage created is added to the Folder List (you might need to scroll down the Folder List to see it). In addition, FrontPage created a file named global.asa, which also appears in the Folder List. This file stores the VBScript that connects the Web site to the requests database. A **VBScript** is a program written in the Visual Basic programming language that contains programming instructions for a Web page. The VBScript is embedded in the HTML document in which it resides so that Web browsers can read and execute its commands.

Trouble? If you do not see the Web site's hidden folders in the Folder List, click Tools on the menu bar, click Site Settings, click the Advanced tab, click the Show hidden files and folders check box to add a check mark to it, click the OK button, and then click the Yes button.

10. Click the **fpdb** folder in the Folder List to display its contents in the Contents pane. The requests database is stored in this folder.

11. If necessary, scroll up the Folder List and click the root folder to display its contents again.

The requests database is stored in the Web site, but you cannot use it until you verify the database connection.

Verifying a Database Connection

After importing the database, you must use the Site Settings dialog box to verify the database connection. When you **verify** a database connection, FrontPage tests the connection to ensure that it is properly configured.

| Reference Window | **Verifying a Database Connection** |

- Click Tools on the menu bar, click Site Settings, and then click the Database tab.
- Click the connection name in the list box, and then click the Verify button.
- Click the OK button.

You'll verify the database connection next.

To verify the database connection:

▶ **1.** Click **Tools** on the menu bar, click **Site Settings**, and then click the **Database** tab. A question mark appears in the Status column for the Requests database connection, indicating that the database connection has not yet been verified.

▶ **2.** Click the **Requests** database connection, and then click the **Verify** button. The question mark in the Status column changes to a green check mark, indicating a valid connection. See Figure 8-7.

| Figure 8-7 ▶ | **Site Settings dialog box** |

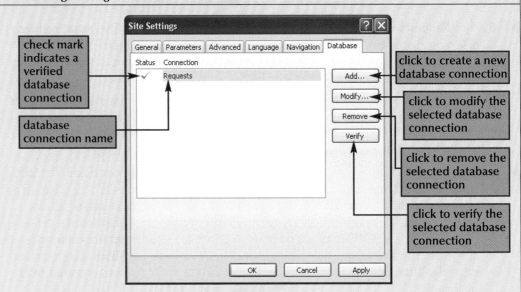

▶ **3.** Click the **OK** button to close the Site Settings dialog box.

The requests database now exists on the server as part of the garden Web site; it also exists as a separate file in the Tutorial.08\Tutorial folder included with your Data Files. These two files have the same name, but they are not linked in any way. As a result, if you open the requests database from the Tutorial.08\Tutorial folder included with your Data Files and make changes to it, the requests database that is stored in the garden Web site will not include these changes. After you import a database into a Web site, it is important that you make changes only to the database that is stored in the fpdb folder in the Web site. To start Access and open the database stored in the Web site, just double-click the database filename in the fpdb folder.

Now that you have imported the requests database into the garden Web site and verified its database connection, you can create a new Web page and use the Database Results Wizard to display the Customer query in the requests database in a Web page.

Setting the Web Site to Run Scripts

Before you can use the Database Results Wizard, the Web site must be enabled to run Active Server Pages (ASP). An **Active Server Page** is a Web page with an .asp filename extension that includes client-side and server-side scripts that process the page. Because these scripts must run on the server, you must also configure your Web site's folder to run scripts. A folder on a Web server that permits the execution of scripts is called an **executable folder**.

Setting a Web Site to Run Scripts

- Open the Web site in Folders view.
- Click Tools on the menu bar, and then click Page Options.
- Click the Authoring tab to display those settings.
- If necessary, click the ActiveX controls and VBScript check boxes to select them, and then click the OK button.
- Right-click the Web site's root folder in the Folder List (the default folder is http://localhost/[Web folder name]) to open the shortcut menu, and then click Properties.
- Click the Allow scripts to be run check box to add a check mark to it.
- Click the Allow files to be browsed check box to add a check mark to it.
- Click the OK button.

You will change the garden Web site's settings before using the Database Results Wizard to create the page. Normally, only the Web site's administrator can change a Web site's settings. If you are working on a server other than a Microsoft IIS, your instructor will provide you with alternative instructions.

To change the Web site's settings to run scripts:

▶ 1. Click **Tools** on the menu bar, and then click **Page Options**. The Page Options dialog box opens.

▶ 2. Click the **Authoring** tab to display those settings.

▶ 3. Make sure that your Authoring tab matches the one shown in Figure 8-8. If your Web site is enabled to support SharePoint Services, the ActiveX controls check box might contain a check mark but will be dimmed out (as shown in Figure 8-8). If your Web site does not support SharePoint Services, then the ActiveX controls check box will be selected and active. Either of these settings is correct.

Figure 8-8 | **Authoring tab settings for the garden Web site**

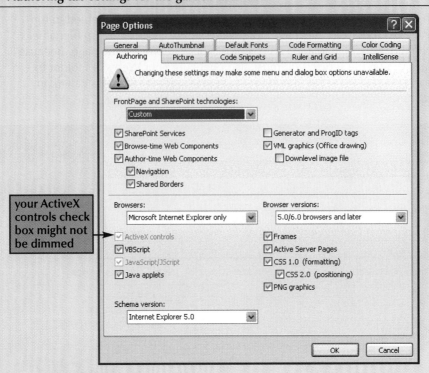

your ActiveX controls check box might not be dimmed

4. Click the **OK** button to close the Page Options dialog box. You also need to configure the Web site's root folder to allow scripts to be run.

5. Right-click the Web site's root folder in the Folder List to open the shortcut menu, and then click **Properties**. The Properties dialog box for the garden Web site opens.

6. If necessary, click the **Allow scripts to be run** and the **Allow files to be browsed** check boxes to add check marks to them, and then click the **OK** button. The Properties dialog box closes.

Now the Web site is configured to run scripts. Next, you will insert the Database Results region into a new Web page.

Inserting a Database Results Region into a Web Page

When you insert data from a database into a Web page, FrontPage calls it a Database Results region. A **Database Results region** is a component in a Web page that contains HTML tags and client-side and server-side scripts that retrieve and display database data in the Web page. After you insert the Database Results region, the Database Results Wizard starts. The **Database Results Wizard** asks you a series of questions about the database, the database object to be inserted, and special filters (if any) to be applied to that database object. A **filter** is a set of restrictions that you place on the records in a table or query to display a subset of a table's or query's records. For example, a filter might display records that contain the value TX in a State field to select only records for people who live in Texas. A filter differs from a query in that a filter only *temporarily* displays a subset of data.

Creating a Database Results Region in a Web Page

- Open the existing page in which to insert the Database Results region in Design view, or create a new page in Design view.
- Position the insertion point where you want to insert the Database Results region.
- Click Insert on the menu bar, point to Database, and then click Results. The Database Results Wizard starts.
- Click the Use an existing database connection option button, and then, if necessary, click the list arrow and select the database connection name. Click the Next button.
- Click the Record source option button, click the list arrow, click the object in the database that contains the data you want to display, and then click the Next button.
- If necessary, click the Edit List button to select and/or reorder the desired fields to display in the Web page, and then click the OK button. To apply a filter to the records, click the More Options button, use the More Options dialog box to create the filter, and then click the OK button. Click the Next button.
- Select a formatting option for displaying the data, and then click the Next button.
- Select an option for displaying returned records in the Web page, and then click the Finish button.

After inserting a Database Results region into a Web page, you can change its properties to customize its default appearance to meet your needs.

To insert a Database Results region into a new Web page:

▶ 1. Close the Folder List, and then click the **Create a new normal page** button ▫ on the Standard toolbar to create a new page and open it in Design view. The new page uses the background picture from the Web site's theme, the Web site's shared borders, and has the filename new_page_1.htm.

   Trouble? If the Layout Tables and Cells task pane opens, click the Close button ☒ to close it.

▶ 2. Click **Insert** on the menu bar, point to **Database**, and then click **Results**. The Database Results Wizard starts. FrontPage selects the Requests database for your Database Results region because the Requests database connection is the only one in the Web site. See Figure 8-9.

Using an existing database connection | Figure 8-9

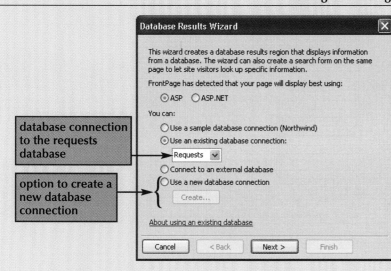

database connection to the requests database

option to create a new database connection

3. Click the **Next** button. The second dialog box lets you specify the database object that contains the data to be used in the Web page. The requests database contains two objects: the Customer Requests table and the Customer query (which appears in the list box as "Customer (VIEW)"). The Customer query is selected in the Record source list box because it is first alphabetically in the list of objects. If you don't find a suitable object in the list, you can open the database from the fpdb folder of the Web site and use Access to create the correct object, or you can click the Custom query option button and click the Edit button to create a query using SQL. You will use the existing Customer query object as the record source.

4. Make sure that **Customer (VIEW)** is selected in the Record source list box, and then click the **Next** button. The third dialog box lets you specify the fields to include in the Web page, their order, and an optional filter, as shown in Figure 8-10.

Figure 8-10	Selecting and ordering the fields to use in the Database Results region

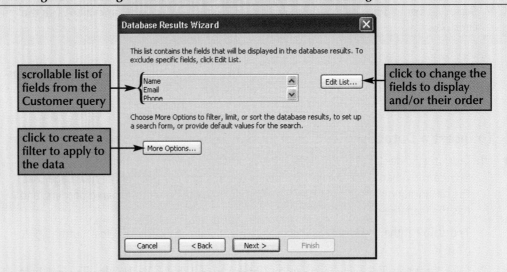

Brett wants the person's phone number to be displayed in the second column of the Database Results region, so you need to change the field order.

5. Click the **Edit List** button. The Displayed Fields dialog box opens. All fields from the Customer query appear in the Displayed fields list box, as shown in Figure 8-11.

Figure 8-11	Displayed Field dialog box

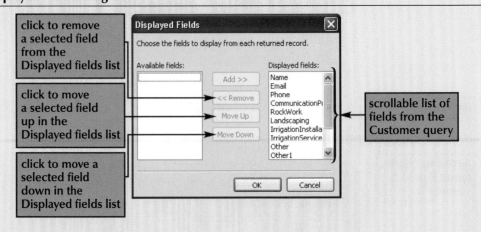

6. Click the **Phone** field in the Displayed fields list box, and then click the **Move Up** button. Now the Phone field appears as the second entry in the list.

7. Click the **OK** button to close the Displayed Fields dialog box. You will not create a filter for the database region, so click the **Next** button to go to the next dialog box. See Figure 8-12. In this dialog box, you select the formatting options to use in the Web page. The default settings are to display one record from the database object in each row, to format the table in the results page using a border and a header row with the object's field names, and to expand the table to the width of the page. You will accept these settings.

Selecting the formatting options for the Database Results region Figure 8-12

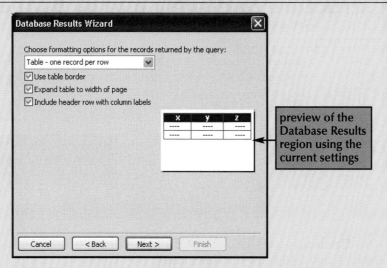

preview of the Database Results region using the current settings

8. Make sure that your settings match the ones shown in Figure 8-12, and then click the **Next** button. The last dialog box lets you set the number of records to display in the results page. The default is to group five records on each results page. You will choose the option to display all records together so users won't need to scroll through the different pages to view the records.

9. If necessary, click the **Display all records together** option button to select it, click the **Finish** button, and then scroll to the beginning of the page. The Web page now contains a Database Results region, as shown in Figure 8-13.

Figure 8-13 | Database Results region in the Web page

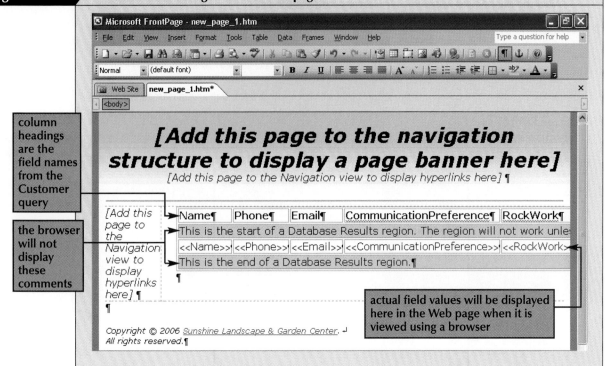

column headings are the field names from the Customer query

the browser will not display these comments

actual field values will be displayed here in the Web page when it is viewed using a browser

The Database Results region created a table in the Web page. Each column in the table represents one field in the Customer query.

Saving and Previewing the Database Results Region

FrontPage used the fonts and styles from the Web site's theme to format the Database Results region. Before previewing the page in the browser, you must save the page.

To save the Web page and preview it in the browser:

1. Click the **Save** button 🖫 on the Standard toolbar. The Save As dialog box opens.

2. Make sure that the **garden** folder appears in the Save in list box, and then type **cust_qry** in the File name text box.

3. Click the **Save as type** list arrow, and then click **ASP Files**. If Windows is configured to show filename extensions, you'll notice that the filename extension .asp is added to the new page, indicating that it is an Active Server Page.

4. Click the **Save** button.

5. Click the **Preview** button 🖾 on the Standard toolbar to open the page in a browser. Each record appears in a row of the table, and all records are displayed in the Web page. See Figure 8-14.

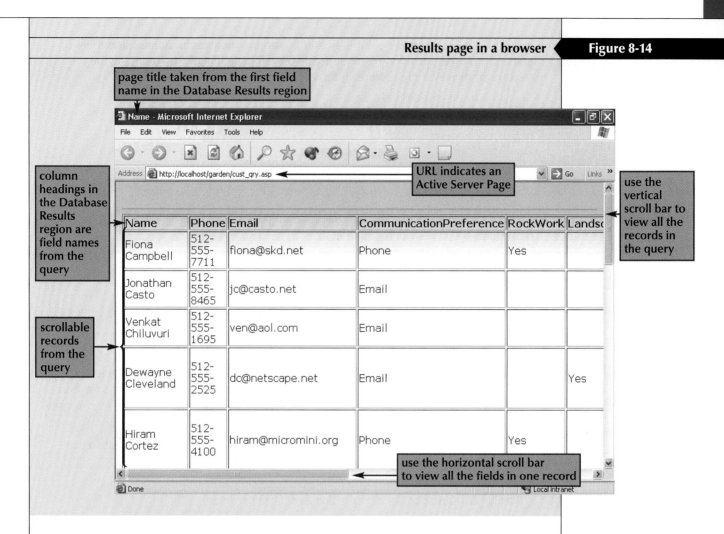

page title taken from the first field name in the Database Results region

column headings in the Database Results region are field names from the query

scrollable records from the query

URL indicates an Active Server Page

use the vertical scroll bar to view all the records in the query

use the horizontal scroll bar to view all the fields in one record

Notice that the Phone column appears as the second column, as you specified using the Wizard. Because you grouped all of the records together, you can use the browser's scroll bars to view them. If you had selected the option to group records, you would see the number of records you specified (for example, five records), and a navigation bar at the bottom of the page so you could scroll to the next group of records, to the previous group of records, or to the first or last group of records.

To scroll the records:

1. Use your browser's horizontal scroll bar to view all of the data for the first record, and then scroll back to the beginning of the first record.

2. Use your browser's vertical scroll bar to scroll to the last record.

3. Close your browser.

After seeing the data, you suggest to Brett that you can improve the appearance of this page. First, you consider the page's title of "Name," which is the first field name displayed in the Database Results region. You can change the page's title in Folders view to "Customer Requests" to better reflect the page's content. Second, you note that the column headings for the Database Results region are the field names from the Customer query. You can change these column headings to more meaningful names, and then format them just as you would any other text in a Web page. Finally, by reducing the font size you can display more records in the browser window at the same time.

Changing the Page Title and Formatting the Database Results Region

Brett asks you to address the issues that you previously identified.

To change the page title and format the Database Results region:

1. In FrontPage, change to Folders view.

2. Right-click **cust_qry.asp** in the Contents pane to select the page and to open the shortcut menu, click **Rename**, and then press the **Tab** key to select the page's title and change to editing mode.

3. Type **Customer Requests** and then press the **Enter** key.

4. Click the **cust_qry.asp** tab on the Contents pane to return to the Customer Requests page in Design view.

   Red, wavy lines appear below some of the column headings, indicating that these words are not in the FrontPage dictionary. You can right-click a column heading to open a shortcut menu for the Spelling dialog box and then click a suggested replacement. Alternatively, you can edit a column heading just like any other text in the page.

5. Click to the left of the word "Preference," and then press **Shift + Enter** to create a line break and move the word "Preference" to the second line.

6. Scrolling the page as necessary, repeat Step 5 to change the headings "RockWork," "IrrigationInstallation," and "IrrigationService" to two lines.

7. Scroll to the beginning of the page, use the ➡ pointer to select the first row in the Database Results region (the one that contains the column headings), click the **Style** list arrow on the Formatting toolbar, and then click **Heading 5**. The column headings change to the Heading 5 style for the theme.

8. With the column headings still selected, click the **Center** button ▤ on the Formatting toolbar to center the headings.

9. Select the third row (which contains the field names from the database, enclosed in angle brackets), click the **Font Size** list arrow on the Formatting toolbar, and then click **2 (10 pt)**. You changed the data displayed in the Database Results region to 10 points.

   The last formatting change you will make is to increase the width of some columns to make the displayed data easier to read. You can do this by using the Distribute Columns Evenly command. Unlike in a regular table, applying this command to a Database Results region will resize each column to make it wide enough to display the data it contains.

10. Select the first row in the Database Results region, click **Table** on the menu bar, and then click **Distribute Columns Evenly**.

11. Save the page and then preview it in a browser. Figure 8-15 shows a portion of the Web page and the new title, column headings, and formatting.

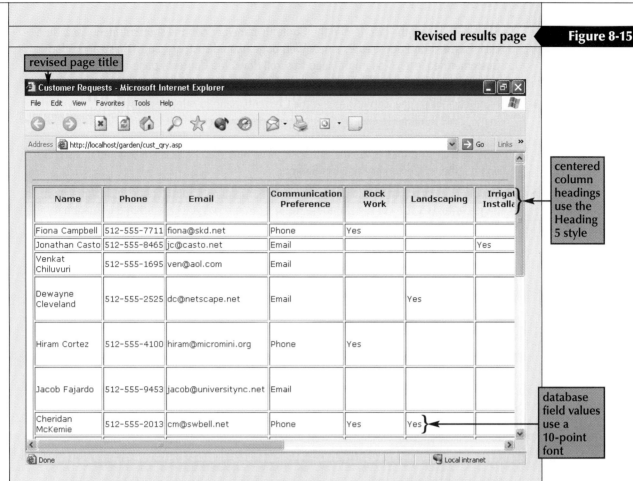

revised page title

centered column headings use the Heading 5 style

database field values use a 10-point font

Trouble? If the phone numbers are displayed on two lines, close your browser, and then repeat Steps 10 and 11.

In addition to displaying all of the records from a database object, such as a query, you might want to let users search for specific records within an object. You can do so by creating a page that contains a Database Results region and a search form.

Using a Web Page to Query a Database

Brett asks you to create another Web page to display only those records from the Customer query that match a category entered by the user. Instead of re-creating the Database Results region, you will copy the existing Customer Requests Web page, rename its filename and title, and then create a search form in the new page.

To create a copy of a Web page and change its filename and title:

1. Close your browser, and then click the **Close** button ⊠ on the Contents pane to close the Customer Requests page.

2. In Folders view, right-click **cust_qry.asp** to open the shortcut menu, and then click **Copy**.

▶ **3.** Right-click below the last item in the Contents pane to open the shortcut menu, and then click **Paste**. FrontPage creates a new Web page named cust_qry_copy(1).asp and titled Customer Requests. (You might need to scroll down the Contents pane to see the new file-name.) You will rename this page, and then open it in Design view.

▶ **4.** Right-click **cust_qry_copy(1).asp** in the Contents pane to select it and to open the shortcut menu, click **Rename** to change to editing mode, type **custsrch.asp**, press the **Tab** key to select the page title and change to editing mode, press the **End** key, press the **spacebar**, type **Search**, and then press the **Enter** key. The new Web page is now named custsrch.asp, and its title is "Customer Requests Search."

▶ **5.** Double-click **custsrch.asp** to open the Customer Requests Search page in Design view. This page contains a copy of the Database Results region that you created in the Customer Requests page.

Now that you have copied and renamed the page, you can run the Database Results Wizard again to create the search form.

Creating a Search Form to Query a Database

The search form that you will create to let users query the database is similar to the search form used to search a Web site for keywords. You must run the Database Results Wizard again to create the search form. FrontPage will program the search form to query the data-base using the object from the database that you specify.

Reference Window	**Creating a Search Form in a Web Page That Queries a Database**

- Open the existing page that contains a Database Results region, right-click the yellow Database Results region to open the shortcut menu, and then click Database Results Properties. If necessary, click the OK button in the message box that opens. The Database Results Wizard starts.

or

- Create a new Web page, click Insert on the menu bar, point to Database, and then click Results. The Database Results Wizard starts.
- Confirm or set the options in the first two dialog boxes.
- In the third dialog box, click the More Options button. The More Options dialog box opens.
- Click the Criteria button to open the Criteria dialog box.
- Click the Add button. The Add Criteria dialog box opens.
- Select the field name and comparison operator to use in the query.
- If necessary, click the Use this search form field check box to add a check mark to it.
- Click the OK button. Click the Add button to specify additional criteria (if necessary), or click the OK button to close the Criteria dialog box.
- Click the OK button to close the More Options dialog box.
- Confirm or set the options in the remaining dialog boxes, and then click the Finish button.

Brett wants to create a search form that identifies customers based on their location so he can get a sense of where his customers are. This information will be useful as he con-siders adding a delivery service to his business, so that customers with orders totaling a certain dollar amount can ask for their purchases to be delivered. To search for customers based on their locations, you need to set the Location field as the search field.

To create a search form in a page that queries a database:

1. Right-click either yellow row in the Database Results region to open the shortcut menu, and then click **Database Results Properties**. The Database Results Wizard starts.

   Trouble? If a message box opens and tells you that you are re-entering the Database Results Wizard, click the OK button.

2. Click the **Next** button twice to advance to the third dialog box.

3. Click the **More Options** button. The More Options dialog box opens.

4. Click the **Criteria** button. The Criteria dialog box opens.

5. Click the **Add** button. The Add Criteria dialog box opens, as shown in Figure 8-16.

Creating a search form field for a Database Results region **Figure 8-16**

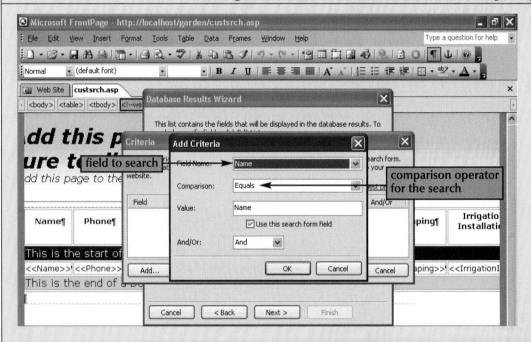

You need to specify the Location field as the search field. Stated in FrontPage language, you must specify that *Location equals Location*, which means that only those records containing a Location field value that matches the one entered by the user in the search text box will be displayed in the results page.

6. Click the **Field Name** list arrow, and then scroll down as necessary and click **Location**. The Comparison list box displays the "Equals" operator and the Value text box displays the value "Location."

7. If necessary, click the **Use this search form field** check box to add a check mark to it, and then click the **OK** button. The Add Criteria dialog box closes, and the Criteria dialog box displays the filter criterion, as shown in Figure 8-17. You could specify additional criteria by clicking the Add button again. However, Brett needs to search using only the Location field, so you can finish the Database Results Wizard now.

Figure 8-17	Criteria dialog box

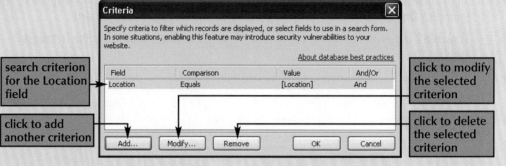

8. Click the **OK** button to close the Criteria dialog box, click the **OK** button to close the More Options dialog box, click the **Next** button twice, click the **Finish** button, and then scroll to the beginning of the page. The Database Results Wizard closes, and the Customer Requests Search page now displays the search form, as shown in Figure 8-18.

Figure 8-18	Customer Requests Search page

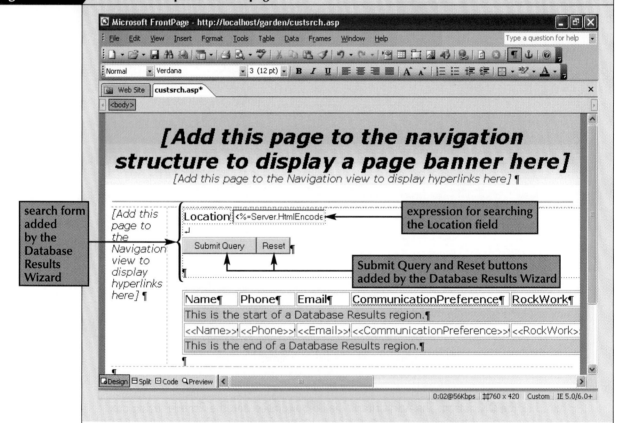

When you ran the Database Results Wizard for the second time, it reset the column headings in the Database Results region to their field-name equivalents from the query. Therefore, you will need to update the formatting and column headings to the same specifications you made when you ran the Database Results Wizard the first time.

To change and format the column heading names:

▶ **1.** Change the CommunicationPreference, RockWork, IrrigationInstallation, and IrrigationService column headings so they contain a line break between words.

▶ **2.** Select the row containing the column headings, change its style to Heading 5, and then click the **Center** button ≣ on the Formatting toolbar.

▶ **3.** Select the third row of the Database Results region (with the field names), and then change its font size to 10 points.

▶ **4.** Select the row containing the column headings, click **Table** on the menu bar, and then click **Distribute Columns Evenly** to set the columns to fit the data.

▶ **5.** Repeat Step 4 to set the columns a second time.

▶ **6.** Save the custsrch.asp page.

You can test the search form by opening it in a browser.

To test the database search form:

▶ **1.** Preview the custsrch.asp page in a browser. Figure 8-19 shows the revised page with the new search form. To list the customers in a specific location, you need to type that location in the text box.

Customer Requests Search page in a browser ◀ **Figure 8-19**

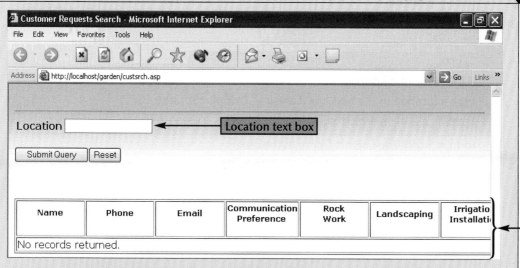

▶ **2.** Click the **Location** text box, and then type **Lakeway**.

▶ **3.** Click the **Submit Query** button. The browser displays seven records that match your request. Each record contains the value "Lakeway" in the Location field. (You'll need to scroll the results to see the Location field.)

Trouble? If an AutoComplete dialog box opens and asks whether you would like to turn on this feature, click the No button.

Trouble? If the "No records returned." message still appears after you click the Submit Query button, make sure that you typed the location name ("Lakeway") correctly in the Location text box. If you typed the location name correctly and you still do not see any records, ask your instructor or technical support person for help.

4. Select the text in the Location text box, type **Dripping Springs**, and then click the **Submit Query** button. The browser displays a message that no records were returned, even though there are customers located in Dripping Springs. The reason that these records weren't included in the results is because the form stores the value "DrippingSprings," without the space between words, instead of "Dripping Springs." Your search expression must *exactly* match the stored value or the search will not display the correct records. As you note this problem, you tell Brett that there are many ways to improve this form so it is easier to use. For example, you might change the Location text box to a drop-down menu that contains the valid choices or provide instructions so users know how to query the database.

5. Delete the space between the words "Dripping" and "Springs" in the Location text box, and then click the **Submit Query** button. This time, the browser displays three records containing the value "DrippingSprings" in the Location field.

Brett asks you to add some instructions for using this page so its users will know what the valid Location values are. You can add the instruction text to the page in Design view.

To add text to the Customer Requests Search page:

1. Close your browser.

2. Press **Ctrl + Home** to move the insertion point to the top of the page, and then press the **Enter** key to insert a paragraph. The insertion point appears in the new paragraph.

3. Type the following text in the new paragraph, adding a line break (Shift + Enter) at the end of the first and second lines:

   Type a location in the text box (Lakeway, DrippingSprings,

   Austin, LagoVista, WestLakeHills, RoundRock, or Other),

   and then click the Submit Query button.

4. Save the page and then preview it in a browser. Figure 8-20 shows the revised page.

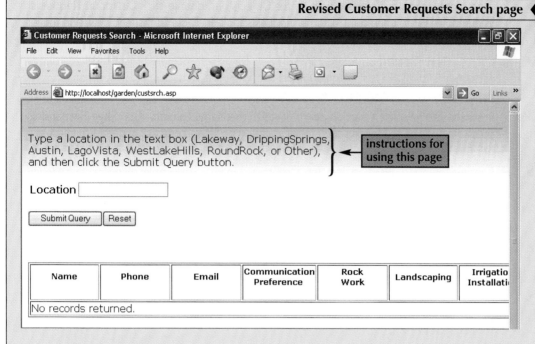

5. Close your browser.

Because of the database connection, any changes made to the data in the Customer query will be reflected in the Customer Requests and Customer Requests Search pages. This means that as new customers use the form in the Requests Web page to request services from Sunshine, the Web page will display their records as well. Next, you will update the database and use the same Web page to view the changes.

Updating a Database and Viewing the Changes in a Web Page

As more people visit the nursery's Web site, more names will be added to the Customer Requests table in the requests database. Brett wants to ensure that the Customer Requests and Customer Requests Search Web pages always reflect the most current data in the database, not the data as it existed when you originally created the Web pages that display the database data. As long as the changes are made in the database that is stored in the Web site, any Web page that uses the database connection will always reflect the most up-to-date data. If you add, change, or delete records in the database, the Web pages that use the database connection will also reflect these changes. Next, you will add a record to the Customer Requests table in Access to simulate the addition of a record by the database connection.

To add a record to the Customer Requests table:

1. Click the **Web Site** tab to change to Folders view, and then double-click the **fpdb** folder in the Contents pane to open it.

2. Double-click **requests.mdb** in the Contents pane. Microsoft Access starts and opens the requests database from the server. You will open the Customer Requests table and add a new record to it.

Trouble? If a Security dialog box opens, click the Open button.

▶ **3.** If necessary, click the **Tables** object on the Objects bar, double-click **Customer Requests** in the tables list to open the Customer Requests table in Table Datasheet view, and then maximize the Table window.

▶ **4.** Click the **New Record** button ▶ on the Table Datasheet toolbar. The current record indicator moves to row 21, the (AutoNumber) text in the CustomerID field is selected, and Access is ready to accept a new record.

▶ **5.** Press the **Tab** key. The insertion point moves to the Name column. Type **Skye Hernandez**, press the **Tab** key to move to the Email column, type **skye@comcast.org**, and then press the **Tab** key to move to the Phone column.

▶ **6.** Continue entering data and pressing the **Tab** key to enter the entire record with the following data: Phone: **512-555-8751**; CommuncationPreference: **Email**; IrrigationInstallation: **Yes**; Location: **LagoVista**; and Visits: **8**. The other columns in the record for Skye will be blank to indicate a "no" response.

▶ **7.** Press the **Tab** key until you return to the selected AutoNumber field in a new row to save the record in the table. The navigation bar at the bottom of the Table window now displays "Record 22 of 22" and "(AutoNumber)" is selected in row 22.

▶ **8.** Click the **Close** button ⊠ on the Access program window title bar to close the table, the requests database, and Access.

Next, you will open the Customer Requests Search page in a browser to confirm that the new record you added to the Customer Requests table appears in the Web page.

To view the new database record in the Web page:

▶ **1.** Click the **custsrch.asp** tab at the top of the Contents pane to return to the Customer Requests Search page in Design view.

▶ **2.** Click the **Preview** button 🔍 on the Standard toolbar to open the Customer Requests Search page in the browser.

▶ **3.** Click the **Location** text box, type **LagoVista**, and then click the **Submit Query** button. The new record for Skye Hernandez appears in the search results, so you know that the database was updated. See Figure 8-21.

New record in the Customer Requests Search page ◀ **Figure 8-21**

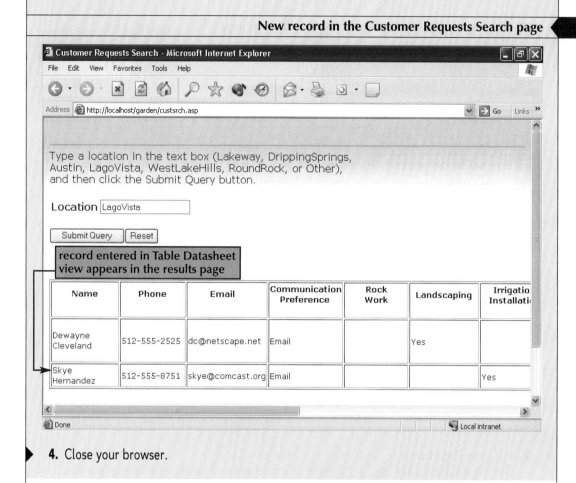

4. Close your browser.

Note: After you close the garden Web site and reopen it, you will need to verify the database connection again for pages containing Database Results regions to work correctly.

Brett wants to examine the HTML document that created the search form and the Database Results region in the Customer Requests Search page.

Viewing the HTML Document for a Page with a Database Connection

The Customer Requests Search Web page contains complex HTML tags that create the querying capability for the Web page, the connection to the Access database, and the capability to display matching field values.

To view an HTML document that contains a database connection:

1. With the **custsrch.asp** page open in Design view, click the **Show Code View** button
   `⊡ Code` at the bottom of the Contents pane to display the HTML document for the page, and then scroll down the page until the opening <form> tag appears at the top of the Contents pane, as shown in Figure 8-22.

Figure 8-22   HTML document for the Customer Requests Search page

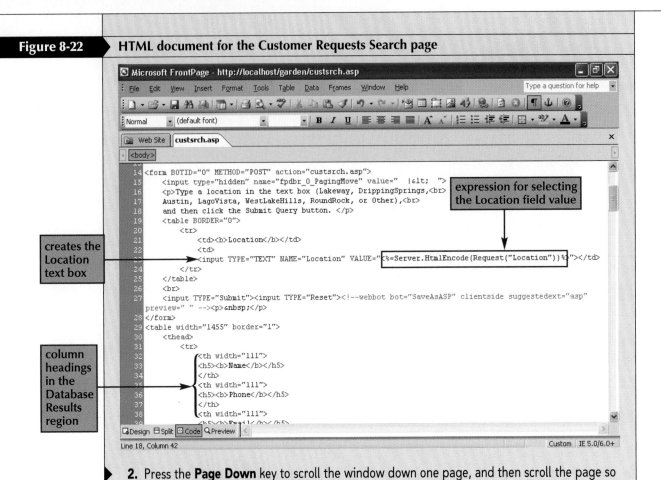

creates the Location text box

expression for selecting the Location field value

column headings in the Database Results region

▶ **2.** Press the **Page Down** key to scroll the window down one page, and then scroll the page so that the <SCRIPT> tag appears at the top of the Contents pane, as shown in Figure 8-23.

HTML document for the Customer Requests Search page, continued | **Figure 8-23**

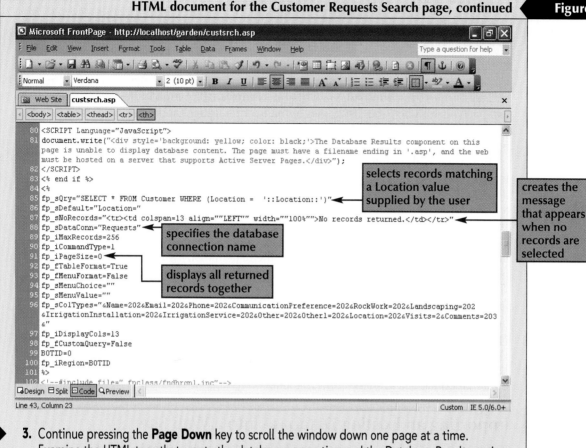

3. Continue pressing the **Page Down** key to scroll the window down one page at a time. Examine the HTML tags that create the database connection and the Database Results region.

4. After you have examined the entire HTML document, return to Design view, and then close the garden Web site and FrontPage.

In the next session, you will create a form into which site visitors can enter information that will be stored in a new database. You will also create a data access page to display the entered data.

Session 8.1 Quick Check

Review

1. What is a database connection?
2. Describe how to import a database into a FrontPage Web site.
3. What must you do before inserting a Database Results region into a Web page?
4. What is a Database Results region?
5. When you temporarily select a subset of records from a database table or query, you are using a(n) _____.
6. True or False: You cannot limit the number of records displayed in a Web page by a Database Results region.
7. True or False: You cannot change the properties of a Database Results region.
8. True or False: If you update a database that has a connection to a FrontPage Web site and is stored in the Web site, any Web pages that use the database connection will display the revised data from the database.

Session 8.2

Creating a Form for Data Input

Brett wants you to create a Web page in the garden Web site that will serve as an electronic guest book and let Web site visitors request promotional materials and advance notices of sales from Sunshine via e-mail or regular mail. A form in this new page will collect each visitor's first and last names, e-mail address, street address, city, state, zip code, and telephone number. The form will also include a form field that asks the visitor's preference for receiving materials via e-mail or regular mail.

The visitor will submit the form to the server, where it will be processed. The form results will be stored in an Access database, which will make the data accessible for many different needs. For example, Brett might use the mailing addresses and e-mail addresses to send printed promotional materials and electronic coupons, or use the phone numbers to contact customers for open-ended marketing research studies. By storing visitor data in an Access database, Brett gains the flexibility to produce reports about the data, query the database for specific records, and manage the data in many ways. These advantages are not easily realized when you collect a form's results in an HTML or text file.

When creating a new database connection, you have the option of importing an existing database into the Web site; in that case, FrontPage will create the database connection. Alternatively, you can use the Database tab in the Site Settings dialog box to add a new database connection to a database that exists on the same file system or server as the Web site. For the guest book, you will import an existing database into the Web site. After importing the database, you will import into the garden Web site a Web page created by Brett that contains a form for collecting data.

Importing an Existing Database into a Web Site

Brett's existing database is stored in the Tutorial.08\Tutorial folder included with your Data Files. The guest database contains one table named Results, which has the structure shown in Figure 8-24.

| Figure 8-24 | Results table design in the guest database |

Field Name	Data Type	Field Size	Description
ID	AutoNumber	Long Integer	An Access AutoNumber field that adds the ID. IDs are assigned sequentially as new records are added to the table.
FirstName	Text	35	The visitor's first name.
LastName	Text	35	The visitor's last name.
Address	Text	65	The visitor's street address.
City	Text	35	The visitor's city.
State	Text	10	The visitor's state.
Zip	Text	10	The visitor's zip code.
Phone	Text	15	The visitor's phone number, including the area code.
Email	Text	55	The visitor's e-mail address.
ReceiveEmail	Text	3	A Yes or No response indicating the visitor's preference to receive promotional materials via e-mail.
ReceiveMail	Text	3	A Yes or No response indicating the visitor's preference to receive promotional materials via regular mail.

To import the guest database into the garden Web site:

1. Start Windows Explorer, open the drive or folder that contains your Data Files, and then open the **Tutorial.08\Tutorial** folder to display its contents.

2. Right-click the **guest.mdb** file to open the shortcut menu, and then click **Copy**.

3. Close Windows Explorer.

4. Start FrontPage, open the **garden** Web site from the server, and then change to Folders view (if necessary). Because the fpdb folder already exists in the Web site, you can paste the file directly into that folder.

5. Double-click the **fpdb** folder in the Contents pane to display its contents, right-click any blank area of the Contents pane to open the shortcut menu, and then click **Paste**. The Importing Files dialog box opens, and then the Add Database Connection dialog box opens on top of it. You will create a database connection named Guest.

6. Type **Guest** in the Name text box, and then click the **Yes** button. The Importing Files dialog box becomes visible again for a few moments, and then it closes. The database is now stored in the fpdb folder of the garden Web site. You can verify the database connection by using the Site Settings dialog box.

7. Click **Tools** on the menu bar, click **Site Settings** to open the Site Settings dialog box, and then click the **Database** tab. The Requests database connection is shown with a verified status (a check mark), and the Guest database connection is shown with an unverified status (a question mark).

8. Click the **Guest** connection, and then click the **Verify** button. The question mark in the Status column changes to a check mark, indicating a valid connection. The garden Web site now has two valid database connections.

9. Click the **OK** button to close the Site Settings dialog box.

Now that you have pasted the guest database in the Web site and verified its database connection, you can use the database connection to send data from a Web page to the database. Brett already created a Web page named guestbk.asp that contains a form for collecting data. You will import this page into the Web site from the Tutorial.08\Tutorial folder included with your Data Files. Then you will configure the form to send data to the guest database.

To import the guestbk.asp Web page into the garden Web site:

1. Click the **Up One Level** button in the Contents pane to display the contents of the Web site's root folder, display the Folder List and make sure the root folder is selected, click **File** on the menu bar, and then click **Import**. The Import dialog box opens.

2. Click the **Add File** button. The Add File to Import List dialog box opens. You need to import the file from the Tutorial.08\Tutorial folder included with your Data Files.

3. If necessary, open the **Tutorial.08\Tutorial** folder, and then double-click **guestbk.asp**. The Import dialog box appears again with guestbk.asp selected.

4. Click the **OK** button to import the Guest Book Web page into the Web site. If necessary, scroll down the Folder List to see the imported file.

Now you can open the Guest Book Web page and set it so the server will send data collected from this Web page to the guest database. You must add this new page to Navigation view so that the page banner and link bar components will appear correctly.

To open the Guest Book Web page and add it to Navigation view:

1. Double-click **guestbk.asp** in the Folder List to open the Guest Book Web page in Design view. The placeholders at the top of the page remind you to add the page to Navigation view.

2. Click the **Web Site** tab, click the **Navigation View** button [Navigation] at the bottom of the Contents pane to change to Navigation view, and then scroll the navigation structure so you can see the Contact Sunshine page icon.

3. Drag the **guestbk.asp** page from the Folder List to the navigation structure, positioning the guestbk.asp page between the Contact Sunshine and Customer Requests page icons as shown in Figure 8-25.

Figure 8-25	Adding the Guest Book page to the navigation structure

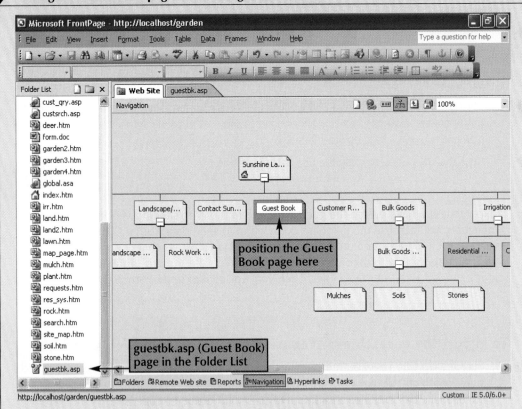

4. Close the Folder List, and then click the **guestbk.asp** tab to return to Design view. Now the page banner and link bar are correct, as shown in Figure 8-26.

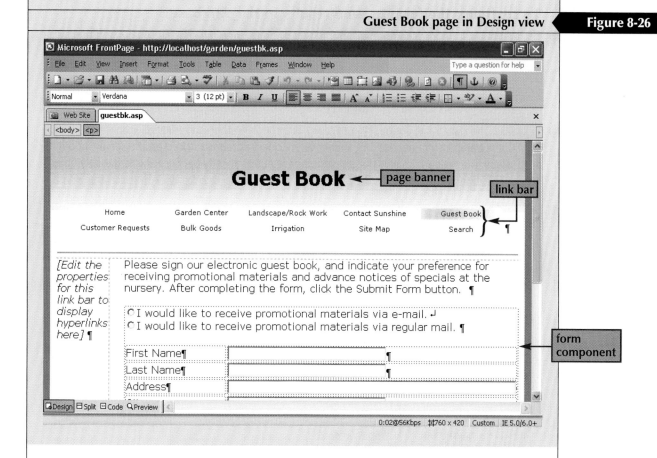

Configuring a Form to Send Results to a Database

Now you can configure the existing form to send its results to the guest database in the Web site.

Configuring a Form to Send Results to a Database	Reference Window

- Right-click the form component in the Web page to open the shortcut menu, and then click Form Properties.
- Click the Send to database option button, and then click the Options button.
- Click the Database Connection to Use list arrow, and then click the name of the database connection. If necessary, click the Table to hold form results list arrow and select the table in the database in which to store the form results.
- Click the Saved Fields tab, and then select the database column name that will store the data for each form field in the form component.
- Click the Additional Fields tab, and then select or remove any additional fields in which to store data.
- Click the OK button.

You'll configure the form to store its results in the Results table of the guest database.

To configure the form to send results to the database:

► 1. Right-click the form component in the Web page to open the shortcut menu, and then click **Form Properties**. The Form Properties dialog box opens.

► 2. Click the **Send to database** option button to select this form handler, and then click the **Options** button. The Options for Saving Results to Database dialog box opens. You need to select the Guest database connection.

► 3. Click the **Database Connection to Use** list arrow, and then click **Guest**. FrontPage uses the Guest database connection to connect to the guest database stored on the server, and it selects the Results table in the guest database automatically because this is the only object in the database. See Figure 8-27.

Figure 8-27	Options for Saving Results to Database dialog box

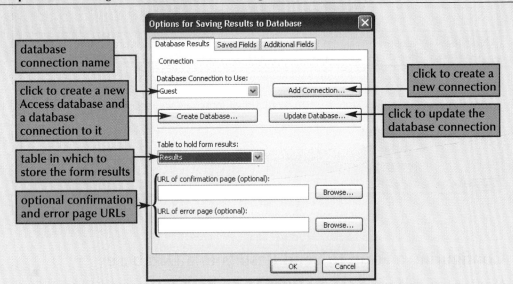

- database connection name
- click to create a new Access database and a database connection to it
- table in which to store the form results
- optional confirmation and error page URLs
- click to create a new connection
- click to update the database connection

► 4. Click the **Saved Fields** tab to display those settings, as shown in Figure 8-28. By default, FrontPage selected each field from the Results table in the guest database. Now you need to tell FrontPage the name of the database column in which to store the values. The values in the Form Field list are the form field names that Brett used when he created the form. For example, the form field name of the text box labeled "Address" is "Address."

Saved Fields for the Results table ◄ Figure 8-28

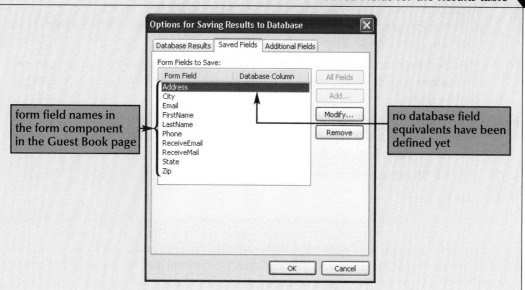

form field names in the form component in the Guest Book page

no database field equivalents have been defined yet

5. Double-click **Address** in the Form Field list. FrontPage connects to the database, reviews the Results table structure, and then opens the Modify Field dialog box. FrontPage selected the Address field in the Results table as the one in which to store form results from the Address field. This selection is correct—the Address form field in the Web page will send data to the Address field in the Results table in the guest database. If you need to change the field in which to save data, you could click the Save to database column list arrow and select a different field.

6. Make sure that **Address** is selected in the Save to database column list box, and then click the **OK** button to close the Modify Field dialog box. The Database Column value for the Address Form Field now displays the Address field. All of the database columns have the same names as the form fields in the form, so FrontPage should correctly select each database field in which to store the data.

7. Repeat Steps 5 and 6 to supply the Database Column value for each field in the database.

8. Click the **Additional Fields** tab to display those settings. See Figure 8-29.

Additional Fields tab ◄ Figure 8-29

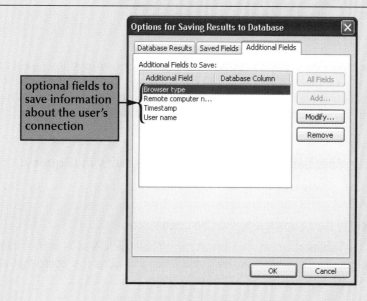

optional fields to save information about the user's connection

Brett doesn't want to save information about the visitor's browser type, his or her user name, or time data, so you will remove these fields from the form results. If you didn't remove these options, the database connection would automatically add these fields to the table structure in the database.

9. Make sure **Browser type** is selected in the Additional Fields to Save list box, and then click the **Remove** button. The Browser type field is deleted, and the Remote computer name field is selected.

10. Click the **Remove** button three times to remove the rest of the fields from the Additional Fields to Save list box, and then click the **OK** button to close the Options for Saving Results to Database dialog box.

11. Click the **OK** button in the Form Properties dialog box to close it.

12. Save the page.

Now you can open the Guest Book Web page in a browser and use it to submit a form to the server. You will examine the guest database to confirm that the server stored the form results as a record in the Results table.

To open the Web page in a browser and submit a form:

1. Click the **Preview** button 🔍 on the Standard toolbar.

2. Click the **I would like to receive promotional materials via e-mail** option button to select it.

3. Click the **First Name** text box, and then type **John**.

4. Press the **Tab** key to move to the Last Name text box, and then type **Samples**.

5. Continue pressing the **Tab** key to enter the following data in the text boxes: Address: **123 Main Street**; City: **Austin**; State: **TX**; Zip: **78704**; Home Phone: **512-555-4650**; and E-mail Address: **john@samples.com**.

6. Click the **Submit Form** button. The default Form Confirmation page opens and confirms that the information was correctly submitted to the server.

7. Click the **Return to the form** hyperlink to return to the Guest Book page. The form fields are cleared, and the page is ready to accept another form submission.

8. Close your browser.

When you submitted the Guest Book page to the server, the server used the Guest database connection that you defined in the garden Web site to send the form results to the guest database. You can open both Access and the guest database from FrontPage to make sure that the form results were correctly stored in the Results table.

To open the Access database and view the form results in a query:

1. Display the Folder List, double-click the **fpdb** folder to display its contents, and then double-click **guest.mdb**. Access starts and opens the guest database.

   Trouble? If a Security dialog box opens, click the Open button.

2. If necessary, click the **Tables** object in the Objects bar, double-click **Results** in the tables list, and then maximize the Table window. The Table window displays the record that you entered using the Guest Book Web page, as shown in Figure 8-30.

record added using the Guest Book page

3. Click the **Close Window** button ☒ on the menu bar to close the Table window. You return to the Database window.

The form you used to store data in the database only accepts user input. If you want to use a Web page to display data from the table on which the form is based, you must use Access to create a data access page.

Creating a Data Access Page

A **data access page** is a Web page that uses a form to display data from the Access table or query on which it is based. You use a data access page in the same way that you would use a form in an Access database. A data access page includes controls that let you add, delete, sort, filter, and change the records displayed. You need Internet Explorer 5.0 or higher (or Netscape Navigator 4.7x or higher) to display data access pages.

Sometimes a data access page is available only on an intranet, or it is stored in a hidden folder in a published Web site so that only authorized users can view its data. For example, in the garden Web site, site visitors should not be able to access the records stored in the Results table in the guest database.

You must use Access to create and format a data access page. You will save the data access page in the garden Web site.

Creating a Data Access Page | Reference Window

- Double-click the database in the fpdb folder in the Web site to start Access and open the database.
- Click the Pages object in the Objects bar of the Database window.
- Double-click Create data access page by using wizard in the pages list.
- Select the table or query on which to base the data access page, select the fields to include in the data access page, and then click the Next button.
- Select an optional grouping level, and then click the Next button.
- Use the drop-down list(s) to select an optional sort order, and then click the Next button.
- Either edit the suggested title or accept the default title, and then click the Finish button.
- Click the Save button on the Page Design toolbar, open the Web site in which to store the page, click the Save button, enter the page's filename, and then click the Save button.

Brett wants you to create a data access page that is based on the Results table. Then, instead of checking the records in the database by starting Access and opening the database and table, he can use the data access page stored in the garden Web site to check the records. Because the data access page will display customer information, you will set this page so that it is not published with the rest of the site on the server. The guest database is already open in Access, so you are ready to create the data access page.

To create a data access page:

▶ 1. Click the **Pages** object in the Objects bar of the Database window, and then double-click **Create data access page by using wizard** in the pages list. The Page Wizard starts and opens the first dialog box. In this dialog box, you can select the table or query in the current database that contains the fields you want to include in your data access page. Because only one object—the Results table—is stored in the guest database, the Tables/Queries list box is already set. The Available Fields list box shows all of the fields in the Results table. See Figure 8-31.

Figure 8-31	Using the Page Wizard to create a data access page

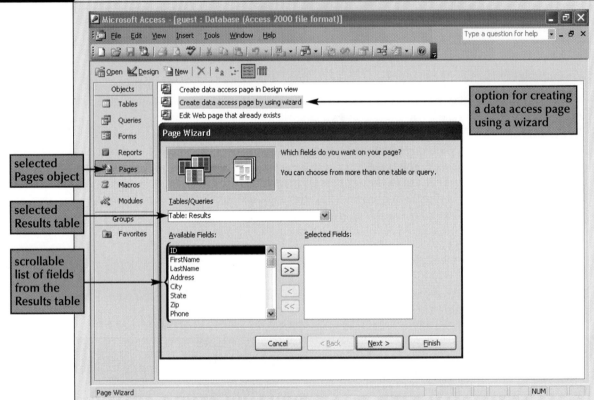

You'll select all fields in the Results table.

▶ 2. Click the >> button to move all available fields to the Selected Fields list box. Use the scroll bar to make sure that the following fields appear in the Selected Fields list box: ID, FirstName, LastName, Address, City, State, Zip, Phone, Email, ReceiveEmail, and ReceiveMail.

 Trouble? If any field besides those listed in Step 2 appears in the Selected Fields list box, click the extra field, and then click the < button to remove it. Repeat this process to remove all extra fields.

▶ 3. Click the **Next** button. The next dialog box asks you to specify an optional grouping level for the data. You will not group the data.

▶ 4. Click the **Next** button. The next dialog box asks you to specify an optional sort order for the data. Brett wants to sort the records alphabetically by last name.

▶ 5. Click the **list arrow** for the first list box, and then click **LastName**. See Figure 8-32. An ascending sort order is already specified, so you can continue to the next dialog box. (Clicking the Ascending button would change the sort order to Descending.)

Specifying the sort order for the data access page Figure 8-32

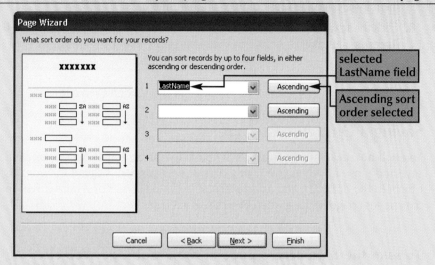

▶ **6.** Click the **Next** button. The final dialog box asks you for a page title. You will accept the default title of "Results."

▶ **7.** Make sure that the **Modify the page's design** option button is selected, and then click the **Finish** button. After a few seconds, Access creates the data access page and opens it in Page Design view. If necessary, click the **Maximize** button 🔲 on the Page Design window to maximize it, as shown in Figure 8-33.

Data access page in Page Design view | Figure 8-33

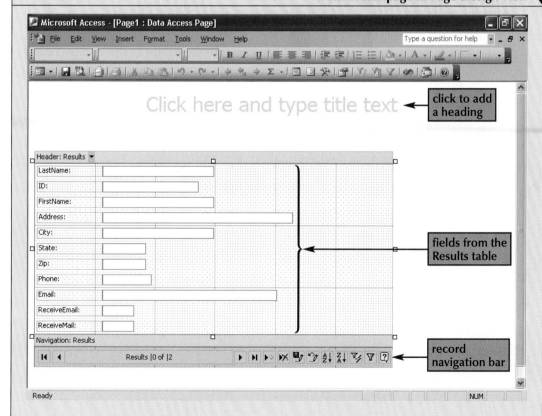

Trouble? If any other windows or toolbars are open in Page Design view, you can close them by clicking the Close buttons on their title bars.

8. Click the text at the top of the page (**Click here and type title text**), type **Guest Book Records**, and then click anywhere outside of the title to deselect it.

Now you can save the data access page in the garden Web site.

Saving a Data Access Page

You will not make any changes to the data access page that Access created, so you can save and close it. When you save a data access page, it is saved in two places: as an object in the database and as an HTML file on the server or a hard drive. You will save the data access page in the garden Web site on the server.

To save the data access page in the FrontPage Web site:

1. Click the **Save** button 🖫 on the Page Design toolbar to open the Save As Data Access Page dialog box.

2. Select the text in the File name text box, type the full path to the garden Web site on your server in the File name text box (the default is http://localhost/garden/), and then click the **Save** button. Access connects to the Web server and displays the contents of the garden Web site. Access suggests the filename Results.htm based on the object on which the data access page is based (the Results table).

   Trouble? If your Web site is stored in another location, type the path to the garden Web site on your server.

3. Select the text in the File name text box (if necessary), type **res_dap**, make sure that the Save as type list box is set to **Microsoft Data Access Pages**, and then click the **Save** button. Access saves the data access page as an object in the database and as an HTML file in the garden Web site.

   Trouble? If a dialog box opens and asks whether you want to set this folder as the default location for data access pages, click the No button.

   Trouble? If a dialog box opens and informs you that the page contains a connection string to an absolute path, click the OK button.

4. Click the **Close** button ☒ on the Access program window title bar to close the data access page, the guest database, and Access.

The data access page is stored in the garden Web site. You can now use FrontPage to open and format the data access page.

Modifying a Data Access Page in FrontPage

You stored the data access page in the garden Web site. You will use FrontPage to open this page so you can edit it. Brett wants you to change the HTML page title to "Guest Book Records," save the page, and then preview it in a browser.

To open the data access page in Design view, change the page title, and preview it in a browser:

1. Close the Folder List, click the **Web Site** tab, change to Folders view, and then click the **Refresh** button 🗿 on the Standard toolbar to refresh the Web site. Depending on your FrontPage settings, double-clicking the res_dap.htm page might cause it to open in Access instead of in FrontPage, so you'll open the page using the shortcut menu and specify FrontPage as the editor.

2. Scroll down the list of files as necessary, right-click **res_dap.htm** to open the shortcut menu, point to **Open With**, and then click **FrontPage (Open as HTML)**. The data access page opens in Design view. The first thing Brett notices is that the LastName field is first. You tell Brett that Access made this the first field in the data access page when you set this field to use an ascending sort order. If you hadn't set a sort order for the LastName field, the ID field would be first, and the remaining fields would appear in the order in which they appear in the table.

   Trouble? If you do not see the res_dap.htm file in the Contents pane, then you may have saved it in the wrong folder of the Web site. Locate the file in one of the other folders of the garden Web site, use drag and drop to move it to the Web site's root folder (http://localhost/garden), and then repeat Step 2.

3. Click **File** on the menu bar, and then click **Properties**. The Page Properties dialog box opens and selects the title of the Web page, Results.

4. With Results selected in the Title text box, type **Guest Book Records**, and then click the **OK** button. FrontPage changes the HTML page title to "Guest Book Records."

5. Save the page, and then preview it in a browser. See Figure 8-34. The record that you entered in the Guest Book Web page appears in the Guest Book Records page. As more records are added to the Results table, Brett will be able to use this data access page to view, delete, sort, and filter records as necessary.

Data access page in a browser ◀ **Figure 8-34**

HTML page title

Guest Book Records - Microsoft Internet Explorer

File Edit View Favorites Tools Help

Address http://localhost/garden/res_dap.htm

Guest Book Records ◀

heading added in Access Page Design view

fields from the Results table in the guest database

LastName:	Samples
ID:	1
FirstName:	John
Address:	123 Main Street
City:	Austin
State:	TX
Zip:	78704
Phone:	512-555-4650
Email:	john@samples.com
ReceiveEmail:	Yes
ReceiveMail:	

text boxes display the data in the first record

record navigation bar

Results 1 of 1

the page is displaying the first record (of a table containing only one record)

Done   Local intranet

Trouble? If a Microsoft Data Access Components dialog box opens and asks if you trust the Web site, click the OK button.

Trouble? If a Microsoft Office Web Components dialog box opens and asks if you trust the Web site, click the OK button.

Trouble? If Internet Explorer opens a page and indicates that you need to change the browser's security settings, ask your instructor or technical support person for help. If you are working on your own computer, follow the directions in the page to change the browser's security settings. Do *not* change the security settings for a public or lab computer.

Trouble? If Internet Explorer opens a Microsoft Data Access Components dialog box that asks if you want to allow the page to access data on another domain, click the Yes button.

The data access page contains the title that you created in Access Page Design view, the fields from the Results table in the guest database, the values for the first record in the Results table, and a record navigation bar.

When a data access page is based on a table, you can use the **record navigation bar** to display, add, change, delete, save, sort, and filter records in the table on which that page is based. If the data access page is based on a query, depending on the type of query, you might not be able to use it to add, change, delete, or save records. Figure 8-35 describes the buttons that appear on the record navigation bar.

Figure 8-35 ▶ **Data access page record navigation bar buttons and their descriptions**

Button	Button Name	Description
◄◄	First	Displays the first record.
◄	Previous	Displays the previous record.
►	Next	Displays the next record.
►►	Last	Displays the last record.
►*	New	Clears the fields in the data access page so that a new record can be entered.
►✕	Delete	Deletes the current record.
🖫	Save	Saves the current record.
↺	Undo	Reverses the previous action.
A↓Z	Sort Ascending	Sorts the records in ascending order based on the current active field.
Z↓A	Sort Descending	Sorts the records in descending order based on the current active field.
▽	Filter by Selection	Lets you set a filter to display a subset of the records using the value in the current active field.
▽	Filter Toggle Button	Removes the currently applied filter.
?	Help	Opens the Microsoft Access Data Pages Help window.

Adding a Record Using a Data Access Page

You can use the data access page to enter a new record in the Results table, just as you would use the Guest Book Web page and its form component to add a new record. A site visitor won't use the data access page to enter a record, but Brett wants you to do so to show him how to use a data access page.

Adding a Record to a Database Table Using a Data Access Page	Reference Window

- Click the New button on the record navigation bar in the Web page.
- Enter the data into the text boxes. Press the Tab key to move the insertion point to the next text box.
- After entering data in all of the text boxes, click the Save button on the record navigation bar to save the record.

To add a record to a table using a data access page:

1. Click the **New** button ▶ on the record navigation bar in the Web page. The browser clears the form fields and positions the insertion point in the LastName text box.

2. Type **Hicks** in the LastName text box, and then press the **Tab** key. The insertion point moves to the FirstName text box, skipping over the ID text box because Access automatically generates the ID field value.

3. Type **Sylvia**, and then press the **Tab** key to move to the Address text box.

4. Enter the following data into the remaining text boxes, using the Tab key to move to the next field: Address: **18 West Enfield**; City: **Austin**; State: **TX**; Zip: **78701**; Phone: **512-555-0004**; Email: **sylviahicks1234@yahoo.com**; and ReceiveEmail: **Yes**. See Figure 8-36.

Adding a new record	Figure 8-36

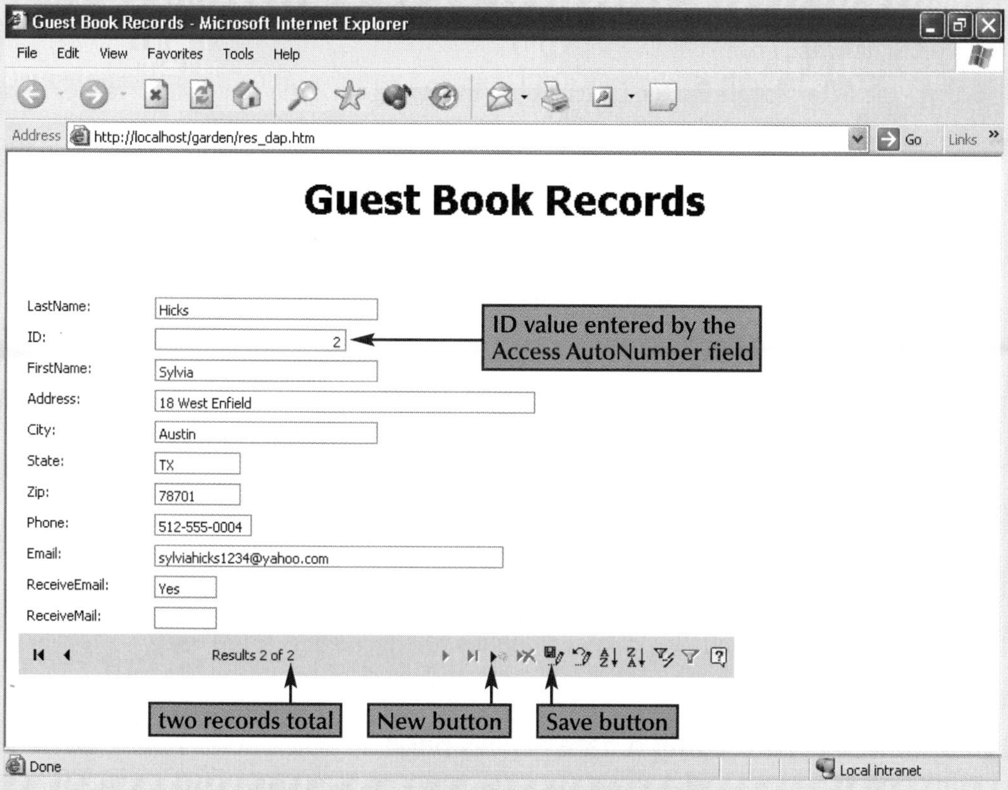

5. Click the **Save** button 🖫 on the record navigation bar.

Viewing Records Using a Data Access Page

The Results table in the guest database currently contains two records, but it will eventually include hundreds of records. Brett wants you to show him how to use the buttons on the record navigation bar to sort and browse the records.

To view the records in the table using the data access page:

► 1. Click your browser's **Refresh** button to refresh the data access page. Sylvia's record is record 1 of 2 because the sort order that you specified—alphabetically by LastName—sorts the record with the LastName "Hicks" before the record with the LastName "Samples."

► 2. Click the **Last** button ▶︎ on the record navigation bar. The browser displays the last record (for John Samples), which has an ID of 1.

► 3. Click the **Previous** button ◀ on the record navigation bar. The browser displays the first record (for Sylvia Hicks), which has an ID of 2.

► 4. Click the **FirstName** text box, and then click the **Sort Ascending** button ᴬ↓ on the record navigation bar. The browser sorts the records in ascending order by the FirstName field and then moves the insertion point to the LastName field. The record for John Samples is displayed because the FirstName "John" comes first in alphabetical order. You can sort records based on any field by clicking the field and then clicking a sort button.

► 5. Click the **Zip** text box, and then click the **Filter by Selection** button 🍥 on the record navigation bar. The filter will select only those records that contain the current value ("78704") in the State field. One record is selected, as indicated by the "Results 1 of 1" text on the record navigation bar.

► 6. Click the **Filter Toggle Button** button ▽ on the record navigation bar to remove the filter.

Now the database on the server contains the record that you added using the browser. You can also use a data access page to change data in the database object on which it is based. Because the data access page is based on the Results table in the guest database, any changes you make to the data in the data access page will also be made to the data in the Results table.

Changing a Record Using a Data Access Page

When you change the data in a data access page, the update is made to the database object on which it is based. Updates that are made in the database object include changes to field values, adding a record, or deleting a record. Other types of changes that affect how the data appears in the data access page, such as sorting records based on a certain field or applying a filter to select a group of records, are not made in the database object.

Sylvia Hicks has changed her preferred method of receiving promotional materials from e-mail to regular mail. You'll show Brett how to update her record next.

To update a record using a data access page:

► 1. Click the **Next** button ▶ on the record navigation bar to display the record for Sylvia Hicks.

► 2. Select the text **Yes** in the ReceiveEmail text box, and then press the **Delete** key. The ReceiveEmail text box is empty, which indicates no response.

► 3. Press the **Tab** key to move to the ReceiveMail text box, and then type **Yes**.

▶ **4.** Click the **Save** button 🖫 on the record navigation bar to save your changes.

▶ **5.** Close your browser.

You can confirm that the change was made in the database by opening the object on which the data access page is based, which, in this case, is the Results table.

To verify that the record was changed:

▶ **1.** Open the **guest.mdb** file in the fpdb folder to start Access and open the guest database.

Trouble? If the Confirm Save dialog box opens, click the Yes button.

▶ **2.** Click the **Tables** object in the Database window (if necessary), and then double-click the **Results** table to open it in Table Datasheet view.

▶ **3.** Scroll the records so you can see the ReceiveMail field for Sylvia's record. The field value "Yes" appears in this field, indicating that the change you made using the data access page was made in the database object.

▶ **4.** Close Access.

Note: FrontPage hardcodes the path to the database in the HTML document of a data access page. After you close the garden Web site and reopen it, you will need to change the path in the Data Source property in the HTML document for the data access page to match the location of the database file on your server. The easiest way to find this property is to open the data access page in FrontPage in Code view, click Edit on the menu bar, click Find, type "Data Source" in the Find what text box, and then search the current page. Change the path that follows the equal sign to the path to your server, and then save the page. Now the data access page will work in the browser.

Brett wants you to open the HTML document for the Guest Book Records page so he can see the HTML tags required to create it.

Viewing the HTML Document for a Data Access Page

When you created the Guest Book Records data access page using Access and then saved it, Access created the HTML document for the page. The data access page includes tags to define each field in the page, including its formatting properties and name, label, and position in the page.

To view the HTML document for the data access page:

▶ **1.** Click the **res_dap.htm** tab at the top of the Contents pane, and then click the **Show Code View** button ▣ Code at the bottom of the Contents pane.

▶ **2.** Press **Ctrl + Home** to scroll to the top of the page, and then scroll down the page so you can see the opening <H1> tag for the heading in the data access page at the top of the Contents pane (this tag appears about three-fourths of the way down the page). See Figure 8-37. Each object in the data access page requires several lines of code to define its properties.

Figure 8-37 | **HTML document for the data access page**

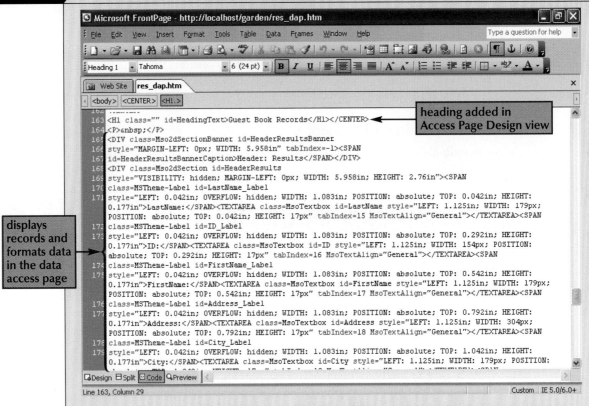

3. Press the **Page Down** key, and then scroll the page so you can see the opening <TBODY> tag at the top of the Contents pane. Figure 8-38 shows the HTML tags that create the buttons in the record navigation bar.

HTML document for the data access page, continued ◄ **Figure 8-38**

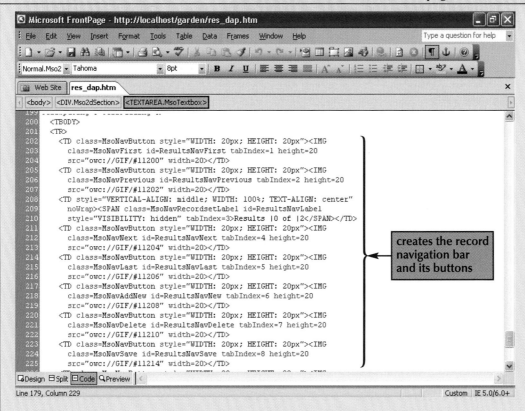

4. Return to Design view, close the garden Web site, and then close FrontPage.

In the next tutorial, you will learn how to create layout tables, styles, and Office components in a Web site.

Session 8.2 Quick Check

Review

1. FrontPage saves database files used with database connections in the _____ folder of the Web site.
2. True or False: You use the Form Properties dialog box to configure the form fields to save in a database table using a database connection.
3. True or False: You can use a form in a Web page to store information about a visitor's browser type and computer name.
4. What is a data access page?
5. True or False: You can use FrontPage to create a data access page.
6. What settings are available when you use the Page Wizard to create a new data access page?
7. To add a new record to a table using a data access page, you click the _____ button on the record navigation bar.

Review

Tutorial Summary

In this tutorial, you learned how to add an Access database to a Web site and use it to store the results collected by a form in a Web page. You also learned how to create a data access page and used it to view, sort, and update records.

The simple example used in this tutorial showed you how to create a database connection and use it to create Web pages that store and display that data. If you are interested in learning more about databases, you should enroll in a course entitled "Database Design" or "Database-Driven Web Sites." In these types of courses, you'll learn how to design and develop a database and how to develop a Web site that displays and stores data in a database. Storing data in a database makes it easy for you to view and use the data in many different ways.

Key Terms

Access	executable folder	query
Active Server Page	field	record
common field	file-based connection	record navigation bar
custom connection	filter	relational database
data access page	fpdb	System Data Source Name
database	Microsoft Office	(DSN) connection
database connection	Access 2003	table
Database Results region	network connection	VBScript
Database Results Wizard	primary key	verify

Practice

Practice the skills you learned in the tutorial using the same case scenario.

Review Assignments

There are no new Data Files needed for these Review Assignments.

The Web pages that you created in this tutorial have the functionality that Brett needs, but the default pages created by the wizards do not have the same appearance as other pages in the garden Web site. Brett asks you to format these Web pages and to finalize their appearance. In addition, you will change the settings for pages that contain customer data so they are not published with the rest of the Web site's pages.

If necessary, start FrontPage, and then do the following:

1. Use My Network Places to open the **garden** Web site from your Web server.
2. Open the Customer Requests page (**cust_qry.asp**) in Design view. Remove the top and left shared borders from the page, and then create a left-aligned heading at the top of the page with the text "Customer List." Apply the Heading 1 style to the heading.
3. Start the Database Results Wizard and use it to make the following changes to the existing Database Results region in the Customer Requests page:
   a. Change the formatting options to display a list with one field per item. Add labels for all field values, place a horizontal separator between records, and use the Paragraphs list option.
   b. Choose the option to display all records together, and then click the Finish button.
4. Change the form fields in the Customer Requests page to add a space between the words in the following field names: CommunicationPreference, RockWork, IrrigationInstallation, and IrrigationService. Then select the text between the yellow paragraphs and change its font size to 10 points.

5. Add a normal, left-aligned paragraph below the heading that you added in Step 2 with the following text: "This page displays current data collected from the Requests Web page. Refresh the page to update the data."

6. Save the page, and then preview it using a browser. Use the browser's Print dialog box to print the first page of the Customer Requests page, and then close your browser.

7. Change the settings for the Customer Requests page to exclude it when publishing the Web site. Save and close the page.

8. Open the Customer Requests Search page (**custsrch.asp**) in Design view. Remove the top and left shared borders from the page, and then create a left-aligned heading at the top of the page with the text "Customer Requests Search." (*Note:* The heading will appear in the search form component in Design view, but it will appear correctly as a heading when viewed in the browser.) Apply the Heading 1 style to the heading.

9. Run the Database Results Wizard again for the **custsrch.asp** page, and change the message that appears when no records are returned in the query to "There are no records matching your request." (*Hint:* Click the More Options button in the third dialog box.)

10. Exclude the **custsrch.asp** page when publishing the Web site, save the page, preview and print the page in a browser, and then close your browser.

11. Open the Guest Book Records page (**res_dap.htm**) in FrontPage in Design view. Change the labels that appear to the left of the LastName, FirstName, ReceiveEmail, and ReceiveMail text boxes to insert a space between words. (*Hint:* Click a label to edit it.) Set the page so it is not published with the Web site, and then save it.

12. Close the **garden** Web site, and then close FrontPage.

Case Problem 1

Create

Create Web pages that are connected to an imported database and that store and display records.

Data File needed for this Case Problem: buffalo.mdb

Buffalo Trading Post Nicole Beirne, president of Buffalo Trading Post, knows that customer service is an important part of BTP's success. She realizes that many of her loyal customers might use a computer for business, but they do not want to receive personal correspondence via their e-mail addresses. In response to customer requests, Nicole wants to create a database of customer information that the promotion department can use to send advertisements about sales and promotions to customers. She asks you to create a Web page that will accept input from the user, a Web page that displays customer information, and a data access page that displays all records in the database and provides functionality to update them.

If necessary, start FrontPage, make sure you have your Data Files, and then do the following:

1. Use My Network Places to open the **buffalo** Web site from your Web server. (If you did not create this Web site in Tutorial 1 and update it in Tutorials 2 through 7, ask your instructor for assistance.)

2. Copy the **buffalo.mdb** database from the Tutorial.08\Case1 folder included with your Data Files and paste it into the root folder of the **buffalo** Web site. Use "Buffalo" as the database connection name, and store all database files in the **fpdb** folder of the Web site.

3. Create an Active Server Page in the Web site using the title "Mailing List" and the filename **mailinfo.asp**.

4. Add the Mailing List page (**mailinfo.asp**) to Navigation view as a child page of the home page. Position the Mailing List page to the left of the What page in the navigation structure.

Explore

5. Enter a brief introductory paragraph in the first paragraph (but not in a shared border of the Web page) of the Mailing List page. Use the information in the case problem description to determine the appropriate content.

Explore

6. Insert a form component below the paragraph that you added in Step 5 using your choice of design and organization. The form component should contain the following text box form fields: First Name, with the name FirstName and a width of 50 characters; Last Name, with the name LastName and a width of 50 characters; Address, with the same name and a width of 70 characters; City, with the same name and a width of 50 characters; State/Province, with the name StateProv and a width of 10 characters; Postal Code, with the name PostalCode and a width of 10 characters; Country, with the same name, a width of 12 characters, and an initial value of USA; Phone, with the same name and a width of 15 characters; and E-mail Address, with the name EmailAddress and a width of 50 characters.

Explore

7. Verify the Buffalo database connection, and then set the form to send its results to the **Customers** table in the buffalo database stored in the **fpdb** folder of the **buffalo** Web site. The database column names and the form field names are the same, except for the StateProv form field, which is State/Prov in the database. Do not collect any additional fields.

8. Save the Mailing List page, and then preview it in a browser. Complete this page using your own name and real or fictitious address information, print the page, and then submit the form to the server. Close your browser.

9. Open the **buffalo.mdb** database stored in the Web site from FrontPage, open the **Customers** table in the Table window, and then confirm that the form handler correctly stored your data. Close Access.

10. Close the Mailing List page, and then create an Active Server Page using the title "Mailing List Info" and the filename **maillist.asp**. Change the settings for the Mailing List Info page to exclude it when publishing the Web site, turn off the top and left shared borders for this page only, and then save the page.

11. Add a centered heading with the Heading 1 style at the top of the page using the text "Mailing List Information." In a new, left-aligned paragraph below the heading, create a Database Results region that displays the records from the **Mailing List** query in the **buffalo.mdb** database. Include all fields in the Database Results region, accept the default formatting options, and display all records together. After inserting the Database Results region in the Web page, change the column headings to more meaningful names, and then apply the Heading 4 style and center them. Select the database fields (in the third row), and then change the font size to 10 points. Save the page, preview it in a browser, use the browser to print the page, and then close your browser. Close the Mailing List Info page.

12. Open the **buffalo.mdb** database stored in the Web site from FrontPage, and then click the Pages object in the Database window. Use a wizard to create a data access page based on the **Customers** table. Include all fields in the page, do not use a grouping level, sort the records in ascending order by ID, and change the default title to "Mailing List Data Access Page."

13. Enter the page heading "Mailing List Data Access Page" at the top of the new data access page, and then save the page as **mail_dap.htm** in the root folder of the **buffalo** Web site. Close Access.

14. Refresh the Web site's root folder, and then use the Open With command to open the **mail_dap.htm** page in Design view. Exclude the page when publishing the Web site. Save the page, and then preview it in a browser. Use the data access page to add a new record to the table using real or fictitious data. Use the browser to save and print this new record, and then close your browser.

15. Close the **buffalo** Web site, and then close FrontPage.

Create

Create Web pages that are connected to an imported database and that store and display records.

Case Problem 2

Data File needed for this Case Problem: grill.mdb

Garden Grill Meghan Elliott and Callan Murphy want to include a new Web page in Garden Grill's Web site that lets customers enter comments into a form whose results are stored in an Access database. Meghan hopes to use this database to gather information about regional trends, which might lead to the introduction of new menu items. The form should contain a text area that lets users enter information about whatever is on their minds—including the restaurant, service, and menu. When the menu is updated, Callan can use the information stored in the database to provide mailing lists to the marketing department, which can then mail coupons and new menus to current and past customers.

If necessary, start FrontPage, make sure you have your Data Files, and then do the following:

1. Use My Network Places to open the **grill** Web site from your Web server. (If you did not create this Web site in Tutorial 1 and update it in Tutorials 2 through 7, ask your instructor for assistance.)
2. Copy the **grill.mdb** database from the Tutorial.08\Case2 folder included with your Data Files and paste it into the root folder of the **grill** Web site. Use "Grill" as the database connection name, and store all database files in the **fpdb** folder of the Web site.
3. Create an Active Server Page using the title "Customer Comments" and the filename **comments.asp**.
4. Add the Customer Comments page (**comments.asp**) to the Web site's navigation structure as a child page of the home page. Position the Customer Comments page between the Job Opportunities and Feedback Web pages.

Explore
5. Open the **jobs.htm** page in Design view, and then copy the picture link bar, Garden Grill logo, and heading at the top of the page. Close the **jobs.htm** page, and then paste the copied material at the top of the **comments.asp** page. Change the heading to "Customer Comments," and then insert a left-aligned paragraph below the heading. Use the information in the case problem description to write a brief introduction for this page.

Explore
6. Insert a form component below the paragraph that you added in Step 5 using your choice of design and organization. The form component should contain the following text box form fields: First Name, with the name First and a width of 50 characters; Last Name, with the name Last and a width of 50 characters; Address, with the same name and a width of 70 characters; City, with the same name and a width of 50 characters; State/Province, with the name StateProv and a width of 10 characters; Postal Code, with the name PostalCode and a width of 10 characters; Country, with the same name, a width of 10 characters, and an initial value of USA; Phone, with the same name and a width of 15 characters; and E-mail Address, with the name Email and a width of 50 characters. Create a text area named Comments, with the same name, a width of 70 characters, and a height of 5 lines.

Explore
7. Verify the Grill database connection, and then set the form to send its results to the **Comments** table in the **grill.mdb** database stored in the **fpdb** folder of the **grill** Web site. The database column names and form field names are the same, except for the StateProv form field, which is State/Prov in the database. Do not collect any additional fields.
8. Save the Customer Comments page, and then preview it in a browser. Complete the Customer Comments page using your own name and real or fictitious address information, print the page, and then submit the form to the server. Close your browser.

9. Open the **grill.mdb** database stored in the Web site from FrontPage, open the **Comments** table in the Table window, and then confirm that the form handler correctly stored your data. Close Access.

10. Close the Customer Comments page, and then create an Active Server Page using the title "Customer Information" and the filename **custinfo.asp**. Change the settings for the Customer Information page to exclude it when publishing the Web site, and then save it.

Explore

11. At the top of the page, add a centered heading that uses the Heading 2 style and the text "Customer Information." In a new, left-aligned paragraph below the heading, create a Database Results region that displays the records from the **Customer Feedback** query in the **grill.mdb** database. Include all fields except ID in the Database Results region. Accept the default formatting options, and display all records together. After inserting the Database Results region in the Web page, change the column headings to more meaningful names, and then apply the Heading 5 style and center them. Select the database fields (in the third row), and then change the font size to 10 points. Save the page, preview it in a browser, use the browser to print the page, and then close your browser.

Explore

12. Open the **grill.mdb** database stored in the Web site from FrontPage, and then click the Pages object in the Database window. Use a wizard to create a data access page based on the **Comments** table. Include all fields in the page except for the ID field, group the records using the State/Prov field, sort the records in ascending order by City, and change the default title to "Customer Comments Data Access Page."

13. Change the heading at the top of the data access page to "Customer Comments Data Access Page," and then save the page as **cust_dap.htm** in the root folder of the **grill** Web site. Close Access.

Explore

14. Refresh the Web site's root folder, and then use the Open With command to open the **cust_dap.htm** page in Design view. Exclude the page when publishing the Web site. Save the page, and then preview it in a browser. How did the grouping option that you set using the Database Results Wizard affect the appearance of the data in the page? What happens when you click the plus box to the left of the State/Prov label? How might Garden Grill use grouping levels to improve a Web page that contains menu items? Print the page, and then close your browser.

15. Close the **grill** Web site, and then close FrontPage.

Create

Create Web pages that are connected to a new database and that store and display records, and then explore the different formatting options for a Database Results region.

Case Problem 3

There are no new Data Files needed for this Case Problem.

Swenson Auctioneers The Mailing List Web page in the Web site for Swenson Auctioneers has generated a lot of interest in the firm's upcoming auctions. In addition, the Web site has generated a few new clients in just a couple of weeks. The Mailing List page currently stores its results in two files in the Web site's _private folder, as comma-separated values and as an HTML document. Scott has been importing the .csv file into a spreadsheet so he can organize the information collected. Because the Web server on which you published the site supports Active Server Pages, you tell Scott that a better way to collect the data is to store it in a database table, where Scott can view, sort, and update records using a Web page. Because you already created the form and form fields in a Web page, you will let FrontPage create the database and database connection for you.

If necessary, start FrontPage, and then do the following:

1. Use My Network Places to open the **swenson** Web site from your Web server. (If you did not create this Web site in Tutorial 1 and update it in Tutorials 2 through 7, ask your instructor for assistance.)

2. Open the Mailing List page (**mail.htm**) in Design view and review the page's contents. Open the Form Properties dialog box, select the option to store the form's results in a database, and then open the Options for Saving Results to Database dialog box.

Explore

3. Select the option to create a new database. Review the options on the Saved Fields tab to make sure that FrontPage correctly associated the fields in the form with the columns in the database. (If necessary, double-click a form field to change the database column associated with it.) Close the Form Properties dialog box.

4. Follow the instructions in the message box that opens to change the filename of the Mailing List page. (*Hint:* Change the filename in Folders view, and click the Yes button to update the hyperlinks.) Save the Mailing List page.

5. Verify the database connection you created.

6. Preview the Mailing List page in a browser, and then use the form to enter a record with your name in the Name text box and data you make up in the remaining text boxes. Choose "Direct Mail" in the list box, select the Business equipment & computers and Special use check boxes, click the No option button, type "This is a comment." in the Other Comments text area, and then submit the form to the server. Close your browser.

7. Open the database you created in Access and examine the table object that FrontPage created, and then close Access.

8. Close the Mailing List page, and then create an Active Server Page using the filename **maillist.asp** and the title "Mailing List Results." Open the home page in Design view, copy the Swenson Auctioneers logo and the user-defined link bar at the top of the page, close the home page, and then paste the copied material at the top of the Mailing List Results page.

Explore

9. In a new, left-aligned paragraph below the link bar, create a Database Results region that displays the records from the table in the database stored in the Web site. Include all fields except ID in the Database Results region. Select the option to format the records in a list, with one field per item, with labels for all field values, and a horizontal separator between records. For the list options, choose the option to create text fields. Display all records together and then save the page and preview it in a browser, noting the way the data is arranged in the page.

Explore

10. Close your browser, and then run the Database Results Wizard again. Change the formatting for the list to a definition list. After you finish the wizard, change the column headings to add spaces between words (when necessary) and to change any underscore characters to spaces (when necessary).

Explore

11. Move each database column to the same line as the form field name, and insert a space after the colon. For example, the first line of the Database Results region would be "**Name:** <<Name>>". Make this change to every form field, delete the empty paragraphs between the form fields, and then delete the last four fields from the Database Results region. (These fields collect the remote computer name, user name, browser type, and timestamp.). When you have finished, select the text between the yellow paragraphs in the Database Results region, and then change the font size to 10 points. Save the page, preview it in a browser, use the browser to print the page, and then close your browser and the Mailing List Results page.

Explore

12. Open the database stored in the Web site from FrontPage, and then click the Tables object in the Database window. You cannot create a data access page from a table unless the table has a primary key specified. Change the ID field in the **Results** table so it is the table's primary key. (*Hint:* Click the **Results** table to select it, click the Design button ⌷ on the Database window toolbar, click the ID field name text box, and then click the Primary Key button ⌷ on the toolbar.) Close the Table window and save your changes.

Explore

13. Click the Pages object in the Database window. Use a wizard to create a data access page based on the table stored in the database. Include all fields in the page except for the ID, Remote_computer_name, User_name, Browser_type, and Timestamp fields. (*Hint:* Select each field and click the button to remove it from the Selected Fields list box.) Do not specify a grouping level or a sort order, and then change the default title to "Mailing List Data Access Page."

14. Change the heading at the top of the data access page to "Mailing List Data Access Page," and then save the page as **mail_dap.htm** in the root folder of the **swenson** Web site. Close Access.

Explore

15. Refresh the Web site's root folder, and then use the Open With command to open the **mail_dap.htm** page in Design view. Exclude the page when publishing the Web site. Save the page, and then preview it in a browser. Change the PermissionToContact field value from "No" to "Yes," save the record, print the page, and then close your browser.

16. Close the **swenson** Web site, and then close FrontPage.

Create

Create Web pages that are connected to existing databases and that store and display records.

Case Problem 4

Data Files needed for this Case Problem: lenders.mdb and mortgage.mdb

Mortgage Services, Inc. Natalie Fuselier wants you to incorporate two databases into the loan Web site for her: one that stores data about clients who use the Application page in the Web site to submit loan applications, and another that stores information about the financial institutions with whom she does business. After you import these databases into the Web site, you will include information from them in Web pages to make it easy for Natalie to access her lists of financial institutions and applicants.

If necessary, start FrontPage, make sure you have your Data Files, and then do the following:

1. Use My Network Places to open the **loan** Web site from your Web server. (If you did not create this Web site in Tutorial 1 and update it in Tutorials 2 through 7, ask your instructor for assistance.)

2. Copy the **mortgage.mdb** database from the Tutorial.08\Case4 folder included with your Data Files and paste it into the root folder of the **loan** Web site. Use "Mortgage" as the database connection name, and store all database files in the **fpdb** folder of the Web site.

3. Copy the **lenders.mdb** database from the Tutorial.08\Case4 folder included with your Data Files and paste it into the **fpdb** folder in the **loan** Web site. Use "Lenders" as the database connection name.

4. Verify the Mortgage and Lenders database connections.

Explore

5. Open the **mortgage.mdb** database stored in the **loan** Web site in Access, and then examine the objects it contains and their contents. Close Access, and then open the **lenders.mdb** database stored in the **loan** Web site in Access and examine the objects it contains and their contents.

6. With the **lenders.mdb** database open in Access, click the Pages object in the Database window, and then use a wizard to create a new data access page that includes all fields in the **Lenders** table. Do not specify a grouping level or sort order, use the page title "Lender Information," and then add the heading "Lender Information" to the data access page in Access Page Design view.

7. Save the data access page in the root folder of the **loan** Web site using the filename **lend_dap.htm**, and then close Access.

8. Refresh the Web site's root folder, and then preview the **lend_dap.htm** page in a browser. Use the page to add a new record to the database using the following information. After adding the record, save it.

      LenderID: 9802
      Name: First United Mortgage
      LenderType: Conventional
      ContactPerson: Cassie Werdenberg
      PhoneNumber: 765-555-4100

9. Use a filter to display only those records with "Conventional" in the LenderType field, and then print the second record. Remove the filter, and then close your browser.

Explore

10. Open the Application (**apply.htm**) page in Design view, and then change the form to store its results in the **Borrower** table of the **mortgage.mdb** database in the **fpdb** folder of the **loan** Web site. On the Saved Fields tab, remove the Authorize form field, and then match the form field names and the database column names for the remaining fields. (*Hint:* The form field names and the database column names are not the same. For example, the BorFirstName form field is BorrowerName1 in the database and the CoBLastName form field is CoBorrowerName2 in the database. If you have trouble matching the form fields to the database column names, click the Cancel button and close the open dialog boxes and then open the **mortgage.mdb** database in Access and study the table so you know how it is designed.) On the Additional Fields tab, remove the four additional fields, and then close the dialog boxes and save the **apply.htm** page. Update the filename and the hyperlinks to the page, and then save the page again.

11. Preview the **apply.asp** page in a browser, type your first and last names in the text boxes for the borrower, and then complete the rest of the form using fictitious data. Click the Yes option button, submit the form to the server, and then close your browser.

12. Close the **apply.asp** page, and then create an Active Server Page using the title "Lender List" and the filename **lenders.asp**. Add the **lenders.asp** page to the Web site's navigation structure as a child page of the home page, positioning it to the right of the Credit Repair page.

13. In the **lenders.asp** page, insert a Database Results region using the Lenders database connection and the **Lenders** table. Choose the option to display one record per row and display all records together. Save the **lenders.asp** page, preview and print it in a browser, and then close your browser.

Explore

14. In the **lenders.asp** page, run the Database Results Wizard again and add a search form to the page that searches the LenderType field for matching values. After finishing the wizard, change the column headings in the Database Results region to insert a space between words (where applicable). Above the LenderType text box, insert a paragraph that describes how to use the page to search for lenders based on their type (Conventional, FHA/VA, Construction, or Problem Credit).

15. Save the **lenders.asp** page, preview it in a browser, and then use the LenderType text box to display only those records for lenders that write Conventional loans. Print the page, and then close your browser.

16. Close the **loan** Web site, and then close FrontPage.

Reinforce

Databases

Lab Assignments

The New Perspectives Labs are designed to help you master some of the key concepts and skills presented in this text. The steps for completing this Lab are located on the Course Technology Web site. Log on to the Internet and use your Web browser to go to the Student Online Companion for New Perspectives Office 2003 at **www.course.com/np/office2003**. Click the Lab Assignments link, and then navigate to the assignments for this tutorial.

Databases   The Databases Lab demonstrates essential concepts of file and database management systems. You will use the Lab to search, sort, and report the data contained in a file of classic books.

Review

Quick Check Answers

Session 8.1

1. A database connection specifies the name, location, and type of database that you want to access from a FrontPage Web site.
2. Copy the database file in Windows Explorer, open the Web site in FrontPage, right-click the root folder in the Folder List, click Paste on the shortcut menu, enter the name of the database connection, and then click the Yes button. Click the Yes button again to store the database's files in the fpdb folder of the FrontPage Web site.
3. You must enable the Web site to run Active Server Pages and to run scripts.
4. a component in a Web page that contains HTML tags and client-side and server-side scripts that retrieve and display data from the database in the Web page
5. filter
6. False
7. False
8. True

Session 8.2

1. fpdb
2. False
3. True
4. a Web page that displays data from the Access object on which it is based; the page includes controls that let you add, delete, sort, filter, browse, and change the data displayed, depending on the type of object on which the page is based
5. False
6. select the table or query on which to base the data access page, select the fields to display in the data access page, select an optional grouping level, select optional sort orders, and enter a title
7. New

Objectives

Session 9.1
- Use a layout table to organize a Web page's contents
- Include a Web page in a layout cell
- Create a layout cell in a layout table
- Format a layout cell

Session 9.2
- Create user-defined styles in a Web page
- Create a cascading style sheet
- Link a cascading style sheet to a Web page
- Use a template to create a cascading style sheet

Session 9.3
- Insert a spreadsheet component into a Web page and import data into it
- Get help for an Office component
- Insert a chart component in a Web page
- Format a chart component

Lab

Spreadsheets

Student Data Files

To complete this tutorial, you will need your ending files from Tutorial 8 and the following Data Files. Additional Data Files needed to complete the end-of-tutorial exercises are listed with the Review Assignments and Case Problems.

Using Layout Tables, Styles, and Office Components

Creating a Layout Table, Styles, and Interactive Components in the Garden Web Site

Case

Sunshine Landscape & Garden Center

Brett Kizer just stopped by your office to report that Chad Schomaker, Sunshine's irrigation specialist, is working on the two pages in the garden Web site that will include information about irrigation services. The existing RainMaker Irrigation page in the Web site is a frames page that includes basic information about the services Sunshine offers. The RainMaker Irrigation page has two child pages, Residential Systems and Commercial Systems, in the Web site's navigation structure. However, because both of these child pages were blank, you had set these pages so they were excluded from the site's navigation bars. When Chad finishes the Residential Systems and Commercial Systems pages, he will send you the files so you can import them into the Web site and activate their links. Because you know that Chad is working on these changes now, you decide this is a good time to replace the current RainMaker Irrigation frames page with a new page that you will design using a tool called a layout table.

During the development of the Web site, you have shown Brett how to format text. You want to make sure that Brett knows how to create and modify styles in a Web page so he can use these skills in the future to make formatting changes to the Web pages. Including styles in a Web page or creating a separate document in which to store all of the styles used in a Web site is a powerful formatting tool in FrontPage that will make Brett's future work much easier.

New gardeners visiting the nursery often ask questions about temperatures in the area, so they can get a sense of when to plant their gardens. Brett's final request for the Web site is to include a Web page that illustrates the previous year's daily high and low temperatures. He wants to update this new Web page each month so that the temperature data reflects the temperatures for the current month of the previous year. Because the home page currently includes gardening activities for the month of February, you will work with data for February in this new Web page. Brett collected the data you need and saved it in a file. You will show Brett how to insert a spreadsheet component in a Web page, insert his temperature data into it, and then create a chart from that data.

Session 9.1

Understanding Layout Tables

In this book, you have used a variety of methods to create and format new Web pages in the garden Web site. For example, you learned how to use the default page templates provided by FrontPage to create blank pages and pages with different content, and you created shared templates and Dynamic Web Templates to create pages with content specific to the garden Web site. You also used a frames page to arrange hyperlinks and to control where the targets of those hyperlinks open. Finally, you used tables to arrange data in a row-and-column format and also to control the appearance of text and pictures in a Web page.

Another way to arrange the content of a Web page is to use a layout table. A **layout table** is a framework that you can use to organize the content of an entire page, or part of a page, creating a simple or sophisticated design. You can create a layout table by using one of several table layout templates provided by FrontPage or by drawing your own layout table. After creating a layout table, you can change its properties just like you can for regular tables.

A layout table's framework is divided into regions called **layout cells**. Figure 9-1 shows an example of a layout table that includes four layout cells. Each layout cell will hold its own content, such as text, images, hyperlinks, and other objects. After you use a table layout template to create a framework, you can edit the layout table properties to customize its appearance. For example, you might add or remove layout cells or change the sizes of the layout cells. You can also draw your own layout table and add cells to it by using the Layout Tables and Cells task pane.

Layout table created from a template ◀ **Figure 9-1**

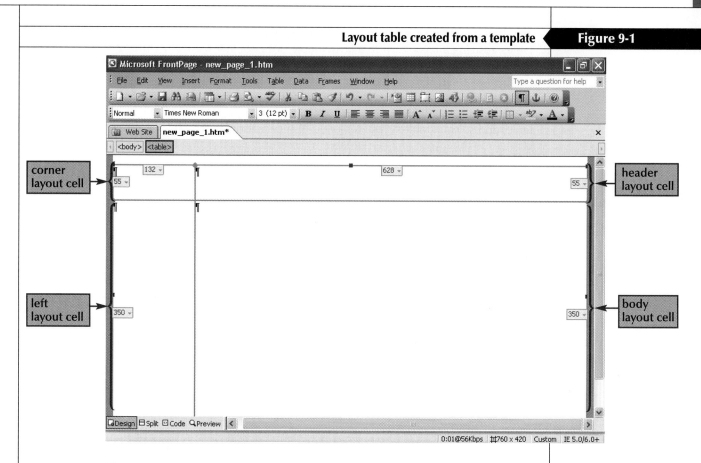

Green and blue lines, which appear only in Design view, indicate the borders of the layout table and its layout cells. The layout table is outlined with green lines; the blue lines within a layout table indicate those individual layout cell borders that do not overlap the layout table's border. When you first create a layout table, the dimensions for each layout cell it contains are displayed as labels appearing on the borders; the number in a label indicates the column width or row height (in pixels) of an individual layout cell. When you click one of these labels, a shortcut menu opens. You can choose the option to change the width or height of a column or row or to set the column or row to autostretch. Changing a column or row to **autostretch** means that the browser will automatically resize the layout cell to fill the available space in the browser window, much like using the In percent option button to size the width of a regular table. You can also set columns to use a spacer image. A **spacer image** is a picture that serves as an empty placeholder to add space between layout cells in the table. Sometimes FrontPage adds a spacer image for you automatically. When you save the page, the spacer image's filename is MsSpacer.gif.

When you select a particular layout cell's border, all borders of that layout cell appear in blue and include sizing handles, indicating that the layout cell is selected. The pointer changes shape as you move around the selected layout cell's border. Clicking ↔ on the border lets you drag the layout cell to a new location. Clicking ⌐, ⊤, ├, or ┤ on a middle-sizing handle lets you drag the border down, up, left, or right to resize the layout cell. Clicking ⌐, ⌐, ⌐, or ∟ on the corner-sizing handle of a layout cell lets you resize the height and width of a layout cell at the same time. When you decrease the size of a layout cell, an area with a beige background color appears in the layout table or around the layout cell, indicating an area of the layout table that contains no layout cells. You can insert a new layout cell into the empty area, or you can leave it empty. Unlike working in regular tables, resizing a layout cell in a layout table does not automatically resize the other layout cells in the layout table. Sometimes you have to experiment with resizing the different layout cells to arrive at the desired appearance for your Web page.

Figure 9-2 shows the Layout Tables and Cells task pane, which includes tools that let you insert a layout table, insert a layout cell, change the width and height of the layout table, and select a table layout template. You can also use the Tables toolbar to make changes to the layout of a layout table by inserting and deleting layout cells, changing the cell alignment, and merging and splitting cells.

Figure 9-2	Layout Tables and Cells task pane

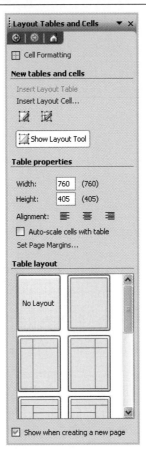

When you select a cell in a layout table and then click the Cell Formatting link on the Layout Tables and Cells task pane, the Cell Formatting task pane shown in Figure 9-3 opens. The Cell Formatting task pane shows the properties for the selected layout cell, and lets you change its width, height, cell padding, vertical alignment, background color, border color and width, borders to apply, and margins (distance between the content of the layout cell and the layout cell's border). Clicking the Cell Header and Footer link lets you change the properties of layout cells that are used as headers and footers. Clicking the Cell Corners and Shadows link lets you change the corners of a layout cell to use rounded edges, colors, and shadows.

Using a layout table to organize a Web page can result in a very simple or very sophisticated design. Because most Web browsers interpret the HTML tags used to create tables in consistent ways, layout tables can be very effective page layout tools because you can be confident that your page's contents will be displayed correctly and consistently.

Because a layout table is an excellent design tool, you want to show Brett how to use one. Instead of creating a new page in the Web site, you decide to change the organization of the RainMaker Irrigation page, which currently includes three frames, to a page formatted by a layout table. You will begin by using one of the table layout templates to create the initial framework for the page, and then you will add the content and format the layout table and its layout cells to achieve the desired appearance.

Using a Layout Table to Organize a New Page

When you create a Web page, the default option is to create a normal, blank page. If you want to use a layout table to format the page's contents, you need to display the Layout Tables and Cells task pane. You can configure FrontPage to display this task pane automatically when you create a Web page.

The table layout template that you select will create a specific number and arrangement of layout cells in the layout table. When selecting a table layout template, choose the one that most closely matches your needs. After inserting the layout table in the page, you can make changes to it by moving, resizing, adding, and deleting layout cells.

The current RainMaker Irrigation Web page is a frames page with three frames. The links in the contents frame on the left open pages in the main frame on the right. The links in the banner frame open pages in the full browser window, outside of the frames page. Figure 9-4 shows the current RainMaker Irrigation page.

Figure 9-4 | **RainMaker Irrigation frames page**

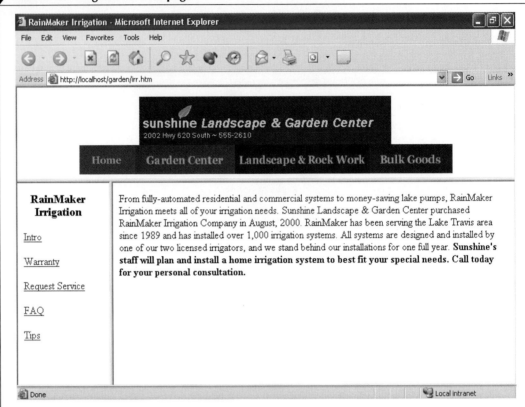

You'll replace this page by creating a new page, using a table layout template to insert a layout table that closely matches the current arrangement of the page's content, and then saving the page with the same filename. Because a page with a layout table cannot use shared borders, you will remove the shared borders from the new page. In addition, because Brett wants this page to have a different appearance from other pages in the garden Web site, you will also remove the page's theme.

Reference Window | **Using a Table Layout Template to Insert a Layout Table in a Web Page**

- Create a new Web page in Design view.
- If necessary, remove any existing shared borders from the new page.
- If necessary, display the Layout Tables and Cells task pane.
- In the Table layout section, scroll the table layout templates until you find one that matches the layout you want to use, and then click it.

You will begin by creating a new page in the garden Web site.

To create a new page, remove its shared borders and theme, and save it:

1. Start FrontPage, and then use My Network Places to open the **garden** Web site from your Web server.

2. Click the **Create a new normal page** button ▯ on the Standard toolbar. A new Web page opens in Design view and the Layout Tables and Cells task pane opens. The Web page uses the Web site's shared borders and theme.

   Trouble? If the Layout Tables and Cells task pane doesn't open automatically, click View on the menu bar, click Task Pane, click the Other Task Panes list arrow on the task pane, and then click Layout Tables and Cells.

3. Click the **Show Code View** button ▯ Code at the bottom of the Contents pane. You will delete the meta tags that insert the Web site's default theme and shared borders into the page. These meta tags have "Microsoft Theme" and "Microsoft Border" as their name values.

4. Select the two meta tags that insert the theme and shared borders, and then press the **Delete** key.

5. Click the **Show Design View** button ▯ Design at the bottom of the Contents pane to return to Design view. Now the new page doesn't use either shared borders or a theme.

   Save the new page as irr.htm, replacing the existing frames page. The existing page has different titles in Navigation and Folders view; the title in Folders view is "RainMaker Irrigation" but the title in Navigation view is "Irrigation" so the page title will fit on the navigation buttons in the site's link bars. You suggest using the title "Irrigation" for the new page so its Navigation view title and Folders view title will match.

6. Click the **Save** button ▯ on the Standard toolbar, and then click the **Change title** button in the Save As dialog box.

7. In the Page title text box of the Set Page Title dialog box, type **Irrigation**, and then click the **OK** button.

8. In the Save As dialog box, make sure the **garden** Web site appears in the Save in list box, click **irr.htm**, and then click the **Save** button. Because the irr.htm page already exists in the Web site, a message box opens and asks if you want to replace the existing file.

9. Click the **Yes** button. The new page you created replaces the old frames page. Because you already added the old irr.htm page to the Web site's navigation structure, the new page simply takes its place.

Now you can examine the table layout templates and find one that matches the design of the old frames page.

To create a layout table in the page:

1. If necessary, point to the **arrow** at the bottom of the Layout Tables and Cells task pane to scroll to the bottom of the task pane.

| Figure 9-5 | New Irrigation page in Design view |

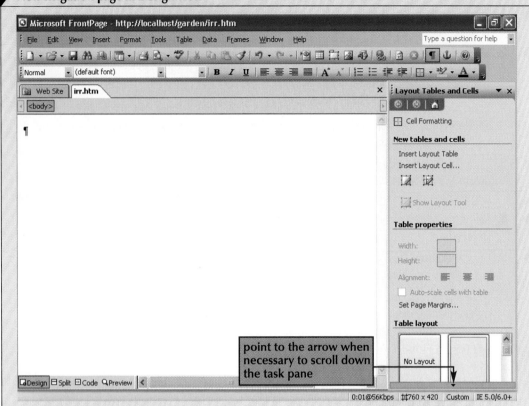

Trouble? Figure 9-5 shows the task pane before it was scrolled to show the entire Table layout section. If your monitor's resolution is set to 1024 × 768 pixels or higher, then you won't see this arrow or need to scroll the Layout Tables and Cells task pane to see all of its content. After you point to this arrow and scroll the task pane down, another arrow appears at the top of the task pane. When you point to this arrow, the task pane scrolls up.

2. Scroll the Table layout section as necessary to view all of the table layout templates. As you are examining the table layout templates, try to find one that will match the organization of the frames page (shown in Figure 9-4). Also notice the different organizations that are available using a table layout template. Some of the table layout templates format content in columns; others format content in rows. Some table layout templates use a combination of cells to provide vertical and horizontal content.

3. After you have viewed all of the table layout templates, scroll back to the top of the Table layout list, and then scroll down and point to the first table layout template in the fourth row. This table layout template has the ScreenTip "Header, Body, Footer, and Left," as shown in Figure 9-6.

| Figure 9-6 | Selecting a table layout template |

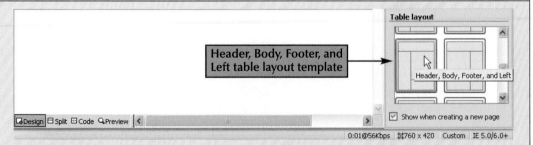

4. Click the **Header, Body, Footer, and Left** table layout template. The layout table is inserted in the blank Web page. A blank paragraph appears above the layout table. Because you won't need to use this blank paragraph, you'll delete it.

5. Press **Ctrl + Home** to scroll to the top of the page, and then press the **Delete** key to delete the blank paragraph that appears above the layout table.

6. Click the **Save** button on the Standard toolbar to save the page.

Now the only content in the Irrigation page is the layout table.

Moving around a Layout Table

You can move the insertion point between layout cells by pressing the Tab key or by using the arrow keys. When the insertion point is positioned in a layout cell, you can type text or insert a picture or other object into that layout cell. Each layout cell has a border; clicking the border of a layout cell selects that layout cell and all other layout cell borders in the layout table. However, only the selected layout cell includes sizing handles on its border (all parts of which appear as blue lines, even when a part of the selected layout cell's border overlaps the layout table's border). When you point to a corner-sizing handle, the pointer changes shape to indicate which direction you can size the selected layout cell. Just like in a regular table, layout cells cannot overlap each other. The layout table is a container and all of the layout cells it includes must fit inside the layout table's border. For example, before you can increase the height of a layout cells at the top of a layout table, you must decrease the height of the layout cells that appear directly below it to create the new space for the other layout cell's new height. Moving the insertion point to a specific layout cell is similar to selecting a regular table cell. To select a layout cell, you can either click in it or press an arrow key or the Tab key to move to it.

Right now, the layout table and its layout cells appear with a dashed border. You want to show Brett how to select the layout table and its layout cells, so you'll practice these skills next.

To move the insertion point around the layout table:

1. Click in the header layout cell, and then press the **Tab** key. The insertion point moves from the header layout cell to the left layout cell.

2. Press the **down arrow** key ↓. The insertion point moves to the footer layout cell.

3. Press **Ctrl + Home**. The insertion point moves to the beginning of the HTML document and blinks along the left side of the layout table.

4. Press the **Enter** key. A new paragraph is created above the layout table. Usually the layout table contains all of the text and other objects, such as pictures and link bars, that appear in the page. However, you might need to include text outside the layout table, so it's important to know how to create a paragraph that is not included in the layout table.

5. Click the **Undo** button on the Standard toolbar to remove the blank paragraph.

Brett also needs to know how to select the layout table and each layout cell it contains, in case he needs to resize the dimensions of the selected object. When you select a layout cell, its border turns blue and includes sizing handles. When you select a layout table, its border turns green.

To select the layout table and layout cells:

1. Position the pointer on the left border of the left layout cell so it changes to a ⬚ shape and the outside border of the layout table turns green.

2. Click the border. The layout table is selected, as shown in Figure 9-7. The labels along the border show the measurements in pixels between the selected points. The layout table's size is set in pixels based on the current page size setting for the Web site and your monitor's size and resolution. In Figure 9-7, the page size is 760×420 pixels; the width of the layout table is 760 pixels (132 pixels plus 628 pixels). The height of the layout table is 405 pixels (55 pixels plus 313 pixels plus 37 pixels). These measurements correspond to the values in the Width and Height text boxes in the Table properties section of the Layout Tables and Cells task pane.

| Figure 9-7 | Selected layout table |

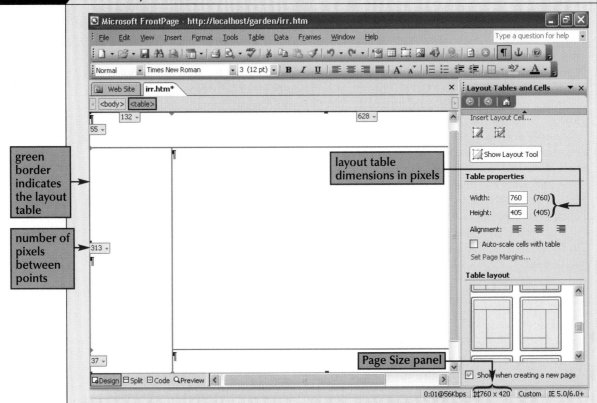

Trouble? If your page size setting is different, your layout table's dimensions might differ. This difference causes no problems, except your content will look slightly different. You can change the page size by clicking the Page Size panel, and then selecting a new page size.

3. Point to the left border of the header layout cell so the pointer changes to a ✛ shape, click the border, and then, if necessary, scroll the page up so you can see the label above the selected header layout cell. The border of the header layout cell is selected, as shown in Figure 9-8. Notice that when you select the header layout cell, the layout table and the other layout cell's borders are also selected. You can identify the selected layout cell because it has sizing handles on it, and its dimensions (in pixels) appear above it.

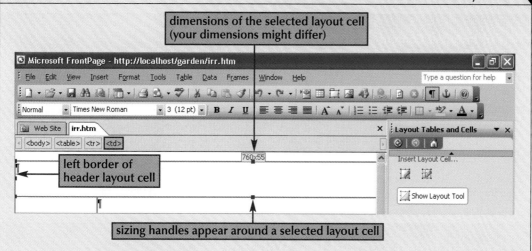

When you are working in a layout table, you might want to close the Layout Tables and Cells task pane so you can see more of the page. You'll close the Layout Tables and Cells task pane for now and then open it again when you need to use its tools.

4. Click the **Close** button ☒ on the Layout Tables and Cells task pane to close it.

Now that you have shown Brett how to select the layout table and its layout cells, you are ready to add content to the cells. Brett wants to include a page banner and link bar to same-level pages in the header layout cell, a link bar to child pages in the left layout cell, a Web page with information about irrigation services in the body layout cell, and the company's copyright information in the footer layout cell. You tell Brett that you could insert all of this content manually by inserting link bar components, a page banner, and copying and pasting the content for the body and footer layout cells. However, because all of this content already exists in separate Web pages that are stored in the garden Web site, you tell Brett that he can set the various layout cells to include page content. In other words, the header layout cell will include the Web page that creates the Web site's top shared border, the left layout cell will include the Web page that creates the Web site's left shared border, and the footer layout cell will include the Web page that creates the Web site's bottom shared border. Brett pasted all of the content that previously existed in the main frame of the frames page into a single Web page and saved it. You will import this page into the Web site and then set the body layout cell to include this page's contents.

Included content is a file or other object that exists elsewhere in a Web site that you set to appear in a second location, such as in a layout cell or shared border. One benefit of using included content in the layout table is that any changes made to the included pages in the site will also automatically be updated in the layout table. Another benefit is that including existing pages in the layout table saves you the time it would otherwise have taken to re-create the content.

Including a Web Page in a Layout Cell

There are several types of included content that you can insert in a Web page; you don't need to use a layout table to include content. Figure 9-9 identifies the different types of included content.

| Figure 9-9 | Types of included content for a Web page |

Type of Included Content	Description
Substitution	Inserts text that includes the page's author, description, author who last modified the page, or URL in a Web page
Page	Displays the content of a Web page in another Web page
Page Based On Schedule	Includes the content of a Web page in another Web page based on a schedule that is set using a starting and ending date and a starting and ending time
Picture Based On Schedule	Includes a picture in a Web page based on a schedule that is set using a starting and ending date and a starting and ending time
Page Banner	Inserts a picture or text page banner in a Web page

Reference Window

Using Included Content in a Web Page

- Position the insertion point in the location in which to insert the content.
- Click the Web Component button on the Standard toolbar.
- In the Component type list box, click Included Content.
- In the Choose a type of content list box, click the option that represents the content you want to include. If you are including a page, use the Include Page Properties dialog box to locate and double-click the page to include. If you are including content based on a schedule, set the starting and ending times.
- Click the OK button.

You'll set the layout cells to include the appropriate page content in them.

To include the top shared border Web page in the header layout cell:

1. Click in the header layout cell so the insertion point appears in it.
2. Click the **Web Component** button 📄 on the Standard toolbar. The Insert Web Component dialog box opens.
3. In the Component type list box, click **Included Content**. See Figure 9-10.

Insert Web Component dialog box ◄ **Figure 9-10**

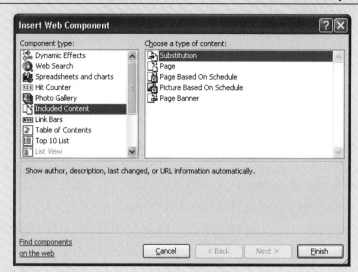

4. In the Choose a type of content list box, click **Page**, and then click the **Finish** button. The Include Page Properties dialog box opens. The Web page that creates the top shared border is a hidden file; you'll need to open it from the _borders folder.

5. Click the **Browse** button in the Include Page Properties dialog box. The Current Web Site dialog box opens and lists the folders and files in the root folder of the garden Web site.

6. Double-click the **_borders** folder to display its contents, and then double-click the **top.htm** page, which creates the top shared border. The Include Page Properties dialog box appears again, with "_borders/top.htm" in the Page to include text box.

7. Click the **OK** button. The Web page that creates the top shared border is inserted in the header layout cell. Because the irr.htm page was already positioned in Navigation view, the page banner includes the page's title and the link bar includes links to the same-level pages and to the home page. The top shared border also includes a horizontal line. Because the irr.htm page does not use a theme, the page banner, link bar, and horizontal line use the default formatting. See Figure 9-11.

Included page in the header layout cell ◄ **Figure 9-11**

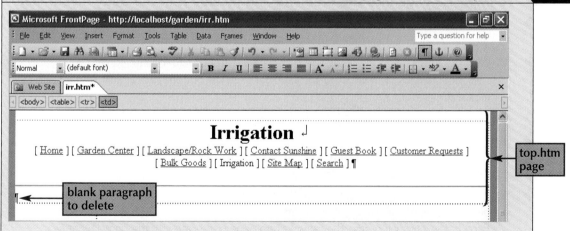

A blank paragraph appears below the horizontal line in the header layout cell. You'll delete this paragraph to close up the blank space.

   8. Click the blank paragraph in the header layout cell, and then delete it.

   9. Save the irr.htm page.

Next, you'll include the content of the Web page that creates the left shared border in the left layout cell and the content of the Web page that creates the bottom shared border in the footer layout cell.

To include content in the left and footer layout cells:

   1. Click in the left layout cell to position the insertion point in it, and then click the **Web Component** button 🖭 on the Standard toolbar.

   2. In the Component type list box, click **Included Content**.

   3. In the Choose a type of content list box, click **Page**, and then click the **Finish** button.

   4. In the Include Page Properties dialog box, click the **Browse** button, open the **_borders** folder, double-click the **left.htm** page, and then click the **OK** button in the Include Page Properties dialog box to close it. The page that creates the left shared border now appears in the left layout cell. Because the Irrigation page doesn't include any active links to child pages, the link bar in the left layout cell displays the default placeholder text.

   5. Scroll down the layout table as necessary, and then click in the footer layout cell to position the insertion point in it.

   6. Click 🖭 ,and then repeat Steps 2 through 4 to include the **bottom.htm** page from the _borders folder in the footer layout cell.

   7. Save the irr.htm page.

The body layout cell will include the new Web page that Brett created. Instead of using the Insert/File menu commands to insert this page's contents into the body layout cell, you'll import Brett's page in the Web site, and then set the body layout cell to include the page content of the imported page.

To import a page into the Web site and include it in the body layout cell:

   1. Display the Folder List, make sure the garden Web site's root folder is selected, click **File** on the menu bar, and then click **Import**. The Import dialog box opens.

   2. Click the **Add File** button, open the **Tutorial.09\Tutorial** folder included with your Data Files, double-click **rainmkr.htm**, and then click the **OK** button. The rainmkr.htm page is added to the Web site.

   3. Close the Folder List, and then click in the body layout cell to position the insertion point in it.

   4. Click the **Web Component** button 🖭 on the Standard toolbar, click the **Included Content** component type, click the **Page** content type, and then click the **Finish** button. The Include Page Properties dialog box opens.

   5. Click the **Browse** button, scroll down the list of folders and files in the root folder of the garden Web site, double-click **rainmkr.htm**, and then click the **OK** button to close the Include Page Properties dialog box. The rainmkr.htm page is inserted into the body layout cell.

   6. Save the irr.htm page.

Now you have included content in each layout cell in the layout table. Brett notices that the content in the left layout cell appears about halfway down the cell and that the content in the body and footer layout cells includes some blank paragraphs. To fix the problem in the left layout cell, you'll need to vertically align the layout cell's contents to top instead of the current default setting, which is middle. You can change the properties of a layout cell by using the Cell Formatting task pane, the Tables toolbar, or the Table command on the menu bar. In general, any command that you can issue for a regular table cell is also permitted in a layout cell.

To change the properties of a layout cell:

1. Right-click the left layout cell to open the shortcut menu, and then click **Cell Properties**. The Cell Properties dialog box opens.

2. Click the **Vertical alignment** list arrow, click **Top**, and then click the **OK** button. The Cell Properties dialog box closes and the vertical alignment of the left layout cell changes from middle to top, causing the link bar placeholder text to move to the top of the cell. The blank paragraph that appears below the placeholder text in the left layout cell isn't going to affect the spacing in the layout cell, so you won't need to delete it.

To delete the blank paragraphs that appear in the body and footer layout cells, you can select and delete them just like any other text. However, when you use included pages in a layout cell (or anywhere else in a Web page), you can change the included page content only by opening the included page. As you'll demonstrate for Brett, some of the blank paragraphs are part of the layout table. Other blank paragraphs, however, are part of the included pages.

To delete the blank paragraphs:

1. Scroll down the irr.htm page so you can see the bottom of the body layout cell, and then delete the blank paragraph that appears below the last bullet in the Warranty Information section.

2. In the footer layout cell, delete the last blank paragraph.

3. In the footer layout cell, try to select the remaining blank paragraph below the copyright information, as shown in Figure 9-12. When you select the paragraph, all of the content in the footer layout cell is selected. The blank paragraphs above and below the copyright information are part of the included page, so you can't delete them from the footer layout cell. To make changes to included page content, you have to open the included page, make the desired changes, and then save the included page.

Figure 9-12 **Selected included page**

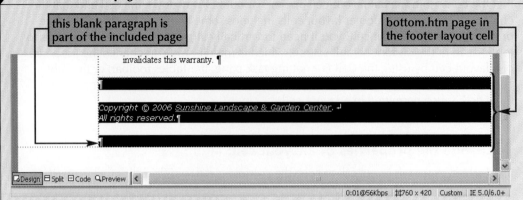

4. Right-click the selected content in the footer layout cell to open the shortcut menu, and then click **Open Page in New Window**. The included page, which is the bottom.htm page in the _borders folder, opens in Design view.

5. Delete the blank paragraph that appears below the copyright information, and then save and close the bottom.htm page. It might take a few seconds for FrontPage to save the page and update it in the pages in the Web site that use it. The footer layout cell now includes only one blank paragraph above the copyright information, which is the effect you want. By including a blank paragraph above the copyright information, you create some space between the copyright information and the content that appears above it in the irr.htm page and also in the pages that use the bottom shared border.

6. Save the irr.htm page.

You must be careful about changing the content in an included page because your changes to that page will be made in every place in the Web site that includes that content. For example, if you changed the copyright information in the bottom.htm page to make it more useful for the layout table, you would also update the bottom shared border in every page in the Web site that uses it. You might be making a change that is appropriate for the bottom shared border, in which case your change is acceptable. However, you might make a change that is acceptable in one place but not in another. If your change is unwanted in one place, it is better to either create a new page to include or to delete the included page and then create original content in the footer layout cell.

Brett wants to preview the page in a browser to check its appearance.

To preview the page in a browser:

1. Click the **Preview** button on the Standard toolbar. The Irrigation page opens in a browser, as shown in Figure 9-13. If necessary, scroll down the page so you can examine the included content.

Irrigation

[Home] [Garden Center] [Landscape/Rock Work] [Contact Sunshine] [Guest Book] [Customer Requests]
[Bulk Goods] [Irrigation] [Site Map] [Search]

top.htm page

Frequently Asked Questions

- **How often should I water my lawn?**
  We recommend a five-day schedule that delivers at least one-half inch of water on an irrigation day. Most pop-up heads can deliver one-half inch of water in 20-25 minutes, depending on your water pressure. Rotor heads require about 50-60 minutes to deliver one-half inch of water, depending on water pressure and the coverage area. Try placing several tuna cans in your yard and check the amount after your system has completed an irrigation cycle to determine the amount of water delivered, and then use your controller to make adjustments.
- **What is the best time to water?**
  We recommend watering in the early morning hours, between 3:00 A.M. and 6:00 A.M. During this time, you will not lose any water to evaporation like you would in the heat of the day, and winds are likely to be calm, reducing the risk of over sprays.
- **My sprinklers water twice on my irrigation day. What is causing this problem?**
  You can program multiple start times for many controllers, so you probably have a second start time programmed for your irrigation day. Check your user manual for information about setting a start time.

left.htm page (no links appear because the irr.htm page has no active links to child pages)

Requesting Service

- We repair most systems, even if we did not install them. If your system is not covered by a warranty, we charge $50 an hour for service work. We will contact you to schedule a convenient day and time to conduct repairs. A technician might call you prior to arriving to confirm the problem you are experiencing so he can arrive with the correct equipment, parts, and crew. Payment is due on completion of service unless other arrangements have been made. Please call 555-2610 to arrange a service visit.

rainmkr.htm page

Tips

- Water deeply and infrequently to establish a deep root system.
- Test your system monthly to look for broken heads and spray problems.
- Set your mower to a height of at least four inches.
- Install a rain sensor so your system will shut off automatically after or during a rain.

Warranty Information

- Our warranty covers material and installation defects, including problems with water coverage, for a full year. During the first year of service, please call us if you have any questions about your new system or the controller, or if you have any problems with coverage that will require adjustments to heads.
- Our warranty is comprehensive, but it does not cover problems caused by city water supply problems, additional landscape installation, landscape growth, or natural disasters.
- RainMaker Irrigation must complete all work during the first year. Any work completed by others invalidates this warranty.

Copyright © 2006 Sunshine Landscape & Garden Center.
All rights reserved.

bottom.htm page

Brett wonders what happened to the link bar in the left layout cell. You tell him that the irr.htm page doesn't have any active links to child pages in Navigation view, so there are no links to display. You remind Brett that Sunshine's irrigation supervisor, Chad Schomaker, asked you to include two pages that would provide information about commercial and residential irrigation systems in the Web site, but you didn't activate these links because

Chad hasn't yet finished these pages. For now, Brett asks you to activate the links so he can see how they look in the layout table. Then you'll ask Chad to finish these pages so the links will open the correct information.

2. Close your browser, click the **Web Site** tab at the top of the Contents pane, and then change to Navigation view.

3. Scroll Navigation view as necessary so you can see the Irrigation page icon in the navigation structure, as shown in Figure 9-14. Notice that the two child pages of the Irrigation page have gray backgrounds, indicating that these pages are not included in the site's link bars.

Figure 9-14	Navigation view

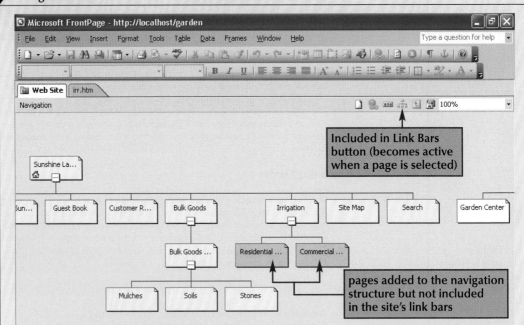

4. Click the **Residential Systems** page icon to select it, and then click the **Included in Link Bars** button 🔲 at the top of the Contents pane. The page icon's background color changes from gray to blue. A blue page icon indicates a selected page; when you select another page in the navigation structure, the background color of the Residential Systems page will change to yellow, which indicates a page that is included in the site's link bars.

5. Repeat Step 4 to change the **Commercial Systems** page so it is included in the site's link bars.

6. Click the **irr.htm** tab at the top of the Contents pane, and then preview the page in a browser. Now the left layout cell contains links to the Residential Systems and Commercial Systems pages, as shown in Figure 9-15.

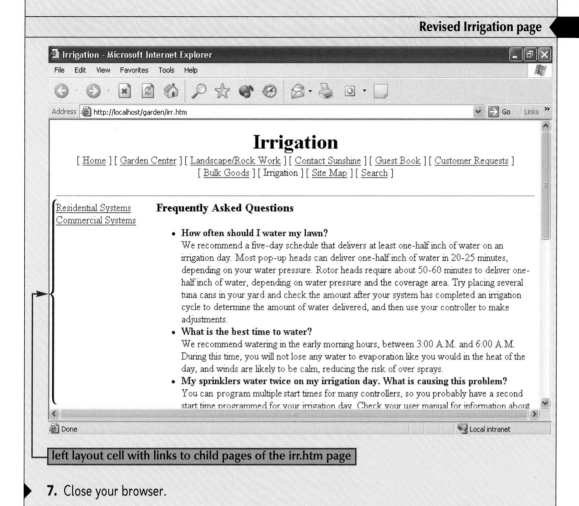

left layout cell with links to child pages of the irr.htm page

7. Close your browser.

Brett is happy with the content of the page. The only thing that he wants you to add is the company's logo, which he wants to appear in the left layout cell. He asks if you can insert several blank paragraphs so the logo will appear at the bottom of the left layout cell. You tell him that inserting blank paragraphs isn't the best approach for controlling the position of the logo. A better way to do this is to create a new layout cell below the left layout cell, and then to insert the logo in the new layout cell.

Creating a Layout Cell in a Layout Table

To create a new layout cell, you have two options. First, you can use the Draw Layout Cell button on the Layout Tables and Cells task pane to draw a new layout cell in the layout table. Second, you can click the Insert Layout Cell link on the Layout Tables and Cells task pane to insert a layout cell by specifying its width, height, and layout orientation (horizontal, vertical, or inline) and location.

Creating a Layout Cell in a Layout Table

- Resize an existing layout cell that borders the layout cell that you want to create to make room for the new layout cell.
- If necessary, display the Layout Tables and Cells task pane.
- Click the Draw Layout Cell button on the Layout Tables and Cells task pane.
- Click and drag the pointer from the upper-left corner of the new layout cell's location to the desired lower-right corner, and then release the mouse button.

Because Brett wants the logo to appear at the bottom of the left layout cell, you will add a new layout cell below the left layout cell in which to store the logo. When you add a layout cell to a layout table, you must make room for it by resizing a layout cell that will border it. In this case, you need to decrease the size of the left layout cell by moving its bottom border up. Then you can add the new layout cell in the space that you created.

To resize the left layout cell:

1. Point to the right border of the left layout cell so the pointer changes to a ✛ shape, and then click the right border of the left layout cell so its border turns blue and sizing handles appear around the left layout cell.

   There are two ways to resize a layout cell. If you need to size the layout cell using exact dimensions in pixels, you can use the Cell Formatting task pane to change the Width and Height values for the selected layout cell. You can also resize the layout cell by dragging a border up or down or right or left with the pointer. It is usually easier to use the pointer to resize a layout cell when you need to make it match the dimensions of another cell by visually repositioning a border. To resize the left layout cell, you'll use the pointer and drag the bottom border up.

2. Scroll down the page as necessary, point to the bottom-middle sizing handle of the selected left layout cell so the pointer changes to a ⊤ shape, and then drag the sizing handle up so it is even with the top of the footer layout cell, as shown in Figure 9-16. Notice that the area you created is beige, which indicates an area in the layout table that does not contain any layout cells.

Resized left layout cell ◄ **Figure 9-16**

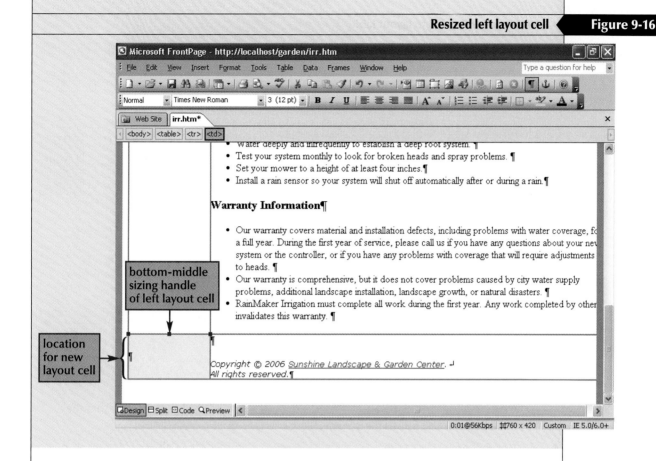

Now that you have made room for the new layout cell, you can use the Draw Layout Cell pointer to create it.

To insert the new layout cell:

▶ 1. Click **View** on the menu bar, click **Task Pane**, and then, if necessary, click the **Other Task Panes** list arrow, and then click **Layout Tables and Cells** to display the Layout Tables and Cells task pane.

▶ 2. Click the **Draw Layout Cell** button 🖳 on the Layout Tables and Cells task pane, and then move the pointer to the upper-left corner of the beige area so the pointer changes to a ✏ shape. You will draw the upper-left corner of the new layout cell in this location.

▶ 3. Click and drag the ✏ pointer from the upper-left corner of the beige area to the lower-right corner. When you release the mouse button, the new layout cell is inserted, as shown in Figure 9-17.

Figure 9-17 ▶ **New layout cell added to layout table**

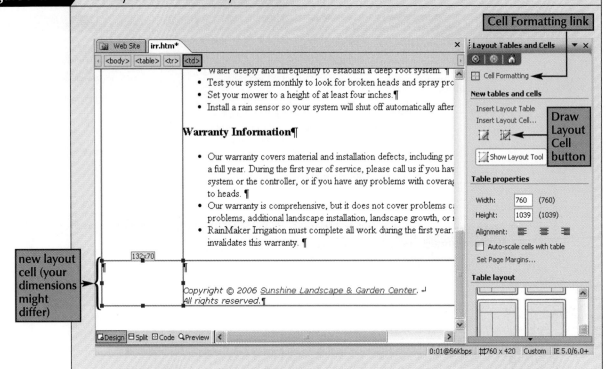

Trouble? The dimensions of your new layout cell might differ. Just make sure that the new layout cell appears in the correct location in the layout table.

▶ **4.** Click in the new layout cell to position the insertion point, click the **Cell Formatting** link at the top of the Layout Tables and Cells task pane to display the Cell Formatting task pane, click the **VAlign** list arrow in the Layout cell properties section of the Cell Formatting task pane, and then click **Bottom**. The vertical alignment of the new layout cell changes to bottom.

▶ **5.** Click the **Insert Picture From File** button 🖾 on the Standard toolbar, open the **images** folder of the garden Web site, double-click the **sun1.gif** file, and then click the **Center** button ☰ on the Formatting toolbar. The picture is inserted in the new layout cell and its alignment changes to centered.

▶ **6.** Save the irr.htm page, and then preview in a browser.

▶ **7.** Scroll down the page and examine the picture that you just inserted, and then close your browser.

Brett likes the position of the logo. He wonders if you can add some color to the page. You tell him that you can format the layout cells with background colors, just like you can format regular table cells with background colors. You'll show Brett how to add background colors next.

Formatting a Layout Cell

After adding content to a layout cell, you can use the Cell Formatting task pane to add cell borders and a background color, to change the cell's alignments, or to change the cell's padding to enhance its appearance. In most cases, any formatting that you can apply to a cell in a regular table is permitted in a layout cell.

Formatting a Layout Cell

- Click the layout cell you want to format.
- If necessary, display the Cell Formatting task pane and use the options on the Cell Formatting task pane to change the cell's borders, background color, padding, alignment, margins, or spacing.

Brett wants you to change the background color of the body layout cell to a light-blue color and the background color of the other layout cells to a light-yellow color.

To change the background color of the layout cells:

1. Click in the body layout cell to select it. Because the layout cell contains an included page, all of its content is selected.

2. Click the **BgColor** list arrow in the Layout cell properties section on the Cell Formatting task pane, click **More Colors**, click the light-blue color with the value Hex={CC,FF,FF}, and then click the **OK** button.

   Trouble? If you cannot find the light-blue color with Hex={CC,FF,FF}, select another light-blue color in the More Colors dialog box, and then click the OK button.

3. Scroll the page as necessary and click in the header layout cell, click the **BgColor** list arrow on the Cell Formatting task pane, click **More Colors**, click the light-yellow color with the value Hex={FF,FF,CC}, and then click the **OK** button.

   Trouble? If you cannot find the light-yellow color with Hex={FF,FF,CC}, select another light-yellow color in the More Colors dialog box, and then click the OK button.

4. Click in the left layout cell, click the **BgColor** list arrow on the Cell Formatting task pane, and then click the light-yellow color in the Document Colors section. The background color of the left layout cell changes to light yellow.

5. Repeat Step 4 to change the background color of the new layout cell and the footer layout cell to light yellow.

6. Save the irr.htm page, and then preview it in a browser. Figure 9-18 shows the completed page.

Figure 9-18   Completed Irrigation page

Irrigation

[Home] [Garden Center] [Landscape/Rock Work] [Contact Sunshine] [Guest Book] [Customer Requests]
[Bulk Goods] [Irrigation] [Site Map] [Search]

Residential Systems
Commercial Systems

Frequently Asked Questions

- **How often should I water my lawn?**
  We recommend a five-day schedule that delivers at least one-half inch of water on an irrigation day. Most pop-up heads can deliver one-half inch of water in 20-25 minutes, depending on your water pressure. Rotor heads require about 50-60 minutes to deliver one-half inch of water, depending on water pressure and the coverage area. Try placing several tuna cans in your yard and check the amount after your system has completed an irrigation cycle to determine the amount of water delivered, and then use your controller to make adjustments.
- **What is the best time to water?**
  We recommend watering in the early morning hours, between 3:00 A.M. and 6:00 A.M. During this time, you will not lose any water to evaporation like you would in the heat of the day, and winds are likely to be calm, reducing the risk of over sprays.
- **My sprinklers water twice on my irrigation day. What is causing this problem?**
  You can program multiple start times for many controllers, so you probably have a second start time programmed for your irrigation day. Check your user manual for information about setting a start time.

Requesting Service

- We repair most systems, even if we did not install them. If your system is not covered by a warranty, we charge $50 an hour for service work. We will contact you to schedule a convenient day and time to conduct repairs. A technician might call you prior to arriving to confirm the problem you are experiencing so he can arrive with the correct equipment, parts, and crew. Payment is due on completion of service unless other arrangements have been made. Please call 555-2610 to arrange a service visit.

Tips

- Water deeply and infrequently to establish a deep root system.
- Test your system monthly to look for broken heads and spray problems.
- Set your mower to a height of at least four inches.
- Install a rain sensor so your system will shut off automatically after or during a rain.

Warranty Information

- Our warranty covers material and installation defects, including problems with water coverage, for a full year. During the first year of service, please call us if you have any questions about your new system or the controller, or if you have any problems with coverage that will require adjustments to heads.
- Our warranty is comprehensive, but it does not cover problems caused by city water supply problems, additional landscape installation, landscape growth, or natural disasters.
- RainMaker Irrigation must complete all work during the first year. Any work completed by others invalidates this warranty.

logo in new
layout cell

Copyright © 2006 Sunshine Landscape & Garden Center.
All rights reserved.

7. Close your browser.

8. Close the garden Web site, and then close FrontPage.

Brett likes the new design of the Irrigation page. In the next session, you'll show Brett how to format this and other Web pages in the site with custom styles that format text and paragraphs.

Session 9.1 Quick Check

1. What is a layout table?
2. What is a layout cell?
3. When a layout table is selected in Design view, what color is its border?
4. When a layout cell is selected in Design view, what color is its border?
5. True or False: The dimensions (height and width) of a layout cell are expressed in pixels.
6. True or False: You can include a Web page in another Web page using a schedule that includes the dates and times to display the included page.
7. Describe how to create a layout cell in an existing layout table.

Session 9.2

Using Inline Styles in a Web Page

A **style** is a collection of formatting commands that you can apply to selected text or paragraphs. In FrontPage, you have used styles to format headings and text; these styles are available in the Style list box on the Formatting toolbar. When you format text or a paragraph with a style, a set of formatting properties, such as font, font size, and alignment, is applied to it. When you want to change a style, you can customize it by changing any of its properties. When you customize an existing style, the customized style is called a **user-defined style** or an **inline style**. You can also create new styles in a Web page for characters and paragraphs. A **character style** includes the properties associated with characters, such as the font, font size, font style (bold, italic, and so on), and font color. A **paragraph style** controls all aspects of a paragraph's appearance, such as line spacing, indentation, and alignment, and it can include character formatting. When viewed in the Style list box on the Formatting toolbar, the ¶ symbol precedes paragraph styles and the **a** symbol precedes character styles. Applying a character style affects only selected text; applying a paragraph style affects the current paragraph (or selected paragraphs). Styles are associated with HTML tags, such as hyperlinks (the HTML a tag) and headings (such as the HTML h1 and h2 tags).

When you create a user-defined style in a Web page, it will format characters or paragraphs in the Web page that contains the user-defined style, but *not* in other Web pages in the same Web site. A user-defined style immediately formats characters or paragraphs with that style in the Web page that contains the user-defined style. In addition, any new text that you type in the page and format with the user-defined style also uses the properties associated with the user-defined style.

Creating a User-Defined Style in a Web Page

Brett wants you to show him how to change the styles in a Web page. Chad Schomaker just sent you the revised Residential Systems and Commercial Systems pages that are linked to the Irrigation page. To show Brett how to work with user-defined styles, you'll import Chad's new pages into the Web site, and then create some user-defined styles in the Residential Systems page.

Creating a User-Defined Style in a Web Page

- Open the page in Design view.
- Click Format on the menu bar, and then click Style.
- In the Styles list box, click the HTML tag that you want to modify, and then click the Modify button.
- Click the Format button in the Modify Style dialog box, and then click the characteristic to be modified (Font, Paragraph, Border, Numbering, or Position).
- Make the desired changes in the dialog box that opens, and then click the OK button.
- Continue modifying the default HTML tags until you have formatted each style you want to customize in the Web page.
- Click the OK button twice to close the dialog boxes.
- Save the Web page.

First, you'll import Chad's new pages into the garden Web site, overwriting the ones you previously created.

To import the pages into the Web site:

1. Start FrontPage, and then use My Network Places to open the **garden** Web site from your Web server.

2. If necessary, display the Folder List and make sure the garden Web site's root folder is selected.

3. Click **File** on the menu bar, click **Import**, click the **Add File** button, open the **Tutorial.09\Tutorial** folder included with your Data Files, select the files **comm_sys.htm** and **res_sys.htm**, and then click the **Open** button.

4. Click the **OK** button, and then click the **Yes to All** button to replace the existing files with the same names.

5. Open the res_sys.htm page in Design view, and then close the Folder List. The page contains headings and some text.

Brett wants the text in this page formatted using the Arial font, with normal text having 10 points and the other text in the page having the default font sizes. In addition, Brett asks you to change the level-one heading to center alignment and the level-two headings to navy blue. When you need to change the normal text in a Web page, you modify the HTML body tag. To make these changes, you'll create user-defined styles for the HTML h1, h2, and body tags.

To create user-defined styles in a Web page:

1. Click **Format** on the menu bar, and then click **Style**. The Style dialog box opens, as shown in Figure 9-19. The Styles list box includes all HTML tags available for use in your document. You might recognize some of the tags immediately—for example, the h1 tag defines a level-one heading in a Web page. Other tags, however, are not as easy to decipher. Unfortunately, FrontPage does not include a detailed resource to help you identify the HTML tags listed in the Styles list box. If you need help in identifying which HTML tag to change in your Web pages, search the Internet for Web sites that describe HTML tags or consult an HTML reference book. In addition, the Student Online Companion page for this tutorial includes links that you can follow to learn more about HTML tags.

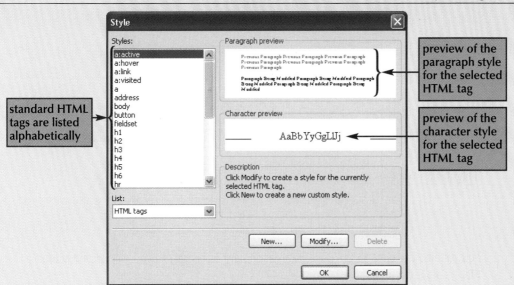

Trouble? If the Style command on the Format menu is dimmed, open the Page Options dialog box, click the Authoring tab, add check marks to the CSS 1.0 (formatting) and CSS 2.0 (positioning) check boxes, click the OK button, and then repeat Step 1.

▶ **2.** In the Styles list box, click **h1**, and then click the **Modify** button. The Modify Style dialog box opens, as shown in Figure 9-20. The HTML tag you selected, h1, appears in the Name (selector) text box.

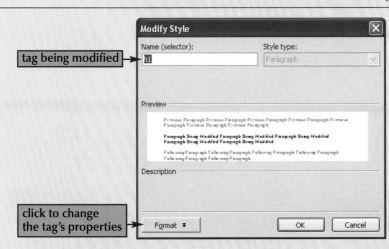

▶ **3.** Click the **Format** button. The Format button list opens and provides options for changing the font, paragraph options, border, numbering, or position of the selected HTML tag. You need to change the font.

▶ **4.** Click **Font** in the Format button list. The Font dialog box opens. You need to change the font to Arial.

▶ **5.** Scroll the Font list box as necessary, and then click **Arial**.

▶ **6.** Click the **OK** button, The Font dialog box closes, and the Modify Style dialog box now displays a preview and description of the change you just made to the h1 tag. See Figure 9-21.

| Figure 9-21 | **Modified h1 tag** |

You still need to change the paragraph alignment to center, so you will not close the Modify Style dialog box yet.

▶ 7. Click the **Format** button, and then click **Paragraph**. The Paragraph dialog box opens.

▶ 8. Click the **Alignment** list arrow, and then click **Center**.

▶ 9. Click the **OK** button to close the Paragraph dialog box, and then click the **OK** button to close the Modify Style dialog box. The h1 tag now appears in the Styles list box as a user-defined style. See Figure 9-22.

| Figure 9-22 | **User-defined styles in the Web page** |

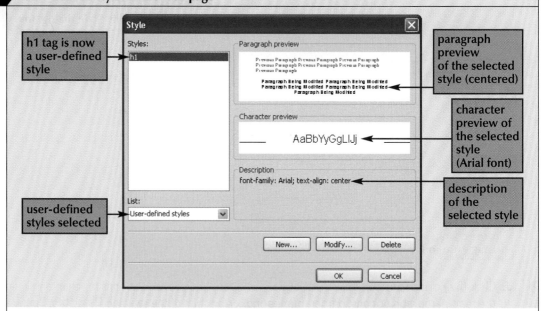

You can modify other styles by changing the List list box to display all HTML tags. Next, you will change the Heading 2 style according to Brett's specifications.

To change the Heading 2 style:

1. Click the **List** list arrow, and then click **HTML tags**. The Styles list box now displays all HTML tags available for use in the document.

2. Click **h2** in the Styles list box, and then click the **Modify** button. The Modify Style dialog box opens. You will change the font.

3. Click the **Format** button, click **Font**, scroll the Font list as necessary and click **Arial**, click the **Color** list arrow, click the **navy** color, and then click the **OK** button. The Font dialog box closes.

   This is the only change you will make to the h2 tag, so you can close the Modify Style dialog box.

4. Click the **OK** button to close the Modify Style dialog box.

5. Click the **OK** button to close the Style dialog box.

The level-one heading in the page now uses the Arial font and is centered; the level-two headings use a navy, Arial font. Next, you will change the normal text to 10 points and the Arial font.

To change the style of normal text:

1. Click **Format** on the menu bar, and then click **Style**. Because this page already contains user-defined styles, the Styles list box automatically displays the user-defined styles in this page. To continue changing the default styles, you need to display the complete list of HTML tags.

2. Click the **List** list arrow, and then click **HTML tags**.

3. In the Styles list box, click **body**, and then click the **Modify** button. The Modify Style dialog box opens.

4. Click the **Format** button, and then click **Font**. The Font dialog box opens.

5. Scroll the Font list and click **Arial**, scroll the Size list and click **10pt**, and then click the **OK** button.

6. Click the **OK** button in the Modify Style dialog box, and then click the **OK** button in the Style dialog box. The normal text changes to 10 points and Arial font, as shown in Figure 9-23.

Figure 9-23 — Residential Systems page formatted by user-defined styles

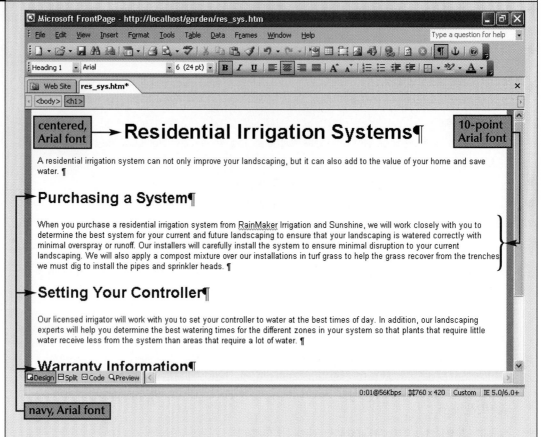

Figure 9-23 — Residential Systems page formatted by user-defined styles

7. Save and close the page.

Now Brett knows how to format styles in a Web page. He asks you to make the same changes in the Commercial Systems Web page so the formatting in these pages will be the same. Instead of changing these pages, however, you decide to show him how to create a cascading style sheet.

Using a Cascading Style Sheet in a Web Site

You have already shown Brett how to create inline styles in a single Web page that format characters and paragraphs. However, the real power of creating styles is to apply formats across all or selected pages in a Web site. To apply styles to more than one page, you create a cascading style sheet. A **cascading style sheet (CSS)**, also called an **external style sheet**, is a file in which you change default styles and create new styles, and then link to other Web pages so they will use the styles you created. To create a cascading style sheet, you start by creating a new, blank page and saving it as a cascading style sheet or use a page template to create a blank cascading style sheet. Instead of adding content to the new page, however, you add the HTML tags for the styles and then save the page. Web pages that have been saved as cascading style sheets have .css filename extensions; Web pages that contain inline styles still have .htm filename extensions. As you add new Web pages to the Web site, you can link them to the cascading style sheet so the styles you defined will format them. If a cascading style sheet does not contain a style for a specific HTML tag, then a browser will format that tag using the default HTML settings.

Before using styles and cascading style sheets in your Web site, make sure that the people who will visit your site are using browsers that can display styles. Internet Explorer 3.01

and higher and Netscape Navigator 4.0 and higher *generally* can display pages that use styles. However, some versions of Internet Explorer and Navigator cannot display some tags generated by styles, or they read the tags unpredictably. As with all Web sites, make sure to test pages that use styles carefully using different browsers, browser versions, operating systems, and monitors to ensure that your content appears as desired. If you know that some of your site's visitors are using older browsers, you can use the Authoring tab in the Page Options dialog box to deselect support for cascading style sheets so FrontPage will disable cascading style sheet commands in your Web site and prevent you from using them.

A cascading style sheet can contain the same kinds of changes that you made to the default HTML styles in the Residential Systems page. You can also create your own styles. For example, you might want to format a company name in a certain way to make it stand out in a Web page. You could create a new inline character style in the Web page and then apply the new style to every occurrence of the company name in the page. If you include this style in a cascading style sheet, then you can use it to format the company name in the same way across multiple pages or the pages in an entire site.

After you create a cascading style sheet and save it in a Web site, you can use it to change the styles in existing or new Web pages by linking the cascading style sheet to them. The styles defined in a cascading style sheet format the content in only those Web pages that are linked to it. If you update a cascading style sheet, the updated styles will be applied automatically to all pages that are linked to the cascading style sheet.

In most cases, you should not link a cascading style sheet to a Web page that uses a theme. The theme provides the styles that format the various HTML tags in the Web page. To change the appearance of HTML tags in a Web page that uses a theme, use the Customize Theme dialog box to make changes to the theme. If you use a cascading style sheet to make changes to a theme, the theme's settings will generally override most of the styles in the cascading style sheet. So it's better to use either a cascading style sheet or a theme, but not both, to format a Web page.

Creating a Cascading Style Sheet

To apply your user-defined styles to other pages, you need to create a cascading style sheet. After saving the cascading style sheet, you can link it to other Web pages by using the Style Sheet Links command on the Format menu. Note that a Web page saved as a cascading style sheet cannot contain any content—it must be blank, except for the user-defined styles.

Creating a Cascading Style Sheet　　　　　　　　　　　　　　Reference Window

- Click File on the menu bar, click New, click the More page templates link on the New task pane, click the Style Sheets tab, click the Normal Style Sheet icon (if necessary), and then click the OK button.
- Click File on the menu bar, click Save, enter the filename in the File name text box, click the Save as type list arrow, click CSS Files, and then click the Save button.
- Click Format on the menu bar, and then click Style.
- In the Styles list box, click the HTML tag that you want to modify, and then click the Modify button.
- Click the Format button in the Modify Style dialog box, and then click the characteristic to be modified (Font, Paragraph, Border, Numbering, or Position).
- Make the desired changes in the dialog box that opens, and then click the OK button.
- Continue modifying the default HTML tags until you have created each style you want to include in the cascading style sheet.
- Click the OK button twice to close the dialog boxes.
- Save the cascading style sheet.

You will use a page template to create a blank cascading style sheet and then add styles to it and use it to format the pages for irrigation services so they will have a consistent appearance.

To create and save a cascading style sheet:

1. Click **File** on the menu bar, and then click **New**. The New task pane opens.

2. On the New task pane, click **More page templates**. The Page Templates dialog box opens.

   Trouble? If a dialog box opens and asks if you want to download custom templates from the garden Web site, click the Yes button.

3. Click the **Style Sheets** tab, make sure the **Normal Style Sheet** icon is selected, and then click the **OK** button, A new cascading style sheet opens and does not contain any content. In addition, the Style toolbar opens, as shown in Figure 9-24.

Figure 9-24	Cascading style sheet in Code view

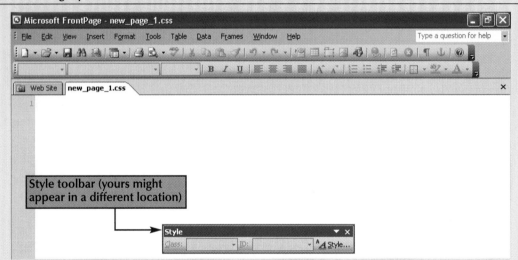

Trouble? If the Style toolbar doesn't open automatically, click View on the menu bar, point to Toolbars, and then click Style.

4. Click the **Save** button 🖫 on the Standard toolbar, and then type **irr_style**.

5. Click the **Save as type** list arrow, scroll down the list, and then click **CSS Files**. If Windows is configured to display filename extensions, the filename in the File name text box changes to irr_style.css. The .css filename extension indicates a cascading style sheet.

6. Click the **Save** button.

You can view a cascading style sheet only in Code view because the file contains only HTML tags.

You will change the Heading 1 style first.

To change the Heading 1 style:

1. Click the **Style** button 🄰ᴬStyle... on the Style toolbar. The Style dialog button opens.

2. In the Styles list box, click **h1**, and then click the **Modify** button. The Modify Style dialog box opens. You will change the font first.

  ▶ **3.** Click the **Format** button, and then click **Font** in the Format button list. The Font dialog box opens. You need to change the font to Arial.

  ▶ **4.** Scroll the Font list as necessary, click **Arial**, and then click the **OK** button. The Font dialog box closes, and the Modify Style dialog box now displays a preview and description of the new style.

      Now you can change the alignment to center.

  ▶ **5.** Click the **Format** button, and then click **Paragraph**. The Paragraph dialog box opens.

  ▶ **6.** Click the **Alignment** list arrow, click **Center**, and then click the **OK** button.

  ▶ **7.** Click the **OK** button to close the Modify Style dialog box.

Next, you will change the level-two headings to navy and Arial.

To change the Heading 2 style:

  ▶ **1.** Click the **List** list arrow in the Style dialog box, and then click **HTML tags**.

  ▶ **2.** In the Styles list box, click **h2**, and then click the **Modify** button.

  ▶ **3.** Click the **Format** button, and then click **Font**. The Font dialog box opens.

  ▶ **4.** Scroll the Font list as necessary and click **Arial**, click the **Color** list arrow, click the **navy** color, and then click the **OK** button.

  ▶ **5.** Click the **OK** button to close the Modify Style dialog box.

Finally, change the style of the normal text to 10 points and Arial.

To change the normal text style:

  ▶ **1.** Click **body** in the Styles list box, and then click the **Modify** button. The Modify Style dialog box opens.

  ▶ **2.** Click the **Format** button, and then click **Font**. The Font dialog box opens.

  ▶ **3.** Scroll the Font list and click **Arial**, scroll the Size list and click **10pt**, and then click the **OK** button.

  ▶ **4.** Click the **OK** button in the Modify Style dialog box to close it. You can view the styles that you modified by changing the Styles list box to display user-defined styles.

  ▶ **5.** Click the **List** list arrow, and then click **User-defined styles**. The Styles list box now includes the h1, h2, and body tags.

  ▶ **6.** Click the **OK** button to close the Style dialog box, and then click the **Save** button to save the page. The only content in the Web page is the styles. See Figure 9-25.

Figure 9-25 | **Cascading style sheet with user-defined styles**

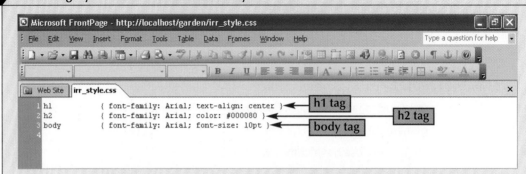

Trouble? If necessary, drag the Style toolbar out of the way so you can see the HTML document.

The cascading style sheet now includes the custom styles you defined. To use the styles to a format a Web page, you need to link the Web page to the cascading style sheet.

Linking a Cascading Style Sheet to a Web Page

When you link a cascading style sheet to a Web page, the HTML link tag is added to the Web page. After you link the page to the cascading style sheet, any HTML tags used in the Web page and defined in the cascading style sheet will use the formatting instructions from the cascading style sheet.

Reference Window | **Linking a Cascading Style Sheet to a Web Page**

- Open the Web page in Design view, or select one or more pages in Folders view.
- Click Format on the menu bar, and then click Style Sheet Links. The Link Style Sheet dialog box opens.
- Click the All Pages option button to link the cascading style sheet to all pages in the Web site, or click the Selected page(s) option button to link the cascading style sheet to only the open page in Design view or the selected pages in Folders view.
- Click the Add button, select the cascading style sheet in the Select Style Sheet dialog box, and then click the OK button.
- Click the OK button.
- If a page is open in Design view, save the page.

You'll link the cascading style sheet to the Commercial Systems page.

To link a Web page to the cascading style sheet:

1. Click the **Close** button ⊗ on the Contents pane to close the irr_style.css page.

2. In Folders view, double-click **comm_sys.htm** to open the Commercial Systems page in Design view.

3. Click **Format** on the menu bar, and then click **Style Sheet Links**. The Link Style Sheet dialog box opens. You can apply a cascading style sheet to all pages in the Web site or to only the selected page. You will apply the cascading style sheet named irr_style.css to the selected page.

4. Make sure that the **Selected page(s)** option button is selected, and then click the **Add** button. The Select Style Sheet dialog box opens.

5. Scroll down the list of folders and files in the garden Web site, and then double-click **irr_style.css** in the list box. The Select Style Sheet dialog box closes, and the Link Style Sheet dialog box displays the irr_style.css page in the URL list box. See Figure 9-26.

Link Style Sheet dialog box ◀ **Figure 9-26**

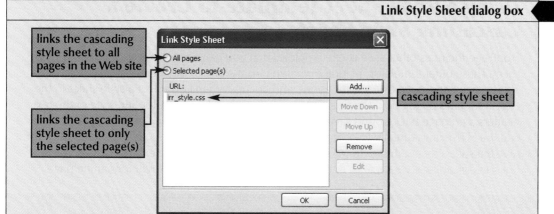

links the cascading style sheet to all pages in the Web site

links the cascading style sheet to only the selected page(s)

cascading style sheet

6. Click the **OK** button. The Link Style Sheet dialog box closes and the text in the Commercial Systems Web page now uses the styles that you defined in the cascading style sheet, as shown in Figure 9-27. Any future text that uses the Heading 1, Heading 2, or Normal style in this Web page will be formatted using the specifications from the cascading style sheet. Any future text that uses any other HTML tag will use the default HTML settings for the tag.

Commercial Systems page formatted by a cascading style sheet ◀ **Figure 9-27**

7. Save and close the page.

Now that Brett has the hang of things, you want to show him a shortcut that he can take when creating a cascading style sheet.

Using a Style Sheet Template to Create a Cascading Style Sheet

FrontPage includes other style sheet templates that you can use to create a cascading style sheet. These other templates include formatting from some of the themes available in the Theme task pane, such as Arcs, Blueprint, and Poetic. When you select a style sheet in the Page Templates dialog box, the Description section identifies the color and style of the text, headers, and page background saved in the style sheet. You can use the Style dialog box or edit the HTML tags directly to change, remove, or add styles to the style sheet, and then you save the style sheet with the desired filename and the .css filename extension. When you link the cascading style sheet to one or more Web pages, the styles will format the page.

Reference Window	**Using a Template to Create a Cascading Style Sheet**

- If necessary, display the New task pane.
- Click More page templates in the New page section. The Page Templates dialog box opens.
- Click the Style Sheets tab.
- Preview each style sheet template and read its description and select one to use.
- Double-click the icon for the style sheet template you selected.
- Click File on the menu bar, click Save, enter the filename in the File name text box, click the Save as type list arrow, click CSS Files, and then click the Save button.
- Link the cascading style sheet to other Web pages as necessary.

You'll show Brett the styles in a style sheet template so he can see how much time he might save by using one to design his pages.

To use a template to create a cascading style sheet:

1. Click **File** on the menu bar, and then click **New**. The New task pane opens.

2. On the New task pane, click **More page templates**. The Page Templates dialog box opens.

   Trouble? If a dialog box opens and asks if you want to download custom templates from the garden Web site, click the Yes button.

3. Click the **Style Sheets** tab.

4. Click a few of the style sheet template icons and read the description of each one to get a sense of the designs they include. Figure 9-28 shows the description for the Poetic style sheet template.

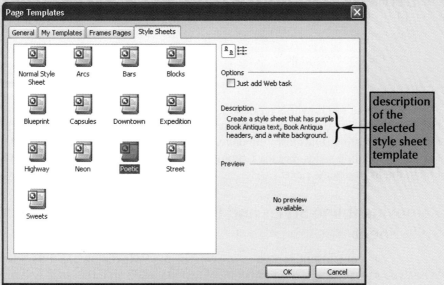

5. If necessary, click the **Poetic** icon, and then click the **OK** button. A new cascading style sheet opens in Code view. See Figure 9-29.

Code view for the new cascading style sheet ◀ **Figure 9-29**

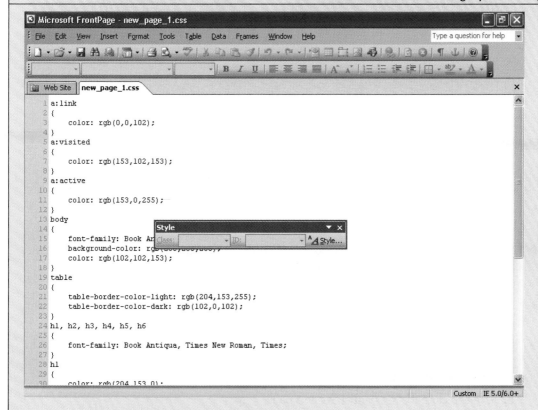

```
1  a:link
2  {
3      color: rgb(0,0,102);
4  }
5  a:visited
6  {
7      color: rgb(153,102,153);
8  }
9  a:active
10 {
11     color: rgb(153,0,255);
12 }
13 body
14 {
15     font-family: Book An
16     background-color: rg
17     color: rgb(102,102,153);
18 }
19 table
20 {
21     table-border-color-light: rgb(204,153,255);
22     table-border-color-dark: rgb(102,0,102);
23 }
24 h1, h2, h3, h4, h5, h6
25 {
26     font-family: Book Antiqua, Times New Roman, Times;
27 }
28 h1
29 {
30     color: rgb(204,153,0);
```

> 6. Scroll down the page and examine the HTML tags that create the styles.
>
> 7. Click the **Save** button 🖫 on the Standard toolbar, type **poetic** in the File name text box, click the **Save as type** list arrow, scroll down the list, click **CSS Files**, and then click the **Save** button.
>
> 8. Close the poetic.css page.

Brett wants to see how this cascading style sheet formats the irrigation pages. However, before you can link these pages to the poetic.css cascading style sheet, you will need to remove the existing styles from the page. For the Residential Systems page, you will need to delete the inline styles. For the Commercial Systems page, you will need to break the link to the irr_styles.css page.

Removing Inline Styles and Breaking the Link to a Cascading Style Sheet

When a page contains inline styles, you can use the Style dialog box to remove them. When you save the page, the formatting of text that used an inline style will revert to the default HTML settings for that tag.

Reference Window | **Removing an Inline Style from a Web Page**

- Open the page in Design view.
- Click Format on the menu bar, and then click Style.
- Click the HTML tag in the Styles list box, and then click the Delete button. Repeat this step as necessary to remove all of the desired HTML tags from the list of user-defined styles.
- Click the OK button.
- Save the page.

You'll open the Residential Systems page in Design view and remove all of the user-defined styles from this page.

To remove inline styles from a Web page:

> 1. In Folders view, double-click **res_sys.htm** to open the Residential Systems page in Design view.
>
> 2. Click **Format** on the menu bar, and then click **Style**. The Style dialog box opens. Because this page contains user-defined styles, the Styles list box displays the user-defined styles in the page.
>
> 3. With **h1** selected in the Styles list box, click the **Delete** button. The h1 tag is removed from the Styles list box, and the user-defined style for this tag is removed from the page.
>
> 4. Repeat Step 3 to remove the **h2** and **body** HTML tags from the Styles list box, and then click the **OK** button. The formatting in the page reverts to the default HTML settings for the h1, h2, and body HTML tags.
>
> 5. Save and close the Residential Systems page.

When you no longer want to use a cascading style sheet to format a Web page, you can remove the link using the Link Style Sheet dialog box or by deleting the HTML link tag that links the cascading style sheet to the Web page in the HTML document.

Breaking the Link to a Cascading Style Sheet

Reference Window

- Open the Web page that contains the link to a cascading style sheet in Design view, or select the pages that contain links to a cascading style sheet in Folders view.
- Click Format on the menu bar, and then click Style Sheet Links. The Link Style Sheet dialog box opens.
- If you are removing the link from only the selected page(s), click the Selected page(s) option button. If you are removing the link to all pages in a Web site, click the All pages option button.
- Click the style sheet to remove in the URL list box, click the Remove button, and then click the OK button.
- If a page was open in Design view, save your changes.

You want to make sure that Brett knows how to break the link to a cascading style sheet, so you'll show him how to do this next.

To remove the link to a cascading style sheet:

1. In Folders view, double-click **comm_sys.htm** to open the Commercial Systems page in Design view.
2. Click **Format** on the menu bar, and then click **Style Sheet Links**. The Link Style Sheet dialog box opens, as shown in Figure 9-30. The URL list box shows the link to the irr_style.css page.

Link Style Sheet dialog box ◁ **Figure 9-30**

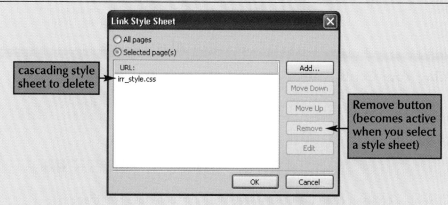

3. Click **irr_style.css** in the URL list box, and then click the **Remove** button.
4. Click the **OK** button. The link to the cascading style sheet is removed from the Commercial Systems page, and the formatting in the Commercial Systems page reverts to the default HTML settings for the h1, h2, and body tags.
5. Save and close the Commercial Systems page.

Now that both pages no longer use any user-defined styles, you can link them to the poetic.css cascading style sheet you created from a style sheet template.

To link the pages to the cascading style sheet:

1. In Folders view, select the pages **comm_sys.htm** and **res_sys.htm**.

2. Click **Format** on the menu bar, and then click **Style Sheet Links**. The Link Style Sheet dialog box opens.

3. Make sure the **Selected page(s)** option button is selected, and then click the **Add** button. The Select Style Sheet dialog box opens.

4. Scroll down the list of folders and files in the garden Web site, and then double-click **poetic.css**. The Link Style Sheet dialog box shows the poetic.css page in the URL list box.

5. Click the **OK** button.

6. In Folders view, click the **comm_sys.htm** page, and then click the **Preview** button 🖾 on the Standard toolbar. Figure 9-31 shows the Commercial Systems page, which is formatted by the poetic.css cascading style sheet.

| Figure 9-31 | Commercial Systems page formatted by poetic.css |

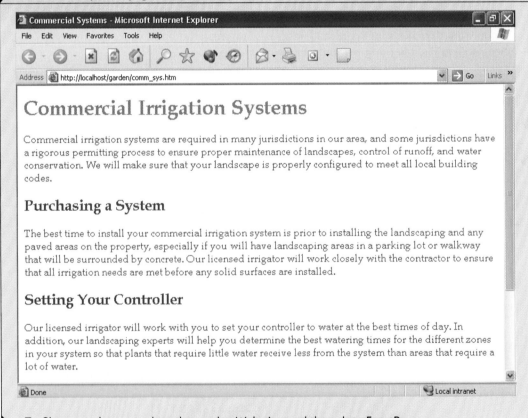

7. Close your browser, close the garden Web site, and then close FrontPage.

When you complete the Review Assignments at the end of this tutorial, you will add the navigation options to the pages with information about irrigation services.

If you want to learn more about using styles in a Web site, the Student Online Companion page for Tutorial 9 includes links that you can follow to locate additional resources on HTML tags and using styles.

In the next session, you will show Brett how to insert a spreadsheet and a chart in a Web page.

Session 9.2 Quick Check

1. What are the five characteristics that you can change for a selected HTML tag using the Modify Style dialog box?
2. True or False: A theme contains a set of styles that you might also find in a cascading style sheet.
3. To save a page as a cascading style sheet, choose the _____ option in the Save as type list box.
4. True or False: You can modify any HTML tag to create a user-defined style.
5. You use the _____ dialog box to link a Web page to a cascading style sheet.
6. A page that is saved as a cascading style sheet has a filename extension of _____.
7. True or False: You can open a cascading style sheet in Design view.

Session 9.3

Using Office Components in a Web Site

Most of the Office 2003 programs—including Word, Excel, and PowerPoint—include commands that let you save their documents as Web pages so that it is easy to include them in a Web site. In many cases, however, you must use the same Office 2003 program to update the Web page that you used to create the page; you cannot use FrontPage to make the changes. To create a Web page that contains a chart, for example, you could use Excel to create the chart and then save the workbook that contains the chart as a Web page in a Web site. In this case, you must use Excel to make any changes to that chart.

You can also use FrontPage to create the chart in the Web page by inserting an Office component into the Web page. An **Office component** is a self-contained object that includes the commands and tools required to use it. Note, however, that an Office component is *not* an embedded object from another Office program. You can create three types of Office components in a Web page: a spreadsheet, a chart, or a PivotTable list. A **spreadsheet**, or **worksheet**, is a tool that lets you analyze and summarize data. A **chart** displays data from a spreadsheet or other data source as a picture—for example, as a pie chart or a bar chart. A **PivotTable list** is an interactive spreadsheet that lets you quickly summarize, organize, and display large amounts of data.

When you insert an Office component in a Web page, FrontPage creates the object and provides the tools and commands needed to use it. When inserted in a Web page, an Office component does not include the same powerful functionality that you will find in Excel, but it does contain tools to perform calculations, format the data's appearance, and change its characteristics.

You insert a component into a Web page by clicking the Web Component button on the Standard toolbar and then clicking the Spreadsheets and charts component type in the list box. If the Spreadsheets and charts component type is dimmed in the Component type list, then you might need to change the Web site's authoring settings to support Office components or install the Office 2003 components on the server.

Brett wants to include a spreadsheet and a chart in a Web page to show the high and low temperatures for February of the previous year. He stored this data in an Excel workbook that you will import into the Web site. Then you can use the data to create a spreadsheet and chart.

Spreadsheets

Inserting a Spreadsheet Component in a Web Page

When you need to display spreadsheet data in a Web page, you can use one of two methods to include the data. The first method is to create a workbook in Excel and then save it as a Web page by clicking File on the menu bar, clicking Save as Web Page, and then saving the file in the desired Web site as a Web page. For this method, you must have Excel installed on your computer.

Alternatively, regardless of whether Excel is installed on your computer, you can create or insert spreadsheet data in a Web page using an Office spreadsheet component. The spreadsheet component allows you to enter, format, and update spreadsheet data using FrontPage. When you insert a spreadsheet component, you are really inserting an object that includes spreadsheet commands and tools similar to those found in Excel. In fact, the object itself looks like a miniature Excel program window, and the commands and tools provided by the spreadsheet component are similar to those found in Excel.

Reference Window	**Inserting and Using a Spreadsheet Component in a Web Page**

- Create a new Web page or open an existing Web page and position the insertion point in the location in which to insert the component.
- Click the Web Component button on the Standard toolbar, click Spreadsheets and charts in the Component type list box, make sure that Office Spreadsheet is selected in the Choose a control list box, and then click the Finish button.
- Click the desired cell and then enter the data that you want to analyze using the spreadsheet component. Use the Tab key or the arrow keys to move to other cells as necessary to enter the data.
- Click the Commands and Options button on the spreadsheet component toolbar to open the Commands and Options dialog box. Use the commands and tools to calculate and format the data.
- Click anywhere outside the spreadsheet component to deselect it.

Your first task is to import Brett's spreadsheet data into the garden Web site. Then you will create a new Web page and insert a spreadsheet component into it. After inserting the spreadsheet component into the Web page, you will import the spreadsheet data into the spreadsheet component.

To import the worksheet data and create a new Web page:

1. Start FrontPage, and then use My Network Places to open the **garden** Web site from your Web server.

2. If necessary, display the Folder List, make sure that the garden Web site's root folder is selected, click **File** on the menu bar, click **Import**, and then click the **Add File** button. The Add File to Import List dialog box opens.

3. Click the **Look in** list arrow, open the **Tutorial.09\Tutorial** folder included with your Data Files, double-click **feb_data.htm**, and then click the **OK** button. The file that contains the spreadsheet data is imported into the Web site.

4. Close the Folder List.

5. Click the **Create a new normal page** button on the Standard toolbar to create a new page and open it in Design view.

Trouble? If the Layout Tables and Cells task pane opens, close it.

6. Save the page using the filename **february.htm** and the title **February Temperature Data**.

Now you can insert a spreadsheet component into the page.

To insert a spreadsheet component into a page:

1. Click the **Web Component** button ⊞ on the Standard toolbar, click **Spreadsheets and charts** in the Component type list box, make sure that **Office Spreadsheet** is selected in the Choose a control list box, and then click the **Finish** button. A spreadsheet component is inserted in the page.

   Trouble? If the Spreadsheets and charts option in the Component type list box is dimmed, click the Cancel button. Click Tools on the menu bar, click Page Options, and then click the Authoring tab. If necessary, click the ActiveX controls and the VBScript check boxes to select them, click the OK button, and then repeat Step 1. If the Spreadsheets and charts option is still dimmed, ask your instructor or technical support person for help.

2. Click the cell in column A, row 1. Sizing handles and a slashed border appear around the component to indicate that it is selected. The dark border around cell A1 indicates that it is the active cell. See Figure 9-32.

Spreadsheet component inserted into the page | Figure 9-32

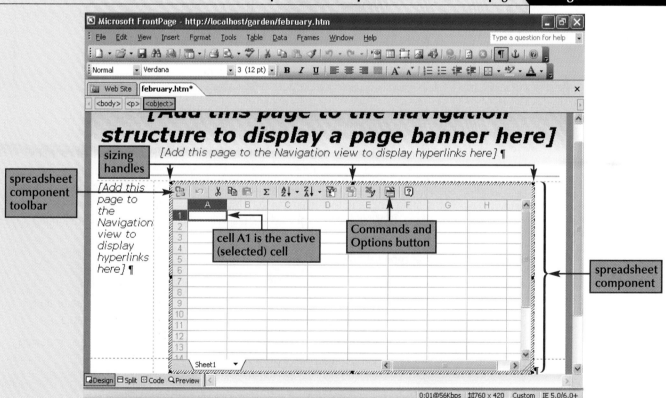

After inserting the spreadsheet component, you can click in a cell and enter data into it just as you would using Excel, or you can use the Commands and Options dialog box to import data into the spreadsheet component. Because you imported Brett's data into the Web site, you can import his data into the spreadsheet component instead of entering it.

Importing Data into a Spreadsheet Component

After you insert a spreadsheet component into a Web page, you can use the Commands and Options dialog box to import data into the spreadsheet component. The Commands and Options dialog box contains commands similar to those found in Excel.

To open the Commands and Options dialog box and import the data:

1. Click the **Commands and Options** button 🖼 on the spreadsheet component toolbar to open the Commands and Options dialog box, and then click the **Import** tab. See Figure 9-33.

| Figure 9-33 | Commands and Options dialog box |

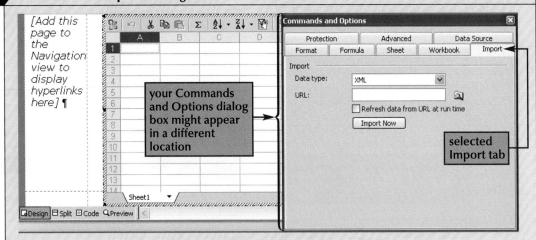

Trouble? The Commands and Options dialog box might appear in a different location on your screen. You can move the dialog box anywhere on the screen by dragging its title bar.

To import the data from a file, you must specify its format and URL. The file that contains Brett's data, feb_data.htm, is stored in the garden Web site as an HTML document. The other file types that you can import are XML and CSV. **XML (Extensible Markup Language)** is a programming language that is similar to HTML, but also permits the author to develop customized tags. **CSV (comma-separated values)** is another name for comma-delimited text, where commas separate data values in a text file.

2. Click the **Data type** list arrow, and then click **HTML**.

3. Click the URL text box, and then type **http://localhost/garden/feb_data.htm**.

   Trouble? If you are storing your Web site on a computer with a different name or on a different server, use the path for your server instead of the one provided in Step 3.

4. Click the **Refresh data from URL at run time** check box to select it. The data is imported into the spreadsheet component. See Figure 9-34.

Data imported into the spreadsheet component | **Figure 9-34**

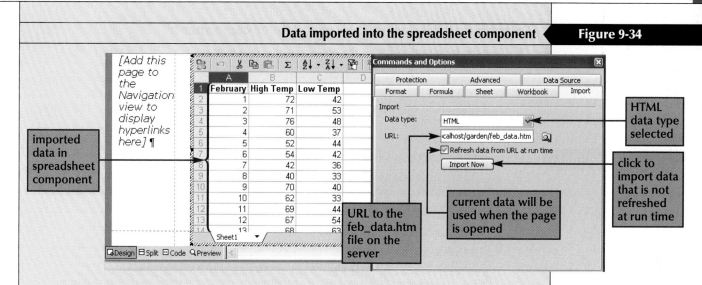

imported data in spreadsheet component

[Add this page to the Navigation view to display hyperlinks here] ¶

URL to the feb_data.htm file on the server

current data will be used when the page is opened

HTML data type selected

click to import data that is not refreshed at run time

Trouble? If a dialog box opens and asks you about importing data from another domain, click the OK button.

Trouble? If a dialog box opens and tells you that it cannot access data on another domain, you must change your computer's security settings to continue. Ask your instructor or technical support person for help.

Selecting the Refresh data from URL at run time check box ensures that the spreadsheet component will display the current data in the data source (feb_data.htm) whenever the Web page is opened or refreshed in the browser. However, the data source must be a file that exists in the Web site on the server. You cannot use this feature when you are importing data from an outside data source because the browser will issue an error message. If you don't select the Refresh data from URL at run time check box, then you click the Import Now button to import the data. If you use FrontPage to change the imported data, then those changes won't appear in the browser. Instead, the browser will use the original data source when loading the component.

Brett decides that he doesn't want to link the spreadsheet component to the data source, so he asks you to disable this feature. When this feature is disabled, any changes that Brett makes to the data in the spreadsheet component will be permanent because the data won't be refreshed from the data source at run time.

5. Click the **Refresh data from URL at run time** check box to clear it. The next time that you display the Import tab, the URL text box will be empty, because no run-time data source will be defined for the spreadsheet component.

6. Click the **Close** button ☒ on the Commands and Options dialog box to close it.

You want to make sure that Brett can make changes to the spreadsheet component, so you will show him how to use the Help system.

Getting Help When Using the Spreadsheet Component

Regardless of your experience using Excel, you might need help using the commands in the Commands and Options dialog box. Fortunately, each Office component has its own Help system to help you find information about your current task. Clicking the Help button on a component's toolbar (or right-clicking the component to open the shortcut menu and then clicking Help) opens the Help window for that component. Brett wants to change the color of the column headings in the spreadsheet component. You decide to show him how to use the Help window to learn how to format data.

To get help while using the spreadsheet component:

▶ **1.** Click the **Help** button 🔲 on the spreadsheet component toolbar. The Microsoft Office 2003 Spreadsheet Component Help window opens.

▶ **2.** If necessary, click the **Maximize** button 🔲 on the Microsoft Office 2003 Spreadsheet Component Help title bar to maximize the window, and then click the **Contents** tab (if necessary). See Figure 9-35.

Figure 9-35 | **Microsoft Office 2003 Spreadsheet Component Help window**

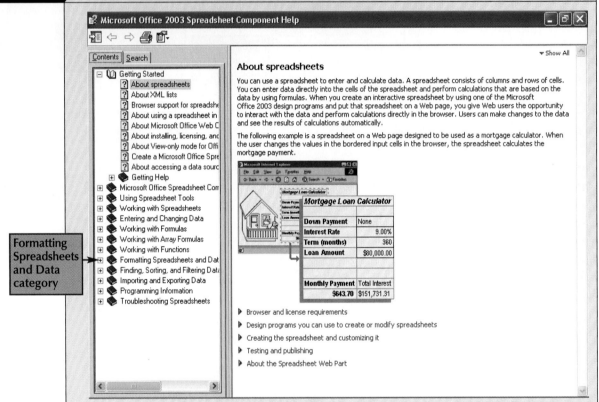

Formatting
Spreadsheets
and Data
category

Like other Microsoft Help windows, the Microsoft Office 2003 Spreadsheet Component Help window has a Contents tab and a Search tab. You use the Contents tab to search for help by category, and you use the Search tab to search for help by entering key terms. You will use the Contents tab to search for help on formatting data.

▶ **3.** Click the **plus box** to the left of the Formatting Spreadsheets and Data category.

▶ **4.** Click **Format cells in a spreadsheet**. The pane on the right displays information and links to pages that describe how to change the format and alignment of data.

▶ **5.** Click some of the links and read the Help pages that open to learn about formatting and aligning spreadsheet data.

▶ **6.** After reading the information about formatting and aligning data, click the **Close** button 🔲 on the Microsoft Office 2003 Spreadsheet Component Help window to close it.

When you need information about other formatting options, performing calculations, or other topics of interest, you can open the Help window to search for information about your task.

Resizing a Spreadsheet Component in a Web Page

The spreadsheet component that you inserted in the Web page is an object, just like a picture or text. It is selected when a slashed border and sizing handles appear around the component. To resize the component, you drag a sizing handle.

Brett thinks that the spreadsheet component might look better if you resized it to fit the data in the worksheet. After resizing the spreadsheet component, it will be narrower and longer to display the data it contains.

To resize the spreadsheet component:

1. Click cell **A1** in the spreadsheet component to select it. Sizing handles and a slashed border appear around the component.

2. Position the pointer on the middle-right sizing handle so the pointer changes to a ↔ shape, and then click and slowly drag it to the left until the right edge of the component is slightly to the right of column C in the worksheet.

3. Position the pointer on the middle-bottom sizing handle so the pointer changes to a ↕ shape, and then click and slowly drag it down until the bottom edge of the component is slightly below row 29 in the worksheet. See Figure 9-36.

Resized spreadsheet component | **Figure 9-36**

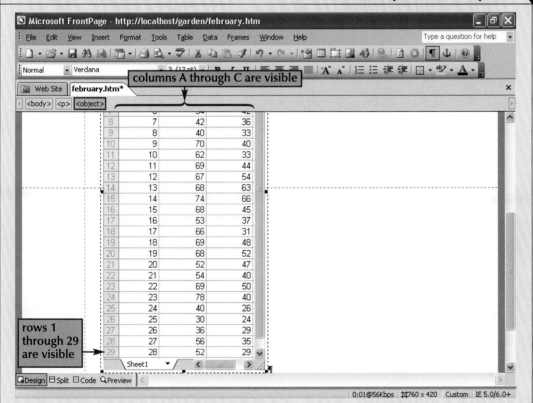

Trouble? If you cannot see all of the data in the worksheet, drag a sizing handle to make the spreadsheet component larger or smaller as necessary so that your component looks like the one shown in Figure 9-36.

4. Click the **Save** button on the Standard toolbar to save the page.

Now you can show Brett how to use the spreadsheet component to create a chart.

Inserting a Chart Component in a Web Page

When you need to display data graphically in a Web page, you can insert an Office chart component, which lets you create many types of charts. The most commonly used data source for a chart is the data contained in a spreadsheet component. For a chart, the data source is an ActiveX control that links a chart component to its data. You use the Chart Wizard to connect to the data source and to specify the chart type, chart subtype, and data range to use for the chart. After inserting the chart component, you can change its properties by using the Commands and Options dialog box. This dialog box has the same name as the one used with a spreadsheet component, but it contains commands for creating and formatting charts.

The spreadsheet component that you added to the page is a valid data source that you will use to create the chart. Brett wants to create a line chart to show the temperature data visually. A **line chart** displays data in a line, with symbols to show each value in the data series you are charting. Brett feels that a line chart will make it easy to interpret the data.

Reference Window	Inserting a Chart Component in a Web Page That Contains a Data Source

- Open the Web page that contains the data source in Design view, and then position the insertion point in the desired location for the chart.
- Click the Web Component button on the Standard toolbar, click Spreadsheets and charts in the Component type list box, click Office Chart in the Choose a control list box, and then click the Finish button. A chart component is inserted in the page, and the Chart Wizard opens the Commands and Options dialog box and selects the Data Source tab.
- Click the Data from the following Web page item option button. If necessary, select the data source in the list box.
- Click the Data Range tab. In the Data range text box, type the range reference for the cells that contain the data you wish to include in the chart.
- Click the option button to identify the data series as appearing in rows or columns, and then click the OK button.
- If necessary, edit the series name and the ranges that represent the category labels and data values.
- Click the Type tab, and then click the desired chart type and chart subtype.
- Close the Commands and Options dialog box.

Brett asks you to create a line chart from the data in the spreadsheet component. Before you start the Chart Wizard, you need to review the organization of the data in the spreadsheet component. The values in cells A1, A2, and A3 are column headings that identify the data in each column. When grouped together, these three cells create a range, which is expressed as A1:A3. When you create the chart, the data in these cells describes the data, but is not actually charted in the line chart. The data to describe the dates in February is in the range A2:A29, with one cell each for each day in February (February 1 though February 28). The data in the range B2:B29 includes the high temperatures for each day in February; the data in the range C2:C29 includes the low temperatures for each day in February. The data that you need to include in the line chart is expressed as B2:C29. The data that will appear in the chart to associate each temperature in the line chart with a day in February is called the category label. The data in the range A2:A29 will appear in the chart to identify each day in February. As you complete the Chart Wizard, you will identify each of these ranges for Brett to help him understand how the data in the spreadsheet component appears in the chart component.

To create the chart component:

1. Click to the right of the spreadsheet component to deselect it and move the insertion point to the end of the paragraph that contains it, and then press the **Enter** key twice.

2. Click the **Web Component** button on the Standard toolbar, click **Spreadsheets and charts** in the Component type list box, click **Office Chart** in the Choose a control list box, and then click the **Finish** button. The Chart Wizard inserts a chart component in the Web page and opens the Commands and Options dialog box. See Figure 9-37.

Chart component inserted into the page — **Figure 9-37**

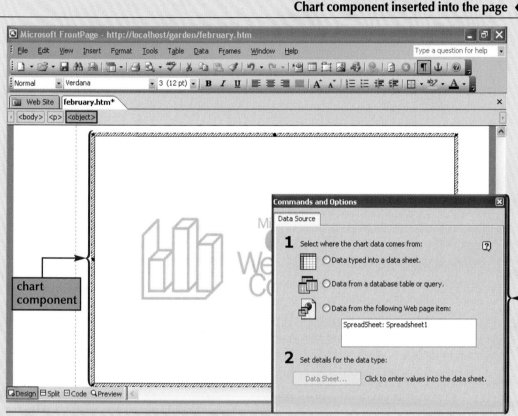

Commands and Options dialog box (yours might appear in a different location)

First, you must create or specify the data source for the chart. You can do so by typing data into a datasheet, by selecting a table or query object in a database, or by selecting an object in the existing Web page. Because you will use the spreadsheet component that you already inserted in the page, you'll select the third option. After specifying the spreadsheet component as the data source, you must identify the data range that contains the data to include in the chart. The data range that you select will vary based on the type of chart you are creating.

To specify the data source for the chart component:

1. On the Data Source tab, click the **Data from the following Web page item** option button. Because there is only one valid data source in the current Web page, the SpreadSheet: Spreadsheet1 item is selected automatically. The appearance of the chart component changes to show that you have selected a data source. See Figure 9-38.

Figure 9-38 | **Data source defined for the chart component**

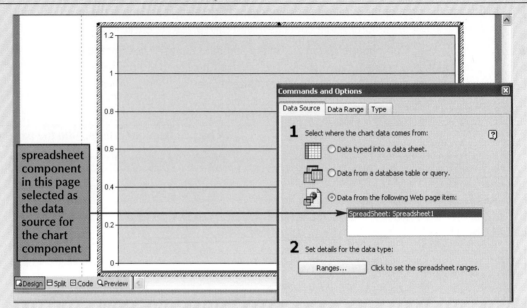

2. Click the **Data Range** tab in the Commands and Options dialog box. You use this tab to specify the data range for the data that you want to chart. The spreadsheet data that you want to chart appears in the range A1:C29. For the lines in the chart, however, you need to provide only the data range containing the values, which in this case is B2:C29.

3. Click the **Data range** text box, and then type **B2:C29**. This range contains the data to chart. The data appears in columns, with the label in the first row and data values in the rows below the labels. You'll use the Columns option button to select this data series.

4. Click the **Columns** option button (if necessary), and then click the **OK** button. The chart component changes to show a bar chart with the high and low temperatures for each day in February. See Figure 9-39.

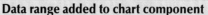

Data range added to chart component — **Figure 9-39**

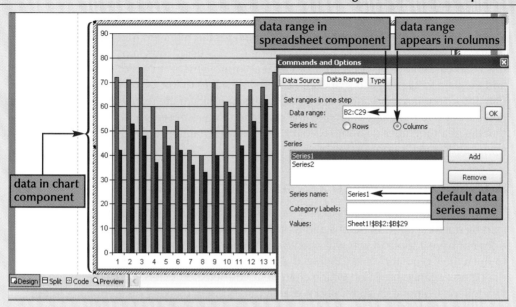

5. Click the **Type** tab. You use the Type tab to indicate the chart type and subtype. As you click the different chart subtypes on the right side of the Type tab, their names and descriptions appear at the bottom of the Type tab.

6. Click the **Line** chart type, and then click the second subtype in the first row, which creates a line chart with markers displayed at each data value. The chart changes to reflect the selections you made. See Figure 9-40.

Chart type and subtype selected — **Figure 9-40**

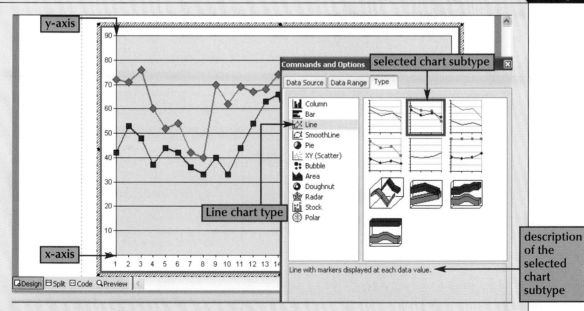

Trouble? Don't worry if the colors used for your lines differ from the ones shown in Figure 9-40; you will change these colors later.

7. Click the **Close** button 🗵 on the Commands and Options dialog box. The dialog box closes and reveals the chart component that you created.

The chart now shows the high temperatures in the upper line and the low temperatures in the lower line. The markers on the y-axis show the temperatures in increments of 10 degrees. The markers on the x-axis show the days in the month of February. For each day, a data marker indicates the point on the line for the high and low temperature, but it's hard to identify the exact temperature for each day using the y-axis markers. To make this chart easier to read, you can make several improvements to it. For example, you can add the data value for each mark on the line, add a title to the x-axis to indicate that this data is for February, and add a title to the y-axis to indicate the temperature. You can also add a legend to the chart to identify the data each line represents and a title to indicate that the chart includes data for February. All of these changes require you to use the Commands and Options dialog box.

Adding Data Labels to a Chart Component

The first change you'll make is to add the data labels to the markers on the lines. You'll start by opening the Commands and Options dialog box. Because the chart component does not have a toolbar, you will need to right-click the chart and use the shortcut menu to open the Commands and Options dialog box. The tabs in the Commands and Options dialog box change based on which chart item you selected when you right-clicked the chart. If the Commands and Options dialog box is open, clicking different parts of the chart changes the tabs to display the options for the selected chart item. Because you want to add data labels to a line, you'll right-click a line in the chart and open the Commands and Options dialog box.

To add data labels to the line markers:

1. Right-click the upper line in the chart component to open the shortcut menu, and then click **Commands and Options**. The Commands and Options dialog box opens and displays the Type tab, which is the last tab you used.

2. Click the **General** tab, and then click the **Add Data Label** button ![icon]. Data labels are added to each marker on the upper line, as shown in Figure 9-41.

Figure 9-41 | **Data labels added to line markers**

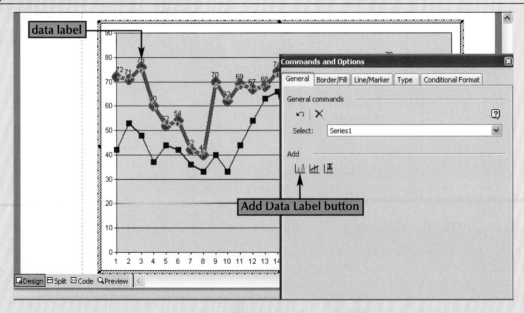

Brett thinks the data labels are difficult to read, and asks you to change them to bold.

3. Click any data label on the upper line to select all of the data labels, and then click the **Format** tab. Notice that the tabs in the Commands and Options dialog box change to reflect the options for data labels. The Format tab includes options for changing the values, including the font, font size, font color, and number style. The number style lets you create percentages, decimals, currency, dates, and other types of number formats,

4. Click the **Bold** button **B** on the Format tab. The data labels change to bold.

Now you can add the data labels to the lower line.

5. Click any marker on the lower line to select all markers on the line, and then click the **Add Data Label** button ⌊ᴬᵢ⌋ on the General tab. The data labels are added to the lower line.

6. Click any data label on the lower line to select all of the data labels, click the **Format** tab, and then click the **Bold** button **B** on the Format tab. Now both lines have bold data labels.

Brett likes these changes. He thinks that most people associate the color red with a high temperature and the color blue with a low temperature, and he asks if you can change the colors of the lines and the line markers so the high temperature values are red and the low temperature values are blue. He feels that this change would make more sense because of the associations of red and blue with warm and cool temperatures. You tell Brett that this change requires you to change the fill colors of the lines and the line markers because they are separate objects in the chart.

To change the line and line marker fill colors:

1. Click the upper line to select it, and then click the **Border/Fill** tab. See Figure 9-42.

Changing the line color ◀ **Figure 9-42**

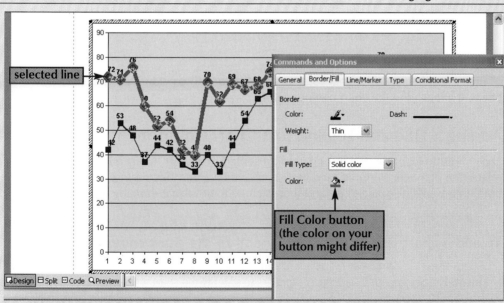

2. Click the **Fill Color** button 🎨▾ to open the color palette, and then click the **red** color (the second color in the second-to-last row). The line markers change to red.

3. Click the **Line/Marker** tab, click the **Line Color** button 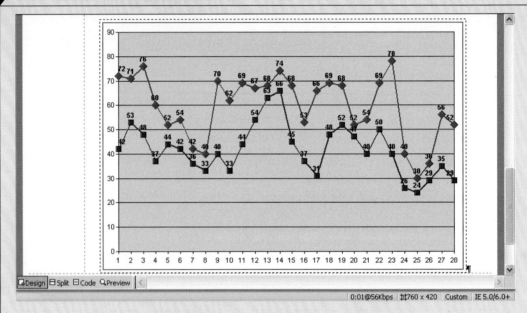, and then click the **red** color (the second color in the second-to-last row). The line changes to red.

4. Click the lower line, click the **Border/Fill** tab, and then use the **Fill Color** button to change the color to blue (the third color in the second row).

5. Click the **Line/Marker** tab, and then use the **Line Color** button to change the line color to **blue** (the third color in the second row).

6. Close the Commands and Options dialog box, and then click outside the chart component to deselect it. Figure 9-43 shows the revised chart.

| Figure 9-43 | **Lines with new colors and data labels** |

7. Save the page.

Brett likes the improvements you made to the lines. The next enhancement is to add a title and a legend to the chart component.

Adding a Title and Legend to a Chart Component

The chart title identifies the information presented in a chart. A **legend** is a box that relates the colors or symbols used in a chart to the values they represent. You can add both of these items to the chart and then change their format in many ways.

To add a chart title and a chart legend to the chart component:

1. Click the chart component to select it, and then point to any white area in the chart component. The ScreenTip "Chartspace" appears to identify the chart workspace area of the chart.

2. Right-click the chartspace to display the shortcut menu, click **Commands and Options**, and then click the **General** tab (if necessary). The General tab contains options for changing the chart component's appearance. See Figure 9-44.

Adding a title to the chart component ◀ Figure 9-44

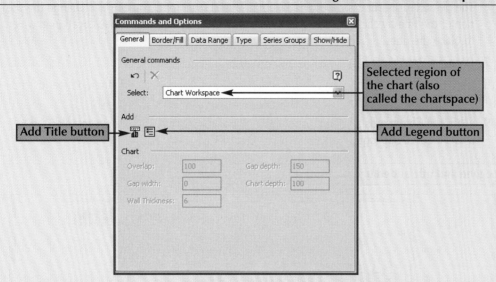

Trouble? Depending on where you right-clicked before opening the Commands and Options dialog box, you might see different tabs in the Commands and Options dialog box. If you do not see the same tabs as shown and described in the steps, click the chartspace to change the tabs in the dialog box.

3. Click the **Add Title** button 🔢 on the General tab. The text "Chart Workspace Title" is added at the top of the chart component. To change the default title, select this place-holder text and then type a new title using the Format tab.

4. Click the **Chart Workspace Title** placeholder in the chart component. A dark border appears around the title, and the tabs in the Commands and Options dialog box change to provide tools for working with titles.

5. Click the **Format** tab in the Commands and Options dialog box.

6. Select the text in the Caption text box, and then type **February Temperature Data**. See Figure 9-45.

Formatting the chart title ◀ Figure 9-45

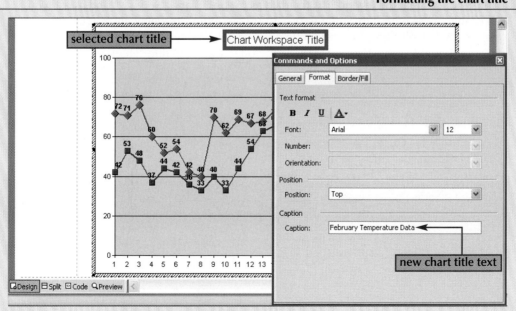

As shown in Figure 9-45, you can use this tab to change the appearance of the title text. The default formatting for a title is 12-point, black, Arial font. You can also change the position of the title by clicking the Position list arrow and then clicking a new location in which to place the title.

▶ **7.** Click the **Bold** button **B** to change the chart title to bold.

▶ **8.** Click the chartspace in the chart component, click the **General** tab in the Commands and Options dialog box, and then click the **Add Legend** button.

▶ **9.** Close the Commands and Options dialog box. The chart component now contains a title and a legend. See Figure 9-46.

| **Figure 9-46** | **Legend and title added to chart component** |

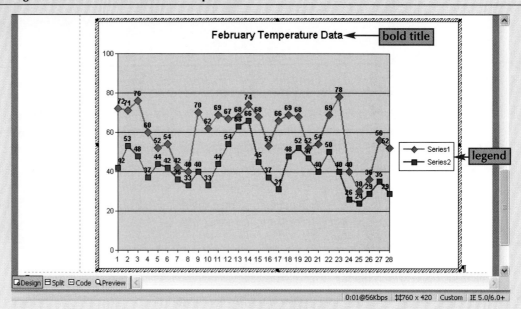

▶ **10.** Save the page.

Brett notices that the legend lists the data as "Series1" and "Series2," and asks if you can change these names to "High Temp" and "Low Temp," respectively. You tell him that you can do this, plus you can add a title on each axis of the chart to describe the values. The x-axis identifies the days in February, so you will use the title "February." The y-axis represents temperatures, so you will use the title "Temperature."

To change the data series names:

▶ **1.** Right-click the chartspace to open the shortcut menu, click **Commands and Options**, and then click the **Data Range** tab.

▶ **2.** If necessary, click **Series1** in the Series list box to select it. The Values text box shows that the data for Series1 is the range B2:B29 in the spreadsheet component. The data in Series1 is for the high temperatures, so you will change the series name from "Series1" to "High Temp."

▶ **3.** Select the text in the Series name text box, and then type **High Temp**. The series name changes to "High Temp." The data in Series2 is for the low temperatures, so you will change this series name to "Low Temp."

4. Select **Series2** in the Series list box, select the value **Series2** in the Series name text box, type **Low Temp**, and then click the **Category Labels** text box to make the change in the chart. Figure 9-47 shows the Commands and Options dialog box and the changes in the legend.

Revised series names added to chart component ◄ **Figure 9-47**

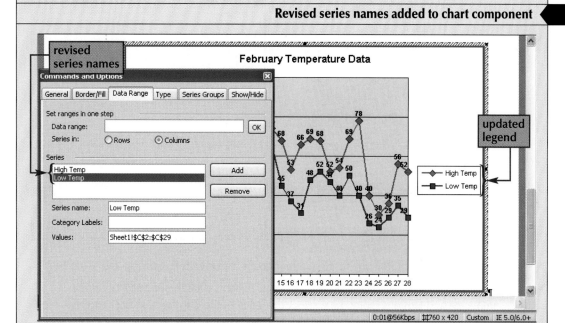

5. Save the page.

Next, you'll add the axis titles to the chart.

To add axis titles to the chart:

1. Click the value **1** on the x-axis to select all of the values on the x-axis, which includes the days in February. Clicking any value on the axis selects all of the category labels on that axis. If you click the value again, you will select only that value.

2. If necessary, click the **General** tab in the Commands and Options dialog box. See Figure 9-48.

Figure 9-48	General tab settings

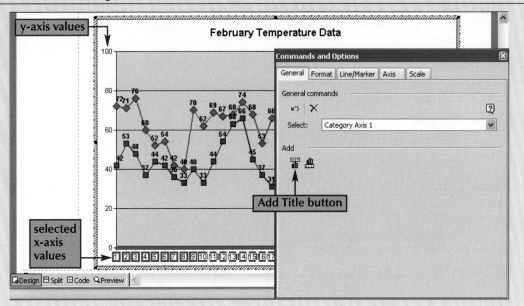

3. Click the **Add Title** button 🔳. A title is added to the x-axis with the default text "Axis Title."

4. Click the **Axis Title** placeholder in the chart component, click the **Format** tab in the Commands and Options dialog box, select the value in the Caption text box, and then type **February**. Brett wants to change the title to 10 points and bold.

5. Click the **Bold** button **B** on the Format tab, click the **Font Size** list arrow on the Formatting tab, and then click **10**. The title changes to bold and 10 points.

6. Click the value **100** on the y-axis to select its category labels, click the **General** tab, and then repeat Steps 3 through 5 to add a y-axis title and change the default text to **Temperature**.

7. Close the Commands and Options dialog box, and then save the page.

When you added the revised series names and the axis titles to the chart component, the size of the chart decreased to make room for these items, and now Brett is concerned that the data in the chart is difficult to read. You tell Brett that you can move the legend from the right side of the chart to below the chart title. This change should allow the chart to fill the space better and make the data more readable.

To move the chart legend:

1. Click the chart to select it, right-click the **legend** to select it and open the shortcut menu, and then click **Commands and Options**.

2. If necessary, click the **Format** tab. The Position list box lets you change the location of the selected item in the chart.

3. Click the **Position** list arrow, and then click **Top**. The legend moves to below the chart title.

4. Close the Commands and Options dialog box, save the page, and then preview it in a browser.

5. Scroll down the page and examine the spreadsheet and chart components. Figure 9-49 shows the completed chart.

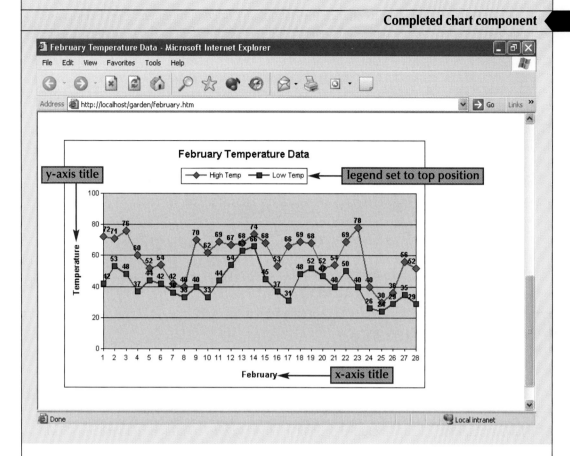

When you insert an Office component in a Web page, users can temporarily change the data in the spreadsheet component. Because the chart component is based on data in the spreadsheet component, changing a value in the spreadsheet component will also change the data displayed in the chart component.

To change data using the browser:

1. Scroll the Web page so you can see row 29 in the spreadsheet component and most of the chart component.

2. Click the spreadsheet component to select it. If the Commands and Options dialog box opens, close it.

3. Select the value **52** in cell B29 in the spreadsheet component, and then type **85**. Watch the chart as you press the **Tab** key. The red marker that represents the high temperature for February 28 changes in the chart component to reflect the increased value in the spread-sheet component.

   You changed the value for the high temperature for February 28 in the Web page that is displayed in the browser. If you refresh the page, your browser will continue to display the changed data, not the original stored value, in the spreadsheet component and in the chart. The spreadsheet component in the Web page in FrontPage, however, still contains the *original* value, 52.

4. Close your browser.

5. Close the garden Web site, and then close FrontPage.

When you use a browser to change the data in an Office component, the changes are temporary, so users of the page can analyze and change the data in the component without changing the original data in the page. To permanently change the data in the spreadsheet component, you must change it using FrontPage.

Review

Session 9.3 Quick Check

1. What are the three types of Office components that you can create in a Web page?
2. When should you use a spreadsheet component to display spreadsheet information in a Web page?
3. True or False: You cannot resize an Office component after inserting it in a Web page.
4. What are the three formats that you can use when importing data into a spreadsheet component?
5. True or False: An ActiveX control links a data source to a chart component.
6. How would you write the cells that appear in cell A1 through cell B5 in a spreadsheet component?

Review

Tutorial Summary

In this tutorial, you learned how to use a layout table to organize the content of a Web page. When you use a layout table to design a Web page, you can control the appearance of text and objects, such as pictures, using HTML tags that almost all browsers interpret consistently. You also learned how to include a Web page's content and other included content in a layout table. You can use included content in other ways to control the information shown in a Web site. For example, you can include a page with current promotions on a schedule that presents the material during or prior to the sale dates.

You also used inline styles and cascading style sheets to control the formatting in Web pages. Styles can be very powerful Web development tools because they are easy to create and tailor to your individual needs. Future changes are automatic when you update the styles or cascading style sheet.

Finally, you used a spreadsheet component to add spreadsheet data to a Web page and a chart component to create a line chart. When you need to present data in a Web page, including the data in a chart can make the results easier to interpret. You might find many different uses for charts in the Web sites you will create in the future.

Key Terms

autostretch	inline style	spacer image
cascading style sheet (CSS)	layout cell	spreadsheet
character style	layout table	style
chart	legend	user-defined style
CSV (comma-separated values)	line chart	worksheet
external style sheet	Office component	XML (Extensible Markup Language)
included content	paragraph style	
	PivotTable list	

Practice

Practice the skills you learned in the tutorial using the same case scenario.

Review Assignments

There are no new Data Files needed for these Review Assignments.

Brett wants you to finish your work in the garden Web site by including navigation options in the pages that include information about irrigation services. He also asks you to make a few changes to the components in the February Temperature Data page.

If necessary, start FrontPage, and then do the following:

1. Use My Network Places to open the **garden** Web site from your Web server.
2. Open the **comm_sys.htm** page in Design view, and then apply the Web site's top, left, and bottom shared borders to the page and save it. Then open the **res_sys.htm** page in Design view, apply the Web site's top, left, and bottom shared borders to the page and save it.
3. Open the Irrigation (**irr.htm**) page in Design view, link it to the **poetic.css** cascading style sheet, save the page, and then preview it in a browser. Use the browser to navigate the pages that include content related to irrigation services. Print the Commercial Systems page, and then close your browser.
4. Add the **february.htm** page to the Web site's navigation structure as a child page of the Garden Center page. Position the **february.htm** page to the right of the Lawn Care page, and then rename the page to "February Temps" so the page title will fit on the navigation buttons used in the Web site's theme.
5. Open the **february.htm** page in Design view. Resize the spreadsheet component's width so the buttons on the spreadsheet component toolbar are visible, and then center the spreadsheet component. (*Hint:* With the spreadsheet component selected, click the Center button on the Formatting toolbar to center the component.)
6. Change the values in column B to red and centered, change the values in column C to blue and centered, and then change the values in column A to centered. (*Hint:* To select a column, click the column header with the column's letter on it.) Click cell A1 to deselect column A.
7. Change the data labels on the x-axis and on the y-axis in the chart component to bold.
8. Change the fill color of the plot area in the chart component to white, and then change the fill color of the chartspace to light cyan. (*Hint:* To select the plot area, click the chartspace, click the General tab, and then use the Select list arrow. Use the ScreenTips to locate the correct color.)
9. Center the chart component, save the page, preview the page in a browser, and then print it.
10. Use the links in the site's pages to navigate all of the pages you created in the garden Web site, and then close your browser.
11. Close the **garden** Web site, and then close FrontPage.

Create

Create a spreadsheet component in a Web page, enter data and formulas into it, illustrate the spreadsheet component data in a bar chart, and create a user-defined style.

Case Problem 1

There are no new Data Files needed for this Case Problem.

Buffalo Trading Post   Nicole Beirne would like to use the Web site for Buffalo Trading Post to track sales in different retail categories. She wants to be able to use a Web page to analyze the data given to her by her accountant, Anna Claire McCannon. Anna Claire doesn't have this data in an electronic format, so Nicole will need to input it manually into a spreadsheet. Instead of using an Excel workbook to create the data, Nicole wants to be able to use a Web page, and she asks you to create this Web page for her. She also wants to display a bar chart in the Web page that shows the relative amounts for each category.

If necessary, start FrontPage, and then do the following:

1. Use My Network Places to open the **buffalo** Web site from your Web server. (If you did not create this Web site in Tutorial 1 and update it in Tutorials 2 through 8, ask your instructor for assistance.)
2. Create a new, normal page with the title "Sales Data" and the filename **salewkbk.htm**.
3. In the first paragraph of the Web page (but not in a shared border), create a heading using the Heading 1 style and the text "Sales Data by Category."

Explore
4. In a new paragraph, insert a centered spreadsheet component. Enter the data shown in Figure 9-50 into the spreadsheet component. Format the column headings (cells B1 through D1) as 10-point, bold, centered, Arial text. Format the row headings (cells A2 through A7) as 10-point, bold, Arial text.

Figure 9-50

	Revenue ($)	Inventory Amount ($)	Sales Percentage
Women's	254,165	354,811	72%
Children's	25,644	84,511	30%
Accessories	10,264	11,265	91%
Men's	1,254	9,558	13%
Hats	157	865	18%
Shoes	2,955	6,988	42%

Explore
5. Resize all columns to their best fit. (*Hint:* Position the pointer on the right edge of column A so it changes to a ✛ shape, and then double-click. Repeat this step until you have resized each column that contains data.)

Explore
6. Insert a formula in cell B8 that computes the total of the values in cells B2 through B7. (*Hint:* Click in cell B8, click the AutoSum button Σ on the spreadsheet component toolbar, and then press the Enter key). Insert a formula in cell C8 that computes the total of the values in cells C2 through C7.

Explore
7. In cell D8, enter a formula that computes the sales percentage, which is the revenue divided by the inventory amount (=B8/C8). Use the Commands and Options dialog box to format the resulting value as a percentage (the percentage will be displayed automatically with two decimal places). In cell A8, enter the label "Totals." Format the values in cells A8 through D8 as 10-point, bold, red, Arial text. (*Hint:* Use the Help button on the spreadsheet component toolbar to get help while completing Step 7.)
8. Resize the spreadsheet component so that only columns A through D and rows 1 through 8 are visible.

Explore
9. Insert a blank paragraph below the spreadsheet component, and then in a new blank, centered paragraph, insert a chart component. Use the spreadsheet component as the data source, chart the data range A1:C7, chart the series in columns, select the Bar chart type, and then select the Clustered Bar subtype.

Explore
10. Use the Commands and Options dialog box to add the minor gridlines to the chart. (*Hint:* With the Commands and Options dialog box open, click a label on the x-axis in the chart component to select all of the axis labels, and then click the Axis tab.)

Explore
11. Change the number format of the x-axis labels to currency.

12. Add the title "Inventory vs. Revenue" to the chart component, change it to bold, and then add a legend to the chart component. (*Hint:* Click the chartspace to change the tabs in the Commands and Options dialog box to add the title and legend.)
13. In Code view, delete the meta tag that inserts the Web site's theme. Create a user-defined style in the Web page that changes the Heading 1 style to centered, 18-point, bold, purple, Book Antiqua font.
14. Change the properties of the Sales Data Web page so it is not published with the Web site, and then save the page.
15. Preview the Sales Data Web page in a browser, print it, and then close your browser.
16. Close the **buffalo** Web site, and then close FrontPage.

Case Problem 2

Data File needed for this Case Problem: g_data.htm

Garden Grill   Garden Grill has always attracted the most qualified applicants for management and staff positions in its restaurants. One of the reasons that it has such a well-trained staff is that Garden Grill pays its employees competitive salaries and rewards them with higher annual performance increases than do other national restaurant chains. To keep employee morale high, management conducts regular salary research to ensure that Garden Grill employees are enjoying higher rewards for their work.

Meghan Elliott just finished a study of starting salaries at three national restaurant chains. She wants to include a page in the Garden Grill Web site that shows her study's results in a spreadsheet and chart. This new page should be available only on the company's intranet, so Meghan asks you to set its properties so it will not be published on the Internet Web site.

If necessary, start FrontPage, make sure you have your Data Files, and then do the following:

1. Use My Network Places to open the **grill** Web site from your Web server. (If you did not create this Web site in Tutorial 1 and update it in Tutorials 2 through 8, ask your instructor for assistance.)
2. Create a new, normal page with the title "Salary Data" and the filename **salary.htm**. At the top of the page, create a heading using the Heading 1 style and the text "Salary Data by Position." In a new paragraph, insert a centered spreadsheet component.
3. Import the file **g_data.htm** from the Tutorial.09\Case2 folder included with your Data Files into the **grill** Web site, and then import the data from this file into the spreadsheet component. Do not select the option to refresh the data at run time.
4. Insert a formula in cell B8 that computes the average of the values in cells B2 through B7. Copy and paste this formula into cells C8, D8, and E8. Use the Format tab in the Commands and Options dialog box to change the number format of the values in cells B2:E8 to currency. In cell A8, enter the text "Average." Use the Format tab to format the values in cells A8 through E8 as bold and red, and then change the font color of the values in the range B2:B7 to blue. (*Hint:* Use the Help button on the spreadsheet component toolbar to get help while completing Step 4. You'll need to learn how to use the AVERAGE function.)
5. Resize the spreadsheet component so that only columns A through E and rows 1 through 8 are visible.
6. In a new, centered paragraph below the spreadsheet component, insert a chart component. Chart the data in the range A1:E8 of the spreadsheet component, chart the series in columns, select the Column chart type, and then select the Clustered Column subtype.

Create

Create a spreadsheet component in a Web page, import data into it, enter formulas into it, and then illustrate the spreadsheet component data in a column chart.

Explore

Explore

Explore

7. Use the Commands and Options dialog box to change the background color of the plot area to white. (*Hint:* Use the Border/Fill tab to change the plot area fill color to white.)
8. Add a legend to the chart, and then change the location of the legend to below the chart.
9. Add the title "Salary Comparisons" to the chart, and then change the chart title text to 14 points, bold, and navy.
10. Change the number format of the values on the y-axis to currency (if necessary), and then change the font style to bold. Change the font style of the values on the x-axis to bold.

Explore

11. Add data labels to the bars for Garden Grill only, and then change the font style of the labels to bold, the font color to blue, and the number format to currency (if necessary). (*Hint:* Select a bar in the chart component that represents data for Garden Grill, and then make the changes.)
12. Save the Salary Data Web page, preview it in a browser, print it, and then close your browser.
13. Set the properties for the **salary.htm** and **g_data.htm** pages so they will not be published with the Web site.
14. Close the **grill** Web site, and then close FrontPage.

Create

Create a Web page that uses a layout table and use a cascading style sheet to format pages in a Web site.

Case Problem 3

Data File needed for this Case Problem: index.htm

Swenson Auctioneers Scott Swenson just found out that the ISP he selected to host his site has changed its filename requirements and now all home pages must have the file-name Default.htm instead of index.htm. Although this is a small change to make and FrontPage will update the content of all pages containing hyperlinks to this page, you decide to use this opportunity to redesign the site's home page using a layout table. Scott likes this idea and wants to see how the home page will look with a black background and red and white text to match the design of the Swenson Auctioneers logo. You agree to make this change to the home page, and also suggest making the same change in the Mailing List, Auction & Appraisal Services, Our Team, and Upcoming Auctions pages. Because the changes affect more than one page, you will create a cascading style sheet to format these pages instead of changing the formatting in individual pages. If Scott likes the new pages, you might redesign the other pages in the site so everything will be consistent, but for now, you'll just work with a few of the site's pages.

If necessary, start FrontPage, make sure you have your Data Files, and then do the following:

1. Use My Network Places to open the **swenson** Web site from your Web server. (If you did not create this Web site in Tutorial 1 and update it in Tutorials 2 through 8, ask your instructor for assistance.)
2. Create a new, normal page, remove the meta tag that inserts the Web site's default theme, and then save it using the filename **Default.htm** and the title "Swenson Auctioneers."

Explore

3. In Folders view, right-click the **Default.htm** page to open the shortcut menu, click Set as Home Page, and then update all pages in the Web site that include a link to the site's home page. FrontPage changes the site's home page to **Default.htm** and renames the site's old home page to **index-old.htm**.
4. Use the Corner, Header, Left, and Body table layout template to insert a layout table in the **Default.htm** page.

Explore

5. Delete the corner and header layout cells, and then increase the height of the left and body layout cells so they reach the top of the layout table. (*Hint:* To delete a layout cell, select it and then press the Delete key.)

6. In the left layout cell, insert the **sw_logo.gif** file from the Web site's **images** folder. In a new paragraph below the picture, insert a navigation bar based on the site's navigation structure. Use the underlined style for links (this style is the last one in the Choose a bar style list box), change the links to vertical orientation, and include links to child-level pages to the link bar.

7. Use the Cell Formatting task pane to change the background color of the left layout cell to black.

8. Click in the body layout cell, and then use the Insert command on the menu bar to insert the contents of the **index.htm** file in the Tutorial.09\Case3 folder included with your Data Files into the body layout cell. Save the page.

Explore

9. Use the Page Templates dialog box and the Normal Style Sheet template to create a new cascading style sheet. Save the page using the filename **sw_style.css**. Then do the following:
   a. Change the h1 tag to Arial font, bold, 18 points, and red.
   b. Change the h2 tag to Arial font, bold, 14 points, and red.
   c. Change the body tag to Arial font, 10 points, and white.
   d. Change the a tag (which creates hyperlinks) to Arial font, bold, 10 points, and white.
   e. Change the table tag (which controls the appearance of text in a table) to Arial font, 10 points, and white.
   f. Create a new character style named swenson with the following characteristics: Arial font, bold, 10 points, and red. (*Hint:* Click the New button in the Style dialog box, type swenson in the Name (selector) text box, and change the style type to Character. Use the Format button to define the new style. Because this is a character style, FrontPage will change its name to "span.swenson" after you create it.)
   g. Save and close the page.

Explore

10. Link the **sw_style.css** page to the **Default.htm** page. Use the Cell Formatting task pane to change the background color of the body layout cell to black. Then change the first paragraph in the body layout cell to the Heading 2 style and change the text "Swenson Auctioneers" in the second and third paragraphs in the body layout cell to the swenson style. (*Hint:* Select the text, and then use the Style list box on the Formatting toolbar to apply the style.) Save the page.

11. Change to Navigation view. Select the **index-old.htm** page, and then remove it from the Web site. Then add the **Default.htm** page to the navigation structure for the custom link bar, positioning it to the left of the Benefit Auctions page.

12. Preview the **Default.htm** page in a browser and use the hyperlinks to test the site's page. There are two problems you must fix: the clients hyperlink on the home page opens the wrong target, and the hotspot in the logo picture points to the wrong page. Close your browser, and return to Design view and update the clients hyperlink so it opens the **benefit.htm** page in the Web site's **frame** folder, and then save the home page.

Explore

13. Use the Replace command to replace all instances of **index-old.htm** with **Default.htm** in the source code for all pages in the Web site. After completing this task, preview the home page in a browser and navigate the site to make sure you made these changes correctly, and then close your browser.

14. In Folders view, select the files **maillist.asp**, **services.htm**, **team.htm**, and **upcoming.htm**, and then remove the Web site's default theme from these pages. (*Hint:* Apply the "No Theme" theme to the selected pages.) With the pages still selected in Folders view, open the Style Sheet Links dialog box and link the **sw_style.css** cascading style sheet to the selected pages.

15. Open the **team.htm** page in Design view. Notice that the change makes the text in this page invisible, because it has white text on a white background.
16. Open the **sw_style.css** page, modify the body tag, and then select the Border option in the Format button list. Click the Shading tab in the Borders and Shading dialog box, click the Background color list arrow, and then click the black color. Close the dialog boxes and save the cascading style sheet, and then click the **team.htm** tab and notice the page's new appearance. Preview the **team.htm** page in a browser and use the hyperlinks to navigate the site.
17. Use your browser to print the home page, and then close your browser.
18. Type your name on line 7 of the **sw_style.css** cascading style sheet, print it, and then close the cascading style sheet without saving your changes.
19. Close the **swenson** Web site, and then close FrontPage.

Use a cascading style sheet to format the pages in a Web site, create formulas to calculate data in a spreadsheet component, and illustrate the data in a spreadsheet component in a chart component.

Case Problem 4

Data Files needed for this Case Problem: calcdata.htm and chart.htm

Mortgage Services, Inc. Natalie Fuselier has decided that she doesn't like certain elements of the theme you created for the Web site. Instead of applying a new theme, you will take the elements of the current theme that Natalie does like and format all pages in the Web site with a cascading style sheet. Natalie also wants to add two pages to the Web site. The first page lets a visitor calculate a monthly mortgage (house) payment by entering a mortgage amount, an interest rate, and a time in years to repay the loan. She also wants you to create a chart to visually illustrate the mortgage rates for the past year so potential homebuyers can get a sense of how the rates are changing. Because the interest rate on a mortgage has a direct impact on the monthly payments, trends that show rates going up or down can play an important role in timing the purchase of a home and securing a loan for its payment.

If necessary, start FrontPage, make sure you have your Data Files, and then do the following:

1. Use My Network Places to open the **loan** Web site from your Web server. (If you did not create this Web site in Tutorial 1 and update it in Tutorials 2 through 8, ask your instructor for assistance.)
2. Use the Theme task pane to delete the site's default theme from all pages in the Web site. (*Hint:* Apply the "No Theme" theme as the default theme.)
3. Use the Page Templates dialog box and the Normal Style Sheet template to create a new cascading style sheet. Save the page using the filename **loan.css**. Then do the following:
   a. Change the h1 tag to Arial Black font, 18 points, and navy. Change the alignment to center.
   b. Change the h2 tag to Arial Narrow font, bold, 18 points, and purple.
   c. Change the h3 tag to Arial Narrow font, bold, and 14 points.
   d. Change the body tag to Tahoma font. Use the Shading tab in the Borders and Shading dialog box to add the **back.gif** file in the Web site's **images** folder as a background picture in the page.
   e. Save and close the page.
4. Use the Link Style Sheets dialog box to link all pages in the Web site to the **loan.css** cascading style sheet. Choose the option to continue in the dialog box that warns that you will overwrite the style information for the Web site. Preview the home page in a browser, and then use the hyperlinks to view other pages in the site. When you are finished, close your browser.

Explore

5. Create a new page and link it to the **loan.css** cascading style sheet. Save the page using the filename **calc.htm** and the title "Mortgage Calculator." Then do the following:

   a. Insert a spreadsheet component in the Mortgage Calculator page, and then import the data in the **calcdata.htm** file in the Tutorial.09\Case4 folder included with your Data Files into the spreadsheet component. Do not choose the option to refresh the data at run time.

   b. Change the text in cell A5 to bold and navy, and then change the fill color of cell D5 to a light-yellow color. Save the page.

   c. In Navigation view, add the **calc.htm** page to the Web site's navigation structure as a child page of the home page, positioning the **calc.htm** page to the right of the Lender List page.

   d. Return to the **calc.htm** page in Design view, save it, and then preview the page in a browser.

   e. In cell D1, enter an amount, enter an interest rate in cell D2 (such as 0.075 for 7.5%), and enter a term in cell D3 (such as 30, for 30 years). Press the Enter key to compute the monthly payment, print the page, and then close your browser.

   f. Close the **calc.htm** page.

Explore

6. Import into the Web site's root folder the **chart.htm** page in the Tutorial.09\Case4 folder, add the page to the site's navigation structure as a child page of the Mortgage Calculator page, open the page in Design view, link the page to the **loan.css** cascading style sheet, and then do the following:

   a. Create a chart component that uses the data in the spreadsheet component.

   b. Chart the data range B1:B12 in columns.

   c. Change the series name from Series1 to "Interest Rate."

   d. Enter the range A1:A12 as the category labels, and then click the Values text box.

   e. Select the SmoothLine chart type and the smooth line with markers subtype.

   f. Add the chart title "Interest Rate Data," and then change its font style to bold and its color to red.

   g. Add a legend below the x-axis to the chart component.

   h. Change the font style of the labels on the x-axis and y-axis to bold.

   i. Add a title to the y-axis using 8-point, bold font and the text "Interest Rate."

   j. Change the fill color of the chartspace to a light-yellow color, and then change the fill color of the plot area to white. (*Hint:* Use the Select list arrow on the General tab in the Commands and Options dialog box to select the plot area.)

   k. Save the page, preview it in a browser, print it, and then close your browser.

7. Close the **loan** Web site, and then close FrontPage.

Lab Assignments

Reinforce

Spreadsheets

The New Perspectives Labs are designed to help you master some of the key concepts and skills presented in this text. The steps for completing this Lab are located on the Course Technology Web site. Log on to the Internet and use your Web browser to go to the Student Online Companion for New Perspectives Office 2003 at **www.course.com/np/office2003**. Click the Lab Assignments link, and then navigate to the assignments for this tutorial.

Spreadsheets The Spreadsheets Lab demonstrates how spreadsheet software works. You will use spreadsheet software to examine and modify worksheets and to create your own worksheets.

Quick Check Answers

Session 9.1

1. a framework that organizes the content of all or part of a Web page, creating a simple or sophisticated design
2. an area in a layout table that stores content, such as a picture or text
3. green
4. blue
5. True
6. True
7. Resize an existing layout cell that borders the layout cell that you want to create to make room for the new layout cell. If necessary, display the Layout Tables and Cells task pane. Click the Draw Layout Cell button on the Layout Tables and Cells task pane. Click and drag the pointer from the upper-left corner of the new layout cell's location to the lower-right corner, and then release the mouse button.

Session 9.2

1. font, paragraph, border, numbering, and position
2. True
3. CSS Files
4. True
5. Link Style Sheet
6. .css
7. False

Session 9.3

1. spreadsheet, chart, and PivotTable list
2. You should use a spreadsheet component in a Web page when you (or other Web site developers and users) do not have Excel installed on your computer but you do have the Office 2003 components and a Web browser that supports them.
3. False
4. CSV, HTML, and XML
5. True
6. A1:B5

Objectives

- Create a new Web site and import pages into it
- Create and format shared borders in a Web site
- Add pictures to Web pages
- Create a cascading style sheet and use it to format pages in a Web site
- Use a layout table to organize a Web page
- Add new pages to a Web site using Navigation view
- Create a form component in a Web page
- Import a database into a Web site
- Create Active Server Pages

In this case, you will use skills you learned in the following tutorials:
- Tutorials 1–4, 6, 8, and 9

Creating a Web Site for Security Shredding, Inc.

Case

Security Shredding, Inc.

When Mary Schmidt retired from her career as a systems analyst, she still wanted to work. Her husband, Bob, was also retiring from his career as a computer programmer. With the help of their two sons, Jeff and Brad, Mary and Bob started a business that shreds documents and other materials. Security Shredding began operations in 1990, at a time when many state agencies and public companies were beginning to realize the benefits of having their sensitive documents destroyed by independent specialists instead of by using in-house resources. At first, Security Shredding primarily shredded documents, including personnel records, classified information, and financial information. The business quickly grew to include the destruction of nonsalable materials such as unsold magazines and paperbacks, expired lottery scratch-off cards, and security videotapes.

Security Shredding soon outgrew its small storage area and relocated to a warehouse that houses several commercial shredders, paper bailers, and the company's offices. The firm also leases several unmarked trucks that are used to pick up materials from clients. Security Shredding's warehouse is unmarked to guarantee the security and privacy of sensitive documents while they are being destroyed.

As business at Security Shredding has continued to expand, Mary has realized that the creation and management of a Web site might increase the efficiency of the company's operations and help market the company's services. Mary wants you to help her create a Web site with the following pages and features:

- A home page that describes the business and includes a picture and a hit counter

- An Experience page that describes the company's shredding experience and lists its professional affiliations

- A 3 S's of Shredding page that answers the question, "What should be shredded?"

Student Data Files

▼**AddCases**

▽ AddCase1 folder

bales1.jpg	email.htm	list.htm	pricing.htm	services.htm	shred.mdb
bales2.jpg	exp.htm	paper.jpg	secure.htm	shred.htm	size.htm
cans.jpg	index.htm	pickup.htm	security.htm		

- A Pickup Request page that lets clients use a form to request pickups
- A Pricing page that identifies the company's pricing policies
- A Size page that describes the company's equipment and facility
- A Services page that describes the company's pickup service, recycling efforts, and policies
- A Security page that describes the company's security measures and policies for ensuring the privacy and protection of materials it handles
- A Recycling Program page that includes information about how recycling efforts benefit the environment
- An E-Mail page that includes the e-mail addresses of the company's managers

In addition to these Web pages, Mary wants to include pictures showing the company's operations. She wants the pages in the Web site to have a consistent appearance. She also wants the company's logo, name, mailing address, phone number, fax number, and e-mail address to appear at the top of each page.

If necessary, start FrontPage, make sure you have your Data Files, and then do the following:

1. Read all the questions for this case problem so you understand the requirements for the Security Shredding Web site.
2. Prepare a Web site plan that shows the planned Web pages and the expected hyperlinks from the home page.
3. Use the Empty Web Site template to create a new Web site named **shred** in the location where your server-based Web sites are stored. (*Hint:* In the Web Site Templates dialog box, type the path to your server in the Specify the location of the new Web site list box, plus the Web site name, such as http://localhost/shred. When you create a Web site directly on a server, you do not need to publish it.) After creating the Web site, import all of the files except for **shred.mdb** from the AddCase1 folder included with your Data Files into the Web site's root folder. If necessary, change the Web site's page options to enable the site for SharePoint Services, Browse-time Web Components, Author-time Web Components (navigation and shared borders), VML graphics, and Internet Explorer versions 5.0/6.0 and later.
4. Move the picture files from the site's root folder to the site's **images** folder.
5. Use Navigation view to create the Web site's navigation structure. Each page in the Web site is a child page of the home page, except for the **list.htm** and **shred.htm** pages, which you will not add to the navigation structure. Position the pages from left to right in alphabetical order by filename.
6. Open the home page in Design view, and then change the default page size to 800 × 600, maximized. Add top and left shared borders to every page in the Web site. The left shared border should include navigation buttons. Select the comment component in the top shared border, type the company's name (Security Shredding, Inc.), format it using the Heading 2 style, and then center it. In a new, normal paragraph below the heading, type the company's mailing address, phone number, and fax number, and create a mailto with the company's e-mail address using the following information: P.O. Box 20996, Cleveland, OH 44123, Phone 440-555-1104, Fax 440-555-0922, mail@securityshreddinginc.com. Format the company's information as centered, 10-point, Arial font. Finally, insert a horizontal line below the address information, and change its color to yellow.
7. Change the **list.htm** and **shred.htm** pages so they do not use the Web site's shared borders.
8. Edit the link bar in the left shared border to include links to child pages, to the home page, and to the parent page. Format the links using the Brackets style. Verify that the top shared border contains only the items that you added in Step 6, and then save the home page.
9. Create appropriate meta description and keywords tags for the home page, and then save the home page.
10. Insert the **paper.jpg** picture from the Web site's **images** folder in a new paragraph between the first and second paragraphs in the home page. Center the picture, resize

it to approximately four inches high and wide, resample the picture, and increase its brightness by clicking the appropriate toolbar button once. Add the alternative text "Paper Shredding" to the picture. Save the page, overwriting the existing picture in the **images** folder, and then close the home page.

11. Use the Highway style sheet template to create a new cascading style sheet. Change the alignment of the Heading 1 and Heading 2 styles to center, save the page as **style.css** in the Web site's root folder, and then close the page. Link the **style.css** cascading style sheet to all pages in the Web site.

12. Create a new, normal page in the Web site and save it using the title "The Three S's of Shredding" and the filename **what.htm**. Remove the shared borders from this page only. Use the Header, Left, Top Right, and Body table layout template to organize the content of the **what.htm** page. If necessary, delete any blank paragraphs that appear above the layout table.

13. Include the **top.htm** page and the **left.htm** page from the Web site's **_borders** folder in the header layout cell and left layout cell, respectively. In the top right layout cell, type "The Three S's of Shredding" and format this text using the Heading 1 style. In a new paragraph below the level-one heading, type "Secure, Smart, Safe," and then format this text using the Heading 2 style. Change the heading "Secure, Smart, Safe" to use an animation effect of your choice that draws attention to these three words when the page is loaded. Save the page and close the DHTML Effects toolbar.

14. Select the body layout cell so that sizing handles appear around its border, and then use the Split Cells button on the Tables toolbar to split the body layout cell into two columns. In the column on the left, include the **shred.htm** page from the Web site's root folder. In the column on the right, insert a paragraph at the top, and then include the **list.htm** page from the Web site's root folder. (There should be only one blank paragraph at the top of the column on the right. If necessary, delete the one that appears in the layout cell.) Select the layout cell on the right, and then reduce the size of its left border by a few pixels to create some space between the columns in the body layout cell.

15. Open the **shred.htm** page in a new window, and then change the "What to Shred?" text to the Heading 2 style and then left-align it. Save and close the **shred.htm** page, save the **what.htm** page, preview it in a browser, and then close your browser.

16. Open each of the remaining pages in the Web site and review their contents. For each page, except for the **what.htm**, **list.htm**, and **shred.htm** pages, format lists using bullets and headings with the Heading 1 style. Insert at least one picture from the Web site's **images** folder in three different Web pages. Make sure that the pictures relate to the content of the pages in which you insert them. Use alternative text to describe each picture, and resize and resample the pictures as necessary to make them fit well in the pages. Save each page, overwriting the existing pictures in the Web site's **images** folder.

17. In the E-Mail Web page (**email.htm**), change the four names listed in the page to mailtos. The e-mail addresses are the person's name in all lowercase letters, with no spaces, followed by the domain securityshreddinginc.com. (*Hint:* In the Insert Hyperlink dialog box, click the E-mail Address button on the Link to bar to create the mailtos.) Use the subject "Web Site." Save the page.

18. Add the **what.htm** page to the Web site's navigation structure, positioning it as a child page of the home page and to the right of the Size page. In Design view, link the **what.htm** page to the **style.css** cascading style sheet, and then save the page.

19. If necessary, save any open Web pages, and then preview the home page in a browser. Use the browser to confirm that the pictures, links, and lists are working as expected. Close your browser.

20. In Navigation view, add a new Web page to the right of the **what.htm** page using the title "Search" and filename **search.htm**. Next, open the Search Web page in Design

view, and add a title with the Heading 1 style and a search component with the default settings. Make sure that the new page uses the Web site's shared borders and is linked to the cascading style sheet. Add text to the Search Web page that describes how to use the search component.

21. In a new paragraph below the search component in the Search page, insert a search component that searches the Internet. Add instructions for using this component to the page, delete the broken link to the picture, and then save the page.

22. Open the Pickup Request Web page (**pickup.htm**) in Design view. Insert a form component in the page, and then cut and paste the information that appears below the first paragraph in the page into the form component. Choose the option to keep the source formatting. Use the existing labels in the page to create appropriate form fields to store the data that the form will collect. (*Hint:* The labels in the first part of the form component are stored in a table with invisible borders. Create the form field for each label in the same row and in the second column.) Change the default form field settings to use appropriately sized form fields and meaningful names. Save the form's results as comma-delimited text in a file named **pickup.csv** in the **_private** folder of the Web site. In addition, save the date and time that the form was submitted to the server using a date and time format of your choice. Save the Pickup Request page, and then open the page in a browser and submit one form to the server. (Use your name as the client's name.) Print the confirmation page that appears, and then close your browser.

23. Add a hit counter to the home page with your choice of specifications, location, and style. Save the home page.

24. Change the filename of the Recycling Program Web page to **recycle.htm**.

25. Copy the **shred** database from the AddCase1 folder and paste it into the **shred** Web site. Use the database connection name "Shred" and store all database files in the **fpdb** folder of the Web site. Verify the database connection.

26. Change the form component in the Pickup Request page (**pickup.htm**) to send its results to the **shred** database in the **fpdb** folder of the Web site. Set the form fields so that their data will be stored in the correct field in the **Results** table of the **shred** database. Do not save any additional fields.

27. Save the Pickup Request page, and then preview it in a browser. Submit a form to the server, using your name as the client name. Print the confirmation page that appears, and then close your browser.

28. Open the **shred** database from FrontPage, open the **Results** table in Table Datasheet view, and then confirm that the form handler correctly stored the record that you added in Step 27. Close Access.

29. Create a new, normal page with the title "Pickup Information" and the filename **pickinfo.asp**. Change the setting for the Pickup Information page to exclude it when the Web site is published. Add a heading with the Heading 1 style at the top of the page using the text "Pickup Information." In a new, normal paragraph below the heading, insert a Database Results region that displays the records from the **Results** table in the **shred** database. Include all fields from the table, accept the default formatting options, and display all records together. After inserting the Database Results region in the Web page, change the column headings so that field names with two words appear on two lines, and then apply the Heading 5 style to these headings and center them. Link this page to the **style.css** cascading style sheet, save the page, preview it in a browser, and then close your browser.

30. Recalculate the hyperlinks in the Web site, verify all hyperlinks in the Web site, and then run a Site Summary report.

31. Use the browser to thoroughly test the Web site. Print any pages as requested to do so by your instructor.

32. Close your browser, the **shred** Web site, and FrontPage.

Objectives

- Create a Web site and import pages into it
- Create a Web site's navigation structure using Navigation view
- Create shared borders in a Web site
- Add pictures to Web pages and create a photo gallery
- Apply a theme to a Web site
- Create a form component in a Web page
- Import a database into a Web site
- Create and format Active Server Pages
- Create spreadsheet and chart components in a Web page

In this case, you will use skills you learned in the following tutorials:
- Tutorials 1–4, 6, 8, and 9

Creating a Web Site for Pet Adoption Services, Inc.

Case

Pet Adoption Services, Inc.

Pet Adoption Services is a not-for-profit organization that cares for lost, abandoned, and neglected dogs and cats in its shelters located throughout the United States. Pet Adoption Services finds caring homes for all healthy, nonaggressive pets brought to its shelters. The organization provides affordable veterinary services through its shelters, and all adopted pets must be neutered before leaving a shelter. To make its clinics more affordable for the entire community, Pet Adoption Services relies on time donations from local veterinarians.

Until recently, Pet Adoption Services has relied on radio advertising to communicate information about its pet adoption weekends across the country. Community reaction to these adoption events has been overwhelming. Madison Somero, president of Pet Adoption Services, has received feedback from many shelter directors indicating the need for a Web site that includes a Web page for each pet offered for adoption in the weekend events. Madison wants the Web site to have a home page, a Dogs page, and a Cats page. Child pages of the Dogs and Cats pages will include brief descriptions of each pet available for adoption, along with each pet's photograph.

Because Pet Adoption Services is a not-for-profit organization, it relies heavily on the generosity of the community to ensure that each animal receives the proper care. Madison wants to include a Guest Book page in the Web site to collect information about potential donors of cash, food, and time. She hopes that the Web site will attract many donors, including veterinarians who will offer their services for free and provide inexpensive vaccines and medications. Because she hopes to collect a lot of information using the Guest Book page, Madison wants to use a form that sends its results to an Access database. She wants to view the data in the

Student Data Files

▼**AddCases**

▽ AddCase2 folder

buster.htm	guest.htm	p_phoebe.jpg	p_tex.jpg	razz.htm	spike.htm
cats.htm	maple.htm	p_razz.jpg	p_zoe.jpg	rocky.htm	tex.htm
chance.htm	p_buster.jpg	p_rocky.jpg	pets.mdb	scout.htm	zoe.htm
default.htm	p_chance.jpg	p_scout.jpg	phoebe.htm		
dogs.htm	p_maple.jpg	p_spike.jpg			

database using an Active Server Page and a data access page. In addition, she wants to create a Web page that shows the dollar amounts for donations received over the past four years by donation category.

Finally, Madison wants the Web site to have a consistent, professional appearance. She asks you to begin work on the new Web site.

If necessary, start FrontPage, make sure you have your Data Files, and then do the following:

1. Read all the questions for this case problem so you understand the requirements for the Pet Adoption Services Web site.
2. Prepare a Web site plan that shows the planned Web pages and the expected hyperlinks from the home page.
3. Use the Empty Web Site template to create a new Web site named **pets** in the location where your server-based Web sites are stored. (*Hint:* In the Web Site Templates dialog box, type the path to your server in the Specify the location of the new Web site list box, plus the Web site name, such as http://localhost/pets. When you create a Web site directly on a server, you do not need to publish it.) Import all of the files except for **pets.mdb** from the AddCase2 folder included with your Data Files into the Web site's root folder. If necessary, change the Web site's page options to enable the site for SharePoint Services, Browse-time Web Components, Author-time Web Components (navigation and shared borders), VML graphics, and Internet Explorer versions 5.0/6.0 and later.
4. Use drag and drop to move all picture files into the Web site's **images** folder.
5. Use Navigation view to create the Web site's navigation structure. The **dogs.htm**, **cats.htm**, and **guest.htm** pages are child pages of the home page. The following are child pages of the **dogs.htm** page: **chance.htm**, **maple.htm**, **rocky.htm**, **scout.htm**, and **spike.htm**. The following are child pages of the **cats.htm** page: **buster.htm**, **phoebe.htm**, **razz.htm**, **tex.htm**, and **zoe.htm**.
6. Open the home page in Design view, and then change the default page size to 800 × 600, maximized. Add a top shared border to all pages in the Web site that includes a centered page banner, and add a left shared border to all pages in the Web site that includes a link bar with links to child pages, the home page, and the parent page. Change the link bar style to use the page's theme.
7. In each of the 10 pages that describe a pet, insert the pet's picture so the pet's description wraps around the right side of the picture. Resize the width of each picture to 200 pixels and resample the picture. The filename of the picture is the same as the Web page's filename, except that it begins with "p_". (All picture files are saved in the Web site's **images** folder.) For each picture, add alternative text using the pet's name. Save and close each page.
8. Open the **dogs.htm** page in Design view. In a new paragraph below the italicized text at the top of the page, insert a photo gallery. Choose the Montage layout. Insert each dog's picture (Chance, Maple, Rocky, Scout, and Spike) in the photo gallery, use the font formatting from the page, and enter the dog's name as the caption. Center the photo gallery component, and then save the page and if necessary, overwrite the picture files in the Web site's **images** folder.

9. Open the **cats.htm** page in Design view. In a new paragraph at the top of the page (but not in the top shared border), insert a Photo Gallery. Choose the Montage layout. Insert each cat's picture (Buster, Phoebe, Razz, Tex, and Zoe) in the Photo Gallery, use the font formatting from the page, and enter the cat's name as the caption. Center the Photo Gallery component, and then save the page and if necessary, overwrite the picture files in the Web site's **images** folder.

10. Create meta description and keywords tags for the home page, and then save the home page.

11. Apply the Nature theme as the Web site's default theme. Select the options to include vivid colors, active graphics, and a background picture. (If you do not have the Nature theme, select another theme.)

12. Open the **guest.htm** page in Design view. Insert a form component in the page, and then cut and paste the existing form field labels from the page into the form component. Choose the option to keep the source formatting. (*Hint:* The labels for some of the form fields are stored in a table; make sure that you paste the entire table into the form component.) Create appropriate form fields; for those labels stored in the table, create the form field in the same row and in the second column. Rename the form fields to have meaningful names, and set each form field to store an appropriate number of characters. Define any necessary validation criteria to ensure that the user enters data correctly. Change the Submit and Reset buttons to have more meaningful form field names, and the labels to "Submit Form" and "Clear Form," respectively. Save the Web page.

13. Copy the **pets** database from the AddCase2 folder and paste it into the **pets** Web site. Use the database connection name "Pets," and store all database files in the **fpdb** folder of the Web site. Verify the database connection.

14. Change the form component in the Guest Book Web page (**guest.htm**) to send its results to the **Guest** table in the **pets** database that is stored in the **fpdb** folder of the Web site. Set the form fields so that their data is stored in the correct field in the **Guest** table. Do not save any additional fields. Save the page.

15. In Navigation view, create a new child page of the home page using the title "Guest Book Info." Change to Folders view, and then change the page's filename to **gst_info.asp**. Open the Guest Book Info page in Design view.

16. Enter the following description at the top of the Guest Book Info Web page: "This page displays data collected from the Guest Book Web page and stored in the Pets database." In a new paragraph, insert a Database Results region that displays the records from the **Guest Book** query in the **pets** database. Change the Database Results region so that it displays fields from the **Guest Book** query in the following order: LastName, FirstName, EmailAddress, Address, City, State, Zip, HomePhone, WorkPhone, Extension, CashDonor, FoodDonor, TimeDonor, and ContactMe. Sort the fields in ascending order using the LastName field. Change the message that is displayed when no records are returned to "There are no records in the database matching your request." Use the default formatting options, and choose the option to display all records together.

17. Change the column headings in the Database Results region so field names with two words appear on two lines, and then change the Extension column heading to "Ext." Select the database fields (the row between the start and end of the Database Results region), and then change their font size to 10 points.
18. Change the Database Results region to use the Grid 3 Table AutoFormat style. (*Hint:* Click anywhere in the Database Results region, display the Tables toolbar, and then set the Table AutoFormat. When you're finished, close the Tables toolbar.)
19. Set the Guest Book Info Web page so that it does not use the Web site's left shared border and will not be published with the Web site. Save the page.
20. Open the Guest Book Web page (**guest.asp**) in a browser, and then complete the form using data that you make up and submit it to the server. Use the Home hyperlink in the Guest Book Web page to open the home page, and then click the Guest Book Info link to open that page. Verify that the record you entered into the database is displayed in the Guest Book Info Web page. (*Note:* You might need to scroll the page to the right to see all of the columns.) Close your browser.
21. Open the **pets** database from FrontPage, and then use a wizard to create a data access page based on the **Guest** table. Include all fields in the page, do not use a grouping level, sort the records in ascending order by LastName, and change the default title to "Guest Book Data Access Page."
22. Enter the title "Guest Book Data Access Page" at the top of the new data access page, and then save this page as **gst_dap** in the root folder of the **pets** Web site. Close Access.
23. Open the Guest Book Data Access Page (**gst_dap.htm**) in Design view. Change the settings to exclude the page when the Web site is published. Save the page, and then preview it in the browser. Use the data access page to add a new record to the database using real or fictitious data. (*Hint:* Enter the value "Yes" or "No" for the CashDonor, FoodDonor, TimeDonor, and ContactMe fields.) Save and print the new record, and then close your browser.
24. Create a new Web page with the title "Donation Data" and the filename **donation.htm**. Add the page to the Web site's navigation structure as a child page of the home page, positioning it to the right of the Guest Book Info page.
25. In the first paragraph of the Web page, enter the following paragraph: "The following spreadsheet shows the total value of donations received by Pet Adoption Services for food, cash, veterinary services, vaccinations, and medications. Veterinary services, vaccinations, and medications are valued at the market rate in the community in which they were donated."
26. In a new, centered paragraph, insert a spreadsheet component. Enter the data shown in Figure AC-1 into the spreadsheet component. Format the column headings (B1:F1) as centered and bold. Format the row headings (A2:A7) as bold. Format numeric data in the range B2:F7 as currency. Change the color of the "Totals" and "Grand Totals" headings to red.

Figure AC-1

	2002	2003	2004	2005	Grand Totals
Food Donations	84,511	95,842	152,132	189,665	
Cash Donations	102,465	118,549	187,456	254,139	
Veterinary Services	167,995	145,884	159,643	162,513	
Vaccinations	94,123	89,569	88,641	87,035	
Medications	54,216	26,843	15,469	38,654	
Totals					

27. Use the AutoSum button on the spreadsheet component toolbar to create totals in the appropriate cells. (*Hint:* Enter the SUM function in cell F2, and then copy and paste cell F2 into cells F3:F7. Next, enter the SUM function in cell B7, and then copy and paste cell B7 into cells C7:E7. Do not include the cell with the year in the range.)

28. Resize the columns containing data to their best fit, and then resize the spreadsheet component to display only those rows and columns containing data.

29. In a new, centered paragraph below the spreadsheet component, insert a chart component. Use the data range A1:E6, chart the series in columns, select the Column chart type, and select the Clustered Column subtype. Add the title "Donation Data" to the chart component. Format the title using 24-point, bold font. Add a legend to the chart component, and then save the page.

30. Recalculate the hyperlinks in the Web site, verify all hyperlinks in the Web site, and then run a Site Summary report.

31. If you have the necessary authorization to do so, set permissions for the **pets** Web site so that you are the administrator, and then add one other user to the Web site as an author. (*Note:* If you cannot change the permissions for a Web site, skip this step.)

32. Save all pages in the Web site as necessary, and then use a browser to thoroughly test the Web site. Print any pages as requested by your instructor.

33. Close your browser, the **pets** Web site, and FrontPage.

Objectives

- Create a Web site and import pages into it
- Create a frames page in a Web site and set pages to open in it
- Animate text in a Web page
- Add pictures to Web pages
- Create meta tags for a Web page
- Apply a theme to a Web site
- Create a Dynamic Web Template and attach pages to it
- Create an interactive button
- Search for information using a browser
- Create a form in a Web page and create a database in which to store its results
- Create an Active Server Page
- Create a site map

In this case, you will use skills you learned in the following tutorials:
- Tutorials 1–8

Creating a Web Site for Marty Sharik, Realtor

Case

Marty Sharik, Realtor

Marty Sharik has been an independent realtor in West Lafayette, Indiana, for more than 25 years. In the past, he has relied on personal and professional referrals as his primary source of listings for residential properties. He has consistently been one of the top agents in West Lafayette.

Recently, Marty began to worry about competitors who were getting new listings from people who normally would work with him. He soon discovered that these agents had Web sites that promoted listings in West Lafayette. Each of these realtors used a Web site to promote his or her services to people moving to West Lafayette and its surrounding areas. When a potential homebuyer indicated an interest in a certain type of neighborhood, the agent could respond immediately with information about listings, the community, and relocation assistance.

Marty has decided to expand his business by creating a Web site that includes information about the community, his services, and his listings in West Lafayette. He wants to include a Web page for each property that he lists. Marty hopes that his new Web site will boost his listings, and that the service he provides will help him to establish relationships with the new residents of his hometown.

If necessary, start FrontPage, make sure you have your Data Files, and then do the following:

1. Read all the questions for this case problem so you understand the requirements for Marty's Web site.
2. Prepare a Web site plan that shows the planned Web pages and the expected hyperlinks from the home page.
3. Use the Empty Web Site template to create a new Web site named **marty** in the location where your server-based Web sites are stored. (*Hint:* In the Web Site

Student Data Files

▼**AddCases**

▽ AddCase3 folder

51642.htm	78456.htm	contact.htm	p_51642.jpg	p_87462.jpg
57495.htm	87462.htm	contents.htm	p_57495.jpg	p_88462.jpg
74862.htm	88462.htm	info.htm	p_75436.jpg	relocate.htm
75436.htm	about.htm	listings.htm	p_78456.jpg	

Templates dialog box, type the path to your server in the Specify the location of the new Web site list box, plus the Web site name, such as http://localhost/marty. When you create a Web site directly on a server, you do not need to publish it.) After creating the Web site, import all of the files from the AddCase3 folder included with your Data Files into the Web site's root folder. If necessary, change the Web site's page options to enable the site for SharePoint Services, Browse-time Web Components, Author-time Web Components (navigation and shared borders), VML graphics, and Internet Explorer versions 5.0/6.0 and later.

4. Move the picture files from the site's root folder to the site's **images** folder.

5. Use the Contents frames page template to create a new Web page. Set the frames page to open the **contents.htm** page in the contents frame and the **contact.htm** page in the main frame. Save the frames page using the filename **Default.htm** and the title "Home Page."

6. Create hyperlinks from the list in the Contents page to open the Contact Us (**contact.htm**), Listings (**listings.htm**), Relocation Services (**relocate.htm**), About Marty Sharik (**about.htm**), and Information Request (**info.htm**) pages in the main frame.

7. Change the text "Over $100 million sold since 1974!" in the Contact Us page (**contact.htm**) to use an animation effect of your choice. Change the "Marty Sharik" text to a WordArt style of your choice, and then center it. Save the page.

8. In Navigation view, create a custom link bar that includes the **Default.htm** and the **listings.htm** pages. Change the default name of the custom link bar to "DWT."

9. Create a Dynamic Web Template named **listing.dwt** by doing the following:

   a. At the top of the page, type "Property Listing Detail," and then change this text to the Heading 1 style.

   b. Insert the DWT custom link bar in a new paragraph below the heading. Choose the option to use the page's theme as the bar style.

   c. Insert two blank paragraphs. Change the alignment of the second paragraph to center, and then create an interactive button using a style of your choice, the text "Request More Information," and a link to the address info@martysharikinc.com. Resize the button so all of the text it contains is visible, and select different hovered and pressed font colors that complement the button you selected.

   d. In a new, left-aligned paragraph below the interactive button, type "Copyright © 2006 Marty Sharik" and then insert a line break and type "Last updated." Add a date field that displays the date in the format May 31, 2006.

   e. Create a body editable region from the blank paragraph that appears below the custom link bar.

   f. Save the Dynamic Web Template, save the images for the interactive button in the Web site's **images** folder, and then close the Dynamic Web Template.

10. Open the Listings page (**listings.htm**) in Design view. Change the listing number in each row of the table to a hyperlink that opens the Web page with the same filename outside of the frames page. For example, create a hyperlink from the 51642 entry in the first row of the table to the **51642.htm** page in the Web site. Some listings do not have associated Web pages yet. In these cases, create a hyperlink from the listing number, and then use the Create New Document button in the Insert Hyperlink dialog box to create the hyperlink and a new Web page at the same time. Use the listing number plus the .htm filename extension as the filename. Choose the option to edit the new page later. When you have finished creating the hyperlinks, save and close the **listings.htm** page.

11. In Folders view, select the files **51642.htm**, **57495.htm**, **74862.htm**, **75436.htm**, **78456.htm**, **84651.htm**, **87462.htm**, **87618.htm**, and **88462.htm**, and then attach them to the **listing.dwt** Dynamic Web Template. Convert the existing body section of these Web pages to the body editable region.

12. For each page attached to the Dynamic Web Template, insert the appropriate picture from the Web site's **images** folder in the second cell of the table. For example, insert the picture file **p_57495.jpg** in the **57495.htm** Web page. Resize the width of each picture to 350 pixels, and then resample the picture. If no picture file is available for a Web page that contains a property description, type the message "Photo Coming Soon!" in the second cell. If the property listing detail is blank, type the message "Coming Soon!" in the body editable region. Save each page as you complete it, and overwrite the existing picture file in the Web site's **images** folder.

13. Create meta description and keywords tags in the home page (**Default.htm**), and then save the page.

14. Apply a theme of your choice to the entire Web site. Make sure that the theme uses vivid colors, active graphics, and a background picture.The theme you select should complement the colors you used in the WordArt object and interactive buttons you created.

15. With the home page open in Design view, use Ctrl + Click to open the Relocation Services page (**relocate.htm**) in the main frame. Use your Web browser and your Internet connection to search for at least four Web sites that provide information about the community of West Lafayette, Indiana. When you locate an appropriate site, enter its URL in the Web page and set the target to the main frame. Format the list of four hyperlinks as a bulleted list. Save the page.

16. Open the Information Request page (**info.htm**) in Design view (outside of the frames page). Insert a form component, and then cut and paste the existing form field labels into the form component. Choose the option to keep the source formatting. Convert the form field labels (First Name, Last Name, E-mail Address, Home Phone, and Work Phone) into a table, insert a new column to the right of the existing column, insert the appropriate form fields for each label, and create appropriate form field names and sizes. Format the table so that it has invisible borders and set its width at 100% of the browser window. Format the options below the "What can I help you with?" text as an option button group, and insert a check box form field to the left of the text that begins "Click here." Save the page.

17. Set the form component that you created in Step 16 to store its results in an Access database that you create when you set the form's properties. Do not include any additional fields. Follow the instructions to finish configuring the page, and then verify the database connection. Save the page.

18. Open the Information Request Web page in a browser, use the page to submit three forms for three different users, and then close your browser.

19. Create a new Active Server Page using the filename **inforeq.asp** and the title "Information Request Data." Set this page so it will not be published with the rest of the Web site. Insert a Database Results region in the Web page using the database connection that you created in Step 17. Remove the ID, Remote_computer_name, User_name, Browser_type, and Timestamp fields from the Database Results region, and then sort the records in ascending order by last name. (*Note:* Even though you chose not to create additional fields in the form, FrontPage created a table with these additional fields in the database.) Create a search form in the Web page that lets Marty filter records using the "What can I help you with?" values. Use a formatting option of your choice, and display all records together. After creating the Database Results region and the search form, add instructions above the search form that tell

Marty how to use the page. (*Hint:* List the values that Marty can use to filter the Database Results region records.)

20. Assign the Web pages in the Web site that include property descriptions to appropriate categories that you create, and then create a new page in the Web site to serve as a site map. Save this Web page using the filename **site_map.htm** and the title "Site Map." Include descriptive text in the Web page to inform Web site visitors how to use the page. Add an appropriate title to the page and format it using the Heading 1 style. After you save the Site Map page, add it to the frames page to open in the main frame. (*Hint:* Create a link to the Site Map page in the contents frame.)

21. Use the Search Page page template to create a new page using the title "Search" and the filename **search.htm**. After creating the page, delete the horizontal line and copyright information at the bottom of the page, and then change the comment component at the top of the page to a "Search" heading using the Heading 1 style. Save the page. Add a link to the **contents.htm** page that opens the Search page in the main frame of the home page, and then save the home page.

22. Recalculate the hyperlinks in the Web site, verify all hyperlinks in the Web site, and then run a Site Summary report.

23. Perform a spell check of all pages in the Web site and correct any errors that you discover.

24. Save all pages in the Web site as necessary, and then use a browser to thoroughly test the Web site to make sure that your targets are set correctly. Print any pages as requested by your instructor.

25. Close the browser, the **marty** Web site, and FrontPage.

Glossary/Index

regions into Web pages

querying using Web pages. *See* querying databases

database connection(s) A specification, including the name, location, and type of database, that serves to connect a Web site to a database. FP 473–478

custom, FP 474

file-based, FP 473

network, FP 474

System DSN, FP 474

verifying, FP 475–476

viewing HTML documents for pages with, FP 493–495

Database Interface Wizard, FP 14

Database Results region(s) A component in a Web page that contains HTML tags and client-side and server-side scripts that retrieve and display database data in the Web page.

formatting, FP 484–485

Database Results Wizard A wizard that inserts a Database Results region in a Web page by asking a series of questions about a database, the database object to insert in a Web page, and special filters (if any) to apply to the database object. FP 478

DAV (Distributed Authoring and Versioning). *See* Web DAV

Decrease Font Size button, FP 31

Decrease Indent button, FP 31

defined term(s) A term being explained in a definition list. The definition (or description) of the defined term appears below the defined term. FP 140

definition list(s) A list in a Web page of defined terms and their definitions. FP 140, FP 151–153

Delete Cells button, FP 271

deleting

custom themes from hard drive, FP 237–238

pages from navigation structure, FP 209–210

table cells, FP 293

tasks, FP 183

descriptions tags, FP 46

Design view, adding comments, FP 165–166

designing Web sites, FP 9

developing Web sites, FP 6–11

building site, FP 10

defining goal and purpose, FP 7–8

designing site, FP 9

determining and preparing contents, FP 8

testing site, FP 11

DHTML. *See* dynamic HTML

Discussion Web Site Wizard, FP 14

disk-based Web site(s) A Web site that is stored on a disk, such as a computer's hard drive. FP 5

Displayed Fields dialog box, FP 480

displaying. *See also* viewing

Pictures toolbar, FP 83

repeated hyperlinks, FP 175

Distribute Columns Evenly button, FP 271

Distribute Rows Evenly button, FP 271

Distributed Authoring and Versioning. *See* WebDAV

drag and drop, creating hyperlinks, FP 97–99

Draw Layout Cell button, FP 271

Draw Layout Table button, FP 271

Draw Table button, FP 271

drawing(s) A canvas object that contains other objects, such as text boxes and arrows, that you can create in a Web page.

inserting into Web pages, FP 247–248

drop-down box(es) A form field that presents choices in a list that the user displays by clicking a list arrow.

adding to forms, FP 350–353

Drop-Down Box Properties dialog box, FP 352

drop-down menu. *See* drop-down box(es)

dynamic HTML An extension of HTML that lets you add interactive elements to a Web page that change dynamically in response to user actions without the transfer of any files from the Web server on which the page is stored. FP 118–121

animated text, FP 119–121

page transitions, FP 118–119

dynamic Web page(s) A Web page that contains data, such as stock market and weather information, that changes on a schedule. FP 5

Dynamic Web Template(s) A file saved with the extension .dwt that includes editable regions and locked areas of content. After creating a Dynamic Web Template, the developer

can attach it to other Web pages to apply the content and formatting contained in the Dynamic Web Template to the other Web pages. FP 438–457

adding locked content, FP 446

adding to Web pages, FP 449–451

attaching to selected pages, FP 455–456

changing font and font size, FP 453–455

creating, FP 445

detaching pages from, FP 456–457

editable regions, FP 440–443, FP 447–449

saving, FP 445

updating, FP 451–452

E

editable region(s) An area in a Dynamic Web Template that is given a standardized name to identify it. When the Dynamic Web Template is attached to other Web pages, authors of the attached pages can edit the content in the editable region.

Dynamic Web Templates, FP 440–443, FP 447–449

Editable Regions dialog box, FP 448

editing

frames in frames pages, FP 312–313

shared borders, FP 204–206

e-mail addresses, creating hyperlinks to, FP 99–101

E-mail Results tab, Saving Results dialog box, FP 365

embedded file(s) In HTML, a file (usually a picture) that is used in a Web page and stored in a file location. An HTML tag in the Web page inserts the embedded file from the specified file location.

saving in Web sites, FP 75–77

Empty Web Site template, FP 14

entering data into tables, FP 283–285

entering text, FP 22–23

Eraser button, FP 271

error correction, spell checking Web pages, FP 24–25

Estimated Time to Download options, FP 84–85

executable folder(s) A folder on a Web server that permits the execution of scripts. FP 477

expanding hyperlinks, FP 173–174

merge(ing) The act of combining a group of selected cells in a table to form a single cell. FP 288–290

Merge Cells button, FP 271

meta tag(s) An HTML tag that includes information about a Web page, such as the character set it uses, the name of its developer, how often it is refreshed, and the keywords and description of the page's content. FP 51–53

Microsoft FrontPage. *See* FrontPage

Microsoft Internet Information Services (IIS) A program that you can install on a personal computer running Windows 2000/XP Professional to make it function as a Web server. FP 372–375, FP 375

    publishing disk-based Web sites to, FP 377–380

    testing, FP 375

Microsoft Office Access 2003 A relational database management program that lets you create and maintain a database. Also called Access. FP 469. *See also* database(s)

    starting, FP 469

Modify Style dialog box, FP 549

More Colors dialog box, FP 40

mouse fly over. *See* mouse over

mouse over The act of moving the pointer over an interactive button or picture. FP 114–117

moving existing data into tables, FP 272–274

multi-level list(s) A list that contains one or more nested lists of information. FP 140

multiple authors, source control to manage, FP 420–421

N

Name option, Frame Properties dialog box, FP 315

navigation structure

    adding new pages, FP 212–215

    adding pages, FP 195–199

    creating custom link bars, FP 221–222

    deleting pages, FP 209–210

Navigation view, FP 162, FP 209–215

    adding new pages to navigation structure, FP 212–215

    changing page titles, FP 235–236

    creating custom link bars, FP 219–224

    creating new pages, FP 210–212

    deleting pages from navigation structure, FP 209–210

    renaming page titles, FP 198

nested list(s) A list that appears within another list, such as a numbered list within a bulleted list. FP 140, FP 149–151

    numbered, FP 149–151

nested table(s) A table that appears within the cell of another table. FP 266

nested tag(s) In HTML, a tag that appears within a one-sided tag or within the opening and closing tags of a two-sided tag. FP 46

network Two or more computers that are connected together for the purposes of resource sharing and communicating. FP 4

network connection(s) A type of database connection that is made to a database server, which is a server that is dedicated to managing a database. FP 474

network server(s) A powerful computer that stores and distributes information and resources across a network to individual computers. FP 4

New Task dialog box, FP 180

No Frames page(s) A Web page that provides instructions and optional alternate content for browsers that cannot display frames pages.

    examining HTML document, FP 309–310

nonprinting characters, FP 78–79

nontext-based bookmarks, FP 159–160

Normal page template, FP 336

Normal push button A form field that initiates a user-defined script. FP 361

numbered list(s) A list of items in a Web page preceded with numbers, letters, or Roman numerals. Also called an ordered list because items are sequentially or alphabetically organized. FP 140, FP 148–151

    nested, FP 149–151

Numbering button, FP 31

Numbers tab, Properties dialog box, FP 148–149

O

Office component(s) A self-contained object in a Web page that includes the commands and tools required to use it. FP 563–582. *See also* chart(s); PivotTable list(s); spreadsheet(s)

Office documents, opening from Web sites, FP 367–369

One Page Web Site template, FP 14

one-sided tag(s) In HTML, a command that requires only one tag; the browser executes the action specified by the tag only while it is interpreting the tag. FP 47

opening

    databases, FP 469–473

    Office documents from Web sites, FP 367–369

    queries, FP 471–473

    tables, FP 471–473

    Web sites, FP 28–29

opening tag(s) In a two-sided HTML tag, the tag that the browser encounters first and that turns on the defined formatting. FP 47

Optimize HTML tab, Remote Web Site Properties dialog box, FP 378

option button(s) A form field that is used to select one option from a group of choices.

    adding to forms, FP 347–350

    changing properties, FP 349–350

option button group name(s) The HTML name that identifies a group of related option buttons in a form. FP 347

Option Button Properties dialog box, FP 349–350

Options dialog box

    Authoring tab, FP 20

    Reports View tab, FP 170–171

Options for Saving Results to Database dialog box, FP 500

ordered list(s), FP 140

outline list(s), FP 140

outside tag(s) In a nested HTML tag, the tag that is processed first by a browser. FP 46

P

page banner(s) Text or a picture object in a Web page that identifies a page's title as shown in Navigation view. FP 201–202, FP 217–219

Page Banner Properties dialog box, FP 218

Page Templates dialog box, FP 306–307, FP 337

page transition(s) An animated effect that you can apply to one or more Web pages in a Web site that runs when the user loads or leaves the page or enters or leaves the site.

    DHTML, FP 118–119

Page Transitions dialog box, FP 118

Task Reference

TASK	PAGE #	RECOMMENDED METHOD
Access database, import into a FrontPage Web site	FP 474	See Reference Window: Importing an Access Database into a Web Site
Access query, open in Query Datasheet view	FP 472	Click the Queries object in the Database window, double-click the query name
Access, start and open an existing database	FP 469	See Reference Window: Starting Access and Opening an Existing Database
Access table, open in Table Datasheet view	FP 471	Click the Tables object in the Database window, double-click the table name
Action, undo previous in a data access page	FP 508	Click
Active Server Page, save	FP 482	Click , type the filename in the File name text box, click the Save as type list arrow, click ASP Files, click Save
Alternative text, add to a picture	FP 85	See Reference Window: Adding Alternative Text to a Picture
Authoring settings, change for a Web site	FP 19	Double-click the Authoring Settings pane on the status bar, select the desired technologies and browsers, click OK
Background color, change for a table or table cell	FP 292	See Reference Window: Changing the Background Color or Picture in a Table or Cell
Background color, set for a Web page	FP 70	See Reference Window: Setting the Background Color of a Web Page
Background picture, insert into a Web Page	FP 74	See Reference Window: Inserting a Background Picture into a Web Page
Bookmark, create hyperlink to	FP 157	See Reference Window: Creating a Hyperlink to a Bookmark
Bookmark, create nontext-based	FP 159	Click the location to create the bookmark, click Insert, click Bookmark, type the bookmark's name in the Bookmark name text box, click OK
Bookmark, create text-based	FP 154	See Reference Window: Creating a Text-Based Bookmark in a Web Page
Caption, add to a table	FP 295	See Reference Window: Adding a Table Caption
Cascading style sheet, break the link to	FP 561	See Reference Window: Breaking the Link to a Cascading Style Sheet
Cascading style sheet, create	FP 553	See Reference Window: Creating a Cascading Style Sheet
Cascading style sheet, create using a template	FP 558	See Reference Window: Using a Template to Create a Cascading Style Sheet
Categories, create for a Web site	FP 430	See Reference Window: Creating Categories and Assigning Pages to Them
Categories report, create	FP 433	Click Reports, click the Site Summary button, point to Workflow, click Categories
Cell, copy contents into adjacent cells in a column in a table	FP 284	Select cell to be copied and cells to copy into, click
Cell, copy contents into adjacent cells in a row in a table	FP 284	Select cell to be copied and cells to copy into, click
Cell, split in a table	FP 290	See Reference Window: Splitting Table Cells
Cells, delete from a table	FP 293	See Reference Window: Deleting Cells from a Table
Cells, merge in a table	FP 289	See Reference Window: Merging Table Cells

TASK	PAGE #	RECOMMENDED METHOD
Chart component, create in a Web page	FP 570	See Reference Window: Inserting a Chart Component in a Web Page That Contains a Data Source
Check box, add to a form	FP 360	Click the desired location, click Insert, point to Form, click Checkbox
Column, insert in a table in a Web page	FP 286	See Reference Window: Inserting a Column in a Table
Column, resize in a table	FP 294	See Reference Window: Resizing a Row or Column in a Table Using the Mouse
Column, select in a table	FP 276	Click the top border of the column
Columns, distribute selected evenly in a table	FP 295	Click ⊞
Comment, insert into a Web page	FP 165	See Reference Window: Inserting a Comment into a Web Page
Custom link bar, create in Navigation view	FP 220	See Reference Window: Creating a Custom Link Bar in Navigation View
Custom theme, delete	FP 237	See Reference Window: Deleting a Custom Theme From Your Hard Drive
Data, import into a spreadsheet component	FP 566	Select the spreadsheet component, click 📋, click the Import tab, click the Data type list arrow, click the file type, click the URL text box, type the path to the data, click Refresh data from URL at run time or click Import Now
Data access page, create	FP 503	See Reference Window: Creating a Data Access Page
Data labels, add to a chart component	FP 574	Select the chart component, right-click the data series, click Commands and Options, click the General tab, click 📊
Database connection, verify in a Web site	FP 476	See Reference Window: Verifying a Database Connection
Database Results region, insert in a Web page	FP 479	See Reference Window: Creating a Database Results Region in a Web Page
Download time, estimate for a Web page	FP 84	Click the Estimated Time to Download pane on the status bar, click the desired transfer rate
Drop-down box, add to a form	FP 350	Click the desired location, click Insert, point to Form, click Drop-Down Box
Dynamic Web Template, attach to a Web page	FP 449	See Reference Window: Attaching a Dynamic Web Template to a Web Page
Dynamic Web Template, detach from a Web page	FP 456	Click Format, point to Dynamic Web Template, click Detach from Dynamic Web Template
Dynamic Web Template, save in a Web site	FP 445	See Reference Window: Saving a Dynamic Web Template
Dynamic Web Template, update	FP 451	See Reference Window: Updating a Dynamic Web Template and Pages Attached to It
Editable region, create in a Dynamic Web Template	FP 447	See Reference Window: Creating an Editable Region in a Dynamic Web Template
Embedded file, save with a Web page	FP 75	See Reference Window: Saving a Web Page That Contains an Embedded File
File, insert into a Web page	FP 23	See Reference Window: Inserting a File into a Web Page
Filter, remove in a data access page	FP 508	Click ▽
Folder List, open or close	FP 17	Click 📑
Folders view, change to	FP 179	Click 📁 Folders

TASK	PAGE #	RECOMMENDED METHOD
Form component, add to a Web page	FP 346	See Reference Window: Creating a Form Component and Adding a Form Field
Form component, send results to a database	FP 499	See Reference Window: Configuring a Form to Send Results to a Database
Form field properties, change	FP 349	Double-click the form field
Form field, validate	FP 358	Double-click the form field, click Validate
Form results file, examine contents of	FP 388	Open the server-based Web site in FrontPage, click the _private folder in the Folder List, double-click the form results file
Format Painter, use to copy and paste text formatting once	FP 41	Select the text whose format you want to copy, click 🖌, select the text to which to copy the format
Format Painter, use to copy and paste text formatting more than once	FP 41	Select the text whose format you want to copy, double-click 🖌, select the text to which to copy the format as needed, click 🖌
Frame, add new to a frames page	FP 320	See Reference Window: Adding a New Frame to an Existing Frames Page
Frame, edit size of in a frames page	FP 312	In Design view, drag a border of the frame to new position
Frames page, create	FP 306	See Reference Window: Creating a Frames Page
Frames page, print in Internet Explorer	FP 322	Click File, click Print, click desired option in the Print frames section, click OK
FrontPage link bar, add to a Web page	FP 216	Click in the desired location, click Insert, Navigation, select the link bar options, click OK
FrontPage link bar, change properties of	FP 206	Double-click the link bar component, make desired changes, click OK
FrontPage, close	FP 28	Click ⊠
FrontPage, start	FP 11	Click Start, point to All Programs, point to Microsoft Office, click Microsoft Office FrontPage 2003
Heading, create in a Web page	FP 32	See Reference Window: Creating a Heading in a Web Page
Help, get in FrontPage	FP 54	Click ⓞ, type a question in the Search for text box, click →
Help, get while using a data access page	FP 508	Click ?
Help, get while using an Office component	FP 568	Click ?
Hit counter, create in a Web page	FP 389	See Reference Window: Creating a Hit Counter in a Web Page
Horizontal line, add to a Web page	FP 91	See Reference Window: Inserting a Horizontal Line and Changing Its Properties
Horizontal line, change properties of	FP 91	See Reference Window: Inserting a Horizontal Line and Changing Its Properties
Hotspot, highlight in a picture	FP 103	See Reference Window: Highlighting Hotspots in a Picture
HTML document, view for a frames page in FrontPage	FP 309	Click ⊡ Code
HTML document, view for a No Frames page	FP 309	Click ⊘ No Frames
HTML document, view using FrontPage	FP 47	In Page view, click ⊡ Code
HTML document, view using Internet Explorer	FP 50	Click View, click Source

TASK	PAGE #	RECOMMENDED METHOD
Hyperlink, create to another Web page	FP 96	See Reference Window: Creating a Hyperlink to an Existing Web Page in the Same Web Site
Hyperlink, create using drag and drop	FP 97	See Reference Window: Creating a Hyperlink Using Drag and Drop
Hyperlink, follow in Design view	FP 97	Press and hold the Ctrl key, click the hyperlink
Hyperlinks view, change to	FP 171	Click ⧉ Hyperlinks
Hyperlinks view, print	FP 176	Press the Print Screen key, click ⬜, click 🖼, click 🖨
Hyperlinks, recalculate	FP 392	Click Tools, click Recalculate Hyperlinks, click the Yes button
Hyperlinks, show or hide links to pictures	FP 172	In Hyperlinks view, right-click the Contents pane, click Hyperlinks to Pictures
Hyperlinks, verify	FP 392	In Reports view, click 📝 on the Contents pane, click the Start button
Image map, create	FP 101	See Reference Window: Creating an Image Map
Included content, insert into a Web page	FP 534	See Reference Window: Using Included Content in a Web Page
Initial page, set for a frame	FP 311	Click the Set Initial Page button, double-click the desired page
Interactive button, create	FP 114	See Reference Window: Creating an Interactive Button in a Web Page
Layout cell, create	FP 542	See Reference Window: Creating a Layout Cell in a Layout Table
Layout cell, format	FP 545	See Reference Window: Formatting a Layout Cell
Layout table, insert in a Web page	FP 528	See Reference Window: Using a Table Layout Template to insert a Layout Table in a Web Page
Legend, add to a chart component	FP 578	Select the chart component, click the General tab, click 📋
Line break, create in a Web page	FP 37	Press Shift + Enter
List, create bulleted	FP 145	See Reference Window: Creating a Bulleted List
List, create definition	FP 151	See Reference Window: Creating a Definition List
List, create nested	FP 150	See Reference Window: Creating a Nested List
List, create numbered	FP 148	See Reference Window: Creating a Numbered List
Mailto, create	FP 99	See Reference Window: Creating a Mailto
Marquee, create in a Web page	FP 78	See Reference Window: Creating a Marquee in a Web Page
Meta tag, insert into a Web page	FP 51	See Reference Window: Inserting a Meta Tag into a Web Page
Navigation structure, create	FP 195	In Navigation view, drag and drop filenames from the Folder List and position them in the navigation structure
Navigation view, change to	FP 195	Click ⧉ Navigation
Nonprinting characters, hide in a Web page	FP 79	Click ¶
Nonprinting characters, show in a Web page	FP 78	Click ¶
Office component, resize in Page view	FP 569	Select the component, drag a sizing handle
Option button, add to a form	FP 348	Click the desired location, click Insert, point to Form, click Option Button
Page banner, create	FP 218	See Reference Window: Creating a Page Banner
Page transition, create	FP 118	See Reference Window: Applying a Page Transition
Permissions, set for a Web site	FP 394	See Reference Window: Setting Permissions for a Web Site
Photo Gallery, change properties of	FP 245	Double-click the photo gallery, change properties as necessary, click OK

TASK	PAGE #	RECOMMENDED METHOD
Photo Gallery, create	FP 242	See Reference Window: Creating a Photo Gallery in a Page
Picture, add to a Web page	FP 81	See Reference Window: Inserting a Picture into a Web Page
Picture, animate in a Web page	FP 119	See Reference Window: Creating Animated Text or an Animated Picture in a Web Page
Picture, bevel	FP 110	Click ▨ on the Pictures toolbar
Picture, change color characteristics	FP 109	Click ▥ on the Pictures toolbar, click desired option
Picture, change color to transparent	FP 89	See Reference Window: Changing a Color in a Picture to Transparent
Picture, convert to another format	FP 88	See Reference Window: Converting a Picture to Another Format
Picture, restore all previously applied, unsaved effects	FP 108	Click ▨ on the Pictures toolbar
Picture, rotate left	FP 110	Click ▨ on the Pictures toolbar
Picture, rotate right	FP 110	Click ▨ on the Pictures toolbar
Program window, maximize	FP 55	Click ▢
Record, add to a database table	FP 492	Click the Tables object in the Database window, double-click the table name, click ▶ , enter the new record
Record, add to a database table using a data access page	FP 509	See Reference Window: Adding a Record to a Database Table Using a Data Access Page
Record, delete from a table using a data access page	FP 508	Display the record, click ▶✗
Record, go to first in a data access page	FP 508	Click ◄
Record, go to last in a data access page	FP 508	Click ►I
Record, go to next in a data access page	FP 508	Click ►
Record, go to previous in a data access page	FP 508	Click ◄
Record, save in a table using a data access page	FP 508	Click ▨
Records, filter by selection in a data access page	FP 508	Click in the field to filter, click ▽⁄
Records, sort in ascending order in a data access page	FP 508	Click in the field to sort, click ⧎↓
Records, sort in descending order in a data access page	FP 508	Click in the field to sort, click ⧎↓
Repeated hyperlinks, show or hide in Hyperlinks view	FP 175	Right-click the Contents pane, click Repeated Hyperlinks
Reports view, change to	FP 169	Click ▣ Reports
Row, insert in a table in a Web page	FP 287	See Reference Window: Inserting a Row in a Table
Row, resize in a table	FP 294	See Reference Window: Resizing a Row or Column in a Table Using the Mouse
Row, select in a table	FP 275	Click the left border of the row

TASK	PAGE #	RECOMMENDED METHOD
Rows, distribute selected evenly in a table	FP 295	Click
Save Results component, configure	FP 363	Right-click the form component, click Form Properties
Search component properties, change	FP 340	Right-click the search component, click Search Form Properties
Search form, add to an Active Server Page	FP 486	See Reference Window: Creating a Search Form in a Web Page That Queries a Database
Search page, create in a Web site	FP 337	Click the list arrow for , click Page, double-click the Search Page icon
Shared border, disable for a Web page	FP 215	See Reference Window: Disabling Shared Borders for a Single Web Page
Shared border, edit	FP 205	In Design view, click the shared border to select it, make the desired changes
Shared borders, create for a Web site	FP 199	See Reference Window: Creating Shared Borders for a Web Site
Shared template, save in a Web site	FP 426	See Reference Window: Saving a Shared Template
Site map, create	FP 435	See Reference Window: Creating a Site Map
Site settings, examine and change for a Web site	FP 166	Click Tools, click Site Settings
Source control, disable	FP 438	Click Tools, Site Settings, click the Use document check-in and check-out check box to clear it, click OK, click Yes
Source control, enable for a Web site	FP 421	See Reference Window: Enabling and Using Source Control for a Web Site
Special character, insert in a Web page	FP 38	Click the desired location, click Insert, click Symbol, select the desired character, click the Insert button, click the Close button
Spreadsheet component, insert in a Web page	FP 564	See Reference Window: Inserting and Using a Spreadsheet Component in a Web Page
Style, create user-defined	FP 548	See Reference Window: Creating a User-Defined Style in a Web Page
Table, align in a Web page	FP 272	See Reference Window: Aligning a Table in a Web Page
Table, apply an AutoFormat to	FP 297	See Reference Window: Applying a Table AutoFormat
Table, create in a Web page	FP 267	See Reference Window: Creating a Table in a Web Page
Target frame, specify	FP 313	Click , click the Target Frame button, select the target frame, click OK, click OK
Task history, show or hide	FP 183	Right-click any blank area in Tasks view, click Show History
Task pane, change	FP 163	Click the Other Task Panes list arrow, click desired task pane
Task pane, close	FP 164	Click on the task pane
Task pane, display	FP 163	Click View, click Task Pane
Task, add in Tasks view	FP 179	See Reference Window: Adding a Task to Tasks View
Task, change in Tasks view	FP 181	Double-click the task, change the settings, click OK
Task, delete from the Tasks list	FP 183	In Tasks view, right-click the task, click Delete Task, click Yes
Task, mark as completed	FP 182	In Tasks view, right-click the task, click Mark Complete
Tasks list, sort	FP 181	In Tasks view, click the column heading on which to sort
Tasks view, change to	FP 181	Click
Text area, add to a form	FP 355	Click the desired location, click Insert, point to Form, click Text Area
Text box, add to a form	FP 353	Click the desired location, click Insert, point to Form, click Textbox
Text, add on top of a picture	FP 110	See Reference Window: Adding Text on a Picture

TASK	PAGE #	RECOMMENDED METHOD
Text, align in a Web page	FP 34	See Reference Window: Aligning a Paragraph in a Web Page
Text, animate in a Web page	FP 119	See Reference Window: Creating Animated Text or an Animated Picture in a Web Page
Text, change color of selected in a Web page	FP 40	Click the list arrow for **A ▾**, click desired color
Text, change font of selected in a Web page	FP 37	Click the Font list arrow, click new font name
Text, change selected to bold	FP 40	Click **B**
Text, change selected to italic	FP 37	Click **I**
Text, change selected to underlined	FP 31	Click **U**
Text, change size of for selected in a Web page	FP 38	Click the Font Size list arrow, click the desired font size
Text, copy and paste in a Web page	FP 26	Select the text to copy, click 🗐, click the location in which to paste the text, click 🗐
Theme, apply to a Web site	FP 226	See Reference Window: Applying a Theme to a Web Site
Theme, create new	FP 238	See Reference Window: Creating a New Theme
Theme, customize	FP 231	See Reference Window: Customizing an Existing Theme
Theme, remove	FP 241	See Reference Window: Removing a Theme From a Page or Web Site
Thumbnail picture, create	FP 108	See Reference Window: Creating a Thumbnail Picture
Title, add to a chart component	FP 576	Select the chart component, click the General tab, click 📊
Title, rename in Folders view	FP 94	Click the title to select it, click it again to change to editing mode, type the new title, press Enter
Title, rename in Navigation view	FP 198	See Reference Window: Renaming a Page's title in Navigation View
Toolbar, show or hide	FP 83	Click View, point to Toolbars, click the toolbar to show or hide
Web page size, set default	FP 21	Click the Page Size pane on the status bar, click the desired page size in the list
Web page, add new to navigation structure	FP 210	See Reference Window: Creating a New Page in Navigation View
Web page, check in	FP 423	Close the Web page in Page view, right-click the Web page in Folders view, click Check In
Web page, check out	FP 423	Double-click the page name in Folders view, click Yes
Web page, check spelling in	FP 25	See Reference Window: Spell Checking a Web Page
Web page, close in Page view	FP 28	Click ✕ on the Contents pane
Web page, delete from navigation structure	FP 209	See Reference Window: Deleting a Page in Navigation View
Web page, import into a Web site	FP 93	See Reference Window: Importing an Existing Web Page into a Web Site
Web page, link to a cascading style sheet	FP 556	See Reference Window: Linking a Cascading Style Sheet to a Web page
Web page, preview	FP 42	See Reference Window: Previewing a Web Page
Web page, print using FrontPage	FP 44	See Reference Window: Printing a Web Page
Web page, remove an inline style from	FP 560	See Reference Window: Removing an Inline Style from a Web Page
Web page, save	FP 28	See Reference Window: Saving a Web Page

TASK	PAGE #	RECOMMENDED METHOD
Web page, scroll to bottom	FP 36	Press Ctrl + End
Web page, scroll to top	FP 40	Press Ctrl + Home
Web page, view in Design view	FP 53	Click ⬚Design
Web page, view in Preview view	FP 42	Click ⬚Preview
Web page, view in Split view	FP 48	Click ⬚Split
Web site, close in FrontPage	FP 28	Click File, click Close Site
Web site, create new	FP 15	Click the Other Task Panes arrow, click New, click the template or Wizard to use to create the Web site, type the Web site's name in the Specify the location of the new Web site text box, click OK
Web site, open in FrontPage	FP 29	See Reference Window: Opening a Web Site
Web site, publish	FP 376	See Reference Window: Publishing a Web Site to Your Computer's Server
Web site, publish changed pages	FP 383	See Reference Window: Publishing Changes to a Server-Based Web Site
Web site, set to run scripts	FP 477	See Reference Window: Setting a Web Site to Run Scripts
WordArt object, create	FP 249	See Reference Window: Creating a WordArt Object in a Page
WordArt object, revise selected	FP 251	Click ⬚ on the WordArt toolbar